A Complete Record 1887-1987

Manchester City

A Complete Record 1887-1987

RAY GOBLE

Breedon Books Sport

© Ray Goble(statistics) 1987

First published in Great Britain by
The Breedon Books Publishing Company Limited
45 Friar Gate, Derby DE1 1DA
1987

ISBN 0 907969 24 0

Printed by Butler and Tanner Limited, Frome
Jacket designed by Graham Hales

CONTENTS

The publishers acknowledge the great help given by Andrew Ward in the compilation of the text of this book.

Photographs supplied by Colorsport, BBC Hulton Picture Library, Steve Hale, *Manchester Evening News.*

Anyone interested in the work of the Association of Football Statisticians should write to the AFS Secretary, Mr Ray Spiller, 22 Bretons, Basildon, Essex SS15 5BY.

Introduction

MANCHESTER CITY FOOTBALL CLUB is one of the most famous names in football and, despite their relegation from the First Division in 1987, there seems no more appropriate time to publish this 'Complete Record' of the club's affairs, since this year also marks something of a centenary.

Although the embryonic City club had been in operation since 1880 — under the Gorton banners — it was in 1887 that the club moved its home to Ardwick, and changed its name at the same time. The Ardwick title meant a change of attitude, away from the club's parochial origins and into the world of commerce and business. Thus, the club which very soon became Manchester City by name was born.

Since then, City and its players have always been at the forefront of British soccer and this book is a celebration of 100 years of football.

The names of Meredith and Turnbull, Brook and Swift, Trautmann and Revie, Oakes and Bell, are just a few of the many which ring out over a century of Manchester City's history. They are all contained within the pages of this book which, the author and the publishers believe, is the definitive story of the Maine Road club.

Tony Book holds the League Cup at Wembley in 1970 during City's greatest era.

THE MANCHESTER CITY STORY

While some Football League clubs were launched systematically — the Portsmouth directors purchased a ground, appointed a manager and took it from there — Manchester City truly evolved from humble origins. There were several changes in name and five changes in address in the first seven years.

The club first saw light as St Mark's of West Gorton in 1880, playing on a piece of rough ground in Clowes Street. The first match, on 13 November 1880, was described thus: 'A match was played between the Baptist Church (Macclesfield) and St Mark's (West Gorton) on Saturday on the ground of the latter, and resulted as follows: Baptist 2 goals, St Mark's 1 goal'. Both teams fielded 12 players.

Together with amalgamations and changes in personnel came the changes in name — to West Gorton (St Mark's) in 1881; to Gorton in 1884 and to Ardwick in 1887, before a financial crisis in 1894 led to the birth of Manchester City.

Ground problems were often at the root of the changes and it is a wonder that the club was not called The Wanderers. Early venues included Clowes Street, Kirkmanshulme Cricket Club, Clemington Park, Pink Bank Lane and Reddish Lane.

Then, in 1887, the Gorton captain, a Scot named McKenzie, happened across an ideal patch of waste ground — home of Ardwick from 1887 to 1894 and Manchester City from 1894 to 1923.

Until Ardwick joined the Alliance in 1891, these early games were mainly friendlies. Cancelled matches were not re-arranged and there was often an element of doubt about whether a fixture would be fulfilled. Manchester was known for its bad weather and poor visibility; opponents might take the wrong train or alight at the wrong station.

It was not always easy to find opponents in the Manchester area, where the major commitment was to rugby football. Nor was there a surplus of committed players. In 1882-3, West Gorton used 26 players to fulfil nine fixtures.

The first professional was Jack Hodgetts — paid five shillings a week by Ardwick in 1887 — and by 1888-9 Ardwick's fixture list had grown to 46 matches. Over 60 goals were scored and only eight games lost.

Ardwick's reputation was enhanced by some excellent results in local cup competitions. They were twice winners of the Manchester Cup, beating Newton Heath 1-0 in 1891 and Bolton Wanderers 4-1 in 1892. In 1891 they also reached the Lancashire Junior Cup Final.

These successes helped the club gain admittance to the Alliance in 1891 and the Football League's Second Division in 1892. But financial problems set in during the second season in the League and the club was forced into bankruptcy.

Ardwick became extinct, only to be restarted as Manchester City Football Club, a limited-liability company. Secretary Josh Parlby persuasively secured the club a position in the Second Division before a ball had been kicked.

After reaching the promotion-deciding test matches in 1896 — an 8-0 defeat by Small Heath crushed their chances — City achieved First Division status in 1899, when the team were presented with gold medals. Star of the side was the famous Welsh winger, Billy Meredith, who scored 29 League goals.

9

Manchester City on the attack during the 1904 FA Cup Final at the Crystal Palace. Dai Davies, the Bolton goal-keeper tries to get back as a high ball is pumped into his goal-mouth. Davies claimed that he was waiting for referee Barker to blow for offside when Meredith went through for the only goal of the game.

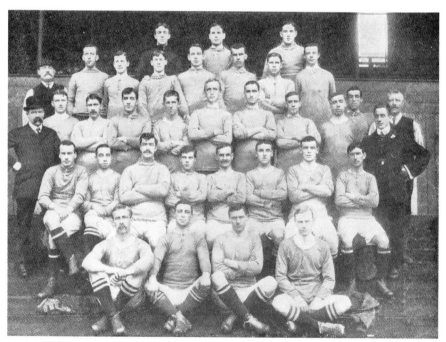

City in 1908-09. Back row (left to right): R.Grieve, J.Blair, W.Smith. Fourth row: W.Iles (asst trainer), F.Davies, A.Winterburn, W.Bottomley, J.Wilkinson, D.Coupe, E.Henderson, R.Harrison. Third row: F.Norgrove, G.Dorsett, B.Jackson, J.Buchan, W.Eadie, T.Kelso, C.Webb, H.Hancock, Bannister, R.Chatt (trainer). Second row: Mr H.J.Newbould (secretary), J.Wood, G.Stewart, C.Broomfield, W.Jones, T.Holford, D.Ross, C.Burgess, J.Conlin, F.McCartan (asst secretary). Front row: F.Buckley, A.Powell, I.Thornley, P.Hill.

City's first-ever spell in Division One started promisingly, but quickly fell away into financial problems. At the end of the 1901-2 season they were relegated.

New direction, and much-needed capital, came from Councillor John Allison, and Edward Hulton, the newspaper magnate. New secretary Tom Maley, from Glasgow Celtic, was provided with funds to secure players and the mid-1900s saw City's first great team.

Fed by Scottish international George Livingstone, Billy Meredith led most of the attacks along City's right wing. Sandy Turnbull and Billy Gillespie queued for the crosses, while left-winger Frank Booth brought variation and was himself an international.

Interest in the Championship was maintained until the last matches of the 1903-4 and 1904-5 seasons, but the only tangible reward was the FA Cup, won for the first time in 1904, when a disputed goal from Meredith was good enough to beat Second Division Bolton Wanderers.

The fall was dramatic. Meredith was suspended for nine months for allegedly attempting to bribe an Aston Villa player. Then came a sustained FA inquiry into payments. Seventeen City players and two directors were suspended for seven months, and two officials, Maley and Forrest, were suspended *sine die*. As if these punishments were not sufficient, there was also the matter of fines — £250 to be paid by the club and £900 spread among the 17 players.

Manchester City barely survived. After a difficult season, though, new secretary-manager Harry Newbould steered City into third place before relegation in 1908-9 formed the prelude for another Second Division Championship success the following season.

City's new First Division era lasted 12 seasons — five before World War One and seven afterwards. For most of this era they were reliant on goals from two expensive signings. Tom 'Boy' Browell joined City for £1,500 from Everton and like his fellow goal-hunter, the lethal left-footed Horace Barnes (£2,500 from Derby County), he notched up 120 League goals in a lengthy spell with the club.

The pinnacles of this period were runners-up spot in the League (1920-21), an appearance in the Cup semi-final (1924) and Cup runners-up at Wembley in 1926 when a late goal from Ted Vizard gave Bolton revenge for that 1904 defeat.

The more evocative moments came when fire destroyed the main stand at Hyde Road in 1920 — the club moved to a newly-built ground in Moss Side in 1923 — and Meredith's return to the team for the Cup run of 1924. Meredith was then in his 50th-year.

City's erratic tradition was evident in the 1925-6 season when they reached Wembley and then a week later needed a point to avoid relegation. They lost 3-2 to Newcastle, Billy Austin missed a penalty (when the score was 2-1) and City went back to Division Two.

Incredibly, the team had scored 120 goals in League and Cup games that season. Barnes had left by now, but Browell was still scoring regularly, helped by £3,400 centre-forward Frank Roberts from Bolton, and the man destined to become City's all-time record League goalscorer — Tom Johnson.

It took City two seasons to leave the Second Division this time, but only because of the narrowest margin ever in a promotion race. Portsmouth's goal average (1.7755) was better than City's only in the third decimal place (1.7705). Had the issue been settled on goal difference, City would have been promoted. Despite an 8-0 win over Bradford City in the last match, it was not enough.

In 1927-28 there was no mistake, however. Once again City scored a century of goals and they registered their fourth Second Division Championship success in their last five seasons in that Division.

Peter Hodge, who had taken over as manager in 1926, assembled a collection of fine players who provided the springboard for the success of the 1930s. The captain,

City's 1927-8 line-up when the club won the Second Division title. Back row (left to right): Pringle, Bennett, Cookson, Gray, McCloy, A.Bell (trainer), Broadhurst. Front: P.Bell, Roberts, McMullan, Johnson, Hicks, Cowan.

An Everton attack on the City goal during the 1933 FA Cup Final.

Manchester City in 1934, pictured with the FA Cup. Back row (left to right): Messrs R.Smith, W.M.Shaw, H.Wood, Dr J.B.Holmes (all directors). Standing: W.Wild (secretary-manager), A.E.Alexander (director), M.Busby, F.Swift, L.Barnett, J.Bray, A.Bell (trainer). Sitting: F.Tilson, W.Dale, S.Cowan, A.H.Hughes (chairman), R.S.Marshall, A.Herd, J.McLuckie. On ground: E.Toseland, E.F.Brook.

Scottish international Jimmy McMullan, was already there. Eric Brook and Fred Tilson were signed from Barnsley, Bobby Marshall from Sunderland, Matt Busby from Denny Hibs, Ernie Toseland from Coventry City and Jackie Bray and Billy Dale from local football.

In 1933 City reached the first of two successive Cup Finals. Fred Tilson missed the first with a leg injury — City lost 3-0 to Everton — but was fit enough to score two goals against Portsmouth the following year. Both came in the last quarter of an hour after Portsmouth had taken a half-time lead, and so veteran City centre-half Sam Cowan was able to collect the FA Cup from King George V.

By this time Alec Herd had arrived from Hamilton Academical; Frank Swift from Fleetwood and Sam Barkas from Bradford City. On 19 February 1936, City paid a mammoth £10,000 for Irish international Peter Doherty, a scheming, scoring inside-forward who would go on to serve the club especially well.

The next season, 1936-7, City won the Championship. On Christmas Day it looked a wild dream — and was probably not even a thought of Wilf Wild, the secretary-manager. City had 20 points from 20 games and were halfway in the League.

But the last 22 matches brought 15 wins and seven draws. And it was done in style. There were two wonderful raiding wingers — the greyhound-like Toseland and the stocky Brook who packed a powerful shot in both feet — and an inside-forward trio of Herd, Tilson and Doherty who blended well. In the last 22 games Doherty scored 18 goals, Tilson 14, Brook 13 and Herd 11 as City swept aside the best teams in the country.

Incredibly, the next season they were relegated....but they did that in style too. They scored more goals than any other team in the First Division, twice hitting seven and twice scoring six in a game. But a late goal and a 1-0 defeat at Huddersfield meant they

Peter Doherty about to score past Arsenal's Frank Boulton to help City towards the 1936-7 League Championship.

City's 1936-7 Championship-winning team. Back row (left to right): W.Chorlton (trainer), Percival, Dale, Swift, Donnelly, Bray, Cassidy. Front row: Herd, Doherty, Marshall, Toseland, Tilson, Brook.

Frank Swift gets his finger-tips to the ball at Highbury in October 1937. George Hunt, transferred from Spurs a few hours earlier, is the Arsenal player overbalancing.

Don Revie receives the 1955 Footballer of the Year trophy from Duggie Livingstone, then manager of Newcastle.

finished next-to-bottom. Ever enigmatic, City used virtually the same players as during the Championship season. No-one could fully explain what had happened. 'Just one of those things,' as they say in football.

In the first post-war season there was another Second Division title to be won. Players had come and gone during the unpredictable wartime seasons, but on the resumption several players continued their careers at City — Frank Swift, Sam Barkas, Les McDowall, Alec Herd and Bert Sproston, who had signed from Spurs for £10,000 in November 1938.

From the earliest days, City had a knack of capturing headlines over the payment of large transfer fees. They created a British record of £450 when Johnny McMahon came from Preston in 1902 and the following year equalled the record with the signing of George Dorsett (West Brom). In 1904, Irvine Thornley almost became the first player to cost a club £1,000. City paid Glossop a basic fee of £450, but infringements of the rules cost them an FA fine of £250, an alleged bribe of £150 went astray, there was a signing-on fee and some advanced wages. The whole lot added up to a few pounds short of five figures.

The tradition of stretching finances, only to come unstuck with an erratic playing season or two, continued in the post-war period. The size of transfer fees escalated incredibly. The amounts City were prepared to pay since the war have been £12,000 (Roy Clarke from Cardiff City), £20,000 (Roy Paul from Swansea), £25,000 (Ivor Broadis from Sunderland and Don Revie from Hull), £55,000 (Denis Law from Huddersfield), £60,000 (Francis Lee from Bolton), £65,000 (Arthur Mann from Hearts), £200,000 (Rodney Marsh from QPR), £275,000 (Dennis Tueart and Dave Watson from Sunderland), £300,000 (Mike Channon from Southampton), £350,000 (Paul Futcher from Luton), £756,000 Mick Robinson from Preston) and over a million (Steve Daley from Wolves, Kevin Reeves from Norwich and Trevor Francis from Nottingham Forest).

The signings either created success or proved unsuccessful in the aftermath of it. In the mid-1950s manager Les McDowall steered City to two successive Cup Finals, with the help of the Revie-plan, a deep-lying centre-forward role modelled on Hungarian tactics. In the days when centre-halves automatically stuck close to centre-forwards, Revie, wearing 'number-nine', forced them to think again.

Although City lost 3-1 to Newcastle in the Wembley Final of 1955 — Jackie Milburn scored for the Magpies in the first minute and City were down to ten men for most of the game after an injury to Jimmy Meadows — there was elation the following year. Ken Barnes and Don Revie prompted the proceedings, Joe Hayes grabbed an early goal, Bobby Johnston put the game beyond doubt at 3-1 and Roy Paul carried away the Cup. The most dramatic news came afterwards. German-born goalkeeper Bert Trautmann had played through the final stages of the game unknowingly nursing a broken neck.

City's 1956 FA Cup-winning team. Back row (left to right): W.Griffiths (secretary), Messrs A.Douglas, R.Smith, W.Smith, F.R.Jolly, E.Gill (all directors). Middle row: L.H.Barnett (trainer), K.H.Barnes, W.E.Leivers, B.Trautmann, D.Ewing, R.Little, L.J.McDowall (manager). Front row: R.Johnstone, J.Hayes, R.Paul, D.Revie, J.Dyson, R.J.Clarke.

17

Alex Dawson sends Bert Trautmann the wrong way with a penalty at Deepdale in March 1964 during City's Second Division days.

That season, 1955-6, City finished fourth in the First Division, but the usual eccentricities were waiting to re-appear. They were grateful to avoid relegation the next season before climbing back to fifth place in 1957-8, one of their oddest-ever seasons. They were the first team to both concede and score over 100 League goals in a season.

McDowall's innovative tactics were partially responsible for the strange results. City won 5-2 at Everton and Blackpool; won 5-4 at Sheffield Wednesday; but went down 9-2 at West Brom and 8-4 at Leicester City.

The next season it was back to fighting relegation. Everything depended on the last match of the season. City beat Leicester 3-1 and were thankful for West Brom's 88th-minute equaliser against Aston Villa which sent Villa down and kept City up.

Despite the signing of Denis Law, City stayed a lower First Division team until 1962-3, when they were relegated along with Leyton Orient. Alex Harley's goals were not enough to keep them up.

City spent three seasons in the Second Division — an exceptionally long time compared with their previous stays — but it was the prelude to an era of the club's greatest achievements. George Poyser had taken City to a League Cup semi-final but they were an ordinary Second Division club when his period of management ended within two years of relegation. He was replaced by Joe Mercer, who brought Malcolm Allison to Maine Road as his assistant.

Captained by Johnny Crossan, City won the Second Division Championship for a record sixth time. Names shortly to become famous were to be found in the Championship-winning team: Harry Dowd; Bobby Kennedy, Cliff Sear, Mike Doyle, George Heslop, Alan Oakes, Mike Summerbee, Johnny Crossan, Glyn Pardoe, Neil Young and Dave Connor.

The addition of Colin Bell — £45,000 from Bury — Franny Lee, Tony Book, Tony Coleman, and goalkeeper Ken Mulhearn, turned this team into a First Division Championship team two years later.

The signing of Tony Book became one of the most romantic stories in post-war

18

football. Allison first signed Book when he took over as manager of Plymouth Argyle. Book was then almost 30, but two seasons later Allison persuaded Mercer that the full-back was good enough to jump from the Second to the First. But Book did more than that. He skippered Manchester City to the League Championship, the FA Cup, the League Cup and the European Cup-winners Cup — all inside four seasons. Later, he would return as manager during the club's 1970s success, taking them within a whisker of a third League Championship and bringing the League Cup to Maine Road again.

In 1968-9 City also won the Charity Shield — the second of three such successes. They beat West Brom 6-1, a record victory margin for Charity Shield games between League clubs, since equalled by Nottingham Forest.

After the League Championship success of 1967-8 City's extra-curriculum activity was phenomenal. In the next three seasons they played 12 FA Cup ties, 11 League Cup ties, 18 European Cup-winners' Cup ties, two European Cup ties and two Charity Shield games — tantamount to more than an extra League programme.

And some of those games were legendary struggles....a frustrating goalless draw with Turkey's Fenerbahce after Malcolm Allison had boasted City would terrorise Europe....Tommy Booth's last-minute FA Cup semi-final winner against Everton....Mike Summerbee following up Alex Stepney's parry to put City and not United into the League Cup Final....Tony Towers' breakthrough in the 209th and last minute of the two-legged European Cup-winners' Cup match against Académica of Coimbra....relying on away goals to put Linfield out of the competition....and four games in four different countries against Górnik Zabrze, the eventual 2-1 win in Vienna, away and home games in Poland and England before a play-off in Copenhagen settled the next season's tie.

Naturally there were casualties from this heavy programme. In 1970-71 City suffered so many injuries that at one time there were seven reserves in the team. The introduction of young players like Willie Donachie, Ian Mellor, Tony Towers and Derek Jeffries — plus an older one in Freddie Hill — gave City a shot at the Championship the following season. But, after the controversial signing of Rodney Marsh, City won only ten points from the last nine games. They missed the Championship by a point.

City with the League Championship trophy. Back row (left to right): Albert Alexander (chairman), Johnny Hart (trainer), G.Pardoe, A.Oaks, K.Mulhearn, M.Doyle, G.Heslop, M.Allison (coach), J.Mercer (manager). Front row: F.Lee, M.Summerbee, C.Bell, T.Book, T.Coleman, N.Young, D.Connor.

19

Joe Mercer shows the FA Cup to City's happy fans at Wembley in 1969.

Joe Mercer left, Malcolm Allison took over but soon gave way to Johnny Hart. Ron Saunders came briefly and took City to a League Cup Final — a late John Richards goal gave Wolves a 2-1 win — before more stability came with the appointment of Tony Book as manager.

For four seasons in the mid-1970s, City chased the Championship. The only trophy collected, however, was the League Cup in 1976, when Dennis Tueart's spectacular overhead kick sealed a 2-1 victory over Newcastle United. City did reach the last eight of the UEFA Cup in 1978-9, but by then the side was on the wane.

The 1970s style differed from that of the 1960s Mercer-Allison team. The build-up was more deliberate, the defence stronger, the goals fewer and therefore more crucial. But no expense was spared for Book to improve the forward-power — Asa Hartford, Joe Royle, Brian Kidd, Jimmy Conway, Paul Futcher, Mick Channon, Colin Viljoen. Yet one of the most pleasing things about the 1976 League Cup triumph was the number of local players in the team.

In 1976-7 City again missed the Championship by a point. Bolstered by two international central defenders, captain Mike Doyle and Dave Watson, City created a club record (for a 42-game season) by conceding only 34 goals, four of them in a vital end-of-season game at Derby County. Paul Power, Gary Owen and Dave Clements established themselves, and Peter Barnes was on the fringes. All four had been scouted without incurring a transfer fee.

Then came the slide. Malcolm Allison returned as team manager, Gary Owen and Peter Barnes went to West Brom, and the signings grew more costly and more perverse

20

Dave Watson leaves Newcastle United's Malcolm Macdonald stranded at Wembley in the 1976 League Cup Final.

Cup fortune failed to smile on City in 1981 when they lost to Tottenham after a replay. Here, Ricky Villa is about to score one of the best goals ever seen at Wembley.

— Kazimiera Deyna, Mick Robinson, Dragoslav Stepanovic, Steve Daley, Steve MacKenzie, Bobby Shinton, Stuart Lee, Barry Silkman, Kevin Reeves, Dennis Tueart (again), Paul Sugrue and so on. But after one very ordinary season which included a Cup exit at Fourth Division Halifax Town, Allison's City started the 1980-81 campaign without a win in the first 12 League games. Allison was dismissed.

The appointment of new manager John Bond was just what the witch-doctor ordered. The television cameras were already following City for a documentary, and Bond was never one to shun publicity. Media attention was attracted by a series of fascinating Cup draws — Allison's new team Crystal Palace, Bond's old team Norwich City, both easily beaten at Maine Road.

Bond's team reached League safety, progressed to the League Cup semi-final and then did Wembley proud in the centenary FA Cup Final. They came within ten minutes of beating Tottenham, Tommy Hutchison deflecting Glenn Hoddle's free-kick past Joe Corrigan after Hutchison himself had given City a first-half lead. The second game will be remembered for Steve MacKenzie's beautifully struck equaliser and Ricky Villa's mazy run and shot which gave Tottenham a 3-2 win.

The promise of Bond's new-look team continued into the 1981-2 season — after the 3-1 Boxing Day win at Liverpool, City were two points behind leaders Swansea — but not much further. The next season brought the end of a 17-year spell in the First Division, ending in a strange, silent anti-climax, when an 86th-minute goal from Radi Antic ensured Luton were safe with a 1-0 win at Maine Road. The goal sent City down by a point.

John Bond had left by now, replaced by John Benson until the end of the season. Billy McNeill came from Celtic to manage City out of the Second Division in two seasons. It was not glorious promotion like some of the past, but third place on goal difference. The sufferers were Portsmouth. Justice was done for the frustrating 8-0 win over Bradford City nearly 60 years earlier.

The 1986-7 season brought an end to the rise. In late-October, when Peter Swales and his directors boycotted Kenilworth Road in protest at Luton's ban on away-club supporters, a few wags suggested City's forwards might as well do the same. The 1-0 defeat meant not a goal had been scored in the first five away games of the season. . . and that was the problem.

In October, Trevor Christie went to Walsall and Imre Varadi came from West Brom — the first transfer action of new manager Jimmy Frizzell, promoted when Billy McNeill left for Aston Villa. McNeill's legacy was what he promised — more stability and dignity, and a First Division team (but not a particularly good one). Frizzell's appointment was the ninth managerial change at Maine Road in 15 years.

After Varadi's equaliser at Watford, McNab's penalty winner against Oxford and the return of Peter Barnes, there was some cause for optimism; City were seventh from bottom and the year was new. But there was not a win in the next 14 League games. Bottom of the division, the best to hope for was a play-off spot.

The signing of Paul Stewart — £200,000 from Blackpool — came too late to avert the goal crisis. The season's total of 36 goals equalled the lowest in the club's history, and a 2-0 defeat at West Ham on the last day of the season meant almost 16 months without an away win.

Ineveitably, relegation meant that there was yet another change of managerial control, although Jimmy Frizzell survived to become general manager. Into Maine Road came Mel Machin, the former Port Vale, Gillingham, Bournemouth and Norwich player, who had been coach at Carrow Road for several years. Machin became City's new team manager.

City began 1987-8 back in Division Two. There is less chance of big spending these days and perhaps the greatest hopes come from the fact that, in 1986, City won the FA Youth Cup for the first time. Young players like Paul Moulden and Paul Simpson impressed and it is with young heads that Manchester City's immediate future lies.

Gordon Davies (left) scored a hat-trick against Leeds in the opening match of the Full Members Cup. Mark Lillis (right) hit two in the Wembley Final.

City in the Football League 1892-93 to 1986-87

		HOME					AWAY						
	P	W	D	L	F	A	W	D	L	F	A	Pts	Pos

DIVISION TWO

	P	W	D	L	F	A	W	D	L	F	A	Pts	Pos
1892-93	22	6	3	2	27	14	3	0	8	18	26	21	5th
1893-94	28	6	1	7	32	20	2	1	11	15	51	18	13th
1894-95	30	9	3	3	56	28	5	0	10	26	44	31	9th
1895-96	30	12	3	0	37	9	9	1	5	26	29	46	2nd
1896-97	30	10	3	2	39	15	2	5	8	19	35	32	6th
1897-98	30	10	4	1	45	15	5	5	5	21	21	39	3rd
1898-99	34	15	1	1	64	10	8	5	4	28	25	52	1st

DIVISION ONE

	P	W	D	L	F	A	W	D	L	F	A	Pts	Pos
1899-1900	34	10	3	4	33	15	3	5	9	17	29	34	7th
1900-01	34	12	3	2	32	16	1	3	13	16	42	32	11th
1901-02	34	10	3	4	28	17	1	3	13	14	41	28	18th

DIVISION TWO

	P	W	D	L	F	A	W	D	L	F	A	Pts	Pos
1902-03	34	15	1	1	64	15	10	3	4	31	14	54	1st

DIVISION ONE

	P	W	D	L	F	A	W	D	L	F	A	Pts	Pos
1903-04	34	10	4	3	35	19	9	2	6	36	26	44	2nd
1904-05	34	14	3	0	46	17	6	3	8	20	20	46	3rd
1905-06	38	11	2	6	46	23	8	3	8	27	31	43	5th
1906-07	38	7	7	5	29	25	3	5	11	24	52	32	17th
1907-08	38	12	5	2	36	19	4	6	9	26	35	43	3rd
1908-09	38	12	3	4	50	23	3	1	15	17	46	34	19th

DIVISION TWO

	P	W	D	L	F	A	W	D	L	F	A	Pts	Pos
1909-10	38	15	2	2	51	17	8	6	5	30	23	54	1st

DIVISION ONE

	P	W	D	L	F	A	W	D	L	F	A	Pts	Pos
1910-11	38	7	5	7	26	26	2	8	9	17	32	31	17th
1911-12	38	10	5	4	39	20	3	4	12	17	38	35	15th
1912-13	38	12	3	4	34	15	6	5	8	19	22	44	6th
1913-14	38	9	3	7	28	23	5	5	9	23	30	36	13th
1914-15	38	9	7	3	29	15	6	6	7	20	24	43	5th
1919-20	42	14	5	2	52	27	4	4	13	19	35	45	7th
1920-21	42	19	2	0	50	13	5	4	12	20	37	54	2nd
1921-22	42	13	7	1	44	21	5	2	14	21	49	45	10th
1922-23	42	14	6	1	38	16	3	5	13	12	33	45	8th
1923-24	42	11	7	3	34	24	4	5	12	20	47	42	11th
1924-25	42	11	7	3	44	29	6	2	13	32	39	43	10th
1925-26	42	8	7	6	48	42	4	4	13	41	58	35	21st

DIVISION TWO

	P	W	D	L	F	A	W	D	L	F	A	Pts	Pos
1926-27	42	15	3	3	65	23	7	7	7	43	38	54	3rd
1927-28	42	18	2	1	70	27	7	7	7	30	32	59	1st

DIVISION ONE

	P	W	D	L	F	A	W	D	L	F	A	Pts	Pos
1928-29	42	12	3	6	63	40	6	6	9	32	46	45	8th
1929-30	42	12	5	4	51	33	7	4	10	40	48	47	3rd
1930-31	42	13	2	6	41	29	5	8	8	34	41	46	8th
1931-32	42	10	5	6	49	30	3	7	11	34	43	38	14th
1932-33	42	12	3	6	47	30	4	2	15	21	41	37	16th
1933-34	42	14	4	3	50	29	3	7	11	15	43	45	5th
1934-35	42	13	5	3	53	25	7	3	11	29	42	48	4th
1935-36	42	13	2	6	44	17	4	6	11	24	43	42	9th
1936-37	42	15	5	1	56	22	7	8	6	51	39	57	1st
1937-38	42	12	2	7	49	33	2	6	13	31	44	36	21st

DIVISION TWO

Season	P	W	D	L	F	A	W	D	L	F	A	Pts	
1938-39	42	13	3	5	56	35	8	4	9	40	37	49	5th
1939-40	3	1	1	0	3	1	0	0	1	3	4	3	-
1946-47	42	17	3	1	49	14	9	7	5	29	21	62	1st

DIVISION ONE

Season	P	W	D	L	F	A	W	D	L	F	A	Pts	
1947-48	42	13	3	5	37	22	2	9	10	15	25	42	10th
1948-49	42	10	8	3	28	21	5	7	9	19	30	45	7th
1949-50	42	7	8	6	27	24	1	5	15	9	44	29	21st

DIVISION TWO

Season	P	W	D	L	F	A	W	D	L	F	A	Pts	
1950-51	42	12	6	3	53	25	7	8	6	36	36	52	2nd

DIVISION ONE

Season	P	W	D	L	F	A	W	D	L	F	A	Pts	
1951-52	42	7	5	9	29	28	6	8	7	29	33	39	15th
1952-53	42	12	2	7	45	28	2	5	14	27	59	35	20th
1953-54	42	10	4	7	35	31	4	5	12	27	46	37	17th
1954-55	42	11	5	5	45	36	7	5	9	31	33	46	7th
1955-56	42	11	5	5	40	27	7	5	9	42	42	46	4th
1956-57	42	10	2	9	48	42	3	7	11	30	46	35	18th
1957-58	42	14	4	3	58	33	8	1	12	46	67	49	5th
1958-59	42	8	7	6	40	32	3	2	16	24	63	31	20th
1959-60	42	11	2	8	47	34	6	1	14	31	50	37	15th
1960-61	42	10	5	6	41	30	3	6	12	38	60	37	13th
1961-62	42	11	3	7	46	38	6	4	11	32	43	41	12th
1962-63	42	7	5	9	30	45	3	6	12	28	57	31	21st

DIVISION TWO

Season	P	W	D	L	F	A	W	D	L	F	A	Pts	
1963-64	42	12	4	5	50	27	6	6	9	34	39	46	6th
1964-65	42	12	3	6	40	24	4	6	11	23	38	41	11th
1965-66	42	14	7	0	40	14	8	8	5	36	30	59	1st

DIVISION ONE

Season	P	W	D	L	F	A	W	D	L	F	A	Pts	
1966-67	42	8	9	4	27	25	4	6	11	16	27	39	15th
1967-68	42	17	2	2	52	16	9	4	8	34	27	58	1st
1968-69	42	13	6	2	49	20	2	4	15	15	35	40	13th
1969-70	42	8	6	7	25	22	8	5	8	30	26	43	10th
1970-71	42	7	9	5	30	22	5	8	8	17	20	41	11th
1971-72	42	16	3	2	48	15	7	8	6	29	30	57	4th
1972-73	42	12	4	5	36	20	3	7	11	21	40	41	11th
1973-74	42	10	7	4	25	17	4	5	12	14	29	40	14th
1974-75	42	16	3	2	40	15	2	7	12	14	39	46	8th
1975-76	42	14	5	2	46	18	2	6	13	18	28	43	8th
1976-77	42	15	5	1	38	13	6	9	6	22	21	56	2nd
1977-78	42	14	4	3	46	21	6	8	7	28	30	52	4th
1978-79	42	9	5	7	34	28	4	8	9	24	28	39	15th
1979-80	42	8	8	5	28	25	4	5	12	15	41	37	17th
1980-81	42	10	7	4	35	25	4	4	13	21	34	39	12th
1981-82	42	9	7	5	32	23	6	6	9	17	27	58	10th
1982-83	42	9	5	7	26	23	4	3	14	21	47	47	20th

DIVISION TWO

Season	P	W	D	L	F	A	W	D	L	F	A	Pts	
1983-84	42	13	3	5	43	21	7	7	7	23	27	70	4th
1984-85	42	14	4	3	42	16	7	7	7	24	24	74	3th

DIVISION ONE

Season	P	W	D	L	F	A	W	D	L	F	A	Pts	
1985-86	42	7	7	7	25	26	4	5	12	18	31	45	15th
1986-87	42	8	6	7	28	24	0	9	12	8	33	39	21st

Summary

	P	W	D	L	F	A	W	D	L	F	A	Pts
Division 1 (65 seasons)	2654	723	309	295	2530	1602	289	335	703	1579	2487	2725
Division 2 (19 seasons)	696	238	59	51	963	369	122	93	133	532	590	913
TOTAL	3350	961	368	346	3493	1971	411	428	836	2111	3077	3638

1891-92

1	Sep 12	(h)	Bootle	D 3-3	Whittle, Davies, Morris	6,000
2	19	(a)	Lincoln C	L 0-3		2,000
3	26	(h)	Burton S	W 1-0	Morris	6,000
4	Oct 10	(a)	Newton Heath	L 1-3	Davies	4,000
5	17	(h)	Birmingham St G	W 4-3	McWhinnie, Bogie (2), Morris	6,000
6	Nov 7	(h)	Walsall Town S	W 6-0	Morris (3),Milne, Milarvie, Bogie	4,500
7	14	(h)	Nottingham F	L 1-3	Morris	11,000
8	19	(a)	Nottingham F	L 0-4		2,000
9	21	(a)	Burton S	D 4-4	Bogie (3), Milarvie	2,000
10	28	(h)	Lincoln C	L 2-3	McWhinnie, Davies	12,000
11	Dec 5	(h)	Sheffield W	L 0-4		5,000
12	19	(h)	Newton Heath	D 2-2	Milne (2),	10,000
13	25	(h)	Grimsby T	W 3-1	Milarvie (2), Morris	6,000
14	26	(a)	Sheffield W	L 0-2		7,000
15	Jan 2	(h)	Small Heath	D 2-2	Morris (2)	4,000
16	23	(a)	Bootle	L 1-2	Parry	3,000
17	30	(a)	Grimsby T	L 0-4		3,000
18	Feb 20	(a)	Small Heath	L 0-4		2,000
19	Mar 1	(h)	Crewe Alex	W 4-0	Milne, Davies (2), Weir	5,000
20	5	(a)	Birmingham St G	W 1-0	Milne	2,000
21	26	(a)	Walsall Town S	D 2-2	Davies, Weir	2,000
22	Apr 6	(a)	Crewe Alex	D 2-2	Davies, Angus	2,000
						Appearances
						Goals

Football Alliance record: P 22 W 6 D 6 L 10 F 39 A 51 Pts 18 Pos 12th

FA Cup

QR1 Oct 3 (a) Newton Heath   L 1-5

Lancashire Senior Cup

R1 Feb 10 (a) Accrington   L 0-6

Manchester Senior Cup

R1	Feb 13	(a)	Heywood Central	W 3-1
SF	Mar 12	(h)	Fairfield	W 4-0
F	Apr 23	(a)	Bolton W	W 4-1

Friendlies

1	Sep 1	(h)	West Manchester	D 2-2
2	5	(h)	Gainsborough T	W 2-1
3	7	(h)	Rossendale	L 1-4
4	21	(h)	Denton	W 3-1
5	28	(h)	Blackburn R	D 1-1
6	Oct 5	(a)	Denton	W 2-0
7	8	(a)	West Manchester	W 3-0
8	24	(h)	Sunderland A	W 2-1
9	31	(h)	Stoke	W 5-2
10	Nov 2	(a)	Chirk	W 3-2
11	Dec 12	(h)	Canadian XI	W 3-1
12	16	(h)	Old Reptonians	W 1-0
13	28	(h)	Sunderland	D 0-0

Friendlies (continued)

14	Jan 1	(h)	West Brom A	W 4-2
15	4	(h)	Airdrieonians	L 1-2
16	9	(h)	Bolton W	L 0-3
17	16	(h)	Heywood Central	W 4-0
18	Feb 6	(h)	Fairfield	W 8-1
19	27	(h)	Blackpool	W 4-0
20	Mar 2	(h)	Heywood Central	D 2-2
21	16	(h)	Third Lanark	D 1-1
22	19	(h)	Preston N E	D 2-2
23	Apr 9	(h)	Inter D'Weirsfifit	D 2-2
24	12	(h)	Gorton Villa	L 1-2
25	15	(h)	Sheffield W	D 0-0
26	16	(h)	Renton	W 5-1
27	18	(h)	Notts C	W 3-1
28	26	(h)	Everton	D 1-1
29	30	(h)	Stoke	W 5-1
30	May 1	(h)	Accrington	D 3-3

Douglas	Ferguson	Weir	Cooke	Robson	Milne	Pearson	Jackson	Whittle	Davidson	Parry	Hopkins	Davies	McWhinnie	Morris	Bogie	Milarvie	Sharpe	Middleton	McVickers	Angus	Powery	Neil	Robinson	Baker	Jones	
1	2	9	3	4				5	6			7	8	10		11										1
1	2	9	3		4			5	6			7	8	11		10										2
1	2		3	10	4			5	6			7	8	9		11										3
1		2	3	9	4			5	6			7		8		11				10						4
1		2	3	5			4		6			7	8	10	9	11										5
1		2	3	8			4	5	6			7		10	9	11										6
1		2	3				4	5	6			7	8	10	9								11			7
1		2	3				4	5	6			7	8	11	9	10										8
1		2	3	5			4		6			7	10	8	9	11										9
1		5	3	6		2	4					7	8	10	9	11										10
1		2	3				4	5	6			7	8	8	9	11										11
1		2	3	9	4			5	6			7		8		11	10									12
1		2	3	4	6			5				7		8	9	11	10									13
1		2	3	9	4			5	6			10		11		7	8									14
1	4	2	3	6				5				7	10	8	9	11										15
1	10	2	3	6	4			5		9		7		8			11									16
1	4	2	3	6				5		9		7		8	10		11									17
1	9	2		4				5	6			7		10	8	11								3		18
1	8	2	3	4				5	6			7		9	10	11										19
1	8	2		6							3	7	11	9		10	5							4		20
1	8			6				5			4	7		10		11		3	2						9	21
1	7		3	4					6				8	9		11				5	2	10				22
22	3	18	9	19	18	4	10	16	5	11	5	22	11	22	11	19	7	2	2	1	1	1	1	1	1	
		2		5			1			1		7	2	10	6	4				1						

1892-93

1	Sep	3	(h)	Bootle	W 7-0	Morris (2), Davies (3), Weir, Angus	4,000
2		10	(a)	Northwich V	W 3-0	Russell (2), Morris	3,000
3		12	(h)	Burslem Port V	W 2-0	Angus, Weir	2,000
4		17	(a)	Walsall Town S	W 4-2	Davies (2), Angus, Lambie	1,000
5		24	(h)	Northwich V	D 1-1	Middleton	2,000
6	Oct	1	(h)	Walsall Town S	W 2-0	Davies, Weir	4,000
7		8	(a)	Darwen	L 1-3	Davies	5,000
8		10	(a)	Burslem Port V	W 2-1	Weir (2)	1,000
9		22	(h)	Small Heath	D 2-2	Weir, Morris	6,000
10	Nov	5	(a)	Grimsby T	L 0-2		2,000
11		26	(h)	Burton S	D 1-1	Russell	3,000
12	Dec	17	(h)	Darwen	W 4-2	Weir (2), Mooney, Milarvie	6,000
13		24	(a)	Lincoln C	L 1-2	Forrester	1,000
14	Jan	14	(a)	Burton S	L 0-2		1,000
15		21	(a)	Bootle	L 3-5	Mooney (2), Middleton	800
16		30	(h)	Grimsby T	L 0-3		1,000
17	Feb	14	(a)	Crewe Alex	L 1-4	Yates	1,000
18		18	(h)	Crewe Alex	W 3-1	Yates, Bowman, Milarvie	3,000
19	Mar	4	(h)	Sheffield U	L 2-3	Whittle, Bowman	2,000
20		25	(a)	Sheffield U	L 1-2	Yates	700
21	Apr	1	(a)	Small Heath	L 2-3	Yates, Carson	800
22		17	(h)	Lincoln C	W 3-1	Yates, Mooney, Morris	2,000

Appearances
Goals

League Division Two record: P 22   W 9   D 3   L 10   F 45   A 40   Pts 21   Pos 5th

FA Cup

QR	Sep	22	(a)	Fleetwood R	D 1-1
R	Oct	5	(h)	Fleetwood R	L 0-2

Lancashire Senior Cup

R1	Jan	28	(h)	Rossendale	W 3-2
R2	Mar	11	(h)	Blackpool	W 3-1
SF	Apr	8	(a)	Bolton W	L 1-5

Manchester Senior Cup

R1	Feb	25	(a)	Bury	L 0-3

Friendlies

1	Sep	1	(h)	Nottingham F	D 2-2
2		28	(a)	Middlesbrough I	L 2-3
3	Oct	15	(h)	West Manchester	L 2-3
4		29	(h)	Middlesbrough	W 6-3
5	Nov	12	(h)	Bolton W	W 3-0
6		19	(a)	Middlesbrough	L 3-6
7	Dec	3	(h)	Notts C	D 3-3
8		10	(h)	Stoke	L 2-6
9		26	(h)	Glasgow Celtic	L 0-5
10		31	(h)	Glasgow Thistle	L 0-1
11	Jan	2	(h)	Newton Heath	L 3-5
12		7	(h)	South Shore	W 5-1
13		11	(h)	International XI	L 0-5

Friendlies (continued)

14	Feb	11	(h)	Middlesbrough I	L 1-3
15		14	(h)	Blackpool	L 2-7
16	Mar	18	(a)	Fairfield	W 2-1
17		20	(h)	Rotherham T	D 2-2
18		27	(a)	Newton Heath	L 2-3
19	Apr	3	(a)	Blackpool	L 1-6
20		10	(a)	Newton Heath	L 1-2
21		20	(h)	Gorton Villa	D 1-1
22		22	(h)	Northwich V	W 1-0
23		24	(a)	Rotherham T	L 0-1
24		29	(h)	Newton Heath	W 3-0

Appearance and scoring grid (numbers denote playing positions by match; match numbers 1–22 shown at right).

Match	Douglas	McVickers	Robson	Middleton	Russell	Hopkins	Davies	Morris	Whittle	Milne	Weir	Angus J.	Mooney	Milarvie	Yates	Forrester	Steele	Carson	Lambie	Bowman	Angus H.	Stones	Turner	Armitt
1	1	2	3	4	5	6	7	8		10	9			11										
2	1	2	3	4	5	6	7	8		10	9			11										
3	1	2	3	4	5	6	7	8		10	9			11										
4	1	2	3	4	5	6	7	8			9			11				10						
5	1	2	3	4	5	6		7		8	9			11				10						
6	1	2	3	4	5		7	8	6	10	9			11										
7	1	2	3	4	5	6	7	8		10	9			11										
8	1	2	3	4	5	6	7	8		9	10			11										
9	1	2	3		5	6	7	8	4	10								9	11					
10	1	2	3	4	5	6	7	8		10	9			11										
11	1	2	3	4	5	6	7	10			9			11			8							
12	1	2	3	4	5	6	7	8			9		10	11										
13	1	2	3	4	5	6		7			9		10	11			8							
14	1		3	4	5	2	8		6	7	9		10	11										
15	1		3	4	5	2	10		6	11	7		9	8										
16	1		3	4	9	6	5			10	11	7	8									2		
17	1		3	2	5		6	4		10	11	7	8									9		
18	1		3	4		2	8	6	9					11	7		5			10				
19	1	2	3	4		6	8	5						10	7					9		11		
20		2	3	4		6	8	5						11	7			9	10		1			
21	1	2	3	4		6	8	5						11	7			9	10					
22		2	3	4		6	8	5					9	11	7				10		1			
Apps	20	17	22	21	17	20	12	19	9	8	14	7	9	17	8	4	4	3	3	2	2	2	1	1
Goals		2	3		7	5	1				8	3	4	2	5	1		1	1	2				

29

1893-94

1	Sep	2	(a)	Burslem Port V	L 2-4	Carson, Robinson	3,000
2		9	(h)	Middlesbrough I	W 6-1	Morris (2), Bowman, Carson, Robinson, Jones	4,000
3		11	(h)	Burton S	L 1-4	Morris	1,000
4		16	(h)	Liverpool	L 0-1		6,000
5		20	(a)	Burton S	L 0-5		3,000
6		23	(a)	Middlesbrough I	L 0-2		1,500
7		30	(h)	Small Heath	L 0-1		5,000
8	Oct	7	(h)	Burslem Port V	W 8-1	Morris (3), Milarvie, Steele, Middleton, Yates, opp.og	4,000
9		21	(h)	Newton Heath	L 2-3	Yates, Morris	3,000
10		28	(h)	Notts C	D 0-0		4,000
11	Nov	11	(a)	W Arsenal	L 0-1		4,500
12		18	(h)	Walsall Town S	W 3-0	Yates (2), Robertson	3,000
13	Dec	2	(a)	Liverpool	L 0-3		4,000
14		9	(h)	Grimsby T	W 4-1	Davies, Bennett, Whittle, Middleton	4,000
15		26	(h)	Rotherham T	W 3-2	Pickford (2), Bennett	4,000
16		30	(h)	W Arsenal	L 0-1		4,000
17	Jan	6	(a)	Newcastle U	L 1-2	Pickford	800
18		13	(h)	Grimsby T	L 0-5		1,000
19		27	(h)	Northwich V	W 4-2	Bennett (2), Whittle, Dyer	3,000
20	Feb	10	(a)	Northwich V	W 4-1	Milarvie (2), Robertson, Milne	2,000
21		24	(a)	Crewe Alex	D 1-1	Bennett	1,000
22	Mar	15	(a)	Notts C	L 0-5		2,500
23		17	(a)	Small Heath	L 2-10	Bennett, Robertson	2,000
24		24	(a)	Lincoln C	L 0-6		1,000
25		26	(h)	Rotherham T	W 3-1	Baker, Milne, Milarvie	2,000
26		31	(h)	Lincoln C	L 0-1		3,000
27	Apr	7	(h)	Crewe Alex	L 1-2	Spittle	2,500
28		14	(a)	Walsall Town S	L 2-5	Milne, Forrester	2,000

Appearances
Goals

League Division Two record P 28 W 8 D 2 L 18 F 47 A 71 Pos 18 Pos 13th

FA Cup

QR Oct 14 (a) West Manchester L 0-3

Lancashire Senior Cup

1 Jan 20 Rossendale   L 2-4

Manchester Senior Cup

1 Feb 3 (h) Bury   L 3-6

Friendlies

1	Sep	4	(h)	Bolton W	L 0-5
2		12	(h)	Darwen	L 0-7
3		18	(a)	Stoke	L 0-4
4		25	(h)	Darwen	L 2-5
5	Oct	16	(h)	Everton	L 2-3
6	Nov	4	(h)	Fairfield	D 1-1
7		6	(h)	Stoke	W 6-3
8		25	(h)	Derby C	W 2-1
9	Dec	23	(h)	Liverpool	L 2-6
10		25	(a)	Newton Heath	L 1-2
11	Jan	1	(h)	Wolves	L 1-2
12		2	(h)	West Manchester	W 1-0
13	Feb	17	(h)	Stockport C	W 3-0

Friendlies (continued)

14	Apr	9	(h)	Newton Heath	L 1-2
15		18	(h)	Sheffield U	L 0-2
16		28	(a)	Stockport C	D 0-0

Player appearances / team sheet grid. Columns are players (left → right); each numbered row is a match, and cell values are the shirt numbers worn. Match number is shown in the right-hand column.

Match	Douglas	Stones	Steele	Dyer	McVickers	Robson	Middleton	Bowman	Whittle	Hopkins	Regan	Yates	Pickford	Morris	Bennett	Robinson	Milarvie	Milne	Hargreaves	Egan	Robertson	Saddington	Forrester	Carson	Willey	Davies	McDowell	Baker	Hughes	Jones	Stenson	O'Brien	Caine
1	1		2	3	4	5		6			7			8	10	11								9									
2	1		2	3	4	5		6			7			9	10							11							8				
3	1		2	3	4	5		6			7			9	10							11							8				
4	1	2		3	4		8	5			6	7					11				10			9									
5	1	2	6	3	4		9	5				7					11						8	10									
6	1	2	4	3			8	5			6	7					11							9								10	
7	1	2		3	4		6	5				7	8	9							11											10	
8	1	9	4	2	3		8		5		6	7		10			11																
9	1		6	2	3		10		5	9	7		8				11																
10	1			2	3	4	9		5		6	7		8	10		11																
11	1	9		2	3	4			5		6	7		8			11									10							
12		1		2	3	4			5		6	7		8			11			9						10							
13	1			2	3	4			5		6		8				11		9				7			10							
14	1			2	3	4			5		6	7	8				11		9							10							
15			1	10	2	3	4		5		6	7	8					11	9														
16	1		10	2	3		4		5		6	7	8				11		9														
17	1		2			3	4	5			6	7	8				11		10	9													
18	1		3				2	5			4	7	8				11	6	10						9								
19		1	2	3				4	5		6	7			8		11			9													
20		1	2	3				4	5		6			7			10	8	11	9													
21		1	2	3				4			6			7			10	5	11	9													
22		1	2	3					5		6			7			10	8	11				4	9									
23		1	2	3				4	5		6			7				8	10		9	11											
24		1		3				4	5		6				8			7	10		9	11										2	
25		1		3					5		6						10	8	11		7			9			2	4					
26		1		4					5	9	3						10	8			7						2	6	11				
27		1		3					4	5							10	7			9						2	6	11				
28			1		3				4	5				7			10	8	11					9							6		
Apps	16	10	13	21	9	17	15	21	21	3	21	12	8	9	12	4	22	10	8	7	7	6	6	6	1	4	4	3	2	2	2	2	
Goals		1	1		2	1	2				4	3	7	6	2	4	3			3		1	2		1		1		1				

*Note: In Match 21, Manchester City played with only 10 men after Whittle and a reserve missed their train.

Match 9 – Caine played 4.

Match 19 – Edge played 10.

Match 27 – Spittle played 8 (and scored 1 goal)

1894-95

1	Sep	1	(a)	Bury	L 2-4	Calvey, Little	7,000
2		3	(h)	Burton W	D 1-1	Little	2,500
3		8	(h)	Burslem Port V	W 4-1	Calvey (2), Mann, Finnerhan	4,000
4		15	(a)	Walsall Town S	W 2-1	Finnerhan, Rowan	4,000
5		22	(h)	Grimsby T	L 2-5	Wallace, Little	5,000
6		29	(a)	W Arsenal	L 2-4	Dyer, Rowan	5,000
7	Oct	1	(a)	Rotherham T	L 2-3	Calvey (2)	1,500
8		6	(h)	Walsall Town S	W 6-1	Sharples (3), Finnerhan, Rowan, Nash	3,000
9		13	(a)	Notts C	W 3-1	Sharples, Finnerhan, Rowan	3,000
10		20	(h)	Darwen	L 2-4	Sharples, Tompkinson	6,000
11		27	(a)	Newcastle U	L 4-5	Sharples (2), Finnerhan, McReddie	2,000
12	Nov	3	(h)	Newton Heath	L 2-5	Meredith (2)	14,000
13		10	(a)	Burton S	L 1-2	Finnerhan	2,000
14	Dec	8	(h)	Bury	D 3-3	McReddie, Rowan, Milarvie	10,000
15		15	(h)	W Arsenal	W 4-1	Meredith (2), McBride, opp.og	5,000
16		26	(a)	Burton W	L 0-8		4,000
17		31	(a)	Crewe Alex	W 3-2	Meredith (2), Finnerhan	450
18	Jan	1	(h)	Rotherham T	W 1-0	Rowan	4,000
19		5	(a)	Newton Heath	L 1-4	Sharples	12,000
20	Feb	2	(a)	Burslem Port V	W 2-1	Finnerhan, McReddie	1,500
21		9	(h)	Newcastle U	W 4-0	Finnerhan (2), Meredith, Rowan	8,000
22	Mar	2	(a)	Lincoln C	W 2-0	Rowan (2)	5,000
23		9	(h)	Notts C	W 7-1	Finnerhan (2), Rowan, McReddie, Sharples, Meredith, Walker	7,000
24		16	(a)	Leicester F	L 1-3	Sharples	4,000
25		23	(h)	Lincoln C	W 11-3	McReddie (4), Finnerhan (2), Meredith (2), Rowan (2), Milarvie	2,000
26		30	(h)	Leicester F	D 1-1	McReddie	4,000
27	Apr	6	(a)	Darwen	L 0-4		2,000
28		12	(h)	Crewe Alex	W 4-1	Meredith, Finnerhan, Sharples, Dyer	4,000
29		13	(h)	Burton S	W 4-1	Meredith, Sharples, Mann, opp.og	4,000
30		20	(a)	Grimsby T	L 1-2	Milarvie	6,000

Appearances
Goals

League Division Two record: P 30   W 14   D 3   L 13   F 82   A 72   Pts 31   Pos 9th

FA Cup

Did not enter.

Lancashire Senior Cup

| 1 | Jan 29 (a) | Nelson | W 2-1 |
| 2 | Feb 9 (a) | Preston N E | L 0-7 |

Manchester Senior Cup

1	Jan 26 (a)	West Manchester	W 4-0
SF	Feb 23 (h)	Bolton W	D 2-2
SFR	Mar 6 (a)	Bolton W	L 1-2

Friendlies

1	Sep 12 (h)	Burnley	L 0-1
2	17 (a)	Stoke	L 1-5
3	26 (h)	Bolton W	L 2-3
4	Oct 15 (h)	Stoke	L 1-4
5	Nov 17 (h)	Heanor T	W 8-2
6	24 (a)	West Manchester	W 3-0
7	Dec 1 (h)	Glasgow Celtic	D 0-0
8	25 (h)	West Manchester	W 5-2

Friendlies (continued)

9	Dec 29 (h)	Fleetwood R	W 1-0
10	Jan 12 (h)	Small Heath	W 2-1
11	Feb 16 (h)	City Comb XI	W 2-0
12	Apr 15 (a)	Millwall	W 1-0
13	17 (h)	Preston N E	L 1-2
14	23 (h)	Everton	W 9-0
15	27 (h)	Fairfield	L 2-3

Williams	Smith	Walker	Dyer	Robson	Mann	Jones	Bowman	Nash	McBride	Meredith	Finnerhan	Rowan	Sharples	McReddie	Wallace	Milarvie	Calvey	Hutchinson	Little	Tompkinson	Ferguson	
1	2	3		4	5		6		8		10	7		9					11			1
1	2	3		4	5		6		8		10	7		9					11			2
1	2	3		4	5		6		8	7	10			9					11			3
1	2			4	5		6		8	9	10	7							11		3	4
1			5	4	6				8	9	10	7		2					11		3	5
	2	3		4	5		6		8	9	10	7						1	11			6
	2			4	5		6	3	8	9	10	7						1	11			7
	2	3		4	5		6		8	9	10						11	1		7		8
	2	3		4	5		6		8	9	10						11	1		7		9
	2	3		4		5	6		8	9	10						11	1		7		10
	2	3	6	4	5	7			8	9	10						11	1				11
	2	3	6	4	5	7			8	9	10						11	1				12
1	2	3		4	6		9	8	5		10						11			7		13
1	4	2	3	5	6	7			8	9	10						11					14
1	4	2	3	5	6	7			8	9	10					11						15
1	2	3	5	4	6	7			8	9	10					11						16
1	4	2	3	5	6	7			8	9	10					11						17
1	4	2	3	5	6	7			8	9	10					11						18
1	4	2	3	5	6	7			8	9	10					11						19
1	2	3	6	5	4				8	9	10					11				7		20
1	4	2	3	5	6	7			8	9	10					11						21
1	2	3	4	5	6	7			8	9	10					11						22
1	4	2	3	5	6	7			8	9	10					11						23
1	4	2	3	5	6				8	9	10					11				7		24
1	2	3	5	4	6	7			8	9	10				11							25
1	2	3	9	5	4	6	7	8			10				11							26
1	2	3	5	4	6	7	8				10			9	11							27
1	2	3	4	5	6	7			8	9	10	11										28
1	2	3	4	5	6	7			8		10	11		9								29
1	2	3	4	5	6	7			8		10	11		9								30
23	18	19	12	17	18	18	10	17	17	18	30	24	24	20	6	10	7	7	7	6	2	
		1	2		2			1	1	12	15	12	12	9	1	3	5		3	1		

1895-96

1	Sep	7	(a)	W Arsenal	W 1-0	Meredith	8,000
2		9	(h)	Rotherham T	W 2-0	Clifford, Little	3,000
3		14	(h)	Leicester F	W 2-0	Finnerhan, Rowan	9,000
4		21	(a)	Grimsby T	L 0-5		3,000
5		28	(h)	W Arsenal	W 1-0	Sharples	9,000
6	Oct	5	(a)	Newton Heath	D 1-1	Rowan	10,000
7		12	(h)	Darwen	W 4-1	Rowan (2), Sharples, Chapman	10,000
8		19	(a)	Crewe Alex	W 2-0	Meredith, Finnerhan	3,000
9		26	(h)	Grimsby T	W 2-1	Rowan, Little	14,000
10	Nov	2	(a)	Darwen	W 3-2	Meredith, Finnerhan, McReddie	4,000
11		4	(a)	Rotherham T	W 3-2	McReddie (2), Rowan	5,000
12		16	(a)	Burton W	L 1-4	Meredith	3,000
13		23	(h)	Burton W	D 1-1	Meredith	12,000
14		30	(a)	Burton S	W 4-1	Rowan (2), Morris (2)	3,000
15	Dec	7	(h)	Newton Heath	W 2-1	Meredith, Hill	20,000
16	Jan	1	(a)	Liverpool	L 1-3	Rowan	15,000
17		4	(h)	Newcastle U	W 5-2	Morris (2), Hill (2), Finnerhan	10,000
18		11	(a)	Lincoln C	W 2-1	Chapman, Meredith	2,000
19	Feb	1	(a)	Loughborough T	W 4-2	Finnerhan (2), Davies, Hill	2,000
20		10	(a)	Burslem Port V	W 1-0	Davies	3,000
21		15	(h)	Crewe Alex	W 4-0	Rowan (2), Meredith, Finnerhan	4,000
22		17	(h)	Burslem Port V	W 1-0	Finnerhan	3,000
23		24	(h)	Loughborough T	W 5-1	Morris (2), Davies, Meredith, Chapman	2,000
24		29	(a)	Notts C	L 0-3		4,000
25	Mar	7	(h)	Burton S	D 1-1	Robertson	9,000
26		14	(h)	Lincoln C	W 4-0	Robertson, Meredith, Morris, Finnerhan	9,000
27		21	(a)	Newcastle U	L 1-4	Davies	12,000
28	Apr	3	(h)	Liverpool	D 1-1	Morris	30,000
29		4	(a)	Leicester F	W 2-1	Meredith, Robson	4,000
30		8	(h)	Notts C	W 2-0	Meredith, Morris	6,000

Appearances
Goals

League Division Two record: P 30   W21   D 4   L 5   F 63   A 38   Pts 46 Pos 2nd

FA Cup

Q Oct 12 (h) Oswaldtwistle R (scr)

Lancashire Senior Cup

1	Jan 18	(h)	Preston N E	W 2-1
2	Feb 8	(h)	Blackburn R	L 1-2

Manchester Senior Cup

1	Jan 25	(h)	Bolton W	W 1-0
SF	Feb 22	(a)	Fairfield	W*2-1
SFR	Mar 10	(a)	Fairfield	D 2-2
SFR	16	(a)	Fairfield	D 2-2
SFR	28	(a)	Fairfield	W 4-0
F	Apr 11	(a)	Bury	L 1-2

*City used ineligible player and
the game was replayed.

Friendlies

1	Sep	2	(h)	Glasgow Celtic	W 3-2
2		3	(a)	Bury	W 3-1
3		4	(a)	Sherton	W 3-1
4	Nov	5	(h)	Bury	L 2-5
5		9	(h)	Chirk	W 9-1
6	Dec	25	(h)	Newton Heath	W 3-1
7		26	(h)	Newtown	L 2-3
8		28	(a)	West Manchester	D 2-2

Williams	Harper	Robson	Mann	Chapman	McBride	Meredith	Finnerhan	Rowan	McReddie	Morris	Davies	Hill	Little	Bowman	Porteous	Sharples	Clifford	Gillies	Robertson	Ditchfield	Miller	Read	Dyer	Espie	Moffatt	McCabe	Maley	Milarvie	#
1	2	3		5	6	7	8	9	10				11			4													1
1	2	3	4	5		7	8	9	10	11							6												2
1	2	3		5	6	7	8	9	11				10			4													3
1	2	3		5	6	7	8	9	11				10			4													4
1	2	3	4	5	6	7	8			11		9			10														5
1	2	3	4	5	6	7	8	9	10	11																			6
1	2	3	4	5	6	7	8	9	10	11																			7
1	2	3	4	5		7	8	9	10	11															6				8
1	2	3	4	5	6	7	8	9	10	11																			9
1	2	3	4	5	6	7	8	9	11				10																10
1	2	3	4	5	6	7	8	9	11				10																11
1	2	3	4	5	6	7	8		10	11	9																		12
1		3	4	5	6	7	8	9	11				10									2							13
1	2	3	4	5	6	7	8	9		10	11																		14
1		3	4	5	6	7	8	9		10	11												2						15
1	2	3	4	5	6	7	8	9		11	10																		16
1	2	3	4	5		7	8			11	10	9													6				17
1	2	3	4	5		7	8			11	10	9			6														18
1	2	3	4	5		7	8			11	10	9			6														19
1		3	4	5	6	7	8	9		11	10				2														20
1		3	4		6	7	8	9		11	10			5	2														21
1		3	4	5	6	7	8	9		11	10				2														22
1		3	4	5		7	8	9		11	10				2											6			23
1		3		5	6		8	9			7			4	2												11	10	24
1	2	3		5	6		8			11	10							9						4					25
1	2	3		5	6	7	8			11				4			10	9											26
1	2	3			6	7	8			11	10			5				9	4										27
1		3	4	5	6	7	8		10		9						11			2									28
1		3	10	5	6	7	8	9						4			11			2									29
1	2	3	4		6	7	8	9	10	11											5								30
30	21	30	23	26	25	29	30	21	11	16	11	9	9	7	5	5	4	3	3	2	2	1	1	1	2	1	1	1	
			1		3	12	9	11		3	9	4	4	2		2	1	2											

Test Matches

Apr 18 v West Brom A (h) D 1-1 (Rowan) Att: 6,000
Williams; Ditchfield, Robson, Mann, Chapman, McBride, Meredith, Finnerhan, Rowan, Gillies, Morris.

Apr 20 v West Brom A (a) L 1-6 (McBride) Att: 8,000
Williams; Harper, Robson, Mann, Chapman, McBride, Meredith, Finnerhan, Hill, Gillies, Morris.

Apr 25 v Small Heath (h) W 3-0 (Meredith, Davies, Rowan) Att: 9,500
Williams; Ditchfield, Robson, Mann, Miller, McBride, Meredith, Finnerhan, Rowan, Davies, Morris.

Apr 27 v Small Heath (a) L 0-8 Att: 2,000
Williams; Ditchfield, Robson, Mann, Miller, McBride, Meredith, Finnerhan, Rowan, Davies, Morris.

1896-97

#	Date			Opponent	Res	Score	Scorers	Att
1	Sep	5	(h)	W Arsenal	D	1-1	Finnerhan	8,000
2		12	(a)	Gainsborough T	D	1-1	Sharples	4,000
3		19	(h)	Darwen	W	4-1	Mann (2), Ditchfield, Lewis	10,000
4		21	(h)	Lincoln C	W	3-0	Finnerhan, Lewis, Sharples	3,000
5		26	(a)	Blackpool	D	2-2	Mann, Hill	5,000
6	Oct	3	(h)	Newton Heath	D	0-0		20,000
7		10	(a)	Notts C	D	3-3	Meredith, Hill, Robinson	7,000
8		17	(h)	Newcastle U	L	1-2	Robinson	10,000
9		24	(a)	Grimsby T	L	1-3	Sharples	3,000
10		31	(h)	Notts C	L	1-4	Meredith	12,000
11	Nov	7	(h)	Blackpool	W	4-2	Bannister, Meredith, Sharples, Lewis	4,000
12		14	(h)	Burton S	W	3-1	Tait (2), Gunn	4,000
13		23	(a)	Walsall	L	2-3	Finnerhan, Mann	3,000
14		28	(h)	Burton W	W	2-1	Williams, Gunn	2,000
15	Dec	19	(h)	Grimsby T	W	3-1	Meredith, Gunn, Williams	12,000
16		25	(h)	Newton Heath	L	1-2	Hill	18,000
17		26	(a)	Burton S	L	0-5		6,000
18	Jan	1	(h)	Small Heath	W	3-0	Bannister, Gunn, Sharples	16,000
19		6	(h)	Walsall	W	5-0	Ray, Mann, Meredith, Lewis, Sharples	500
20		9	(a)	Darwen	L	1-3	Gillespie	1,000
21	Feb	6	(a)	Newcastle U	L	0-3		4,000
22		13	(a)	Lincoln C	W	1-0	Gillespie	1,000
23		27	(h)	Gainsborough T	W	4-1	Gillespie, Williams (2), Meredith	9,000
24	Mar	6	(a)	Burton W	D	1-1	Read	3,000
25		13	(h)	Leicester F	W	4-0	Holmes, Meredith, Gillespie, Williams	6,000
26		17	(a)	Loughborough T	L	0-2		2,000
27	Apr	12	(a)	Leicester F	D	3-3	Meredith (2), opp.og	1,000
28		16	(h)	Loughborough T	D	1-1	Foster	2,000
29		19	(h)	Small Heath	L	1-3	Meredith	500
30		28	(a)	W Arsenal	W	2-1	Hill (2)	2,000

Appearances
Goals

League Division Two record: P 30   W 12   D 8   L 10   F 58   A 50   Pts 32   Pos 6th

FA Cup

1	Jan 30	(a)	Preston N E	L 0-6

Lancashire Senior Cup

1	Dec	5	(a)	Bury	W 1-0
2	Jan	23	(h)	Blackburn R	W 1-0
SF	Feb	20	(h)	Bolton W	W 2-1
F	Mar	27	(n)	Everton	L 0-2

Manchester Senior Cup

1	Jan 16	(h)	Newton Heath	L 0-1

Friendlies

1	Sep	1	(h)	Preston N E	L 0-1
2		8	(h)	Everton	L 0-1
3	Dec	9	(h)	South Shore	W 6-0
4		12	(h)	Sheffield U	L 1-3
5	Mar	20	(h)	Sunderland	W 2-1
6	Apr	3	(a)	Stockport C	L 1-4
7		7	(h)	West Manchester*	W 5-0
8		10	(a)	Oldham C	L 0-2
9		17	(a)	Blackpool	L 1-2
10		26	(h)	Blackpool	L 1-2
11		30	(h)	Newton Heath**	L 2-5

*Manchester & Salford Cup semi-final
**Manchester & Salford Cup Final.

36

Williams C.	Ditchfield	Harper	Ray	Mann	Moffatt	Bannister	Holmes	McBride	Meredith	Finnerhan	Gillespie	Sharples	Gunn	Williams F.	Hill	Lewis	Read	Foster	Tait	Robinson	Townley	Bowman	Hesham	McConnell	Tonge	Patterson	Platt	
1	2	3				5	6	7	8						9				4	11					10			1
1	2	3	4				6	7	8		10									11	5					9		2
1	2	3	4	5			6	7	8		10						9	11										3
1	2	3	4	5			6	7	8		10						9	11										4
1	2	3	4	5			6	7	8				9	10				11										5
1	2	3	4	5			6	7	8				9	10							11							6
1	2	3	4	5			6	7	8					10	9						11							7
1	2	3	4	5			6	7	8					10	9						11							8
1	2	3	4	5			6	7	9			8		10							11							9
1	2	3	4			5	6	7	8			10			9	11												10
1	2	3		5			6	7				8		10	9				4				11					11
1	2	3		5			6	7				8		10	9				4				11					12
1	2	3	9	5			6	7	8			11		10					4									13
1	2	3	4	5	6			7	8					10	11	9												14
1	2	3	4	5			6	7	8					10	11	9												15
1	2	3	4	5			6	7	8					10	11	9												16
1	2	3	4	5			6	7	8			11		10	9													17
1	2	3	4	5			6	7	8			11		10		9												18
1	2	3	4	5			6	7	8			11		10		9												19
1	2	3	4	6	5				8		9	11	10												7			20
1		3	4	5	6						9	10	11					2					8		7			21
1		3	4	5	6	7	8	9				10	11					2										22
1		3	4	5	6	7	8	9				10	11					2										23
1		3	4	5	6		8	9				10	11					2					7					24
1		3	4	5	6	7	8	9				10	11					2										25
1		3	4	5	6	7	8	9				10	11					2										26
1		3	4	5	6	7	8	9				10	11					2										27
1		3	4	5	6	7	8	9				10						2	11									28
1		3	2	5	6	7		9				10			8			11				4						29
1	2	4	3	5	6	7		9				10			8			11										30
30	10	10	30	18	11	18	12	28	27	25	11	10	21	11	12	12	8	6	4	3	3	2	2	2	2	1	1	
	1		1	5		2	1		10	3	4	6	4	5	5	4	1	1		2	2							

1897-98

1	Sep	1	(h)	Gainsborough T	W 3-0	Meredith, Gillespie, F.Williams	2,000
2		4	(a)	Darwen	W 4-2	S.Smith (2), Gillespie, Leonard	1,000
3		11	(h)	Loughborough T	W 3-0	S.Smith (2), Gillespie	7,000
4		18	(a)	Blackpool	W 2-0	S.Smith, F.Williams	4,000
5		25	(h)	W Arsenal	W 4-1	S.Smith (3), F.Williams	7,000
6	Oct	2	(a)	Loughborough T	W 3-0	Gillespie, F.Williams (2)	5,000
7		9	(h)	Grimsby T	W 3-0	B.Smith, Meredith, Gillespie	7,000
8		16	(a)	Newton Heath	D 1-1	Ray	20,000
9		23	(h)	Darwen	W 5-0	Gillespie (2), F.Williams (2), Whitehead	7,000
10		30	(a)	Burnley	L 1-3	opp.og	10,000
11	Nov	20	(h)	Burnley	D 1-1	Gillespie	20,000
12	Dec	11	(h)	Leicester F	W 2-1	Gillespie, Meredith	9,000
13		18	(a)	Grimsby T	W 4-3	Leonard (2), Meredith, Gillespie	5,000
14		25	(h)	Newton Heath	L 0-1		16,000
15		27	(a)	Small Heath	W 1-0	Leonard	10,000
16	Jan	1	(a)	Luton T	L 0-3		4,000
17		3	(h)	Walsall	W 3-2	Gillespie (2), Meredith	7,000
18		8	(h)	Newcastle U	D 1-1	Whitehead	16,000
19		15	(a)	Walsall	D 2-2	Gillespie, S.Smith	10,000
20		24	(h)	Lincoln C	W 3-1	Meredith, Gillespie, opp.og	2,000
21	Feb	5	(a)	W Arsenal	D 2-2	Holmes, Gillespie	8,000
22		26	(a)	Gainsborough T	L 0-1		2,000
23	Mar	16	(a)	Newcastle U	L 0-2		20,000
24		19	(a)	Lincoln C	L 1-2	Dougal	3,000
25		26	(h)	Luton T	W 2-1	Meredith (2)	5,000
26		30	(h)	Blackpool	D 3-3	S.Smith, Gillespie, Dougal	4,000
27	Apr	2	(a)	Leicester F	D 0-0		6,000
28		9	(a)	Burton S	D 0-0		3,000
29		11	(h)	Small Heath	D 3-3	B.Smith, Meredith, Gillespie	2,000
30		16	(h)	Burton S	W 9-0	Meredith (3), Whitehead (3), S.Smith (2), Gillespie	4,000

Appearances
Goals

League Division Two record: P 30   W 15   D 9   L 6   F 66   A 36   Pts 39   Pos 3rd

FA Cup

1	Jan	29	(h)	Wigan C	W 1-0
2	Feb	12	(a)	Bolton W	L 0-1

Lancashire Senior Cup

1	Dec	4	(a)	Liverpool	W 3-1
2.	Jan	22	(a)	Newton Heath	L 0-1

Manchester Senior Cup

1	Feb	7	(h)	Stalybridge C	W 3-2
SF	Mar	5	(a)	Newton Heath	D 1-1
SFR		12	(a)	Newton Heath	W 2-1
F	Apr	8	(n)	Stockport C	W*4-0
FR		18	(n)	Stockport C	L 1-2

*Final ordered to be replayed because
Dougal of City was not registered.

Friendlies

1	Sep	13	(a)	Stoke	W 5-0
2	Nov	6	(a)	Casuals	W 3-2
3	Nov	8	(a)	Burslem Port V	L 0-2
4		13	(a)	Notts C	W 3-2
5		29	(h)	Burslem Port V	W 3-2
6	Feb	19	(a)	Preston N E	L 0-4
7	Mar	21	(a)	Burnley	D 2-2
8	Apr	13	(a)	Macclesfield H	W 2-1
9		21	(h)	Sunderland	D 0-0
10		23	(a)	Bury	W 2-1
11		27	(a)	Newton Heath**	W 4-2
12		30	(a)	Everton	W 4-2

**Healey Cup Final

Williams C.	Read	Ray	Moffatt	Smith B.	Holmes	Meredith	Smith S.	Gillespie	Whitehead	Williams F.	Leonard	Dougal	Munn	Chappell	Bowman	Dyer	Harper	Clare	Foster	Wilson	
1	2	3	4	5	6	7	8	9		10	11										1
1	2	3	4	5	6	7	8	9		10	11										2
1	2	3	4	5	6	7	8	9		10	11										3
1	2	3	4	5	6	7	8	9		10	11										4
1	2		4	5	6	7	8	9		10	11				3						5
1	2	3	4	5	6	7	8	9		10	11										6
1	2	3	4	5	6	7	8	9		10	11										7
1	2	3	4	5	6	7	8	9		10	11										8
1	2	3	4	5	6	7	8	9	11	10											9
1	2	3	4	5	6	7	8	9		10	11										10
1	2	3	4	5	6	7	8	9	10	11											11
	2	3	4	5	6	7		9	8	11	10		1								12
	2	3	4	5	6	7		9	8	11	10		1								13
1	2	3	4	5	6	7		9	8	10	11										14
1	2	3	4	5	6	7		9	8	10	11										15
1		3	4	5	6	7		9	8	10	11					2					16
1		3	4	5	6	7		9	8	10	11							2			17
1	2	3	4	5	6	7	11	9	8	10											18
1	2	3	4	5	6	7	10	9	8	11											19
1	2	3	4	5	6	7	10	9	8	11											20
1	2		4	5	6	7	10	9	8	11							3				21
1		3	4	5	6	7	8	9		10						2					22
1	2		4	5		7	10	9	8		11	6							3	11	23
1	3	2	5	6	7	8	9	11			10	4									24
1	3	2		6	7	8	9	10		11		4		5							25
	3	2		6	7	8	9	10		11		4	1	5							26
	3	2	5	6	7	8	9	10		11		4	1								27
	3	2	5	6	7	8	9	10		11		4	1								28
	3	2	5	6	7	8	9	10		11		4	1								29
	3	2	5	6	7	8	9	10		11		4	1								30
23	27	20	30	28	29	30	24	30	20	22	15	8	8	7	2	2	2	1	1	1	
	1	2	1	12	12	18	5	7	4	2											

1898-99

#	Date		Opponent	Result	Scorers	Attendance
1	Sep 3	(h)	Grimsby T	W 7-2	Meredith (3), Gillespie (3), Whitehead	10,000
2	10	(a)	Newton Heath	L 0-3		15,000
3	17	(h)	New Brighton	D 1-1	Cowie	6,000
4	24	(a)	Lincoln C	L 1-3	Whitehead	3,000
5	Oct 1	(h)	W Arsenal	W 3-1	Read, S.Smith, Dougal	6,000
6	8	(a)	Luton T	W 3-0	Meredith, S.Smith, Cowie	10,000
7	15	(h)	Leicester F	W 3-1	Meredith, S.Smith, Gillespie	8,000
8	22	(a)	Darwen	W 2-0	Meredith, S.Smith	7,000
9	Nov 5	(a)	Barnsley	D 1-1	Cowie	4,000
10	12	(a)	Glossop N E	W 2-1	Meredith, Gillespie	6,000
11	19	(h)	Walsall	W 2-0	Jones, Gillespie	10,000
12	26	(a)	Burton S	D 3-3	Meredith, Moffatt, Gillespie	5,000
13	Dec 3	(h)	Burslem Port V	W 3-1	Meredith (2), Dougal	10,000
14	10	(a)	Loughborough T	W 3-1	B.Smith, Meredith, F.Williams	10,000
15	17	(h)	Loughborough T	W 5-0	Meredith (3), Ray, S.Smith	4,000
16	24	(a)	Blackpool	W 4-2	Moffatt (2), Meredith, Gillespie	8,000
17	26	(h)	Newton Heath	W 4-0	Meredith, Gillespie, Dougal, F.Williams	20,000
18	27	(a)	Small Heath	L 1-4	Dougal	10,000
19	Jan 2	(h)	Glossop N E	L 0-2		7,000
20	14	(a)	New Brighton	W 1-0	Gillespie	10,000
21	Feb 4	(h)	Luton T	W 2-0	S.Smith, Gillespie	8,000
22	11	(a)	Leicester F	D 1-1	F.Williams	10,000
23	18	(h)	Darwen	W 10-0	F.Williams (5), Meredith (3), Dougal, S.Smith	8,000
24	22	(h)	Lincoln C	W 3-1	S.Smith, Gillespie, F.Williams	5,000
25	25	(a)	Gainsborough T	L 1-3	Meredith	5,000
26	Apr 4	(a)	Barnsley	W 5-0	Meredith (3), Ross (2)	12,000
27	18	(a)	Walsall	D 1-1	Ross	6,000
28	25	(h)	Burton S	W 6-0	Meredith (2), Ross (2), Moffatt, Dougal	6,000
29	31	(h)	Gainsborough T	W 4-0	Gillespie (2), Dougal, Ross	15,000
30	Apr 1	(a)	Burslem Port V	D 1-1	Meredith	12,000
31	3	(a)	W Arsenal	W 1-0	Gillespie	5,000
32	8	(h)	Small Heath	W 2-0	F.Williams (2)	20,000
33	11	(a)	Grimsby T	W 2-1	Meredith, Gillespie	5,000
34	22	(h)	Blackpool	W 4-1	Meredith (2), Gillespie, Ross	10,000

Appearances
Goals

League Division Two record: P 34 W 23 D 6 L 5 F 92 A 35 Pts 52 Pos 1st

FA Cup

1	Jan 28	(a)	Small Heath	L 2-3

Lancashire Senior Cup

1	Dec 19	(h)	Fleetwood R	W 6-1
2	Jan 18	(h)	Preston N E	L 0-2

Manchester Senior Cup

1	Feb 8	(a)	Bolton W	W 9-3
SF	Mar 11	(a)	Bury	L 0-1

Friendlies

1	Sep 1	(a)	Seedley	W 4-0
2	Oct 29	(h)	Newton Heath	W 2-1
3	Jan 7	(a)	Newton Heath	L 0-2
4	Mar 6	(a)	Liverpool	W 1-0
5	13	(a)	Druids	W 6-1
6	Apr 15	(h)	Stockport C*	W 2-0
7	24	(a)	Newton Heath**	W 2-1
8	25	(h)	Hibernian	L 1-3
9	26	(h)	Glossop N E	W 2-1
10	28	(a)	Glossop N E	L 0-2
11	29	(h)	Burnley	D 2-2

*Healey Cup semi-final
**Healey Cup Final

Williams C.	Read	Ray	Jones	Moffatt	Smith B.	Holmes	Meredith	Smith S.	Gillespie	Williams F.	Dougal	Cowie	Ross	Munn	Whitehead	Bowman	Chappell	No.
1	2	3		6	5	4	7	8	9		11			10				1
1	3		2	5	4		7	8	9	11		6		10				2
1	3			2	5		7	8	9		11	4		10	6			3
1	2	3		4	5		7		9	10	11			8	6			4
1	2	3		4	5		7	8	9	10	11				6			5
1	2	6	3	4	5		7	8	9	10	11							6
1	2	6	3	4	5		7	8	9	10	11							7
1	2	6	3	4	5		7	8	9	10	11							8
1	2		3	4	5	6	7	8	9	10	11							9
1	2		3	4	5	6	7	8	9	10	11							10
1	2		3	4	5	6	7	8	9	10	11							11
	2		3	4	5	6	7	8	9	11	10				1			12
1	2		3	4	5	6	7	8	9	10	11							13
1	2		3	4	5	6	7	8	9	10	11							14
1	2	8	3	4	5	6	7		9	10	11							15
1	2		3	4	5	6	7	8	9	10	11							16
1	2		3	4	5	6	7	8	9	10	11							17
1	2	7	3	4	5	6		8	9	10	11							18
1	2		3	4	5	6	8	7	9	10	11							19
1	2		3	4	5	6	8	7	9	10	11							20
1	2		3	4	5	6	7	8	9	10	11							21
1	2		3	4	5	6	7	8	9	10	11							22
1	2	3	4	5	6		7	8	9	10	11							23
1	2	3		4	5		7	8	9	10	11	6						24
1	2		3	4	5		7	8	9	10	11	6						25
1	2		3	4	5		7	8		10	11	6	9					26
1	2		3	4	5	6	7		9	10	11		8					27
1	2		3	4	5	6	7		9	10	11		8					28
1	2		3	4	5	6	7		9	10	11		8					29
1	2		3	4	5	6	7		9	10	11		8					30
1	2		3	4	5	6	7		9	10	11		8					31
1	2		3	4	5	6	7		9	10	11		8					32
1	2		3	4	5		7		9	10	11	6	8					33
1	2		3	4	5	6	7		9	10	11		8					34
33	20	24	27	34	34	24	33	25	30	25	31	11	9	6	4	3	1	
	1	1	1	4	1		29	8	17	11	7	3	7		2			

41

1899-1900

1	Sep	2	(a)	Blackburn R	L 3-4	Meredith, Ross, F.Williams	10,000
2		9	(h)	Derby C	W 4-0	Meredith (2), Ross, Gillespie	22,000
3		16	(a)	Bury	W 4-1	Meredith, Ross, F.Williams, Leonard	13,000
4		23	(h)	Notts C	W 5-1	Ross (2), Moffatt, B.Smith, Gillespie	22,000
5		30	(h)	Wolves	D 1-1	Ross	14,000
6	Oct	7	(a)	Sheffield U	L 0-3		18,000
7		14	(h)	Newcastle U	W 1-0	Ross	25,000
8		21	(a)	Aston Villa	L 1-2	F.Williams	20,000
9		28	(h)	Liverpool	L 0-1		25,000
10	Nov	4	(a)	Burnley	L 0-2		5,000
11		11	(h)	Preston N E	W 3-1	Meredith, Gillespie, F.Williams	8,000
12		25	(h)	Glossop N E	W 4-1	Meredith, Ross, F.Williams, Dougal	16,000
13	Dec	2	(a)	Stoke	L 0-1		10,000
14		9	(h)	Sunderland	W 2-1	Moffatt, Meredith	20,000
15		16	(a)	West Brom A	D 0-0		2,429
16		23	(h)	Everton	L 1-2	Meredith	20,000
17		25	(h)	Sheffield U	L 1-2	F.Williams	3,000
18		27	(a)	Nottingham F	L 0-2		5,000
19		30	(h)	Blackburn R	D 1-1	Gillespie	10,000
20	Jan	6	(a)	Derby C	D 0-0		5,000
21		13	(h)	Bury	D 2-2	S.Smith (2)	15,000
22		20	(a)	Notts C	D 1-1	Gillespie	8,000
23	Feb	3	(a)	Wolves	D 1-1	Meredith	2,000
24	Mar	3	(a)	Liverpool	L 2-5	Meredith, Gillespie	20,000
25		10	(h)	Burnley	W 1-0	Meredith	13,000
26		19	(h)	Aston Villa	L 0-2		15,000
27		31	(a)	Glossop N E	W 2-0	Harvey, Davidson	7,000
28	Apr	7	(h)	Stoke	W 1-0	F.Williams	16,000
29		9	(h)	Nottingham F	W 2-0	Meredith (2)	5,000
30		13	(a)	Newcastle U	D 0-0		20,000
31		14	(a)	Sunderland	L 1-3	C.Williams	6,000
32		16	(h)	Preston N E	W 2-0	Gillespie, Dougal	5,000
33		21	(h)	West Brom A	W 4-0	Ross (2), Meredith, Gillespie	15,000
34		28	(a)	Everton	L 0-4		20,000

Appearances
Goals

League Division One record: P 34 W 13 D 8 L 13 F 50 A 40 Pts 34 Pos 7th

FA Cup

1	Jan	27	(h)	Aston Villa	D 1-1
1R		31	(a)	Aston Villa	L 0-3

Lancashire Senior Cup

1	Dec	18	(a)	Bury	L 0-3

Manchester Senior Cup

1	Feb	10	(h)	Stalybridge R	W 4-0
SF	Mar	12	(h)	Bolton W	L 3-5

Friendlies

1	Sep	11	(a)	Stoke	W 1-0
2	Oct	4	(h)	Kaffirs	W 4-3
3	Nov	29	(a)	Newton Heath	W 1-0
4	Dec	6	(a)	Corinthians	D 1-1
5		28	(h)	Corinthians	D 2-2
6	Jan	1	(h)	Newton Heath	W 2-1
7	Feb	24	(h)	Wolves	L 1-2
8		27	(a)	Newton Heath	L 0-1
9	Mar	17	(h)	Glasgow Rangers	L 0-3
10	Apr	17	(a)	Burslem Port V	W 3-2

Williams C.	Read	Ray	Jones	Moffatt	Smith B.	Holmes	Meredith	Ross	Gillespie	Williams F	Dougal	Threlfall	Munn	Smith S.	Davidson	Harvey	Tonge	Cassidy	Dartnell	Leonard	
1		2	3	4	5	6	7	8	9	10	11										1
1	2		3	4	5	6	7	8	9	10	11										2
1	2		3	4	5	6	7	8	9	10									11		3
1	2		3	4	5	6	7	8	9	10	11										4
1	2		3	4	5	6	7	9	10	11	8										5
1	2		3	4	5	6	7	8	9	10	11										6
1	2		3	4	5	6	7	8	9	10		11									7
1	2		3	4	5	6	7	8	9	10	11										8
1	2		3	4	5	6	7	8	9	10		11									9
1	2		3	4	5	6	7	8	9	10			11								10
1	2		3	4	5	6	7	8	9	10	11										11
1	2		3	4	5	6	7	8	9	10	11										12
1	2		3	4	5	6	7	8	9	10	11										13
1	2		3	4	5	6	7	8	9	10	11										14
1	2		3	4	5	6	7	8	9	10	11										15
1	2		3	4	5	6	7	8	9	10	11										16
1	2		3	4	5	6	7	8	9	10	11										17
1		2	3	4	5	6		8	9		11		10				7				18
1		2	3	4	5	6	7		9		10	11	8								19
1		2	3		5	6	7		9	10		11	4	8							20
1	4	2	3		5	6	7			10	11		8			9					21
1		2	3	4	5	6	7		9	10		11		8							22
1	4	2	3		5	6	7		9	10	11			8							23
1	4	2	3		5	6	8		9	10	11						7				24
1		2	3	4	5	6	7	8	9	10	11										25
1	2		3	4	5	6	7	8	9		10	11									26
1	2		3	4	5	6	7			10	11			9	8						27
1	2		3	4	5	6	7			10	11			9	8						28
1	2		3		5	6	7	8		10	11		4			9					29
1	2		3		5	6	7	8		10	11		4			9					30
1	2		3		5	6	7	8		10	11		4			9					31
1	2		3		5	6	7	8	9	10	11		4								32
1	2		3		5	6	7	8	9	10			4						11		33
1	2		3	4	5	6	7	8	9		11							10			
34	28	9	34	25	34	34	33	26	28	31	23	9	6	5	5	5	2	1	1	1	
1			2	1			14	10	8	7	2		2	1	1				1		

1900-01

#	Date		Venue	Opponent	Result	Scorers	Attendance
1	Sep	1	(h)	Sheffield W	D 2-2	Ross, Dougal	18,000
2		8	(a)	Bury	L 0-4		17,000
3		15	(h)	Nottingham F	W 1-0	Cassidy	20,000
4		22	(a)	Blackburn R	L 0-1		10,000
5		29	(h)	Stoke	W 2-0	Meredith, Davies	20,000
6	Oct	6	(a)	West Brom A	L 2-3	Holmes, Moffatt	5,000
7		13	(h)	Everton	W 1-0	Cassidy	15,000
8		20	(a)	Sunderland	L 0-3		10,000
9		27	(h)	Derby C	W 2-0	F.Williams (2)	15,000
10	Nov	3	(a)	Bolton W	D 0-0		20,000
11		10	(h)	Notts C	W 2-0	Gillespie, Cassidy	16,000
12		17	(a)	Preston N E	W 4-0	Cassidy (2), Gillespie, F.Williams	5,000
13		24	(h)	Wolves	W 3-2	Meredith, Ross, Cassidy	16,000
14	Dec	1	(a)	Aston Villa	L 1-7	Cassidy	12,000
15		8	(h)	Liverpool	L 3-4	Cassidy (2), Smith	18,000
16		15	(a)	Newcastle U	L 1-2	F.Williams	16,000
17		22	(h)	Sheffield U	W 2-1	Meredith, Gillespie	15,000
18		25	(h)	Sunderland	D 1-1	Gillespie	20,000
19		26	(a)	Sheffield U	D 1-1	Gillespie	20,000
20		29	(a)	Sheffield W	L 1-4	Cassidy	15,000
21	Jan	5	(h)	Bury	W 1-0	Cassidy	23,000
22		12	(a)	Nottingham F	L 2-4	Gillespie, Cassidy	8,000
23		19	(h)	Blackburn R	L 1-3	Meredith	8,000
24		26	(a)	Stoke	L 1-2	Cassidy	3,000
25	Feb	16	(a)	Everton	L 2-5	Meredith, Cassidy	20,000
26		23	(h)	Preston N E	W 3-1	Meredith, F.Williams, Dougal	10,000
27	Mar	2	(a)	Derby C	L 0-2		5,000
28		9	(h)	Bolton W	D 1-1	Holmes	15,000
29		16	(a)	Notts C	D 0-0		6,000
30		30	(a)	Wolves	L 0-1		3,000
31	Apr	5	(h)	West Brom A	W 1-0	Gillespie	23,000
32		13	(a)	Liverpool	L 1-3	Meredith	15,000
33		20	(h)	Newcastle U	W 2-1	Gillespie (2)	20,000
34		27	(h)	Aston Villa	W 4-0	Scotson (2), Threlfall, Ross	15,000

Appearances
Goals

League Division One record: P 34   W 13   D 6   L 15   F 48   A 58   Pts 32   Pos 11th

FA Cup

1	Feb 9	(a) West Brom A	L 0-1

Lancashire Senior Cup

1	Oct 1	(h) Nelson	W 7-0
2	22	(h) Newton Heath	W 2-0
SF	Nov 12	(h) Burnley	D 2-2
SFR	26	(h) Burnley	L 1-2

Manchester Senior Cup

1	Mar 13	(h) Bolton W	W 2-0
SF	Apr 17	(n) Bury	W 2-1
F	29	(h) Newton Heath	W 4-0

Friendlies

1	Sep	3	(h)	Wellingborough	W 10-1
2		12	(a)	Bolton W	L 0-2
3		18	(a)	Southport C	L 1-3
4		26	(a)	Newton Heath	D 0-0
5	Feb	19	(h)	Liverpool	L 0-8
6	Mar	25	(a)	Chirk	W 4-0
7	Apr	6	(h)	Liverpool	W 3-2
8		8	(h)	Stockport C*	W 5-1
9		23	(a)	Grimsby T	L 1-2

*Healey Cup Final

44

Appearance and scoring grid (columns = players; right-hand column = match number):

Williams C.	Read	Jones	Moffatt	Smith	Holmes	Meredith	Ross	Gillespie	Cassidy	Williams F.	Dougal	Davies	Meecham	Scotson	Threlfall	Slater	Hosie	Dartnell	Davidson	Harvey	Hunter	Cox	Hallows	Hesham	No.
1	2	3	4	5	6	7	8		10	11									9						1
1	2	3	4	5	6	7	8	9	10	11															2
1	2	3	4	5	6	7		9	10		8							11							3
1	2	3	4	5	6	7		9	10	11	8														4
1	2	3	4	5	6	7		9	10	11	8														5
1	2	3	4	5	6	7		9	10	11	8														6
1	2	3	4	5	6	7		9	10	11	8														7
1	2	3	4	5	6	7		9	10	11	8														8
1		3	4	5	6	7	8	9	10					11	2										9
1	2	3	4	5	6	7	8	9	10	11															10
1	2	3	4	5	6	7	8	9	10	11															11
1	2	3	4	5	6	7	8	9		11	10														12
1	2	3	4	5	6	7	8	9		11		10													13
1	2	3	4	5	6	7	8	9		11	10														14
1	2	3	4	5	6	7	8	9		11								10							15
1	2	3	4	5	6	7	8		10	11									9						16
1		3	4	5	6	7	8	9		11	10		2												17
1		3	4	5	6	7	8	9		11	10		2												18
1		3	4	5		7	8	9		11	10	6		2											19
1		3	4	5	6	7	8	9		11	10		2												20
2	5	3	4		6	7	8	9	10	11			2												21
1		3	4		6	7	8	9	10				2					11			5				22
1		3	4	5	6	7	8	9	10	11			2												23
1	2	3	4	5	6	7	8	9	10														11		24
1	2	3	4	5		7		9	10	11						6				8					25
	2	3	4	5	6	7	8	9	10	11											1				26
1	2	3	4	5	6	7	8	9	10	11															27
1	2	3	4	5	6	7	8	9	10	11															28
1	2	3		5		7	8	9		11	6									10	4				29
1	2	3		5		7		9	8	6				10	11						4				30
1	2	3	4	5	6	7	8	9						10	11										31
1	2	3	4	5	6	7		9	10	11				8											32
1	2	3	4	5		7	8	9		11				10				6							33
1	2		4	5		7	8	9						10	11		3		6						34
33	27	33	32	32	28	34	25	23	30	23	13	8	6	5	4	3	3	3	2	2	2	1	1	1	
			1	1	2	7	3	9	14	5	2	1		2	1										

45

1901-02

1	Sep	2	(a)	Everton	L 1-3	Meredith	20,000
2		7	(a)	Sunderland	L 0-1		14,000
3		14	(h)	Small Heath	L 1-4	Scotson	18,000
4		21	(a)	Derby C	L 0-2		10,000
5	Oct	5	(a)	Notts C	L 0-2		12,000
6		12	(h)	Bolton W	W 1-0	F.Williams	20,000
7		19	(h)	Grimsby T	W 3-0	Meredith, Gillespie, F.Williams	18,000
8		26	(a)	Wolves	D 0-0		8,000
9	Nov	2	(h)	Liverpool	L 2-3	Gillespie, F.Williams	22,000
10		9	(a)	Newcastle U	L 0-3		8,000
11		23	(a)	Sheffield U	L 0-5		10,000
12		30	(h)	Nottingham F	W 3-1	Meredith, Morgan, R.Jones	15,000
13	Dec	7	(a)	Bury	L 0-3		9,000
14		14	(h)	Blackburn R	D 1-1	Meredith	10,000
15		26	(a)	Sheffield W	L 1-2	R.Jones	10,000
16	Jan	1	(a)	Bolton W	D 3-3	Meredith, Ross, Henderson	19,853
17		4	(h)	Sunderland	L 0-3		15,000
18		11	(a)	Small Heath	L 0-1		12,000
19		13	(a)	Stoke	L 0-3		5,000
20		18	(h)	Derby C	D 0-0		18,000
21	Feb	1	(h)	Notts C	W 1-0	Threlfall	20,000
22		15	(a)	Grimsby T	L 2-3	Gillespie (2)	4,000
23		17	(h)	Aston Villa	W 1-0	Hosie	17,000
24		22	(h)	Wolves	W 3-0	Gillespie (2), McOustra	16,269
25	Mar	1	(a)	Liverpool	L 0-4		20,000
26		8	(h)	Newcastle U	W 2-0	Hynds (2)	20,000
27		17	(h)	Everton	W 2-0	Meredith, McOustra	22,000
28		22	(h)	Sheffield U	W 4-0	Gillespie (2), Meredith, Hosie	20,000
29		28	(h)	Sheffield W	L 0-3		25,000
30		29	(a)	Nottingham F	L 1-3	Hosie	10,000
31		31	(a)	Aston Villa	D 2-2	Gillespie, Drummond	18,000
32	Apr	5	(h)	Bury	W 2-0	Gillespie, Meredith	7,000
33		12	(a)	Blackburn R	W 4-1	Gillespie (4)	3,000
34		19	(h)	Stoke	D 2-2	Gillespie, Drummond	12,000
							Appearances
							Goals

League Division One record: P 34 W 11 D 6 L 17 F 42 A 58 Pts 28 Pos 18th

FA Cup

1	Jan	25	(a)	Preston N E*	D 1-1
1R		29	(h)	Preston N E	D 0-0
1R	Feb	3	(a)	Preston N E	W 4-2
2		8	(h)	Nottingham F	L 0-2

*Abandoned in extra-time

Lancashire Senior Cup

1	Sep	28	(h)	Southport C	L 0-1

Manchester Senior Cup

1	Jan	14	(a)	Glossop	W 1-0
SF	Mar	12	(h)	Stalybridge R	W 4-2
F	Apr	26	(h)	Newton Heath	L 1-2

Friendlies

1	Oct	1	(a)	Macclesfield	W 7-1
2	Dec	25	(h)	Glasgow Celtic	W 2-1
3	Mar	15	(h)	Blackburn R	L 1-2
4	Apr	1	(a)	Belfast & District	W 3-1
5		7	(a)	Chirk XI	W 2-1

Williams C.	Orr	Jones D	Moffatt	Hynds	Hosie	Meredith	Gillespie	Morgan	McOustra	Drummond	Williams F	Threlfall	Smith	Hurst	Hillman	Slater	Ross	Jones R	Holmes	Barrett	Henderson	Hunter	Read	Scotson	Bevan	Frost	Watson	
1		4			6	7							5	11	3								2	10	9	8		1
1	3				6	7	8				10		5	11								4	2		9			2
1	3				6	7		9					5	11		8						4	2	10				3
1	2	3	4			7	9				10		5	11					6						8			4
1	2		4		6	7	9	8			10		5	11	3													5
1	2	3	4	5	6	7	9	8		10				11														6
1	2	3	4	5	6	7	9	8		10				11														7
1	2	3	4	5	6	7	9	8			10	11																8
1	2	3	4	5	6	7	9	8			10	11																9
1	2	3	4		6		9	7			10	11	5			8												10
1	2	3	4	5	6	7	9			10				11											8			11
1	2			5	6	7	9	8					4	11			10	3										12
1	2			5	6	7	9	8					4	11			10	3										13
1	2	3		5	6	7	9					8	4	11			10											14
	2			5	6	7							4	11		8	10			1	9	3						15
	2			5	6	7							4	11	3	8	10			1	9							16
1	2	3		5	6	7							4	11		8	10				9							17
	2			5	6	7					10	11	4		3	8				1	9							18
				5	6	7		9				11	4		2	8	10	3	1									19
	2			5	6	7		9				11	4		3	8	10		1									20
	2			5	6	7			8			11	4	1	3						9			10				21
	2		4	5	6	7	9	8	10	11			1		3													22
	2	3	4	5	6	7	9		8	11			1	11														23
	2	3	4	5	6	7	9		8	10		11	1															24
	2	3	4	5	6	7	9		8	10		11	1															25
		3	4	5	6	7	9	8		10		11	1	2														26
		3	4	5	6	7	9	8		10		11	1	2														27
		3	4	5	6	7	9	8		10		11	1	2														28
		3	4	5	6	7	9	8		10		11	1	2														29
	2		4	5	6	7	9	8		10		11	1		3													30
	2		4	5	6	7	9	8		10		11	1				3											31
			4	5	6	7	9	8		10		11	1				3				2							32
		3	4	5	6	7	9	8		10		11	1								2							33
		3	4	5	6	7	9	8		10		11	1								2							34
15	23	20	21	29	33	33	24	12	13	13	13	18	16	15	14	13	7	9	6	5	5	4	3	2	2	1		
	2	3	8	15	1	2	2	3	1					1	2						1		1	2				

47

1902-03

1	Sep	6	(h)	Lincoln C	W 3-1	McOustra (2), Bevan	16,000
2		13	(a)	Small Heath	L 0-4		12,000
3		20	(h)	Leicester F	W 3-1	Meredith, Gillespie, opp.og	12,000
4		27	(a)	Chesterfield	W 1-0	Meredith	15,000
5	Oct	4	(a)	Burnley	D 1-1	Miller	4,000
6		11	(h)	Preston N E	W 1-0	Gillespie	16,000
7		18	(a)	Burslem Port V	W 4-1	Gillespie (2), Meredith, Drummond	5,000
8		22	(a)	Gainsborough T	W 3-0	Gillespie (2), Miller	4,000
9	Nov	1	(a)	W Arsenal	L 0-1		11,000
10		8	(h)	Burton U	W 2-0	Gillespie, McOustra	13,000
11		15	(a)	Bristol C	L 2-3	Turnbull, Drummond	13,000
12		22	(h)	Glossop	W 5-2	Gillespie (3), Turnbull, opp.og	8,000
13		24	(h)	Barnsley	W 3-2	Gillespie (2), Meredith	8,000
14	Dec	6	(h)	Stockport C	W 5-0	Meredith (2), Turnbull (2), Gillespie	12,000
15		13	(a)	Blackpool	W 3-0	Meredith, Turnbull, Gillespie	5,000
16		20	(h)	W Arsenal	W 4-1	Gillespie (3), Turnbull	25,000
17		25	(a)	Manchester U	D 1-1	Bannister	40,000
18		26	(a)	Preston N E	W 2-0	Gillespie, Drummond	10,000
19		27	(a)	Doncaster R	W 2-1	Hynds, Gillespie	30,000
20	Jan	1	(h)	Doncaster R	W 4-1	Bannister (2), Meredith, Turnbull	25,000
21		3	(a)	Lincoln C	L 0-1		6,000
22		17	(a)	Leicester F	D 1-1	Threlfall	7,000
23		24	(h)	Chesterfield	W 4-2	Meredith (3), Turnbull	15,000
24		31	(h)	Burnley	W 6-0	Meredith (2), Gillespie (2), Threlfall, Bannister	16,000
25	Feb	14	(h)	Burslem Port V	W 7-1	Meredith (2), Gillespie (2), Turnbull, Meredith,McOustra	12,000
26		23	(h)	Small Heath	W 4-0	Meredith (2), Gillespie, Threlfall	20,000
27		28	(h)	Gainsborough T	W 9-0	Bannister (3), Gillespie (2), Turnbull (2), Meredith, Threlfall	15,000
28	Mar	7	(a)	Burton U	W 5-0	Bannister (2), Gillespie (2), Meredith	5,000
29		14	(h)	Bristol C	D 2-2	Meredith, Threlfall	20,000
30		21	(a)	Glossop	W 1-0	Bannister	7,000
31	Apr	4	(a)	Stockport C	W 2-0	Gillespie, Turnbull	10,000
32		10	(h)	Manchester U	L 0-2		30,000
33		11	(h)	Blackpool	W 2-0	Meredith (2),	8,000
34		14	(a)	Barnsley	W 3-0	Meredith, Bannister, Gillespie	5,000

Appearances
Goals

League Division Two record: P 34   W 25   D 4   L 5   F 95   A 29   Pts 54   Pos 1

FA Cup

1 Feb 7 (a) Preston N E   L 1-3

Lancashire Senior Cup

1 Sep 29 (h) Accrington   W 5-2
2 Oct 27 (h) Everton   D 2-2
R Nov 10 (a) Everton   D 2-2
2R   17 (a) Everton   L 0-3

Manchester Senior Cup

1 Mar 16 (h) Glossop   W 4-0
SF   28 (h) Stockport C   W 7-0
F Apr 29 (n) Bury   D 2-2

Friendlies

1 Sep 1 (h) Glasgow Celtic   W 1-0
2   9 (h) Bolton W   W 3-1
3 Mar 25 (h) Northern Nomads   D 2-2
4 Apr 15 (a) Aberdare   W 1-0
5   25 (a) Ayr U   W 2-1
6   27 (a) Glasgow Celtic   D 0-0

Hillman	Orr	McMahon	Davidson	Frost	Hynds	McOustra	Meredith	Bannister	Gillespie	Turnbull	Threlfall	Drummond	Holmes	Booth	Miller	Bevan	Dearden	Edmondson	Hosie	Slater	Moffatt	
1		2	4	5	10	7							3	11	8	9			6			1
1		2	4	5	9	7					10		3	11	8				6			2
1	2	3	4	5	8	7		9			10			11					6			3
1	2	3	4	5	6	7		9	10	11					8							4
1	2	3	4	5	6	7		9	10	11					8							5
1	2	3	4	5	6	7		9	10	11					8							6
1	2	3	4	5	6	7		9	10	11					8							7
1	2	3	4	5	6	7		9		11	10				8							8
1	2	3	4	5	6	7		9		11	10					8						9
1	2	3	4	5	6	7		9		11	10				8							10
1	2	3	4	5	6	7		9	8	11	10											11
1	2	3	4	5	6	7		9	8	11	10											12
1	2	3	4	5	6	7		9	8	11	10											13
1	2	3	4	5	6	7	8	9	10	11												14
1		3	4	5	6	7	8	9	10	11			2									15
		3	4	5	6	7	8	9	10	11							1	2				16
1	2	3	4	5	6	7	8	9	10	11												17
1		3	4	5	6	7	8	9		11	10		2									18
1	2	3	4	5	6	7	8	9		11	10											19
1	2	3		5	6	7	8	9	10	11			4									20
1	2	3		5	6	7	8	9	10	11			4									21
1	2	3	4	5	6	7	8	9	10	11												22
1	2	3	4	5		7	8	9	10	11					6							23
1	2	3	4	5		7	8	9	10	11					6							24
1	2	3	4	5	6	7	8	9	10	11												25
1	2	3	4	5	6	7	8	9	10	11												26
1	2		4	5	6	7	8	9	10	11			3									27
1	2		4	5	6	7	8	9	10	11			3									28
1	2			5	6	7	8	9	10	11			3		4							29
	2		4	5	6	7	8	9	10	11			3					1				30
	2		4		6	7	8	9	10	11			3				5	1				31
1	2		4	5	6	7	8	9	10	11			3									32
1	3	2	4		6	7	8	9	10				11		5							33
1		2			6	7	8	9	10				11	4	5				3			34
31	13	17	26	30	31	32	34	21	32	22	25	14	11	9	8	6	3	3	3	2	1	
		1	4	22	13	30	12	5	3					2	1							

49

1903-04

1	Sep	5	(a)	Stoke	W 2-1	Livingstone, opp.og	16,000
2		12	(h)	Derby C	W 2-1	Turnbull (2)	28,000
3		19	(h)	Wolves	W 4-1	Meredith, Turnbull (2), Booth	25,000
4		26	(a)	Notts C	W 3-0	Hynds, Meredith, Pearson	15,000
5	Oct	3	(h)	Sheffield U	L 0-1		28,000
6		10	(a)	Newcastle U	L 0-1		19,730
7		17	(h)	Aston Villa	W 1-0	Gillespie	30,000
8		24	(a)	Middlesbrough	L 0-6		14,000
9		31	(h)	Liverpool	W 3-2	Booth, Turnbull, Gillespie	25,000
10	Nov	7	(a)	Bury	W 3-1	Gillespie (2), Meredith	19,371
11		14	(h)	Blackburn R	W 1-0	Meredith	20,000
12		21	(a)	Nottingham F	W 3-0	Frost, Hynds, Gillespie	12,000
13		28	(h)	Sheffield W	D 1-1	Livingstone	8,000
14	Dec	5	(a)	Sunderland	D 1-1	Hynds	18,000
15		12	(h)	West Brom A	W 6-3	Meredith (2), Gillespie (2), Turnbull, Livingstone	14,000
16		19	(a)	Small Heath	W 3-0	Turnbull (2), Gillespie	12,000
17		26	(h)	Everton	L 1-3	Gillespie	28,000
18		28	(a)	Sheffield U	L 3-5	Gillespie (2), Threlfall	35,000
19	Jan	1	(h)	Middlesbrough	D 1-1	Meredith	30,000
20		2	(h)	Stoke	D 2-2	Frost, Turnbull	16,000
21		9	(a)	Derby C	W 3-2	Gillespie (2), Meredith	12,000
22		23	(a)	Notts C	W 3-0	Gillespie, Booth, Frost	15,000
23	Feb	13	(a)	Aston Villa	W 1-0	Gillespie	16,000
24		27	(a)	Liverpool	D 2-2	Gillespie, Hynds	20,000
25	Mar	12	(a)	Blackburn R	W 5-2	Meredith (2), Dennison (2), Turnbull	12,000
26		21	(a)	Wolves	W 6-1	Livingstone (2), Gillespie (2), Meredith, Turnbull	6,000
27		26	(a)	Sheffield W	L 0-1		25,000
28	Apr	1	(h)	Newcastle U	L 1-3	Turnbull	28,000
29		2	(h)	Sunderland	W 2-1	Turnbull (2)	15,000
30		9	(a)	West Brom A	L 1-2	Jones	14,000
31		11	(h)	Bury	W 3-0	Turnbull (2), Bannister	10,000
32		13	(h)	Nottingham F	D 0-0		10,000
33		16	(h)	Small Heath	W 4-0	Bannister (2), J.Moffatt (2)	15,000
34		25	(a)	Everton	L 0-1		12,000

Appearances
Goals

League Division One record: P 34 W 19 D 6 L 9 F 71 A 45 Pts 44 Pos 2nd

FA Cup

1	Feb	6	(h)	Sunderland	W 3-2
2		20	(a)	W Arsenal	W 2-0
3	Mar	5	(h)	Middlesbrough	D 0-0
R		9	(a)	Middlesbrough	W 3-1
SF		19	(n)	Sheffield W	W 3-1
F	Apr	23	(n)	Bolton W	W 1-0

Lancashire Senior Cup

1	Jan	18	(a)	Burnley	L 1-2

Manchester Senior Cup

1	Jan	30	(a)	Glossop	W 1-0
SF	Apr	4	(h)	Manchester U	D 1-1
R		7	(a)	Manchester U	W 2-1
F		30	(h)	Bury	D 0-0
R*	Dec	5	(h)	Bury	L 0-4

*Final replay held over to 1904-05

Friendlies

1	Sep	1	(a)	Glasgow Rangers	D 1-1
2		7	(a)	Liverpool	L 5-6
3		15	(a)	Glossop	L 1-3
4	Apr	26	(a)	Hyde District XI	L 0-2

Hillman	McMahon	Burgess	Frost	Hynds	Ashworth	Meredith	Livingstone	Gillespie	Turnbull	Booth	Threlfall	Holmes	Bannister	Davidson	Dearden	Edmondson	Lyon	Moffatt	Thornley	Pearson	McOustra	Slater	Dennison	Drummond	Jones	Norgrove	Robinson	No.
1	2	3	6	5		7	8		10	11								9		4								1
1	2	3	4	5		7	8		10	11								9		6								2
1	2	3	4	5	6	7	8	9	10	11																		3
1	2	3	4	5	6	7	8		10	11								9										4
1	2	3	4	5	6	7	8		10	11								9										5
1	2	3		5		7	4	9	10	11			8		6													6
1	2	3		5		7	4	9		11			8		6					10								7
1	2	3		5		7	4	9	10	11			8		6													8
1	2	3	4	5		7	8	9	10	11					6													9
1		3	4	5		7	8	9		11				2	6								10					10
1	2		4	5		7	8	9	10		11				6							3						11
1	2	3	4	5	6	7	8	9	10		11																	12
1	2	3	4	5	6	7	8	9	10		11																	13
1	2	3	4	5	6	7	8		10	11							9											14
1	2	3	4	5	6	7	8	9	10		11																	15
1	2	3	4	5	6	7	8	9	10		11																	16
1			4	5	6	7	8	9	10		11			2								3						17
1		3	4	5	6	7	8	9	10		11			2														18
1		3	4	5	6	7	8	9	10		11			2														19
1		3	4	5	6	7	8	9	10		11			2														20
1	2	3	4	5		7	8	9	10		11						6											21
1	2	3	4	5		7	8	9	10	11							6											22
1	2	3	4		6	7	8	9	10	11							5											23
1	2	3	4	5	6	7	8	9	10	11																		24
	2		4	5		7	8		10	11		3				1								9				25
	2	3	4	5		7	8	9	10	11		6				1												26
	2	3	4	5		7	8	9	10	11		6				1												27
	2	3	4	5		7	8	9	10	11		6				1												28
			4	5		7		9	10	11		3	8	2	6	1												29
1	2		4	5		7			10	11		3					6		8						9			30
1	2		4	5	6	7			10	11		3	8						9									31
	2		4	5	6	7			10	11		3	8			1			9									32
1	2				6	7			10	11			8					5	9							3	4	33
1	2	3	4	5	6	7	8	9	10	11																		34
28	27	27	30	32	18	34	29	24	32	24	10	8	7	6	6	6	6	4	4	3	2	2	1	1	1	1	1	
			3	4		11	5	18	16	3	1			3				2	1					2	1			

51

1904-05

1	Sep	3	(h)	Small Heath	W	2-1	Livingstone, Booth	30,000
2		10	(a)	Stoke	L	0-1		12,000
3		17	(a)	Notts C	D	1-1	Thornley	10,000
4		24	(h)	Sheffield U	D	1-1	Thornley	23,000
5	Oct	1	(a)	Newcastle U	L	0-2		22,000
6		8	(h)	Preston N E	W	6-1	Turnbull (2), Livingstone (2), Booth, Gillespie	23,000
7		15	(a)	Middlesbrough	W	1-0	Gillespie	12,000
8		29	(a)	Bury	W	4-2	Gillespie, Meredith, Turnbull, Booth	12,000
9	Nov	9	(h)	Aston Villa	W	2-1	Turnbull, Booth	8,000
10		12	(a)	Blackburn R	L	1-3	Turnbull	10,000
11		14	(h)	Wolves	W	5-1	Meredith, Booth (2), Livingstone, Gillespie	11,000
12		19	(h)	Nottingham F	D	1-1	Booth	16,000
13		26	(a)	Sheffield W	L	1-2	Turnbull	15,000
14	Dec	3	(h)	Sunderland	W	5-2	Turnbull (3), Gillespie, Booth	27,000
15		10	(a)	W Arsenal	L	0-1		16,000
16		17	(h)	Derby C	W	6-0	Turnbull (4), Gillespie (2)	22,000
17		24	(a)	Everton	D	0-0		16,000
18		26	(a)	Preston N E	W	1-0	Turnbull	17,000
19		31	(a)	Small Heath	L	1-3	Turnbull	11,000
20	Jan	7	(h)	Stoke	W	1-0	Meredith	12,000
21		14	(h)	Notts C	W	2-1	Turnbull, Dorsett	10,000
22		21	(a)	Sheffield U	W	3-0	Dorsett (2), Turnbull	15,000
23		28	(h)	Newcastle U	W	3-2	Hynds, Dorsett, Jones	40,000
24	Feb	11	(h)	Middlesbrough	W	3-2	J.Moffatt, Dorsett, opp.og	18,000
25		25	(h)	Bury	W	3-2	Bannister (2), Meredith	16,000
26	Mar	4	(a)	Derby C	W	1-0	Bannister	7,000
27		11	(h)	Blackburn R	W	2-1	Meredith, Turnbull	12,000
28		18	(h)	Nottingham F	L	1-2	Meredith	10,000
29	Apr	1	(a)	Sunderland	D	0-0		9,000
30		8	(h)	W Arsenal	W	1-0	Meredith	18,000
31		15	(h)	Sheffield W	D	1-1	Meredith	20,000
32		21	(h)	Everton	W	2-0	Hynds, Livingstone	40,000
33		24	(a)	Wolves	W	3-0	Livingstone, Jones, Pearson	15,000
34		29	(a)	Aston Villa	L	2-3	Turnbull, Livingstone	20,000

Appearances
Goals

League Division One record: P 34   W 20   D 6   L 8   F 66   A 37   Pts 46   Pos 3rd

FA Cup

1	Feb	4	(a)	Lincoln C	W 2-1
2		18	(h)	Bolton W	L 1-2

Lancashire Senior Cup

1	Oct	10	(h)	Bury	D 2-2
R	Nov	23	(a)	Bury	L 3-4

Manchester Senior Cup

1	Feb	14	(a)	Glossop	L*0-3
1		20	(h)	Glossop	L 1-4

*Match restaged because Glossop used
an unregistered player.

Friendlies

1	Sep	1	(h)	Ripley A	W 3-0
2		28	(a)	Altrincham	L 1-3
3	Dec	12	(a)	Brentford	W 2-0
4		14	(h)	Lancs Fusilrs	W 2-1
5	Jan	23	(h)	G.Robey's XI	L 0-3
6	Feb	4	(h)	Hull C	W 1-0
7	Mar	25	(a)	Hull C	D 0-0
8	Apr	17	(a)	Hearts	L 1-2

Hillman	McMahon	Burgess	Frost	Hynds	Moffatt	Meredith	Livingstone	Gillespie	Turnbull	Booth	Jones	Norgrove	Dorsett	Dearden	Buchan	Bannister	Holmes	Thornley	Pearson	Edmondson	McOustra	Christie	Threlfall	
1	2	3	4	5		7	8	9	10	11											6			1
	2	3	4	5		7	8		10	11								9		1	6			2
1	2	3	4	5		7	8		10	11						6		9						3
1	2		4	5			8		10	11				6		3		9				7		4
1		3	4	5		7	8		10	11				6		2		9						5
1	2	3	4	5		7	8	9	10	11				6										6
1	2		4	5		7	8	9	10	11		3		6										7
1	2	3	4	5		7	8	9	10	11				6										8
1	2	3	4	5		7	8	9	10	11				6										9
1	2	3	4	5		7	8	9	10	11				6										10
1		3	4	5		7	10	9		11		2		6	8									11
1	2	3	4	5		7	10	9		11					8	6								12
1	2	3	4	5	6	7	8	9	10	11														13
1	2	3	5	4		7	8	9	10	11		6												14
1	2	3	5	4		7	8	9	10	11									6					15
1	2	3	4	5	6	7	8	9	10	11														16
1	2	3	4	5	6	7		9	10	11							8							17
1	2	3	4	5	6	7	8	9	10	11														18
1	2	3	4	5	6	7	8	9	10	11														19
	2	3	4	5	8				10	11	9		7							1	6			20
1	2	3	4	5	6	7		9	10	11			8											21
1	2	3	4	5	6	7			10	11	9		8											22
1	2	3	4	5	6	7			10	11	9		8											23
1		3	4	5	6	7			10	11		2	9				8							24
1	2		4	5	6	7			10		9	3	11				8							25
1	2	3	4	5		7			10	11	9		6				8							26
1	2		4	5		7	8		10	11	9	3		6										27
1	2	3	4	5		7	8		10	11	9			6										28
1	2	3	4	5		7	8		10	11	9		6											29
1	2	3	4	5		7	10			11	9		6		8									30
1	2		4	5		7	8		10	11	9	3		6										31
1	2		4	5		7	8		10	11	9	3		6										32
1	2		4	5		7	8			11	9	3		6					10					33
1	2		4	5		7	8		10	11	9	3		6										34
32	31	26	32	33	13	33	26	16	30	33	12	10	9	8	7	6	4	4	3	2	2	1	1	
				2	1	8	7	7	19	8	2		5			3		2	1					

53

1905-06

1	Sep	2	(a)	Sheffield W	L 0-1		25,000
2		6	(a)	Newcastle U	D 2-2	Thornley, Dorsett	22,000
3		9	(h)	Nottingham F	W 5-0	Dorsett (2), Livingstone, Jones, Booth	16,000
4		16	(h)	Wolves	W 4-0	Jones (2), Livingstone, Booth	20,000
5		23	(a)	Bury	W 4-2	Thornley (2), Livingstone, Dorsett	24,000
6		30	(h)	Middlesbrough	W 4-0	Dorsett (2), Jones, McMahon	20,000
7	Oct	7	(a)	Preston N E	L 0-2		10,000
8		21	(a)	Aston Villa	L 1-2	Livingstone	30,000
9		28	(h)	Liverpool	L 0-1		30,000
10	Nov	4	(a)	Sheffield U	W 3-1	Dorsett, Thornley, Jones	8,000
11		11	(h)	Notts C	W 5-1	Thornley (2), Turnbull, Dorsett, Buchan	14,000
12		18	(a)	Stoke	D 0-0		8,000
13		25	(h)	Bolton W	W 3-1	Thornley, Jones, Booth	38,000
14	Dec	2	(a)	W Arsenal	L 0-2		15,000
15		9	(h)	Blackburn R	D 1-1	Dorsett	16,000
16		16	(a)	Sunderland	L 0-2		15,000
17		23	(h)	Birmingham	W 4-1	Thurnbull (2), Livingstone, opp.og	15,000
18		25	(a)	Derby C	W 2-1	Dorsett, Frost	12,000
19		26	(h)	Newcastle U	L 1-4	Burgess	35,000
20		30	(h)	Sheffield W	W 2-1	Banks, Booth	16,000
21	Jan	1	(h)	Everton	W 1-0	Thornley	25,000
22		6	(a)	Nottingham F	W 1-0	Thornley	4,000
23		20	(a)	Wolves	W 3-2	Thornley, Livingstone, Booth	5,000
24		27	(h)	Bury	W 5-2	Thornley (2), Dorsett, Booth, Turnbull	16,000
25	Feb	10	(a)	Preston N E	D 0-0		12,000
26	Mar	3	(a)	Liverpool	W 1-0	Booth	30,000
27		10	(h)	Sheffield U	L 1-2	Bannister	18,000
28		14	(h)	Aston Villa	L 1-4	Dorsett	10,000
29		17	(a)	Notts C	L 0-3		12,000
30		24	(h)	Stoke	W 2-0	Dorsett, Thornley	8,000
31		31	(a)	Bolton W	W 3-1	Thornley (2), Livingstone	40,000
32	Apr	7	(a)	W Arsenal	L 1-2	Dorsett	12,000
33		13	(h)	Derby C	L 1-2	Dorsett	15,000
34		14	(a)	Blackburn R	D 1-1	Turnbull	12,000
35		16	(a)	Everton	W 3-0	Thornley (2), Turnbull	10,000
36		17	(a)	Middlesbrough	L 1-6	J.Moffatt	8,000
37		21	(h)	Sunderland	W 5-1	Thornley (3), Whittaker, Bannister	3,000
38		28	(a)	Birmingham	L 2-3	Burgess, Thornley	6,000

Appearances
Goals

League Division One record: P 38 W 19 D 5 L 14 F 73 A 54 Pts 43 Pos 5th

FA Cup

1 Jan 15 (a) Sheffield U L 1-4

Lancashire Senior Cup

1 Sep 18 (h) Darwen   W 2-1
2 Oct 4 (h) Accrington S L 2-3

Manchester Senior Cup

1   Feb 21 (a) Bolton W   D 1-1
R   26 (h) Bolton W   D 1-1
R   Mar 28 (n) Bolton W   D 1-1
R   Apr 4 (n) Bolton W   L 0-1

Friendlies

1 Sep 27 (a) Altrincham   L 2-3
2 Feb 3 (a) Corinthians L 1-4
3   24 (a) Bristol R   W 5-3

Edmondson	McMahon	Burgess	Buchan	Hynds	Banks	Dorsett	Livingstone	Thornley	Jones	Turnbull	Booth	Bannister	Hillman	Norgrove	Frost	McOustra	Whittaker	Christie	Dearden	Steele	Gregory	Moffatt	Pearson	Young	#
	2	3	6	5		7	8		9		11	1							4			10			1
		3	4	5		7	8	10	9		11	1	2			6									2
1		3	4	5		7	8	10	9		11			2		6									3
1		3	4	5		7	8	10	9		11			2		6									4
1	2	3	4	5		7	8	10	9		11					6									5
1	2	3	4	5		7	8	10	9		11					6									6
1	2		4	5		7	8	10	9							6	11				3				7
1	2	3	4	5		7	8	10	9		11					6									8
1	2	3	6	5		7	8	10	9		11											4			9
1	2	3	4	5		7	6	8	9	10	11														10
1	2	3	4	5		7	6	8	9	10	11														11
1	2	3	6	5		7	8	10	9		11			4											12
1	2	3		5		7	6	8	9	10	11			4											13
1	2	3	6	5		7		8	9	10	11			4											14
1	2	3		5		11	8	7	9	10				4					6						15
1		3	4	5		7	8		9	10	11			2					6						16
1	2	3		5	6	7	8	9		10	11			4											17
1	2	3		5	6	7	8	9		10	11			4											18
1	2	3		5	6		8	9		10	11	7		4											19
1		3	4	5	6	7		9		10	11	8			2										20
1		3		5	6	7		9		10	11	8		4	2										21
1		3		5	6	7		8	9	10	11			4	2										22
1	2	3	6	5	4	11	10		9	8	7														23
	2	3	4	5	6	7	8		9	10	11		1												24
	2	3	4		6	7	8		9	10	11		1				5								25
1	2	3	4	5	6	7	8		9	10	11														26
1	2	3	4	5	6	7	8		9		11	10													27
1	2		4	5	6	11	8	7	9	10				3											28
1	2		4	5	6	11		7	9	10		8		3											29
	2		4		6	11	8	7	9	10			1	3							5				30
	2	3	4	5	6	7	8		9	10	11		1												31
	2		4	5	6	7			9	10	11	8	1	3											32
		3		5	6	7	8	9	10	11			1							2	4				33
		3		5	6	7		9	10	8			1				11	2	4						34
		3		5	6		9	7	10	8			1				11	2	4						35
		3	4	5			9	7	10	8			1				11	2			6				36
1				5	6		9	7	10	8							11	3	4	2					37
1		3		5	6	7		9	10	8							11	2	4						38
27	25	32	29	33	21	34	26	36	25	26	28	11	11	11	9	7	6	5	4	4	3	3	1	1	
1	2	1		1	15	7	21	6	6	7	2			1		1						1			

1906-07

1	Sep 1	(h)	W Arsenal	L 1-4	Dorsett		18,000
2	3	(a)	Everton	L 1-9	Fisher		16,000
3	8	(a)	Sheffield W	L 1-3	Conlin		12,000
4	15	(h)	Bury	D 2-2	Jones, Thornley		20,000
5	22	(a)	Derby C	D 2-2	Dorsett (2)		8,000
6	29	(a)	Middlesbrough	W 3-2	Stewart, Thornley, Fisher		22,000
7	Oct 6	(h)	Preston N E	D 1-1	Thornley		25,000
8	13	(a)	Newcastle U	L 0-2			22,000
9	20	(h)	Aston Villa	W 4-2	Thornley (2), Stewart, Conlin		30,600
10	27	(a)	Liverpool	L 4-5	Thornley (2), Stewart, Jones		20,000
11	Nov 3	(h)	Bristol C	L 0-1			20,000
12	10	(a)	Notts C	D 0-0			10,000
13	17	(h)	Sheffield U	L 0-2			20,000
14	24	(a)	Bolton W	D 1-1	Thornley		30,000
15	Dec 1	(h)	Manchester U	W 3-0	Stewart (2), Jones		40,000
16	8	(a)	Stoke	L 0-3			5,000
17	15	(h)	Blackburn R	D 0-0			12,000
18	22	(a)	Sunderland	D 1-1	Thornley		12,000
19	25	(h)	Birmingham	W 1-0	Dorsett		24,000
20	26	(h)	Everton	W 3-1	Steele, Thornley, Jones		25,000
21	29	(a)	W Arsenal	L 1-4	Thornley		15,000
22	Jan 2	(h)	Middlesbrough	W 3-1	Jones (2), Thornley		8,000
23	5	(h)	Sheffield W	L 0-1			25,000
24	19	(a)	Bury	L 1-3	Grieve		16,000
25	26	(h)	Derby C	D 2-2	Thornley, Jones		20,000
26	Feb 9	(a)	Preston N E	W 3-1	Dorsett, Grieve, Jones		10,000
27	16	(h)	Newcastle U	D 1-1	Jones		35,000
28	23	(a)	Aston Villa	L 1-4	Stewart		15,000
29	Mar 2	(h)	Liverpool	W 1-0	Grieve		20,000
30	9	(a)	Bristol C	L 0-2			12,000
31	16	(h)	Notts C	W 2-1	Grieve, Ross		18,000
32	23	(a)	Sheffield U	W 4-1	Grieve (2), Dorsett (2)		15,000
33	29	(a)	Birmingham	L 0-4			10,000
34	30	(h)	Bolton W	D 1-1	Jones		30,000
35	Apr 6	(a)	Manchester U	D 1-1	Dorsett		35,000
36	13	(h)	Stoke	D 2-2	Stewart, Jones		12,000
37	20	(a)	Blackburn R	L 0-4			5,000
38	27	(h)	Sunderland	L 2-3	Stewart, Eyres		15,000

Appearances
Goals

League Division One record: P 38   W 10   D 12   L 16   F 53   A 77   Pts 32   Pos 17th

FA Cup

1	Jan 12	(a)	Blackburn R	D 2-2
R	16	(h)	Blackburn R	L 0-1

Lancashire Senior Cup

1	Oct 1	(a)	Bolton W	L 3-4

Manchester Senior Cup

1	Feb 2	(h)	Atherton Church	W 5-1
SF	Apr 17	(h)	Manchester U	W 2-1
F	29	(h)	Stockport C	W 2-0

Friendlies

1	Apr 1	(a)	Ilford	D 3-3
2	2	(a)	Norwich C	D 2-2
3	3	(a)	King's Lynn	W 4-0
4	30	(a)	Northwich District XI	L 0-4

56

Smith	Kelso	Hill	Norgrove	Steele	Eadie	Buchan	Stewart	Dorsett	Grieve	Thornley	Jones	Conlin	Ross	Hall	Blair	McOustra	Davies	Fisher	Banks	Christie	Farrell	Rankin	Wilkinson	Baldwin	Blew	Eyres	Hamblett	
	3		4	5		7	6	9		8	10	11			1					2								1
		3	4	5		7	6	9			10	11			1	8				2								2
	2	3	4	5	6	7	10			9		11		1									8					3
		3	4	5	6	7				9	8	11		1			10						2					4
	2	3	4	5	6	7	8			9		11		1			10											5
	2	3	4	5	6	7	8			9		11		1			10											6
	2	3	4	5	6	7	8			9		11		1			10											7
	2	3	4	5		7	8			9	10	11		1				6										8
	2	3	4	5		7	8			9	10	11		1				6										9
	2	3	4	5		7	8			9	10	11		1				6										10
		3	4	5		7	8			9	10	11		1				6	2									11
	2	3	4	5	6	7	10			9	8	11		1														12
	5	2	3	4	6	7	10			9	8	11		1														13
1	2	3		5	6	7	4			9	8	11	10															14
1	2	3		5	6	7	4			9	8	11	10															15
1	2	3		5	6	7	4			9	8	11	10															16
1	2	3		5	4	7	8			9		11	10			6												17
1	2	3		5	4	7	8			9	10	11				6												18
1	2	3		5	4	7	8			9	10	11				6												19
1	2	3	4	5	6	7	8			9	10	11																20
1	2	3	4	5	6	7			9	8	10	11																21
1		2	3	4	5	6	7		8	9	10	11																22
1		2	3	4	5	7	8			9		11				6					10							23
1	2	3	4	5	6	7	11	8	9	10																		24
1	2	3		5	4	7	8			9	10	11				6												25
1	2	3		5			4	8		9	10	11				6						7						26
1	2	3		5		7	4			9	10	11				6					8							27
1	2			5		7	4	8	9		10					6			3	11								28
	3	2			6	7	4	8		9		11	10		1									5				29
1	3	2		5	6	7	4	8	9			11	10															30
	3	2		5	4	7		8	9			11	10		1	6												31
	3	2	4	5	6	7		9	8			11	10		1													32
1	3	2	4	5	6	7		9	8			11	10															33
1	3	2	4	5		7		9	8		10	11				6												34
1	3	2		5	4	7	8			9	10	11				6												35
1	3	2		4		7		8	9		10	11				6					5							36
1		2	3	4	5	7		9	8		10					6						11						37
1	3	2		4		7		10	8			11				6										9	5	38
22	24	21	27	23	31	28	36	32	19	29	27	35	6	11	9	9	5	5	4	4	3	2	2	1	1	1	1	
			1			8	8	6	13	11	2	1						2						1				

57

1907-08

1	Sep	2 (a)	Sunderland	W 5-2	Grieve (3), Stewart, Conlin	20,000
2		7 (a)	Everton	D 3-3	Thornley (3)	30,000
3		14 (h)	Sunderland	D 0-0		30,000
4		21 (a)	W Arsenal	L 1-2	Thornley	12,000
5		28 (h)	Sheffield W	W 3-2	Ross (2), Thornley	30,000
6	Oct	5 (a)	Bristol C	L 1-2	Thornley	12,000
7		12 (h)	Notts C	W 2-1	Grieve (2)	10,000
8		19 (h)	Newcastle U	W 1-0	Thornley	28,000
9		26 (a)	Preston N E	W 4-2	Dorsett, Grieve, Thornley, Conlin	14,000
10	Nov	2 (h)	Bury	D 2-2	Jones, Wood	30,000
11		9 (a)	Aston Villa	D 2-2	Thornley (2)	20,000
12		16 (h)	Liverpool	D 1-1	Dorsett	25,000
13		23 (a)	Middlesbrough	L 0-2		10,000
14	Dec	7 (a)	Chelsea	D 2-2	Buchan, Jones	40,000
15		14 (h)	Nottingham F	W 4-2	Wood (2), Eadie, Thornley	18,000
16		21 (a)	Manchester U	L 1-3	Eadie	35,000
17		25 (a)	Birmingham	L 1-2	Dorsett	20,000
18		26 (h)	Bolton W	W 1-0	Grieve	35,000
19		28 (h)	Blackburn R	W 2-0	Dorsett, Thornley	22,000
20	Jan	1 (a)	Bolton W	L 0-2		26,000
21		4 (h)	Everton	W 4-2	Grieve (2), Ross, Conlin	9,000
22		18 (h)	W Arsenal	W 4-0	Eadie, Wood, Grieve, Jones	25,000
23		25 (a)	Sheffield W	L 1-5	Dorsett	11,000
24	Feb	8 (a)	Notts C	L 0-1		8,000
25		15 (h)	Newcastle U	D 1-1	Conlin	25,000
26		29 (a)	Bury	D 0-0		10,000
27	Mar	7 (h)	Aston Villa	W 3-2	Dorsett (3)	25,000
28		11 (h)	Sheffield U	L 0-2		18,000
29		14 (a)	Liverpool	W 1-0	Dorsett	18,000
30		21 (h)	Middlesbrough	W 2-1	Webb, Thornley	35,000
31		28 (a)	Sheffield U	W 2-1	Thornley, Conlin	12,000
32	Apr	4 (h)	Chelsea	L 0-3		25,000
33		6 (h)	Preston N E	W 5-0	Buchan (2), Webb (2), Wilkinson	10,000
34		11 (a)	Nottingham F	L 1-3	Dorsett	10,000
35		17 (h)	Birmingham	W 2-1	Jones, Conlin	27,000
36		18 (h)	Manchester U	D 0-0		40,000
37		21 (h)	Bristol C	D 0-0		2,500
38		25 (a)	Blackburn R	D 0-0		10,000

Appearances
Goals

League Division One record: P 38   W 16   D 11   L 11   F 62   A 54   Pts 43   Pos 3rd

FA Cup

1	Jan	11 (a)	Glossop	D 0-0	
R		15 (h)	Glossop	W 6-0	
2	Feb	1 (h)	New Brompton	D 1-1	
R		5 (a)	New Brompton	W 2-1	
3		22 (h)	Fulham	D 1-1	
R		26 (a)	Fulham	L 1-3	

Lancashire Senior Cup

1	Sep 23 (a)	Manchester U	L 0-3	

Manchester Senior Cup

1	Mar 18 (a)	Manchester U	L 0-1	

Friendlies

1	Dec 11 (h)	George Robey's Old City XI		W 4-3
2	Apr 28 (a)	Aston Villa		D 2-2

Smith	Kelso	Hill	Jackson	Norgrove	Buchan	Eadie	Blair	Stewart	Dorsett	Grieve	Wood	Thornley	Jones	Conlin	Webb	Ross	Buckley	Steele	Callaghan	Holford	Baldwin	Bannister	Wilkinson	
1	3	2			4	5	6	7	8			9	10	11										1
1	2		3		4	5	6	7	8			9	10	11										2
1	2		3		4	5	6	7	8			9	10	11										3
1	3	2			4	5	6	7	8			9	10	11										4
1	3	2			4	5	6		7		8	9		11	10									5
1	3	2			4	5	6		7	8		9		11	10									6
1	3	2				5	6		7	9	8			11	10			4						7
1	2		3			5	6	7	8	10		9		11				4						8
1	2		3			5	6	7	8	10		9		11			4							9
1	2	4	3				6			8	10	9	7	11			5							10
1	2		3				6		7	8	4	9	10	11			5							11
1	2		3				6		7	8	4	9	10	11			5							12
1		2	3				6		7		4	9	10	11		8	5							13
1		2		3	4	5	6		7			9	10	11		8								14
1		2		3	4	5	6		7		8	9		11	10									15
1		2		3	4	5	6		7		8	9	10	11										16
1		2		3		5	6		7	10	8	9		11				4						17
1		2		3		5	6	7	4	10	8	9		11										18
1		2		3		5	6	7	4	10	8	9		11										19
1		2		3		5	6	7	4	10	8	9		11										20
1		2		3	4	5		7	6	9	8			11		10								21
1	2		3		4	5		7	6	9	8		10	11										22
1	2		3		4			7	6	9	8		10	11			5							23
1	2		3		5		6		4		8	9		11		10			7					24
1	2		3		4	5	6		7		8	9	11			10								25
1	2		3		4	5			11		8	10							7	9	6			26
1	2		3		4	5	6		9		10	8		11	7									27
1	2		3		4	5	6		9			8	10	11	7									28
1	2		3		4	5	6		9			8	10	11	7									29
1	2		3		4	5	6		9			8	10	11	7									30
1	2		3		4	5	6		9			8	10	11	7									31
1	2		3		4	5	6		9			8		11	7	10								32
1	2		3		4		6		9			8		11	7		5						10	33
1	2		3		4	5	6		9	8			10	11	7									34
1	2		3		4	5	6		9			8	10	11	7									35
1		2	3		4	5	6		9			8	10	11	7									36
1		2	3		4		6		7			8	9	10	11					5				37
1	2		3		4		6		9			8	10	11	7					5				38
38	25	17	21	14	27	29	34	10	34	17	22	31	24	37	11	10	7	3	2	2	1	1	1	
								3	3	1	10	10	4	14	4	6	3	3			1			

1908-09

1	Sep	1	(h)	Sunderland	W 1-0	Eadie	25,000
2		5	(h)	Blackburn R	D 3-3	Thornley (2), Jones	30,000
3		12	(a)	Bradford C	D 0-0		30,000
4		19	(h)	Manchester U	L 1-2	Thornley	40,000
5		26	(a)	Everton	L 3-6	Thornley (3)	20,000
6	Oct	3	(h)	Leicester F	W 5-2	Grieve (2), Ross (2), Dorsett	15,000
7		10	(a)	W Arsenal	L 0-3		10,000
8		17	(h)	Notts C	W 1-0	Thornley	20,000
9		24	(a)	Newcastle U	L 0-2		25,000
10		31	(h)	Bristol C	W 5-1	Thornley (2), Buchan, Dorsett, Wood	20,000
11	Nov	7	(a)	Preston N E	L 0-3		10,000
12		14	(h)	Middlesbrough	D 0-0		18,000
13		21	(a)	Sheffield W	L 1-3	Thornley	11,000
14		28	(a)	Liverpool	W 3-1	Dorsett, Conlin, Jones	15,000
15	Dec	5	(h)	Bury	W 6-1	Thornley (3), Dorsett (2), Stewart	30,000
16		12	(a)	Sheffield U	L 0-4		12,000
17		19	(h)	Aston Villa	W 2-0	Dorsett, Holford	18,000
18		25	(h)	Chelsea	L 1-2	Dorsett	25,000
19		26	(a)	Chelsea	W 2-1	Jones, Ross	40,000
20		28	(a)	Nottingham F	W 2-0	Holford, Ross	10,000
21	Jan	2	(a)	Blackburn R	L 2-3	Wood, Conlin	12,000
22		9	(h)	Bradford C	W 4-3	Holford (3), Conlin	10,000
23		23	(a)	Manchester U	L 1-3	Conlin	40,000
24		30	(h)	Everton	W 4-0	Holford (3), Wilkinson	30,000
25	Feb	13	(a)	W Arsenal	D 2-2	Buchan, Holford	20,000
26		20	(a)	Notts C	L 1-5	Dorsett	4,000
27		27	(h)	Newcastle U	L 0-2		30,000
28	Mar	11	(a)	Leicester F	L 1-3	Thornley	8,000
29		13	(h)	Preston N E	W 4-1	Thornley (2), Yuill, Jones	12,000
30		20	(a)	Middlesbrough	L 0-3		10,000
31		27	(h)	Sheffield W	W 4-0	Holford (3), Jones	12,000
32	Apr	3	(h)	Liverpool	W 4-0	Buchan, Jones, Ross, Dorsett	15,000
33		9	(a)	Sunderland	L 0-2		15,000
34		10	(a)	Bury	L 0-1		16,000
35		13	(h)	Nottingham F	W 2-1	Thornley, Conlin	3,000
36		17	(h)	Sheffield U	L 1-3	Thornley	10,000
37		26	(a)	Aston Villa	L 1-2	Buchan	15,000
38		28	(a)	Bristol C	L 0-1		8,000

Appearances
Goals

League Division One record: P 38   W 15   D 4   L 19   F 67   A 69   Pts 34   Pos 19th

FA Cup

1	Jan 16	(h)	Tottenham H	L 3-4

Lancashire Senior Cup

1	Oct 12	(h)	Preston N E	W 1-0
2	26	(a)	Southport C	W 2-1
SF	Nov 23	(h)	Blackburn R	D 3-3
R	Dec 7	(a)	Blackburn R	L 0-7

Manchester Senior Cup

1	Oct 10	(h)	Northern Nomads	D 1-1
R	Nov 18	(a)	Northern Nomads	W 5-2*
R	30	(n)	Northern Nomads	D 2-2
R	Feb 6	(h)	Northern Nomads	W 7-0
SF	Apr 5	(a)	Bolton W	L 0-1

*Abandoned in extra-time.

Friendlies

1	Sep 16	(h)	Northern Nomads	W 9-1
2	Mar 6	(a)	Q.P.R. (postponed at KO)	
3	Apr 26	(a)	Plymouth A	W 3-2
4	29	(a)	Merthyr	W 4-2
5	30	(a)	Munster Assn	W 4-2

60

Match	Smith	Burgess	Kelso	Jackson	Buchan	Holford	Blair	Dorsett	Webb	Jones	Thornley	Ross	Conlin	Wilkinson	Eadie	Grieve	Stewart	Norgrove	Wood	Broomfield	Brown	Buckley	Yuill	Hendren	Bottomley	Hitchcock	Mansfield	Ramsey	Match
1	1	2	3	4		6			7	10	9		11		5	8													1
2	1	2	3	4		6			7	10	9		11		5	8													2
3	1	2	3	4		6			7	10	9		11		5	8													3
4	1	2	3	4		6	11		7	8	9	10			5														4
5	1	2	3	4	5	6			7		9	10	11			8													5
6	1	2	3	4				8	7			10	11		5	9						6							6
7	1	2	3	4				8	7			10	11		5	9						6							7
8	1	2	3	4		6				9	8		10	11			7								5				8
9	1	2	3	4	5	6				9	8		10	11			7												9
10	1	3	2	4			11		7	10	9				5				8		6								10
11	1	3	2	4			11		7	10	9				5				8		6								11
12	1	3	2	4	5	6			7	10	9		11						8										12
13		3	2	4	5	6		10			9		11			8	7			1									13
14		3	2	4	5	6	7		10	8			11						9	1									14
15	1	3	2	4	5	6		10		8	9		11				7												15
16	1	3	2	4	5	6		10		8	9		11				7												16
17	1	2		4	5	6	11			8	9			10			7	3											17
18	1	2		4	5	6	11			8	9			10			7	3											18
19	1		2	4	5	6	7			8	9		10	11				3											19
20	1		2	4	9	6	7						10	11	5			3	8										20
21	1	2		4	5	6	7				9		10	11				3	8										21
22	1		2	4	9	6	7			8			10	11	5			3											22
23		2		4	9	6	7				8		10	11	5			3		1									23
24	1	3	2	4	9	6				8			10	11	5		7												24
25	1	3	2	4	9	6				8		7	10	11	5														25
26	1	3	2	4	9	6	7			8			10	11	5														26
27		2	3	4	5				7	10	9		11	6		9				1									27
28	1	2	3	4		6					9		10		5							11	7	8					28
29	1	2	3	4	5	6				8	9		10									11	7						29
30	1	2	3	4	5	6					9		10									11	7				8		30
31	1	2	3	4	5	6				8		7	10		5							11							31
32	1	2	3	4	9	6	11			8		7	10		5														32
33	1	2	3	4	9	6	11			8		7	10		5														33
34	1	2	3	4	9	10				8		7		11	5													6	34
35	1	2	3	4	9	6				10		7		11	5									8					35
36	1	2	3	4	8	6				8		7		11	5											10			36
37	1	2	3	4		6				8		7	10	11	9	5													37
38	1	2	3	4		6	7			8	9		10	11	5														38
Totals	34	26	21	22	38	26	31	22	11	29	32	22	27	17	10	8	8	7	6	4	4	4	3	2	1	1	1	1	
			4	12					9			6	18	5	5	1	1	2	1		2		1						

61

1909-10

1	Sep	2 (h)	Blackpool	L 1-2	Thornley	10,000
2		4 (a)	Leicester F	W 3-1	Stewart, Ross, Conlin	9,000
3		11 (h)	Lincoln C	W 6-2	Jones (2), Thornley (2), Dorsett, Conlin	8,000
4		18 (a)	Clapton O	L 2-3	Dorsett, Ross	15,000
5		25 (a)	Blackpool	D 0-0		8,000
6	Oct	2 (a)	Hull C	W 2-1	Jones, Dorsett	12,000
7		9 (h)	Derby C	W 2-1	Holford, Conlin	20,000
8		16 (a)	Stockport C	W 2-1	Eadie, Conlin	12,000
9		23 (h)	Glossop	D 3-3	Ross (2), Holford	14,000
10		27 (a)	Gainsborough T	W 3-1	Jones (3)	6,000
11		30 (a)	Birmingham	D 1-1	Thornley	18,000
12	Nov	6 (h)	West Brom A	W 3-2	Holford (2), Thornley	24,000
13		13 (a)	Oldham A	L 0-1		22,000
14		27 (a)	Fulham	D 1-1	Thornley	12,000
15	Dec	4 (h)	Burnley	W 4-0	Jones (2), Thornley, Dorsett	12,000
16		11 (a)	Leeds C	W 3-1	Thornley (2), Ross	3,000
17		18 (h)	Wolves	W 6-0	Thornley (3), Dorsett (2), Ross	20,000
18		25 (a)	Bradford	L 0-2		18,000
19		27 (h)	Grimsby T	W 2-0	Wynn, Holford	20,000
20	Jan	1 (h)	Bradford	W 3-1	Wynn, Dorsett (2)	25,000
21		8 (h)	Leicester C	W 2-0	Jones, Holford	25,000
22		22 (a)	Lincoln C	W 2-0	Wynn, Conlin	9,000
23	Feb	12 (h)	Hull C	W 3-0	Conlin, Wynn, Holford	30,000
24		26 (h)	Stockport C	W 2-1	Wynn (2)	16,000
25	Mar	9 (h)	Barnsley	D 0-0		15,000
26		12 (h)	Birmingham	W 3-0	Eadie, Jones, Conlin	15,000
27		16 (a)	Derby C	L 1-3	Dorsett	12,000
28		19 (a)	West Brom A	D 0-0		10,000
29		25 (a)	Grimsby T	W 1-0	Jones	8,000
30		26 (h)	Oldham A	L 0-2		40,000
31		28 (h)	Gainsborough T	W 3-1	Dorsett, Holford, Jones	15,000
32	Apr	2 (a)	Barnsley	D 1-1	Dorsett	10,000
33		6 (a)	Glossop	W 3-0	Conlin (2), Gould	5,000
34		9 (h)	Fulham	W 3-1	Holford (2), Wynn	16,000
35		13 (h)	Clapton O	W 2-1	Dorsett, Wynn	8,000
36		16 (a)	Burnley	D 3-3	Gould, Holford, Wynn	7,000
37		23 (h)	Leeds C	W 3-0	Dorsett, Wynn, Conlin	16,000
38		30 (a)	Wolves	L 2-3	Holford, Conlin	10,000

Appearances
Goals

League Division Two record: P 38   W 23   D 8   L 7   F 81   A 40   Pts 54   Pos 1st

FA Cup

1 Jan 15 (a) Workington   W 2-1
2 Feb 5 (a) Southampton   W 5-0
3   19 (a) Aston Villa   W 2-1
4 Mar 5 (a) Swindon T   L 0-2

Lancashire Senior Cup

1 Oct 11 (h) Southport C   W 3-0
2   25 (h) Burnley   W 4-1
SF Nov 22 (a) Blackburn R   L 1-4

Manchester Senior Cup

1 Feb 2 (h) Manchester U   L 2-6

Friendlies

1 Aug 28 (h) Local Amateur XI W 5-1
2 Apr 18 (a) Chirk/Wrexham XI D 4-4

Tour

1 May 15 (a) Hamburg Vic   W 2-0
2   16 (a) Danish XI   W 3-2
3   18 (a) Danish XI   L 2-5
4   21 (a) Gothenburg Org W 3-2
5   23 (a) Gothenburg Org W 6-0

Lyall	Kelso	Jackson	Buchan	Eadie	Dorsett	Stewart	Wynn	Holford	Thornley	Jones	Conlin	Bottomley	Ross	Wilkinson	Norgrove	Chapelow	Gould	Burgess	Furr	Smith	Blair	Brown	James	Coupe	Davies	Swann	
	2		4		6	7			9	8	11			5		10		3	1								1
	2		4		6	7	5		9	8	11	10			3				1								2
	2		4		6	7	5		9	8	11	10			3				1								3
	2		4		6	7	5		9	8	11	10			3										1		4
1	2		4		6	7	5		9	8	11	10			3												5
1	2		4	5	6				9	8	10	11			3	7											6
1	2		4	5	6	7			9	8	10	11			3												7
	2		4	5	6	7			9	8	10	11			3											1	8
1	2		4	5	6			9	7	10	11	8			3												9
1	2	3	4	5	6	7		9		8	10											11					10
1	2	3	4	5	6	7				8	10											11	9				11
1	2	3	4	5	6	7			9	8	10	11															12
1	2	3	4	5	6	7			9	8	10	11															13
1	2	3			5	6			9	10	11	4	8			7											14
1		3			5	6			9	10	11	4	8			7		2									15
1	2	3			5	6			9	10	11	4	8			7											16
1	2	3			5	6			9	10	11	4	8			7											17
1	2	3			5	6	8	9		10	11	4				7											18
1					5	6	7	8	9	10	11	4						3						2			19
1	2	3			5	6	7	8	9	10	11	4															20
1	2	3			5	6	7	8	9	10	11	4															21
1	2	3			5	6	7	8	9	10	11	4															22
1	2	3			5	6	7	8	9	10	11	4															23
1	2	3	4	5	6	7	8	9		10	11																24
1	2	3	4	5	6	7	8	9		10	11																25
1	2	3	4	5	6	7	8	9		10	11																26
1	2	3	4	5	6	7	8	9		10	11																27
1	2	3	4	5	6	7			9	10	11	8															28
1	2	3	4		6	7	8	5	9	10	11																29
1	2		4			7	8	5	9	10	11							3			6						30
1	2	3	4					8	9	10	11			5						7	6						31
1	2	3	6					8	4	11	10			5						7			9				32
1	2	3	6					8	9	10	11	4		5			7										33
1	2	3	6					8	9	10	11	4		5			7										34
1	2	3	6					8	9	10	11	4		5			7										35
1	2	3	6					8	9	10		4		5			11	7									36
1	2	3	6					8	9	4	10	11		5			7										37
1	2	3	6					8	9	4	10	11		5			7										38
33	28	35	20	23	38	22	20	30	23	37	35	14	11	9	8	7	6	4	3	3	2	2	2	1	1	1	
		2			13	1		10	12	12	12	11		6			2										

1910-11

1	Sep	1	(h)	Bury	W 5-1	Wynn (3), Holford, Conlin	18,000
2		3	(a)	Preston N E	D 1-1	Holford	10,000
3		10	(h)	Notts C	L 0-1		30,000
4		17	(a)	Manchester U	L 1-2	Jones	60,000
5		24	(h)	Liverpool	L 1-2	J.Dorsett	40,000
6	Oct	1	(a)	Bury	L 2-5	G.Dorsett, Wynn	20,000
7		8	(h)	Sheffield U	L 0-4		20,000
8		15	(a)	Aston Villa	L 1-2	Wall	20,000
9		22	(h)	Sunderland	D 3-3	Norgrove, G.Dorsett, Thornley	25,000
10		29	(a)	W Arsenal	W 1-0	J.Dorsett	10,000
11	Nov	5	(h)	Bradford C	L 1-3	J.Dorsett	12,000
12		12	(a)	Blackburn R	L 0-2		10,000
13		19	(h)	Nottingham F	W 1-0	Conlin	20,000
14		26	(h)	Oldham A	W 2-0	Thornley, Conlin	25,000
15	Dec	3	(a)	Everton	L 0-1		8,000
16		10	(h)	Sheffield W	L 1-2	Thornley	20,000
17		17	(a)	Bristol C	L 1-2	J.Smith	6,000
18		24	(h)	Newcastle U	W 2-0	Wynn, Conlin	25,000
19		26	(a)	Middlesbrough	D 0-0		30,000
20		27	(a)	Tottenham H	D 1-1	J.Smith	25,000
21		31	(h)	Preston N E	L 0-2		30,000
22	Jan	3	(h)	Tottenham H	W 2-1	Ross, Jones	20,000
23		7	(a)	Notts C	W 1-0	Ross	10,000
24		21	(h)	Manchester U	D 1-1	Jones	40,000
25		28	(a)	Liverpool	D 1-1	J.Smith	16,000
26	Feb	11	(a)	Sheffield U	D 2-2	J.Smith, Ross	12,000
27		18	(h)	Aston Villa	D 1-1	Jones	25,000
28		25	(a)	Sunderland	L 0-4		10,000
29	Mar	4	(h)	W Arsenal	D 1-1	Thornley	20,000
30		14	(a)	Bradford C	L 0-1		7,000
31		18	(h)	Blackburn R	D 0-0		35,000
32		25	(a)	Nottingham F	D 0-0		7,000
33	Apr	1	(a)	Oldham A	D 1-1	J.Smith	25,000
34		8	(h)	Everton	W 2-1	Wynn, Thornley	25,000
35		14	(h)	Middlesbrough	W 2-1	Thornley, Jones	35,000
36		15	(a)	Sheffield W	L 1-4	Jones	9,000
37		22	(h)	Bristol C	L 1-2	Wynn	30,000
38		29	(a)	Newcastle U	D 3-3	Wynn (2), Ross	11,000
						Appearances	
						Goals	

League Division One record: P 38   W 9   D 13   L 16   F 43   A 58   Pts 31   Pos 17th

FA Cup

1	Jan 14 (a) Stoke	W 2-1
2	Feb 4 (a) Wolves	L 0-1

Lancashire Senior Cup

1	Oct 10 (a) Blackpool	L 0-2

Manchester Senior Cup

1	Oct 3 (a) Bury	1-1
R	17 (h) Bury	W 5-0
SF	Nov 7 (a) Stockport C	W 2-1
F	Dec 14 (h) Manchester U	W 3-1

Friendlies

1	Oct 31 (a) Southampton	D 3-3
2	Mar 11 (a) Huddersfield T	L 2-3

Smith W.	Kelso	Norgrove	Chaplin	Bottomley	Dorsett G.	Eadie	Holford	Dorsett J.	Wynn	Thornley	Smith J.	Jones	Conlin	Stewart	Jackson	Ross	Wall	Nelson	Lyall	Buchan	Codling	Humphreys R.	Gould	Wilkinson	Brown	Burgess	Brooks	Salt	#
	2		4	6	5	9		8				10	11	7	3				1										1
	2		4	6	5	9	7	8				10	11		3				1										2
	2		4		5	9	7	8				10	11		3				1	6									3
	2		4		5	9	7					10	11		3	8			1	6									4
	2		4			9	7					10	11		3	8			1	6				5					5
	2			5	6		7	8				9	11		3	10			1	4									6
			4	11	5		7	8				10			3		9		1	6						2			7
1		3	4	6	5		7	8				10	11		2		9												8
1	2	3	4	6				8	9					7										5					9
1	2	3	4	6	5		7	8	9			10	11																10
1		3	4	6	5		7	8	9			10	11	2															11
1		3	4		5	9	10				8	6	11	7	2														12
1	2	3			5			8	9			6	11	7				10			4								13
1	2	3			5			8	9			6	11	7				10			4								14
1	2				5			8	9			6	11	7	3			10			4								15
1	2	3		6	5	9	7	8					11					10			4								16
1		3	4	8	5	6	7				9		11					10					2						17
1	2	3	4		5	6	7	8				9	10	11															18
1	2	3			5		11				8	9	10	7							4					6			19
1	2	3			5		10				8	9	6	11				7							4				20
1	2	3				6	11			8	5	9	10	7						4									21
1	2	3	4			6	11					9	10	7		8	5												22
1	2	3	4			6	11					9	10	7		8	5												23
1	2	3	4		5	6	11					9	10	7		8													24
1	2	3	4		5	6					9	10	11	7		8													25
1			4	6	5			8			9		11		3	10		7					2						26
1	2	3	4		5	6					9	10	11					7									8		27
1	2	3	8	4	5	6					9	10	11					7											28
1	2	3	4		5	6					9	10	11			8		7											29
1	2		4		5	6						9	10			8		7						11	3				30
1	2	3	4		5	6	11				8	9	10	7															31
1	2	3	4		5	6	11				8	9	10	7															32
1	2	3	4		5	6	7	8				9	10	11															33
1	2	3	4		5	6	7	8	9			10	11																34
1	2	3	4		5	6		8	9			10	11					7											35
1		3			5	6						9	10	11	2			4			7	8							36
1	2	3	4		5	6		8	9			10						7										11	37
1	2	3	4		5	6		8	9			10	11	7															38
31	31	13	15	19	23	29	29	26	20	18	14	34	27	17	13	10	10	8	7	6	5	3	2	2	2	2	1	1	
		1		2		2	3	9	6	5	6	4			4	1													

65

1911-12

1	Sep	2	(h)	Manchester U	D 0-0		25,000
2		9	(a)	Liverpool	D 2-2	Kelso (2)	15,000
3		16	(h)	Aston Villa	L 2-6	Holford, Jones	30,000
4		23	(a)	Newcastle U	L 0-1		10,000
5		30	(h)	Sheffield U	D 0-0		25,000
6	Oct	7	(a)	Oldham A	L 1-4	Thornley	15,000
7		14	(h)	Bolton W	W 3-1	Wall, Wynn, Keary	25,000
8		21	(a)	Bradford C	L 1-4	Thornley	12,000
9		28	(h)	W Arsenal	D 3-3	Wynn (2), Thornley	25,000
10	Nov	4	(a)	Preston N E	L 1-2	Kelso	10,000
11		11	(a)	Everton	L 0-1		15,000
12		18	(h)	West Brom A	L 0-2		12,000
13		25	(a)	Sunderland	D 1-1	J.Dorsett	4,000
14	Dec	2	(h)	Blackburn R	W 3-0	Wynn (2), J.Dorsett	40,000
15		9	(a)	Sheffield W	L 0-3		12,000
16		16	(h)	Bury	W 2-0	Wynn, Thornley	14,000
17		23	(a)	Middlesbrough	L 1-3	J.Dorsett	10,000
18		25	(h)	Notts C	W 1-0	Young	15,000
19		26	(h)	Notts C	W 4-0	Fletcher, Wynn, Young, Jones	35,000
20		30	(a)	Manchester U	D 0-0		41,743
21	Jan	6	(h)	Liverpool	L 2-3	Wynn (2)	10,000
22		20	(a)	Aston Villa	L 1-3	J.Dorsett	10,000
23		27	(h)	Newcastle U	D 1-1	Wynn	30,000
24	Feb	10	(h)	Oldham A	L 1-3	J.Smith	25,000
25		17	(a)	Bolton W	L 1-2	Brooks	20,000
26		26	(a)	Sheffield U	L 2-6	Thornley (2)	5,000
27	Mar	2	(a)	W Arsenal	L 0-2		12,000
28		9	(h)	Preston N E	D 0-0		13,000
29		16	(h)	Everton	W 4-0	Holford (4)	25,000
30		23	(a)	West Brom A	D 1-1	Bottomley	8,000
31		28	(h)	Bradford C	W 4-0	Holford (2), Wynn, Jones	10,000
32		30	(h)	Sunderland	W 2-0	Wynn, Holford	20,000
33	Apr	5	(h)	Tottenham H	W 2-1	Jones, J.Dorsett	10,000
34		6	(a)	Blackburn R	L 0-2		14,000
35		8	(a)	Tottenham H	W 2-0	Jones, J.Dorsett	15,000
36		13	(h)	Sheffield W	W 4-0	Wynn (3), Jones	30,000
37		20	(a)	Bury	W 2-1	Wynn (2)	18,000
38		27	(h)	Middlesbrough	W 2-0	Jones, J.Dorsett	20,000

Appearances
Goals

League Division One record: P 38   W 13   D 9   L 16   F 56   A 58   Pts 35   Pos 15th

FA Cup

1	Jan 13	(a)	Preston N E	W 1-0
2	Feb 3	(h)	Oldham A	L 0-1

Lancashire Senior Cup

| 1 | Oct 9 | (a) | Bury | L 0-4 |

Manchester Senior Cup

| 1 | Oct 16 | (h) | Oldham A | W 2-1 |
| SF | Nov 27 | (a) | Rochdale | L 0-2 |

Friendly

| 1 | Sep 27 | (a) | Altrincham | W 1-0 |

Smith W.	Goodchild	Henry	Fletcher	Lawrence	Bottomley	Eadie	Holford	Hoad	Wynn	Thornley	Jones	Dorsett J.	Wall	Young	Beeby	Kelso	Keary	Kelly	Davies	Booth	Smith J.	Norgrove	Ross	Brooks	Bentley	Dorsett G.	Eden	
1						5	6	7	8	9	10	11		2			4					3						1
1						5	6	7	8	9	10	11		2			4					3						2
1						5	6	7	8	9	10			2			4	11				3						3
		3				2	6	7			10	5		1			4	11	9				8					4
		3				3	6	7	8			5		1			4	11	9				10					5
		3	4			5		7	8			11	6	1	2	10					9							6
		3	4				6	7	8	9		11	5	1	2	10												7
		3	4			5		7	8	9	6	11		1	2	10												8
		3	4			2	6	7	8	9		11	5	1		10												9
		3				4	6	7	8		10	11	5	1	2	9												10
		3					6	7			10	11	5	1	2	9	8	4										11
		3	4					7	8		6	11	5	1	2	10	9											12
1	2	3	4			5	6	7	8	9		11		10														13
1	2	3	4			5	6	7	8	9		11		10														14
1	2	3	4			5	6	7	8	9		11		10														15
1	2	3	4			5	6	7	8	9		11		10														16
1	2	3	4			5	6	7	8		10	11		9														17
1	2	3	4			5	6	7	8		10	11		9														18
1	2	3	4			5	6	7	8		10	11		9														19
1	2	3	4			5	6	7	8		10	11		9														20
1	2	3	4			5	6		8		7	11		9	10													21
1	2	3	4			5	6	7	8	9		11		10														22
1	2	3	4			5	6	7	8	9		11		10														23
1	2	3	4			5	6	7						10		8					9				11			24
	2	3	4			6		7				5		10	1	8	11							9				25
	2	3	4					7	8	9		11	5	1	10									6		3		26
1	2		4			5	6	7		9	10	11								8							3	27
1	2	3	4			5	6	7	8	9		11									10							28
1	2	3	4			5	9	7	8		10	11	6															29
1	2	3	4			5	9	7	8		10	11	6															30
1	2	3	4			5	9	7	8		10	11	6															31
1	2	3	4			5	9	7	8		10	11	6															32
1	2	3	5	4			9	7	8		10	11	6															33
1	2	3	5	4			9	7	8		10	11	6															34
1	2	3	5	4			9	7	8		10	11	6															35
1	2	3	5	4			9	7	8		10	11	6															36
1	2	3	5	4				7	8	9	10	11	6			9												37
1	2	3	5	4				7	8	9	10	11	6															38
12	15	25	35	19	19	26	32	37	31	18	24	33	20	13	11	9	8	7	6	4	4	3	2	2	1	1	1	
	1				1		8		17	6	7	7	1	2		3	1						1		1			

67

1912-13

1	Sep	2 (a)	Notts C	W 1-0	Henry	12,000
2		7 (a)	Manchester U	W 1-0	Wynn	38,911
3		14 (h)	Aston Villa	W 1-0	Wynn	32,000
4		21 (a)	Liverpool	W 2-1	Wynn, Dorsett	35,237
5		28 (h)	Bolton W	W 2-0	Hoad, Jones	30,000
6	Oct	5 (a)	Sheffield U	D 1-1	Wallace	25,000
7		12 (h)	Newcastle U	L 0-1		40,000
8		19 (a)	Oldham A	L 1-2	Wynn	10,000
9		26 (h)	Chelsea	W 2-0	Taylor, Jones	15,000
10	Nov	2 (a)	W Arsenal	W 4-0	Wynn, Taylor (2), Jones	8,000
11		9 (h)	Bradford C	L 1-3	Wynn	30,000
12		16 (h)	Sunderland	W 1-0	Wynn	16,000
13		23 (a)	West Brom A	W 2-0	Jones, Wallace	20,000
14		30 (h)	Everton	W 1-0	Wallace	20,000
15	Dec	7 (a)	Sheffield W	L 0-1		20,000
16		14 (h)	Blackburn R	W 3-1	Dorsett, Wynn, Jones	20,000
17		21 (a)	Derby C	L 0-2		15,000
18		25 (h)	Tottenham H	D 2-2	Bottomley, Wynn	30,000
19		26 (a)	Tottenham H	L 0-4		12,000
20		28 (h)	Manchester U	L 0-2		36,223
21	Jan	2 (h)	Notts C	W 4-0	Wynn (2), Jones, Wallace	22,000
22		4 (a)	Aston Villa	L 0-2		10,000
23		18 (h)	Liverpool	W 4-1	Howard (4)	20,000
24		25 (a)	Bolton W	D 2-2	Wynn, Howard	25,000
25	Feb	8 (h)	Sheffield U	W 3-0	Howard, Jones, Wallace	18,000
26		15 (a)	Newcastle U	W 1-0	Wynn	30,000
27	Mar	1 (a)	Chelsea	L 1-2	Dorsett	40,000
28		8 (h)	W Arsenal	L 0-1		15,000
29		12 (h)	Oldham A	W 2-0	Dorsett, Jones	16,000
30		15 (a)	Bradford C	L 1-2	Wallace	6,000
31		21 (a)	Middlesbrough	D 0-0		15,000
32		22 (a)	Sunderland	L 0-1		20,000
33		24 (h)	Middlesbrough	W 3-0	Howard (2), Taylor	26,000
34		29 (h)	West Brom A	W 2-1	Wallace (2)	20,000
35	Apr	5 (a)	Everton	D 0-0		12,000
36		12 (h)	Sheffield W	D 2-2	Howard, Jones	30,000
37		19 (a)	Blackburn R	D 2-2	Howard (2)	8,000
38		26 (h)	Derby C	D 1-1	Wynn	15,000

Appearances
Goals

League Division One record: P 38   W 18   D 8   L 12   F 53   A 37   Pts 44   Pos 6th

FA Cup

1	Jan	11 (h)	Birmingham	W 4-0	
2	Feb	1 (h)	Sunderland	D 0-0*	
R		5 (a)	Sunderland	L 0-2	

*Abandoned in extra-time

Lancashire Senior Cup

1	Oct	7 (a)	Everton	D 0-0	
R		16 (h)	Everton	W 4-2	
2		21 (a)	Barrow	W 2-1	
SF	Nov	11 (a)	Blackburn R	L 1-6	

Manchester Senior Cup

1	Feb	25 (a)	Rochdale	L 1-2	

Friendly

1	Nov	4 (a)	West Ham U	W 4-2	

Goodchild	Henry	Fletcher	Bottomley	Eadie	Holford	Hoad	Dorsett	Wynn	Taylor	Jones	Howard	Wallace	Smith	Wall	McGuire	Hughes	Kelly	Webb	Jobling	Garner	Lawrence	#
1	2	3	4	5	6	7	11	8		10							9					1
1	2	3	4	5	6	7	11	8		10							9					2
1	2	3	4	5	6	7	11	8	9	10												3
1	2	3	4	5	6	7	11	8	9	10												4
1	2	3	4	5	6	7		8	9	10		11										5
1	2	3	4	5	6	7		8		10		11				9						6
1	2	3	4	5	9	7	11	8		10		6										7
1	2	3	4	5	6		7	8	9	10		11										8
1	2	3	4	5	6	7	11	8	9	10												9
1	2	3	4	5	6	7	11	8	9	10												10
1	2	3	4	5	6	7	11	8	9	10												11
1	2	3	4	5	6	7	11	8	9	10												12
1	2	3	4	5	6	7			9	10		11			8							13
1	2	3	4	5	6	7		8	9	10		11										14
1	2	3	4	5	6	7		8	9	10		11										15
1	2	3	4	5	6		7	8	9	10		11										16
1	2	3	4	5	6		7	8	9	10		11										17
1	2	3	4	5	6		7	8	9	10		11										18
1	2	3	4	5	6	7			9	10		11								8		19
1	2	3	4	5	9	7	11	8		10		6										20
	2	3	4	5	6			8	9	10		11	1					7				21
	2	3	4		6			8	9	10		11	1					7	5			22
	2	3		5	6		7	8		10	9	11	1		4							23
	2	3		5	6		7	8		10	9	11	1		4							24
	2	3		5	6		7			10	9	11	1				8			4		25
	2	3		5	6		7	8		10	9	11	1		4							26
	2		4	5	6		7	8		10	9	11	1		3							27
	2	3	4	5	6		7	8		10	9	11	1									28
	2	3	4	5	6		7	8		10	9	11	1									29
		3	4		6		7	8		10	9	11	1	5	2							30
1	2	3	4	5	6		7	8		10	9	11										31
1	2			5	6		7	8		10	9	11			3	4						32
1	2				6		7	8		10	9	11		5	3	4						33
1	2		4		6		7	8		10	9	11		5	3							34
1	2		4	5	6		7	8		10	9	11			3							35
1	2	3	4		6		7	8		10	9	11		5								36
1	2	3	4		6		7	8		10	9	11		5								37
1	2	3	4	5	6		7	8		10	9	11										38
28	37	33	33	31	38	16	30	31	22	37	16	28	10	7	6	5	3	2	2	2	1	
	1		1		1	4	14	4	9	11	8											

69

1913-14

1	Sep	1	(a)	Aston Villa	D 1-1	Taylor	10,000
2		6	(h)	Middlesbrough	D 1-1	Taylor	30,000
3		13	(a)	Sheffield U	W 3-1	Abbott, Jones, Taylor	15,000
4		20	(h)	Derby C	L 1-2	Abbott	25,000
5		27	(a)	Tottenham H	L 1-3	Jones	30,513
6	Oct	4	(a)	Bradford C	L 2-3	Wynn (2)	20,000
7		11	(h)	Blackburn R	L 1-2	Hughes	40,000
8		18	(a)	Sunderland	D 0-0		28,000
9		25	(h)	Everton	D 1-1	Taylor	30,000
10	Nov	1	(a)	West Brom A	D 0-0		12,000
11		8	(h)	Sheffield W	L 1-2	Browell	25,000
12		15	(a)	Bolton W	L 0-3		25,000
13		22	(h)	Chelsea	W 2-1	Browell, Wallace	30,000
14		29	(a)	Oldham A	W 3-1	Cumming, Howard, Browell	18,000
15	Dec	6	(h)	Manchester U	L 0-2		40,000
16		13	(a)	Burnley	L 0-2		20,000
17		20	(h)	Preston N E	D 1-1	Browell	20,000
18		25	(a)	Liverpool	L 2-4	Howard (2)	22,000
19		26	(h)	Liverpool	W 1-0	Howard	25,000
20		27	(a)	Middlesbrough	L 0-2		12,000
21	Jan	1	(a)	Newcastle U	W 1-0	Browell	15,000
22		3	(h)	Sheffield U	W 2-1	Taylor, Browell	25,000
23		17	(a)	Derby C	w 4-2	Howard (3), Taylor	8,000
24		24	(h)	Tottenham H	W 2-1	Cumming, Taylor	30,000
25	Feb	7	(h)	Bradford C	W 1-0	Browell	25,000
26		14	(a)	Blackburn R	L 1-2	Browell	10,000
27		28	(a)	Everton	L 0-1		20,000
28	Mar	14	(a)	Sheffield W	D 2-2	Hughes, Taylor	17,000
29		18	(h)	Sunderland	W 3-1	Howard (2), Hindmarsh	20,000
30		21	(h)	Bolton W	L 0-1		30,000
31		25	(h)	West Brom A	L 2-3	A.Fairclough, Browell	15,000
32		28	(a)	Chelsea	L 0-1		30,000
33	Apr	4	(h)	Oldham A	W 2-1	Jones (2)	25,000
34		10	(h)	Aston Villa	W 3-1	Browell (2), Dorsett	30,000
35		11	(a)	Manchester U	W 1-0	Cumming	36,440
36		13	(h)	Newcastle U	L 0-1		35,000
37		18	(h)	Burnley	W 4-1	Browell (2), Howard, Wynn	18,000
38		25	(a)	Preston N E	D 2-2	Hanney, Howard	8,000

Appearances
Goals

League Division One record: P 38   W 14   D 8   L 16   F 51   A 53   Pts 36   Pos 13th

FA Cup

1	Jan	10	(h)	Fulham	W 2-0
2		31	(h)	Tottenham H	W 2-1
3	Feb	21	(a)	Blackburn R	W 2-1
4	Mar	7	(h)	Sheffield U	D 0-0
R		12	(a)	Sheffield U	D 0-0
R		16	(n)	Sheffield U	L 0-1

Lancashire Senior Cup

1	Oct	6	(a)	Eccles Borough	W 3-0
2		20	(a)	Burnley	W 2-1
SF	Nov	10	(h)	Manchester U	D 1-1
R		24	(h)	Manchester U	L 0-2

Manchester Senior Cup

1	Feb	18	(h)	Stockport C	D 1-1
R	Mar	9	(a)	Stockport C	L 1-4

Friendly

1	Apr	30	(a)	Northwich & Witton XI	W 5-3

70

Smith	Henry	Fletcher	Hughes	Hanney	Hindmarsh	Cumming	Taylor	Howard	Browell	Dorsett	Holford	Wallace	Jones	Wynn	Bottomley	Cartwright	McGuire	Spottiswood	Eadie	Hoad	Wall	Abbott	Fairclough A.	Garner	Goodchild	
	2	3					9			7	6	11	10	8	4			5						1		1
	2	3					9			7	6	11	10	8	4				5					1		2
1	2	3					9				6	11	10		4					7	5	8				3
1	2	3					9				6	11	10		4					7	5	8				4
1	2	3					9				6	11	10		4					7	5	8				5
1		3									6		10	8	4	2	11	5		7			9			6
1	2	3	4					9			6	11	10	8				5		7						7
1	2	3	4					9		7	6		10	8	5		11									8
1	2		4				8	9			6	7	10		5	11	3									9
1	2	3					8	9			6	7	10		4	11		5								10
1	2	3						9		7	6		10	8	4	11		5								11
1		3	4				8	9	10	7	6	11				2		5								12
1	2	3	4		6	7	8	9	10	11															5	13
1	2	3	4	5	6	7	8	9	10	11																14
1	2	3	4	5	6	7	8	9	10	11																15
1		3	4	5	6		8	9	10	7		11					2									16
1	2	3	4	5	6	7	8		10	11				9												17
1	2	3	4	5	6	7	8	9	10							11										18
1		3	4	5	6	7	8	9	10							2	11									19
1		3	4	5	6	7	10	9						8		2	11									20
1	2	3	4	5	6	7	8	9	10	11																21
1	2	3	4	5	6	7	8	9	10	11																22
1	2	3	4	5	6	7	8	9	10	11																23
1	2	3	4	5	6	7	8	9	10	11																24
1	2	3	4	5	6	7		9	10					8		11										25
1	2	3	4	5	6	7	8	9	10	11																26
1	2		4	5	6	7	8	9	10	11							3									27
1	2	3	4		6		8	9	10			11	7												5	28
1	2	3	4	5	6	7	8	9	10	11																29
1	2	3	4	5	6	7	8	9	10	11																30
1	2	3	4	5		7	8		10	11		6											9			31
1	2	3	4	5	6	7	8	9	10	11																32
1	2	3	4	5	6	7		9	10	11		8														33
1	2	3	4	5	6	7		9	10	11			8													34
1	2	3	4	5	6	7		9	10	11			8													35
1	2	3	4	5				9	10	11		6	7	8												36
1	2	3	4	5	6	7		9	10	11				8												37
1	2	3	4	5	6	7		9	10	11				8												38
36	33	36	30	24	24	23	27	29	27	17	15	15	14	12	11	9	6	6	6	5	4	3	2	2	2	
	2	1	1	3	8	11	13	1		1	4	3											2	1		

1914-15

#	Date		Venue	Opponent	Result	Scorers	Attendance
1	Sep	1	(h)	Bradford C	W 4-1	Taylor, Howard, Barnes, Dorsett	9,000
2		5	(a)	Manchester U	D 0-0		20,000
3		12	(h)	Burnley	W 1-0	Howard	10,000
4		19	(a)	Bolton W	W 3-2	Howard, Barnes, opp.og	20,000
5		26	(h)	Tottenham H	W 2-1	Taylor, Howard	20,000
6	Oct	3	(a)	Blackburn R	W 1-0	Cartwright	22,000
7		10	(h)	Newcastle U	D 1-1	Barnes	24,000
8		17	(a)	Notts C	w 2-0	Howard (2)	14,000
9		24	(h)	Middlesbrough	D 1-1	Howard	25,000
10		31	(a)	Sunderland	W 2-0	Howard (2)	10,000
11	Nov	7	(h)	Sheffield U	D 0-0		25,000
12		14	(a)	Sheffield W	L 1-2	Taylor	24,000
13		25	(h)	Aston Villa	W 1-0	Howard	16,000
14		28	(a)	West Brom A	W 1-0	Browell	10,000
15	Dec	5	(a)	Liverpool	D 1-1	Howard	12,000
16		12	(a)	Everton	L 1-4	Howard	20,000
17		19	(h)	Bradford	L 2-3	Taylor, Howard	7,000
18		25	(h)	Chelsea	D 0-0		15,000
19		26	(h)	Chelsea	W 2-1	Taylor, Howard	25,000
20	Jan	1	(a)	Oldham A	D 0-0		22,000
21		2	(h)	Manchester U	D 1-1	Howard	30,000
22		18	(a)	Burnley	W 2-1	Dorsett, Barnes	8,000
23		23	(h)	Bolton W	W 2-1	Taylor, Barnes	20,000
24	Feb	6	(h)	Blackburn R	L 1-3	Taylor	25,000
25		13	(a)	Newcastle U	L 1-2	Taylor	18,000
26		22	(h)	Notts C	D 0-0		20,000
27		27	(a)	Middlesbrough	L 0-1		8,000
28	Mar	6	(h)	Sunderland	W 2-0	Cartwright, opp.og	20,000
29		13	(a)	Liverpool	L 2-3	Barnes, Howard	20,000
30		15	(a)	Tottenham H	D 2-2	Taylor, Barnes	7,000
31		20	(h)	Sheffield W	W 4-0	Howard (2), Barnes (2)	20,000
32		29	(a)	Sheffield U	D 0-0		18,000
33	Apr	3	(h)	West Brom A	W 4-0	Taylor (2), Barnes (2)	15,000
34		5	(h)	Oldham A	D 0-0		40,000
35		6	(a)	Bradford C	D 0-0		15,000
36		17	(h)	Everton	L 0-1		30,000
37		21	(a)	Aston Villa	L 1-4	Barnes	8,000
38		24	(a)	Bradford	L 1-3	Jones	12,000

Appearances
Goals

League Division One record: P 38   W 15   D 13   L 10   F 49   A 39   Pts 43   Pos 5th

FA Cup

1	Jan	9	(a)	Preston N E	D 0-0
R		16	(h)	Preston N E	W 3-0
2		30	(h)	Aston Villa	W 1-0
3	Feb	20	(h)	Chelsea	L 0-1

Lancashire Senior Cup

1	Oct	5	(h)	Liverpool	L 3-6

Manchester Senior Cup

1	Nov	14	(h)	Eccles Borough	W 6-0
2	Mar	17	(a)	Manchester U	L 1-3

Friendly

1	Aug	29	(h)	Local Amateur XI	W 2-0

Smith	Henry	Fletcher	Hughes	Hanney	Brennan	Taylor	Howard	Barnes	Cartwright	Dorsett	Jones	Cumming	Browell	Gaughan	Hoad	Hindmarsh	McGuire	Bottomley	Fairclough A.	Fairclough P.	Garner	Gartland	Goodchild	Hall	Henderson	Wynn	
1	2	3	4	5		8	9	10		11					7	6											1
1	2	3	4	5		8	9	10		11					7	6											2
1	2	3	4	5	6	8	9	10		11					7												3
1	2	3	4	5	6	8	9	10		11	7																4
1	2	3	4	5	6	8	9	10		11	7																5
1	2	3	4	5	6	8	9	10	7	11																	6
1	2	3	4	5	6	8	9	10	7	11																	7
1	2	3	4	5	6	8	9						10	11	7												8
1	2	3	4	5	6	8	9						10	11	7												9
1	2	3	4	5	6	8	9					7	10	11													10
1	2	3	4	5	6	8	9					7	10	11													11
1	2	3	4	5	6	8	9	10				7		11													12
1	2	3	4	5	6	8	9					7	10	11													13
1		3	4	5	6	8	9					7	10	11			2										14
1	2	3	4	5	6	8	9					7	10	11													15
1		3	4	5	6	8	9					7	10	11			2										16
1		3	4	5	6	8	9		11		10	7					2										17
1	2	3	4	5	6	8	9		11	7	10																18
1	2		4	5		8	9		11	7	10					6		3									19
1	2	3		5	6	8	9		11	7	10					4											20
1	2	3		5	6	8	9		11	7	10					4											21
1	2	3	4	5	6	8	9	10	11	7																	22
1	2	3	4	5	6	8	9	10	11	7																	23
1	2	3	4	5		8	9	10	11	7		6															24
1	2	3	4	5	6	8		10	11	7			9														25
1	2	3	4	5	6	8		10	11			7	9														26
1	2	3	4	5	6	8		10	11	7									9								27
1	2	3	4	5	6	8	9	10	11	7																	28
1	2	3	4	5	6	8	9	10	11	7																	29
1	2	3	4	5	6	8	9	10	11	7																	30
	2	3	4	5	6	8	9	10	11	7													1				31
1	2	3	4	5	6	8	9	10	11	7																	32
1	2	3	4	5	6	8	9	10	11	7																	33
1	2	3	4	5	6	8	9	10	11	7																	34
1	2	3	4	5	6			9	10			8	7	11													35
1	2	3	4	5	6	8	9	10	11	7																	36
1	2	3	4	5	6				10		11	7							9							8	37
1	2	3	4						10		11	8			7						6			9	5		38
37	35	37	36	37	33	35	33	25	21	18	17	12	10	10	6	4	3	1	1	1	1	1	1	1	1	1	
						11	18	12	2	2	1		1														

73

1919-20

1	Aug 30	(h)	Sheffield U	D 3-3	Barnes (2), Browell	30,000
2	Sep 1	(a)	Oldham A	W 3-1	Browell (2), Cartwright	3,000
3	6	(a)	Sheffield U	L 1-3	Wynn	30,000
4	8	(h)	Oldham A	W 3-1	Browell (2), Barnes	22,000
5	13	(h)	Bolton W	L 1-4	Crawshaw	20,000
6	20	(a)	Bolton W	L 2-6	Taylor, Browell	30,000
7	27	(h)	Notts C	W 4-1	Barnes (3), Taylor	20,000
8	Oct 4	(a)	Notts C	L 1-4	Barnes	16,000
9	11	(h)	Manchester U	D 3-3	Barnes (2), Taylor	32,000
10	18	(a)	Manchester U	L 0-1		45,000
11	25	(h)	Sheffield W	W 4-2	Browell (2), Taylor, Goodwin	20,000
12	Nov 1	(a)	Sheffield W	D 0-0		20,000
13	8	(h)	Blackburn R	W 8-2	Browell (3), Barnes (2), Murphy (2), Crawshaw	25,000
14	15	(a)	Blackburn R	W 4-1	Browell (2), Barnes (2)	6,000
15	22	(h)	Derby C	W 3-1	Cranshaw (2), Barnes	15,000
16	29	(a)	Derby C	D 0-0		7,000
17	Dec 6	(h)	West Brom A	L 2-3	Browell (2)	30,000
18	13	(a)	West Brom A	L 0-2		20,000
19	20	(a)	Sunderland	L 1-2	Reid	20,000
20	25	(h)	Everton	D 1-1	Barnes	25,000
21	26	(a)	Everton	L 0-2		26,000
22	27	(h)	Sunderland	W 1-0	Murphy	30,000
23	Jan 1	(h)	Bradford C	W 1-0	Murphy	30,000
24	3	(a)	Arsenal	D 2-2	Murphy, Barnes	32,000
25	17	(h)	Arsenal	W 4-1	Browell (3), Goodwin	25,000
26	24	(h)	Middlesbrough	W 1-0	Browell	28,000
27	Feb 7	(h)	Burnley	W 3-1	Barnes (2), Crawshaw	30,000
28	14	(a)	Burnley	L 0-2		20,000
29	18	(a)	Middlesbrough	W 2-0	Johnson (2)	15,000
30	28	(a)	Preston N E	D 1-1	Fletcher	17,000
31	Mar 13	(h)	Bradford	W 4-1	Barnes (2), Johnson, Crawshaw	10,000
32	17	(h)	Preston N E	W 1-0	Godfrey	18,000
33	20	(a)	Liverpool	L 0-1		30,000
34	22	(a)	Bradford	L 1-2	Johnson	8,000
35	27	(h)	Liverpool	W 2-1	Barnes (2)	35,000
36	Apr 3	(a)	Chelsea	L 0-1		45,000
37	5	(a)	Bradford C	L 0-1		20,000
38	10	(h)	Chelsea	W 1-0	Barnes	25,000
39	17	(a)	Newcastle U	L 0-3		36,000
40	24	(h)	Newcastle U	D 0-0		25,000
41	26	(a)	Aston Villa	W 1-0	Browell	45,000
42	May 1	(h)	Aston Villa	D 2-2	Johnson, Barnes	23,000
						Appearances
						Goals

League Division One record: P 42   W 18   D 9   L 15   A 71   A 62   Pts 45   Pos 7th

FA Cup

1	Jan 10	(h)	Clapton	0	W 4-1
2	31	(a)	Leicester C		L 0-3

Friendlies

None played.

Manchester Senior Cup

3	Apr 7	(h)	Hurst		L 0-3

In the Lancashire Senior Cup, City were second in Group 3, League games against Manchester United and Oldham Athletic counting towards the final positions. The top teams only in each group met in the knockout competition.

Smith	Goodchild	Henry	Cookson	Fletcher	Brennan	Hughes	Lamph	Scott	Woosnam	Tyler	Broad	Goodwin	Dorsett	Crawshaw	Browell	Johnson	Barnes	Murphy	Cartwright	Godfrey	Hanney	Sharp	Sugden	Taylor	Fairclough P.	Henderson	Wynn	Reid	Allen	Fairclough A.	Gray	Match
1	2	3	6	4						7					9		10	11	5								8					1
1			6	4					2	7					9		10	11	5								8					2
1			6	4					2	7					9		10	11	5								8					3
1	2		6	4					3	7					9		10	11										5	8			4
1	2		6	4					3	7				8	9		10	11	5													5
1	2	3	6	4					5	7					9		10	11					8									6
1		3							2	7					9		10	11	5					8	6	4						7
1		3							2	7					9		10	11	5					8	6	4						8
1	2	3							4	7					9		10	11	5				8									9
1	2	3						5	4	7					9		10	11					8									10
1	2	3					4	5	6	7					9		10	11					8									11
1	2	3					4	5	6	7				8	9		10	11														12
1	2	3					4	5	6	7				8	9		10	11														13
1	2	3					4	5	6	7				8	9		10	11														14
1	2	3					4	5	6	7				8	9		10	11														15
1	2	3					4	5	6	7					9		10	11		8												16
1	2	3					4	5	6	7					9		10	11		8												17
1		3					4	5	6	7				8				11				2								9		18
1		3					4	5	6	7							10	11				2					8			9		19
1		3					4	5	6	7				8	9		10	11				2										20
1		3					4	5	6	7				8	9		10	11				2										21
1		3			6					7				8			10	11				2		5				9			4	22
1	2	3	4					5	6	7				8	9		10	11														23
1		3	4					5	6	7				8	9		10	11				2										24
1	2	3	4					5	6		7			8	9		10	11														25
1	2	3	4					5	6		7			8	9		10	11														26
1	2	3	4					5	6		7			8			10	11														27
1	2	3	4					5	6		7			8			10	11										9				28
1	2	3						5	6		7				9		10	11		8		4										29
1	2	3	4					5	6		7				9		10	11		8												30
1	2	3	4					5	6		7			8	9		10	11														31
1	2	3	4						6		7				9		10	11		8											5	32
1	2	3						5	6		7				9		10	11		8		4										33
1	2	3						5	6		7				9		10	11		8		4										34
1	2	3	4					5	6		7			8	9		10	11														35
1	2	3	4					5	6		7			8			10	11		9												36
1	2	3	4					5	6		7			8			10	11		9												37
1	2	3	4					5	6		7			8	9		10	11														38
1	2	5						3			7			8	9		10	11				4		6								39
1	2							5	6		7			8	9		10	11												3		40
1	2							5	6		7			8	9		10	11							4					3		41
1	2	3						5			7			8	9		10	11						6	4							42
9	33	13	20	34	20	6	11	13	16	41	19	15	8	21	30	10	39	36	6	9	7	6	6	6	4	4	4	3	2	2	2	
	1										2			6	22	5	22	5	1	1						4		1	1			

Knowles played 6 in Matches 9 & 10.
Newton played 3 in Matches 2 & 3.
Howard played 9 in Match 27.
Jarvis played 4 in Match 40.
Leivesley played 10 in Match 18.

1920-21

1	Aug 28	(a)	Liverpool	L 2-4	Goodwin, Browell	30,000
2	30	(h)	Aston Villa	W 3-1	Browell (2), Murphy	40,000
3	Sep 4	(h)	Liverpool	W 3-2	Browell (3)	30,000
4	6	(a)	Aston Villa	L 1-3	Murphy	14,000
5	11	(a)	Arsenal	L 1-2	Browell	42,000
6	18	(h)	Arsenal	W 3-1	Browell, Barnes, Murphy	30,000
7	25	(a)	Bolton W	L 0-3		50,000
8	Oct 2	(h)	Bolton W	W 3-1	Woodcock, Fayers, Browell	40,000
9	9	(a)	Derby C	L 0-3		20,000
10	16	(h)	Derby C	D 0-0		35,000
11	23	(a)	Blackburn R	W 2-0	Woodcock, Johnson	30,000
12	30	(h)	Blackburn R	D 0-0		35,000
13	Nov 6	(a)	Huddersfield T	W 1-0	Barnes	22,000
14	13	(h)	Huddersfield T	W 3-2	Browell (2), Fayers	30,000
15	20	(a)	Manchester U	D 1-1	Barnes	66,000
16	27	(h)	Manchester U	W 3-0	Browell, Barnes, Murphy	40,000
17	Dec 4	(a)	Bradford C	W 2-1	Murphy, Browell	20,000
18	11	(h)	Bradford C	W 1-0	Browell	30,000
19	18	(a)	Sunderland	L 0-1		18,000
20	25	(h)	West Brom A	W 4-0	Browell (2), Barnes (2)	30,000
21	27	(a)	West Brom A	D 2-2	Browell (2)	40,000
22	Jan 1	(h)	Sunderland	W 3-1	Murphy (2), Browell	40,000
23	15	(a)	Chelsea	L 1-2	Murphy	35,000
24	22	(h)	Chelsea	W 1-0	Browell	30,000
25	Feb 5	(a)	Everton	L 0-3		35,000
26	12	(a)	Tottenham H	L 0-2		35,000
27	23	(h)	Everton	W 2-0	Browell (2)	33,000
28	26	(a)	Oldham A	L 0-2		30,000
29	Mar 5	(h)	Oldham A	W 3-1	Browell, Johnson, Barnes	33,000
30	9	(h)	Tottenham H	W 2-0	Browell, Barnes	30,000
31	12	(h)	Preston N E	W 1-0	Fayers	18,000
32	25	(h)	Middlesbrough	W 2-1	Johnson, Barnes	25,000
33	26	(h)	Burnley	W 3-0	Barnes (2), Johnson	40,000
34	28	(a)	Middlesbrough	L 1-3	Browell	29,000
35	Apr 2	(a)	Burnley	L 1-2	Fayers	40,000
36	9	(h)	Sheffield U	W 2-1	Browell, Johnson	20,000
37	16	(a)	Sheffield U	D 1-1	Barnes	23,000
38	20	(a)	Preston N E	W 5-1	Browell (3), Barnes (2)	20,000
39	23	(h)	Bradford	W 1-0	Browell	25,000
40	30	(a)	Bradford	W 2-1	Fayers, Barnes	10,000
41	May 2	(h)	Newcastle U	W 3-1	Barnes (2), Warner	18,000
42	7	(a)	Newcastle U	D 1-1	Browell	40,000
						Appearances
						Goals

League Division One record: P 42 W 24 D 6 L 12 F 70 A 50 Pts 54 Pos 2nd

FA Cup

1 Jan 8 (a) Crystal P   L 0-2

Lancashire Senior Cup

City topped Group 3 in the Qualifying
Competition where League matches against
Manchester United and Oldham Athletic
counted towards the positions.

SF May 9 (h) Burnley   W 2-0
F   14 (n) Bolton W   W 2-1

Manchester Senior Cup

2 Mar 15 (a) Bury   L 0-1

Friendly

1 Jan 29 (h) The Corinthians   W 2-0

No.	Goodchild	Cookson	Fletcher	Fayers	Woosnam	Hamill	Broad	Woodcock	Browell	Barnes	Murphy	Kelly	Carroll	Johnson	Allan	Edelston	Goodwin	Sharp	Warner	Tyler	Brennan	Cartwright	Crawshaw	Scott	Thompson J.	Gray	Jarvis	Leyland	Taylor
1	1	2	3	5				8	9	10	11				6	7	4												
2	1	2	3	5				8	9	10	11				6	7	4												
3	1	2	3	5				8	9	10	11				6	7			4										
4	1	2	3	5				8	9	10	11				6	7			4										
5	1	2	3					8	9	10	11				4	7				5	6								
6	1	2	3			5	7		9	10	11				6							8							4
7	1	2	3	6	5		7		9	10	11						4					8							
8	1	2	3	6	5		7	8	9	10	11						4												
9	1	2	3	4	5	6	7	8	9	10	11																		
10	1	2	3	4	5	6	7	8		10	11			9															
11	1	2	3	4	5	6	7	8	10		11			9															
12	1	2	3	4	5	6	7	8		10				9									11						
13	1	2	3	4		6			9	10		7	8										11					5	
14	1	2	3	4	5	6			9	10	11	7	8																
15	1	2	3	4	5	6	7		9	10	11		8																
16	1	2	3	4	5	6	7		9	10	11		8																
17	1	2	3	4	5	6	7		9	10	11		8																
18	1	2	3	4	5	6	7		9	10	11		8																
19	1	2	3	4		6	7		9	10	11		8											5					
20	1	2	3	4	5	6			9	10	11	7	8																
21	1	2	3	4	5			8	9	10	11	7	6																
22	1	2	3	6	5				9	10	11	7	8				4												
23	1	2	3	4					9	10	11	7	6											5	8				
24	1	2	3	4	5				9	10	11	7													6		8		
25	1	2	3	4	5		7	8	9	10	11						6												
26	1	2	3	4	5	6	7	8	9	10	11																		
27	1	2	3	4	5	6	7	8	9	10	11																		
28	1	2	3	6	5		7	8	9	10	11			4															
29	1	2		4	5	6		8		10	11	7		9	3														
30	1	2	3	4	5	6		8		10	11	7		9															
31	1	2	3	4	5	6		8		10	11	7		9															
32	1	2	3	4	5	6		8		10	11	7		9															
33	1	2	3	4	5	6	7	8		10	11			9															
34	1	2	3	4	5	6		8		10	11	7		9															
35	1	2	3	4	5	6		8		10	11	7		9															
36	1	2	3	4	5	6		8		10	11			9												7			
37	1	2		4	5	6	7	8		10	11			9	3														
38	1	2		4	5	6	7		9	10	11				3			8											
39	1	2		4	5	6	7		9	10	11				3			8											
40	1	2		4	5	6	7		9	10	11				3			8											
41	1	2		4	5	6	7		9	10	11				3			8											
42	1	2		4	5	6	7		9	10	11				3			8											
	42	42	35	40	34	28	23	13	42	41	40	13	12	12	7	6	5	5	5	3	2	2	2	2	2	1	1	1	1
			5					2	31	17	8			5			1	1											

1921-22

#	Date			Opponent	Result	Scorers	Attendance
1	Aug	27	(h)	Aston Villa	W 2-1	Barnes (2)	35,000
2		31	(a)	Liverpool	L 2-3	Barnes, Murphy	25,000
3	Sep	3	(a)	Aston Villa	L 0-4		30,000
4		7	(h)	Liverpool	D 1-1	Murphy	25,000
5		10	(h)	Arsenal	W 2-0	Warner, Barnes	25,000
6		17	(a)	Arsenal	W 1-0	Barnes	25,000
7		24	(h)	Blackburn R	D 1-1	Browell	35,000
8	Oct	1	(a)	Blackburn R	L 1-3	Browell	25,000
9		8	(h)	Oldham A	W 2-1	Browell, Murphy	35,000
10		15	(a)	Oldham A	W 1-0	Browell	25,000
11		22	(h)	Manchester U	W 4-1	Barnes (3), Warner	20,000
12		29	(a)	Manchester U	L 1-3	Murphy	56,000
13	Nov	5	(a)	Cardiff C	W 2-0	Browell, Barnes	35,000
14		12	(h)	Cardiff C	D 1-1	Murphy	25,000
15		19	(h)	West Brom A	W 6-1	Barnes (3), Browell (2), Woosnam	25,000
16		26	(a)	West Brom A	L 0-2		30,000
17	Dec	3	(h)	Bolton W	L 2-3	Browell, Barnes	35,000
18		10	(a)	Bolton W	L 0-5		40,000
19		17	(h)	Everton	W 2-1	Browell, Murphy	20,000
20		24	(a)	Everton	D 2-2	Johnson (2)	30,000
21		26	(a)	Huddersfield T	L 0-2		26,000
22		31	(a)	Sunderland	W 3-0	Browell, Johnson, Murphy	10,000
23	Jan	2	(h)	Huddersfield T	W 2-1	Johnson, Kelly	30,000
24		14	(a)	Sunderland	W 3-2	Browell, Barnes, Murphy	5,000
25		21	(h)	Middlesbrough	D 2-2	Barnes, Browell	25,000
26	Feb	1	(a)	Middlesbrough	L 1-4	Browell	20,000
27		4	(h)	Tottenham H	D 3-3	Browell, Johnson, Barnes	20,000
28		11	(a)	Tottenham H	L 1-3	Barnes	45,000
29		22	(h)	Bradford C	W 3-2	Browell, Barnes, Woosnam	20,000
30		25	(a)	Bradford C	W 2-1	Murphy, Browell	25,000
31	Mar	11	(a)	Preston N E	L 0-1		20,000
32		18	(a)	Chelsea	D 0-0		40,000
33		25	(h)	Chelsea	D 0-0		26,000
34	Apr	1	(a)	Sheffield U	L 0-1		20,000
35		5	(h)	Preston N E	W 2-0	Browell, Barnes	20,000
36		8	(h)	Sheffield U	D 2-2	Browell (2)	12,000
37		14	(h)	Birmingham	W 1-0	Warner	35,000
38		15	(a)	Burnley	L 2-5	Woosnam, opp.og	15,000
39		18	(a)	Birmingham	L 1-3	opp.og	39,000
40		22	(h)	Burnley	W 2-0	Browell, Barnes	25,000
41		29	(a)	Newcastle U	L 1-5	Ingham	25,000
42	May	6	(h)	Newcastle U	W 1-0	Browell	18,000

Appearances
Goals

League Division One record: P 42   W 18   D 9   L 15   F 65   A 70   Pts 45   Pos 10th

FA Cup

1	Jan	7	(h)	Darlington	W 3-1
2		28	(a)	Bolton W	W 3-1
3	Feb	18	(a)	Tottenham H	L 1-2

Manchester Senior Cup

2	Mar	7	(a)	Bury	W 3-2
3		29	(h)	Hurst	W 5-0
SF	May	2	(a)	Eccles U	L 1-2

Lancashire Senior Cup

City topped Group 3 in the Qualifying
Competition when League matches against
Manchester United and Oldham Athletic
counted towards the final positions.

| SF | May | 8 | (n) | Bolton W | D 0-0 |
| R | | 13 | (n) | Bolton W | L 0-1 |

Friendlies

None played.

Blair	Cookson	Fletcher	Sharp	Woosnam	Hamill	Meredith	Warner	Browell	Barnes	Murphy	Fayers	Johnson	Kelly	Carroll	Ford, Alf	Goodchild	Albinson	Thompson	Allen	Crawshaw	Etherington	Ingham	Leyland	Lievesley	Mulligan	Woodcock	Brennan	Pearson	Royle	Simpson	Wilson	
	2	3			6	7	8	9	10	11	4					1							5									1
	2	3			6	7	8	9	10	11	4					1							5									2
	2	3		5	6	7	8	9	10	11	4					1																3
1	2	3	4			7	8	9	10	11	5						6															4
1	2	3	5		6	7	8		10	11	4	9																				5
1	2	3	4		6	7	8		10	11	5	9																				6
1	2	3		5	6	7	8	9	10	11	4																					7
1	2	3	4	5		7	8	9		11	6												10									8
1	2	3	4	5		7	8	9	10	11							6															9
1	2	3	4	5		7	8	9	10	11							6															10
1	2	3	4	5		7	8	9	10	11	6																					11
1	2	3	4	5		7	8	9	10	11	6																					12
1	2	3	4	5		7	8	9	10	11	6																					13
1	2	3	4			7	8	9	10	11	5									6												14
1	2	3	4	5		7	8	9	10	11	6																					15
1	2	3	4	5		7	8	9	10	11	6																					16
1	2	3	4	5		7	8	9	10	11	6																					17
1	2	3	4	5		7		9	10	11	6																8					18
1	2	3		5	6	7		9	10	11	4																8					19
1	2	3		5	6		8		10	11	4	9	7																			20
1	2	3	4	5	6		8		10	11		9	7																			21
1	2	3		5			8		10	11	6	9	7	4																		22
1	2	3		5			8		10	11	6	9	7	4																		23
1	2	3		5			8		10	11	6	9	7	4																		24
1	2	3			5		8		10	11	6	9	7	4																		25
1		3			5	6	8		10	11	3	9	7					2														26
1		3			5		8		10	11	4	9	7					2													6	27
1		3			5		8		10	11	4	9	7					2									6					28
1	2	3		5	6		8		10	11	4	9	7																			29
1	2	3		5	6		8		10	11	4	9		7																		30
1	2		4	5	6		8		10	11		9		7					3													31
1	2	3	4	5	6					11		10	8	7									9									32
1	2	3	4	5	6		8		10	11		9		7																		33
1	2	3	4	5	6			9	10	11																			8	7		34
1	2	3	4	5	6	7	8		10	11		9																				35
1	2	3	4	5	6	7	8		10	11		9																				36
1	2	3	4	5	6	7	8	9		11		10																				37
1	2	3	4	5		7	8	9		11	6												10									38
1	2	3	4		6	7	8			11	5	9																		10		39
1	2			5	6		8	9	10	11	4									7				3								40
1	2			5	6		8		10	11	4									7		9		3								41
	2			5	6	7	8	9	10	11	4					1		3														42
38	39	38	25	33	24	25	22	38	37	42	32	20	11	4	4	4	3	3	2	2	2	2	2	1	2	2	1	1	1	1	1	
			3				3	21	20	9		5	1								1											

79

1922-23

1	Aug	26	(a)	Sheffield U	L 0-2		25,000
2		28	(h)	Middlesbrough	W 2-1	Browell, Barnes	25,000
3	Sep	2	(h)	Sheffield U	D 3-3	Browell, Doran, Murphy	25,000
4		4	(a)	Middlesbrough	L 0-5		15,000
5		9	(h)	Birmingham	L 0-1		22,000
6		16	(a)	Birmingham	W 1-0	Johnson	30,000
7		23	(h)	Huddersfield T	W 3-1	Johnson (2), Barnes	28,000
8		30	(a)	Huddersfield T	D 0-0		16,200
9	Oct	7	(a)	Stoke	D 1-1	Johnson	21,000
10		14	(h)	Stoke	W 2-1	Johnson, Barnes	28,000
11		21	(a)	Preston N E	W 2-0	Barnes (2)	12,000
12		28	(h)	Preston N E	W 2-1	Johnson, Barnes	20,000
13	Nov	4	(a)	West Brom A	L 0-2		18,000
14		11	(h)	West Brom A	D 1-1	Johnson	25,000
15		18	(h)	Bolton W	W 2-0	Roberts, Johnson	30,000
16		25	(a)	Bolton W	L 1-2	Barnes	30,000
17	Dec	2	(a)	Blackburn R	D 0-0		20,000
18		9	(h)	Blackburn R	W 2-1	Barnes (2)	26,000
19		16	(a)	Cardiff C	L 1-3	Barnes	15,000
20		23	(h)	Cardiff C	W 5-1	Barnes (3), Roberts, Johnson	18,000
21		25	(a)	Everton	D 0-0		35,000
22		26	(h)	Everton	W 2-1	Roberts, Barnes	30,000
23		30	(h)	Oldham A	W 3-2	Johnson (2), Roberts	20,000
24	Jan	6	(a)	Oldham A	W 3-0	Barnes (2), Roberts	18,000
25		20	(a)	Arsenal	L 0-1		25,000
26		27	(h)	Arsenal	D 0-0		30,000
27	Feb	3	(a)	Aston Villa	L 0-2		20,000
28		10	(h)	Aston Villa	D 1-1	Roberts	15,000
29		17	(a)	Burnley	L 0-2		14,000
30		24	(h)	Burnley	W 1-0	Barnes	20,000
31	Mar	3	(a)	Tottenham H	L 1-3	Browell	35,000
32		14	(h)	Tottenham H	W 3-0	Roberts (2), Johnson	25,000
33		17	(h)	Liverpool	W 1-0	Barnes	35,000
34		24	(a)	Liverpool	L 0-2		25,000
35		30	(a)	Sunderland	L 0-2		35,000
36		31	(h)	Chelsea	W 3-0	Johnson (2), Barnes	15,000
37	Apr	2	(h)	Sunderland	W 1-0	Barnes	32,000
38		7	(a)	Chelsea	D 1-1	Barnes	22,000
39		14	(h)	Nottingham F	D 1-1	Roberts	14,000
40		21	(a)	Nottingham F	L 0-2		12,000
41		28	(h)	Newcastle U	D 0-0		20,000
42	May	5	(a)	Newcastle U	L 1-3	Roberts	15,000
						Appearances	
						Goals	

League Division One record: P 42 W 17 D 11 L 14 A 50 A 49 Pts 45 Pos 8th

FA Cup

1 Jan 13 (a) Charlton A   L 1-2

Lancashire Senior Cup

City topped Group 3 of the Qualifying
Competition after League games against
Oldham Athletic counted towards the
final positions.

SF Apr 25 (a) Preston N E   W 3-0
F   May 12 (n) Liverpool   W 1-0

Manchester Senior Cup

3	Mar	12	(a)	Oldham A	D 0-0
R		19	(h)	Oldham A	W 1-0
SF	Apr	30	(a)	Stockport C	L 1-4

Friendlies

1	Sep	13	(h)	International XI	W 3-1
2	Nov	21	(h)	Stalybridge & Stockport XI	W 1-0
3	Mar	10	(h)	Manchester U	W 5-0

Goodchild	Mitchell	Cookson	Allen	Sharp	Hammill	Pringle	Morris	Roberts	Johnson	Barnes	Murphy	Browell	Wilson	Daniels	Etherington	Thompson	Warner	Fletcher	Calderwood	Doran	Fayers	Kelly	Meredith	Mulligan	Utley	
1	2		4	6	5	7				10	11	8						3	9							1
1	2		4	6	5	7				10	11	8						3	9							2
1	2		4	6	5	7				10	11	8						3	9							3
1	2		4	6	5	7				10	11	9					8	3								4
	1	2	4	5	6	7				10	11	9					8	3								5
	1	2	3	4	5	6	7		9	10	11						8									6
1	2	3	4	5	6	7			9	10	11						8									7
	1	2	3	4	5	6	7		9	10	11						8									8
	1	2	3	4	5	6	7		9	10	11						8									9
	1	2	3	4	5	6	7		9	10	11						8									10
	1	2	3	4	5	6	7	8	9	10	11															11
	1	2	3	4		6	7	8	9	10	11													5		12
	1	2	3	4	5	6		8	9	10	11												7			13
	1	2	3	4	5	6	7	8	9	10	11															14
	1	2	3	4	5	6	7	8	9	10	11															15
1	2	3	4	5	6	7	8	9	10	11																16
	1		3	4	5	6	7	8	9	10	11			2												17
	1		3	4	5	6	7	8	9	10	11			2												18
	1		3	4	5	6		8	9	10	11	7		2												19
	1		3	4	5	6		8	9	10	11	7	2													20
	1		3	4	5	6		8	9	10	11	7	2													21
	1		4	5	6			8	9	10	11	7	2	3												22
	1		4	5	6			8	9	10	11	7	2												3	23
	1		4	5	6			8	9	10	11		2	3												24
	1		4	5	6			8	9	10	11		2	3								7				25
	1		4	5	6	7			9	10	11	8	2	3												26
	1		4	5	6	7		9	10		11	8	2	3												27
	1		4	5	6			8	10		11	9	2	3		7										28
1			4	5	6			8	10		11	9	2	3		7										29
1		3	4	5	6			8		10	11	9	2			7										30
1		3		5	6			8	9	10			2		11	7			4							31
1	2	3	4	5	6			8	9	10					11	7										32
1	2	3	4	5	6			8	9	10					11	7										33
1	2	3	4	5	6			8	9	10					11	7										34
1	2	3	4	5	6			8	9	10					11	7										35
1	2	3	4	5	6	7		8	9	10					11											36
1	2	3	4	5	6	7		8	9	10					11											37
1	2	3	4	5	6	7		8	9	10					11											38
1	2	3	4	5	6	7		8	9	10					11											39
1	2		4	5	6	7		8	9	10					11				3							40
1		2	4	5	6			8	9	10	11					7			3							41
1			4	5	6			8	9	10	11	7	2						3							42
20	22	25	27	41	41	42	26	32	35	38	32	15	12	10	10	10	7	5	4	3	1	1	1	1	1	
							10	14	21	1	3									1						

1923-24

1	Aug 25	(h)	Sheffield U	W 2-1	Johnson, Barnes	56,993
2	29	(a)	Aston Villa	L 0-2		15,000
3	Sep 1	(a)	Sheffield U	L 0-3		30,000
4	5	(h)	Aston Villa	L 1-2	Barnes	32,038
5	8	(h)	Bolton W	D 1-1	Roberts	43,601
6	15	(a)	Bolton W	D 0-0		35,000
7	22	(h)	Sunderland	W 4-1	Barnes (2), Johnson, Hamill	33,952
8	29	(a)	Sunderland	L 2-5	Barnes (2)	15,000
9	Oct 6	(h)	Arsenal	W 1-0	Roberts	23,477
10	13	(a)	Arsenal	W 2-1	Barnes (2)	32,000
11	20	(a)	Blackburn R	W 1-0	Barnes	30,000
12	27	(h)	Blackburn R	W 3-1	Roberts (2), Barnes	32,498
13	Nov 3	(h)	Newcastle U	D 1-1	Barnes	27,652
14	10	(a)	Newcastle U	L 1-4	Murphy	30,000
15	17	(h)	Cardiff C	D 1-1	Murphy	20,200
16	24	(a)	Cardiff C	D 1-1	Roberts	30,000
17	Dec 1	(h)	Notts C	W 1-0	Roberts	22,990
18	8	(a)	Notts C	L 0-2		12,000
19	15	(h)	Everton	W 2-1	Roberts, Barnes	35,000
20	22	(a)	Everton	L 1-6	Barnes	20,000
21	26	(a)	Birmingham	L 0-3		30,000
22	29	(h)	West Brom A	D 3-3	Barnes (2), Roberts	20,000
23	Jan 1	(h)	Tottenham H	W 1-0	Johnson	40,000
24	5	(a)	West Brom A	L 1-2	Barnes	15,000
25	19	(h)	Liverpool	L 0-1		22,000
26	26	(a)	Liverpool	D 0-0		25,000
27	Feb 9	(a)	Nottingham F	W 2-1	Johnson, Browell	10,000
28	13	(a)	Nottingham F	L 1-3	Roberts	3,000
29	16	(h)	Burnley	D 2-2	Roberts, Hicks	24,000
30	Mar 1	(h)	Middlesbrough	W 3-2	Barnes (2), Roberts	20,000
31	15	(a)	Preston N E	L 1-4	Barnes	18,000
32	17	(a)	Burnley	L 2-3	Warner, Browell	12,000
33	22	(h)	Preston N E	D 2-2	Barnes, Johnson	22,000
34	Apr 2	(a)	Middlesbrough	D 1-1	Johnson	10,000
35	5	(h)	Chelsea	W 1-0	Johnson	17,000
36	12	(a)	Huddersfield T	D 1-1	Roberts	11,000
37	18	(h)	Birmingham	W 1-0	Roberts	30,000
38	19	(h)	Huddersfield T	D 1-1	Warner	35,000
39	21	(a)	Tottenham H	L 1-4	Johnson	18,000
40	26	(a)	West Ham U	W 2-1	Roberts, Browell	16,000
41	30	(a)	Chelsea	L 1-3	Browell	3,600
42	May 3	(h)	West Ham U	W 2-1	Warner, Johnson	12,000

Appearances
Goals

League Division One record: P 42   W 15   D 12   L 15   F 54   A 71   Pts 42   Pos 11th

FA Cup

1	Jan 12	(h)	Nottingham F	W 2-1
2	Feb 2	(a)	Halifax T	D 2-2
R	6	(h)	Halifax T	D 0-0
R	11	(n)	Halifax T	W 3-0
3	23	(h)	Brighton & H A	W 5-1
4	Mar 8	(h)	Cardiff C	D 0-0
R	12	(a)	Cardiff C	W 1-0
SF	29	(n)	Newcastle U	L 0-2

Friendly

1	Apr 28	(h)	Glentoran	W 7-2

Lancashire Senior Cup

2	Oct 1	(h)	Accrington S	W 2-1
3	15	(a)	Burnley	D 2-2
R	22	(h)	Burnley	W 4-0
SF	Nov 7	(n)	Oldham A	W 2-1
F	Dec 12	(h)	Liverpool	D 1-1
R	May 10	(a)	Liverpool	L 0-2

Manchester Senior Cup

3	Mar 12	(h)	Manchester N E	W 12-0
SF	Apr 28	(a)	Wigan B	W 1-0
F	May 10	(a)	Manchester U	L 0-3

Mitchell	Cookson	Fletcher	Sharp	Hamill	Pringle	Morris	Roberts	Johnson	Barnes	Murphy	Warner	Wilson	Allen	Browell	Calderwood	Daniels	Elwood	Donaldson	Goodchild	Smith	Harper	Carroll	Hicks	Meredith	Thompson	Woosnam	Leslie	No.
1	2	3		4	6		8	9	10	11								7							5			1
1	2	3	4	5	6		8	9	10	11								7										2
1	2		4	5	6		8	9	10	11			3					7										3
1	2	3	4	5				9	10	11				8				7	6									4
1	2		4	5			8	9	10	11			3					7	6									5
1	2		4	5	6		8	9	10	11			3					7										6
1	2		4	5	6	7	8	9	10				3		11													7
	2		4	5	6	7	8	9	10				3		11				1									8
1		3	4	5	6	7		9	10	11	8	2																9
1			4	5	6	7		9	10	11	8	2	3															10
1			4	5	6	7		9	10	11	8	2	3															11
1			4	5		7		9	10	11	8	2	3						6									12
1			4	5		7		9	10	11	8	2	3						6									13
			4	5		7		9	10	11	8	2	3						1	6								14
1	2	3	4	5		7		9	10	11	8	6																15
1	2	3	4	5		7		9	10	11	8	6																16
1	2	3	4	5	6	7		9	10	11	8																	17
1	2	3	4	5	6	7		9	10	11	8																	18
1	2	3	4	5	6	7		9	10	11	8																	19
1	2		4	5	6	7		9	10	11	8		3															20
1	2		4	5	6	7		9	10	11	8		3															21
1	2		4	5		7		9	10	11		6	3	8														22
1	2		4	5		7		9	10	11		6	3	8														23
1	2		4	5		7	8	9	10	11		6	3															24
1	2		4	5	6	7	8	9	10	11			3															25
1	2		4	5	6			9	10	11	8		3					7										26
1	2		4	5		7	8		10	11		6	3	9														27
	2		4	5		7	8		10			6	3	9							1		11					28
	2	3	4			7	8		10			6		9							1		11					29
1	2	3		5	6		8		10				4	9	11									7				30
	2		4	5		7	8		10	11		6	3	9					1									31
		3				7			10		8		4	9	11	5			6		1					2		32
	2	3	4	5			8		10	11		6		9					1					7				33
	2	3	4			7		9	10		8	6			11	5			1									34
	2	3	4			7		9	10		8	6			11	5			1									35
1	2	3				7		9	10	11	8	6								5		4						36
1	2		4			7		9	10		8	6	3		11	5												37
1	2		4			7		9	10		8	6	3		11	5												38
1	2					7		9	10		8	6	3		11							4					5	39
1	2	3	4			7			10		8	6		9	11	5												40
	2	3	4	5		7			10		8	6		9	11				1									41
	2	3	4			7		9		11	8	6	10			5			1									42
31	34	20	34	25	28	31	41	30	23	26	23	21	14	14	15	11	8	7	7	6	4	2	2	2	1	1	1	
				1			14	9	20	2	3								1									

1924-25

1	Aug 30	(a)	Bury	W 2-0	Roberts (2)	40,000
2	Sep 1	(a)	Arsenal	L 0-1		25,000
3	6	(h)	Nottingham F	W 4-2	Barnes (2), Murphy, Roberts	31,000
4	13	(a)	Liverpool	L 3-5	Roberts (2), Barnes	30,000
5	17	(h)	Arsenal	W 2-0	Johnson, Barnes	34,000
6	20	(h)	Newcastle U	W 3-1	Roberts (2), Johnson	35,000
7	27	(a)	Sheffield U	W 5-0	Roberts (3), Johnson, Barnes	20,000
8	Oct 4	(h)	West Ham U	W 3-1	Roberts (2), Barnes	46,000
9	11	(a)	Blackburn R	L 1-3	Barnes	30,000
10	18	(h)	Huddersfield T	D 1-1	Barnes	50,000
11	25	(h)	Bolton W	D 2-2	Roberts, Johnson	50,000
12	29	(a)	Everton	L 1-3	Johnson	20,000
13	Nov 1	(a)	Notts C	L 0-2		12,000
14	8	(h)	Everton	D 2-2	Austin, Roberts	30,000
15	10	(a)	Tottenham H	D 1-1	Roberts	11,000
16	15	(a)	Sunderland	L 2-3	Johnson, Murphy	20,000
17	22	(h)	Cardiff C	D 2-2	Roberts (2)	18,000
18	29	(a)	Preston N E	W 3-2	Austin, Roberts, Warner	22,000
19	Dec 6	(h)	Burnley	D 3-3	Austin, Roberts, Browell	20,000
20	13	(a)	Leeds U	W 3-0	Roberts, Browell, Murphy	15,000
21	20	(h)	Birmingham	D 2-2	Austin, Browell	40,000
22	25	(h)	West Brom A	L 1-2	Browell	35,000
23	26	(a)	West Brom A	L 1-3	Johnson	50,000
24	Jan 3	(a)	Nottingham F	W 3-0	Johnson (2), Cowan	8,000
25	17	(h)	Liverpool	W 5-0	Roberts (4), Woosnam	25,000
26	24	(a)	Newcastle U	L 0-2		25,000
27	31	(h)	Bury	D 0-0		15,000
28	Feb 7	(a)	West Ham U	L 0-4		25,000
29	14	(h)	Blackburn R	L 1-3	Roberts	31,000
30	21	(a)	Huddersfield T	D 1-1	Roberts	18,000
31	23	(h)	Sheffield U	W 2-1	Roberts (2)	12,000
32	28	(a)	Bolton W	L 2-4	Daniels, Hicks	25,000
33	Mar 7	(h)	Notts C	W 2-1	Roberts (2)	25,000
34	21	(h)	Sunderland	L 1-3	Roberts	30,000
35	Apr 1	(a)	Cardiff C	W 2-0	Austin, Johnson	8,000
36	4	(h)	Preston N E	W 2-1	Warner, Browell	20,000
37	10	(a)	Aston Villa	L 1-2	Hicks	20,000
38	11	(a)	Burnley	L 0-1		14,000
39	13	(h)	Aston Villa	W 1-0	Warner	25,000
40	18	(h)	Leeds U	W 4-2	Austin, Browell, Johnson, Hicks	14,000
41	25	(a)	Birmingham	L 1-2	Johnson	13,000
42	May 2	(h)	Tottenham H	W 1-0	Warner	15,000

Appearances
Goals

League Division One record: P 42   W 17   D 9   L 16   F 76   A 68   Pts 43   Pos 10th

FA Cup

1 Jan 10 (a) Preston N E   L 1-4

Lancashire Senior Cup

2 Oct 20 (h) Blackpool   D 2-2
R Nov 3 (a) Blackpool   L 0-2

Manchester Senior Cup

3 Mar 18 (a) Manchester U   D 2-2
R   25 (h) Manchester U   W 7-4
SF Apr 23 (h) Ashton National W 4-1
F May 9 (n) Bury   L 0-1

Friendlies

1 Sep 10 (h) Everton &
            Liverpool XI   L 2-3
2 Nov 24 (h) Sth African XI   W 3-1
3 Mar 28 (a) Bolton W   L 0-3
4 Apr 29 (h) Rangers & Celtic XI D 2-2

84

Mitchell	Cookson	Fletcher	Sharp	Elwood	Cowan	Pringle	Austin	Roberts	Johnson	Murphy	Hicks	Barnes	Browell	Calderwood	Goodchild	Warner	Wilson	Daniels	Thompson	McCourt	Woosnam	Benzie	
1	2	3	4		6	7	8	9	11	10										5			1
1	2	3	4		6	7	8	9	11	10										5			2
1	2	3	4		6	7	8	9	11	10										5			3
1	2	3	4	5		7	8	9	11	10						6							4
1	2		4	5	6	7	8	9	11	10				3									5
1	2		4	5	6	7	8	9	11	10				3									6
1	2		4	5		7	8	9	11	10				3		6							7
1	2		4	5	6	7	8	9	11	10				3									8
	2		4	5	6	7	8	9	11	10				3	1								9
1	2	3	4	5	6	7	8	9	11	10													10
1	2	3	4	5	6	7	8	9		10								11					11
	2		4	5	6	7	8			10		9			1		3	11					12
1			4	5		7	8		11	10	9			3		6			2				13
1	2		4	5		7	8	9	11	10				3		6							14
		3	4	5	6	7	8	9	11	10					1				2				15
		3	4	5	6		8	9	11	7					1			10	2				16
1		3	4	5	6		8	9	11	7								10	2				17
1	2	3	4		6	7	8	10	11				9							5			18
	2	3	4	5	6	7	8	10	11				9		1								19
1	2	3	4	5	6	7	8	10	11				9										20
1	2	3	4	5	6	7	8	10	11				9										21
1	2	3	4	5	6	7	8	10					9					11					22
1	2	3	7		5	4		10				11	9			8	6						23
1		3	4		6	7	8	10				11	9						2		5		24
1	2	3	4			7	9	10	11							6	8				5		25
1	2	3	4	5		7	9	10	11							6	8						26
1	2	3	4	5		7	9	10	11							6	8						27
	2	3	4	5		7	9	10	11						1	6	8						28
1	2		4	5	6	7	8	9	11	10				3									29
1	2	3	8	5	4	7	9	10								6	11						30
	2		8	5	4	7	9	10							1	6	11	3					31
1	2	3	8	5	4	7	9		11							6	10						32
1	2	3	8	5	4	7	9	10	11							6							33
1	2	3	4	5	6	7	8	10	11				9										34
	2	3	4	5	6	7		10	11				9		1	8							35
	2	3	4	5	6	7		10	11				9		1	8							36
	2	3	4	5	6	7	9	10	11						1	8							37
1	2		4	5	6	7	9	10	11							8	3						38
	2		4	5	6	7	9	10	11						1	8	3						39
	2		4	5	6	7	8	10	11				9		1		3						40
	2		4	5	6	7	8	10	11				9	3	1								41
1	2		5	4		7	9	10	11					3		8						6	42
29	37	27	40	15	21	35	38	38	41	24	15	14	14	14	13	12	12	9	7	4	2	1	
				1		6	31	12	3	3	8	6				4		1		1			

1925-26

1	Aug 29	(h)	Cardiff C	W 3-2	Austin, Warner, Johnson		42,000
2	31	(a)	Birmingham	L 0-1			20,000
3	Sep 5	(a)	Tottenham H	L 0-1			45,000
4	12	(h)	Manchester U	D 1-1	Cowan		70,000
5	19	(h)	Everton	D 4-4	Browell (4)		17,000
6	23	(a)	West Brom A	L 1-4	Roberts		8,000
7	26	(a)	Huddersfield T	D 2-2	Warner, Johnson		18,000
8	Oct 3	(h)	Sunderland	W 4-1	Austin (2), Warner, Browell		40,000
9	10	(a)	Blackburn R	D 3-3	Browell (2), Roberts		20,000
10	17	(a)	Liverpool	L 1-2	Johnson		18,000
11	24	(h)	Burnley	W 8-3	Browell (5), Roberts, Johnson, Hicks		16,000
12	26	(a)	Sheffield U	L 3-8	Cowan, Roberts, Johnson		8,000
13	31	(a)	West Ham U	L 1-3	Browell		23,000
14	Nov 4	(h)	Sheffield U	L 2-4	Austin, Roberts		7,000
15	7	(h)	Arsenal	L 2-5	Warner, Browell		10,000
16	14	(a)	Bolton W	L 1-5	Roberts		20,000
17	21	(h)	Notts C	D 1-1	Coupland		20,000
18	28	(a)	Aston Villa	L 1-3	Dennison		24,000
19	Dec 5	(h)	Leicester C	W 5-1	Roberts (2), Johnson (2), Dennison		20,000
20	12	(a)	Leeds U	W 4-3	Bradford, Dennison, Johnson, Roberts		18,000
21	19	(h)	Newcastle U	D 2-2	Johnson, Murphy		35,000
22	25	(a)	Bury	L 5-6	Browell (2), Coupland, Johnson, Roberts		25,000
23	26	(h)	Bury	L 0-2			50,000
24	Jan 1	(h)	West Brom A	W 3-1	Austin, Dennison, Johnson		25,000
25	2	(a)	Cardiff C	D 2-2	Roberts (2)		10,000
26	16	(h)	Tottenham H	D 0-0			25,000
27	23	(a)	Manchester U	W 6-1	Austin (2), Roberts (2), Johnson, Hicks		50,000
28	Feb 6	(h)	Huddersfield T	L 1-5	Roberts		40,000
29	10	(a)	Everton	D 1-1	Roberts		20,000
30	13	(a)	Sunderland	L 3-5	Austin, Browell, Hicks		25,000
31	27	(h)	Liverpool	D 1-1	Browell		40,000
32	Mar 13	(h)	West Ham U	W 2-0	Roberts, Murphy		35,000
33	17	(h)	Blackburn R	L 0-1			20,000
34	20	(a)	Arsenal	L 0-1			30,000
35	29	(h)	Bolton W	D 1-1	Austin		30,000
36	Apr 2	(h)	Birmingham	L 2-4	Austin, Hicks		60,000
37	3	(a)	Notts C	L 0-1			12,000
38	6	(a)	Burnley	W 2-1	Johnson, Hicks		18,000
39	10	(h)	Aston Villa	W 4-2	Austin, Browell, Roberts, Johnson		40,000
40	17	(a)	Leicester C	W 3-2	Roberts (2), Browell		20,000
41	27	(h)	Leeds U	W 2-1	Austin, Johnson		20,000
42	May 1	(a)	Newcastle U	L 2-3	Browell, Roberts		15,000
						Appearances	
						Goals	

League Division One record: P 42 W 12 D 11 L 19 F 89 A 100 Pts 35 Pos 21st

FA Cup

3	Jan 9	(a)	Corinthians	D 2-2
R	13	(h)	Corinthians	W 4-0
4	30	(h)	Huddersfield T	W 4-0
5	Feb 20	(h)	Crystal P	W 11-4
6	Mar 6	(a)	Clapton O	W 6-1
SF	27	(n)	Manchester U	W 3-0
F	Apr 24	(n)	Bolton W	L 0-1

Lancashire Senior Cup

2	Nov 18	(h)	Liverpool	W 5-0
3	Dec 2	(h)	Manchester U	W 3-2
SF	May 3	(n)	Accrington S	L 1-2

Manchester Senior Cup

3	Mar 1	(h)	Hurst	W 5-1
SF	Apr 12	(h)	Crewe A	D 0-0
R	28	(a)	Crewe A	W 2-0
F	May 6	(a)	Manchester U	L 0-2

Friendlies

None played.

86

Goodchild	Mitchell	Cookson	McCloy	Coupland	Cowan	Pringle	Austin	Roberts	Browell	Johnson	Hicks	McMullan	Murphy	Sharp	Thompson	Benzie	Dennison	Warner	Bradford	Elwood	Calderwood	Appleton	Daniels	Fletcher	Phillips	
1	2	3		5	6	7		9	10	11				4			8									1
	1	2	3	5	6	7		9	10	11				4			8									2
1	2	3		5	6	7		9	10	11				4			8									3
1	2	3		5	6	7		9	10	11				4			8									4
1	2	3		5	6	7	8	9	10	11				4												5
		3		5		7	8	9	10	11				4		2	6						1			6
	1		3	4	5	7		9	10	11						2	6	8								7
	1		3	4	5	7		9	10	11						2	6	8								8
	1		3	4	5	7	8	9	10	11						2	6									9
1	2	3	4	5	6	7	8	9	10	11																10
1	2	3	4	5	6		8	9	10	11								7								11
1	2			5	6	7	8	9	10	11				4									3			12
1	2			5	4	7	8	9	10	11						3	6									13
1	2		4	5		7	8	9		11						3	6	10								14
	1		3		6	7	9	10		11				4		2		8	5							15
	1		3	5	4	7	8	9	10	11						2	6									16
1	2	3	4	5	6	7	8	9	10			11														17
1	2	3	4	5	6	7		9	10			11					8									18
1	2	3	4	5	6			9	10			11					8	7								19
1	2	3	4	5	6			9	10			11					8	7								20
1	2	3	4	5	6			9	10			11					8	7								21
1	2	3	4	5	6		8	9	10			11						7								22
1	2	3	4	5	6		8	9	10	7		11														23
1	2		4	5	6	7		9	10	11							8				3					24
1	2	3	4	5		7		9	10	11							8				6					25
1		3	4	5	6	7		9	10			11				2	8									26
1	2	3	4	5	6	7	9	8	10	11																27
1	2	3	4	5	6	7	9	8	10	11																28
1	2	3	4	5	6	7	9	8		11												10				29
1	2	3	4	5	6	7	9	8	10	11																30
1	2	3		5	4	7	9	8	10	11	6															31
1	2			5	4	7	9	8		10	6	11										3				32
1	2	3		5	4	7	9	8	10	11	6															33
1	2	3		5	4	7	9	8	10	11	6															34
1	2	3		5	4	7	9	8	10	11	6															35
1	2	3		5	4	7	9	8	10	11	6															36
	1	2	3	5	4	7	9	8	10	11	6															37
	1	2	3	4	9	5	7	8	10	11										6						38
	1	2	3	4		7	9	8	10	11	6									5						39
1		2	3	4	6	7	9	8	10	11										5						40
1	2	3		5	4	7	9	8	10	11	6															41
1	2	3		5	4	7	9	8	10	11	6															42
24	17	35	37	23	38	36	36	38	32	38	35	10	9	8	9	7	8	7	5	4	2	1	1	1	1	
			2	2		12	21	21	15	5			2			4	4	1								

87

1926-27

1	Aug	28	(h)	Fulham	W 4-2	Austin, Barrass, Roberts, Hicks	40,000
2	Sep	1	(h)	Portsmouth	W 4-0	Roberts (2), Johnson, Hicks	25,000
3		4	(a)	Grimsby T	D 2-2	Roberts, Johnson	16,000
4		6	(a)	Oldham A	W 2-1	Pringle, Austin	25,000
5		11	(h)	Blackpool	W 2-1	Austin, Johnson	30,000
6		18	(a)	Reading	L 0-1		24,000
7		22	(h)	Oldham A	W 3-0	Roberts, Johnson, Hicks	25,000
8		25	(h)	Swansea T	W 3-1	Roberts, Johnson, Hicks	35,000
9	Oct	2	(a)	Nottingham F	D 3-3	Johnson (2), W.Cowan	15,000
10		9	(h)	Barnsley	D 1-1	Hicks	18,000
11		16	(h)	Southampton	L 3-4	McMullan, Austin, Johnson	25,000
12		23	(a)	Port Vale	W 2-0	McMullan, Johnson	14,000
13		30	(h)	Clapton O	W 6-1	Barrass (3), Roberts (2), Johnson	25,000
14	Nov	6	(a)	Notts C	L 0-1		6,000
15		13	(h)	Wolves	W 2-1	McMullan, Austin	15,000
16		20	(a)	Hull C	L 2-3	Barrass, Johnson	12,000
17		27	(h)	South Shields	L 1-2	Barrass	12,000
18	Dec	4	(a)	Preston N E	W 4-2	Austin (3), Barrass	25,000
19		11	(h)	Chelsea	W 1-0	Bell	25,000
20		18	(a)	Bradford C	L 3-4	Hicks (2), Roberts	17,000
21		25	(h)	Middlesbrough	L 3-5	S.Cowan, W.Cowan, Johnson	35,000
22		26	(a)	Middlesbrough	L 1-2	Roberts	40,000
23	Jan	1	(a)	Portsmouth	L 1-2	Johnson	20,000
24		15	(a)	Fulham	W 5-2	Gibson (2), Austin, W.Cowan, S.Cowan	10,000
25		22	(h)	Grimsby T	W 2-0	Johnson, Hicks	17,000
26		29	(a)	Blackpool	W 4-2	Hicks (2), W.Cowan, Johnson	9,000
27	Feb	5	(h)	Reading	W 3-0	Roberts, Hicks, opp.og	30,000
28		12	(a)	Swansea T	W 3-1	Johnson (2), Hicks	20,000
29		19	(h)	Nottingham F	D 1-1	W.Cowan	45,000
30		26	(a)	Barnsley	D 1-1	W.Cowan	14,000
31	Mar	12	(h)	Ports Vale	W 4-1	Johnson (2), W.Cowan, Hicks	30,000
32		19	(a)	Clapton O	W 4-2	Hicks (3), Austin	16,000
33		26	(h)	Notts C	W 4-1	W.Cowan (2), Hicks (2)	15,000
34	Apr	2	(a)	Wolves	L 1-4	W.Cowan	10,000
35		9	(h)	Hull C	D 2-2	W.Cowan, Bell	20,000
36		15	(a)	Darlington	D 2-2	Broadhurst, Johnson	10,000
37		16	(a)	South Shields	D 2-2	Roberts, Hicks	6,000
38		18	(h)	Darlington	W 7-0	Broadhurst (4), Johnson (2), Bell	40,000
39		23	(h)	Preston N E	W 1-0	Hicks	49,000
40		25	(a)	Southampton	D 1-1	Roberts	8,000
41		30	(a)	Chelsea	D 0-0		50,000
42	May	7	(h)	Bradford C	W 8-0	Johnson (3), Broadhurst (2), Hicks, Bell, Roberts	50,000
							Appearances
							Goals

League Division Two record: P 42   W 22   D 10   L 10   F 108   A 61   Pts 54   Pos 3rd

FA Cup   Friendlies

3 Jan 8 (a) Birmingham   L 1-4   None played.

Lancashire Senior Cup

2 Oct 13 (h) Oldham A   W 8-4
3   25 (a) Accrington S   W 5-3
SF Nov 24 (n) Bolton W   L 1-6

Manchester Senior Cup

3 Mar 9 (a) Wigan B   L 0-4

88

Goodchild	Gray	Cookson	McCloy	Pringle	Cowan S.	McMullan	Austin	Cowan W.	Roberts	Johnson	Hicks	Barrass	Bell	Bennett	Finnegan	Broadhurst	Sharp	Elwood	Benzie	Thompson	Allen	Gibson	Wilson	Coupland	
1	2	3	4	5	6	7	10	9			11	8													1
1	2	3	4	5	6	7			9	10	11	8													2
1	2	3	4	5	6	7			9	10	11	8													3
1	2	3	4		6	7	8		9	10	11	5													4
1	2	3	4		6	7			9	10	11	8						5							5
1	2	3			6		8		9	10	11	5	7						4						6
1	2	3			6		8		9	10	11	5	7			4									7
1	2	3			6		8		9	10	11	5	7			4									8
1	2	3			6		8		9	10	11	5	7			4									9
1	2	3	4		6		8		9	10	11	5	7												10
1	2	3	8		6	7			9	10	11	5				4									11
	2		4	5	6	7			9	10	11	8		3	1										12
	2		6	5		7			9	10	11	8		3	1	4									13
	2		4	5	6	7			9	10	11	8		3	1										14
	2		4	5	6	7			9	10	11	8		3	1										15
	2		4	5	6	7	8			10	11	9		3	1										16
1	2			5	6	7	8			10	11	9		3					4						17
	2			5	6	7			9	11	10	8		3	1								4		18
	2		4		6		8	9		11	10	7		3	1					5					19
	2				6		8	9		11	10	7		3	1					5				4	20
1	2			5		7	8		9	10	11	4		3					6						21
1	2					7	8		9	10	11	4		3					6	5					22
1	2		4			7				10	11	8		3				5	6			9			23
1	2	3	4	5	6	7	8			10	11											9			24
1	2	3	4	5	6	7	8		9		11	11													25
1	2	3	4	5	6		8		9	10	11												7		26
1	2	3	4	5	6				9	10	11	8	7												27
1	2	3	4	5	6				9	10	11	8	7												28
1	2	3	4	5	6		8		9	10	11		7												29
1	2	3	4	5	6	9	8			10	11		7												30
1	2	3	4	5	6	7	8		9	10	11														31
1	2	3	4	5	6	7	8		9	10	11														32
1	2	3			6	7	8		9	10	4	11					5								33
1	2	3	4			7	8		9	10	5	11						6							34
1	2	3	4	5	6	7	8		9	10	11														35
1	2	3	4	5	6		8			10	11		7				9								36
1	2	3		5	6		8			10	11		7				9	4							37
1	2	3	4	5	6					10	11		7				9				8				38
1	2	3	4	5	6					10	11		7				9				8				39
1	2	3	4	5	6		8			10	11		7				9								40
1	2	3	4	5	6		8			10	11		7				9								41
1	2	3	4	5	6		8			10	11		7				9								42
15	19	42	30	34	27	35	26	22	27	38	42	27	26	12	8	7	6	4	5	3	2	2	2	1	
			1	2	3	10	11	14	25	21	7	4		7						2					

1927-28

1	Aug	27	(a)	Wolves	D 2-2	McMullan, Hicks	30,000
2		29	(h)	Swansea T	W 7-4	Johnson (3), Broadhurst, Hicks, Roberts, Bell	40,000
3	Sep	3	(h)	Port Vale	W 1-0	Johnson	34,000
4		5	(a)	Swansea T	L 3-5	Bell, Johnson, Hicks	13,000
5		10	(a)	South Shields	W 1-0	McMullan	9,000
6		17	(h)	Leeds U	W 2-1	Johnson (2)	35,000
7		24	(a)	Nottingham F	W 5-4	Johnson (2), Hicks (2), Broadhurst	15,000
8	Oct	1	(h)	Oldham A	W 3-1	Broadhurst (2), Johnson	20,000
9		8	(h)	Hull C	W 2-1	Barrass (2)	45,000
10		15	(a)	Preston N E	L 0-1		28,000
11		22	(a)	Blackpool	D 2-2	Roberts, Hicks	17,000
12		29	(h)	Reading	W 4-1	Austin (2), Roberts, Johnson	35,000
13	Nov	5	(a)	Grimsby T	L 1-4	Smelt	14,000
14		12	(h)	Chelsea	L 0-1		60,000
15		19	(a)	Clapton O	W 2-0	Austin, Roberts	16,000
16		26	(h)	Stoke C	W 4-0	Austin, Allen, Roberts, Johnson	40,000
17	Dec	3	(a)	Bristol C	L 0-2		30,000
18		10	(h)	West Brom A	W 3-1	Austin, Broadhurst, Johnson	25,000
19		17	(a)	Southampton	D 1-1	Broadhurst	12,000
20		24	(h)	Notts C	W 3-1	Broadhurst (2), Hicks	20,000
21		26	(a)	Barnsley	W 3-0	Broadhurst (2), Roberts	17,000
22		31	(h)	Wolves	W 3-0	Johnson (2), Broadhurst	20,000
23	Jan	2	(h)	Barnsley	W 7-3	Austin (2), Gorringe (2), McMullan, Roberts, Johnson	30,000
24		7	(a)	Port Vale	W 2-1	Roberts, Hicks	15,000
25		21	(h)	South Shields	W 3-0	Austin, Broadhurst, Johnson	30,000
26	Feb	4	(h)	Nottingham F	D 3-3	Broadhurst, Austin, Hicks	25,000
27		11	(a)	Oldham A	L 2-3	Bell, Broadhurst	25,000
28		25	(h)	Preston N E	D 2-2	Roberts (2)	60,000
29	Mar	3	(h)	Blackpool	W 4-1	Roberts (4)	45,000
30		10	(a)	Reading	D 1-1	Marshall	12,000
31		17	(h)	Grimsby T	W 2-0	Roberts, McMullan	40,000
32		24	(a)	Chelsea	W 1-0	Roberts	50,000
33		31	(h)	Clapton O	W 5-3	Roberts (3), Horne, Brook	35,000
34	Apr	6	(h)	Fulham	W 2-1	Marshall, Roberts	45,000
35		7	(a)	Stoke C	L 0-2		30,000
36		9	(a)	Fulham	D 1-1	Tait	27,000
37		14	(h)	Bristol C	W 4-2	Tait, Johnson, Marshall, Hicks	30,000
38		16	(h)	Hull C	D 0-0		6,000
39		21	(a)	West Brom A	D 1-1	Brook	15,000
40		25	(a)	Leeds U	W 1-0	Tait	12,000
41		28	(h)	Southampton	W 6-1	Marshall (3), Johnson, Tait, Horne	50,000
42	May	5	(a)	Notts C	L 1-2	Marshall	6,000
						Appearances	
						Goals	

League Division Two record: P 42   W 25   D 9   L 8   F 100   A 59   Pts 59   Pos 1st

FA Cup

3	Jan	16	(h)	Leeds U	W 1-0
4		28	(a)	Sunderland	W 2-1
5	Feb	18	(h)	Stoke C	L 0-1

Lancashire Senior Cup

2	Sep	21	(h)	Newton	W 10-2
3	Oct	26	(h)	Oldham A	W 3-2
SF	Nov	23	(h)	Liverpool	W 3-2
F	May	12	(h)	Bury	W 3-1

Manchester Senior Cup

SF	Apr	11	(a)	Wigan B	W 2-0
F	May	9	(h)	Manchester U	W 4-2

Friendlies

None played.

Gray	Ridley	McCloy	Pringle	Cowan	McMullan	Austin	Roberts	Broadhurst	Barrass	Hicks	Johnson	Bell	Marshall	Brook	Sharp	Cookson	Barber	Horne	Tait	Allen	Tilson	Bennett	Gibbons	Foster	Smelt	Appleton	Gorringe	Robertson	#
1		3	4	5	6		8	9		11	10	7				2													1
1		3	4	5	6		8	9		11	10	7				2													2
1		3	4	5	6		8	9		11	10	7				2													3
1		3	4	5	6			9	8	11	10	7				2													4
1	2	3	4	5	6			9	8	11	10	7																	5
1	2	3	4	5	6			9	8	11	10	7																	6
1	2	3	4	5	6			9	8	11	10	7																	7
1	2	3	4		6			9	8	11	10	7											5						8
1	2	3	4		6			9	8	11	10	7											5						9
1	2	3	4	5				9	8	11		7						10									6		10
1	2	3	4	5	6		8	9		11	10	7																	11
		3	4	5		7		9	6		10	11					1							8	2				12
1	2	3		5	6	7		9			10	11												8	4				13
1	2	3	4	5	6	7		9		8	11	10																	14
1		3	4	5	6	7		9		11	10					2		8											15
1		3	4	5	6	7		9			10	11				2		8											16
1		3	4	5	6	7		9			10	11				2		8											17
1		3	4	5	6	7		9		11	10					2		8											18
1		3	4		6	7		9	5	11	10					2		8											19
1		3	4	5	6	7	8	9		11	10					2													20
1		3		5	6	7	8	9	4		10					2					11								21
1	2	3		5	6	7	8	9	4		10										11								22
1	2	3		5	6	7	8		4		10										11					9			23
1	2	3	4		6	7	8	9	5	11	10																		24
	2	3		5	6	7	8	9	4	11	10						1												25
	2	3		5	6	7	8	9	4	11	10						1												26
1	2	3		5	6		8	9	4	11	10	7																	27
1	2	3		5	6	7	8	9		11	10											4							28
1	2	3	5		6	7		9		11	10		8		4														29
1	2	3		5	6	7		9		11	10		8		4														30
1	2	3		5	6			9					8	11	4			7	10										31
1	2	3			6			9				5	8	11	4			7	10										32
1	2	3			6			9				5	8	11	4			7	10										33
1	2	3			6			9				5	8	11	4			7	10										34
1	2				6			9				5	8	11	4			7	10				3						35
	2			5	6				4	7			8	11			1	9	10				3						36
	2			5	6	7					10		8	11	4		1	9					3						37
	2				6				5	7	10		8	11	4		1	9					3						38
	2	3			6				5	7	10		8	11	4		1	9											39
	2	3			6				5	7	10		8	11	4		1	9											40
	2	3			6				5		10		8	11			1	7	9									4	41
	2	3			6				5		10		8	11			1	7	9									4	42
32	30	38	22	28	38	18	26	21	28	28	35	16	14	12	11	11	10	7	7	6	6	5	4	3	2	1	1	2	
		4	9	20	14	2	10	19	3	7	2					2	4	1				1		2					

1928-29

1	Aug 25	(a)	Birmingham	L 1-4	Tait	45,000
2	Sep 1	(h)	Manchester U	D 2-2	Roberts, Johnson	60,000
3	5	(a)	Portsmouth	L 0-1		26,000
4	8	(h)	Huddersfield T	W 3-2	Johnson (2), Marshall	40,000
5	15	(a)	Everton	W 6-2	Johnson (5), Brook	45,000
6	22	(h)	Arsenal	W 4-1	Broadhurst (2), Tilson (2)	35,000
7	29	(a)	Blackburn R	D 2-2	Tilson, Brook	30,000
8	Oct 1	(h)	Portsmouth	W 2-1	Austin, Johnson	20,000
9	6	(h)	Sunderland	W 5-3	Broadhurst, Barrass, Johnson, Marshall, Brook	40,000
10	13	(a)	Derby C	D 1-1	Brook	20,000
11	20	(a)	Leeds U	L 1-4	Barrass	30,000
12	27	(h)	Leicester C	L 2-3	Roberts (2)	30,000
13	Nov 3	(a)	West Ham U	L 0-3		30,000
14	10	(h)	Newcastle U	L 2-4	Johnson (2)	16,000
15	17	(a)	Burnley	W 3-2	Cowan, Roberts, Brook	12,000
16	24	(h)	Cardiff C	D 1-1	Broadhurst	15,000
17	Dec 1	(a)	Sheffield U	W 3-1	Johnson (2), Roberts	22,000
18	19	(a)	Aston Villa	L 1-5	Roberts	17,000
19	22	(h)	Liverpool	L 2-3	Bacon, Johnson	17,000
20	25	(a)	Sheffield W	L 0-4		45,000
21	26	(h)	Sheffield W	D 2-2	Johnson (2)	55,000
22	29	(h)	Birmingham	L 2-3	Marshall, Johnson	35,000
23	Jan 5	(a)	Manchester U	W 2-1	Johnson, Austin	50,000
24	19	(a)	Huddersfield T	D 2-2	Tait, Brook	18,000
25	26	(h)	Everton	W 5-1	Tilson (2), Austin, Brook, opp.og	35,000
26	30	(h)	Bury	W 6-4	Johnson (2), Tait, Brook, Tilson, Austin	20,000
27	Feb 2	(a)	Arsenal	D 0-0		18,000
28	9	(h)	Blackburn R	L 1-2	Johnson	40,000
29	16	(a)	Sunderland	L 1-3	Johnson	10,000
30	23	(h)	Derby C	L 2-3	Johnson (2)	30,000
31	Mar 2	(h)	Leeds U	W 3-0	Johnson, Tilson, Brook	40,000
32	9	(a)	Leicester C	L 2-3	Johnson, Tilson	15,000
33	16	(h)	West Ham U	W 4-2	Brook (2), Johnson, Austin	30,000
34	23	(a)	Newcastle U	L 0-4		25,000
35	29	(h)	Bolton W	W 5-1	Johnson (3), Marshall, Tilson	50,000
36	30	(h)	Burnley	W 4-1	Johnson (2), Marshall, Brook	40,000
37	Apr 1	(a)	Bolton W	D 1-1	Marshall	23,000
38	6	(a)	Cardiff C	W 3-1	Johnson (2), Tilson	10,000
39	13	(h)	Sheffield U	W 3-1	Marshall, Tilson, Brook	20,000
40	20	(a)	Bury	W 2-1	Johnson, Tilson	15,000
41	27	(h)	Aston Villa	W 3-0	Toseland, Johnson, Brook	25,000
42	May 4	(a)	Liverpool	D 1-1	Johnson	20,000
						Appearances
						Goals

League Division One record: P 42   W 18   D 9   L 15   F 95   A 86   Pts 45   Pos 8th

FA Cup

3	Jan 12	(a)	Birmingham	L 1-3

Lancashire Senior Cup

1	Sep 19	(h)	Bolton W	D 1-1
R	Oct 17	(a)	Bolton W	L 1-3

Manchester Senior Cup

3	Feb 27	(h)	Rochdale	W 3-2
SF	Apr 24	(a)	Wigan B	W 1-0
F	May 11	(h)	Bolton W	W 2-0

Friendly

1	Sep 12	(h)	Queen's Park	W 4-1

Barber	Ridley	McCloy	Barrass	Cowan	McMullen	Austin	Marshall	Roberts	Johnson	Tilson	Brook	Gray	Felton	Tait	Bacon	Broadhurst	Heinemann	Horne	Gibbons	Toseland	Bennett	Hicks	#
	2	3	4	5	6	7	8		10		11	1		9									1
	2	3	4	5	6	7	8	9	10		11	1											2
	2	3	4	5	6	7	8		10		11	1		9									3
	2	3	4	5	6	7	8		10		11	1		9									4
	2	3	4	5	6	7	8	9	10		11	1											5
	2	3	4	5	6	7	8		10		11	1			9								6
	2	3	4	5	6	7	8	9	10		11	1											7
	2	3	4	5	6	7	8	9			11	1								10			8
	2	3	4	5	6	7	8	9			11	1				10							9
	2	3	4	5	6	7	8		10		11	1			9								10
	2	3	4	5	6	7	8		10		11	1			9								11
1		3	6	5		7	8	9			11							10	4	2			12
	2	3		5	6	7	4	9			11	1						8					13
	2	3		5	6	7	4	8	9		11	1						10					14
1	2	3	4	5	6	7	8	9	10		11												15
	2	3	4	5	6	7		9	10		11	1			8								16
	2	3	4	5	6	7	8	9	10		11	1											17
	2	3	4	5	6	7		9	10		11	1			8								18
	2	3	4	5	6			9	10		11	1			8			7					19
1	2	3	4	5	6	7	8	9	10		11												20
1	2	3	4	5	6	7	8	9			11				10								21
1	2	3	4	5	6	7	8	9			11				10								22
1	2	3	4	5	6	7	8	9	10		11												23
1	2	3	4	5	6	7	8		10		11			9									24
1	2	3	4	5	6	7			10	8	11			9									25
1		3	2	5	6	7			10	8	11			9					4				26
1	2	3		5	6	7			10	8	11			9					4				27
1	2		4	5	6	7			10	8	11			9						3			28
1	2	3	4		6	7	5	9	10		11				8								29
1	2	3	4	5		7	8	9	10		11						6						30
1	2	3	4	5	6	7	8	9	10		11												31
1	2	3	4		6	7	5	8	9	10	11												32
1	2		4	5	6	7	8	9	10		11		3										33
1	2		4	5	6	7	8	9	10		11		3										34
1	2		4	5	6	7	8	9	10		11		3										35
1	2		4	5	6	7	8	9	10		11		3										36
1	2		4	5		7	8	9	10		11		3				6						37
1	2		4	5	6	7	8	9	10		11		3										38
1	2		4	5		7	8	9	10		11		3				6						39
1	2		4	5	6		8	9	10		11		3							7			40
1	2		4	5	6		8	9	10		11		3							7			41
1	2			5	6		8	9	10		11		3					4		7			42
25	40	31	40	38	38	38	33	14	39	22	42	17	10	8	5	5	4	4	3	3	2	1	
			2	1			5	7	6	38	12	14		3	1	4				1			

1929-30

1	Aug 31	(h)	Burnley	D 2-2	Marshall, Johnson		30,000
2	Sep 4	(h)	Arsenal	W 3-1	Tilson (2), Marshall		50,000
3	7	(a)	Sunderland	L 2-5	Johnson, Tilson		35,000
4	11	(a)	Arsenal	L 2-3	McMullan, Brook		27,000
5	14	(h)	Bolton W	W 2-0	Brook (2)		40,000
6	21	(a)	Everton	W 3-2	Marshall (2), Tilson		30,000
7	28	(h)	Derby C	W 3-0	Tilson (3)		40,000
8	Oct 5	(a)	Manchester U	W 3-1	Marshall, Johnson, Brook		50,000
9	12	(a)	Portsmouth	D 2-2	Tait, Johnson		20,000
10	19	(h)	West Ham U	W 4-3	Tait (3), Marshall		25,000
11	26	(a)	Liverpool	W 6-1	Tait (2), Johnson (2), Brook (2)		40,000
12	Nov 2	(h)	Middlesbrough	W 3-1	Toseland, Tait, Harrison		35,000
13	9	(a)	Grimsby T	D 2-2	Tait, Brook		16,000
14	16	(h)	Newcastle U	W 3-0	Marshall, Tait, Brook		30,000
15	23	(a)	Sheffield U	W 2-1	Marshall, Brook		12,000
16	30	(h)	Huddersfield T	D 1-1	Tait		25,000
17	Dec 7	(a)	Birmingham	L 0-3			15,000
18	14	(h)	Leicester C	W 3-2	Johnson (2), Brook		10,000
19	21	(a)	Blackburn R	W 3-1	Marshall (3)		25,000
20	25	(a)	Aston Villa	W 2-0	Tait (2)		40,000
21	26	(h)	Aston Villa	L 1-2	Tait		70,000
22	28	(a)	Burnley	L 2-4	Johnson, Cowan		17,000
23	Jan 1	(h)	Sheffield W	D 3-3	McMullan, Marshall, Brook		54,516
24	4	(h)	Sunderland	D 2-2	Marshall (2)		30,000
25	18	(a)	Bolton W	W 2-1	Johnson, Brook		40,111
26	Feb 1	(a)	Derby C	L 2-4	Tait, Brook		16,000
27	5	(h)	Everton	L 1-2	Marshall		20,000
28	8	(h)	Manchester U	L 0-1			63,018
29	22	(a)	West Ham U	L 0-3			28,000
30	26	(h)	Portsmouth	W 5-2	Tait (3), Toseland, Brook		20,000
31	Mar 1	(h)	Liverpool	W 4-3	Tait (2), Johnson, Brook		25,000
32	8	(a)	Middlesbrough	L 0-1			14,000
33	15	(h)	Grimsby T	W 3-1	Tait (2), Barrass		25,000
34	22	(a)	Newcastle U	D 2-2	Tait, Busby		30,000
35	29	(h)	Sheffield U	W 2-1	Brook, Hedley		25,000
36	Apr 5	(a)	Huddersfield T	D 1-1	Busby		15,000
37	12	(h)	Birmingham	L 1-4	Hedley		25,000
38	19	(a)	Leicester C	L 1-3	Tait		10,000
39	21	(h)	Leeds U	W 4-1	Tait (3), Ridding		25,000
40	22	(a)	Leeds U	L 2-3	Ridding, Busby		12,000
41	26	(h)	Blackburn R	D 1-1	Tait		15,000
42	May 3	(a)	Sheffield W	L 1-5	Tait		33,000
							Appearances
							Goals

League Division One record: P 42   W 19   D 9   L 14   F 91   A 81   Pts 47   Pos 3rd

FA Cup

3	Jan 11	(a)	Tottenham H	D 2-2
	15	(h)	Tottenham H	W 4-1
4	25	(a)	Swindon T	D 1-1
R	29	(h)	Swindon T	W 10-1
5	Feb 15	(h)	Hull C	L 1-2

Lancashire Senior Cup

2	Sep 24	(a)	Southport	D 3-3
R	Oct 21	(h)	Southport	W 7-0
3	Nov 13	(a)	Liverpool	W 5-4
SF	Dec 11	(h)	Manchester U	W 3-1
F	May 10	(h)	Burnley	W 3-0

Manchester Senior Cup

3	Mar 5	(h)	Bury	W 1-0
SF	Apr 28	(h)	Oldham A	W 2-1
F	May 7	(h)	Wigan B	L 2-3

Friendlies

1	Apr 28	(a)	Portsmouth	L 1-2
2	30	(a)	Torquay U	W 3-1

Barber	Ridley	Felton	Barrass	Cowan	McMullen	Toseland	Marshall	Tait	Johnson	Brook	Heinemann	McCloy	Tilson	Busby	Robertson	Ridding	Wrightson	Gibbons	Harrison	Hedley	Bray	Cann	
1	2	3	4	5	6	7	8		9	11			10										1
1	2	3	4	5	6	7	8		9	11			10										2
1	2		4	5	6	7	8		9	11		3	10										3
1	2		4	5	6	7	8		9	11		3	10										4
1	2		4	5	6	7	8		9	11		3	10										5
1	2		4	5	6	7	8		9	11		3	10										6
1		3	4	5	6	7	8		9	11			10		2								7
1	2	3	4	5		7	8		9	11	6		10										8
1	2	3	4	5		7	8	9	10	11	6												9
1	2	3	4	5	6	7	8	9	10								11						10
1	2	3	4	5	6	7	8	9	10	11													11
1	2	3	4	5		7	8	9			6		10				11						12
1	2	3		5		7	8	9	10	11	6					4							13
1	2	3		5		7	8	9	10	11	6					4							14
1	2	3	4	5		7	8	9	10	11	6												15
1	2	3	4	5		7	8	9	10	11	6												16
1	2	3	4	5		7	8	9	10	11	6												17
1	2	3	4	5		7	8	9	10	11	6												18
1	2	3	4	5		7	8	9	10	11	6												19
1	2		4	5		7	8	9	10	11	6	3											20
1	2		4	5		7	8	9	10	11	6	3											21
1	2		4	5	6	7	8	9	10	11		3											22
1	2	3	4	5	6	7	8	9	10	11													23
1	2	3	4	5	6	7	8	9	10	11													24
1		2	4	5		7	8		9	11	6	3	10										25
1		2	4	5		7	8	9	10	11	6	3											26
1		2	4	5		7	8		9	11	6	3	10										27
1		2	4	5		7	8	9	10	11		3							6				28
1	2	3	4	5	6	7	8	9		11				10									29
1	2	3		5	6	7	8	9	10	11							4						30
1	2		4	5	6	7	8	9	10	11					3								31
1	2		4	5	6	7		9		11			10	8	3								32
1	2	3	4	5	6	7		9		11				10				8					33
1	2	3	4	5	6	7		9		11				10				8					34
1	2	3	4	5	6	7		9		10							8		11				35
1	2	3	4	5	6	7		9		11				10				8					36
1	2	3	8	5	6	7		9		10										11	4		37
1	2		4	5	6	7		9		11				10	3	8							38
1	2		4	5	6	7		9		11				10	3	8							39
1	2		4	5	6	7		9		11				10	3	8							40
1	2		4	5		7		9		11				10	3	8				6			41
1	2		4	5	6	7		9		11				10	3	8							42
42	37	28	41	40	25	42	31	31	30	40	15	11	11	11	8	5	4	3	2	2	2	1	
		1	1	2	2	15	28	11	16		7	3					2		1	2			

95

1930-31

1	Aug	30	(a)	Sunderland	D 3-3	Barrass, Tait, Brook	30,000
2	Sep	3	(h)	Blackpool	L 2-4	Toseland, Brook	32,000
3		6	(h)	Leicester C	L 0-2		25,000
4		8	(a)	Leeds U	L 2-4	Brook (2)	14,000
5		13	(a)	Birmingham	L 2-3	Tait, Brook	18,000
6		17	(h)	Leeds U	W 1-0	Brook	15,000
7		20	(h)	Sheffield U	L 0-4		20,000
8		27	(a)	Derby C	D 1-1	Tait	14,000
9	Oct	4	(h)	Manchester U	W 4-1	Marshall (2), Tait (2)	45,000
10		11	(h)	Portsmouth	L 1-3	Marshall	30,000
11		18	(a)	Sheffield W	D 1-1	Tait	20,000
12		25	(h)	Grimsby T	W 1-0	Marshall	25,000
13	Nov	1	(a)	Liverpool	W 2-0	Austin, Tilson	15,000
14		8	(h)	Middlesbrough	W 4-2	Tait (2), Race, Marshall	25,000
15		15	(a)	Chelsea	L 0-2		25,000
16		22	(h)	Bolton W	W 3-0	Halliday (2), Marshall	20,000
17		29	(a)	Huddersfield T	D 1-1	Brook	12,000
18	Dec	6	(h)	Newcastle U	W 2-0	Halliday, Tilson	18,000
19		13	(a)	West Ham U	L 0-2		22,000
20		20	(h)	Aston Villa	W 3-1	Toseland, Halliday, Brook	30,000
21		25	(h)	Arsenal	L 1-4	Tilson	58,000
22		26	(a)	Arsenal	L 1-3	Marshall	22,000
23		27	(h)	Sunderland	W 2-0	Marshall, Ridding	20,000
24	Jan	1	(a)	Blackburn R	W 1-0	Toseland	25,000
25		3	(a)	Leicester C	L 2-3	Halliday (2)	15,000
26		17	(h)	Birmingham	W 4-2	Brook (2), Tilson, Wrightson	18,000
27		28	(a)	Sheffield U	D 2-2	Toseland, Halliday	8,000
28		31	(h)	Derby C	W 4-3	Halliday (2), Toseland, Roberts	15,000
29	Feb	7	(a)	Manchester U	W 3-1	Brook, Toseland, Halliday	50,000
30		18	(a)	Portsmouth	D 1-1	Halliday	5,000
31		21	(h)	Sheffield W	W 2-0	Halliday (2)	25,000
32		28	(a)	Grimsby T	W 5-3	Toseland, Marshall, Halliday, Roberts, Brook	15,000
33	Mar	7	(h)	Liverpool	D 1-1	Barrass	18,000
34		14	(a)	Middlesbrough	L 1-4	Cowan	10,000
35		21	(h)	Chelsea	W 2-0	Marshall, Wrightson	25,000
36		28	(a)	Bolton W	D 1-1	Brook	10,000
37	Apr	3	(h)	Blackburn R	W 3-0	Brook (2), Toseland	30,000
38		4	(h)	Huddersfield T	L 0-1		25,000
39		11	(a)	Newcastle U	W 1-0	Brook	18,000
40		18	(h)	West Ham U	D 1-1	Cowan	15,000
41		25	(a)	Aston Villa	L 2-4	Toseland, Wrightson	17,000
42	May	2	(a)	Blackpool	D 2-2	Toseland, Ridding	20,000

Appearances
Goals

League Division One record: P 42   W 18   D 10   L 14   F 75   A 70   Pts 46   Pos 8th

FA Cup

3 Jan 10 (a) Burnley   L 0-3

Lancashire Senior Cup

2 Oct 7 (a) Bolton W   L 1-2

Manchester Senior Cup

3 Mar 4 (h) Rochdale   L 0-1

Friendlies

1 Apr 13 (a) Doncaster R   W 3-0
2   27 (a) Linfield   W 4-1

Langford	Ridley	Barnett	Barrass	Busby	Cowan	McMullan	Bray	Toseland	Marshall	Halliday	Tilson	Brook	Barber	Tait	Felton	Wrightson	Roberts	Race	Ridding	Robertson	Heinemann	Austin	
	2	4		5	6		7	8			10	11	1	9	3								1
	2	4		5	6		7	8			10	11	1	9	3								2
	2	4		5	6		7				10	11	1	9	3	8							3
	2	4		5	6		7	8				11	1	9						3			4
	2	4		5	6		7	8				11	1	9				10		3			5
	2	3	4			10	6	7				11	1	9				8		5			6
	2	3		5	6	4	7				10	11	1	9				8					7
	2	4		5		10	6	7	8			11	1	9	3								8
	2	4		5		10	6	7	8			11	1	9	3								9
	2	4		5		10	6	7	8			11	1	9	3								10
	2	4		5		10	6	7	8			11	1	9	3								11
	2	4		5		10	6		8			11	1	9	3							7	12
	2	4		5	6			8			10	11	1	9	3							7	13
	2	4		5	6			8				11	1	9	3			10				7	14
	1	4		5	6			8				11	1	9	3			10				7	15
1	2	4		5	6		7	8	9	10		11			3								16
1	2	3	4	5	6		7	8	9	10		11											17
1	2	3	4	5	6		7	8	9	10		11											18
1	2	3	4	5	6		7	8	9	10		11											19
1	2	3	4	5	6		7	8	9	10		11											20
1	2	3	4	5	6		7	8	9	10		11											21
1	2	3	4	5	6		7	8	9	10		11											22
1	2	3	4	5	6		7	8		10		11						9					23
1	2	3	4	5	6		7	8		10		11						9					24
1	2	3	4	5	6		7	8	9	10		11											25
1	2	3	4	5				7	9	10		11				8					6		26
1	2	3	4	5	6		7		9			11				8	10						27
1	2	3	4	5	6		7	8	9			11					10						28
1	2	3	4	5	6		7	8	9			11					10						29
1	2	3		5	6		7	8	9			11					10		4				30
1	2	3	4	5	6		7	8	9			11					10						31
1	2	3	4	5	6		7	8	9			11					10						32
1	2	3	4	5	6		7	8	9			11					10						33
1	2	3	4	5	6		7	8	9			11					10						34
1	2	3	4	5	6		7	8	9			11				10							35
1	2	3	4	5	6		7	8	9			11				10							36
1	2	3	4	5	6		7	8	9			11				10							37
1	2	3	4	5	6		7	8	9			11				10							38
1	2	3	4	5	6		7	8	9			11				10							39
1	2	3	4	5	6		7	8	9			11				10							40
1	2	3	4	5	6		7	8	9			11				10							41
1	2	3	4	5	6		7	8				11				10					9		42
27	42	28	21	20	40	27	21	38	37	24	17	42	15	15	12	11	8	5	3	3	2	4	
		2		2				10	10	14	4	16		8		3	2	1	2			1	

97

1931-32

					Result	Scorers	Attendance
1	Aug	29	(h)	Sunderland	D 1-1	Marshall	40,000
2	Sep	2	(a)	Derby C	L 1-2	Halliday	11,000
3		5	(a)	Leicester C	L 0-4		12,000
4		9	(h)	Derby C	W 3-0	Halliday (3)	16,000
5		12	(a)	Everton	W 1-0	Halliday	25,000
6		14	(a)	West Brom A	D 1-1	Cowan	24,000
7		19	(h)	Arsenal	L 1-3	Bray	50,000
8		23	(h)	West Brom A	L 2-5	Cowan, Halliday	18,000
9		26	(a)	Blackpool	D 2-2	Wrightson	25,000
10	Oct	3	(h)	Sheffield U	D 1-1	Marshall	25,000
11		10	(a)	Blackburn R	D 2-2	Halliday, Tilson	12,000
12		17	(h)	West Ham U	L 0-1		18,000
13		24	(a)	Newcastle U	L 1-2	Marshall	23,000
14		31	(h)	Huddersfield T	W 3-0	Halliday (2), Marshall	18,000
15	Nov	7	(a)	Middlesbrough	D 3-3	Toseland, Halliday, Tilson	8,000
16		14	(h)	Grimsby T	W 4-1	Halliday (2), Marshall, Brook	18,000
17		21	(a)	Liverpool	L 3-4	Marshall, Halliday, Tilson	30,000
18		28	(h)	Aston Villa	D 3-3	Halliday (2), Tilson	30,000
19	Dec	5	(a)	Chelsea	L 2-3	Tilson, Toseland	30,000
20		12	(h)	Bolton W	W 2-1	Halliday, Tilson	18,000
21		19	(a)	Sheffield W	D 1-1	Brook	10,000
22		26	(a)	Portsmouth	L 2-3	Halliday, Tilson	35,000
23	Jan	1	(h)	Portsmouth	D 3-3	McMullan, Marshall, opp.og	30,000
24		2	(a)	Sunderland	W 5-2	Halliday (3), Rowley (2)	18,000
25		16	(a)	Leicester C	W 5-1	Marshall (2), Halliday, Tilson, Brook	20,000
26		27	(h)	Everton	W 1-0	Halliday	20,000
27		30	(a)	Arsenal	L 0-4		45,000
28	Feb	6	(h)	Blackpool	W 7-1	Halliday (2), Brook (2), Toseland, Tilson, Cowan	25,000
29		15	(a)	Sheffield U	L 1-2	Rowley	10,000
30		20	(h)	Blackburn R	W 3-1	Marshall (2), Brook	20,000
31	Mar	2	(a)	West Ham U	D 1-1	Busby	18,000
32		5	(h)	Newcastle U	W 5-1	Tilson (2), Toseland, Marshall, Brook	25,000
33		19	(h)	Middlesbrough	L 1-2	Tilson	20,000
34		26	(a)	Grimsby T	L 1-2	Brook	17,000
35		28	(h)	Birmingham	W 2-1	Marshall, Brook	20,000
36		29	(a)	Birmingham	W 5-1	Halliday (3), Payne, Tilson	12,000
37	Apr	2	(h)	Liverpool	L 0-1		20,000
38		6	(h)	Huddersfield T	L 0-1		15,000
39		9	(a)	Aston Villa	L 1-2	Brook	30,000
40		16	(h)	Chelsea	D 1-1	Rowley	18,000
41		23	(a)	Bolton W	D 1-1	Halliday	10,000
42		30	(h)	Sheffield W	L 1-2	Toseland	15,000

Appearances
Goals

League Division One record: P 42 W13 D 12 L 17 F 83 A 73 Pts 38 Pos 14th

FA Cup

3	Jan	9	(a)	Millwall	W 3-2
4		23	(h)	Brentford	W 6-1
5	Feb	13	(h)	Derby C	W 3-0
6		27	(a)	Bury	W 4-3
SF	Mar	12	(n)	Arsenal	L 0-1

Lancashire Senior Cup

1	Oct	7	(a)	Manchester U	W 3-2
2	Nov	2	(h)	Oldham A	W 3-1
SF	Apr	20	(h)	Burnley	W 4-1
F	May	14	(h)	Bolton W	L 2-3

Manchester Senior Cup

3	Feb	24	(h)	Rochdale	W 6-0
SF	Apr	27	(a)	Bury	W 3-0
F	May	14	(a)	Oldham A	W 1-0

Friendlies

None played.

Tour (of France)

1	May	5	(a)	Racing Club de Paris	W 4-3
2		7	(a)	Red Star Olympique	W 5-0
3		8	(a)	Les Diables Rouges	W 5-1

Langford	Ridley	Felton	Dale	Busby	Cowan	McMullen	Bray	Toseland	Marshall	Halliday	Tilson	Brook	Rowley	Barnett	Cann	Wrightson	Gregory	Barrass	Payne	Walmsley	Race	Ridding	Syme	No.
1	2			4	5	6		7	8	9	10	11		3										1
1	2			4	5	6		7	8	9	10	11		3										2
1	2			4	5	6		7	8	9	10	11		3										3
1	2			4	5		6	7		9	10	11		3		8								4
1	2			4	5		6	7		9	10	11		3		8								5
1	2			4	5		6	7		9	10	11		3		8								6
1	2			4			6	7		9	10	11		3		8	5							7
1	2			4	5		6	7		9	10	11		3		8								8
1	2			4	5		6	7		9	10	11		3		8								9
1	2	3		4	5		6	7	8			11									10	9		10
1	2			4	5			7	8	9	10	11		3			6							11
1	2			4	5		6	7	8	9	10	11		3										12
1	2	3		4	5		6	7	8	9	10	11												13
1	2	3		4	5		6	7	8	9	10	11												14
1	2	3		4	5		6	7	8	9	10	11												15
1	2	3		4	5		6	7	8	9	10	11												16
1	2	3		4	5		6	7	8	9	10	11												17
1	2	3		4	5		6	7	8	9	10	11												18
1	2	3		4	5		6	7	8	9	10	11												19
1	2	3		4	5		6	7	8	9	10	11												20
1	2	3		4	5		6	7		9	10	11				8								21
1		2	3	4	5	6		7	8	9	10	11												22
1		2	3	4	5	6		7	8	9	10	11												23
1		2	3	4	5		6	7	8	9		11	10											24
1		2	3	4	5	6		7	8	9	10	11												25
1		2	3	4		6		7	5	9	8	11	10											26
1		2	3	4	5	6		7	8	9	10	11												27
1		2	3	4	5	6		7		9	8	11	10											28
1		2	3				6	7	5	9	8	11	10				4							29
1		2	3	4	5	6		7	8	9	10	11												30
1		2	3	4	5	6		7	8	9	10	11												31
1		2	3	4	5	6		7	8	9	10	11												32
1	2	3	4	5	6			7	8	9	10	11												33
			3	4	5	6		7	8	9		11	10		2				1					34
			3	4	6			7	5	9	8	11	10		2				1					35
1			3	4	6				5	9	8	11	10		2					7				36
1			3	4	6				8	9		11	10		2			5		7				37
1	2	3	4		6			7	8	9		11	10		2			5						38
1			3	4	6			7	5	9	8	11	10		2									39
1			3	4	6			7	5		8	11	10		2								9	40
1			3	4	6			7	5	9	8	11	10		2									41
1			3	4	6			7	5	9	8	11	10		2									42
40	21	23	21	41	31	21	20	40	34	40	37	42	13	11	8	7	3	2	2	2	1	1	1	
				1	3	1	1	5	13	28	13	10	4				1		1					

1932-33

1	Aug	27	(a)	Sunderland	L	2-3	Brook (2)	33,000
2		31	(h)	Birmingham	W	1-0	Marshall	26,000
3	Sep	3	(h)	Middlesbrough	L	2-3	Marshall (2)	25,000
4		7	(a)	Birmingham	L	0-3		20,000
5		10	(h)	Arsenal	L	2-3	Tilson, Busby	40,000
6		17	(a)	Everton	L	1-2	Toseland	35,000
7		24	(h)	Blackpool	W	5-1	Toseland (2), Halliday (2), Brook	25,000
8	Oct	1	(a)	Derby C	L	0-4		13,000
9		8	(h)	Blackburn R	L	2-3	Halliday, Tilson	6,000
10		15	(a)	Leeds U	L	1-2	Tilson	14,000
11		22	(a)	Bolton W	L	1-2	Tilson	10,000
12		29	(h)	Liverpool	D	1-1	Marshall	10,000
13	Nov	5	(a)	Sheffield U	W	5-2	Race (2), Toseland, Marshall, Brook	15,000
14		12	(h)	Wolves	W	4-1	Marshall (2), Comrie, Brook	25,000
15		19	(a)	Newcastle U	L	0-2		14,000
16		26	(h)	Aston Villa	W	5-2	Tilson (4), Brook	20,000
17	Dec	3	(a)	Leicester C	W	2-1	Tilson, Brook	15,000
18		10	(h)	Portsmouth	W	3-1	Tilson (2), Cowan	10,000
19		17	(a)	Chelsea	L	1-3	Tilson	25,000
20		24	(h)	Huddersfield T	W	3-0	Toseland, Tilson, Brook	18,000
21		26	(h)	Sheffield W	D	2-2	Cowan, Brook	35,000
22		27	(a)	Sheffield W	L	1-2	Cowan	35,000
23		31	(h)	Sunderland	L	2-4	Toseland, Tilson	18,000
24	Jan	7	(a)	Middlesbrough	L	0-2		10,000
25		21	(a)	Arsenal	L	1-2	Tilson	35,000
26	Feb	1	(h)	Everton	W	3-0	Toseland, Tilson, Brook	10,000
27		4	(a)	Blackpool	L	0-1		20,000
28		11	(h)	Derby C	W	2-1	Toseland, Herd	32,590
29		23	(a)	Blackburn R	L	0-1		12,000
30	Mar	8	(h)	Bolton W	W	2-1	Cowan, Herd	20,000
31		11	(a)	Liverpool	D	1-1	Herd	28,000
32		22	(h)	Sheffield U	W	1-0	Tilson	20,000
33		25	(a)	Wolves	W	2-1	Herd, Brook	30,000
34	Apr	1	(h)	Newcastle U	L	1-2	Brook	30,000
35		5	(h)	Leeds U	D	0-0		15,000
36		8	(a)	Aston Villa	D	1-1	Marshall	20,000
37		14	(h)	West Brom A	W	1-0	Brook	48,000
38		15	(h)	Leicester C	W	4-1	Herd (2), Toseland, Marshall	22,000
39		17	(a)	West Brom A	L	0-4		20,000
40		22	(a)	Portsmouth	W	2-1	Herd, Brook	12,000
41	May	3	(h)	Chelsea	L	1-4	Brook	25,000
42		6	(a)	Huddersfield T	L	0-1		5,000

Appearances
Goals

League Division One record: P 42   W16   D 5   L 21   F 68   A 71   Pts 37   Pos 16

FA Cup

3	Jan	14	(a)	Gateshead	D	1-1
R		18	(h)	Gateshead	W	9-0
4		28	(h)	Walsall	W	2-0
5	Feb	18	(a)	Bolton W	W	4-2
6	Mar	4	(a)	Burnley	W	1-0
SF		18	(n)	Derby C	W	3-2
F	Apr	29	(n)	Everton	L	0-3

Lancashire Senior Cup

1	Sep	26	(a)	Blackpool		L 1-4

Manchester Senior Cup

SF	Apr	10	(h)	Rochdale		W 4-0
F	May	13	(h)	Manchester U		W 2-0

Friendlies

None played.

Langford	Cann	Dale	Busby	Cowan	Bray	Toseland	Marshall	Tilson	McMullan	Brook	Herd	Comrie	Nicholls	Corbett F.	Halliday	Gregory	Rowley	Ridley	Race	Barnett	Barrass	Syme	Fletcher	Higgs	Naylor	Robertson	#
1	2	3	4	5		7	8	10	6	11					9												1
1	2	3	4			7	8		6	11					9	5	10							1			2
	2	3	4			7	8		6	11					9	5	10										3
1	2	3	4			7	8	10	6	11						5							9				4
1	2	3	4	5		7	8	10	6	11					9												5
	2	3	4	5		7	8	10	6	11		1			9												6
	2	3		5		7	8	10	6	11		1			9					4							7
	2	3		5		7	8	10		11		1			9					4					6		8
	2	3		5		7	8	10	6	11		1			9			4									9
	2	3	4			7	5	8	6	11	10	1			9							–					10
	2	3	4			7	5	8	6	11	10	1			9												11
	2	3	4	5	6	7	8			11		1					10						9				12
	2	3	4	5	6	7	8			11		1			9		10										13
	2	3	4	5	6	7	8			11	10	1			9												14
	2	3	4	5	6	7	8	10		11		1			9												15
		3	4	5	6	7	8	9		11	10	1		2													16
		3	4	5	6	7	8	9		11	10	1		2													17
1		3	4	5	6	7	8	9		11	10			2													18
		3	4	5	6	7	8	9		11	10	1		2													19
1			4	5	6	7	8	9		11	10			2					3								20
1			4	5	6	7	8	9		11	10			2					3								21
1		3	4	5	6	7	8	9		11	10			2													22
1		3	4	5	6	7	8	9		11	10			2													23
1		3	4	5		7		9		11			8	2			10								6		24
1		3	4	5	6	7	8	9	10	11				2													25
1		3	4	5	6	7	8		10	11				2									9				26
1		3	4		6	7		9	10	11			8	2		5											27
1		3	4		6	7		9	10	11			8	2		5											28
1	2	3	4		6	7	8	9		11	10					5											29
1	2	3	4	5	6	7		9	10	11	8																30
1	2	3	4	5	6	7		9	10	11	8																31
1	2	3	4	5	6	7		9	10	11	8																32
1	2	3	4	5	6	7	8		10	11	9																33
1	2	3	4	5	6	7		9	10	11	8																34
1	2	3	4	5	6	7		9	10	11	8																35
1	2	3	4	5	6	7	8		10	11	9																36
1	2	3	4	5	6	7	8		10	11	9																37
1	2	3	4	5	6	7	8			11	9		10														38
1	2		4		6	7	8		10	11	9					5			3								39
1	2	3	4		6	7	8		10	11	9		8														40
1	2	3	4	5	6	7	8		10	11	9																41
		3	4	5	6	7		9	10	11	8	1									2						42
27	28	39	39	32	30	42	33	29	26	42	16	14	14	9	8	7	5	4	4	4	3	1	1	1	1	1	
		1	4			9	9	17		15	7	1				3					2						

1933-34

1	Aug	26	(h)	Sheffield W	L	2-3	Herd, Tilson	35,000
2		30	(a)	Birmingham	W	1-0	Tilson	30,000
3	Sep	2	(a)	Leicester C	D	0-0		25,000
4		6	(h)	Birmingham	W	1-0	Syme	20,000
5		9	(a)	Arsenal	D	1-1	Herd	45,000
6		16	(h)	Everton	D	2-2	Herd, Brook	40,000
7		23	(a)	Middlesbrough	L	1-2	Marshall	7,000
8		30	(h)	Blackburn R	W	3-1	Cowan, Halliday, Brook	30,000
9	Oct	7	(a)	Newcastle U	D	2-2	Halliday, Herd	20,000
10		14	(h)	Leeds U	L	0-1		20,000
11		21	(h)	Aston Villa	W	1-0	Marshall	35,000
12		28	(a)	Sheffield U	D	1-1	Tilson	14,000
13	Nov	4	(h)	Sunderland	W	4-1	Brook (2), Toseland, Marshall	25,000
14		11	(a)	Stoke C	W	1-0	Toseland	20,000
15		18	(h)	Huddersfield T	D	2-2	Toseland, Tilson	30,000
16		25	(a)	Portsmouth	L	0-2		15,000
17	Dec	2	(h)	Tottenham H	W	2-0	Brook, Herd	40,000
18		9	(a)	Chelsea	W	2-1	Herd, Gregory	15,000
19		16	(h)	Liverpool	W	2-1	Tilson, Herd	15,000
20		23	(a)	Wolves	L	0-8		20,000
21		25	(a)	Derby C	L	1-4	Toseland	32,786
22		26	(h)	Derby C	W	2-0	Gregory, Brook	58,000
23		30	(a)	Sheffield W	D	1-1	Busby	24,000
24	Jan	1	(h)	West Brom A	L	2-7	Herd, Bray	20,000
25		6	(h)	Leicester C	D	1-1	Herd	20,000
26		20	(h)	Arsenal	W	2-1	Marshall, Herd	50,000
27	Feb	3	(h)	Middlesbrough	W	5-2	Tilson (2), Brook (2), Busby	16,000
28		7	(a)	Everton	L	0-2		18,000
29		10	(a)	Blackburn R	L	0-3		20,000
30		24	(a)	Leeds U	L	1-3	Syme	15,000
31	Mar	7	(a)	Aston Villa	L	0-0		20,000
32		10	(h)	Sheffield U	W	4-1	Tilson (2), Herd, Busby	18,000
33		21	(h)	Newcastle U	D	1-1	Wright	16,000
34		24	(h)	Stoke C	W	4-2	Herd (2), Cowan, Bray	20,000
35		31	(a)	Huddersfield T	L	0-1		21,000
36	Apr	2	(a)	West Brom A	L	0-4		20,000
37		7	(h)	Portsmouth	W	2-1	Busby, Herd	35,000
38		11	(a)	Sunderland	D	0-0		10,000
39		14	(a)	Tottenham H	L	1-5	Toseland	20,000
40		21	(h)	Chelsea	W	4-2	Tilson (3), Toseland	20,000
41	May	2	(a)	Liverpool	L	2-3	Herd, Heale	20,000
42		5	(h)	Wolves	W	4-0	Herd (2), Cowan, Heale	22,000

Appearances
Goals

League Division One record: P 42   W17   D 11   L 14   A 65   A 72   Pts 45   Pos 5th

FA Cup

3	Jan	13	(h)	Blackburn R	W 3-1
4		27	(a)	Hull C	D 2-2
R		31	(h)	Hull C	W 4-1
5	Feb	17	(a)	Sheffield W	D 2-2
R		21	(h)	Sheffield W	W 2-0
6	Mar	3	(h)	Stoke C	W 1-0
SF		17	(n)	Aston Villa	W 6-1
F	Apr	28	(n)	Portsmouth	W 2-1

Lancashire Senior Cup

1	Sep	13	(h)	Blackpool	W 4-1
2	Oct	11	(h)	Bury	D 1-1
R		31	(a)	Bury	W 3-1
SF	Nov	15	(a)	Bolton W	L 2-3

Manchester Senior Cup

3	Feb	14	(h)	Oldham A	W 4-2
SF	Apr	25	(h)	Bolton W	W 4-0
F	May	7	(a)	Manchester U	L 0-1

Friendly

1	Dec	18	(h)	FK Austria	W 3-0

Tour (to France and Italy)

1	May	10	(a)	Racing Club France	W 3-1
2		13	(a)	Fiorentina	D 3-3
3		20	(a)	Milan	L 0-5
4		21	(a)	Admira Wein	W 5-3
5		27	(a)	Marseilles Olympique	D 4-4

Player appearance / position grid (positions 1–11 by match). Player columns read left-to-right; the final column is the match number.

Langford	Swift	Barnett	Dale	Busby	Cowan	McLuckie	Toseland	Marshall	Herd	Tilson	Brook	Bray	Heale	Gregory	Syme	Cann	Corbett V.	Percival J.	Halliday	Comrie	Lloyd	Barkas	Dunne	Nicholls	Payne	Percival R.	Corbett F.	Wright	No.
		2	3	4	5	10	7	8	9		11	6												1					1
1		2	3	4	5	6	7	8	10	11	9																		2
1		2	3	4	5	6	7	8	10	11	9																		3
1		2	3	4	5	6	7	8	10	11	9																		4
1			3	4	5	6	7	8	10	11	9						2												5
1		2	3	4	5	6	7	8	10	11	9																		6
1		2	3	4	5	6	7	8	10	11									9										7
1		2	3	4	5	6	7	8	10	11									9										8
1		2	3	4	5	6	7	8	10	11									9										9
1		2	3	4	5	6	7	8											9	10					11				10
1		2	3		5	6	7	8	9	11	10							4											11
1		2	3	4	5	6	7	8	10	9	11																		12
1		2	3	4	5	6	7	8	9	10	11																		13
1		2	3	4	5	6	7	8	9	10	11																		14
1		2	3	4	5	6	7	8	9	10	11																		15
1		2			5	6	7	8	10	9	11							4					3						16
1		2	3	4	7	5	8	10	11	6	9																		17
1		2	3	4	7	5	8	10	11	6	9																		18
1		2	3	4	7	5	8	10	11	6	9																		19
		2		4	7	5	10	11	6	9										8			3	1					20
	1	2		4	7	5	8	10	11	6	9					3													21
	1	2		10	7	5	8		11	6	9					3		4											22
	1	2		10	7	5	8		11	6	9					3		4											23
	1	2	3	10	7	5	8		11	6	9							4											24
	1	2	3	4	6	7	5	8	10	11	9																		25
	1	2	3	4	5	6	7	8	10	9	11																		26
	1	2	3	4	5	6	7	8	9	11	10																		27
	1	2	3	4	5	6	7	8	11	10	9																		28
	1	2		4	5	6	7	8	11	10	9															3			29
	1	3		5	6	8	11	4	10						9	2										7			30
	1	3	4	5		8	9	11	6	10						2										7			31
	1	3	4	5		7	8	10	9	11	6						2												32
	1	2	3	4	5		7	8	9	6	10																	11	33
	1	2	3	4	5		7	8	9	11	6	10																	34
	1	2	3	4	5		7	8	9	11	10										6								35
	1	3	4	5		7	8	11	10						9		2				6								36
	1	2	3	4	5	6	7	8	9	11	10																		37
	1	3	4	5	6	7	8	9	11	10							2												38
	1	3	4	5	6	7	8	9	10								2								11				39
	1	2	3	4	5		7	8	10	9	11										6								40
	1	2		4	6	7	5	9	11	10										8		3							41
	1	2		4	5	6	7	8	9	11	10											3							42
18	22	38	31	39	32	27	40	34	37	21	38	16	14	11	7	5	5	5	4	3	3	2	2	2	2	2	2	1	
			4	3		6	4	17	12	8		2	2	2	2	2	2										1		

1934-35

1	Aug 25	(a)	West Brom A	D 1-1	Barkas	30,000
2	29	(h)	Liverpool	W 3-1	Marshall, Brook, opp.og	30,000
3	Sep 1	(h)	Sheffield W	W 4-1	Herd (2), Marshall, Brook	50,000
4	5	(a)	Liverpool	L 1-2	Tilson	35,000
5	8	(a)	Birmingham	W 3-1	Tilson, Herd, Brook	20,000
6	15	(h)	Stoke C	W 3-1	Tilson (3)	50,000
7	22	(a)	Leicester C	W 3-1	Herd (2), Busby	25,000
8	29	(a)	Middlesbrough	W 2-1	Herd, Fletcher	10,000
9	Oct 6	(h)	Blackburn R	D 3-3	Brook (2), Heale	25,000
10	13	(a)	Arsenal	L 0-3		70,000
11	20	(h)	Derby C	L 0-1		50,000
12	27	(a)	Aston Villa	L 2-4	Herd, Tilson	27,000
13	Nov 3	(h)	Tottenham H	W 3-1	McLuckie, Herd, Heale	35,000
14	10	(a)	Sunderland	L 2-3	Brook (2)	9,000
15	17	(h)	Huddersfield T	D 0-0		35,000
16	24	(a)	Everton	W 2-1	Tilson, Heale	35,000
17	Dec 1	(h)	Grimsby T	W 1-0	Toseland	30,000
18	8	(a)	Preston N E	W 4-2	Tilson (3), Brook	20,000
19	15	(h)	Chelsea	W 2-0	Tilson, Heale	25,000
20	22	(a)	Wolves	L 0-5		25,000
21	25	(a)	Leeds U	W 2-1	Toseland, Heale	24,000
22	26	(h)	Leeds U	W 3-0	Heale (2), Brook	49,478
23	29	(h)	West Brom A	W 3-2	Brook (2), Herd	30,000
24	Jan 5	(a)	Sheffield W	L 0-1		35,000
25	19	(h)	Birmingham	D 0-0		25,000
26	26	(a)	Stoke C	L 0-2		25,000
27	Feb 2	(h)	Leicester C	W 6-3	Brook (2), Bray, Toseland, Herd, Tilson	20,000
28	9	(a)	Middlesbrough	W 6-2	Toseland, Tilson, Herd, Brook, opp.og (2)	25,000
29	23	(h)	Arsenal	D 1-1	Brook	77,582
30	Mar 2	(a)	Derby C	W 2-1	Dellow, Herd	23,000
31	4	(a)	Blackburn R	L 0-1		22,000
32	9	(h)	Aston Villa	W 4-1	Dellow (2), Heale, Brook	25,000
33	16	(a)	Tottenham H	D 0-0		50,000
34	30	(a)	Huddersfield T	L 0-3		18,000
35	Apr 6	(h)	Everton	D 2-2	Heale, Tilson	25,000
36	10	(h)	Sunderland	W 1-0	Heale	18,000
37	13	(a)	Grimsby T	D 1-1	Herd	14,000
38	19	(h)	Portsmouth	L 2-4	Tilson (2)	35,000
39	20	(h)	Preston N E	L 1-2	Herd	18,000
40	22	(a)	Portsmouth	L 2-4	Dellow, Tilson	17,000
41	27	(a)	Chelsea	L 2-4	Heale, Tilson	35,000
42	May 4	(h)	Wolves	W 5-0	Heale (2), Marshall, Toseland, Brook	15,000

Appearances
Goals

League Division One record: P 42 W 20 D 8 L 14 F 82 A 67 Pts 48 Pos 4th

FA Cup

3 Jan 12 (a) Tottenham H L 0-1

Lancashire Senior Cup

1	Sep 11	(a)	Southport	W 4-3
2	29	(h)	Everton	D 2-2
R	Oct 10	(a)	Everton	L 2-5

Manchester Senior Cup

SF Apr 24 (a) Manchester U L 1-3

FA Charity Shield

1 Nov 28 (a) Arsenal L 0-4

Friendlies

1	Sep 18	(a)	Glasgow Rangers	L 0-1
2	19	(a)	Ayr United	W 4-1
3	Oct 3	(h)	Glasgow Rangers	W 4-2

Tour (to Austria and Switzerland)

1	May 7	(a)	Rapide Wein	W 5-3
2	9	(a)	Slava/Sparta	L 1-5
3	16	(a)	FK Austria	L 3-4
4	18	(a)	Zurich	W 3-2
5	22	(a)	FC Basle	W 5-1

Swift	Dale	Barkas	Busby	Cowan	Bray	Toseland	Marshall	Tilson	Herd	Brook	Heale	Dellow	Percival J.	McLuckie	Fletcher	Barnett	Shadwell	Wright	Corbett F.	Dunne	
1	2	3	4	5	6	7	8	9	10	11											1
1	2	3	4	5	6	7	8	9	10	11											2
1	2	3	4	5	6	7	8	9	10	11											3
1	2	3	4	5	6	7	8	9	10	11											4
1	2	3	4	5	6	7	8	9	10	11											5
1	2	3	4	5	6	7	8	9	10	11											6
1	2	3	8	5	6	7		9	10	11								2			7
1	2	3	4	5		7		8		10			6	9			11				8
1		3	4	5	6	7		9	8	11	10			2							9
1	2	3	4	5	6	7	8	9	10	11											10
1		3	4	5	6	7	8	9	10	11				2							11
1	2	3	4	5	6	7		9	8	11	10										12
1	2	3	4	5	6			9	7	11	10	8									13
1	2	3	4	5	6	7		9		11	10	8									14
1	2	3	4	5	6	7	8		11	9		10									15
1	2	3	4	5	6	7		9		11	10	8									16
1	2		4	5	6	7		9	8	11	10			3							17
1	2	3	4	5	6	7		9	8	11	10										18
1	2	3	4	5	6	7		9	8	11	10										19
1	2	3	4	5	6	7	10	8	11	9											20
1	2	3	4	5	6	7	10	8	11	9											21
1	2	3	4	5	6	7		9	10	11	8										22
1	2	3	4	5	6	7		9	10	11	8										23
1	2	3	4	5	6	7		9	10	11	8										24
1	2	3	4	5	6	7		9	10	11	8										25
1	2	3	4	5	6	7	8	9	10	11											26
1	2	3	4	5	6	7	8	9	10	11											27
1	2	3	4	5	6	7	8	9	10	11											28
1	2	3	4	5	6	7	8	9	10	11											29
1	2	3	4	5	6		8	9	10	11		7									30
1	2	3	4	5	6		8		10	11	9	7									31
1		3		5	6		8		11	10	7	4		9				2			32
1	2	3		5	6			10	11	8	7		4	9							33
1	2	3	4	5				10	11	8		7			9	6					34
1	2	3	4	5				9	10		8	7				6	11				35
1	2	3		5	6			9	10	11	8	7	4								36
1	2	3		5	6			9	10	11	8	7	4								37
1	2	3		5	6			9	10	11	8	7	4								38
1	2	3		5	6	7		9	10	11	8		4								39
1	2	3		5	6	7		9	10	11		8	4								40
1	2	3		5	6	7		9	10	11	8		4								41
1	2	3		5	6	7	8		10	11	9		4								42
42	39	41	33	42	39	32	19	34	37	40	27	10	9	5	4	3	2	2	1	1	
		1	1		1	5	3	18	14	17	13	4		1	1						

105

1935-36

1	Aug	31	(h)	West Brom A	W 1-0	Herd	39,826
2	Sep	4	(a)	Liverpool	W 2-0	Tilson, Brook	35,000
3		7	(a)	Sunderland	L 0-2		45,000
4		11	(h)	Liverpool	W 6-0	Toseland (2), Heale (2), Busby, Herd	45,000
5		14	(h)	Birmingham	W 3-1	Bray, Toseland, Tilson	30,000
6		21	(a)	Arsenal	W 3-2	Toseland, Herd, Tilson	65,000
7		28	(h)	Portsmouth	D 0-0		40,000
8	Oct	5	(h)	Stoke C	L 1-2	Heale	35,000
9		12	(a)	Blackburn R	L 1-4	Toseland	23,000
10		19	(a)	Preston N E	L 0-4		18,000
11		26	(h)	Brentford	W 2-1	Marshall, Owen	25,000
12	Nov	2	(a)	Derby C	L 0-3		29,092
13		9	(h)	Everton	W 1-0	Herd	38,000
14		16	(a)	Bolton W	D 3-3	Brook (2), Tilson	40,000
15		23	(h)	Sheffield W	W 3-0	Owen (2), McCullough	30,000
16		30	(a)	Middlesbrough	L 0-2		18,000
17	Dec	7	(h)	Aston Villa	W 5-0	Toseland (2), Tilson (2), Brook	35,000
18		14	(a)	Wolves	L 3-4	Tilson (2), Brook	20,000
19		25	(h)	Chelsea	D 0-0		26,000
20		26	(a)	Chelsea	I 1-2	Herd	30,000
21		28	(a)	West Brom A	L 1-5	McLeod	30,000
22	Jan	1	(h)	Grimsby T	L 0-3		30,000
23		4	(h)	Sunderland	L 0-1		45,000
24		15	(h)	Huddersfield T	L 1-2	Brook	30,000
25		18	(a)	Birmingham	W 1-0	McLeod	20,000
26	Feb	1	(a)	Portsmouth	W 2-1	McLeod (2)	20,000
27		8	(a)	Stoke C	L 0-1		30,000
28		19	(h)	Blackburn R	W 2-0	McLeod (2)	30,000
29		22	(h)	Preston N E	L 1-3	Brook	39,364
30		29	(a)	Everton	D 2-2	Tilson, Toseland	17,000
31	Mar	7	(h)	Middlesbrough	W 6-0	Herd (2), Toseland, Doherty, Brook, Tilson	18,000
32		11	(h)	Arsenal	W 1-0	Percival	38,000
33		14	(a)	Brentford	D 0-0		35,000
34		21	(h)	Bolton W	W 7-0	Brook (3), Doherty (2), Herd, Toseland	35,000
35		28	(a)	Sheffield W	L 0-1		22,000
36	Apr	4	(h)	Derby C	W 1-0	McLeod	25,000
37		10	(h)	Leeds U	L 1-3	Herd	30,000
38		11	(a)	Aston Villa	D 2-2	Marshall, Percival	40,000
39		13	(a)	Leeds U	D 1-1	Brook	15,000
40		18	(h)	Wolves	W 2-1	Herd, Tilson	22,000
41		25	(a)	Huddersfield T	D 1-1	Doherty	8,253
42	May	2	(a)	Grimsby T	L 1-3	Brook	10,000

Appearances
Goals

League Division One record: P 42   W 17   D 8   L 17   F 68   A 60   Pts 42   Pos 9th

FA Cup

3	Jan 11	(h)	Portsmouth	W 3-1
4	25	(h)	Luton T	W 2-1
5	Feb 15	(a)	Grimsby T	L 2-3

Lancashire Senior Cup

1	Sep 23	(a)	Lancaster T	L 0-1

Manchester Senior Cup

SF	Apr 30	(h)	Oldham A	D 1-1
R	May 4	(a)	Oldham A	L 1-5

Friendlies

1	Sep 23	(a)	St Johnstone	W 4-3
2	Nov 13	(h)	Slovan/Sparta	W 4-1
3	Apr 27	(a)	Blackpool	W 4-1

106

Swift	Dale	Barkas	Percival	Donnelly	Bray	Toseland	Herd	Tilson	Marshall	Brook	Busby	McCullough	Doherty	McLeod	Owen	Heale	Corbett	Neilson	Rodger	Cassidy	Rogers	
1	2	3		5	6	7	8	10		11	4					9						1
1	2	3		5	6	7	8	10		11	4					9						2
1	2	3		5	6	7	8	9		11	4			10								3
1	2	3		5	6	7	8	9		11	4			10								4
1	2	3		5	6	7	8	9		11	4			10								5
1	2	3		5	6	7	8	9		11	4			10								6
1	2	3		5	6	7	8	9		11	4			10								7
1	2	3		5	6	7	8	9		11	4			10								8
1	2	3		5	6	7	8	10		11	4		9									9
1	2	3	6	5		7		11	10	11	4		9							8		10
1	2	3		5	6	7	10		8	11	4		9									11
1	2	3		5	6	7	10			11	4	8	9									12
1	2	3		5	6	7	10	9		11	4	8										13
1	2	3		5	6	7	10	9		11	4	8										14
1	2	3		5	6	7	10			11	4	8	9									15
1	2	3			6	7	8	10		11	5	4	9									16
1	2	3		5	6	7	10	9	8	11		4										17
1	2	3		5	6	7	10	9	8	11		4										18
1	2	3		5	6	7	10	9		11	4	8										19
1	2	3		5	6	7	10		8	11		4	9									20
1	2	3	4	5		7	10			11		6	9						8			21
1	2	3	4	5	6	7			8	11		10	9									22
1		3	4	5	6	7			10	11		8	9	2								23
1	2	3	4		6	7	8			11					9			5	10			24
1	2		4		6	7	10		8	11					9			3	5			25
1	2	3	4		6	7			8	11	5				9				10			26
1	2	3	4		6	7	10		8	11					9			5				27
1		3	8		6	7	10		5	11	4				9			2				28
1	2		7		6		8		5	11	4		10		9			3				29
1	2	3	4		6	7	8	9	5	11		10										30
1	2	3	4		6	7	8	9	5	11		10										31
1	2	3	4		6	7	8	9	5	11		10										32
1	2	3	4	5	6	7		9	8	11		10										33
1	2	3	4		6	7	8	9	5	11		10										34
1	2	3	4	5	6	7	10		8	11			9									35
1	2	3	4	5		7	10		8				9						11	6		36
1	2	3	4	5	6	7	8	9		11									10			37
1	2	3	4	5		7	10	9	8	11										6		38
1	2	3	4	5	6	7	10	9	8	11												39
1	2	3	4	5	6	7	8	9		11		10										40
1	2	3	4		6	7	8	9		11		10						5				41
1	2	3	4	5	6	7	8	9		11		10										42
42	41	39	23	30	38	41	33	32	21	40	19	12	9	9	9	8	4	4	4	2	2	
			2			1	10	10		11	2	13	1	1	4	7	3	3				

1936-37

#	Date		Opponent	Result	Scorers	Attendance
1	Aug 29	(a)	Middlesbrough	L 0-2		40,000
2	Sep 2	(h)	Leeds U	W 4-0	Herd, Tilson, Doherty, Brook	30,000
3	5	(h)	West Brom A	W 6-2	Herd (2), Doherty (2), Heale, Brook	30,000
4	9	(a)	Leeds U	D 1-1	Heale	20,000
5	12	(a)	Manchester U	L 2-3	Bray, Heale	69,000
6	16	(h)	Birmingham	D 1-1	Doherty	20,000
7	19	(a)	Portsmouth	L 1-2	McLeod	25,000
8	26	(h)	Chelsea	D 0-0		30,000
9	Oct 3	(a)	Stoke C	D 2-2	Heale, Doherty	36,000
10	10	(h)	Charlton A	D 1-1	Heale	28,000
11	17	(h)	Derby C	W 3-2	Toseland, Heale, Doherty	18,000
12	24	(a)	Wolves	L 1-2	Doherty	20,000
13	31	(h)	Sunderland	L 2-4	McLeod, Doherty	35,000
14	Nov 7	(a)	Huddersfield T	D 1-1	Brook	18,438
15	14	(h)	Everton	W 4-1	Rodger (2), Toseland, Brook	25,000
16	21	(a)	Bolton W	W 2-0	Herd, Brook	30,000
17	Dec 5	(a)	Arsenal	W 3-1	Rodger (2), Doherty	45,000
18	12	(h)	Preston N E	W 4-1	Toseland (2), Doherty, Brook	15,000
19	19	(a)	Sheffield W	L 1-5	Doherty	30,000
20	25	(a)	Grimsby T	L 3-5	Rodger, Doherty, Brook	15,000
21	26	(h)	Middlesbrough	W 2-1	Rodger, Brook	50,000
22	28	(h)	Grimsby T	D 1-1	Tilson	12,000
23	Jan 2	(a)	West Brom A	D 2-2	Herd, Tilson	20,000
24	9	(h)	Manchester U	W 1-0	Herd	62,895
25	23	(h)	Portsmouth	W 3-1	Toseland, Herd, Brook	25,000
26	Feb 3	(a)	Chelsea	D 4-4	Doherty (2), Bray, Tilson	12,000
27	6	(h)	Stoke C	W 2-1	Tilson, Doherty	30,000
28	13	(a)	Charlton A	D 1-1	Herd	45,000
29	24	(a)	Derby C	W 5-0	Tilson (3), Rodger, Brook	15,000
30	27	(h)	Wolves	W 4-1	Tilson (3), Herd	40,000
31	Mar 13	(h)	Huddersfield T	W 3-0	Doherty (2), Brook	25,000
32	20	(a)	Everton	D 1-1	Percival	20,000
33	26	(a)	Liverpool	W 5-0	Brook (3), Herd, Doherty	45,000
34	27	(h)	Bolton W	D 2-2	Herd, Doherty	40,000
35	29	(h)	Liverpool	W 5-1	Herd (2), Neilson, Tilson, Brook	40,000
36	Apr 3	(a)	Brentford	W 6-2	Doherty (2), Toseland, Herd, Brook, Tilson	37,000
37	7	(h)	Brentford	W 2-1	Doherty, Brook	25,000
38	10	(h)	Arsenal	W 2-0	Toseland, Doherty	76,000
39	14	(a)	Sunderland	W 3-1	Doherty (2), Brook	15,000
40	17	(a)	Preston N E	W 5-2	Doherty (3), Herd, Donnelly	16,000
41	24	(h)	Sheffield W	W 4-1	Brook (2), Tilson, Doherty	55,000
42	May 1	(a)	Birmingham	D 2-2	Tilson, Doherty	25,000

Appearances
Goals

League Division One record: P 42 W 22 D 13 L 7 F 107 A 61 Pts 57 Pos 1st

FA Cup

3	Jan 16	(a)	Wrexham	W 3-1
4	30	(h)	Accrington S	W 2-0
5	Feb 20	(a)	Bolton W	W 5-0
6	Mar 6	(a)	Millwall	L 0-2

Lancashire Senior Cup

| 1 | Sep 16 | (h) | Southport | W 3-0 |
| 2 | Nov 16 | (a) | Blackpool | L 2-3 |

Manchester Senior Cup

| SF | Apr 26 | (h) | Bury | L 1-2 |

Friendly

| 1 | Apr 28 | (a) | Blackpool | L 0-1 |

Tour (to Germany)

1	May 6	(a)	Duisberg XI	D 0-0
2	9	(a)	Wuppertal	D 1-1
3	12	(a)	Schiveinfurt	W 3-2
4	19	(a)	German XI	L 2-3
5	22	(a)	German XI	L 2-3

Swift	Dale	Barkas	Percival	Marshall	Bray	Toseland	Herd	Tilson	Doherty	Brook	Clark	Heale	Rodger	Donnelly	Regan	McLeod	McCullough	Neilson	Rogers	Cassidy	Freeman	No.
1	2	3	4		6	7	8	9	10	11							5					1
1	3		4	5	6	7	8	9	10	11	2											2
1	3		4	5	6	7	8		9	11	2	10										3
1	2		4		6	7	8		9	11	2	10	5									4
1	2	3	4		6	7	8		10	11		9	5									5
1	3		4	5	6	7			10	11	2	9				8						6
1	3	8	5		6	7			10	11	2				9	4						7
1	3		4	5	6	7			9	11	2	10							8			8
1	3		4	5	6	7			10		2	8		11								9
1	2	3	4	5	6	7			10	9		8		11								10
1	2	3	4	5	6	7			10	9		8		11								11
1	2	3	4	5	6	7			10	9		8		11								12
1	2	3	4	5	6	7			10	11		8			9							13
1	2	3	4	5	6	7	8		10	11					9							14
1	2	3	4	5	6	7	8		10	11			9									15
1	2	3	4	5	6	7	8		10	11			9									16
1	2	3	4	5	6	7	8		10	11			9									17
1	2	3	4	5	6	7	8		10	11			9									18
1	2	3	4	5	6	7	8		10	11			9									19
1	2	3	4	5	6	7	8		10	11			9									20
1	2		4	5	6	7	8		10	11			9	3								21
1			4	5	6	7	8	9	10	11	2			3								22
1	2		4	5	6	7	8	9	10	11				3								23
1	2	3	4	5	6	7	8	9	10	11												24
1	2	3	4	5	6	7	8	9		11									10			25
1	2	3	4	5	6	7	8	9	10	11												26
1	2	3	4	5	6	7	8	9	10	11												27
1	2	3	4	5	6	7	8	9	10	11												28
1	2	3	4	5	6	7		9	8	11			10									29
1		3	4	5	6	7	8	9	10	11	2											30
1	2	3	4	5	6	7	8	9	10	11												31
1	2	3	4	5	6	7	8	9	10	11												32
1	2	3	4	5	6	7	8	9	10	11												33
1	2	3	4	5	6	7	8	9	10	11												34
1	2	3	4		6	7	8	9	10	11								5				35
1	2	3	4	5	6	7	8	9	10	11												36
1	2	3	4	5	6	7	8	9	10	11												37
1	2	3	4	5	6	7	8	9	10	11												38
1			4	5		7		9	8	11	2		10	3					6			39
1			4	5		7	8	9	10	11	2			3					6			40
1		3	4	5	6	7	8	9	10	11	2											41
1		3	4	5	6	7	8	9	10	11	2											42
42	36	30	42	38	40	42	32	23	41	42	13	10	9	7	4	3	2	2	2	1	1	
		1		2	7	15	15	30	20		6	7	1		2		1					

1937-38

1	Aug 28	(a)	Wolves	L 1-3	Herd		49,000
2	Sep 1	(h)	Everton	W 2-0	Herd, Doherty		30,000
3	4	(h)	Leicester C	W 3-0	Bray, Herd, Brook		40,000
4	8	(a)	Everton	L 1-4	Brook		28,000
5	11	(a)	Sunderland	L 1-3	Doherty		30,000
6	15	(h)	Huddersfield T	W 3-2	Herd (2), Percival		18,000
7	18	(h)	Derby C	W 6-1	Doherty (2), Brook (2), Clayton, Percival		28,000
8	25	(a)	Portsmouth	D 2-2	Doherty, Barr		20,000
9	Oct 2	(a)	Arsenal	L 1-2	Clayton		70,000
10	9	(h)	Blackpool	W 2-1	Herd, Brook		40,000
11	16	(h)	Stoke C	D 0-0			40,000
12	23	(a)	Middlesbrough	L 0-4			18,000
13	30	(h)	Birmingham	W 2-0	Doherty (2)		20,000
14	Nov 6	(a)	Preston N E	D 2-2	Doherty, Brook		32,000
15	13	(h)	Liverpool	L 1-3	Toseland		25,000
16	20	(a)	Chelsea	D 2-2	Herd, Brook		40,031
17	27	(h)	Grimsby T	W 3-1	Percival (2), Herd		30,000
18	Dec 18	(a)	Leeds U	L 1-2	Doherty		22,000
19	25	(h)	Brentford	L 0-2			35,000
20	27	(a)	Brentford	L 1-2	Herd		40,000
21	Jan 1	(h)	Wolves	L 2-4	Herd, Doherty		40,000
22	15	(a)	Leicester C	W 4-1	Doherty (3), Heale		16,000
23	29	(a)	Derby C	W 7-1	Heale (3), Doherty (2), Brook, Toseland		12,000
24	Feb 2	(h)	Sunderland	D 0-0			19,000
25	5	(h)	Portsmouth	W 2-1	Rogers, Brook		30,000
26	8	(h)	Arsenal	L 1-2	Heale		30,000
27	19	(a)	Blackpool	L 1-2	Tilson		25,000
28	26	(a)	Stoke C	L 2-3	Toseland, Doherty		30,000
29	Mar 9	(h)	Middlesbrough	L 1-6	Milsom		15,000
30	12	(a)	Birmingham	D 2-2	Doherty, Brook		25,000
31	16	(a)	West Brom A	D 1-1	Dunkley		15,000
32	19	(h)	Preston N E	L 1-2	Doherty		45,000
33	26	(a)	Liverpool	L 0-2			30,000
34	Apr 2	(h)	Chelsea	W 1-0	Pritchard		25,000
35	6	(h)	Charlton A	W 5-3	Milsom (3), Bray, Pritchard		18,000
36	9	(a)	Grimsby T	L 1-3	Doherty		12,000
37	15	(h)	Bolton W	L 1-2	Milsom		50,000
38	16	(h)	West Brom A	W 7-1	Brook (4), Herd (2), Doherty		35,000
39	18	(a)	Bolton W	L 1-2	Brook		26,788
40	23	(a)	Charlton A	D 0-0			31,000
41	30	(h)	Leeds U	W 6-2	Doherty (3), Percival, Heale, Brook		25,000
42	May 7	(a)	Huddersfield T	L 0-1			35,100
						Appearances	
						Goals	

League Division One record: P 42   W 14   D 8   L 20   F 80   A 77   Pts 36   Pos 21st

FA Cup

3	Jan 8	(a)	Millwall	D 2-2	
R	12	(h)	Millwall	W 3-1	
4	22	(h)	Bury	W 3-1	
5	Feb 12	(a)	Luton T	W 3-1	
6	Mar 5	(a)	Aston Villa	L 2-3	

Lancashire Senior Cup

1	Apr 25	(h)	Everton	L 0-1	

Manchester Senior Cup

SF	Mar 23	(h)	Bolton W	D 1-1	
R	May 2	(a)	Bolton W	L 0-1	

FA Charity Shield

1	Nov 4	(h)	Sunderland	W 2-0	

Friendlies

None played.

Tour (to Denmark and Sweden)

1	May 15	(a)	Esbjorg		W	2-0
2	18	(a)	Aarhus		W	11-1
3	24	(a)	Gothenburg Combined XI		D	2-2
4	27	(a)	Copenhagen XI		W	4-1
5	30	(a)	Copenhagen XI		W	4-1
6	Jun 1	(a)	Copenhagen XI		W	8-0

110

Football appearances and goals grid. Players are columns; match numbers (1–42) are in the final column. Blank cells indicate the player did not appear in that match.

Swift	Dale	Barkas	Percival	Marshall	Bray	Toseland	Herd	Doherty	Brook	Clark	Milsom	Tilson	McDowall	Pritchard	Heale	Rogers	Neilson	Rodger	Wardle	Emptage	Clayton	Dunkley	McCullough	Gregg	Allmark	Barr	No.
1	2	3	4	5	6	7	8	10	11			9															1
1	2	3	4	5	6	7	8	10	11			9															2
1	2	3	4	5	6	7	8	10	11			9															3
1	2	3	4	5	6	7	8	10	11															9			4
1		3	4	5	6	7	8	10	11	2								9									5
1		3	4	5	6	7	8	10	11	2								9									6
1		3	4	5	6	7	8	10	11	2											9						7
1	3		4	5	6	7		8	11	2	9														10		8
1	2	3	4	5	6	7		10	11												9	8					9
1	2	3	4	5	6	7	8	10	11												9						10
1	2	3	4	5	6	7	8	10	11			9															11
1			4	5	6	7	8			2	9					10	11					3					12
1		3	4	5	6	7	8	10	11	2	9																13
1		3	4	5	6	7	8	10	11	2	9																14
1		3	4	5	6	7	8	10	11	2								9									15
1	2	3	4	5	6	7	8	10	11									9									16
1	2	3	4	5		7	8	10							6		9	11									17
1	2	3	4	5	6	7	8	10									9	11									18
1	2		4	5	6	7	8	10									9	11				3					19
1	2			5	6	7	8	10		2							9	11		4							20
1		3		5	6	7	8	10		2							9	11		4							21
1	3		4			7		10	11	2				9	6	5			8								22
1	2	3	4	5		7		10	11					9	6				8								23
1	2	3	4	5		7		10	11	2				9	6				8								24
1		3	4	5		7		10	11	2				9	6				8								25
1	2	3	4	5		7	8	10	11					9	6												26
1	2	3	4	5		7	8	10	11			9			6												27
1	2	3	4	5	6	7	8	10	11		9																28
1	2	3	4		6	7	8	10	11		9						5										29
1	3		4	5	6		8	10	11	2	9		7														30
1	3		4		6		8	10	11	2	9		5										7				31
1	3		4		6		8	10	11	2	9		5										7				32
1	3		4				8	10	11	2	9		6				5						7				33
1	3		4		6		8	10	11	2	9		5	7													34
1	3		4		6			10	11	2	9		5	7	8												35
1	3		4		6		8	10	11	2	9		5	7													36
1	2	3	4	5			8	10	11			9	6	7													37
1	2	3	4	5			8	10	11			9	6	7													38
1	2	3	4	5		7	8	10	11			9			6												39
1		3	4				8	10	11	2			6	7	9		5										40
1		3	4				8	10	11	2			6	7	9		5										41
1		3	4				8	10	11	2		9	6	7			5										42
42	30	30	40	31	28	30	35	41	36	22	13	13	12	9	8	7	6	6	6	4	3	3	3	2	1	1	
		5		2	3	12	23	16		5	1			2	6	1					2	1			1		

111

1938-39

1	Aug 27	(h)	Swansea T	W 5-0	Herd (2), Doherty (2), Howe		30,889
2	29	(a)	Chesterfield	W 3-0	Howe (2), Brook		15,000
3	Sep 3	(a)	Bradford	L 2-4	Herd, Brook		16,000
4	7	(h)	West Ham U	L 2-4	Howe, Herd		18,671
5	10	(h)	Luton T	L 1-2	Howe		29,627
6	17	(h)	Millwall	L 1-6	Bray		27,437
7	24	(a)	Blackburn R	D 3-3	Herd, Heale, McDowall		20,000
8	Oct 1	(h)	Fulham	L 3-5	McDowall (2), Barr		27,975
9	8	(a)	Sheffield W	L 1-3	Brook		25,000
10	15	(a)	Plymouth A	D 0-0			24,710
11	22	(h)	Sheffield U	W 3-2	Toseland, Milsom, Brook		29,848
12	29	(a)	West Brom A	L 1-3	Milsom		25,000
13	Nov 5	(h)	Tottenham H	W 2-0	Milsom, Doherty		46,302
14	12	(a)	Southampton	W 2-1	Milsom, Brook		20,000
15	19	(h)	Coventry C	W 3-0	Doherty (2), Herd		38,712
16	26	(a)	Nottingham F	W 4-3	Brook (3), Herd		15,000
17	Dec 3	(h)	Newcastle U	W 4-1	Herd (2), Milsom (2)		41,418
18	10	(h)	Burnley	D 1-1	Milsom		20,000
19	17	(h)	Norwich C	W 4-1	Doherty (2), Herd (2)		17,907
20	24	(a)	Swansea T	L 0-2			15,000
21	26	(a)	Tranmere R	W 9-3	Milsom (4), Toseland (2), Doherty (2), Herd		14,000
22	27	(h)	Tranmere R	W 5-2	Milsom (3), Doherty, Pritchard		43,894
23	31	(h)	Bradford	W 5-1	Herd (3), Milsom, Pritchard		32,033
24	Jan 14	(a)	Luton T	L 0-3			16,000
25	28	(h)	Blackburn R	W 3-2	Heale (2), Doherty		45,378
26	Feb 4	(a)	Fulham	L 1-2	opp.og		25,000
27	18	(h)	Plymouth A	L 1-3	Brook		28,784
28	25	(a)	Sheffield U	L 0-1			40,000
29	Mar 4	(h)	West Brom A	D 3-3	Herd, Doherty, Brook		27,099
30	11	(a)	Tottenham H	W 3-2	Sproston (2), Freeman		25,000
31	13	(a)	Millwall	L 1-3	Doherty		14,000
32	18	(h)	Southampton	W 2-1	McLeod, McDowall		17,976
33	25	(a)	Coventry C	W 1-0	Heale		20,088
34	Apr 1	(h)	Nottingham F	W 3-0	Herd (2), opp.og		23,047
35	7	(a)	Bury	W 5-1	Heale (2), Herd, Doherty, Brook		24,520
36	8	(a)	Newcastle U	W 2-0	Heale, Doherty		22,000
37	10	(h)	Bury	D 0-0			36,816
38	15	(h)	Burnley	W 2-0	Doherty (2),		17,519
39	22	(a)	Norwich C	D 0-0			12,000
40	26	(h)	Sheffield W	D 1-1	Pritchard		24,244
41	29	(h)	Chesterfield	W 3-1	Herd, Heale, McLeod		12,258
42	May 6	(a)	West Ham U	L 1-2	Heale		30,000

Appearances
Goals

League Division Two record: P 42 W21 D 7 L 14 F 96 A 72 Pts 49 Pos 5th

FA Cup

3	Jan 12	(a)	Norwich C	W 5-0
4	21	(a)	Sheffield U	L 0-2

Lancashire Senior Cup

1	Sep 22	(h)	Barrow	W 4-1
2	Oct 26	(h)	New Brighton	W 3-0
SF	Feb 11	(a)	Bolton W	L 0-4

Manchester Senior Cup

SF	Apr 19	(h)	Manchester U	L 0-1

Friendly

1	Aug 20	(h)	Manchester U	W 2-1

112

Swift	Clark	Sproston	Westwood	Percival	Cardwell	McDowall	Bray	Toseland	Herd	Milsom	Heale	Doherty	Brook	Dunkley	Pritchard	Emptage	Gregg	Eastwood	Howe	McLeod	Neilson	Barr	Blackshaw	Freeman	Robinson	
1	2				4	6		8				10	11	7			3	9		5						1
1	2				4	6		8				10	11	7			3	9		5						2
1	2				4	6		8				10	11	7			3	9		5						3
1	2				4	6	7	10	8				11				3	9		5						4
1	2		4	5	6		7	10	8				11				3	9								5
	2			5	4	6		8	10				11				3	9							1	6
1			4	5	10	6		8	9				11	7			3	2								7
1			4	5	10	6							11	7	8		3	2			9					8
1	2		4	5	6					9			11	7	8		3				10					9
1	2		4	5	6		7	8	10				11				3				9					10
1	2		4	5	6		7		9			10	11		8		3									11
1	2		4	5	6		7		9			10	11		8		3									12
1	2	3	4	5	6		7	8	9			10	11													13
1	2	3	4	5	6		7	8	9			10	11													14
1	2	3	4	5	6		7	8	9			10	11													15
1	2	3	4	5	6		7	8	9			10	11													16
1	2	3	4	5	6		7	8	9			10	11													17
1	2	3	4	5	6		7	8	9			10	11													18
1	2	3	4	5	6		7	8	9			10	11													19
1	2	3	4	5	6		7	8	9			10	11													20
1	2	3	4	5	6		7	8	9			10			11											21
1	2	3	4	5	6		7	8	9			10			11											22
1	2	3	4	5	6		7	8	9			10			11											23
1	2	3	4	5	6		7	8	9			10	11													24
1	2	3	4	5	6			8			9	10	11		7											25
1	2	3	4	5	6			8			9	10	11		7											26
1	2	3	4	5	6		7		9			10	11			8										27
1	2	3	5	4	6						9	10	11	7		8										28
1	2	3	5	4	6			8				10	11	7										9		29
1	2	3	5	4	6			8				10	11	7										9		30
1	2	3	4	5	6						9	10	11	7		8										31
1	2	3	5	4	6			8	10				11	7					9							32
1	2	3	5	4	6			8	9			10	11	7												33
1	2	3	5	4	6			8	9			10	11	7												34
1	2	3	5	4	6			8	9			10	11	7												35
1	2	3	5	4	6			8	9			10	11	7												36
1	2	3	5	4	6			8	9			10	11	7												37
1	2	3	5	4	6			8				10		7	11									9		38
1	2	3	5	4	6			8	9					7	11						10					39
1	2	3	4	5	6			8	9						11	10						7				40
1	2	3	4	5	6			8	9						11					10		7				41
1	2	3	4	5	6				9						11	8				10		7				42
41	20	20	30	26	37	38	23	18	35	19	17	28	34	16	13	9	7	7	6	4	4	3	3	3	1	
	2				4	1		3	20	15		9	17	11		3				5	2		1		1	

1946-47

1	Aug 31	(a)	Leicester C	W 3-0	McDowall, Walsh, Jackson	20,000
2	Sep 4	(h)	Bury	W 3-1	Dunkley, Black, Smith	28,000
3	7	(h)	Chesterfield	D 0-0		47,319
4	14	(a)	Millwall	W 3-1	Constantine (3)	30,000
5	18	(a)	Bury	D 2-2	Herd (2)	11,000
6	21	(h)	Bradford	W 7-2	Black (3), Smith (2), Constantine, Sproston	38,330
7	28	(a)	Tottenham H	D 0-0		55,253
8	Oct 5	(a)	West Ham U	L 0-1		32,000
9	12	(h)	Sheffield W	W 2-1	Herd, Constantine	36,413
10	19	(h)	Swansea T	D 1-1	Sproston	34,436
11	26	(a)	Newcastle U	L 2-3	Black, Westwood	65,798
12	Nov 2	(h)	West Brom A	W 5-0	Black (3), Dunkley, Herd	38,821
13	9	(a)	Birmingham C	L 1-3	Smith	30,000
14	16	(h)	Coventry C	W 1-0	Dunkley	25,569
15	23	(a)	Nottingham F	W 1-0	Smith	22,000
16	30	(h)	Southampton	D 1-1	Constantine	24,867
17	Dec 7	(a)	Newport C	W 3-0	Dunkley, Black, Constantine	15,000
18	14	(h)	Barnsley	W 5-1	Constantine (2), Smith (2), opp.og	22,210
19	21	(a)	Burnley	D 0-0		35,000
20	25	(h)	Plymouth A	W 4-3	Smith (2), Herd, Constantine	24,532
21	26	(a)	Plymouth A	W 3-2	Constantine, Smith, opp.og	27,000
22	28	(h)	Leicester C	W 1-0	Constantine	43,910
23	Jan 1	(h)	Fulham	W 4-0	Herd (2), Black (2)	47,658
24	4	(a)	Chesterfield	W 1-0	Jackson	20,000
25	18	(h)	Millwall	W 1-0	Capel	36,635
26	Feb 1	(h)	Tottenham H	W 1-0	Westwood	39,000
27	22	(a)	Swansea T	W 2-1	Smith, Herd	26,584
28	Mar 1	(a)	Fulham	D 2-2	Smith, Herd	32,000
29	15	(h)	Birmingham C	W 1-0	Smith	59,535
30	22	(a)	Coventry C	D 1-1	Herd	26,629
31	29	(h)	Nottingham F	W 2-1	Smith, Wharton	26,354
32	Apr 4	(h)	Luton T	W 2-0	Woodroffe, Smith	57,592
33	5	(a)	Southampton	W 1-0	Smith	25,000
34	7	(a)	Luton T	D 0-0		24,000
35	19	(a)	Barnsley	W 2-0	McDowall, Black	26,274
36	May 3	(h)	Newcastle U	L 0-2		46,972
37	10	(h)	Burnley	W 1-0	Herd	67,672
38	14	(a)	Bradford	D 1-1	Smith	15,162
39	24	(h)	West Ham U	W 2-0	McDowall, Smith	31,980
40	26	(a)	Sheffield W	L 0-1		30,000
41	31	(a)	West Brom A	L 1-3	Black	25,000
42	Jun 14	(h)	Newport C	W 5-1	Smith (5)	24,300

Appearances
Goals

League Division Two record: P 42   W 26   D 10   L 6   F 78   A 35   Pts 62   Pos 1st

FA Cup

3	Jan 11	(h)	Gateshead	W 3-0
4	25	(a)	Bolton W	D 3-3
R	29	(h)	Bolton W	W 1-0
5	Feb 8	(a)	Birmingham C	L 0-5

Lancashire Senior Cup

1	Oct 16	(h)	Bolton W	L 0-1*
1	30	(a)	Bolton W	W 3-2**
R	Nov 6	(h)	Bolton W	D 0-0
R	27	(h)	Bolton W	L 1-2

*1st leg   **2nd leg

Manchester Senior Cup

None played.

Friendly

| 1 | Apr 26 | (h) | Glasgow Rangers W 2-1 |

Tour (to Ireland)

| 1 | Jun 6 | (a) | Shelbourne | L 2-4 |
| 2 | 9 | (a) | Linfield | D 1-1 |

114

Football appearances and goals grid — shirt numbers worn by each player per match (matches 1–42). Appearances and goals totals at foot.

Swift	Sproston	Barkas	Percival	Fagan	McDowall	Emptage	Dunkley	Herd	Black	Smith	Westwood	Constantine	Walsh	Woodroffe	Eastwood	Jackson	Williams	Hope	Thurlow	Capel	Wharton	Rudd	Clarke	Hodgson	Murray	Oakes.	Robinson J.	Robinson P.	Cardwell	Rigby	McCormack	No.
1	2	3	**4**		5	7	8		10	11	6	9																				1
1	2	3	4		5	7	8		10	11	6	9																				2
1	2	3	4		5	7			10	8	6	9					11															3
1	2	3	4		5				8	10	9	6	7				11															4
	2	3	4		6				8	10	9		7				11										1	5				5
1	2	3	4						8	10	9	6	7				11													5		6
	2	3	4		5				8	10	9	6	7				11	1														7
1	2	3	4		5				8	10	9	6	7				11															8
1	2	3	4		5	7	8		10	11	9	6																				9
1	2	3	4			7	8		10	11	9	6	5																			10
1	2	3	4			7	8	9	10	11	6		5																			11
1	2		4		6	7	8	9	10	11	5										11											12
1	2		4		6	7	8	9	10	3	5										11											13
1	2		4		6	8	7		10	3	9	5									11											14
1	2		4		6	7	8		10	3	9	5										11										15
1	2		4		6	7	8		10	3	9	5										11										16
1	2	3	6	4		7	8		10	11	9	5																				17
1	2	3	6	4		7	8		10	11	9	5																				18
1	2	3	6	4		7	8		10	11	9	5																				19
1	2	3	5	4			8		10	11	9	7																	6			20
1	2	3	5	4		7	8		10	11	9	6																				21
1	2	3	5	4		7	8		10	11	9	6																				22
1	2	3	4	5	6	7	8	9	10	11																						23
1		3	4	5	6	7	8			11								9	2	10												24
1		3	4	5	6	7		9	8	11									2	10												25
1	2	3	4	5	6	7		9	8	11										10												26
1	2	3	4	5	6	7	8	9	10											11												27
1	2	3	4	5	6	7	8	9	10											11												28
1	2		4	5	6	7	8	9	10	11	3																					29
1	2	3	4	5	6	7	8	9	10										11													30
1	2	3	4	5	6	7	8	9	10										11													31
1	2	3	4	5	6		8		10		9		7						11													32
1	2	3	4	5	6		8		10	11	9												7									33
1	2	3	4	5	6			9	10	11			7												8							34
1	2		4	5	6	7	8	9	10	11	3																					35
	2		4		6	7	8	9	10	11	3							1						5								36
	2	3	4	5	6	7	8	9	10	11								1														37
		3	4	5	6	7	8	9	10	11								1	2													38
	2	3	4	5	6	7	8	9	10	11								1														39
	2	3	4	5	6	7	8	9	10	11								1														40
1			4	5	6		8	9	10	11									2							7			11			41
1	2	3	4	5		7	8	9	10			6																			11	42
35	38	33	16	20	35	29	32	28	34	38	28	18	13	9	9	7	7	7	6	5	3	2	1	1	1	1	1	1	2	1	1	
	2				3		4	11	13	23	2	12	1	1		2				1	1											

1947-48

1	Aug	23	(a)	Wolves	W 4-3	Black, McMorran, Smith, Clarke	67,800
2		27	(a)	Everton	L 0-1		53,822
3		30	(a)	Aston Villa	D 1-1	Clarke	50,000
4	Sep	3	(h)	Everton	L 0-1		44,000
5		6	(h)	Sunderland	W 3-0	Black, McMorran, Clarke	53,263
6		10	(a)	Derby C	D 0-0		31,000
7		13	(a)	Grimsby T	L 0-1		20,000
8		17	(h)	Derby C	W 3-2	Smith, McMorran, Capel	35,000
9		20	(h)	Manchester U	D 0-0		78,000
10		27	(h)	Blackburn R	L 1-3	Smith	44,900
11	Oct	4	(a)	Blackpool	D 1-1	Wharton	30,000
12		11	(a)	Preston N E	L 1-2	Black	32,000
13		18	(h)	Stoke C	W 3-0	Smith (2), Herd	42,408
14		25	(a)	Burnley	D 1-1	Fagan	41,626
15	Nov	1	(h)	Portsmouth	W 1-0	Smith	43,000
16		8	(a)	Middlesbrough	L 1-2	Black	40,000
17		15	(h)	Charlton	W 4-0	Black (3), McMorran	40,000
18		22	(a)	Bolton W	L 1-2	Linacre	30,000
19		29	(h)	Liverpool	W 2-0	McMorran, Smith	37,464
20	Dec	6	(a)	Arsenal	D 1-1	Black	43,000
21		13	(h)	Sheffield U	W 4-3	Smith (2), McMorran, Black	27,058
22		20	(a)	Wolves	L 0-1		33,000
23		26	(h)	Huddersfield T	D 1-1	Linacre	56,460
24		27	(a)	Huddersfield T	D 1-1	Black	32,634
25	Jan	3	(h)	Aston Villa	1 0-0		50,080
26		17	(a)	Sunderland	W 1-0	Black	35,659
27		31	(h)	Grimsby T	W 3-1	McMorran (2), Smith	34,362
28	Feb	14	(a)	Blackburn R	L 0-1		31,000
29		21	(h)	Blackpool	W 1-0	Smith	28,838
30	Mar	6	(a)	Stoke C	L 0-3		28,000
31		13	(h)	Burnley	W 4-1	Smith (2), Clarke (2)	29,605
32		20	(a)	Portsmouth	L 0-1		29,000
33		26	(a)	Chelsea	D 2-2	Linacre. Black	64,396
34		27	(h)	Middlesbrough	W 2-0	McMorran, Black	39,688
35		29	(h)	Chelsea	W 1-0	Black	29,034
36	Apr	3	(a)	Charlton A	W 1-0	McMorran	37,000
37		7	(a)	Manchester U	D 1-1	Linacre	71,960
38		10	(h)	Bolton W	L 0-2		33,800
39		17	(a)	Liverpool	D 1-1	Black	39,348
40		21	(h)	Preston N E	L 0-3		18,393
41		24	(h)	Arsenal	D 0-0		20,782
42	May	1	(a)	Sheffield U	L 1-2	Black	24,000

Appearances
Goals

League Division One record: P 42   W 15   D 12   L 15   F 52   A 47   Pts 42   Pos 10th

FA Cup

3	Jan 10	(h)	Barnsley	W 2-1
4	24	(h)	Chelsea	W 2-0
5	Feb 7	(h)	Preston N E	L 0-1

Lancashire Senior Cup

| 1 | Oct 22 | (a) | Liverpool | L 0-2 |

Manchester Senior Cup

| 1 | Apr 20 | (a) | Oldham A | L 1-3 |

Friendlies

1	Nov 12	(a)	Western Command	W 8-2
2	Apr 14	(a)	Chester	W 1-0

116

Swift	Sproston	Westwood	Fagan	Walsh	McDowall	Emptage	Linacre	Wharton	Black	McMorran	Smith	Clarke	Thurlow	Murray	Williams	Munro	Capel	Herd	Hart	Oxford	Jackson	No.
1	2	3	4		5	6		7	8	9	10	11										1
1	2	3	4		5	6		7	8	9	10	11										2
1	2	3	4		5	6		7	8	9	10	11										3
1	2	3	4		5	6		7	8	9	10	11										4
1	2	3	4		5	6		7	8	9	10	11										5
1	2	3	4		5	6		7	8	9	10	11										6
1	2	3	4		5	6		7	8	9	10	11										7
1	2	3	5	4		6	7		9	8		11				10						8
	2	3	5	4		6	7		9	8		11	1			10						9
1	2	3	5	4		6	7		9	8		11				10						10
1	2	3	4		5	6		11	8		10	7				9						11
1		3	5	4		6		7	8	9	10	7		2								12
	2	3	5	4		6		7		9	10	11	1		8							13
1	2	3	5	4		6	7	11		9	10				8							14
1	2	3	5	4		6	7			9	10	11			8							15
1		3	5	4		6	7		8		10	11		2				9					16
1		3	5	4		6	7	11	8	9	10			2								17
1		3	5	4		6	7	11	8	9	10			2								18
		3	4		5	6	7		8	9	10	11	1	2								19
1	2	3	4		5	6	7		8	9	10	11										20
1	2	3	4		5	6	7		8	9	10	11										21
1	2	3	4		5	6	7		8	9	10	11										22
1	2	3	5	4		6	7		8	9	10	11										23
1	2	3	5	4		6	7		8	9	10	11										24
1	2	3	5	4		6	7	11	8	9	10											25
1	2	3	5	4		6	7	11	8	9	10											26
	2	3	5	4		6	7	11	8	9	10		1									27
1	2	3	4	6	5	7				9	10	11				8						28
1	2	3	9	4	5	6	7				10	11	8									29
1	2	3	5	4		6	7		8		10	11				9						30
1	2	3	4	6	5	8	7			9	10	11										31
1	2	3	4	6	5	8	7			9	10	11										32
1	2	3	5	6		4	7			9	10	11				8						33
1	2	3	5	6		4	7		8	9	10	11										34
1	2	3	5	6		4	7		8	9	10	11										35
1	2	3	5	6		8		10		9		11	4			7						36
	2	3	5	6		10		9	8			11	1	4		7						37
	2	3	5	6		10			9			11	1	4		7		8				38
	2	3	5	6			7		8	9	10	11	1	4								39
	2	3	5	6			7		8	9	10	11	1	4								40
	2	3	5	4		6	7		8	9	10	11							1			41
1	2	3	5	4		6	9	7	8		10	11										42
33	37	42	42	30	16	39	27	20	37	29	39	36	8	6	5	5	4	4	1	1	1	
			1					4	1	16	10	13	5				1	1				

117

1948-49

1	Aug	21	(a)	Burnley	L 0-1		28,000
2		25	(h)	Preston N E	W 3-2	Sproston, McDowall, McMorran	45,000
3		28	(h)	Stoke C	D 0-0		42,450
4	Sep	1	(a)	Preston N E	W 3-1	Black, Godwin, Linacre	35,000
5		4	(a)	Charlton A	L 2-3	Godwin (2)	45,000
6		8	(h)	Birmingham C	W 1-0	Black	26,841
7		11	(h)	Manchester U	D 0-0		64,502
8		15	(a)	Birmingham C	L 1-4	Smith	40,000
9		18	(h)	Portsmouth	D 1-1	McMorran	48,376
10		25	(a)	Newcastle U	D 0-0		58,000
11	Oct	2	(h)	Middlesbrough	W 1-0	Oakes	42,000
12		9	(a)	Sheffield U	W 2-0	Oakes, Black	26,000
13		16	(h)	Aston Villa	W 4-1	Smith (3), Oakes	38,024
14		23	(a)	Sunderland	L 0-3		46,879
15		30	(h)	Wolves	D 3-3	Oakes, Black, Linacre	44,130
16	Nov	6	(a)	Bolton W	L 1-5	Smith	37,931
17		13	(h)	Liverpool	L 2-4	Black, Clarke	21,659
18		20	(a)	Blackpool	D 1-1	Smith	28,000
19		27	(h)	Derby C	W 2-1	Black, Clarke	42,225
20	Dec	4	(a)	Arsenal	D 1-1	Oakes	45,000
21		11	(h)	Huddersfield T	W 3-1	Clarke (2), Emptage	37,717
22		18	(h)	Burnley	D 2-2	Smith, opp.og	30,000
23		25	(a)	Everton	D 0-0		45,000
24		27	(h)	Everton	D 0-0		30,000
25	Jan	1	(a)	Stoke C	W 3-2	Smith (2), Clarke	25,000
26		15	(h)	Charlton A	L 0-1		20,000
27		22	(a)	Manchester U	D 0-0		66,485
28	Feb	5	(a)	Portsmouth	L 1-3	Smith	34,167
29		19	(h)	Newcastle U	W 1-0	Black	48,624
30		26	(a)	Middlesbrough	W 1-0	Black	35,000
31	Mar	5	(h)	Sheffield U	W 1-0	Black	16,502
32		12	(a)	Aston Villa	L 0-1		35,000
33		19	(h)	Blackpool	D 1-1	Hart	35,857
34		26	(a)	Derby C	L 0-2		29,125
35	Apr	2	(h)	Bolton W	W 1-0	Black	28,000
36		9	(a)	Liverpool	W 1-0	Smith	31,389
37		15	(h)	Chelsea	W 1-0	Smith	30,000
38		16	(h)	Sunderland	D 1-1	Clarke	31,345
39		18	(a)	Chelsea	D 1-1	Munro	25,864
40		23	(a)	Wolves	D 1-1	Black	45,000
41		27	(h)	Arsenal	L 0-3		27,955
42	May	7	(a)	Huddersfield T	L 0-1		27,507

Appearances
Goals

League Division One record: P 42   W 15   D 15   L 12   F 47   A 51   Pts 45   Pos 7th

FA Cup

3	Jan	8	(a)	Everton	L 0-1

Lancashire Senior Cup

1	Oct	19	(a)	Oldham A	W 2-1
2	Nov	10	(h)	Burnley	D 1-1
R		16	(a)	Burnley	W 2-1
SF	May	3	(h)	Rochdale	L 0-2

Manchester Senior Cup

SF	May	5	(h)	Bolton W	D 0-0
R		11	(a)	Bolton W	W 2-0
F		14	(a)	Bury	W 2-1

Friendlies

1	Jan	29	(a)	Coventry C	L 1-2
2	Feb	12	(a)	Bournemouth	W 4-2

Tour (to Denmark)

1	May	19	(a)	Copenhagen Select	L 1-2
2		21	(a)	Copenhagen Select	D 3-3
3		24	(a)	Esjberg	W 4-1
4		26	(a)	Alborgand Aallorg	W 5-1
5		29	(a)	Randers	W 4-1
6	Jun	1	(a)	Jutland Select	L 1-2

Swift	Sproston	Westwood	Fagan	Walsh	Emptage	Oakes	Black	Smith	Linacre	Clarke	McDowall	Williams	Hart	Godwin	Thurlow	McMorran	Munro	Phillips	Hogan	Jones	Bootle	Gill	Greenwood	No.
1	2	3	4	6			8	10	7	11	5				9									1
1	2	3	4	6			8	10	7	11	5				9									2
1	2	3	4	6		7	8	10	9	11	5													3
1	2	3	4	6		7	8		10	11	5			9										4
1		3	4	6		7	8		10	11	5	2		9										5
1		3	4	6		7	8		10	11	5	2		9										6
1		3	4	6		7	8		10	11	5	2		9										7
	2	3	4	6		7		8	10	11	5				1	9								8
1	2	3	4	6		7		8	10	11	5				9									9
	2	3	4	6			8	10	7	11	5			9	1									10
1	2	3	4	6		7	8		10	11	5			9										11
	2	3	4		6	7	8	9	10	11	5			1										12
1	2	3	4	6		7	8	9	10	11	5													13
1		3	4	6		7	8	9	10	11	5	2												14
1		3	4	6		7	8	9	10	11	5	2												15
1	2	3	4	6		7	8	9	10	11	5													16
		3	5	4	6	7	8	9	10	11		2					1							17
		3	5	4	6	7	8	9	10	11		2					1							18
1		3	5	4	6	7	8	9	10	11		2												19
1		3	5	4	6	7	8	9	10	11		2												20
1		3	5	4	6	7	8	9	10	11		2												21
1		3	5	4	6	7	8	9	10	11		2												22
1		3	5	4	6	7		9	10	11		2	8											23
1		3	5	4	6	7		9	10	11		2	8											24
		3	5	4	6	7		9	10	11		2	8				1							25
1		3	5	4	6		10	9	7	11		2	8											26
1	2	3	5	4	6		9	10	7	11			8											27
1	2	3	5	4	6	7		9	10	11			8											28
1	2	3	5	4	6	7	10	9					8							11				29
1	2	3	5	4	6	7	10	9	11				8											30
1	2	3	5	4	6	7	10	9	11				8											31
1	2	3	5		6	7	10	9	11				8									4		32
1	2	3	5	4	6	7	10	9					8							11				33
1	2	3	5	4	6	11	10	9	7				8											34
1	2	3	5	4	6	11	8	10	7					9										35
	2	3	5	4	6	11	10	9	7					1		8								36
1	2	3	5	4	6	7	8	9	10	11														37
1		3	5	4	6	7			10	11				9			8	2						38
1		3	5	4	6	7		9	10	11							8	2						39
1	2	3	5		6		8		10	11									7	9		4		40
1	2	3	5	4	6		8		10	11									7	9				41
1	2	3	5	4	6		8		10	11									9	7				42
35	25	42	42	39	27	34	35	32	40	34	16	15	12	8	7	4	3	3	3	2	2	1	1	
	1						1	5	11	12	2	6	1	1		3	2	1						

119

1949-50

1	Aug	20	(h)	Aston Villa	D	3-3	Smith (2), Black	39,594
2		24	(a)	Portsmouth	D	1-1	Munro	44,294
3		27	(a)	Charlton A	L	1-3	Fagan	31,000
4		31	(h)	Portsmouth	W	1-0	Smith	32,631
5	Sep	3	(a)	Manchester U	L	1-2	Munro	47,706
6		7	(h)	Everton	D	0-0		27,265
7		10	(h)	Fulham	W	2-0	Turnbull, Clarke	42,192
8		17	(a)	Newcastle U	L	2-4	Turnbull, Clarke	58,141
9		24	(h)	Blackpool	L	0-3		57,815
10	Oct	1	(a)	Middlesbrough	D	0-0		45,000
11		8	(a)	Chelsea	L	0-3		45,153
12		15	(h)	Stoke C	D	1-1	Munro	31,151
13		22	(a)	Burnley	D	0-0		25,063
14		29	(h)	Sunderland	W	2-1	Murray, Turnbull	43,026
15	Nov	5	(a)	Liverpool	L	0-4		50,536
16		12	(h)	Arsenal	L	0-2		28,288
17		19	(a)	Bolton W	L	0-3		35,000
18		26	(h)	Birmingham C	W	4-0	Black (2), Clarke (2)	30,501
19	Dec	7	(a)	Derby C	L	0-7		23,681
20		10	(h)	West Brom A	D	1-1	Black	29,544
21		17	(a)	Aston Villa	L	0-1		30,000
22		24	(h)	Charlton A	W	2-0	Black, Clarke	32,092
23		26	(a)	Huddersfield T	L	0-1		29,989
24		27	(h)	Huddersfield T	L	1-2	Clarke	45,000
25		31	(h)	Manchester U	L	1-2	Black	63,704
26	Jan	14	(a)	Fulham	L	0-1		30,000
27		21	(h)	Newcastle U	D	1-1	Clarke	42,986
28	Feb	4	(a)	Blackpool	D	0-0		25,000
29		18	(h)	Middlesbrough	L	0-1		59,252
30		25	(h)	Chelsea	D	1-1	Hart	32,824
31	Mar	4	(a)	Stoke C	L	0-2		30,000
32		11	(h)	Bolton W	D	1-1	Black	46,648
33		18	(a)	Birmingham C	L	0-1		30,000
34		29	(h)	Liverpool	L	1-2	opp.og	20,000
35	Apr	1	(a)	Arsenal	L	1-4	Hart	42,000
36		8	(h)	Burnley	W	1-0	Westcott	31,182
37		10	(h)	Wolves	W	2-1	Smith, Turnbull	36,723
38		11	(a)	Wolves	L	0-3		50,000
39		15	(a)	Sunderland	W	2-1	Oakes, Clarke	40,404
40		22	(h)	Derby C	D	2-2	Smith (2)	52,928
41		29	(a)	West Brom A	D	0-0		16,760
42	May	6	(a)	Everton	L	1-3	Clarke	29,627

Appearances
Goals

League Division One record: P 42   W 8   D 13   L 21   F 36   A 68   Pts 29   Pos 21st

FA Cup

3 Jan 7 (h) Derby C   L 3-5

Lancashire Senior Cup

1 Oct 12 (a) Manchester U   L 1-2

Manchester Senior Cup

1 Apr 26 (h) Bury   W 3-0
SF May 4 (a) Bolton W   W 1-0
F   8 (a) Oldham A   L 1-2

Friendlies

1 Jan 28 (a) Reading   D 0-0
2 Feb 11 (a) Barnsley   D 0-0
3 Apr 27 (a) St Helens   W 2-0

120

Trautmann	Phillips	Westwood	Walsh	Fagan	Emptage	Oakes	Munro	Turnbull	Smith	Clarke	Black	Westcott	Murray	Spurdle	Powell	Williams	Alison	Hart	Linacre	Gill	Rigby	Sproston	Swift	Williamson	Cunliffe	Bootle	Jones	
	3	4	5	6		8		9	11	10									7			2	1					1
	3	4	5	6		8		9	11	10					1	2			7									2
	3	4	5	6		8		9	11	10					1	2			7									3
	3	4	5	6		8		9	11	10						2			7					1				4
	3	4	5	6	11	8		9		10						2			7					1				5
	3	4	5		11	8		9		10		6				2			7					1				6
	3	4	5				7	9		11	8	6			1	2			10									7
	3	4	5				7	9		11	8	6			1	2			10									8
	3	4	5			7	8	9	11	10		6			1	2												9
	3	4	5			7	8	9	11	10		6			1						2							10
	3	4	5			7	8	9	10	11		6			1	2												11
	2	3	4	5	6	7	8	9	11	10					1													12
	2	3	4	5	6	7	8	9	11	10					1													13
	2	3	4	5	6	7		9		10	8				1										11			14
	2	3	4	5	6	7		9		10	8				1										11			15
	2	3	4	5	6	7		9	11	10	8				1													16
1	2	3	4	5		11	7	9	10		8	6																17
1	3	11	6				7	9		10	8					4				5		2						18
1	3	11	6	5			7	9		10	8					4						2						19
1	2	3			6			9		10	8						11			4	5					7		20
1	2	3		4	6			9		10	8						11				5					7		21
1	2	3			6	7	8	9	11	10										4	5							22
1	2	3		4				9	11	10		6					8				5					7		23
1	2	3		4	8		7		11	9							10			6	5							24
1	2	3	6	5			7	9		11	8						10			4								25
1	2	3	6	5		11	7	9			8						10			4								26
1		3	6	5	10		7	9	11		8									4	2							27
1	2	3	6	5			7		11	10						4		8									9	28
1	2	3	4	5	6		7		11	10		9	8															29
1	2	3	6	5				7	11	10		9				4		8										30
1	2	3	6	5				7	11	10		9				4		8										31
1	2	3		5	6			7	11		8	9				4	10											32
1	2	3		5	6		8		11			9				4	7	10										33
1	2	3	4	5	6			10	11		8	9					7											34
1	2	3		5	6			9	11		8					4	7	10										35
1	2	3		5	6		7		10	11		9				4		8										36
1	2	3		5	6		7		10	11		9				4		8										37
1	2			5	6		7		10	11	8	9				4	3											38
1	2			5	6	7			10	11		9				4	3								8			39
1	2	3		5	6	7			10	11		9				4									8			40
1	2	3		5	6	7			10	11		9				4		8										41
1	2	3		5	6		7		10	11		9				4		8										42
26	30	40	27	39	27	22	17	29	15	37	33	13	13	13	12	11	10	9	8	7	6	5	4	3	2	3	1	
				1			1	3	4	6	9	7	1	1					2									

1950-51

#	Date		Opponent	Result	Scorers	Attendance
1	Aug 19	(a)	Preston N E	W 4-2	Smith (2), Westcott, Clarke	36,294
2	23	(h)	Cardiff C	W 2-1	Westcott, Smith	14,858
3	26	(h)	Bury	W 5-1	Westcott (3), Hart, Oakes	40,778
4	28	(a)	Cardiff C	D 1-1	Oakes	32,817
5	Sep 2	(a)	Q.P.R.	W 2-1	Smith, Clarke	21,593
6	6	(a)	Grimsby T	D 4-4	Westcott (2), Spurdle, Clarke	18,529
7	9	(h)	Chesterfield	W 5-1	Smith (2), Hart (2), Westcott	43,485
8	16	(a)	Leicester C	W 2-1	Turnbull, Smith	32,856
9	23	(h)	Luton T	D 1-1	Paul	42,333
10	30	(h)	Coventry C	W 1-0	Spurdle	40,839
11	Oct 7	(a)	Doncaster R	L 3-4	Smith (3)	32,832
12	14	(h)	Brentford	W 4-0	Westcott (2), Hart, Clarke	39,497
13	21	(a)	Swansea T	W 3-2	Westwood, Westcott, Cunliffe	26,000
14	28	(h)	Hull C	D 0-0		45,693
15	Nov 4	(a)	Leeds U	D 1-1	Haddington	30,500
16	11	(h)	West Ham U	W 2-0	Haddington, Westcott	41,734
17	18	(a)	Blackburn R	L 1-4	Haddington	37,400
18	25	(h)	Southampton	L 2-3	Haddington, Westcott	38,972
19	Dec 2	(a)	Barnsley	D 1-1	Westcott	29,615
20	9	(h)	Sheffield U	W 5-3	Smith (2), Westcott, Spurdle, Hart	33,172
21	16	(h)	Preston N E	L 0-3		30,413
22	25	(h)	Birmingham C	W 3-1	Paul (2), Westcott	40,064
23	26	(a)	Birmingham C	L 0-1		32,000
24	Jan 13	(a)	Chesterfield	W 2-1	Smith, Clarke	12,309
25	20	(h)	Leicester C	D 1-1	Hart	30,198
26	27	(a)	Bury	L 0-2		25,439
27	Feb 3	(a)	Luton T	D 2-2	Smith (2)	12,087
28	17	(a)	Coventry C	W 2-0	Spurdle, Clarke	29,205
29	24	(h)	Doncaster R	D 3-3	Westcott (2), Oakes	38,572
30	Mar 3	(a)	Brentford	L 0-2		24,290
31	14	(h)	Swansea T	L 1-2	Cunliffe	10,000
32	17	(a)	Hull C	D 3-3	Westcott (2), Hart	25,000
33	24	(h)	Leeds U	W 4-1	Meadows, Westcott, Smith, Hart	35,000
34	26	(h)	Notts C	D 0-0		31,948
35	31	(a)	West Ham U	W 4-2	Smith (2), Westcott, Hart	22,000
36	Apr 4	(h)	Q.P.R.	W 5-2	Westcott (2), Hart (2), Clarke	21,474
37	7	(h)	Blackburn R	W 1-0	Hart	37,754
38	14	(a)	Southampton	L 1-2	Hart	24,579
39	21	(h)	Barnsley	W 6-0	Smith (2), Clarke (2), Meadows, Hart	42,741
40	28	(a)	Sheffield U	D 0-0		24,500
41	30	(a)	Notts C	D 0-0		13,873
42	May 5	(h)	Grimsby T	D 2-2	Westcott, Smith	30,284

Appearances
Goals

League Division Two record: P 42   W 19   D 14   L 9   F 89   A 61   Pts 52   Pos 2nd

FA Cup

3 Jan 6 (a) Birmingham C   L 0-2

Lancashire Senior Cup

1 Oct 19 (a) Barrow   W 2-1
2 Jan 16 (a) Southport   W 3-1
SF Apr 18 (h) Manchester U D 0-0
R May 7 (a) Manchester U L 1-2

Manchester Senior Cup

SF Apr 11 (a) Bury   D 2-2
R   30 (h) Bury   L 2-3

Friendlies

1 Mar 10 (a) Hearts   L 0-1
2 May 2 (a) St Helens   W 6-0
3 May 9 (h) FC Wacker   W 2-1

122

Trautmann	Phillips	Westwood	Spurdle	Paul	Rigby	McCourt	Oakes	Hart	Westcott	Smith	Clarke	Meadows	Branagan	Alison	Gunning	Haddington	Williamson	Fagan	Cunliffe	Turnbull	Emptage	
1	2	3	4	6	5		7	8	9	10	11											1
1	2	3	4	6	5		7	8	9	10	11											2
1	2	3	4	6	5		7	8	9	10	11											3
1	2	3	4	6	5		7	8	9	10	11											4
1	2	3	4	6	5		7	8	9	10	11											5
1	2	3	4	6	5		7	8	9	10	11											6
1	2	3	4	6	5		7	8	9	10	11											7
1	2	3	4	6	5			8	9	10	11								7			8
1	2	3	4	6	5		7		9	10	11			8								9
1	2	3	4	6	5		7		9	10	11			8								10
1	2	3	4	6	5		7		9	10	11			8								11
1	2	3	4	6	5			8	9	10	11			7								12
1	2	3	4		5			8	9	10				7					11	6		13
1	2	3	4	6	5			8	9	10	11			7								14
1	2	3	4	6	5				9	10	11		8	7								15
1	2	3	4	6	5		7		9	10	11			8								16
1	2	3	4	6	5			7	9	10	11			8								17
1	2	3	4	6	5		7		9	10	11			8								18
1	2	3	6	4	5		7		9	10	11			8								19
1		3	6	4	5	11	8	9	10				2		7							20
1		3	6	4		11	8	9	10				2		7	5						21
1		3	6	4				9		11			2	10	7		8	5				22
1		3	6	4				9		11			2	10	7		8	5				23
1		3	6	4			7	8	9	10	11		2					5				24
1		3	6	4			7	8	9	10	11		2					5				25
1		3	6	4	5		7	8	9	10	11		2									26
1		3	4	8	5	6			9	10	11		2	7								27
1		3	8	4	5	6	7		9	10	11		2									28
1		3	8	4	5	6	7		9	10	11		2									29
1	2	3	8	4	5	6	7		9	10	11											30
1	2	3		4	5	6	7		9	8	10						11					31
1	2	3		4	5	6		8	9	10	11	7										32
1	2	3		4	5	6		8	9	10	11	7										33
1	2	3		4	5	6		8	9	10	11	7										34
1	2	3		4	5	6		8	9	10	11	7										35
1	2	3		4	5	6		8	9	10	11	7										36
1	2	3		4	5	6		8		10	11	7					9					37
1	2	3		4	5	6		8	9	10	11	7										38
1	2	3		4	5	6		8	9	10	11	7										39
1	2	3		4	5	6		8	9	10	11	7										40
1	2	3	10	4	5	6					11	7				8	9					41
1	2	3		4	5	6			9	10	11	7					8					42
42	37	37	31	41	37	16	21	27	40	39	39	11	10	9	4	6	6	5	2	1	1	
		1	4	3			3	14	25	21	9	2				4			2	1		

123

1951-52

1	Aug 18	(h)	Wolves	D 0-0		45,748
2	22	(a)	Huddersfield T	L 1-5	Westcott	25,653
3	25	(a)	Sunderland	L 0-3		45,396
4	29	(h)	Huddersfield T	W 3-0	Meadows, Hart, Westcott	30,863
5	Sep 1	(h)	Aston Villa	D 2-2	Paul, Westcott	31,503
6	5	(a)	Portsmouth	L 0-1		30,018
7	8	(a)	Derby C	W 3-1	Meadows, Hart, Williamson	22,073
8	15	(h)	Manchester U	L 1-2	Hart	52,571
9	22	(h)	Arsenal	L 0-2		48,367
10	29	(a)	Blackpool	D 2-2	Hart, Westcott	33,858
11	Oct 6	(a)	Tottenham H	W 2-1	Clarke (2)	57,550
12	13	(h)	Preston N E	W 1-0	opp.og	57,566
13	20	(a)	Burnley	D 0-0		30,977
14	27	(h)	Charlton A	W 4-2	Meadows, Westcott, Broadis, Clarke	44,348
15	Nov 3	(a)	Fulham	W 2-1	Broadis, Revie	35,000
16	10	(h)	Middlesbrough	W 2-1	Meadows, Westcott	47,422
17	17	(a)	West Brom A	L 2-3	Hart, opp.og	28,000
18	24	(h)	Newcastle U	L 2-3	Meadows, Clarke	39,328
19	Dec 1	(a)	Bolton W	L 1-2	Meadows	45,008
20	8	(h)	Stoke C	L 0-1		20,397
21	15	(a)	Wolves	D 2-2	Westcott, Clarke	30,000
22	22	(h)	Sunderland	W 3-1	Westcott (2), Clarke	28,535
23	25	(a)	Chelsea	W 3-0	Westcott, Broadis, Meadows	34,850
24	26	(h)	Chelsea	W 3-1	Meadows, Revie, Westcott	49,700
25	29	(a)	Aston Villa	W 2-1	Meadows, Williamson	40,000
26	Jan 1	(h)	Portsmouth	L 0-1		40,412
27	5	(h)	Derby C	W 4-2	Hart (2), Broadis, Clarke	37,572
28	19	(a)	Manchester U	D 1-1	McCourt	54,254
29	26	(a)	Arsenal	D 2-2	Hart, Phoenix	54,527
30	Feb 9	(h)	Blackpool	D 0-0		47,437
31	16	(h)	Tottenham H	D 1-1	Revie	38,989
32	Mar 1	(a)	Preston N E	D 1-1	Hart	38,000
33	12	(h)	Burnley	L 0-1		20,132
34	15	(a)	Charlton A	D 0-0		25,000
35	22	(h)	Fulham	D 1-1	Hart	30,945
36	29	(a)	Middlesbrough	D 2-2	Hart, Revie	18,000
37	Apr 5	(a)	West Brom A	L 1-2	Revie	13,842
38	11	(h)	Liverpool	L 1-2	Clarke	35,305
39	12	(a)	Newcastle U	L 0-1		40,000
40	14	(a)	Liverpool	W 2-1	Williamson, Clarke	34,404
41	19	(h)	Bolton W	L 0-3		28,297
42	26	(a)	Stoke C	L 1-3	Branagan	27,000

Appearances
Goals

League Division One record: P 42   W 13   D 13   L 16   F 58   A 61   Pts 39   Pos 15th

FA Cup

3	Jan 12	(h)	Wolves	D 2-2
R	16	(a)	Wolves	L 1-4

Lancashire Senior Cup

1	Oct 18	(a)	Barrow	D 2-2
R	25	(a)	Barrow	L 0-2

Manchester Senior Cup

1	Mar 26	(h)	Bury	L 0-2

Friendlies

1	Feb 2	(h)	River Plate FC	L 3-4
2	23	(a)	Manchester U	L 2-4
3	Mar 8	(h)	Hibernian	L 1-4
4	Apr 29	(a)	Sheffield W	D 1-1

Tour (to Spain)

1	May 18	(a)	Seville	L 1-5
2	25	(a)	Zaragoza	W 3-1
3	Jun 2	(a)	Barcelona	L 1-5

124

Trautmann	Branagan	Hannaway	Paul	Rigby	McCourt	Meadows	Revie	Westcott	Broadis	Clarke	Hart	Phoenix	Williamson	Phillips	Spurdle	Westwood	Cunliffe	Davies	Gunning	Smith	Barnes	Williams	
1		3	4	5	6	7		9		10	8			2			11						1
1		3	4	5	6	7		9		11	8			2					10				2
1		3	4	5	6	7		9		11	8			2					10				3
1		3	4	5	6	7		9		10	8			2			11						4
1		3	4	5	6	7		9		10	8			2			11						5
1		3	4	5	6	7		9		11	8			2					10				6
1		3	4	5	6	7				11	8		9	2	10								7
1		3	4	5	6	7	10			11	8		9	2									8
1		3	4	5	6	7	10			11	8		9	2									9
1		3	4	5	6	7	10			11	8		9	2									10
1	2	3	4	5	6	7			10	11	8		9										11
1	2	3	4	5	6	7			10	11	8		9										12
1	2	3		5	6	7	8		10				9		4		11						13
1	2	3	4	5	6	7	8	9	10	11													14
1	2	3	4	5		7	8	9	10	11					6								15
1	2	3	4	5	6	7	8	9	10	11													16
1	2	3	4	5	6	7		9	10	11	8												17
1	2	3	4	5	6		9	8	10	11	7												18
1	2	3	4	5	6		9	8	10	11	7												19
1	2	3	4	5	6	7	8		10	11			9										20
1	2	3		5	6	7	8	9	10	11					4								21
1	2	3		5	6	7	8	9	10	11					4								22
1	2	3		5	6	7	8	9	10	11					4								23
1	2	3		5	6	7	8	9	10	11					4								24
1	2	3	4	5	6	7	8		10	11			9										25
1	2	3	4	5	6	7	8	9	10	11													26
1	2	3	6	5			8	9	10	11	7										4		27
1	2	3		5	6		9	8	10	11	7				4								28
1	2	3		5	6		9		8	11	7	10			4								29
	2	3	4	5		7	8		10	11		6	9									1	30
1	2	3	4	5		7	8		10	11		9	6										31
1	2	3	4	5		7	10		8	11		9	6										32
1	2		4	5					8	11		9	6			3		10		7			33
1	2		4	5			10		8	11		9	6			3				7			34
1	2		4	5			10		8	11		9	6			3				7			35
1	2	3	4	5			9	10	8	11	7		6										36
1	2	3	4	5		7	8			11		9	6					10					37
1	2	3	4	5		7	10		8	11		9	6										38
1	2		4	5		7	10		8	11		6	9			3							39
1	2		4	5		7	10		8	11		6	9			3							40
1	2		4	5		7			8	11		6	9			3		10					41
1	2		4	5	6				8	11	7	10	9			3							42
41	32	35	35	38	31	37	26	19	31	41	26	14	15	10	9	7	4	3	3	3	1	1	
	1		1		1	9		5	11		4	9	11		1	3							

125

1952-53

1	Aug	23	(a)	Stoke C	L 1-2	Smith	37,644
2		27	(h)	Tottenham H	L 0-1		33,521
3		30	(h)	Manchester U	W 2-1	Broadis, Clarke	56,140
4	Sep	1	(a)	Tottenham H	D 3-3	Sowden (2), Meadows	40,870
5		6	(h)	Liverpool	L 0-2		42,965
6		8	(a)	Burnley	L 1-2	Meadows	27,083
7		13	(a)	Middlesbrough	L 4-5	Revie (2), Broadis, Meadows	36,000
8		17	(h)	Burnley	D 0-0		24,884
9		20	(h)	West Brom A	L 0-1		33,043
10		27	(a)	Newcastle U	L 0-2		48,110
11	Oct	4	(h)	Cardiff C	D 2-2	Revie, Branagan	35,000
12		11	(a)	Portsmouth	L 1-2	Williamson	33,644
13		18	(h)	Bolton W	L 1-2	Revie	42,270
14		25	(a)	Aston Villa	D 0-0		30,000
15	Nov	1	(h)	Sunderland	L 2-5	Hart, Williamson	33,121
16		8	(a)	Wolves	L 3-7	Williamson (2), Davies	33,832
17		15	(h)	Charlton A	W 5-1	Meadows (3), Williamson, Clarke	23,362
18		22	(a)	Arsenal	L 1-3	Meadows	39,161
19		29	(h)	Derby C	W 1-0	Hart	22,918
20	Dec	6	(a)	Blackpool	L 1-4	Williamson	19,496
21		13	(h)	Chelsea	W 4-0	Meadows, Hart, Clark, opp.og	20,633
22		20	(h)	Stoke C	W 2-1	Williamson, Hart	13,562
23		26	(a)	Preston N E	L 2-6	Hart (2)	38,000
24	Jan	3	(a)	Manchester U	D 1-1	Broadis	47,883
25		17	(a)	Liverpool	W 1-0	Hart	41,191
26		24	(h)	Middlesbrough	W 5-1	Spurdle (3), Williamson, Revie	26,715
27	Feb	7	(a)	West Brom A	L 1-2	Revie	25,000
28		14	(h)	Newcastle U	W 2-1	Meadows, Phoenix	25,000
29		21	(a)	Cardiff C	L 0-6		28,000
30		28	(h)	Portsmouth	W 2-1	Meadows, Cunliffe	38,736
31	Mar	7	(a)	Bolton W	L 0-1		36,405
32		14	(h)	Aston Villa	W 4-1	Spurdle (3), Anders	32,566
33		21	(a)	Sunderland	D 3-3	Broadis (2), Williamson	26,270
34		28	(h)	Wolves	W 3-1	Spurdle, Whitfield, McCourt	27,127
35	Apr	3	(h)	Sheffield W	W 3-1	Broadis, Whitfield, Cunliffe	55,485
36		4	(a)	Charlton A	W 2-1	Hart, McCourt	26,242
37		6	(a)	Sheffield W	D 1-1	Hart	43,520
38		11	(h)	Arsenal	L 2-4	Spurdle (2)	53,418
39		18	(a)	Derby C	L 0-5		15,618
40		22	(h)	Preston N E	L 0-2		45,000
41		25	(h)	Blackpool	W 5-0	Spurdle (2), McCourt, Cunliffe, Williamson	38,507
42		29	(a)	Chelsea	L 1-3	Williamson	48,594
							Appearances
							Goals

League Division One record: P 42   W 14   D 7   L 21   F 72   A 87   Pts 35   Pos 20th

FA Cup

3	Jan	10	(h)	Swindon T	W 7-0
4		31	(h)	Luton T	D 1-1
R	Feb	4	(a)	Luton T	L 1-5

Lancashire Senior Cup

1	Oct	22	(h)	Liverpool	W 2-1
2	Feb	24	(a)	Southport	W 1-0
SF	Apr	8	(h)	Preston N E	W 2-0
F	May	6	(a)	Chester	W 5-1

Manchester Senior Cup

SF	Apr	23	(a)	Oldham A	L 1-2

Friendlies

None played.

126

Trautmann	Branagan	Westwood	Paul	Rigby	Spurdle	Meadows	Revie	Hart	Williamson	Broadis	Clarke	Cunliffe	Ewing	Hannaway	McCourt	Sowden	Anders	Whitfield	Phoenix	Gunning	Davies	Little	Smith F.	Webster	Woosnam	No.
1	2	3	4	5	7		8			10	11				6								9			1
1	2	3	4	5	7		8			10	11				6								9			2
1	2	3	4	5	6	7	8			10	11					9										3
1	2	3	4	5	6	7	8			10	11					9										4
1	2		4	5	6	7	8			10	11		3			9										5
1	2		4	5	6	7	8			10	11		3			9										6
1		3	4	5	6	7	8			10	11		2			9										7
1	2	3	4	5	6	7	8			10	11					9										8
1	2	3	4	5	6	7	8			10	11					9										9
1	2	3	4	5	6	7	10	8		11						9										10
1	2	3	4	5	6	7	10	8		11						9										11
1	2	3		5	4	7	10	8	9	11									6							12
1	2	3			4	5	10	7	9	8	11								6							13
1	2	3	5			7	4	8	9	11									6	10						14
1	2	3	5			7	4	8	9	11									6	10						15
1	2	3	5			7	4	8	9	11									6	10						16
1	2	3	4	5		7	6	8	9	10	11															17
1	2	3	4	5		7	6	8	9	10	11															18
1	2	3	6	5		7	4	8	9	11											10					19
1	2	3	6	5		7	4	8	9	11											10					20
1	2	3		5	6	7	4	8	9	10	11															21
1	2	3	6	5		7	4	8	9	10	11															22
1	2	3	6			5	4	8	9	10	11									7						23
1	2	3	6			7	4	8	9	10	11	5														24
1	2		6				4	8	9	10	11	5								7	3					25
1	2		6		8		4		9	10	11	5								7	3					26
1	2		6		8		4		9	10	11	5								7	3					27
1	2		6				9	4		8	11	5	3						10	7						28
1	2						9	4		8	11	5	3							7				6	10	29
1	2		4				7	10		8	11	5	3	6			9									30
1	2		4				9		10	8	11	5	3	6	7											31
1	2		4		8					10	11	5	3	6	7		9									32
1	2		4		8				9	10	11	5	3	6	7											33
1	2		4		8					10	11	5	3	6	7		9									34
1	2		4		8					10	11	5	3	6	7		9									35
1	2		4		8			9		10	11	5	3	6	7											36
1	2		4		8			9		10	11	5	3	6	7											37
1	2		4		8			9		10	11	5	3	6	7											38
1	2		6		8	4	10				11	5	3		7		9									39
1	2		6		8	4				10	11	5	3		7		9									40
1	2		4		8				9	10	11	5	3	6	7											41
1	2		4		8				9	10	11	5	3	6	7											42
42	41	22	38	18	27	26	32	20	19	34	22	20	19	18	13	9	12	6	6	6	5	3	2	1	1	
	1				11	10	6	9	11	6	3	3		3	2	1	2	1			1		1			

127

1953-54

1	Aug	19	(a)	Sheffield W	L 0-2		48,000
2		22	(h)	Wolves	L 0-4		20,039
3		24	(a)	Aston Villa	L 0-3		30,000
4		29	(a)	Sunderland	W 5-4	Hart (2), Whitfield, Clarke, Anders	49,434
5	Sep	2	(h)	Aston Villa	L 0-1		24,918
6		5	(h)	Manchester U	W 2-0	Revie, Hart	53,097
7		9	(a)	Huddersfield T	D 1-1	Little	24,341
8		12	(h)	Cardiff C	D 1-1	opp.og	31,915
9		16	(h)	Huddersfield T	L 0-1		24,580
10		19	(a)	Arsenal	D 2-2	Spurdle, Hart	65,869
11		26	(h)	Portsmouth	W 2-1	Revie, Hart	35,691
12	Oct	3	(a)	Blackpool	L 0-2		31,765
13		10	(a)	Bolton W	L 2-3	Revie (2)	29,403
14		17	(h)	Preston N E	L 1-4	Anders	43,295
15		24	(a)	Tottenham H	L 0-3		37,577
16		31	(h)	Burnley	W 3-2	Meadows (2), Cunliffe	32,353
17	Nov	7	(a)	Liverpool	D 2-2	Hart, Meadows	30,917
18		14	(h)	Newcastle U	D 0-0		34,150
19		21	(a)	Middlesbrough	W 1-0	opp.og	25,000
20		28	(h)	West Brom A	L 2-3	Hart, Revie	40,753
21	Dec	5	(a)	Charlton A	L 1-2	Meadows	17,813
22		12	(h)	Sheffield W	W 3-2	Little, Revie, Davies	27,639
23		19	(a)	Wolves	L 1-3	Davies	27,606
24		25	(a)	Sheffield U	D 2-2	Revie, Hart	35,000
25		26	(h)	Sheffield U	W 2-1	Hart, opp.og	35,783
26	Jan	2	(h)	Sunderland	W 2-1	McAdams, Revie	23,742
27		16	(a)	Manchester U	D 1-1	McAdams	46,379
28		23	(a)	Cardiff C	W 3-0	Revie, Clarke, Anders	22,000
29	Feb	6	(h)	Arsenal	D 0-0		39,026
30		13	(a)	Portsmouth	L 1-4	McAdams	30,135
31		24	(h)	Blackpool	L 1-4	Clarke	22,515
32		27	(h)	Bolton W	W 3-0	McAdams, Meadows, Revie	39,340
33	Mar	6	(a)	Preston N E	L 0-4		21,000
34		17	(h)	Tottenham H	W 4-1	Hart, McAdams, Revie, Clarke	10,841
35		20	(a)	Burnley	L 1-3	Hart	23,054
36	Apr	3	(a)	Newcastle U	L 3-4	Hart, McAdams, Clarke	27,760
37		7	(h)	Liverpool	L 0-2		12,593
38		10	(h)	Middlesbrough	W 5-2	Meadows (2), Clarke (2), Revie	28,445
39		16	(a)	Chelsea	W 1-0	Meadows	59,794
40		17	(a)	West Brom A	L 0-1		35,000
41		19	(h)	Chelsea	D 1-1	Branagan	30,620
42		24	(h)	Charlton A	W 3-0	McAdams (2), Spurdle	19,549

Appearances
Goals

League Division One record: P 42   W 14   D 9   L 19   F 62   A 77   Pts 37   Pos 17th

FA Cup

| 3 | Jan | 9 | (a) | Bradford | W 5-2 |
| 4 | | 30 | (h) | Tottenham H | L 0-1 |

Lancashire Senior Cup

1	Nov	4	(h)	Barrow	W 2-1
2	Mar	24	(a)	Preston N E	W 2-1
SF	Apr	26	(a)	Liverpool	L 0-1

Manchester Senior Cup

| SF | Dec | 16 | (h) | Manchester U | L 0-2 |

Friendlies

1	Oct	14	(h)	Hearts	W 6-3
2		21	(h)	Fenerbahce	W 5-1
3		28	(h)	Celtic	D 1-1
4	Nov	25	(h)	Admira Vienna	W 3-2
5	Jan	5	(a)	Army XI	D 5-5
6	Feb	20	(h)	East Fife	W 2-1
7	Mar	9	(a)	Bury	L 1-3
8		13	(a)	Oldham A	D 0-0
9	Apr	28	(h)	Manchester U	W 3-2

Tour (to West Germany)

See opposite page.

Trautmann	Branagan	Little	Revie	Ewing	Paul	Spurdle	Hart	Meadows	Clarke	McTavish	Anders	McAdams	Hayes	Cunliffe	Broadis	Whitfield	Williamson	Fagan	Hannaway	Sowden	Davies	McCourt	Davidson	No.
1	2		4	5	6		8				7			11	10		9		3					1
1	2		4	5	6		8			11	7				10		9		3					2
1	2	3	4	5	6		8			11	7				10		9							3
1	2	3	4	5	6	10	8			11	7						9							4
1	2	3	4	5	6	10	8			11	7						9							5
1	2	3	4	5	6	10	8			11	7						9							6
1	2	3	4	5	6	10	8			11	7						9							7
1	2	3	4	5	6	10	8			11	7						9							8
1	2	3	4	5	6	10	8			11	7						9							9
1	2	3	4	5	6	7	8			11					10	9								10
1	2	3	4	5	6	7	8			11					10	9								11
1	2	3	4	5	6	7	8			11					10	9								12
1	2	3	4	5		7	8			11					10	9					6			13
1	2	3	4	5	6		8			11	7				10	9								14
1	2	3	4	5	6		8			11		7			10	9								15
1	2	3	4	5	6		8	9	10			7		11										16
1	2	3	4	5	6		8	9	10			7		11										17
1	2	3	4	5	6		8	9	10			7		11										18
1	2	3	10	5	6		8	9		4		7		11										19
1	2	3	4	5	6		8	9	10	7				11										20
1	2	3		5	6			9	10	4	7	8		11										21
1	2	3	8	5	6			9	11	4		7								10				22
1	2	3	4	5	6		8	9	11			7								10				23
1	2	3	10	5	6		8	9	11	4	7													24
1	2	3	10	5	6		8	9	11	4								7						25
1	2	3	10	5	6		8		11	4		9						7						26
1	2		10	5	6		8	3	11	4		9						7						27
1	2		10	5	6		8	3	11	4	7	9												28
1	2		10	5	6	7	8	3		4	9		11											29
1	2		10	5	6	7	8	3		4	9		11											30
1	2	3	10	5		7	8		11	4		9									6			31
1	2		10	5	6			9	11	4		7	8						3					32
1	2			5	6	10			11	4	7		8					9	3					33
1	2		10	5	6	7	8		11	4								9	3					34
1	2		10	5	6		8	3	11	4	7	9												35
1	2		5	4	6		8	10	9	11								7	3					36
1	2	3	10	5	4	6		9	11			7	8											37
1	2	3	10	5	6	7		9	11	4			8											38
1	2	3	10	5	6	7		9	11	4			8											39
1	2	3		5	6	7	10			4			9	8	11									40
1	2	3	10	5	6	7			11	4			9	8										41
1	2	3		5	6	7	10		11	4			9	8										42
42	42	31	37	42	39	24	32	20	35	20	19	17	11	10	9	7	7	6	6	2	2	1	1	
	1	2	12			2	12	8	7		3	8		1	1				2					

Tour (to West Germany)

1	Aug	2	(a)	Frankfurt	D 2-2
2	May	9	(a)	Bayern Munich	D 3-3
3		12	(a)	Furth FC Nu'burg	W 2-0
4		15	(a)	Stuttgart K	D 2-2
5		16	(a)	PSV Wurnburg Frankfurt	W 1-0
6		19	(a)	Wuppertal Combined XI	W 2-0

1954-55

1	Aug 21	(a)	Preston N E	L 0-5			35,000
2	25	(h)	Sheffield U	W 5-2	Revie (2), Hart (2), Clarke		23,856
3	28	(h)	Burnley	D 0-0			38,201
4	30	(a)	Sheffield U	W 2-0	Revie, Hart		25,000
5	Sep 4	(a)	Leicester C	W 2-0	McAdams, Hart		32,825
6	8	(h)	Arsenal	W 2-1	Hart, opp.og		38,146
7	11	(h)	Chelsea	D 1-1	Paul		35,971
8	14	(a)	Arsenal	W 3-2	McAdams, Hart, Clarke		33,898
9	18	(a)	Cardiff C	L 0-3			30,000
10	25	(h)	Manchester U	W 3-2	Fagan, McAdams, Hart		54,105
11	Oct 2	(h)	Everton	W 1-0	Clarke		45,737
12	9	(a)	Wolves	D 2-2	Fagan (2)		41,601
13	16	(h)	Aston Villa	L 2-4	Spurdle (2)		36,384
14	23	(a)	Bolton W	D 2-2	McAdams, Revie		30,123
15	30	(h)	Huddersfield T	L 2-4	Revie (2)		34,246
16	Nov 6	(a)	Sheffield W	W 4-2	Williamson (2), Hart, Clarke		19,152
17	13	(h)	Portsmouth	L 1-2	Fagan		24,564
18	20	(a)	Blackpool	W 3-1	McAdams (2), Williamson		21,734
19	27	(a)	Charlton A	L 1-5	Davies		25,799
20	Dec 4	(a)	Sunderland	L 2-3	Hart (2)		33,733
21	11	(h)	Tottenham H	D 0-0			27,052
22	18	(h)	Preston N E	W 3-1	Hart (2), Hayes		26,615
23	25	(h)	Newcastle U	W 3-1	Hayes, Spurdle (2)		26,664
24	27	(a)	Newcastle U	L 0-2			52,850
25	Jan 1	(a)	Burnley	L 0-2			25,931
26	15	(h)	Leicester C	D 2-2	Hayes, Clarke		13,648
27	22	(a)	Chelsea	W 2-0	Hayes, Clarke		34,160
28	Feb 5	(h)	Cardiff C	W 4-1	Fagan, Hayes, Revie, Clarke		31,922
29	12	(a)	Manchester U	W 5-0	Fagan (2), Hayes (2), Hart		47,914
30	23	(a)	Everton	L 0-1			20,457
31	Mar 5	(a)	Tottenham H	D 2-2	Hart, Hayes		35,358
32	16	(h)	Bolton W	W 4-2	Hayes (3), Fagan		27,413
33	19	(a)	Huddersfield T	D 0-0			31,065
34	30	(h)	Sheffield W	D 2-2	Hayes, Davies		14,825
35	Apr 2	(a)	Portsmouth	L 0-1			24,286
36	8	(h)	West Brom A	W 4-0	Johnstone, Spurdle, Hayes, Fagan		57,663
37	9	(h)	Sunderland	W 1-0	Revie		60,611
38	11	(a)	West Brom A	L 1-2	Spurdle		30,000
39	16	(a)	Charlton A	D 1-1	Johnstone		25,064
40	20	(h)	Wolves	W 3-0	Fagan, Meadows, Williamson		50,705
41	23	(h)	Blackpool	L 1-6	Fagan		44,339
42	30	(a)	Aston Villa	L 0-2			25,000

Appearances
Goals

League Division One record: P 42 W 18 D 10 L 14 F 76 A 69 Pts 46 Pos 7th

FA Cup

3	Jan 8	(a)	Derby C	W 3-1
4	29	(h)	Manchester U	W 2-0
5	Feb 19	(a)	Luton T	W 2-0
6	Mar 12	(a)	Birmingham C	W 1-0
SF	26	(n)	Sunderland	W 1-0
F	May 7	(n)	Newcastle U	L 1-3

Lancashire Senior Cup

1	Nov 3	(h)	Barrow	D 2-2
R	Jan 3	(a)	Barrow	L 2-4

Manchester Senior Cup

SF	Mar 21	(h)	Oldham A	L 1-3

Friendlies

1	Sep 28	(h)	England XI*	D 0-0
2	28	(h)	England XI**	D 2-2
3	Oct 6	(h)	Aberdeen	W 4-3
4	18	(a)	Millwall	W 1-0
5	27	(a)	Rangers	W 4-1

*Trial match played with morning KO
**Trial match played with afternoon KO.

Tour (to West Germany & France)
See opposite page.

	Trautmann	Meadows	Little	Barnes	Ewing	Paul	Fagan	Hayes	Revie	Hart	Clarke	McAdams	Spurdle	Branagan	Williamson	Johnstone	Davies	McTavish	Leivers	Savage	Anders	Hannaway	
	1	3			5	6			9	10	11	8	7					4	2				1
	1	2	3	4	5	6			9	10	11	8	7										2
	1	2	3	4	5	6	7		9	10	11	8											3
	1	2	3	4	5	6	7		9	10	11	8											4
	1	2	3	4	5	6	7		9	10	11	8											5
	1	2	3	4	5	6	7		9	10	11	8											6
	1	2	3	4	5	6	7		9	10	11	8											7
	1	2	3	4	5	6	7		9	10	11	8											8
	1	2	3	4	5	6	7		9	10	11	8											9
	1	2	3	4	5	6	7		9	10	11	8											10
	1	2	3	4	5	6	7			10	11	8			9								11
	1	2	3	4	5	6	7		9	10	11				8								12
	1	2	3	4	5			11	9	10		8	7					6					13
	1	2	3	4	5	6	7		9	10	11	8											14
	1	2	3	4	5	6	7		9	10	11	8											15
	1	2	3	4	5	6				10	11	8	7		9								16
	1	2	3	4	5	6	11	8			10	7			9								17
	1	2	3	4	5	6	7			10	11	8			9								18
	1	2	3	4	5	6	7				11	8			9	10							19
	1		3	4	5	6	7			10	11	8		2	9								20
	1		3	4	5	6	7		9	10	11	8		2									21
	1		3	4	5	6	7	8	9	10	11			2									22
	1		3	4	5	6		8	9	10	11		7	2									23
			3	4	5	6		8	9	10	11		7	2						1			24
		5	3	4		6	11	8	9	10			7	2						1			25
	1		3	4		6	7	8	9	10	11			2				5					26
	1	2	3	4	5	6	7	8	9	10	11												27
	1	2	3	4	5	6	7	8	9	10	11												28
	1	2	3	4	5	6	7	8	9	10	11												29
	1	2	3	4	5	6	7	8	9	10	11												30
	1	2	3	4	5	6	7	8	9	10	11												31
	1	2	3	4	5	6	7	8	9		11					10							32
	1	2	3	4	5	6	7		9	10	11					8							33
	1		3	4	5	6	11	8						2	9	10					7		34
	1				5	6	11	8					7	2	9	10	4					3	35
	1	2	3	4	5	6	11	8	9			7				10							36
	1	2	3	4	5	6	11	8	9			7				10							37
	1	2	3	4	5	6	11	8	9			7				10							38
	1	2	3	4	5	6	7		9		11	8				10							39
	1	8	3	4	5	6	7				11			2	9	10							40
	1	10	3	4	5	6	11	8	9				7	2									41
	1	2	3	4	5	6	7	8	9		11					10							42
Apps	40	36	38	40	40	41	36	20	32	31	33	19	16	11	9	8	3	3	2	2	1	1	
Goals		1					1	11	13	8	14	7	6	6	4	2	2						

Tour (to West Germany & France)

1	May 15	(a)	RSD Strasbourg	L	2-3
2	19	(a)	FC Mainz	L	1-2
3	21	(a)	Saarbrucken	D	4-4
4	22	(a)	SV Eintracht Trier	W	5-1
5	25	(a)	Alemannia Aachen	L	2-4

1955-56

1	Aug 20	(h)	Aston Villa	D 2-2	Revie, Cunliffe	38,099
2	27	(a)	Wolves	L 2-7	Hayes, Revie	38,000
3	31	(h)	Arsenal	D 2-2	Hayes (2)	36,955
4	Sep 3	(h)	Manchester U	W 1-0	Hayes	59,192
5	6	(a)	Arsenal	D 0-0		30,864
6	10	(h)	Cardiff C	W 3-1	Hayes (2), Johnstone	33,240
7	17	(a)	Huddersfield T	D 3-3	Fagan, Johnstone, Clarke	20,443
8	24	(h)	Blackpool	W 2-0	Revie, Johnstone	63,925
9	Oct 1	(a)	Chelsea	L 1-2	Meadows	44,538
10	8	(a)	Sheffield U	D 1-1	Dyson	24,000
11	15	(h)	Preston N E	L 0-2		33,187
12	22	(a)	Birmingham C	L 3-4	Hayes, Dyson, Faulkner	28,500
13	29	(h)	West Brom A	W 2-0	Cunliffe, opp.og	25,081
14	Nov 5	(a)	Charlton A	L 2-5	Hayes, Cunliffe	24,655
15	12	(h)	Tottenham H	L 1-2	Hayes	24,094
16	19	(a)	Everton	D 1-1	Faulkner	34,632
17	26	(h)	Newcastle U	L 1-2	Clarke	32,860
18	Dec 3	(a)	Burnley	D 2-2	Hayes, Dyson	26,227
19	10	(h)	Luton T	W 3-2	Spurdle, Hayes, Clarke	14,499
20	17	(a)	Aston Villa	W 3-0	Spurdle, Dyson (2)	20,000
21	24	(h)	Wolves	D 2-2	Spurdle, Hayes	32,935
22	26	(a)	Bolton W	W 3-1	Spurdle, Dyson, opp.og	43,706
23	27	(h)	Bolton W	W 2-0	Paul, Clarke	38,405
24	31	(a)	Manchester U	L 1-2	Dyson	60,956
25	Jan 2	(h)	Portsmouth	W 4-1	Johnstone (3), Hayes	43,133
26	14	(a)	Cardiff C	L 1-4	Johnstone	27,000
27	21	(h)	Huddersfield T	W 1-0	Spurdle	21,076
28	Feb 4	(a)	Blackpool	W 1-0	Faulkner	17,014
29	11	(h)	Chelsea	D 2-2	Hayes (2)	26,642
30	25	(a)	Preston N E	W 3-0	Johnstone (2), Hayes	22,664
31	Mar 7	(h)	Everton	W 3-0	Spurdle, Johnstone, Clarke	15,227
32	10	(a)	West Brom A	W 4-0	Johnstone (2), Hayes, Dyson	32,000
33	21	(h)	Charlton A	L 0-2		13,998
34	24	(a)	Tottenham H	L 1-2	Hayes	31,622
35	30	(a)	Sunderland	W 3-0	Hayes, Revie, opp.og	40,394
36	31	(h)	Birmingham C	D 1-1	Hayes	44,777
37	Apr 2	(h)	Sunderland	W 4-2	Hayes (2), Dyson (2)	40,915
38	7	(a)	Newcastle U	L 1-3	Dyson	25,999
39	11	(h)	Sheffield U	W 3-1	Spurdle, Hayes, Faulkner	16,991
40	14	(h)	Burnley	L 1-3	Spurdle	29,087
41	21	(a)	Luton T	L 2-3	Barnes, Clarke	18,189
42	28	(a)	Portsmouth	W 4-2	Dyson (2), Spurdle, Hart	24,684

Appearances
Goals

League Division One record: P 42 W 18 D 10 L 14 F 82 A 69 Pts 46 Pos 4th

FA Cup

3	Jan 7	(h)	Blackpool	D 1-1* (abandoned)
3	11	(h)	Blackpool	W 2-1
4	28	(a)	Southend U	W 1-0
5	Feb 18	(h)	Liverpool	D 0-0
R	22	(h)	Liverpool	W 2-1
6	Mar 3	(h)	Everton	W 2-1
SF	17	(n)	Tottenham H	W 1-0
F	May 5	(n)	Birmingham C	W 3-1

Lancashire Senior Cup

1	Dec 14	(h)	Burnley	D 2-2
R	19	(a)	Burnley	W 4-3
2	Apr 5	(a)	Barrow	L 2-3

Manchester Senior Cup

SF	Apr 30	(a)	Bolton W	L 0-5

Friendlies

1	Aug 10	(h)	Gt Britain XI	D 2-2
2	Oct 12	(h)	Rangers	L 1-2
3	Nov 1	(a)	Hibernian	L 1-2

Tour (to West Germany)

1	May 10	(a)	P Munster	W 3-1
2	12	(a)	Eintracht Nordhern	D 1-1
3	13	(a)	Werder Bremen	W 4-1
4	16	(a)	Munchen 1860	D 0-0
5	20	(a)	PSV Peforzheim	W 3-1
6	23	(a)	Sterk.D'dorf	W 6-1

No.	Trautmann	Leivers	Little	Barnes	Ewing	Paul	Spurdle	Hayes	Revie	Johnstone	Dyson	Clarke	Fagan	Branagan	Faulkner	Cunliffe	Phoenix	McTavish	Hannaway	Savage	Hart	Marsden	Murray
1	1		3	4	5	2	6	8	9	10			7			11							
2	1		3	4	5	2	6	8	9	10			7			11							
3	1		3	4	5	6	7	8	9	10		11	2										
4	1		3	4	5	6	7	8	9	10		11	2										
5	1		3	4	5	6	7	8	9	10		11	2										
6	1		3	4	5	6		8	9	10		11	7	2									
7	1		3	4	5			8	9	10		11	7	2		6							
8	1		3	4	5			8	9	10		11	7	2		6							
9	1		3	4	5		7	8		9		11	2			6						10	
10	1		3	4	5	6	7	8		9		11	2		10								
11	1		3	4	5	6	7	8	9	10		11	2										
12	1		3	4	5			8		9		7	2		10	11	6						
13	1		3	4	5	6	7	8	9				2		10	11							
14	1		3	4	5		7	8	9	10			2		11	6							
15	1	5	3	4		6	7	8	9	10		11	2										
16	1	5	3	4				8		9		11	7	2	10		6						
17	1	5	3	4				8		9		11	7	2	10		6						
18	1	5	3	4	2	6	7	8		9	10	11											
19	1	5	3	4	2	6	7	8		9	10	11											
20	1	2	3	4	5	6	7	8		9	10	11											
21	1	2	3	4	5	6	7	8		9	10	11											
22	1	2	3	4	5	6	7	8		9	10	11											
23	1	2	3	4	5	6	7	8		9	10	11											
24	1	2	3	4	5	6	7	8		9	10	11											
25	1	2	3	4	5	6	7	8		9	10	11											
26	1	2	3	4	5	6	7	8		9	10			11									
27	1	2	3	4	5	6	7	8		9	10	11											
28	1	2	3	4	5	6	7	8	9			11		10									
29	1	2	3	4	5	6		8	9	7	10	11											
30	1	2	3	4	5	6	7	8		9	10	11											
31	1	2	3	4	5	6	7	8		9	10	11											
32	1	2	3	4	5	6	7	8		9	10	11											
33	1	2	3	4	5	6	7	8	9		10	11											
34	1	2	3	4	5	6	7	8		9	10	11											
35	1	2	3	4	5	6	7	8	9		10	11											
36	1	2	3	4	5	6	7	8	9		10	11											
37	1		3		5	6	7	8		9	10	11						4	2				
38	1		3	4	5	6	7	8		9	10	11							2				
39	1	2	3	4	5		7	8	9					10			6						11
40		2	3	4	5	6	7	8	9			11			10					1			
41		2	3	4	5	6	7	8	9		10	11								1			
42	1		3	4	5	2	7	8	9		10						6				11		
	40	25	42	39	39	36	35	42	21	31	25	25	16	15	7	6	6	5	2	2	1	1	1
			1			1	9	23	4	12	13	6	1		4	3					1	1	

133

1956-57

1	Aug 18	(a)	Wolves	L 1-5	Revie	43,407
2	22	(h)	Tottenham H	D 2-2	Clarke (2)	32,718
3	25	(h)	Aston Villa	D 1-1	Clarke	24,326
4	29	(a)	Tottenham H	L 2-3	Johnstone, Paul	33,083
5	Sep 1	(a)	Luton T	L 2-3	Hayes, McAdams	21,625
6	5	(h)	Leeds U	W 1-0	McAdams	34,185
7	8	(h)	Sunderland	W 3-1	McAdams, Revie, Hayes	35,753
8	12	(a)	Leeds U	L 0-2		35,000
9	15	(a)	Charlton A	L 0-1		18,533
10	22	(a)	Manchester U	L 0-2		53,515
11	29	(h)	Blackpool	L 0-3		39,528
12	Oct 6	(a)	Arsenal	L 3-7	Clarke (2), Dyson	32,651
13	13	(h)	Burnley	L 0-1		35,981
14	20	(a)	Newcastle U	W 3-0	Fagan, Johnstone, Dyson	34,310
15	27	(h)	Sheffield W	W 4-2	Fagan, Hayes (2), Johnstone	29,259
16	Nov 3	(a)	Cardiff C	D 1-1	Dyson	28,000
17	10	(h)	Birmingham C	W 3-1	Johnstone (2), Hayes	21,005
18	17	(a)	West Brom A	D 1-1	Dyson	25,780
19	24	(h)	Portsmouth	W 5-1	Fagan, Hayes (2), Johnstone, Clarke	24,364
20	Dec 1	(a)	Preston N E	L 1-3	opp.og	25,433
21	8	(h)	Chelsea	W 5-4	Johnstone (3), Hayes (2)	24,412
22	15	(h)	Wolves	L 2-3	Johnstone (2)	30,329
23	25	(h)	Bolton W	L 1-3	Fagan	19,731
24	26	(a)	Bolton W	L 0-1		20,865
25	29	(h)	Luton T	W 3-2	Dyson (2), Clarke	27,253
26	Jan 12	(a)	Sunderland	D 1-1	Fagan	34,119
27	19	(h)	Charlton A	W 5-1	Dyson (3), Johnstone, Fagan	22,108
28	Feb 2	(h)	Manchester U	L 2-4	Hayes, Clarke	63,872
29	4	(a)	Aston Villa	D 2-2	McClelland, Hayes	11,000
30	9	(a)	Blackpool	L 1-4	Johnstone	21,105
31	23	(a)	Sheffield W	D 2-2	Paul, Hayes	11,271
32	Mar 2	(h)	Newcastle U	L 1-2	Barnes	25,229
33	9	(a)	Chelsea	L 2-4	Fagan, Hayes	35,664
34	16	(h)	Cardiff C	W 4-1	Johnstone (3), Dyson	26,395
35	20	(h)	Arsenal	L 2-3	Barnes, Clarke	27,974
36	30	(h)	West Brom A	W 2-1	Paul, Fagan	26,361
37	Apr 6	(a)	Portsmouth	W 1-0	Dyson	24,949
38	13	(h)	Preston N E	L 0-2		31,305
39	19	(h)	Everton	L 2-4	Fagan, Clarke	28,009
40	20	(a)	Burnley	W 3-0	Hayes, Dyson, Clarke	16,746
41	22	(a)	Everton	D 1-1	McAdams	28,887
42	27	(a)	Birmingham C	D 3-3	Kirkman (2), opp.og	23,700

Appearances
Goals

League Division One record: P 42 W 13 D 9 L 20 F 78 A 88 Pts 35 Pos 18th

FA Cup

3	Jan 5	(a)	Newcastle U	D 1-1
R	9	(h)	Newcastle U	L 4-5

FA Charity Shield

	Oct 24	(h)	Manchester U	L 0-1

Lancashire Senior Cup

1	Nov 19	(h)	Everton	D 2-2
R	Dec 10	(a)	Everton	L 1-3

Manchester Senior Cup

SF	Nov 28	(h)	Manchester U	L 1-9

Friendlies

1	Nov 19	(a)	Hearts	W 4-3
2	Dec 6	(h)	MTK Budapest	L 2-3
3	Jan 26	(a)	Stoke C	L 1-4
4	Feb 16	(a)	Notts C	W 2-1
5	Mar 11	(h)	Werder Bremen	W 4-0

Tour (to West Germany & Spain)

1	May 8	(a)	Barcelona	L 2-3
2	15	(a)	Eintracht/Frankfurt Select XI	L 0-2
3	19	(a)	SV Werder Bremen	W 6-3
4	22	(a)	Borussia Dortmund	L 1-4
5	24	(a)	Lloret de Mar	W 9-0

Savage	Trautmann	Leivers	Little	Barnes	Ewing	Paul	Fagan	Hayes	Johnstone	Dyson	Clarke	Revie	McAdams	Marsden	Phoenix	McTavish	Spurdle	Hart	McClelland	Hannaway	Thompson	Sear	Kirkman	No.
		2	3	4	5	6		8	10		11	9					7			1				1
		2	3	4	5	6		8	7		11	9					10			1				2
1		2	3	4	5	6		8	7		11	9					10							3
1		2	3	4	5	6		8	9		11						10		7					4
1		2	3	4	5	6		8	7		11	9	10											5
1		2	3		5	4			10		11	9	8			6		7						6
1		2	3		5	4			10		11	9	8			6		7						7
1		2	3		5	4			10		11	9	8			6		7						8
1		2	3		5	4	11		10			9	8			6		7						9
1		2		4	5	6			10		11	9	8					7				3		10
1		2		4	5	3	7	8	10		11	9				6								11
1		2		4	5	3	7	8	9	10	11					6								12
1		2			5	6	7	8	9	10	11	4									3			13
1		2	3		5	6	7	8	9	10	11	4												14
1		2	3		5	6	7	8	9	10	11	4												15
1		2	3		5	6	7	8	9	10	11	4												16
1		2	3	4	5	6	7	8	9	10	11													17
1		2	3	4	5	6	7	8	9	10	11													18
1		2	3	4	5	6	7	8	9	10	11													19
1		2	3	4	5	6	7	8	9	10	11													20
1		2	3	4	5		7	8	9	10	11					6								21
	1	2	3	4	5	6	7	8	9	10	11													22
	1	2	3	4	5	6	7	8	9	10	11													23
	1	2	3	4	5	6	7	8	9	10	11													24
	1	2	3	4	5	6	7	8	9	10	11													25
	1	2	3	4	5	6	7		9	10	11		8											26
	1	2	3	4	5	6	11	8	9	10									7					27
	1	2	3	4	5	6	7	8	9	10	11													28
	1	2	3	4	5	6		8	9	10	11								7					29
	1	2	3	4	5	6	7	8	9	10	11													30
	1	2	3	4	5	6	7	8	9		11		10											31
	1	2	3	4	5	6	7	10	9		11		8											32
	1	2	3	9	5	4	7	10			11		8			6								33
	1	2	3	9		6	7	8		10	11			5	4									34
	1	2	3	9		6	7	8		10	11			5	4									35
	1	2	3	9		6	7	8		10	11			5	4									36
	1	2	3	9		6	7	8		10	11			5	4									37
	1	2	3	9		6	7	8		10	11			5	4									38
	1	2	3	4		6	7	8	9	10	11			5										39
	1	2	3			6	7	8	9	10	11			5	4									40
	1	2	3			6	7	8		10	11	9		5	4									41
	1	2		5						10	11	9	4	6					7			3	8	42
19	21	42	37	31	34	40	31	34	31	32	40	14	12	9	8	8	5	4	4	2	2	1	1	
			2		3	9		14	16	12	11	2	4					1				2		

135

1957-58

1	Aug 28	(a)	Chelsea	W 3-2	Barlow, Hayes, McAdams	43,722
2	31	(a)	Manchester U	L 1-4	Barnes	63,103
3	Sep 4	(h)	Chelsea	W 5-2	Barlow (2), Fagan (2), McAdams	27,943
4	7	(a)	Nottingham F	L 1-2	Hayes	37,041
5	11	(h)	Preston N E	W 2-0	Hayes, Fagan	24,439
6	14	(h)	Portsmouth	W 2-1	Johnstone, Ewing	28,798
7	18	(a)	Preston N E	L 1-6	Fagan	22,034
8	21	(a)	West Brom A	L 2-9	Fagan, Clarke	25,900
9	28	(h)	Tottenham H	W 5-1	Johnstone (2), Hayes (2), Barlow	22,497
10	Oct 5	(a)	Birmingham C	L 0-4		28,500
11	9	(h)	Sheffield W	W 2-0	Barlow, McAdams	24,016
12	12	(h)	Leicester C	W 4-3	Hayes (2), McAdams, Barlow	29,884
13	19	(a)	Blackpool	W 5-2	Hayes (2), Barnes, Barlow, McAdams	28,322
14	26	(h)	Luton T	D 2-2	Barlow, McAdams	30,633
15	Nov 2	(a)	Arsenal	L 1-2	McAdams	43,664
16	9	(h)	Bolton W	W 2-1	McAdams, Hayes	34,147
17	16	(a)	Leeds U	W 4-2	Hayes (2), McAdams, Barnes	23,000
18	23	(h)	Wolves	L 3-4	Barnes (2), McAdams	45,121
19	30	(a)	Sunderland	L 1-2	McAdams	35,442
20	Dec 7	(h)	Everton	W 6-2	Barnes (3), McAdams (2), Hayes	20,912
21	14	(a)	Aston Villa	W 2-1	Hayes, opp.og	24,000
22	21	(a)	Sheffield W	W 5-4	Hayes (2), Kirkman (2), Johnstone	23,073
23	25	(a)	Burnley	L 1-2	Fagan	27,966
24	26	(h)	Burnley	W 4-1	Barlow, Kirkman, Hayes, Fagan	47,285
25	28	(h)	Manchester U	D 2-2	Hayes, opp.og	70,493
26	Jan 11	(a)	Nottingham F	D 1-1	Johnstone	34,837
27	18	(a)	Portsmouth	L 1-2	Sambrook	26,254
28	Feb 1	(h)	West Brom A	W 4-1	McAdams (3), Barlow	38,702
29	8	(a)	Tottenham H	L 1-5	Hayes	37,539
30	22	(a)	Leicester C	L 4-8	Johnstone (2), McAdams, Barnes	31,017
31	Mar 1	(h)	Blackpool	W 4-3	Barnes, Barlow, McAdams, opp.og	30,621
32	5	(h)	Birmingham C	D 1-1	Barlow	30,565
33	8	(a)	Luton T	W 2-1	Sambrook, opp.og	16,004
34	15	(h)	Arsenal	L 2-4	Barlow, Hayes	31,645
35	22	(a)	Wolves	D 3-3	Barlow (2), opp.og	34,932
36	29	(h)	Leeds U	W 1-0	McAdams	21,962
37	Apr 5	(a)	Bolton W	W 2-0	Barlow (2)	27,733
38	7	(H)	Newcastle U	W 2-1	Warhurst, Hayes	33,995
39	12	(h)	Sunderland	W 3-1	Hayes (2), Hart	31,166
40	14	(a)	Newcastle U	L 1-4	Warhurst	53,280
41	19	(a)	Everton	W 5-2	Hart (2), Hayes, Sambrook, Barnes	35,000
42	26	(h)	Aston Villa	L 1-2	Hayes	28,278

Appearances
Goals

League Division One record: P 42 W 22 D 5 L 15 F 104 A 100 Pts 49 Pos 5th

FA Cup

3	Jan 4	(a)	West Brom A	L 1-5

Lancashire Senior Cup

1	Dec 2	(a)	Rochdale	W 2-0
2	Mar 24	(h)	Barrow	L 0-3

Manchester Senior Cup

SF	Mar 26	(h)	Bolton W	W 1-0
F	May 5	(a)	Oldham A	L 0-1

Friendlies

1	Nov 4	(a)	Hearts	W 5-3
2	11	(a)	Coventry C	L 1-3
3	18	(h)	Hibernian	W 1-0
4	25	(a)	Hibernian	L 2-5
5	Dec 16	(a)	Army XI	W 3-1
6	Jan 14	(a)	England XI	D 2-2
	(private trial match)			
7	Mar 17	(a)	Derby C	W 5-0
8	Apr 28	(h)	Great Britain XI	L 2-4

Tours (to Holland, & USA and Canada)

(See opposite page)

Trautmann	Leivers	Sear	Barnes	Ewing	Warhurst	Barlow	Hayes	Johnstone	McAdams	Fagan	Little	Sambrook	Savage	Branagan	McTavish	Clarke	Hart	Marsden	Kirkman	McClelland	Cheetham	Pheonix	Fleet	Taylor	Fidler	№
1	2		4	5	6	7	8	9	10		3					11										1
1	2		4	5	6	7	8	9	10		3					11										2
1	2		4	5	6	7	8	9	10	11	3															3
	2		4	5	6	7	8	9	10	11	3		1													4
	2		4	5	6	7	8	9		11	3		1			10										5
1	2		4	5	6	7	8	9		11	3					10										6
	2		4	5	6	7	8	9		11	3		1			10										7
			4	5			8	9		7	3	1	2	6	11	10										8
		3	4	5	6	7	8	9	10	11		1	2													9
		3	4	5	6	10	8	9				1	2	11	7											10
	2		4	5	6	7	8	9	10	11	3		1													11
1	2	3	4	5	6	7	8	9	10	11																12
1	2	3	4	5	6	7	8	9	10	11																13
1	2	3	4	5	6	7	8	9	10															11		14
1	2	3	4	5	6	7	8	9	10	11																15
1	2	3	4	5	6	7	8	9	10	11																16
1	2		4	5	6	7	8		10		3				11							9				17
	2	3	4	5	6	7	8	9	10	11													1			18
1	2	3	4	5	6	7	8	9	10						11											19
1	2	3	4	5	6	7	8	9	10	11																20
1	2	3	4	5	6	7	8	9	10	11																21
1	2		4	5	6	7	10	9		11	3				8											22
1	2		4	5	6	7	10	9		11	3				8											23
1	2		4	5	6	7	10			11	3				8							9				24
1	2		4	5	6	7	10	9		11	3				8											25
1	2	3	4	5	6	8	10		9	11										7						26
1	2	3	4	5		8	10		9	11					6					7						27
1	2	3	4	5	6	7	8	9	10	11																28
1	2	3	4	5	6	7	8	9	10	11																29
1	2		4	5	6	7	8	9	10	11	3															30
1	2	3	4			7	8	9	10	11					6										5	31
1	2	3	5	4		7	8	9	10	11					6											32
1	2	3		5		7	8	9	10	11					6				4							33
1	2			5		7	8	9	10	11	3				6				4							34
1	2	3	4	5	6		8	9	10	7		11														35
1	2	3	4	5	6		8	9	10	7		11														36
1	2	3	4	5	6	8	10		9	7		11														37
1	2	3	4	5	6	8	10		9	7		11														38
1	2	3	4	5	6	8	10			7		11						9								39
1	5	3	4		6	8	10			7		11		2				9								40
1	5	3	4		6	8	10			7		11		2				9								41
1	5	3	4		6	8	10			7		11		2				9								42
34	36	29	39	38	37	39	40	33	28	29	16	16	7	6	6	6	5	4	4	3	2	2	1	1	1	
			11	1	2	17	25	7	19	7	3				1	3				3						

Tours (to Holland, and USA & Canada)

#	Date		Opponent	Result	
1	Aug 10	(a)	Twente Enschede	W 4-1	
2	May 18	(a)	Pennsylvania Uk	W 6-1	
3	21	(a)	USA Am.Soccer Stars	W 7-2	
4	25	(a)	Hearts	L 5-6	(in New York)
5	28	(a)	St Louis All Stars	W 6-2	
6	Jun 1	(a)	Hearts	L 2-5	(in Vancouver)
7	4	(a)	San Francisco All Stars	W 9-1	
8	7	(a)	Hearts	W 7-1	(in Toronto)
9	8	(a)	Ulster United	W 8-2	
10	11	(a)	Hearts	L 0-6	(in Montreal)

1958-59

1	Aug	23	(a)	Burnley	W 4-3	Hayes (2), Johnstone (2)	31,000
2		27	(h)	Bolton W	D 3-3	Barnes, Barlow, Sambrook	40,844
3		30	(h)	Preston N E	D 1-1	McClelland	42,576
4	Sep	3	(a)	Bolton W	L 1-4	Hayes	39,727
5		6	(a)	Leicester C	L 1-3	McAdams	29,053
6		10	(h)	Luton T	D 1-1	Fagan	30,771
7		13	(h)	Everton	L 1-3	Barlow	35,437
8		17	(a)	Luton T	L 1-5	Johnstone	18,160
9		20	(a)	Arsenal	L 1-4	Sambrook	47,878
10		27	(h)	Manchester U	D 1-1	Hayes	62,812
11	Oct	4	(h)	Leeds U	W 2-1	Barlow, Hayes	31,989
12		11	(a)	Wolves	L 0-2		33,769
13		18	(h)	Portsmouth	W 3-2	Cheetham, Hayes, Fagan	31,330
14		25	(a)	Newcastle U	L 1-4	Hannah	54,330
15	Nov	1	(h)	Tottenham H	W 5-1	Barlow (3), Hannah, Hayes	30,601
16		8	(a)	Nottingham F	L 0-4		31,004
17		15	(h)	Chelsea	W 5-1	Leivers, Fagan, Barlow, Hayes, Sambrook	19,778
18		22	(a)	Blackpool	D 0-0		19,200
19		29	(h)	Blackburn R	L 0-1		16,405
20	Dec	6	(a)	Aston Villa	D 1-1	Kirkman	19,000
21		13	(h)	West Ham U	W 3-1	Barlow (3)	22,250
22		20	(h)	Burnley	L 1-4	Barnes	22,328
23		26	(a)	Birmingham C	L 1-6	Barlow	24,263
24		27	(h)	Birmingham C	W 4-1	Hayes (2), Barlow, Sambrook	29,276
25	Jan	3	(a)	Preston N E	L 0-2		21,208
26		31	(a)	Everton	L 1-3	Barlow	43,360
27	Feb	7	(h)	Arsenal	D 0-0		31,819
28		14	(a)	Manchester U	L 1-4	Johnstone	59,604
29		21	(a)	Leeds U	W 4-0	Barlow (2), Barnes, Fidler	18,500
30		28	(h)	Wolves	L 1-4	Hayes	42,776
31	Mar	7	(a)	Portsmouth	W 4-3	Fagan, McAdams, Hayes, Sambrook	19,919
32		14	(h)	Newcastle U	W 5-1	Hayes (2), Sambrook (2), Barnes	25,417
33		21	(a)	Tottenham H	L 1-3	McAdams	34,493
34		28	(h)	Nottingham F	D 1-1	Barlow	28,164
35		30	(h)	West Brom A	L 0-2		25,551
36		31	(a)	West Brom A	L 0-3		31,600
37	Apr	4	(a)	Chelsea	L 0-2		32,554
38		11	(h)	Blackpool	L 0-2		27,118
39		18	(a)	Blackburn R	L 1-2	Hayes	24,616
40		20	(a)	West Ham U	L 1-5	Barlow	23,500
41		25	(h)	Aston Villa	D 0-0		39,661
42		29	(h)	Leicester C	W 3-1	McAdams, Hayes, Sambrook	46,936

Appearances
Goals

League Division One record: P 42   W 11   D 9   L 22   F 64   A 95   Pts 31   Pos 20th

FA Cup

| 3 | Jan 10 | (a) | Grimsby T | D 2-2 |
| R | 24 | (h) | Grimsby T | L 1-2 |

Lancashire Senior Cup

| 1 | Oct 27 | (a) | Manchester U | L 4-5 |

Manchester Senior Cup

| F | Apr 13 | (a) | Manchester U | L 0-4 |

Friendlies

None played.

Trautmann	Leivers	Sear	Barnes	Ewing	Barlow	Hayes	Fagan	Hannah	McAdams	Sambrook	Johnstone	Cheetham	Branagan	McTavish	Pheonix	Fidler	Shawcross	Warhurst	Lister	Kirkman	Horridge	Fleet	Little	McClelland	Pennington	No.
1	2	3	4	5	7	8			10	11	9			6												1
1	2	3	4	5	7	8			10	11	9			6												2
1	2	3	4	5	8	10				11	9			6										7		3
1	2	3	4	5	7	10			8	11	9			6												4
1		2	4	5	7	10			8	11	9			6									3			5
	2	3	4	5	8	10	7		9	11						6				1						6
1	2	3	4	5	8	10	7		9	11						6										7
1	5	3	4		7	10	11	8			9		2			6										8
1	2	3	4	5	7	10			8	11	9					6										9
1	2	3	6	5	8	10	7		9	11				4												10
1	2	3	6	5	7	8	11		9	10				4												11
1	2	3	6	5	7	8	11		9					4					10							12
1	2	3	6	5	7	10	11		9			8		4												13
1	2	3	6	5	7	10	11		9			8		4												14
1	2	3	6	5	8	10	7		9	11				4												15
1	2	3	6	5	8	10	7		9	11				4												16
1	2	3	6	5	8	10	7		9	11				4												17
1	2		6	5	8	10	7		9	11				4							3					18
1	2	3	6	5	8	10	7		9	11				4												19
1		2	6	5	10		7		9	11				4							3	8				20
1	2	3	6	5	8		7	11	9	10				4												21
1	2	3	6	5	8		7		9	10	11			4												22
1		3	6	5	8	10	7		9	11			4	2												23
1		3	6	5	8	10	7		9	11			2		4											24
1		3		5	8	10	7		9	11		6	2		4											25
1	2		6	5	10		7		9	11		8		4							3					26
1	2	3	4		10	7					9			5	6		11		8							27
1	2		4		8	10	7				9		3	5	6		11									28
1	2		4		9	10	8	7					3	5	6		11									29
1	2		4		9	10	8	7					3	5	6		11									30
1		3	4		10	7	8		9	11			2	5	6											31
1	2		4		10	7	8		9	11			3	5	6											32
1	2		4		10	7	8		9	11			3	5	6											33
1	2	3	4		7	10	8		9	11				5	6											34
1	2	3	4		7	10	8		9	11				5	6											35
1		3	4	5	10	7			9	11			2		6				8							36
1		3	4	5	9	10	7		8				2		6			11								37
1	2	3	4	5	9	10	7		8						6			11								38
1	2		4	5	9	10	11		8				3		6										7	39
1	2			5	7	10		8	9	11			3	6	4											40
1	2		6		8	10	7		9	11			3	5	4											41
1	2		6		7	10		8	9	11			3	5	4											42
41	34	31	40	30	38	40	25	23	21	33	18	18	16	16	16	4	4	3	2	2	3	1	1	1	1	
	1		4		17	16	4	2	4	8	4	1				1				1				1		

1959-60

1	Aug	22	(h)	Nottingham F	W 2-1	Fagan, Johnstone	38,974
2		26	(a)	Fulham	L 2-5	Barlow, Colbridge	27,000
3		29	(a)	Sheffield W	L 0-1		33,479
4	Sep	2	(h)	Fulham	W 3-1	McAdams (2), Colbridge	37,485
5		5	(h)	Wolves	L 4-6	McAdams (3), Barlow	43,650
6		9	(a)	Luton T	W 2-1	Hannah, Hayes	13,122
7		12	(a)	Arsenal	L 1-3	McAdams	38,392
8		16	(h)	Luton T	L 1-2	Colbridge	29,309
9		19	(h)	Manchester U	W 3-0	Hayes (2), Hannah	58,300
10		26	(h)	Blackburn R	W 2-1	McAdams, Hayes	41,687
11	Oct	3	(a)	Blackpool	W 3-1	Barlow, Hayes, Colbridge	33,226
12		10	(a)	Preston N E	W 5-1	McAdams (3), Barlow, Cheetham	31,546
13		17	(h)	Leicester C	W 3-2	McAdams (2), Hayes	33,896
14		24	(a)	Burnley	L 3-4	Hannah (2), Colbridge	28,653
15		31	(h)	Tottenham H	L 1-2	Leivers	45,506
16	Nov	7	(a)	West Ham U	L 1-4	Hayes	25,243
17		14	(h)	Chelsea	D 1-1	Dyson	24,364
18		21	(a)	West Brom A	L 0-2		24,600
19		28	(h)	Newcastle U	L 3-4	McAdams (3)	29,416
20	Dec	5	(a)	Birmingham C	L 2-4	Hayes, Colbridge	18,661
21		12	(h)	Leeds U	D 3-3	Barlow (2), McAdams	19,715
22		19	(a)	Nottingham F	W 2-1	Barlow, opp.og	13,363
23		26	(a)	Everton	L 1-2	Barlow	30,580
24		28	(h)	Everton	W 4-0	Fagan, Barlow, McAdams, Hayes	43,531
25	Jan	2	(h)	Sheffield W	W 4-1	McAdams (2), Barlow, Hayes	44,167
26		16	(a)	Wolves	L 2-4	Barlow, Colbridge	27,864
27		23	(h)	Arsenal	L 1-2	opp.og	28,441
28	Feb	6	(a)	Manchester U	D 0-0		59,490
29		13	(a)	Blackburn R	L 1-2	Barlow	23,731
30		27	(h)	Birmingham C	W 3-0	Hayes (2), Barlow	23,479
31	Mar	5	(a)	Leicester C	L 0-5		24,009
32		9	(h)	Blackpool	L 2-3	Barlow, Haydock	19,653
33		19	(a)	Leeds U	L 3-4	Barlow, Law, opp.og	32,545
34		30	(h)	West Ham U	W 3-1	Barlow, Law, McAdams	29,572
35	Apr	2	(a)	Chelsea	L 0-3		36,044
36		9	(a)	West Brom A	L 0-1		24,342
37		15	(h)	Bolton W	W 1-0	Barlow	50,053
38		16	(a)	Tottenham H	W 1-0	McAdams	49,767
39		18	(h)	Bolton W	L 1-3	Barlow	35,591
40		23	(h)	Preston N E	W 2-1	Barlow, Colbridge	29,812
41		30	(a)	Newcastle U	W 1-0	Hayes	27,812
42	May	2	(h)	Burnley	L 1-2	Colbridge	65,981

Appearances
Goals

League Division One record: P 42   W 17   D 3   L 22   F 78   A 84   Pts 37   Pos 15th

FA Cup

3 Jan 9 (h) Southampton   L 1-5

Lancashire Senior Cup

1 Nov 23 (a) Burnley   L 1-5

Manchester Senior Cup

None played.

Friendlies

1	Aug	1	(a)	St Mirren	L 0-3
2	Oct	7	(h)	Grenchan	D 1-1
3		15	(h)	St Mirren	W 6-1
4	Jan	30	(h)	Hibernian	D 1-1
5	Mar	12	(h)	Manchester U	L 1-3

Tour (to West Germany)

1 Aug 15 (a) SC Tasmania 1900 W 2-1

140

Trautmann	Leivers	Branagan	Sear	Barnes	McTavish	Oakes	Barlow	Hannah	Hayes	McAdams	Colbridge	Cheetham	Fagan	Kerr	Law	Ewing	Dyson	Shawcross	Sambrook	Haydock	Leigh	Johnstone	Fleet	Phoenix	
1	2		4	5			9		10		11		7	3				6				8			1
1	2		4	5			9		10		11		7	3				6				8			2
1	2		4	5			7		10	9	11			3				6				8			3
1	2			6	5		7	8	10	9	11	4		3											4
1	2			6	5		7	8	10	9	11	4		3											5
1	2	3			5		7	8	10	9	11	4		6											6
1	2	3			5		7	8	10	9	11	4		6											7
1	2			6	5		7	8		9	11	4	10	3											8
1	2	3		6	5		7	8	10	9	11	4													9
1	2	3		6	5		7	8	10	9	11	4													10
1	2	3		6	5		7	8	10		11	4			9										11
1	2	3		6	5		7	8	10	9	11	4													12
1	2	3		6	5		7	8	10	9	11	4													13
1	2	3		6	5		7	8	10	9	11	4													14
1	2	3			5		9	8	10		11		7					6					4		15
1	2	3			5		7	8	10		11	4			9			6							16
1	2	3			5	6	7	9	8		11	4					10								17
1	2	3		6	5		7	8	10	9	11	4													18
1	2	3		6	5		7	8	10	9		4	11												19
1	2	3		6	5		7	8	10	9	11	4													20
1	2	3		6	5		7	8	10	9		4	11												21
1	2	3		6	5		7	8		9	11	4					10								22
1	2	3		6	5		7	8		9	11	4					10								23
1	2	3		6	5		8		10	9	11	4	7												24
1	2	3		6	5	4	8		10	9	11		7												25
1	2	3	4	5	6		8		10	9	11		7												26
1	2	3	4	5	6		8		10	9	11		7												27
1	2	3	4	5	6		8		10	9	11							7							28
1	2	3	4	5	6		9	8	10		11							7							29
	2	3	4	5	6	7	8	9			11						10							1	30
1	2	3	4	5	6	7	8	9			11						10								31
1	2	3		6	5		7		8		11	4					10		9						32
1	2	3	4	5	6	7			10	9	11				8										33
1	2	3	4	5	6	7			10	9	11				8										34
1	2	3	4	5	6				10	9	11				8					7					35
1	2	3	4			6	8			9	11	7				5			10						36
1	2	3	4			6	7		10	9	11				8	5									37
1	2	3	4			6	7		10	9	11				8	5									38
1	2		4			6	7	8	10	9	11					5					3				39
1	2		4			6	7	8	10	9	11					5					3				40
1	2	3	4			6	8			9		7				5	10		11						41
1	2	3	4			6	7	8		9	11					5	10								42
41	28	23	25	37	35	18	39	26	41	30	40	21	10	10	7	7	6	6	3	2	2	3	1	1	
	1						19	4	13	21	9	1	2		2		1			1		1			

1960-61

1	Aug 20	(a)	Nottingham F	D	2-2	Law, Hayes	30,133
2	24	(h)	Burnley	W	2-1	Barlow, Hayes	26,941
3	30	(h)	Burnley	W	3-1	Barlow, Law, Colbridge	28,547
4	Sep 3	(h)	Arsenal	D	0-0		36,656
5	7	(h)	Sheffield W	D	1-1	Law	35,180
6	10	(a)	Newcastle U	W	3-1	Law, Hannah, Hayes	25,904
7	14	(a)	Sheffield W	L	1-3	Wagstaffe	28,796
8	17	(h)	Cardiff C	W	4-2	Hayes (2), Barlow (2)	30,932
9	24	(a)	West Brom A	L	3-6	Barlow, Hannah, Hayes	24,800
10	Oct 1	(h)	Birmingham C	W	2-1	Barlow, Law	27,665
11	10	(a)	Tottenham H	D	1-1	Colbridge	58,916
12	15	(h)	Leicester C	W	3-1	Barlow, Hayes, Sambrook	30,193
13	24	(a)	Everton	L	2-4	Barlow, Hayes	53,781
14	29	(h)	Blackburn R	W	4-0	Hayes (2), Law, Hannah	33,641
15	Nov 5	(a)	Bolton W	L	1-3	Law	34,005
16	12	(h)	West Ham U	L	1-2	Barlow	33,721
17	19	(a)	Chelsea	L	3-6	Betts, Law, Baker	37,346
18	Dec 3	(a)	Aston Villa	L	1-5	Law	25,093
19	10	(h)	Wolves	L	2-4	Baker, Law	30,078
20	17	(h)	Nottingham F	L	1-2	Betts	18,252
21	24	(h)	Fulham	W	3-2	Baker (2), Colbridge	18,469
22	26	(a)	Fulham	L	0-1		20,240
23	31	(a)	Manchester U	L	1-5	Barlow	61,123
24	Jan 14	(a)	Arsenal	L	4-5	Hayes (2), Betts, Barlow	36,400
25	21	(h)	Newcastle U	D	3-3	Barlow, Hayes, Law	19,746
26	Feb 4	(a)	Cardiff C	D	3-3	Hayes, Baker	15,478
27	11	(h)	West Brom A	W	3-0	Barlow (2), Betts	21,252
28	25	(h)	Tottenham H	L	0-1		40,278
29	Mar 4	(h)	Manchester U	L	1-3	Wagstaffe	50,479
30	11	(h)	Everton	W	2-1	Shawcross, Baker	29,571
31	18	(a)	Blackburn R	L	1-4	Hayes	19,733
32	22	(a)	Birmingham C	L	2-3	Law (2)	18,092
33	25	(h)	Bolton W	D	0-0		21,816
34	31	(h)	Preston N E	L	2-3	Law (2)	31,164
35	Apr 1	(a)	Wolves	L	0-1		25,365
36	3	(a)	Preston N E	D	1-1	Baker	25,358
37	8	(h)	Chelsea	W	2-1	Law, opp.og	27,720
38	15	(a)	West Ham U	D	1-1	Barlow	17,982
39	19	(h)	Blackpool	D	1-1	Law	28,269
40	22	(h)	Aston Villa	W	4-1	Law (2), Barlow, Hayes	25,235
41	26	(a)	Leicester C	W	2-1	Baker (2)	22,248
42	29	(a)	Blackpool	D	3-3	Barlow, Hayes, Wagstaffe	20,838

Appearances
Goals

League Division One record: P 42   W 13   D 11   L 18   F 79   A 90   Pts 37   Pos 13

FA Cup

3	Jan 7	(a)	Cardiff C	D	1-1	
R	11	(h)	Cardiff C	D	0-0	
2R	16	(n)	Cardiff C	W	2-0	
4	28	(a)	Luton T	W	6-2	(abandoned)
4	Feb 1	(a)	Luton T	L	1-3	

League Cup

2	Oct 18	(h)	Stockport C	W	3-0
3	Nov 21	(a)	Portsmouth	L	0-2

Lancashire Senior Cup

1	Nov 14	(h)	Rochdale	L	0-1

Manchester Senior Cup

None played.

Friendlies

1	Aug 6	(a)	St Mirren	W	4-3
2	Feb 17	(a)	Huddersfield T	L	2-5

Tour (to Austria & Italy)

1	May 17	(a)	Steirischer Graz	L	2-3
2	22	(a)	Wacker Innsbruck	W	4-1
3	Jun 7	(a)	Torino	D	1-1
			(abandoned)		

142

Trautmann	Betts	Sear	Barnes	Plenderleith	Oakes	Barlow	Law	Hannah	Hayes	Wagstaffe	Shawcross	Baker	Colbridge	Leivers	Ewing	Cheetham	Sambrook	Fleet	Hart	Haydock	
1	2	3	4	5	6	7	8	9	10				11								1
1	2	3	4	5	6	7	8	9	10				11								2
1	2	3	4	5	6	7	8	9	10				11								3
1	2	3	4	5	6	7	8	9	10				11								4
1	2	3	4	5	6	7	8	9	10	11											5
1	2	3	4	5	6	7	8	9	10	11											6
1	2	3	4	5	6	7	8	9	10	11											7
1	2	3	4	5	6	7	8	9	10	11											8
1	2	3	4	5	6	7	8	9	10	11											9
1	2	3	4	5	6	7	8	9	10	11											10
1	2	3	4	5		7	8	9	10		6		11								11
1	2	3	4	5		7	8	9	10		6						11				12
1	2	3	4	5		7	8	9	10		6		11								13
1	2	3	4	5		7	8	9	10		6		11								14
1	2	3	4	5		7	8	9			6	10	11								15
1	2	3	4	5		7	8	9			6	10	11								16
1	2	3	4	5		7	8	9			6	10	11								17
1	2	3	4	5			8	9	7		6	10	11								18
1	2	3	4	5			8	9	10		6	7	11								19
1		3		5			8	9	10	11	6	7		2		4					20
1	2	3	4	5			8	10	11		6	9	7								21
1	2	3	4	5			8	10	11		6	9							7		22
1	2	3	4	5		7	10	8	11		6	9									23
1		3	4	5		7	8	9	10		6		11	2							24
1		3	4	5		7	10	8	9		6		11	2							25
1		3				7	8		10		6	9	11	2	5	4					26
1		3		5	6	7	8		10		4	9	11	2							27
		3		5	6		9	8	10	11	4	7		2			1				28
		3		5	6		9	10	8	11	4	7		2			1				29
1		3	4	5		7	8		10	11	6	9		2							30
1	2	3	4	5		7	8		10	11	6	9									31
1	2	3	4	5			9	8	10	11	6						7				32
1	2	3	4	5		7	9	8	10		6						11				33
1	2	3		5	6		8		10	11		9				4	7				34
1	2	3			6		8		11	10		9			5	4	7				35
1	2	3			6	7			10			9			5	4	11	8			36
1	2	3			6	7	8		10	11		9			5	4					37
1	2	3			6	7	8		10	11		9			5	4					38
1	2	3	4		6	7	8		10	11		9			5						39
1	2	3	4		6	7	8		10	11		9			5						40
1	2	3	4		6	7	8		10	11		9			5						41
1		3	4		6	7	8		10	11		9		2	5						42
40	42	33	31	34	22	33	37	30	38	22	24	22	19	9	9	7	6	2	1	1	
	4							17	19	3	18	3	1	9	3	1					

1961-62

1	Aug 19	(h)	Leicester C	W 3-1	Kennedy, Barlow, Hayes	28,899
2	23	(a)	Fulham	W 4-3	Cheetham (2), Betts, Hayes	16,175
3	26	(a)	Ipswich T	W 4-2	Dobing (2), Barlow, Hayes	21,473
4	30	(h)	Fulham	W 2-1	Baker, Hayes	36,775
5	Sep 2	(h)	Burnley	L 1-3	Baker	38,171
6	6	(a)	Everton	W 2-0	Dobing, Baker	38,023
7	9	(a)	Arsenal	L 0-3		42,746
8	16	(h)	Bolton W	W 2-1	Baker, Hayes	27,275
9	20	(h)	Everton	L 1-3	Hayes	35,102
10	23	(a)	Manchester U	L 2-3	Kennedy, opp.og	55,933
11	30	(a)	West Brom A	D 2-2	Baker, opp.og	20,900
12	Oct 7	(h)	Cardiff C	L 1-2	Sambrook	20,143
13	14	(a)	Tottenham H	L 0-2		40,344
14	21	(h)	Nottingham F	W 3-0	Dobing, Barlow, Hayes	20,258
15	28	(a)	Wolves	L 1-4	Barlow	22,821
16	Nov 4	(h)	West Ham U	L 3-5	Dobing (3)	18,839
17	11	(a)	Sheffield U	L 1-3	Hannah	18,135
18	18	(h)	Chelsea	D 2-2	Kennedy, Barlow	16,583
19	25	(a)	Aston Villa	L 1-2	Dobing	26,617
20	Dec 2	(h)	Blackpool	L 2-4	Dobing, Barlow	15,971
21	9	(a)	Blackburn R	L 1-4	Kennedy	13,892
22	16	(a)	Leicester C	L 0-2		15,196
23	23	(h)	Ipswich T	W 3-0	Young, Dobing, Hayes	18,376
24	26	(a)	Birmingham C	D 1-1	Dobing	21,902
25	Jan 13	(a)	Burnley	L 3-6	Young, Dobing, Hayes	22,728
26	20	(h)	Arsenal	W 3-2	Young (2), opp.og	20,414
27	Feb 3	(a)	Bolton W	W 2-0	Hayes, Wagstaffe	18,454
28	10	(h)	Manchester U	L 0-2		49,959
29	21	(h)	West Brom A	W 3-1	Oakes, Dobing, Young	17,225
30	24	(a)	Cardiff C	D 0-0		19,600
31	Mar 3	(h)	Tottenham H	W 6-2	Dobing (3), Young, Hayes, opp.og	31,706
32	10	(a)	Nottingham F	W 2-1	Young, Hayes	20,199
33	17	(h)	Wolves	D 2-2	Dobing (2)	28,407
34	24	(a)	West Ham U	W 4-0	Dobing (3), Hayes	25,808
35	31	(h)	Sheffield U	D 1-1	Hayes	19,157
36	Apr 7	(a)	Chelsea	D 1-1	Hayes	18,629
37	11	(h)	Birmingham C	L 1-4	opp.og	21,941
38	14	(h)	Aston Villa	W 1-0	Young	18,564
39	20	(h)	Sheffield W	W 3-1	Kennedy, Dobing, Hayes	32,131
40	21	(a)	Blackpool	L 1-3	Leivers	19,954
41	23	(a)	Sheffield W	L 0-1		22,084
42	28	(h)	Blackburn R	W 3-1	Young (2), Kennedy	22,253

Appearances
Goals

League Division One record: P 42   W 17   D 7   L 18   F 78   A 81   Pts 41   Pos 12th

FA Cup

3	Jan 6	(a)	Notts C	W 1-0
4	27	(a)	Everton	L 0-2

League Cup

1	Sep 11	(a)	Ipswich T	L 2-4

Lancashire Senior Cup

1	Oct 23	(h)	Bolton W	L 3-4

Manchester Senior Cup

F	Mar 27	(a)	Bury	L 0-1

Friendlies

1	Aug 2	(a)	Bury	W 2-1
2	9	(a)	Bury	W 4-0
3	Oct 11	(h)	Torino	W 4-3
4	Feb 17	(a)	Dundee U	L 1-2

144

Trautmann	Betts	Kennedy	Sear	Ewing	Leivers	Young	Dobing	Barlow	Hayes	Wagstaffe	Oakes	Cheetham	Baker	Benson	Hannah	McDonald	Pardoe	Sambrook	Colbridge	Aimson	Dowd	Gomersall	Plenderleith	Shawcross	
1	2	6		5	3		8	7	10	11		4	9												1
1	2	6		5	3		8	7	10	11		4	9												2
1	2	6		5	3		8	7	10	11		4	9												3
1	2	6	3	5			8	7	10	11		4	9												4
1	2	6		5	3		8	7	10	11		4	9												5
1	2	6	3	5			8		10	11		4	9						7						6
1	2	6	3	5			8	9	10	11		4							7						7
1	2	6	3	5			8		10	11		4	7	9											8
1	2	6	3	5			8		10	11		4	7	9											9
1	2	4	3	5			8		10	11	6		9					7							10
1	2	4	3	5			8		10	11	6		9					7							11
1	2	4	3	5			8		10	11	6		9					7							12
1	2	4	3	5			8		10	11	6		9					7							13
1		4	3	5			8	9	10	11	6		7			2									14
1	2	4	3	5			8	9	10	11	6		7												15
1	2	4	3	5			8	9	10	11	6		7												16
1	2	4		5	3		8	9	7	11	6					10									17
1	2	4		5			8	9		11	6					10			7				3		18
1	2	4	3	5		7	8	9		11	6					10									19
1	2	4	3	5		7	8	9	10	11	6														20
	2	4	3			7	8		10	11	6								9	1				5	21
1	2	6	3	5			7	9	10	11		4		8											22
1	2	6	3	5			7	9	10	11		4		8											23
1	2	6	3	5			7	9	10	11		4		8											24
		6	3	5			7	9	10	11		4		8			2			1					25
1		6	3	5			7	9	10	11		4		8			2								26
1		6		5			7	9	10	11		4		8			2					3			27
1		6	3	5			7	9	10	11		4		8			2								28
1	2	3	5			7	8	9	10	11	6		4												29
1	2	3	5			7	8	9		11	6		4						10						30
1	2	3	5			7	8	9	10	11	6		4												31
1	2	3	5			7	8	9	10	11	6		4												32
1	2	3	5			7	8	9	10	11	6		4												33
1	2	3	5			7	8	9	10	11	6		4												34
1	2	3	5			7	8	9	10	11	6		4												35
1	2	3	5			7	8	9	10	11	6		4												36
1	2	3	5			7	8		10	11	6		4					9							37
1	2	3				7			10	11	6		4	8				9						5	38
1	2	3	5			7	8		10	11	6		4					9							39
1	2	3	5			7	8		10	11	6		4					9							40
1	2	3	5			7	8	9		11	6		4										10		41
1	2	6	3	5		7	8	9		11			4										10		42
40	24	42	35	21	24	24	41	21	39	42	25	16	15	14	13	5	4	4	3	2	2	2	2	2	
	1	6					1	10	22		6	16	1	1	2	5			1					1	

145

1962-63

1	Aug	18	(a)	Wolves	L 1-8	opp.og	26,986
2		22	(h)	Liverpool	D 2-2	Young (2)	33,165
3		25	(h)	Aston Villa	L 0-2		29,524
4		29	(a)	Liverpool	L 1-4	Dobing	46,073
5	Sep	1	(a)	Tottenham H	L 2-4	Dobing, Harley	48,558
6		5	(h)	Ipswich T	W 2-1	Harley (2)	24,825
7		8	(h)	West Ham U	L 1-6	Barlow	24,069
8		11	(a)	Ipswich T	D 0-0		18,849
9		15	(a)	Manchester U	W 3-2	Dobing, Harley, Hayes	49,193
10		22	(a)	Blackpool	D 2-2	Harley, Young	29,961
11		29	(h)	Blackburn R	L 0-1		23,249
12	Oct	6	(h)	Leyton O	W 2-0	Harley, Hannah	19,706
13		13	(a)	Birmingham C	D 2-2	Young, Harley	21,114
14		20	(h)	Sheffield W	W 3-2	Harley (3)	20,756
15		27	(a)	Burnley	D 0-0		30,505
16	Nov	3	(h)	Everton	D 1-1	Dobing	40,336
17		10	(a)	Bolton W	L 1-3	Oakes	21,700
18		17	(h)	Leicester C	D 1-1	Leivers	21,053
19		24	(a)	Fulham	W 4-2	Harley (2), Dobing, Hannah	17,871
20	Dec	1	(h)	Arsenal	L 2-4	Harley (2)	25,454
21		8	(a)	West Brom A	L 1-2	Dobing	12,400
22		15	(h)	Wolves	D 3-3	Hayes, Dobing, Hannah	14,170
23	Feb	23	(a)	Leyton O	D 1-1	Harley	12,464
24	Mar	2	(h)	Birmingham C	W 2-1	Harley, Gray	28,798
25		9	(a)	Sheffield W	L 1-4	Harley	17,424
26		23	(a)	Everton	L 1-2	Wagstaffe	46,101
27		26	(h)	Burnley	L 2-5	Harley (2)	21,985
28		29	(h)	Fulham	L 2-3	Barlow, Gray	12,789
29	Apr	3	(a)	Sheffield U	L 1-3	Gray	16,710
30		6	(a)	Leicester C	L 0-2		27,092
31		12	(h)	Notts C	W 1-0	Gray	25,793
32		13	(h)	Bolton W	W 2-1	Young, Dobing	18,551
33		15	(a)	Nottingham F	D 1-1	Harley	14,989
34		20	(a)	Arsenal	W 3-2	Gray (2), Hayes	20,569
35		24	(h)	Sheffield U	L 1-3	Hayes	19,277
36		27	(h)	West Brom A	L 1-5	Harley	14,995
37	May	1	(a)	Blackburn R	L 1-4	Oakes	12,900
38		4	(h)	Blackpool	L 0-3		19,062
39		8	(a)	Aston Villa	L 1-3	Dobing	17,707
40		11	(h)	Tottenham H	W 1-0	Harley	27,784
41		15	(h)	Manchester U	D 1-1	Harley	52,424
42		18	(a)	West Ham U	L 1-6	Oakes	16,600

Appearances
Goals

League Division One record: P 42   W 10   D 11   L 21   F 58   A 102   Pts 31   Pos 21st

FA Cup

3	Mar	6	(a)	Walsall	W 1-0
4		13	(h)	Bury	W 1-0
5		16	(h)	Norwich C	L 1-2

League Cup

2	Sep	24	(h)	Blackpool	D 0-0
R	Oct	8	(a)	Blackpool	D 3-3
2R		15	(h)	Blackpool	W 4-2
3		24	(a)	Newport C	W 2-1
4	Nov	14	(h)	Luton T	W 1-0
5	Dec	11	(a)	Birmingham C	L 0-6

Lancashire Senior Cup

1	Oct 24	(h)	Manchester U	D 0-0
R	Nov 12	(a)	Manchester U	L 0-2

Manchester Senior Cup

None played.

Friendly

1	Oct 12	(a)	Burnley	D 1-1
			(Played in Dublin)	

Appearances and goals grid (numbers indicate the shirt number worn by each player in each match; matches numbered 1–42 at right).

Dowd	Kennedy	Sear	Benson	Leivers	Oakes	Young	Dobing	Harley	Hayes	Wagstaffe	Gray	Betts	Trautmann	Cheetham	Hannah	Barlow	Pardoe	Plenderleith	Shawcross	Chadwick	Wood	Batty	No.
	2		4	5		7	8		10	11		3	1				9		6				1
	3		4		6	7	8		10	11		2	1			9	5						2
	3		4		6	7	8	9		11		2	1					5	10				3
	3		4		6	7	8	9		11		2	1				10	5					4
	3		4		6	10	8	9		11		2	1			7		5					5
	3		4	5	6	10	8	9		11		2	1			7							6
	3		4	5	6	10	8	9		11		2	1			7							7
	4	3		5		7	8	9	10	11		2	1						6				8
	4	3		5		7	8	9	10	11		2	1						6				9
	4	3		5		7	8	9	10	11		2	1						6				10
	4	3		5		7	8	9	10	11		2	1						6				11
1	4	3	6	5		7	8	9		11		2		10									12
1	2	3	4	5	6	7	8	9		11				10									13
1	2	3	4	5	6	7	8	9		11				10									14
1	2	3	4	5	6	7	8	9		11				10									15
1	2	3	4	5	6	7	8	9		11				10									16
1	2	3	4	5	6	7	8	9		11				10									17
1	2	3	4	5	6	7	8	9		11				10									18
1	2	3	4	5	6	7	8	9		11				10									19
	2	3	4	5	6	7	8	9		11			1	10									20
	2	3	4	5	6	7	8	9		11			1	10									21
1	3		4	5	6		8	9	7	11		2			10								22
1	8	3	4	5	6	7		9				2			10	11							23
1	8	3	4	5		7		9		11		2			10				6				24
1	8	3	4	5		7		9		11		2			10				6				25
1	3		4	5	6	7	8	9		11		2			10								26
1	2	3	4		6	7	8	9		11					10			5					27
1	2	3		5	6		8	9		11				4	10	7							28
1	2	3	4	5	6		8	9		11					10	7							29
1	2	3		5	6	11	8	9						4	10	7							30
1	2	3		5	6	11	8	9						4	10	7							31
1	2	3			6	7	8	9		11				4	10					5			32
1	2	3			6	7	8	9	10	11				4						5			33
1	2	3		5	6	7	8	9		11				4	10								34
1	2	3		5	6	7	8	9		11				4	10								35
1	2	3		5	6	7	8	9		11				4	10								36
	2	3	5	4			8	9		11			1		10	7			6				37
	3	2	4				8	9		11			1		10	7			6	5			38
1	6	3	2	4		7	8	9		11					10					5			39
1	2	3	5	4		7	8	9		11		6		10									40
1	2	3	5	4		7	8	9	10	11		6											41
1	2	3	5	4		7	8	9	10	11		6											42
27	41	33	24	35	34	31	41	40	21	31	18	17	15	10	13	9	5	5	4	4	3	1	
			1	3	5	9	23	4	1	6				3	2								

147

1963-64

1	Aug 24	(h)	Portsmouth	L 0-2			21,822
2	28	(a)	Cardiff C	D 2-2	Hannah, Kevan		25,352
3	31	(a)	Rotherham U	W 2-1	Kevan (2)		11,418
4	Sep 4	(h)	Cardiff C	W 4-0	Aimson (2), Young, Kevan		22,138
5	7	(h)	Leeds U	W 3-2	Young, Hannah, Kevan		29,186
6	10	(a)	Swindon T	L 0-3			28,291
7	14	(a)	Sunderland	L 0-2			39,298
8	18	(h)	Swindon T	D 0-0			23,103
9	21	(h)	Northampton T	W 3-0	Oakes, Young, Wagstaffe		21,340
10	28	(a)	Bury	D 1-1	Hodgkinson		18,032
11	Oct 5	(h)	Charlton A	L 1-3	Gray		16,138
12	9	(h)	Plymouth A	D 1-1	Cunliffe		13,456
13	12	(a)	Grimsby T	D 1-1	opp.og		9,754
14	19	(h)	Preston N E	L 2-3	Aimson, Kevan		23,153
15	26	(a)	Derby C	W 3-1	Aimson, Oakes, Young		15,675
16	Nov 2	(h)	Swansea T	W 1-0	Oakes		16,770
17	9	(a)	Southampton	L 2-4	Kevan, Murray		17,142
18	23	(a)	Newcastle U	L 1-3	Gray		21,200
19	30	(h)	Huddersfield T	W 5-2	Murray (2), Kevan (2), Gray		16,192
20	Dec 7	(a)	Leyton O	W 2-0	Murray, Kevan		9,610
21	14	(a)	Portsmouth	D 2-2	Murray, Kevan		13,206
22	21	(h)	Rotherham U	W 6-1	Murray (3), Kevan (2), Young		11,060
23	26	(h)	Scunthorpe U	W 8-1	Gray (3), Murray (3), Kevan (2)		26,365
24	28	(a)	Scunthorpe U	W 4-2	Murray (2), Kevan, Wagstaffe		9,085
25	Jan 14	(a)	Leeds U	L 0-1			33,737
26	18	(h)	Sunderland	L 0-3			31,136
27	Feb 1	(a)	Northampton T	L 1-2	Kevan		12,330
28	8	(h)	Bury	D 1-1	Dowd		14,698
29	15	(a)	Charlton A	L 3-4	Frost, Gray, Kevan		18,961
30	22	(h)	Grimsby T	L 0-4			11,411
31	29	(a)	Middlesbrough	D 2-2	Gray, Kevan		12,763
32	Mar 7	(h)	Derby C	W 3-2	Kevan (2), Murray		11,908
33	14	(a)	Plymouth A	L 1-2	Kevan		11,761
34	17	(h)	Middlesbrough	W 1-0	Kevan		8,053
35	21	(h)	Southampton	D 1-1	Murray		13,481
36	27	(h)	Norwich C	W 5-0	Kevan (3), Murray, Wagstaffe		20,212
37	28	(a)	Preston N E	L 0-2			24,796
38	30	(a)	Norwich C	W 2-1	Murray, Shawcross		17,842
39	Apr 4	(h)	Newcastle U	W 3-1	Kevan (2), Murray		15,450
40	11	(a)	Huddersfield T	W 2-0	Pardoe, Murray		13,250
41	18	(h)	Leyton O	W 2-0	Murray, Kevan		15,144
42	25	(a)	Swansea T	D 3-3	Pardoe, Murray, Kevan		10,862

Appearances
Goals

League Division Two record: P 42   W 18   D 10   L 14   F 84   A 66   Pts 46   Pos 6th

FA Cup

2 Jan 4 (a) Swindon T   L 1-2

League Cup

2	Sep 25	(h)	Carlisle U	W 2-0
3	Oct 16	(a)	Hull C	W 3-0
4	Nov 27	(h)	Leeds U	W 3-1
5	Dec 17	(a)	Notts C	W 1-0
SF	Jan 15	(a)	Stoke C	L 0-2
SF	Feb 5	(h)	Stoke C	W 1-0

Lancashire Senior Cup

1	Nov 14	(a)	Morecambe	W 4-1
2	Jan 15	(a)	Chester	D 0-0
R	22	(h)	Chester	W 3-1
SF	Apr 13	(a)	Blackburn R	L 1-5

Manchester Senior Cup

F May 12 (h) Manchester U   L 3-5
(City's last season in this Cup)

Friendlies

1	Jan 25	(a)	Blackpool	L 1-4
2	Apr 15	(h)	International XI	W 5-4
3	27	(a)	International XI	L 4-5

148

#	Dowd	Kennedy	Sear	Cheetham	Oakes	Young	Gray	Murray	Kevan	Wagstaffe	Pardoe	Betts	Leivers	Aimson	Wood	Hannah	Chadwick	Gomersall	Ogley	Benson	Trautmann	Hayes	Cunliffe	Shawcross	Batty	Frost	McAlinden	Hodgkinson	Panter	#
1	1	3		6	7	8		10				2			5	9			4	11										1
2	1		5	6	7			10	11			2		9			8	4	3											2
3	1		5	6	7			10	11			2		9			8	4	3											3
4	1		5	6	7			10	11			2		9			8	4	3											4
5	1		5	6	7			10	11			2		9			8	4	3											5
6	1		5	6	7			10	11			2		9			8	4	3											6
7	1		3	5	6	7	4	10	11			2		9			8													7
8	1		3	5	6	7	4	10	11			2		9			8													8
9	1		3	5	6	7	4	10	11			2		9									8							9
10	1		3	5	6		4	10	11			2		9									8					7		10
11	1		3	4	6	7	8	10	11			2	5	9																11
12	1		3	5	6	7	4	9	11			2					8					10								12
13	1		3	5	6	7	4	9	11	8		2										10								13
14	1	4	3	5		7	8	10						9			2			6							11			14
15	1	4	3	5	6	11	8	10			7	2		9																15
16	1	4	3	5	6	11	8	10			7	2		9																16
17	1	4	3	5	6	11	8	9	10		7						2													17
18	1	4	3	5	6	7	8	9	10	11		2																		18
19	1	4	3		6	7	8	9	10	11		2	5																	19
20	1	4	3		6	7	8	9	10			2	5										11							20
21	1	4	3		6	7	8	9	10	11		2	5																	21
22	1	4	3		6	7	8	9	10	11		2	5																	22
23	1	4	3		6	7	8	9	10	11		2	5																	23
24	1	4	3		6	7	8	9	10	11		2	5																	24
25	1	4	3		6	7	8		9	11		2	5											10						25
26	1	4	3		6	7	8	10	11			2		9	5															26
27	1	4	3		6	7	8	10	11			2	5																9	27
28	1	4	3		6	7	9	10	11	8		2	5																	28
29		4		6		8		10	11	9		2	5					3			1					7				29
30		4	3	6		8		10	11	9		2	5								1					7				30
31	1		3	5	6	7	8	10	11	9		2								4										31
32	1		3	5	6		8	9	10	11	7	2								4										32
33	1		3	5	6	11	8	9	10		7	2								4										33
34	1	2	3	5	6		8	9	10	11	7									4										34
35		2	3	5	6	7	4	9	10	11	8								1											35
36		2	3	5	6	7	4	9	10	11	8								1											36
37		2			6	7	4	9	10	11	8							3	1						5					37
38		2	3		6	7	4	9		11	8								1					10	5					38
39		2	3	5	6	7	4	9	10	11	8								1											39
40		2	3	5	6	7	4	9	10	11	8								1											40
41		2	3	5	6	7	4	9	10	11	8								1											41
42		2	3	5	6	7	4	9	10	11	8										1									42
	32	26	35	27	41	37	37	19	40	35	20	18	15	14	11	9	8	7	7	6	3	3	3	2	2	2	1	1	1	
	1				3	5	8	21	30	3	2		4	2		1	1						1				1			

1964-65

1	Aug 22	(a)	Charlton A	L 1-2	Kevan	19,299
2	26	(h)	Leyton O	W 6-0	Murray (3), Oakes, Pardoe, Kevan	21,085
3	29	(h)	Northampton T	L 0-2		20,935
4	31	(a)	Leyton O	L 3-4	Gray, Pardoe, Kevan	11,512
5	Sep 5	(h)	Portsmouth	W 2-0	Murray, Kevan	16,527
6	9	(h)	Norwich C	L 0-2		16,191
7	12	(a)	Swindon T	W 1-0	Kevan	17,353
8	16	(a)	Norwich C	L 1-4	Gray	22,309
9	19	(h)	Derby C	W 2-0	Stobart, Kevan	16,214
10	26	(a)	Swansea T	L 0-3		10,862
11	Oct 3	(h)	Rotherham U	W 2-1	Gray, Kevan	15,211
12	10	(a)	Southampton	L 0-1		18,412
13	14	(h)	Newcastle U	W 3-0	Kevan, Young, Oakes	10,215
14	17	(h)	Huddersfield T	L 2-3	Kevan (2)	15,704
15	24	(a)	Coventry C	D 2-2	Young, opp.og	28,693
16	31	(h)	Cardiff C	W 2-0	Murray (2)	13,146
17	Nov 7	(a)	Preston N E	W 5-2	Kevan (3), Young (2)	19,374
18	14	(h)	Ipswich T	W 4-0	Murray (2), Kevan (2)	16,835
19	21	(a)	Plymouth A	L 2-3	Gray, Kevan	19,468
20	28	(h)	Bolton W	L 2-4	Ogden, Young	21,895
21	Dec 5	(a)	Middlesbrough	W 1-0	Kevan	13,873
22	19	(a)	Northampton T	L 0-2		12,665
23	26	(h)	Bury	D 0-0		22,299
24	28	(a)	Bury	W 2-0	Murray, Kevan	11,279
25	Jan 2	(a)	Portsmouth	D 1-1	Young	12,500
26	16	(h)	Swindon T	L 1-2	Oakes	8,015
27	30	(a)	Derby C	L 0-2		14,765
28	Feb 6	(h)	Swansea T	W 1-0	Murray	11,931
29	13	(a)	Rotherham U	D 0-0		10,917
30	20	(h)	Southampton	W 3-1	Young, Kennedy, Crossan	10,470
31	27	(a)	Huddersfield T	L 0-1		14,405
32	Mar 6	(h)	Middlesbrough	D 1-1	Ogden	14,231
33	12	(a)	Cardiff C	D 2-2	Connor, Gray	9,094
34	20	(h)	Preston N E	W 4-3	Murray (2), Connor, Crossan	12,884
35	27	(a)	Ipswich T	L 1-4	Crossan	12,709
36	Apr 3	(h)	Plymouth A	W 2-1	Ogden, Oakes	10,929
37	10	(a)	Bolton W	L 0-4		14,546
38	16	(a)	Crystal P	L 0-2		15,885
39	17	(h)	Coventry C	D 1-1	Connor	10,804
40	19	(a)	Crystal P	D 1-1	Pardoe	12,175
41	24	(a)	Newcastle U	D 0-0		33,259
42	28	(h)	Charlton A	W 2-1	Murray, Young	8,409

Appearances
Goals

League Division Two record: P 42 W 16 D 9 L 17 F 63 A 62 Pts 41 Pos 11th

FA Cup

3	Jan 9	(h)	Shrewsbury T	D 1-1		
R	13	(a)	Shrewsbury T	L 1-3		

League Cup

2	Sep 23	(h)	Mansfield T	L 3-5	

Lancashire Senior Cup

1	Nov 3	(a)	Everton	D 0-0	
R	17	(h)	Everton	L 0-2	

Friendlies

1	Aug 9	(a)*Stoke C	L 1-2
2	15	(h) Stoke C	W 3-0

*Played in the Isle of Man

150

Dowd	Ogley	Bacuzzi	Gomersall	Kennedy	Oakes	Connor	Kevan	Murray	Gray	Young	Crossan	Gratrix	Pardoe	Stobart	Wagstaffe	Cheetham	Batty	Wood	Ogden	Sear	Doyle	Shawcross	Hayes	
1		3	2	6	11	10	9	4					7	8		5								1
1	2	3		6	11	10	9	4					7	8		5								2
1	2	3		6	11	10	9	4					7	8		5								3
1	2	3		6	11	10	9	4					7	8		5								4
1	2	3		6	11	10	9	8						7				5			4			5
	1	2	3	6	11	10		8	9					7				5			4			6
	1	2	3	6	11	10	8	9						7		5					4			7
	1	2	3	6	11	10	8	9						7		5					4			8
	1	2	3	6		10	9	8				5	7	11							4			9
1		2	3	6		10	9	4	7			5	8	11										10
	1	2	3	4	6	10	9	8					7	11				5						11
	1	2	3	4	6	10	9	8		11		5	7											12
	1	2	3	4	6	10	9	8		11		5	7											13
	1	2	3	4	6	10	9	8		11		5	7											14
	1	2	3	4	6	10	9	8		11		5		7										15
	1	2	3	4	6	10	9	8		11		5		7										16
	1	2	3	4	6	10	9	8		11		5		7										17
	1	2	3	4	6	10	9			11		5	8	7										18
	1	2	3	4	6	10	9	8		11		5		7										19
	1	2	3	4	6	10		8		11		5		7					9					20
1		2		4	6	10	9	8		11				7				5		3				21
1		2		4	6	10	9	8		11				7				5		3				22
1		2		4	6	10	9	8		11			7					5		3				23
1		2		4	6	10	9	8		11			7					5		3				24
1		2		4	6	10	9	8		11			7					5		3				25
1		2		4	6	11	10	8				5	7						9	3				26
1		2		4	6	11	10	9				7	8	5						3				27
	1	2	3	4	6	7		9	10	11	8					5								28
	1	2	3		6	7		9	10	11	8			4		5								29
	1	2	3	4	10	7		9		11	8						6	5						30
	1	2	3	4	10			9		11	8						6	5					7	31
	1	2	3	4	6	7			10	11	8							5	9					32
1		2	3	4		7			10	11	8							5	9		6			33
1		2	3	4	6	7	8		10	11								5	9					34
1		2	3	4	6	7	8		10	11		5							9					35
1		2	3	4	10	7				11	8	5					6		9					36
1		2	3	4	10	7				11	8						6	5	9					37
1		2	3	5	6	7			10	11									9			4	8	38
	1	2	3	5	6	7			10	11	8								9			4		39
	1	2	3	5	6	7			10	11	8								9			4		40
	1	2	3	5	6	7			10	11	8								9			4		41
	1	2	3	5	6	7		9	10	11	8											4		42
21	21	41	29	38	41	24	27	30	27	31	16	15	14	14	14	11	10	9	9	7	6	5	2	
	1	4	3	18	13	5	8	3			3	1						3						

151

1965-66

1	Aug 21	(a)	Middlesbrough	D 1-1	Murray	17,982
2	25	(h)	Wolves	W 2-1	opp.og (2)	25,572
3	28	(h)	Bristol C	D 2-2	Brand, opp.og	19,349
4	30	(a)	Wolves	W 4-2	Doyle, Crossan, Murray, opp.og	22,799
5	Sep 4	(a)	Coventry C	D 3-3	Young (2), Murray	29,403
6	11	(h)	Carlisle U	W 2-1	Pardoe (2)	22,891
7	15	(a)	Norwich C	D 3-3	Pardoe (2), Crossan	16,381
8	18	(a)	Cardiff C	L 3-4	Murray, Pardoe, Gray	11,520
9	25	(h)	Derby C	W 1-0	Murray	20,834
10	Oct 2	(a)	Southampton	W 1-0	Young	21,504
11	9	(a)	Huddersfield T	D 0-0		31,876
12	16	(h)	Crystal P	W 3-1	Pardoe (2), Young	24,765
13	23	(a)	Preston N E	W 3-0	Young (2), Brand	25,117
14	27	(h)	Norwich C	D 0-0		34,091
15	30	(h)	Charlton A	D 0-0		23,102
16	Nov 6	(a)	Plymouth A	L 0-1		15,954
17	13	(h)	Portsmouth	W 3-1	Murray (2), Pardoe	22,106
18	20	(a)	Bolton W	L 0-1		22,968
19	27	(h)	Ipswich T	W 2-1	Crossan (2)	19,416
20	Dec 4	(a)	Birmingham C	L 1-3	Summerbee	10,442
21	11	(h)	Leyton O	W 5-0	Young (3), Summerbee, Crossan	16,202
22	18	(a)	Crystal P	W 2-0	Doyle (2)	12,847
23	Jan 1	(h)	Huddersfield T	W 2-0	Doyle, Crossan	47,171
24	8	(a)	Portsmouth	D 2-2	Doyle, Summerbee	17,352
25	12	(h)	Rotherham U	W 3-1	Doyle (2), Crossan	25,526
26	15	(h)	Preston N E	D 0-0		26,668
27	29	(h)	Middlesbrough	W 3-1	Summerbee (2), Young	25,278
28	Feb 5	(a)	Bristol C	D 1-1	Young	25,723
29	19	(h)	Coventry C	W 1-0	Crossan	40,190
30	26	(a)	Carlisle U	W 2-1	Summerbee, Pardoe	9,000
31	Mar 12	(h)	Cardiff C	D 2-2	Connor, Young	29,642
32	19	(a)	Derby C	W 2-1	Bell, Young	22,533
33	Apr 2	(h)	Plymouth A	D 1-1	Crossan	24,087
34	8	(h)	Bury	W 1-0	Summerbee	43,104
35	12	(a)	Bury	L 1-2	Summerbee	21,437
36	16	(h)	Bolton W	W 4-1	Kennedy, Sear, Crossan, Connor	29,459
37	23	(a)	Ipswich T	D 1-1	Crossan	15,995
38	30	(h)	Birmingham C	W 3-1	Bell, Young, Crossan	28,409
39	May 4	(a)	Rotherham U	W 1-0	Bell	11,376
40	7	(a)	Leyton O	D 2-2	Bell, opp.og	6,109
41	13	(a)	Charlton A	W 3-2	Oakes, Crossan, Connor	13,687
42	18	(h)	Southampton	D 0-0		34,653

Appearances
Sub Appnces
Goals

League Division Two record: P 42   W 22   D 15   L 5   F 76   A 44   Pts 59   Pos 1st

FA Cup

3	Jan 22	(a)	Blackpool	D 1-1
R	24	(h)	Blackpool	W 3-1
4	Feb 12	(h)	Grimsby T	W 2-0
5	Mar 5	(h)	Leicester C	D 2-2
R	9	(h)	Leicester C	W 1-0
6	26	(h)	Everton	D 0-0
R	29	(a)	Everton	D 0-0
2R	Apr 4	(n)	Everton	L 0-2

League Cup

2	Sep 22	(h)	Leicester C	W 3-1
3	Oct 13	(h)	Coventry C	L 2-3

Lancashire Senior Cup

1	Nov 2	(a)	Rochdale	L 0-1

Friendlies

1	Aug 7	(h)	Dundee	L 1-2
2	10	(a)	Walsall	D 1-1
3	14	(a)	Tranmere R	W 3-2
4	Oct 18	(a)	Coventry C	L 2-4
5	Dec 6	(h)	Moscow Dynamo	W 2-0

Dowd	Kennedy	Sear	Doyle	Heslop	Oakes	Summerbee	Crossan	Pardoe	Connor	Young	Brand	Horne	Bacuzzi	Murray	Cheetham	Bell	Ogley	Gray	Gomersall	Wood	
1			4		6	7	8		11		10		2	9	5				3		1
1			4		6	7	8	11	3		10		2	9	5						2
1			4		6	7	8	11	3		10		2	9	5						3
1	6	3	4		5	7*	8	10	11				2	9	12						4
1	5				6	7	8	10	3	11				9	2			4			5
1			4			7	8	9	3	11	10		2		5			6			6
1				5	6	7	8	9	3*	11	10		2		12			4			7
		3	4		6	7	8*	10		11			2	9	5		1	12			8
	2			5	6	7	8	10	3	11		4		9			1				9
1	2	3		5	6	7		10	12	11	8	4*		9							10
1	2	3		5	6	7	8	9		11	10				4						11
1	2	3		5	6	7	8	9		11	10				4						12
1	2	3*		5	6	7	8	9		11	10		12		4						13
1	2	3		5	6	7	8	9		11	10				4						14
1	2	3			6	7	8	9		11	10*				4			12		5	15
1	2	3		5	6	7	8	9	10	11					4						16
1	2			5	6	7	8	10		11		4	3	9							17
1	2			5	6	7	8	10		11		4	3	9							18
1	2			5	6	7*	8	12		11	10	4	3	9							19
1	2			5	6	7	8	10		11*	9	4	3					12			20
1	2	3	4	5	6	7	8	9	10	11											21
1	2	3	4	5	6	7	8	9	10	11											22
1	2	3	4	5	6	7	8	9	10	11											23
1	2	3	4	5	6	7	8	9	10	11											24
	2	3	4	5	6	7	8	9		11	10						1				25
	2		4*	5	6	7	8	9		11	10		3				1			12	26
1		3	4	5	6	7	8	9	10	11			2								27
1	2	3	4	5	6	7	8	9	10	11											28
1	2		4	5	6	7	8	9	10	11			3								29
1	2		4	5	6	7	8	9	10*	11			3		12						30
1	2		9	5	6	7	8	4	10	11		3									31
1	2			5	6	7	8	4	11	9		3				10					32
1	2		4	5	6	9	10	7	11			3				8					33
1	2			5	6	7	8	4	10		11	3				9					34
1	2	3		5	6	7	8	4	10	11						9					35
1	2	3	9	5	6	7	8	4	11							10					36
1	2	3		5	6	7	10	4	11	9						8					37
1	2			5	6	7	10	4	11	9		3				8					38
1	2			5	6	7	10	4	11	9		3				8					39
1	2			5	6	7		4	11	9	10	3				8					40
1	2			5	6	7	10	4	11	9		3				8					41
1	2		12	5	6	7	10	4	11*	9		3				8					42
38	35	19	19	34	41	42	40	40	29	35	17	15	15	11	12	11	4	3	1	1	
			1					1	1				1		3			3		1	
	1	1	7		1	8	13	9	3	14	2			7		4		1			

1966-67

#	Date			Opponent	Result	Scorers	Attendance
1	Aug 20	(a)	Southampton	D 1-1	Summerbee	19,900
2	24	(h)	Liverpool	W 2-1	Bell, Murray	50,320
3	27	(h)	Sunderland	W 1-0	Oakes	34,948
4	30	(a)	Liverpool	L 2-3	Murray, Gray	51,645
5	Sep 3	(a)	Aston Villa	L 0-3		15,118
6	7	(h)	West Ham U	L 1-4	Bell	31,079
7	10	(h)	Arsenal	D 1-1	Pardoe	27,948
8	17	(a)	Manchester U	L 0-1		62,500
9	24	(a)	Blackpool	W 1-0	Crossan	25,761
10	Oct 1	(h)	Chelsea	L 1-4	Young	31,989
11	8	(h)	Tottenham H	L 1-2	Summerbee	32,551
12	15	(a)	Newcastle U	L 0-2		16,510
13	29	(a)	Burnley	W 3-2	Crossan (2), Bell	25,996
14	Nov 5	(h)	Newcastle U	D 1-1	Young	26,137
15	12	(a)	Stoke C	W 1-0	Summerbee	27,803
16	19	(h)	Everton	W 1-0	Bell	39,572
17	26	(a)	Fulham	L 1-4	Young	14,579
18	Dec 3	(h)	Nottingham F	D 1-1	Kennedy	24,013
19	10	(a)	West Brom A	W 3-0	Pardoe, Jones, Crossan	16,908
20	17	(h)	Southampton	D 1-1	Bell	20,104
21	27	(a)	Sheffield W	L 0-1		34,005
22	31	(a)	Sunderland	L 0-1		28,826
23	Jan 2	(h)	Sheffield W	D 0-0		32,198
24	14	(a)	Arsenal	L 0-1		22,392
25	21	(h)	Manchester U	D 1-1	opp.og	63,000
26	Feb 4	(h)	Blackpool	W 1-0	Bell	27,840
27	11	(a)	Chelsea	D 0-0		28,633
28	25	(a)	Tottenham H	D 1-1	Connor	33,822
29	Mar 4	(h)	Burnley	W 1-0	Bell	32,692
30	18	(a)	Leeds U	D 0-0		34,366
31	24	(a)	Leicester C	L 1-3	Crossan	35,396
32	25	(h)	West Brom A	D 2-2	Hince (2)	22,780
33	28	(a)	Leicester C	L 1-2	Jones	17,361
34	Apr 1	(a)	Sheffield U	L 0-1		16,976
35	12	(h)	Stoke C	W 3-1	Bell (3)	22,714
36	19	(h)	Aston Villa	D 1-1	Summerbee	21,817
37	22	(h)	Fulham	W 3-0	Oakes, Bell, Crossan	22,752
38	29	(a)	Everton	D 1-1	Coleman	33,239
39	May 2	(a)	Nottingham F	L 0-2		32,000
40	6	(h)	Sheffield U	D 1-1	Crossan	21,267
41	8	(h)	Leeds U	W 2-1	Crossan, Young	24,316
42	13	(a)	West Ham U	D 1-1	Bell	17,186

Appearances
Sub Appnces
Goals

League Division One record: P 42   W 12   D 15   L 15   F 43   A 52   Pts 39   Pos 15th

FA Cup

3	Jan 28	(h)	Leicester C	W 2-1
4	Feb 18	(a)	Cardiff C	D 1-1
R	22	(h)	Cardiff C	W 3-1
5	Mar 11	(h)	Ipswich T	D 1-1
R	14	(a)	Ipswich T	W 3-0
6	Apr 8	(a)	Leeds U	L 0-1

League Cup

| 2 | Sep 14 | (h) | Bolton W | W 3-1 |
| 3 | Oct 5 | (a) | West Brom A | L 2-4 |

Lancashire Senior Cup

| 1 | Oct 24 | (a) | Barrow | L 2-5 |

Friendlies

1	Aug 6	(a)	Aberdeen	L 1-2
2	9	(a)	Walsall	L 1-2
3	15	(h)	Bolton W	D 0-0
4	Oct 24	(a)	Wigan A	W 4-0
5	Dec 7	(a)	Bath City	W 5-0
6	12	(a)	Altrincham	W 4-0
7	May 15	(a)	Crewe A	W 4-0
8	17	(a)	Stockport C	L 0-1

Tour (To West Germany and Belgium)

| 1 | May 21 | (a) | Eintracht B'wick | W 2-1 |
| 2 | 23 | (a) | Standard Liege | W 1-0 |

154

Dowd	Book	Pardoe	Horne	Heslop	Oakes	Summerbee	Bell	Crossan	Connor	Young	Kennedy	Ogley	Doyle	Murray	Coleman	Brand	Jones	Gray	Cheetham	Hince	No.
1	2	4		5	6	7	8		10	11	3			9							1
1	2	4		5	6	7	8	10		11	3			9							2
1	2	4		5	6	7*	8	10	12	11	3			9							3
1	2	4		5	6		8		7	11	3			9				10			4
1	2	4		5	6	7	8	10		11	3			9							5
1	2	4		5	6	9	8	10	7	11	3										6
1	2	9	4	5	6	7	8	10*	12	11	3										7
1	2	10	4	5	6	9	8		7	11	3*		12								8
1	2	9	4	5	6	7	8	10	3	11											9
1	2	9		5	6	7	8	10	3	11			4								10
1	2	3	4	5	6	7	8	10		11				9							11
1	2	3	4	5	6	7	8	10		11				9							12
1	2	3	4	5	6	7	8	10		11				9							13
1	2	3	4	5	6	7	8	10		11				9							14
1	2	3	4	5		7	8	10	9	11	6										15
1	2	3	4		6	9	8	10	7	11	5										16
1	2	3	4	5		9	8	10	7	11	6										17
	2	3	4	5			8	10	11	7	6	1					9				18
	2	3	4	5	6	7	8	10	11			1					9				19
	2	3	4	5	6	9	8	10	7			1					11				20
	2	3	4	5	6	9	8	10	7	11	8	1									21
	2		4	5	6	9	8	10	7	11	8	1	7								22
	2		4	5	6		8	10*	7	11	3	1			9			12			23
	2	3	4	5	6	7*	8	10		11	12	1			9						24
	2	3	4	5	6	7	8	9	11			1	10								25
	2	3	4	5	6	7	8	10		11		1			9						26
	2	3	4	5	6	7	8	10		11		1			9						27
	2	3	4	5	6		8	10	11	7		1			9						28
	2	3	4		6	7*	8	10	12	11	5	1			9						29
	2	3	4		6		8	10	11		5	1			9	7					30
	2	3	4		6		8	10	7	11	5	1			9						31
	2	3	4	5	6		8	10		11		1			9				7		32
	2*	3	4	5	6		8	10	7	11		1			9			12			33
		3	4		6		8	10	7			1	5		9	11			2		34
1	2	3	4	5	6	7	8	9	10						11						35
1	2	3	4	5	6	7	8	9	12	10*					11						36
1	2	3	12	5	6	7	8	9	10*				4		11						37
1	2	3		5	6	7	8	9	10				4		11						38
1	2	3		5	6	7	8	9	10				4		11						39
1	2	3		5	6	7	8	9	10				4		11						40
1	2	3		5	6	7	8	9	10				4		11						41
1	2	3		5	6	7	8	9*	10				4		11	12					42
25	41	40	29	37	39	32	42	38	20	38	20	17	14	10	9	3	4	2	1	1	
					1					4	1	2					1	1			
	2				2	4	12	8	1	4	1			2	1		2	1		2	

1967-68

1	Aug 19	(h)	Liverpool	D 0-0		49,343
2	23	(a)	Southampton	L 2-3	Bell, Coleman	23,675
3	26	(a)	Stoke C	L 0-3		22,426
4	30	(h)	Southampton	W 4-2	Bell (2), Young (2)	22,002
5	Sep 2	(h)	Nottingham F	W 2-0	Summerbee, Coleman	29,547
6	6	(h)	Newcastle U	W 2-0	Hince, Young	29,978
7	9	(a)	Coventry C	W 3-0	Hince, Bell, Summerbee	34,578
8	16	(h)	Sheffield U	W 5-2	Bowles (2), Summerbee, Young, Bell	31,922
9	23	(a)	Arsenal	L 0-1		41,567
10	30	(h)	Manchester U	L 1-2	Bell	62,942
11	Oct 7	(a)	Sunderland	L 0-1		27,885
12	14	(h)	Wolves	W 2-0	Young, Doyle	36,476
13	21	(a)	Fulham	W 4-2	Summerbee (2), Lee, Young	22,108
14	28	(h)	Leeds U	W 1-0	Bell	39,713
15	Nov 4	(a)	Everton	D 1-1	Connor	47,144
16	11	(h)	Leicester C	W 6-0	Young (2), Lee (2), Doyle, Oakes	29,039
17	18	(a)	West Ham U	W 3-2	Lee (2), Summerbee	25,595
18	25	(h)	Burnley	W 4-2	Coleman (2), Summerbee, Young	37,098
19	Dec 2	(a)	Sheffield W	D 1-1	Oakes	38,207
20	9	(h)	Tottenham H	W 4-1	Summerbee, Coleman, Young, Bell	35,792
21	16	(a)	Liverpool	D 1-1	Lee	53,268
22	23	(a)	Stoke C	W 4-2	Lee (2), Young, Coleman	40,121
23	26	(a)	West Brom A	L 2-3	Summerbee, Lee	44,897
24	30	(h)	West Brom A	L 0-2		45,754
25	Jan 6	(a)	Nottingham F	W 3-0	Summerbee, Young, Coleman	39,581
26	20	(a)	Sheffield U	W 3-0	Doyle, Bell, Lee	32,142
27	Feb 3	(h)	Arsenal	D 1-1	Lee	42,392
28	24	(h)	Sunderland	W 1-0	Lee	28,624
29	Mar 2	(a)	Burnley	W 1-0	Lee	23,486
30	9	(h)	Coventry C	W 3-1	Bell, Summerbee, Young	33,310
31	16	(h)	Fulham	W 5-1	Young (2), Summerbee, Bell, Lee	30,773
32	23	(a)	Leeds U	L 0-2		51,818
33	27	(a)	Manchester U	W 3-1	Heslop, Lee, Bell	63,400
34	Apr 6	(a)	Leicester C	L 0-1		24,925
35	12	(h)	Chelsea	W 1-0	Doyle	47,132
36	13	(h)	West Ham U	W 3-0	Young (2), Doyle	38,754
37	16	(a)	Chelsea	L 0-1		37,171
38	20	(a)	Wolves	D 0-0		39,622
39	27	(h)	Sheffield W	W 1-0	opp.og	32,999
40	29	(h)	Everton	W 2-0	Book, Coleman	37,776
41	May 4	(a)	Tottenham H	W 3-1	Bell (2), Summerbee	51,242
42	11	(a)	Newcastle U	W 4-2	Young (2), Summerbee, Lee	46,300

Appearances
Sub Appnces
Goals

League Division One record: P 42   W 26   D 6   L 10   F 86   A 43   Pts 58   Pos 1st

FA Cup

3	Jan 27	(h)	Reading	D 0-0	
R	31	(a)	Reading	W 7-0	
4	Feb 17	(h)	Leicester C	D 0-0	
R	19	(a)	Leicester C	L 3-4	

League Cup

2	Sep 13	(h)	Leicester C	W 4-0	
3	Oct 11	(h)	Blackpool	D 1-1	
R	18	(a)	Blackpool	W 2-0	
4	Nov 1	(a)	Fulham	L 2-3	

Lancashire Senior Cup

1	Nov 28	(a)	Oldham A	L 1-2	

Friendlies

1	Aug 7	(a)	Portsmouth	W 2-0	
2	11	(h)	Borussia Dortmund	W 4-0	
3	May 14	(h)	Bury	W 4-2	

Tour (to USA)

1	May 18	(a)	Dunfermline A	D 1-1	
2	19	(a)	Dunfermline A	D 1-1	
3	22	(a)	Rochester Lan.	W 4-0	
4	26	(a)	Atlanta Chiefs	L 2-3	
5	30	(a)	Borussia Dortmund	L 1-2	
6	Jun 2	(a)	Dunfermline A	D 0-0	
7	5	(a)	Dunfermline A	D 0-0	
8	9	(a)	Oakland Clippers	L 0-3	
9	15	(a)	Atlanta Chiefs	L 1-2	

Mulhearn	Book	Pardoe	Doyle	Heslop	Oakes	Lee	Bell	Summerbee	Young	Coleman	Connor	Dowd	Hince	Horne	Kennedy	Bowles	Cheetham	Jones	Ogley	Clay	#
	2	3		5	6		8	7	9	11	4							10	1		1
	2	3	10	5	6		8	7	9	11	4								1		2
	2	3	10	5	6		8	7		11	9	1				4					3
	2	3	12	5	6		8	9	10	11		1	7			4*					4
	2	3	4	5	6		8	9	10	11		1	7								5
	2	3	4	5	6		8	9	10	11		1	7								6
	2	3	4	5	6		8	9	10	11		1	7								7
	2	3	4	5	6		8	9	10			1	7*	11							8
	2	3	4	5	6		8	9	10	11	12	1	7*								9
1	2	3	4	5	6		8	9	10*	11				12		7					10
1	2	3		5	6		8	9	10	11				4		7					11
1	2	3	4	5	6	7	8	9	10	11*								12			12
1	2		4	5	6	7	8	9	10	11	3										13
1	2	3	4	5	6	7	8	9	10	11											14
1	2	3	4	5	6	7	8	9		11	10										15
1	2	3	4		6	7	8	9	10	11				5							16
1	2	3	4	5	6	7	8	9	10	11											17
1	2	3	4	5	6	7	8	9	10	11											18
1	2	3	4	5	6	7	8	9	10	11											19
1	2	3	4	5	6	7	8	9	10	11											20
1	2	3	4	5	6	7	8	9*	10	11				12							21
1	2	3	4	5	6	7	8	9	10	11											22
1	2	3		5	6	7		9	10	11*				4	8		12				23
1	2	3		5	6	7		9	10	11				4				8			24
1	2	3	4	5	6	7		9	10	11	8										25
1	2	3	4	5	6	7	8	9	10	11*	12										26
1	2	3	4	5	6	7	8	9	10	11											27
1	2	3	4	5	6	7	8			11	10						9				28
1	2	3	4	5	6	7	8	9	10	11											29
1	2	3	4	5	6*	7	8	9	10	11					12						30
1	2	3	4	5		7	8	9	10	11					6						31
1	2	3	4	5	6	7	8	9	10	11											32
1	2	3	4	5	6	7	8*	9	10	11	12										33
1	2	3	4	5	6	7		9	10	11	8										34
1	2	3	8	5	6	7		9	10	11					4						35
1	2	3	8	5	6	7		9	10	11					4						36
1	2	3	8	5	6	7		9	10		11				4						37
1	2	3	4	5	6	7	8	9	10		11										38
1	2	3	4	5	6	7	8	9	10	11											39
1	2	3	4	5	6	7	8	9	10	11											40
1	2	3	4	5	6	7	8	9	10	11											41
1	2	3	4	5	6	7	8	9	10	11											42
33	42	41	37	41	41	31	35	41	40	38	10	7	6	4	4	4	2	2	2	1	
			1								3		1	2	1					1	
	1		5	1	2	16	14	14	19	8	1		2			2					

1968-69

1	Aug	10	(a)	Liverpool	L 1-2	Young	51,236
2		14	(h)	Wolves	W 3-2	Summerbee (2), Lee	35,835
3		17	(h)	Manchester U	D 0-0		63,052
4		21	(a)	Leicester C	L 0-3		30,076
5		24	(a)	Q.P.R.	D 1-1	Doyle	19,716
6		27	(a)	Arsenal	L 1-4	Bell	40,767
7		31	(h)	Ipswich T	D 1-1	Bell	31,303
8	Sep	7	(a)	Stoke C	L 0-1		22,015
9		14	(h)	Southampton	D 1-1	Coleman	29,031
10		21	(a)	Sunderland	W 4-0	Lee (2), Bell, Summerbee	31,687
11		28	(h)	Leeds U	W 3-1	Bell (2), Young	46,431
12	Oct	5	(a)	Everton	L 0-2		55,649
13		9	(h)	Arsenal	D 1-1	Bell	33,830
14		12	(h)	Tottenham H	W 4-0	Lee (2), Connor, Coleman	38,019
15		19	(a)	Coventry C	D 1-1	opp.og	30,670
16		26	(h)	Nottingham F	D 3-3	Bell, Young, opp.og	32,937
17	Nov	2	(a)	Chelsea	L 0-2		40,700
18		9	(h)	Sheffield W	L 0-1		23,861
19		16	(a)	Newcastle U	L 0-1		36,400
20		23	(h)	West Brom A	W 5-1	Young (2), Bell (2), Doyle	24,667
21		30	(a)	West Ham U	L 1-2	Lee	33,082
22	Dec	7	(h)	Burnley	W 7-0	Bell (2), Young (2), Doyle, Lee, Coleman	31,009
23		14	(a)	Tottenham H	D 1-1	Lee	28,462
24		21	(h)	Coventry C	W 4-2	Young (2), Booth, opp.og	27,760
25		26	(h)	Everton	L 1-3	Bell	53,549
26	Jan	11	(h)	Chelsea	W 4-1	Owen (2), Lee, Young	35,606
27		18	(a)	Sheffield W	D 1-1	Young	33,074
28	Mar	4	(a)	Burnley	L 1-2	Bell	18,348
29		8	(a)	Manchester U	W 1-0	Summerbee	63,388
30		11	(a)	Ipswich T	L 1-2	Doyle	24,312
31		15	(h)	Q.P.R.	W 3-1	Lee, Young, Bowyer	28,869
32		24	(a)	Nottingham F	L 0-1		24,613
33		29	(h)	Stoke C	W 3-1	Bell, Owen, Doyle	27,337
34	Apr	4	(h)	Leicester C	W 2-0	Summerbee (2)	42,022
35		5	(a)	Leeds U	L 0-1		43,176
36		8	(a)	Wolves	L 1-3	Lee	28,533
37		12	(h)	Sunderland	W 1-0	Young	22,842
38		16	(a)	West Brom A	L 0-2		25,030
39		19	(a)	Southampton	L 0-3		26,254
40		30	(h)	West Ham U	D 1-1	Pardoe	31,846
41	May	5	(h)	Newcastle U	W 1-0	Young	20,108
42		12	(h)	Liverpool	W 1-0	Lee	28,309

Appearances
Sub Appnces
Goals

League Division One record: P 42   W 15   D 10   L 17   F 64   A 55   Pts 40   Pos 13th

FA Cup

3	Jan	4	(h)	Luton T	W 1-0
4		25	(a)	Newcastle U	D 0-0
R		29	(h)	Newcastle U	W 2-0
5	Feb	24	(a)	Blackburn R	W 4-1
6	Mar	1	(h)	Tottenham H	W 1-0
SF		22	(n)	Everton	W 1-0
F		26	(n)	Leicester C	W 1-0

League Cup

2	Sep	4	(a)	Huddersfield T	D 0-0
R		11	(h)	Huddersfield T	W 4-0
3		25	(a)	Blackpool	L 0-1

Lancashire Senior Cup

1	Oct	22	(h)	Morecambe	W 2-1
2	Dec	11	(a)	Bolton W	W 2-1
SF	Mar	10	(h)	Liverpool	L 0-1

Friendlies

1	Jul	27	(a)	Chester	D 4-4
2	Oct	31	(h)	Ajax A'dam	W 3-0
4	Dec	18	(a)	Crook T	W 6-1
5	Apr	1	(a)	Hull C	L 0-2
6		28	(a)	Bury	L 5-6
7	May	10	(a)	Bath City XI	D 5-5
8		16	(a)	Crewe A	W 5-2

Dowd	Connor	Book	Pardoe	Doyle	Booth	Oakes	Lee	Bell	Summerbee	Young	Coleman	Heslop	Owen	Mulhearn	Kennedy	Mann	Corrigan	Bowyer	Bowles	Towers	Mundy	Glennon	#
	2	3*	4		6	7	8	9	11	12	5	10		1									1
		3	4		6	7	8	9	11		5	10		1	2								2
		3	4		6	7	8	9	11		5	10		1	2								3
		3	4		6	7	8	9	10	11	5			1	2								4
	2	3	4		6	7	8	9	10	11	5			1									5
	2	3	4		6	7	9	8	10	11	5			1									6
	2	3	4		6	7	8	9	10	11	5			1									7
		3	4		6	7	8	9	10	11	5			1	2								8
		3	4		6	7	8	9		11	5	10		1	2								9
		3	4		6	7	8	9	10	11	5			1	2								10
	2	3	4		6	7	8	9	10	11	5			1									11
1	2	3	4		6	7	8	9	10	11	5												12
1	2	3	4	5	6	7	8	9	10	11													13
1	2	3	4	5	6	7	8	9	10	11													14
1	2	3	4	5	6	7	8	9	10	11													15
1	2	3	4	5	6	7	8	9	10	11													16
1		3	4	5	6	7	8	9		11			10		2								17
1		3	4	5	6	7	8	9	10	11*	12				2								18
1		3	4	5	6	7	8	9	10				12		2			11*					19
1	11	3	4	5	6	7	8	9	10						2								20
1	11	2	4	5	6	7	8	9	10							3							21
1	12	2	4	5	6	7	8	9*	10	11						3							22
1		2	4	5	6	7	8		10	11			9			3							23
1		2	4	5	6	7	8		10	11			9			3							24
1		2	4	5	6	7	8	9	10	11*			12			3							25
1	2	3	4	5	6	7	8*		10	11	12		9										26
1	2	3	4	5	6	8	7		10	11			9										27
1	2	3	4	5	6		8	7	10	11			9										28
1	2	3	4	5	6	9*	8		7	10	11		12										29
8	2	6	4	5					7	10	11*		9			3	1	12					30
1	2	3	4*	5	6	9	8		7	10			12										31
	2	3			6	4			7	10*	5		9				1	11	8		12		32
1	2	3	4	5	6		8	7		10			9					11					33
1	2	3	4	5	6	9	8		7	10	11*							12					34
11	2*	3	4	5	6	9	8		7	10							1			12			35
1	2	3	4	5	6	9	8		7	10	11												36
1	2	3	4		6	9	8		7	10	11*	5	12										37
1	4	2					7	9	5	8	11	6	10			3							38
1	2	3*	4	5			8	9	7	10	11		12						6				39
1		2	3	4	5	6	9	8	7	10	11												40
1		2	3	4	5	6			7	10	11	8									9		41
11	2	3	4	5	6	9	8		7	10							1						42
27	20	15	39	40	28	39	37	39	39	40	30	15	16	11	10	7	4	3	1	1	1	0	
	1										1	1	4			1		3	1		1	1	
	1		1	5	1		12	14	6	14	3		3				1						

159

1969-70

1	Aug	9	(h)	Sheffield W	W 4-1	Young (2), Bell, Lee	32,583
2		12	(a)	Liverpool	L 2-3	Bowyer, opp.og	51,959
3		16	(a)	Newcastle U	L 0-1		46,850
4		20	(h)	Liverpool	L 0-2		47,888
5		23	(h)	Everton	D 1-1	Bowyer	43,676
6		27	(a)	Sunderland	W 4-0	Bowyer (2), Oakes, Bell	21,515
7		30	(a)	Burnley	D 1-1	Bowyer	26,341
8	Sep	6	(h)	Chelsea	D 0-0		35,995
9		13	(a)	Tottenham H	W 3-0	Oakes, Bell, Bowyer	41,644
10		20	(h)	Coventry C	W 3-1	Bell (2), Lee	34,320
11		27	(a)	Stoke C	L 0-2		29,739
12	Oct	4	(h)	West Brom A	W 2-1	Bell, Young	34,329
13		8	(h)	Newcastle U	W 2-1	Young, Lee	32,172
14		11	(a)	Nottingham F	D 2-2	Lee (2)	30,037
15		18	(a)	Derby C	W 1-0	Lee	40,788
16		25	(h)	Wolves	W 1-0	Doyle	34,425
17	Nov	1	(a)	Ipswich T	D 1-1	Lee	24,124
18		8	(h)	Southampton	W 1-0	Bell	27,069
19		15	(a)	Manchester U	W 4-0	Bell (2), Young, opp.og	63,013
20		22	(a)	Arsenal	D 1-1	Bowyer	42,939
21		29	(h)	Leeds U	L 1-2	Lee	44,590
22	Dec	6	(a)	West Ham U	W 4-0	Bowyer (2), Lee, Doyle	27,440
23		13	(h)	Tottenham H	D 1-1	Oakes	29,216
24		20	(a)	Chelsea	L 1-3	Summerbee	34,791
25		23	(a)	Everton	L 0-1		51,864
26	Jan	6	(h)	Burnley	D 1-1	Lee	22,074
27		10	(a)	Coventry C	L 0-3		29,386
28		17	(h)	Stoke C	L 0-1		31,565
29		31	(a)	West Brom A	L 0-3		30,722
30	Feb	7	(h)	Nottingham F	D 1-1	Doyle	27,077
31		18	(h)	Arsenal	D 1-1	Bowyer	25,504
32		21	(a)	Wolves	W 3-1	Summerbee (2), Bell	30,373
33		28	(h)	Ipswich T	W 1-0	Lee	29,376
34	Mar	11	(h)	Crystal P	L 0-1		25,381
35		21	(h)	West Ham U	L 1-5	Lee	28,353
36		27	(h)	Derby C	L 0-1		42,316
37		28	(a)	Manchester U	W 2-1	Lee, Doyle	60,286
38	Apr	4	(h)	Sunderland	L 0-1		22,006
39		6	(a)	Crystal P	L 0-1		27,704
40		8	(a)	Southampton	D 0-0		24,384
41		18	(a)	Leeds U	W 3-1	Towers, Bell, Young	22,932
42		22	(a)	Sheffield U	W 2-1	Bowyer (2)	45,258

Appearances
Sub Appnces
Goals

League Division One record: P 42   W 16   D 11   L 15   F 55   A 48   Pts 43   Pos 10th

FA Cup

3	Jan	3	(a)	Hull C	W 1-0
4		24	(a)	Manchester U	L 0-3

League Cup

2	Sep	3	(a)	Southport	W 3-0
3		24	(h)	Liverpool	W 3-2
4	Oct	15	(h)	Everton	W 2-0
5		29	(h)	Q.P.R.	W 3-0
SF	Dec	3	(h)	Manchester U	W 2-1
SF		17	(a)	Manchester U	D 2-2
F	Mar	7	(n)	West Brom A	W 2-1

Lancashire Senior Cup

1	Sep	16	(a)	Chorley	W 2-1
2	Oct	21	(a)	Oldham A	D 1-1
R	Nov	3	(h)	Oldham A	D 1-1
2R	Jan	14	(a)	Oldham A	L 0-1

Friendlies

1	Jul	19	(a)	Caernarfon Select	D 1-1
2		26	(a)	Ajax A'dam	D 3-3
3	Apr	17	(a)	Birmingham C	W 3-2

Tour (to Australia)

(see opposite page)

Appearances (shirt numbers by match):

Corrigan	Book	Pardoe	Doyle	Booth	Oakes	Summerbee	Bell	Lee	Young	Bowyer	Bowles	Mann	Connor	Heslop	Mulhearn	Towers	Carrodus	Jeffries	Coleman	Glennon	Owen	Dowd	Donachie	Mundy	
1	2	3	4	5	6	7	8	9	10										11						1
1	2	3	4	5	6	7	8	9		10									11						2
1	2	3	4	5	6	7	8	9		10									11						3
1	2	3	4	5		7	8	9		10	6								11						4
1	2	3	4	5		7		9		10	6		8						11						5
1	2	3	4	5	6	7	8	9	10	11															6
1	2		4	5	6	7	8	9	10	11			3												7
1	2	3	4	5	6	7	8	9	10	11															8
1	2	3	4	5	6	7	8	9	10	11															9
1	2	3	4		6	7	8	9	10	11				5											10
1	2	3	4	5*	6	7		9	10	11					12					8					11
1	2	3	4	5	6	7	8	9*	10	11							12								12
1	2	3	4	5	6	7	8	9	10	11															13
1	2	3	4	5	6	7	8	9	10	11															14
1	2	3	4	5	6	7	8	9	10	11															15
1	2	3	4	5	6	7	8		10	11												9			16
1	2	3	4	5	6	7	8	9	10*	11							12								17
1	2	3	4	5	6	7	8	9		11				10											18
1	2	3	4	5	6	7	8	9	10	11															19
1	2	3	4	5	6	7	8	9	10	11															20
	2	3	4	5	6	7	8	9	10	11					1										21
1	2	3	4	5	6	7	8	9	10*	11		12													22
	2	3	4	5	6	7		9	10	11		8		1											23
1	2		4		6	7			10	11	8		3	5						9					24
1	2	8	4		6	7		9	10	11			3	5											25
1	2*	3	4	5	6	7	8	9		11	10		12												26
1		3	4	5	6	7	8	9		11	10	2													27
	2*	3	4	5	6	7	8	9	10	11	12			1											28
		3*	4	5	6		8	9	10	11	7		2		1		12								29
	2*		4	5	6		8	9	10	11	7	3			1								12		30
	2		4	5	6		8		10	11	9	3			1		7								31
1	2	11	4	5	6	9	8		10			3					7								32
1	2	11	4	5	6	9	8		10			3					7								33
1		11	9	4			8	10				3	2	5			7								34
1	2	11	4	5	6		8		10	9		3					7								35
1	2	11	4	5	6		8		10			3					7			9					36
1	2	11	4	5	6			9	10	8		3					7								37
1	2	8	4	5	6				10			3				7	11				9*		12		38
1	2	3	4	5	6	12				11				10		7					9*			8	39
1	2	3	4	5	6	9	8	10	11				7												40
	2	3	4	5	6		8		10	9		11	7									1			41
	2	3	4	5	6	9*			10	12		11	8	7										1	42
34	38	38	41	41	40	32	31	36	29	33	10	9	8	6	6	6	6	4	5	3	2	2	1	1	
								1				1	1		1	1					3			2	
			4			3	3	11	13	6	12				1										

Tour (to Australia)

1	May 10	(a)	Western Australia	D	1-1
2	13	(a)	South Australia	W	4-0
3	16	(a)	New South Wales	W	2-1
4	17	(a)	Queensland	W	3-0
5	24	(a)	Victoria	W	3-0
6	27	(a)	Northern NSW	W	4-1
7	30	(a)	New South Wales	W	4-0

161

1970-71

1	Aug	15	(a)	Southampton	D 1-1	Bell	24,599
2		19	(a)	Crystal P	W 1-0	Oakes	33.118
3		22	(h)	Burnley	D 0-0		36,599
4		26	(h)	Blackpool	W 2-0	Bell, Lee	37,598
5		29	(a)	Everton	W 1-0	Bell	50,724
6	Sep	5	(h)	West Brom A	W 4-1	Bell (2), Summerbee, Lee	30,549
7		12	(a)	Nottingham F	W 1-0	Doyle	28,896
8		19	(h)	Stoke C	W 4-1	Book, Lee, Young, opp.og	35,473
9		26	(a)	Tottenham H	L 0-2		42,490
10	Oct	3	(h)	Newcastle U	D 1-1	Doyle	33,159
11		10	(a)	Chelsea	D 1-1	Bell	51,903
12		17	(h)	Southampton	D 1-1	Lee	31,998
13		24	(a)	Wolves	L 0-3		32,700
14		31	(h)	Ipswich T	W 2-0	Bell, Lee	27,317
15	Nov	7	(a)	Coventry C	L 1-2	Bell	25,287
16		14	(h)	Derby C	D 1-1	Bell	31,817
17		21	(h)	West Ham U	W 2-0	Lee (2)	28,485
18		28	(a)	Leeds U	L 0-1		43,511
19	Dec	5	(h)	Arsenal	L 0-2		33,027
20		12	(a)	Manchester U	W 4-1	Lee (3), Doyle	52,636
21		19	(a)	Burnley	W 4-0	Bell (2), Summerbee, Lee	19,917
22		26	(h)	Huddersfield T	D 1-1	Bell	40,091
23	Jan	9	(h)	Crystal P	W 1-0	Book	27,442
24		12	(a)	Liverpool	D 0-0		45,985
25		16	(a)	Blackpool	D 3-3	Summerbee (2), Bell	29,356
26		30	(h)	Leeds U	L 0-2		43,517
27	Feb	6	(a)	Arsenal	L 0-1		46,122
28		20	(a)	West Ham U	D 0-0		30,168
29		26	(a)	Ipswich T	L 0-2		20,685
30	Mar	6	(h)	Wolves	D 0-0		24,663
31		13	(a)	Derby C	D 0-0		31,987
32		20	(h)	Coventry C	D 1-1	Lee	22,120
33		27	(a)	West Brom A	D 0-0		20,100
34	Apr	3	(h)	Everton	W 3-0	Doyle, Booth, Hill	26,885
35		9	(h)	Nottingham F	L 1-3	Doyle	33,772
36		10	(a)	Huddersfield T	L 0-1		21,992
37		12	(a)	Newcastle U	D 0-0		29,040
38		17	(h)	Chelsea	D 1-1	Lee	26,120
39		24	(a)	Stoke C	L 0-2		14,836
40		26	(h)	Liverpool	D 2-2	Carter, opp.og	17,975
41	May	1	(h)	Tottenham H	L 0-1		19,674
42		5	(h)	Manchester C	L 3-4	Mellor, Lee, Hill	43,636

Appearances
Sub Appnces
Goals

League Division One record: P 42 W 12 D 17 L 13 F 47 A 42 Pts 41 Pos 11th

FA Cup

3	Jan	2	(h)	Wigan A	W 1-0
4		23	(a)	Chelsea	W 3-0
5	Feb	17	(h)	Arsenal	L 1-2

League Cup

2	Sep	9	(a)	Carlisle U	L 1-2

Lancashire Senior Cup

2	Oct	19	(h)	Bolton W	W 2-1
3	Dec	1	(a)	Oldham A	D 1-1
R	Jan	2	(a)	Oldham A	L 1-4

Friendlies

1	Aug	1	(a)	Oxford U	L 1-4
2		4	(a)	Celtic	D 0-0
3		8	(a)	Bury	W 5-4
4	Nov	10	(a)	Manchester U	W 3-0
5		18	(a)	Anderlecht	L 0-1
6		25	(h)	Australian Tourists	W 2-0
7	Dec	2	(a)	International XI	W 7-5

Corrigan	Book	Pardoe	Doyle	Booth	Oakes	Summerbee	Bell	Lee	Young	Towers	Hill	Heslop	Jeffries	Mann	Connor	Donachie	Healey	Bowyer	Carrodus	Mellor	Johnson	Carter	White	Brennan	
1	2	3	4		6	9	8	10		7	11	5													1
1	2	3	4		6	9	8	10		7	11	5													2
1	2	3	4		6	9	8	10		7	11	5													3
1	2	3	4	5	6	7	8	9	10	11															4
1	2	3	4	5	6	7	8	9	10	11															5
1	2	3	4	5	6	7	8	9	10	11															6
1	2	3	4	5	6	7	8	9	10	11															7
1	2	3	4	5	6	7*	8	9	10	11			12												8
1	2	3	4		6	7	8	9*	10	11		5						12							9
1		3	4		6	7	8	9		11	10*	5	12	2											10
1	2	3	4		6	7	8	9		11	10	5													11
1	2	3	4		6	7	8	9		11	10	5													12
1	2	3	4			7	8	9		11	10	5	6												13
1	2	3	4		6	7	8	9		11	10	5													14
1		3	4		6		8	9		11	10	5		2					7						15
1	2		4		6	7	8	9		11	10	5		3											16
1	2*	3	4		6	7	8	9		11		5	12	10											17
1	2	3	4		6	7	8	9		10		5		11											18
1	2	3	4		6	7	8	9		12		5*	11	10											19
1	2	3*	4	5	6	7	8	9	10	11			12												20
1	2		4	5	6	7	8	9	10	11						3									21
1	2		4	5*	6	7	8	9	10	11						3		12							22
1	2		4	5	6	9	8		10*	11						3			7						23
1	2		4	5	6	9	8			10			11			3		12	7*						24
1	2		4	5	6	7	8	9*	10				11			3		12							25
1	2		4	5	6		8	9			7		11			3		12	10*						26
1			4	5	6		8	9		10	7		2			3				11					27
1	2		4	5	6			9	10	3	8	7								11					28
	2		4	5	6			9	10	3	11	7					1	8							29
1	2		4	5	6	7		9	10	3			11					12	8*						30
	2*		4	5	6	7	8	9	10	3		11					1							12	31
			4	5			8	9	10	3		7		2	6		1			11					32
			4	5			8	9	10	3	12	7		2	6		1			11*					33
			4	5			8	9	10	3*	11	7		2	6		1			12					34
	12		4	5			8	9	10	3	11	7*		2	6		1								35
1	2		4	5			8	9	10	7	11*		12	3	6										36
1		4*	5				8			2		11	3	6					9	7	10		12		37
1	2			5			9	10	4*	12		11	3	6					7	8					38
1	2			5			9	10	4	8		11	3	6					7						39
				5*				2		4		10		3	1	9	7	12	8	11	6				40
	2						9	10	4	8	5		3	6	1	11*			7	12					41
	2						9	10	4	11	5		3	6	1				8	7					42
33	33	19	37	26	30	26	34	38	24	33	20	19	18	16	11	11	9	6	5	5	4	4	1	0	
1											1	3	1	2	2	1		3	1	1	1	1		2	
2		5	1	1	4	13	14	1		2															

1971-72

#	Date		Opponent	Result	Scorers	Attendance
1	Aug 14	(h)	Leeds U	L 0-1		38,566
2	18	(h)	Crystal P	W 4-0	Lee (2), Davies, Booth	27,103
3	21	(a)	Chelsea	D 2-2	Lee (2)	38,425
4	24	(a)	Wolves	L 1-2	Lee	26,663
5	28	(h)	Tottenham H	W 4-0	Bell, Summerbee, Davies, Lee	36,483
6	Sep 1	(h)	Liverpool	W 1-0	Mellor	45,144
7	4	(a)	Leicester C	D 0-0		25,238
8	11	(h)	Newcastle U	W 2-1	Bell, Lee	32,710
9	18	(a)	Nottingham F	D 2-2	Davies, Lee	21,488
10	25	(h)	Southampton	W 3-0	Bell, Davies, Lee	27,897
11	Oct 2	(a)	West Brom A	W 2-0	Lee, Connor	25,834
12	9	(h)	Everton	W 1-0	Lee	33,538
13	16	(a)	Leeds U	L 0-3		36,004
14	23	(h)	Sheffield U	W 2-1	Doyle, Lee	41,688
15	30	(a)	Huddersfield T	D 1-1	Carter	20,153
16	Nov 6	(h)	Manchester U	D 3-3	Summerbee, Bell, Lee	63,326
17	13	(a)	Arsenal	W 2-1	Mellor, Bell	47,443
18	20	(a)	West Ham U	W 2-0	Davies, Lee	33,694
19	27	(h)	Coventry C	W 4-0	Bell (2), Lee (2)	31,003
20	Dec 4	(a)	Derby C	L 1-3	Lee	35,354
21	11	(h)	Ipswich T	W 4-0	Bell, Davies, Lee, Mellor	26,900
22	18	(h)	Leicester C	D 1-1	Lee	29,524
23	27	(a)	Stoke C	W 3-1	Book, Lee, Towers	43,007
24	Jan 1	(h)	Nottingham F	D 2-2	Davies, Lee	38,777
25	8	(a)	Tottenham H	D 1-1	Davies	36,470
26	22	(a)	Crystal P	W 2-1	Lee, opp.og	31,480
27	29	(h)	Wolves	W 5-2	Lee (3), Booth, Towers	37,639
28	Feb 12	(a)	Sheffield U	D 3-3	Lee (2), Bell	38,184
29	19	(h)	Huddersfield T	W 1-0	Booth	36,421
30	26	(a)	Liverpool	L 0-3		50,074
31	Mar 1	(h)	West Brom A	W 2-0	Bell (2)	25,677
32	4	(h)	Arsenal	W 2-0	Lee (2)	44,213
33	11	(a)	Everton	W 2-1	Hill, opp.og	44,646
34	18	(h)	Chelsea	W 1-0	Booth	53,322
35	25	(a)	Newcastle U	D 0-0		37,460
36	Apr 1	(h)	Stoke C	L 1-2	Lee	49,392
37	3	(a)	Southampton	L 0-2		27,374
38	8	(h)	West Ham U	W 3-1	Marsh (2), Bell	38,491
39	12	(a)	Manchester U	W 3-1	Lee (2), Marsh	56,000
40	15	(a)	Coventry C	D 1-1	Towers	34,225
41	18	(a)	Ipswich T	L 1-2	Summerbee	24,365
42	22	(h)	Derby C	W 2-0	Lee, Marsh	55,026

Appearances
Sub Appnces
Goals

League Division One record: P 42   W 23   D 11   L 8   F 77   A 45   Pts 57   Pos 4th

FA Cup

| 3 | Jan 15 | (h) | Middlesbrough | D 1-1 |
| R | 18 | (a) | Middlesbrough | L 0-1 |

League Cup

| 2 | Sep 8 | (h) | Wolves | W 4-3 |
| 3 | Oct 5 | (a) | Bolton W | L 0-3 |

Lancashire Senior Cup

| 1 | Sep 20 | (a) | Wigan A | L 0-2 |

Friendlies

1	Jul 28	(a)	Chester	W 4-0
2	31	(a)	Port Vale	W 1-0
3	Aug 9	(a)	Doncaster R	W 2-0
4	Sep 21	(h)	Hertha BSC	D 1-1
5	Nov 15	(a)	Preston N E	W 3-2
6	Dec 15	(a)	Floriania	D 0-0
7	Apr 26	(a)	Olympiakos	D 0-0
8	May 1	(a)	Altrincham	W 1-0
9	3	(h)	Manchester U	L 1-3
10	5	(a)	Oxford U	W 3-2

Tour (to West Germany)

| 1 | Aug 3 | (a) | Hertha BSC | L 0-1 |
| 2 | 4 | (a) | Arm. Bielefeld | L 0-1 |

Corrigan	Book	Donachie	Doyle	Booth	Oakes	Summerbee	Bell	Davies	Lee	Mellor	Towers	Jeffries	Connor	Heslop	Healey	Marsh	Hill	Young	Carter	Johnson	Henson	
1	2		4	5	6	7*		9	10	11			3	8			12					1
1	2		4	5	6			9	10	11			3	8			7					2
1	2*	12	4	5	6			9	10	11			3	8			7					3
1			4	5	6	7		9	10	11		2	3	8								4
1		12	4*	5		7	6	9	10	11		2	3	8								5
1	2		4	5		7	6	9	10	11	12		3*	8								6
1	2		4	5		7	6	9	10	11			3	8								7
1	2	3	4	5		7	6	9	10	11				8								8
1	2	3	4	5		7	6	9	10	11				8								9
1	2	3	4	5		7	6*	9	10	11				8			12					10
1	2	3	4	5		7		9	10	11	6	8										11
1	2	8	4	5		7			10	11	6	12	3*					9				12
1	2	3	4	5		7		9	10*	11	6			8			12					13
1	2	3	4	5	6	7	8	9	10	11												14
1	2	3	4	5	6	7	8	9	10	11*								12				15
1	2	3	4	5	6	7	8	9	10	11												16
1	2	3	4*	5	6	7	8	9	10	11			12									17
1	2	3	4	5	6	7	8	9	10	11												18
1	2	3	4	5	6	7	8	9	10	11												19
1	2	3	4	5	6	7	8	9	10	11												20
1	2	3	4	5	6	7	8	9	10	11												21
1	2	3	4	5	6	7	8	9	10	11												22
1	2	3	4	5	6	7	8	9	10		11											23
1	2	3	4	5	6	7	8	9	10		11											24
1	2	3	4	5	6	7	8	9	10		11											25
1	2	3	4	5	6	7	8*	9	10		11								12			26
1	2	3	4	5	6	7*	8	9	10		11			12								27
1	2	3	4	5	6	7	8	9	10		11											28
1	2	3	4	5	6	7		9	10		11			8								29
1	2	3	4	5	6	7		9	10		11			8								30
1	2	3	4	5*	6	7	8	9	10		11			12								31
1	2	3	4		6	7	8	9	10		11						5					32
1	2	3	4		6	7	8	9	10	12	11						5*					33
1	2	3	4	5	6	7	8	9	10							12	11*					34
	2	3	4	5	6	7	8	9	10						1	11						35
	2	3	4	5	6	7	8	9	10						1	11						36
	2	3	4	5	6	11*	8	9	7		12				1	10						37
	2	3		5	6	11	8	9	7		4				1	10						38
	2	3	4*	5	6	7	8	9	10	11					1	12						39
	2	3	4	5	6	7	8	9	10	11					1							40
	2	3	4	5	12	7	8	9*	6	11					1	10						41
1	2	3	4	5			9	8	7	11	6					10						42
35	40	35	41	40	31	40	33	40	42	21	19	9	8	7	7	7	4	3	0	0	0	
	2			1							1	2	3			1	2	2	1	1	1	
		1		1	4		3	12	8	33	3	3		1		4	1		1			

165

1972-73

1	Aug 12	(a)	Liverpool	L 0-2		55,383
2	16	(h)	Everton	L 0-1		38,676
3	19	(h)	Norwich C	W 3-0	Lee (2), Bell	31,171
4	23	(a)	Derby C	L 0-1		31,173
5	26	(a)	Chelsea	L 1-2	Mellor	30,845
6	29	(a)	Crystal P	L 0-1		24,731
7	Sep 2	(h)	Leicester C	W 1-0	Marsh	27,233
8	9	(a)	Birmingham C	L 1-4	Towers	32,983
9	16	(h)	Tottenham H	W 2-1	Marsh (2)	31,755
10	23	(a)	Stoke C	L 1-5	Lee	26,448
11	30	(h)	West Brom A	W 2-1	Booth, Lee	27,332
12	Oct 7	(h)	Wolves	D 1-1	Marsh	31,201
13	14	(a)	Coventry C	L 2-3	Summerbee, Marsh	24,560
14	21	(h)	West ham U	W 4-3	Marsh (2), Summerbee, Towers	30,890
15	28	(a)	Arsenal	D 0-0		45,536
16	Nov 4	(h)	Derby C	W 4-0	Bell, Marsh, Carrodus, opp.og	35,829
17	11	(a)	Everton	W 3-2	Lee (2), opp.og	32,924
18	18	(h)	Manchester U	W 3-0	Bell (2), opp.og	52,050
19	25	(a)	Leeds U	L 0-3		39,879
20	Dec 2	(h)	Ipswich T	D 1-1	Lee	27,839
21	9	(a)	Sheffield U	D 1-1	Bell	19,208
22	16	(h)	Southampton	W 2-1	Marsh (2)	24,825
23	23	(a)	Newcastle U	L 1-2	Mellor	28,249
24	26	(h)	Stoke C	D 1-1	Mellor	36,334
25	30	(a)	Norwich C	D 1-1	Towers	24,203
26	Jan 20	(a)	Leicester C	D 1-1	Bell	18,761
27	27	(h)	Birmingham C	W 1-0	Donachie	31,882
28	Feb 10	(a)	Tottenham H	W 3-2	Lee (2), Marsh	30,944
29	17	(h)	Liverpool	D 1-1	Booth	41,709
30	Mar 3	(a)	Wolves	L 1-5	Marsh	25,047
31	6	(a)	Southampton	D 1-1	Lee	16,188
32	10	(h)	Coventry C	L 1-2	Booth	30,448
33	17	(a)	West ham U	L 1-2	Doyle	30,156
34	24	(h)	Arsenal	L 1-2	Booth	32,031
35	27	(h)	Chelsea	L 0-1		23,973
36	31	(h)	Leeds U	W 1-0	Towers	35,772
37	Apr 7	(a)	Ipswich T	D 1-1	Oakes	19,109
38	14	(h)	Sheffield U	W 3-1	Bell, Marsh, Lee	26,811
39	18	(h)	Newcastle U	W 2-0	Booth, Marsh	25,156
40	21	(a)	Manchester U	D 0-0		61,500
41	25	(a)	West Brom A	W 2-1	Lee, Towers	21,193
42	28	(h)	Crystal P	L 2-3	Lee (2)	34,784

Appearances
Sub Appnces
Goals

League Division One record: P 42   W 15   D 11   L 16   F 57   A 60   Pts 41   Pos 11th

FA Cup

3	Jan 13	(h)	Stoke C	W 3-2
4	Feb 3	(a)	Liverpool	D 0-0
R	7	(h)	Liverpool	W 2-0
5	24	(h)	Sunderland	D 2-2
R	27	(a)	Sunderland	L 1-3

League Cup

2	Sep 6	(h)	Rochdale	W 4-0
3	Oct 3	(a)	Bury	L 0-2

Lancashire Senior Cup

2	Oct 16	(a)	Rochdale	D 1-1
R	Nov 8	(h)	Rochdale	L 2-4

Friendlies

1	Jul 31	(a)	Bradford C	W 5-0
2	Aug 1	(a)	Bury	W 2-0
3	7	(a)	Swansea C	W 2-0
4	Nov 28	(a)	Doncaster R XI	L 3-4
5	Dec 12	(a)	Q.P.R.	W 1-0
6	Apr 9	(a)	Oldham A	W 4-1
7	May 2	(a)	Plymouth A	D 2-2

Tours (to Sweden and Greece)

1	Jul 18	(a)	Hammarby IF	D 3-3
2	20	(a)	Hull C*	W 1-0
3	23	(a)	Partick T*	W 5-0
4	27	(a)	Ope IF	W 8-0
5	May 8	(a)	Olympiakos	L 1-2
6	15	(a)	Olympiakos	D 0-0

*played in Sweden

Corrigan	Book	Donachie	Doyle	Booth	Jeffries	Summerbee	Bell	Marsh	Lee	Towers	Barrett	Oakes	Healey	Mellor	Pardoe	Carrodus	Hill	Davies	Whelan	Brennan	No.
1	2	3	4	5		7	6	10	8	11								9			1
1	2	3	4	5	12	7	6	10*	8	11								9			2
1		3	4	5	11	7	8		10	6	2			12				9*			3
1	12	3	4	5	11	7	8		10*	6	2			9							4
1		3	4	5	11	7	8		10	6	2			9							5
1		2	4	5	11	7	8	10	9	6	2										6
1	2	3		5	4	7	8	10		6				11				9			7
1		3	4	5	2	7	8	11	10	6				12				9*			8
		3	4	5	2	7	8*	9	10	11		6	1				12				9
1		3	4	5	2*		8	9	10	11		6				7	12				10
	2	3		5		7	8	9	10	4	12	6*	1	11							11
	2	3	4*	5			8	9	10			6	1	11		7			12		12
	2	3	12	5	6	7	8	9	10	4			1	11*							13
	2	3	4	5	6	7	8	9	10	11			1								14
1	2	3	4	5	6	7	8	9	10					11							15
1		3	4		6	7	8	9	10		5			11		2					16
1	2	3	4		6	7	8	9	10		5			11							17
1	2	3	4		6	7	8	9	10	11	5										18
1	2	3	4		6	7	8	9	10	11	5										19
1	2	3	4		6		8	9	10	11	5					7*	12				20
1	2	3	4		6	7	8	9	10	11	5										21
1	2	3	4*		6	7	8	9	10	11	5						12				22
1		3	4	5	6	7	8	9		11				10		2					23
1			4	5	2	7		9		11		6		10	3	8					24
1			4	5	2	7		9		11		6		10	3	8					25
1	2	3	12	5	6	7	8	9	10	4				11*							26
1	2	3	4	5	6	7	8	9	10	11											27
1	2	3	4	5	6	7	8	9	10	11											28
1	2	3	4	5	6	7	8	9	10	11											29
1	2	3	4	5	6		8	9		11				7					10		30
1		3	4	5	6	7	8	9	10	11						2					31
1		3	4*	5	6	7	8	9	10	11						2	12				32
1	2	3	4	5	6*	7	8		10	11						12		9			33
1	2	3	4	5	6	7	8	9		11									10		34
1	2	3	4	5	6	7		9		11						8			10		35
	2	3	4	5		7	8	9	10	11		6	1								36
	2	3	4	5	10	7	8		9	11		6	1								37
	2	3	4	5		7	8	9	10	11		6	1								38
	2	3	4	5		7*	8	9	10	11		6	1			12					39
	2	3	4	5		7	8	9	10	11		6	1								40
	2	3	4	5		7*	8	9	10	11		6	1			12					41
	2	3	4		5	7	8	9	10	11		6	1								42
30	29	40	38	34	33	38	39	37	35	35	14	13	12	10	6	6	4	5	3	1	
	1		2		1						1	1		2	4	2			1		
		1	1	5		2	7	14	14	5		1		3	1						

167

1973-74

1	Aug	25	(h)	Birmingham C	W 3-1	Law (2), Bell	34,178
2		29	(a)	Derby C	L 0-1		31,295
3	Sep	1	(a)	Stoke C	D 1-1	Law	22,434
4		5	(h)	Coventry C	W 1-0	Marsh	30,931
5		8	(h)	Norwich C	W 2-1	Bell, Lee	31,209
6		11	(a)	Coventry C	L 1-2	Marsh	27,394
7		15	(a)	Leicester C	D 1-1	Bell	28,466
8		22	(h)	Chelsea	W 3-2	Lee (2), Towers	32,118
9		29	(a)	Burnley	L 0-3		24,492
10	Oct	6	(h)	Southampton	D 1-1	Marsh	27,727
11		13	(a)	Newcastle U	L 0-1		35,225
12		20	(a)	Sheffield U	W 2-1	Law, opp.og	25,234
13		27	(h)	Leeds u	L 0-1		45,346
14	Nov	3	(a)	Wolves	D 0-0		21,499
15		10	(h)	Arsenal	L 1-2	Lee	31,041
16		17	(h)	Q.P.R.	W 1-0	Lee	30,486
17		24	(a)	Ipswich T	L 1-2	Leman	19,143
18	Dec	8	(a)	West Ham U	L 1-2	Lee	20,790
19		15	(a)	Tottenham H	W 2-0	Bell, Booth	17,066
20		22	(h)	Burnley	W 2-0	Doyle, Bell	28,114
21		26	(a)	Everton	L 0-2		36,007
22		29	(a)	Norwich C	D 1-1	Law	24,303
23	Jan	1	(h)	Stoke C	D 0-0		35,009
24		12	(h)	Leicester C	W 2-0	Marsh, Law	27,488
25		19	(a)	Birmingham C	D 1-1	Law	31,401
26	Feb	2	(h)	Tottenham H	D 0-0		24,652
27		6	(h)	Derby C	W 1-0	Bell	22,845
28		9	(a)	Chelsea	L 0-1		20,206
29		23	(a)	Southampton	W 2-0	Law, Marsh	19,234
30	Mar	9	(a)	Leeds U	L 0-1		36,578
31		13	(h)	Manchester U	D 0-0		51,331
32		16	(h)	Sheffield U	L 0-1		26,220
33		23	(a)	Arsenal	L 0-2		25,319
34		27	(h)	Newcastle U	W 2-1	Lee (2)	21,590
35		30	(h)	Wolves	D 1-1	Lee	25,236
36	Apr	2	(h)	Everton	D 1-1	Tueart	22,918
37		6	(h)	Ipswich T	L 1-3	Summerbee	22,269
38		9	(a)	Q.P.R.	L 0-3		20,461
39		12	(h)	Liverpool	D 1-1	Lee	43,248
40		16	(a)	Liverpool	L 0-4		50,781
41		20	(h)	West Ham U	W 2-1	Booth, Bell	29,700
42		27	(a)	Manchester U	W 1-0	Law	56,966

Appearances
Sub Appnces
Goals

League Division One record: P 42   W 14   D 12   L 16   F 39   A 46   Pts 40   Pos 14th

FA Cup

3	Jan	5	(a)	Oxford U	W 5-2
4		26	(a)	Notts C	L 1-4

League Cup

2	Oct	2	(a)	Walsall	D 0-0
R		22	(h)	Walsall	D 0-0
2R		30	(n)	Walsall	W 4-0
3	Nov	6	(a)	Carlisle U	W 1-0
4		21	(a)	York C	D 0-0
R	Dec	5	(h)	York C	W 4-1
5		19	(a)	Coventry C	D 2-2
R	Jan	16	(h)	Coventry C	W 4-2

League Cup (cont)

SF	Jan	23	(a)	Plymouth A	D 1-1
SF		30	(h)	Plymouth A	W 2-0
F	Mar	3	(n)	Wolves	L 1-2

Lancashire Senior Cup

2	Oct	30	(a)	Oldham A	W 2-1
3	Jan	8	(a)	Bury	W 3-1
SF	Apr	30	(a)	Bolton W	W 3-1
F	May	11	(n)	Morecambe	W 3-0

(played at Burnden Park)

This was Manchester City's last
season in the Lancashire Senior Cup

168

MacRae	Pardoe	Donachie	Doyle	Booth	Oakes	Summerbee	Bell	Marsh	Law	Lee	Towers	Barrett	Carrodus	Corrigan	Leman	Tueart	Horswill	Book	Healey	Daniels	Lester	Henson	Whelan	#
		3	4	5	6	7	8	11	9	10			12	1				2*						1
	2	3	4	5	6	7	8	11	9	10				1										2
	2	3	4	5	6	7	8	11	9	10*			12	1										3
	2	3	4	5	6*	7	8	11	9	12			10	1										4
	2	3	4	5		7	8	11	9*	10	6		12	1										5
	2	3	4	5		7	8	11		10	6		9	1										6
		3	4	5	6	7	8	11		10	9			1		2								7
		3	4	5	6	7	8	9		10	11			1		2								8
		3	4	5	6	7	8	9		10	11			1		2								9
	2	3	4*	5	6	7	8	9			11				10	1						12		10
	2	3	4	5	6	7	8	12	9	10	11*						1							11
1	2	3	4	5	6	7	8	11	9	10														12
1	2	3	4	5	6	7	8		9*	10	11		12											13
1	2	3	4*	5	6	9	8	12	10	11	7													14
1	2	3		5	6*	7	8		9	10			11	12						4				15
1	2	3		5		7	8	11	9	10	6	4												16
1	2	3	4	5		9	8	11			6	7			10									17
1	2	3	4	5		7	8	9		10	6				11									18
1	2*	3	4	5		7	8	10	9		6	12			11									19
1	2	3	4	5		7	8	9		10	6				11									20
1	2	3	4	5		7	8	9	12	10	6				11*									21
1		3	4	5			8	9	10		6	2	7		11									22
		3	4	5		7	8	9	10		6	2		1	11									23
1		3	4	5		7	8	9	10*	11	6	2			12									24
1	12	3	4	5		7	8	11	10	9	6*	2												25
1	7	3	4	5	10		8				6	2	11		9									26
1	7	3	4	5	10		8				6	2	11							9				27
1	10	3	4	5	6	7	8				12	2	11							9*				28
1	2	3	4	5		7	8	11	10		6		9											29
	2	3	4	5		7	8	11	10	9	6			1										30
	2	3	4	5	10	7	8						9	1		11	6							31
		3	4	5	10	7	8						2	9*	1	12	11	6						32
1	2	3	4	5	10	7	8	9									11	6						33
1	2	3	4	5	10	7	8	9									11	6*				12		34
1	2	3	4	5	10	7	8	9								11		6						35
1	2	3	4		10	7		9*				5	7				11	6				12		36
1	2	3	4		10	7	8					5	9				11	6						37
1	2	3	4	5*	6	7	8		10	9						11	12							38
1	2	3		5	6	7	8		10	9		4	11											39
1	2	3	4	5	6	7	8		10*	9	11									12				40
		3	4	5	6	7	8		10	9		2		1	11									41
		3	4	5	6	7	8		10*	9		2		1	11							12		42
25	31	42	39	40	28	39	41	23	22	29	23	16	16	15	9	8	7	4	2	2	1	0	0	
	1											1	2	1	1	1	3	4	1		1	1	3	
		1	2		1	7	5	9	10	1				1	1									

Friendlies

1	Aug	1	(a)	Aberdeen	W 1-0
2		6	(a)	St Johnstone	W 1-0
3		11	(a)	Oldham A	D 2-2
4		15	(a)	Blackpool	D 0-0
5	Oct	24	(a)	Manchester U	W 2-1
6	May	1	(h)	Stoke C	W 3-1
7		6	(a)	All Stars XI	W 4-2
8		7	(a)	Nthn Prem Lge XI	D 2-2
9		16	(a)	Panathinaikos	W 2-0

1974-75

1	Aug 17	(h)	West Ham U	W 4-0	Marsh (2), Tueart, Doyle		30,240
2	21	(h)	Tottenham H	W 1-0	Hartford		31,549
3	24	(a)	Arsenal	L 0-4			27,143
4	28	(a)	Tottenham H	W 2-1	Bell, Booth		20,079
5	31	(h)	Leeds U	W 2-1	Summerbee, Bell		37,919
6	Sep 7	(a)	Coventry C	D 2-2	Oakes, Marsh		15,440
7	14	(h)	Liverpool	W 2-0	Marsh, Tueart		45,194
8	21	(a)	Middlesbrough	L 0-3			30,256
9	24	(a)	Carlisle U	D 0-0			17,900
10	28	(h)	Q.P.R.	W 1-0	Marsh		30,674
11	Oct 5	(h)	Chelsea	D 1-1	Bell		32,412
12	12	(a)	Burnley	L 1-2	Tueart		23,406
13	16	(h)	Arsenal	W 2-1	Tueart (2)		26,658
14	19	(h)	Luton T	W 1-0	Summerbee		30,649
15	26	(a)	Ipswich T	D 1-1	Bell		25,171
16	Nov 2	(a)	Everton	L 0-2			43,905
17	9	(h)	Stoke C	W 1-0	Marsh		36,966
18	16	(a)	Birmingham C	L 0-4			35,143
19	23	(h)	Leicester C	W 4-1	Daniels (2), Bell, Tueart		31,628
20	30	(a)	Newcastle U	L 1-2	Marsh		37,600
21	Dec 7	(h)	Sheffield U	W 3-2	Hammond, Marsh, Bell		29,675
22	14	(a)	West Ham U	D 0-0			33,908
23	21	(h)	Wolves	D 0-0			29,326
24	26	(a)	Liverpool	L 1-4	Bell		46,062
25	28	(h)	Derby C	L 1-2	Bell		40,180
26	Jan 11	(a)	Sheffield U	D 1-1	Booth		25,190
27	18	(h)	Newcastle U	W 5-1	Tueart (3), Bell, Hammond		32,021
28	Feb 1	(a)	Stoke C	L 0-4			32,007
29	8	(h)	Everton	W 2-1	Bell, Tueart		44,718
30	22	(h)	Birmingham C	W 3-1	Bell, Royle, Tueart		33,240
31	Mar 1	(a)	Leeds U	D 2-2	Oakes, Donachie		47,489
32	8	(a)	Leicester C	L 0-1			23,059
33	15	(a)	Q.P.R.	L 0-2			22,102
34	19	(h)	Carlisle U	L 1-2	Barnes		24,047
35	22	(h)	Coventry C	W 1-0	Tueart		25,903
36	28	(h)	Middlesbrough	W 2-1	Bell, Marsh		37,772
37	29	(a)	Wolves	L 0-1			21,716
38	Apr 1	(a)	Derby C	L 1-2	Bell		32,966
39	12	(a)	Chelsea	W 1-0	Hartford		26,249
40	19	(h)	Burnley	W 2-0	Bell, Tueart		30,723
41	23	(h)	Ipswich T	D 1-1	Bell		29,391
42	26	(a)	Luton T	D 1-1	Tueart		20,768

Appearances
Sub Appnces
Goals

League Division One record: P 42   W 18   D 10   L 14   F 54   A 54   Pts 46   Pos 8th

FA Cup

3 Jan 4 (a)*Newcastle U   L 0-2
*City drawn away but game played at
Maine Road because of FA ruling.

League Cup

2 Sep 10 (h) Scunthorpe U   W 6-0
3 Oct 9 (a) Manchester U   L 0-1

Friendlies

1	Jul 26	(a)	Bangor C	W 6-2
2	Nov 12	(a)	Barcelona	L 2-3
3		27	(h)	All Stars XI	L 4-6
4	Dec 10	(a)	Ashton U	W 8-1
5	Jan 21	(a)	Israel National XI	W 2-0
6	Jan 24	(a)	Bristol C	D 2-2
7	Feb 12	(a)	Moroccan National XI	L 2-3
8	Feb 14	(a)	Portsmouth	D 3-3
9	Apr 28	(h)	All Stars XI	D 4-4

Tour (to Nigeria)

1 May 7 (a) Shooting Stars   W 1-0
2   11 (a) Nigerian Forces   W 2-1

MacRae	Hammond	Donachie	Doyle	Booth	Oakes	Summerbee	Bell	Marsh	Hartford	Tueart	Barrett	Royle	Corrigan	Clarke	Henson	Daniels	Pardoe	Horswill	Keegan	Barnes	Leman	
1		3	4		6		8	9	10	11	2			5	7							1
1		3	4		6		8	9	10	11	2			5	7							2
1		3	4		6		8	9	10	11	2			5	7							3
1		3	4	5	6	7	8	9	10	11	2											4
1		3	4	5	6	7	8	9	10	11	2											5
1		3	4	5	6	7	8	9	10	11	2											6
1		3	4		6	7	8	9*	10	11	2			5	12							7
1		3	4		6	7	8	9	10	11	2			5								8
1	2	3	4*		6	7	8	9	10	11	5				12							9
1	2	3	4		6	7	8	9	10	11	5											10
1	2		4		6	7	8	9	10	11	5*					3	12					11
1	2		4		6	9	8			11	5				7	3			10			12
1	2	3	4		6	7	8	9		11*	5				10					12		13
1	2	3	4		6	7	8	9			5				10				11			14
1	2	3	4		6	7	8	9		11	5				10							15
1	2*	3	4		6	7	8	9	10	11	5				12							16
1	2	3	4		6	7	8	9	10	11	5											17
1	2	3	4		6	7	8	9		11	5				10							18
1	2	3	5		6		8	9	10	11				4	7							19
1	2*	3	5		6		8	9	10	11	12			4	7							20
1	2	3	5		6	12	8	9	10	11				4	7*							21
1	2	3	5*		6		8	9	10	11				4	12	7						22
		3			6		8	9	10	11	2		1	5	7	4						23
		3			6	7	8	9	10	11	2		1	5		4						24
	2	3	5		6		8	9	10	11			1		7	4						25
	2	3	4	5	6	7	8	9	10	11			1									26
	2	3	4	5	6	7	8	9	10	11			1									27
1	2	3	4	5	6	7	8	10	11			9										28
1		3	4	5*	6	7	8	9	10	11							12	2				29
1		3	4	5	6	7	8	9	10	11								2				30
1		3	4	5	6	7	8	9	10	11								2				31
1*		3	4	5	6	7	8	9	10	11		12						2				32
	2	3	4	5	6	7	8	9	10	11			1									33
	2	3	4		6	7*	8	9		11			1	5					10	12		34
	2	3	4	5	6	7	8			11		9	1		10							35
	2	3	4	5	6		8	9	10	11			1		7							36
	2	3	4		6		8		10	11	5	9	1		7*		12					37
	2	3	4	5	6	7	8	9	10	11			1									38
	2	3	4	5	6	7	8		10	11		9*	1				12					39
	2	3	4	5	6	7	8	9		11			1		10							40
	2	3	4	5	6	7	8	9		11			1		10							41
	2	3	4	5	6	7	8	9*		11			1		10		12					42
27	26	40	42	18	40	26	42	37	29	39	17	16	15	13	12	7	6	4	3	3	0	
				1				1		1				2	3			2	2		1	
2	1	1	2	2	2	15	9	2	14		1				2				1			

171

1975-76

#	Date		Opponent	Result	Scorers	Attendance
1	Aug 16	(h)	Norwich C	W 3-0	Tueart (2), Bell	29,103
2	20	(h)	Leicester C	D 1-1	opp og	28,557
3	23	(a)	Coventry C	L 0-2		21,097
4	27	(a)	Aston Villa	L 0-1		35,212
5	30	(h)	Newcastle U	W 4-0	Royle (2), Tueart (2)	31,875
6	Sep 6	(a)	West Ham U	L 0-1		29,752
7	13	(h)	Middlesbrough	W 4-0	Marsh (2), Royle, Tueart	30,353
8	20	(a)	Derby C	L 0-1		23,250
9	24	(h)	Stoke C	W 1-0	Marsh	28,915
10	27	(h)	Manchester U	D 2-2	Royle, opp.og	46,931
11	Oct 4	(a)	Arsenal	W 3-2	Hartford, Royle, Marsh	24,928
12	11	(h)	Burnley	D 0-0		35,003
13	18	(a)	Tottenham H	D 2-2	Bell, Watson	30,502
14	25	(h)	Ipswich T	D 1-1	Bell	30,644
15	Nov 1	(a)	Sheffield U	D 2-2	Barnes, Booth	24,670
16	8	(h)	Birmingham C	W 2-0	Bell (2)	28,329
17	15	(a)	Everton	D 1-1	Booth	32,077
18	22	(h)	Tottenham H	W 2-1	Oakes, Tueart	31,456
19	29	(a)	Wolves	W 4-0	Hartford (2), Barnes, Tueart	20,867
20	Dec 6	(h)	Q.P.R.	D 0-0		36,066
21	13	(h)	Coventry C	W 4-2	Oakes, Barnes, Booth, Tueart	27,256
22	20	(a)	Norwich C	D 2-2	Royle, Tueart	19,692
23	26	(h)	Leeds U	L 0-1		48,077
24	27	(a)	Liverpool	L 0-1		53,386
25	Jan 10	(a)	Middlesbrough	L 0-1		23,000
26	17	(h)	West.Ham U	W 3-0	Royle (2), Oakes	32,147
27	31	(a)	Leicester C	L 0-1		21,723
28	Feb 7	(h)	Aston Villa	W 2-1	Hartford, Booth	32,331
29	14	(a)	Birmingham C	L 1-2	Hartford	22,445
30	21	(h)	Everton	W 3-0	Hartford, Royle, Tueart	33,148
31	Mar 6	(h)	Sheffield U	W 4-0	Hartford (2), Royle, Tueart	33,510
32	13	(a)	Burnley	D 0-0		24,278
33	20	(h)	Wolves	W 3-2	Keegan, Doyle, Tueart	32,761
34	27	(a)	Q.P.R.	L 0-1		29,883
35	Apr 2	(a)	Stoke C	D 0-0		18,798
36	7	(a)	Ipswich T	L 1-2	Keegan	21,290
37	10	(h)	Derby C	W 4-3	Tueart (2), Royle, Power	42,061
38	14	(a)	Newcastle U	L 1-2	Royle	21,095
39	17	(a)	Leeds U	L 1-2	Bell	33,154
40	19	(h)	Liverpool	L 0-3		50,439
41	24	(h)	Arsenal	W 3-1	Hartford, Booth (2)	31,003
42	May 4	(a)	Manchester U	L 0-2		59,528
					Appearances	
					Sub Appnces	
					Goals	

League Division One record: P 42   W 16   D 11   L 15   F 64   A 46   Pts 43   Pos 8th

FA Cup

3	Jan 3	(h)	Hartlepools	W 6-0
4	28	(a)	Stoke C	L 0-1

League Cup

2	Sep 10	(a)	Norwich C	D 1-1
R	17	(h)	Norwich C	D 2-2
2R	29	(n)	Norwich C	W 6-1
3	Oct 8	(h)	Nottingham F	W 2-1
4	Nov 12	(h)	Manchester U	W 4-0
5	Dec 3	(h)	Mansfield T	W 4-2
SF	Jan 13	(a)	Middlesbrough	L 0-1
SF	21	(h)	Middlesbrough	W 4-0
F	Feb 28	(n)	Newcastle U	W 2-1

Friendlies

1	Aug 11	(a)	Macclesfield T	D 1-1
2	Sep 2	(h)	Manchester U XI	L 3-4
3	Oct 13	(a)	Stockport C	W 5-0
4	Apr 26	(a)	Lancaster C	W 1-0
5	May 10	(a)	Stafford R	W 3-1
6	11	(a)	Great Harwood	D 2-2

Tour (to Far East)

1	May 21	(a)	Japan National XI	W 3-0
2	23	(a)	Japan National XI	W 1-0
3	26	(a)	Japan National XI	W 1-0
4	28	(a)	Japan National XI	W 2-0
5	30	(a)	South Korea 'B' XI	L 2-4
6	Jun 1	(a)	South Korea Ntl XI	W 3-0
7	3	(a)	South Korea Ntl XI	W 3-0

Corrigan	Clements	Donachie	Doyle	Watson	Oakes	Hartford	Barnes	Bell	Booth	Tueart	Royle	Keegan	Power	Hammond	Marsh	Owen	Barrett	MacRae	Leman	Docherty	Telford	No.
1		3	4	5	6	7		8		11	10		2	9								1
1		3	4	5	6	7		8		11	10		2	9								2
1		3	4	5	6	7		8		11	9*		2	10						12		3
1	2	3	4	5	6	7		8		11		10		9								4
1	2	3	4	5	6	7		8		11	9			10								5
1	2	3	4	5	6	7		8		11				10	9							6
1	2	3	4	5	6	7		8		11	9			10								7
1	2	3	4	5	6	7		8		11	9			10								8
1	2	3	4	5	6	7		8		11	9			10								9
1	2	3	4	5	6	7		8		11	9*			10	12							10
1	2	3	4	5	6	7		8		11*	9	12		10								11
1	2	3	4	5	6	7	11	8			10*			9	12							12
1	2	3	4	9	6	10	7	8	5	11												13
1	2	3	4	9	6	10	7	8	5	11												14
	2	3	4	5	6	10	7	8	9	11								1				15
1	2	3	4	5	6	10	7	8		11	9											16
1	2	3	4	5	6	10	7		8	11*	9	12										17
1	2	3	4	5	6	10	7			11	9		8									18
1	2	3	4	5	6	10	7			11	9		8									19
1	2	3	4	5	6	10	7		8	11	9											20
1		3	4	5	6	10	7		8*	11	9	12	2									21
1	2	3	4	5	6	10	7		8	11	9											22
1	2	3	4	5	6	10	7*		8	11	9	12										23
1	2	3	4	5	6*	10			8	11	9	12	7									24
1		3	4	5	6	10			8		9		7	10			2					25
1	5	3	4		6	10	11				9	8	7				2					26
1		3	4	5	6*	10	12		8	11	9		7				2					27
1	2*	3	4	5	6	10	7	12		11	9	8										28
1	2	3	4	5	6	10	11		8		9	7										29
1		3	4	5	6	10	7		8	11	9	2										30
1		3	4	5	6	10	7		8	11	9	2										31
1		3	4	5	6	10	7		8	11	9	2										32
1	5	3	4			10	7		8	11	9	2				6						33
1	12	3	4		6	10	7		5	11	9*	2				8						34
1		3	4		6	7			5	11	9		8	10	2							35
1		3	4			10	7		5	11	9		8	6	2							36
1		3	4		6	7*	8	5		11	9		2	10	12							37
1	4	3					7		5	11	9		8	10	2	6						38
1		2	4		3	10		8	5	11	9		6	7								39
1		2	4		3*	10	7	8	5	11	9		6	12								40
1		3	4			10	7	8	5	12	9		2	6*		11						41
1	2		4*		12	10	7		5	11	9		6	8					3			42
41	26	40	41	31	38	39	27	20	25	37	37	17	14	7	12	4	3	1	1	1	0	
	1			1		1		1	1		1	5	1				2		1			
		1	1	3	9	3	6	6	14	12	2	1		4								

1976-77

1	Aug 12	(a)	Leicester C	D 2-2	Royle, Tueart	22,612
2	25	(h)	Aston Villa	W 2-0	Tueart, Watson	41,007
3	28	(h)	Stoke C	D 0-0		39,878
4	Sep 4	(a)	Arsenal	D 0-0		35,132
5	11	(h)	Bristol C	W 2-1	Barnes, Tueart	35,891
6	18	(a)	Sunderland	W 2-0	Royle, Tueart	37,397
7	25	(h)	Manchester U	L 1-3	Tueart	48,861
8	Oct 2	(h)	West Ham U	W 4-2	Tueart (2), Owen, Hartford	37,795
9	5	(a)	Everton	D 2-2	Hartford, Power	31,370
10	16	(h)	Q.P.R.	D 0-0		40,751
11	23	(a)	Ipswich T	L 0-1		25,041
12	30	(a)	Norwich C	W 2-0	Kidd, Royle	22,861
13	Nov 6	(h)	Newcastle U	D 0-0		40,049
14	20	(h)	West Brom A	W 1-0	Tueart	36,656
15	27	(a)	Birmingham C	D 0-0		29,722
16	Dec 4	(h)	Derby C	W 3-2	Kidd (2), Tueart	34,179
17	7	(a)	Middlesbrough	D 0-0		18,000
18	11	(a)	Tottenham H	D 2-2	Kidd, Power	24,608
19	18	(h)	Coventry C	W 2-0	Kidd, Tueart	32,227
20	27	(a)	Leeds U	W 2-0	Kidd (2)	48,708
21	29	(h)	Liverpool	D 1-1	Royle	50,020
22	Jan 22	(h)	Leicester C	W 5-0	Kidd (4), Doyle	37,609
23	Feb 5	(a)	Stoke C	W 2-0	Royle, Tueart	27,139
24	12	(h)	Arsenal	W 1-0	Royle	45,368
25	16	(a)	Newcastle U	D 2-2	Kidd, Tueart	27,920
26	19	(a)	Bristol C	L 0-1		27,601
27	Mar 1	(h)	Norwich C	W 2-0	Tueart (2)	36,021
28	5	(a)	Manchester U	L 1-3	Royle	58,595
29	9	(h)	Sunderland	W 1-0	Tueart	44,439
30	12	(a)	West Ham U	L 0-1		24,974
31	22	(a)	Q.P.R.	D 0-0		17,619
32	Apr 2	(h)	Ipswich T	W 2-1	Kidd, Watson	42,780
33	8	(h)	Leeds U	W 2-1	Kidd (2)	47,727
34	9	(a)	Liverpool	L 1-2	Kidd	55,283
35	11	(h)	Middlesbrough	W 1-0	Hartford	37,735
36	16	(a)	West Brom A	w 2-0	Kidd, Tueart	24,889
37	19	(h)	Birmingham C	W 2-1	Kidd (2)	36,203
38	30	(a)	Derby C	L 0-4		29,127
39	May 4	(a)	Aston Villa	D 1-1	Tueart	36,190
40	7	(h)	Tottenham H	W 5-0	Booth, Barnes, Kidd, Tueart, Hartford	37,919
41	10	(h)	Everton	D 1-1	Kidd	38,004
42	14	(a)	Coventry C	W 1-0	Conway	21,429

Appearances
Sub Appnces
Goals

League Division One record: P 42   W 21   D 14   L 7   F 60   A 34   Pts 56   Pos 2nd

FA Cup

3	Jan 8	(h)	West Brom A	D 1-1
R	11	(a)	West Brom A	W 1-0
4	29	(a)	Newcastle U	W 3-1
5	Feb 26	(a)	Leeds U	L 0-1

League Cup

2	Sep 1	(a)	Aston Villa	L 0-3

Friendlies

1	Nov 2	(h)	Man City Triple Championship XI	W 2-1
2	22	(a)	Stockport C	W 2-0
3	Mar 25	(h)	Manchester U	W 4-2
4	May 16	(a)	Blackburn R	L 1-2
5	17	(a)	Oldham A	L 1-3
6	23	(a)	Wolves	W 2-1

Tour (to Spain)

1	Aug 14	(a)	Atletico Madrid	L 0-2
2	15	(a)	Real Betis	D 1-1

Appearance and scoring grid (player columns left-to-right; match number at right):

Corrigan	Clements	Donachie	Doyle	Watson	Power	Owen	Barnes	Kidd	Royle	Hartford	Tueart	Booth	Conway	Keegan	Docherty	Henry	Lester	#
1		3	4	5	6			8	9	10	11		7		2			1
1		3	4	5	6			8	9	10	11		7		2			2
1		3	4	5	6	7			9	10	11		8		2			3
1		3	4	5	7				9	10	11	6	8		2			4
1		3	4	5		7		8	9	10	11		6		2			5
1		3	4	5	7			8	9	10	11		6*		2		12	6
1		3	4	5	6			8	9	10	11	12	7*		2			7
1	2	3	4	5		6	7	8	9	10	11							8
1	2	3	4	5	7	6		8	9	10	11							9
1	2	3	4	5	7	6		8	9*	10	11					12		10
1	2	3	4	5	7	6		8	9	10	11							11
1	2	3	4	5		6	7	8	9	10	11							12
1	2	3	4	5	6*	7	12	8	9	10	11							13
1	2	3	4	5	12	7		8	9*	10	11		6					14
1	2	3	4	5		6	7	8	9	10	11							15
1	2*	3	4	5	6	7	12	8	9	10	11							16
1	2	3	4	5	6			8	9	10	11		7					17
1	2	3	4	5	6	7		8	9	10	11							18
1	2	3	4	5	6	7		8	9	10	11							19
1	2	3	4	5	6	7		8	9	10	11							20
1	2	3	4	5	6	7		8	9	10	11							21
1	2	3	4	5	6	7	12	8	9	10	11*							22
1	2	3	4	5	6	7		8	9	10	11							23
1	2	3	4	5	6	7		8	9	10	11							24
1	2	3	4	5	6	7		8	9	10	11							25
1	2	3	4	5	6	7		8	9	10	11							26
1	2	3	4	5	6	7		8	9	10	11							27
1	2	3	4	5	6*	7	12	8	9	10	11							28
1	2	3	4			6	7	8	9	10	11	5						29
1	2	3	4*	5	12	7		8	9	10	11		6					30
1	2	3		5		7		8	9	10	11	4	6					31
1	2	3		5	11*	7		8	9	10		4	6			12		32
1	2	3	4	5		7		8	9	10	11		6					33
1	2	3	4	5	11		12	8	9*	10			6	7				34
1	2	3		5		6	7		9	10	11	4		8				35
1	2	3		5		6	7		9	10	11	4		8				36
1	2	3		5		6	7	8		10	11	4		8				37
1	2	3	6	5	12	10	7	8	9*			4	11					38
1	2	3		5		6	7	8*	9		11	4	12	10				39
1	2	3		5		6	7	8	9*	10	11	4	12					40
1	2	3		5		6	7	8	9	10	11	4						41
1	2	3		5	11	6	7		9	10		4		8				42
42	35	42	33	41	27	30	16	39	39	40	38	14	11	8	7	0	0	
					2	1	5						1	2		2	1	
			1	2	2	1	2	21	7	4	18	1	1					

175

1977-78

1	Aug 20	(h)	Leicester C	D 0-0			45,963
2	24	(a)	Aston Villa	W 4-1	Tueart (3), Booth		40,121
3	27	(a)	West Ham U	W 1-0	Royle		25,278
4	Sep 3	(h)	Norwich C	W 4-0	Channon (2), Hartford, Power		41,269
5	10	(h)	Manchester U	W 3-1	Kidd (2), Channon		50,856
6	17	(a)	Q.P.R.	D 1-1	Royle		24,668
7	24	(h)	Bristol C	W 2-0	Barnes, Owen		41,897
8	Oct 1	(a)	Everton	D 1-1	Hartford		43,286
9	4	(a)	Coventry C	L 2-4	Barnes, Tueart		19,586
10	8	(h)	Arsenal	W 2-1	Barnes, Tueart		43,177
11	15	(a)	Nottingham F	L 1-2	Kidd		35,572
12	22	(h)	Wolves	L 0-2			42,730
13	29	(h)	Liverpool	W 3-1	Channon, Royle, Kidd		49,207
14	Nov 5	(a)	Ipswich T	L 0-1			23,636
15	12	(h)	Leeds U	L 2-3	Barnes, Channon		42,651
16	19	(a)	West Brom A	D 0-0			27,159
17	26	(h)	Chelsea	W 6-2	Tueart (3), Barnes, Channon, opp.og		34,345
18	Dec 3	(a)	Derby C	L 1-2	Power		26,888
19	10	(h)	Birmingham C	W 3-0	Owen, Channon, Tueart		36,671
20	17	(a)	Leeds U	L 0-2			37,380
21	26	(h)	Newcastle U	W 4-0	Tueart (3), Kidd		45,811
22	27	(a)	Middlesbrough	W 2-0	Hartford, Owen		26,879
23	31	(h)	Aston Villa	W 2-0	Kidd, Barnes		46,074
24	Jan 2	(a)	Leicester C	W 1-0	Owen		24,041
25	14	(h)	West Ham U	W 3-2	Barnes, Booth, Kidd		43,627
26	21	(a)	Norwich C	W 3-1	Kidd (2), Owen		20,397
27	Feb 11	(h)	Q.P.R.	W 2-1	Channon, Bell		39,860
28	17	(a)	Bristol C	D 2-2	Kidd, Booth		25,834
29	25	(h)	Everton	W 1-0	Kidd		46,817
30	Mar 4	(a)	Arsenal	L 0-3			34,003
31	15	(a)	Manchester U	D 2-2	Barnes, Kidd		58,426
32	18	(a)	Wolves	D 1-1	Bell		20,583
33	25	(h)	Middlesbrough	D 2-2	Channon (2)		37,944
34	29	(a)	Newcastle U	D 2-2	Palmer (2)		20,246
35	Apr 1	(h)	Ipswich T	W 2-1	Channon, Palmer		34,975
36	11	(h)	Nottingham F	D 0-0			43,428
37	15	(h)	West Brom A	L 1-3	Kidd		36,521
38	22	(a)	Birmingham C	W 4-1	Kidd (2), Owen, Power		25,294
39	25	(h)	Coventry C	W 3-1	Owen, Kidd, Hartford		32,412
40	29	(a)	Derby C	D 1-1	Channon		39,175
41	May 2	(a)	Liverpool	L 0-4			44,528
42	5	(a)	Chelsea	D 0-0			18,782

Appearances
Sub Appnces
Goals

League Division One record: P 42   W 20   D 12   L 10   F 74   A 51   Pts 52   Pos 4th

FA Cup

3	Jan 7	(a)	Leeds U	W 2-1
4	31	(a)	Nottingham F	L 1-2

League Cup

2	Aug 31	(a)	Chesterfield	W 1-0
3	Oct 25	(a)	Luton T	D 1-1
R	Nov 1	(h)	Luton T	D 0-0
2R	9	(n)	Luton T	W 3-2
4	29	(a)	Ipswich T	W 2-1
5	Jan 18	(h)	Arsenal	D 0-0
R	24	(a)	Arsenal	L 0-1

Friendlies

1	Jul 30	(a)	Walsall	W 4-1
2	Sep 19	(a)	Wigan A	W 2-1
3	Apr 18	(a)	Tranmere/Everton XI	D 2-2
4	May 9	(h)	England XI	W 4-3

Tour (to Holland & Belgium)

1	Aug 3	(a)	Vitesse Arnhem	W 2-1
2	6	(a)	Zwolle PEC	D 1-1
3	9	(a)	Lokeren	D 1-1

Match	Corrigan	Clements	Donachie	Booth	Watson	Owen	Barnes	Channon	Kidd	Hartford	Tueart	Power	Bell	Doyle	Royle	Palmer	Henry	Keegan
1	1	2	3	6	5	7		8		10	11			4	9			
2	1	2	3	6	5			8	7	10	11			4	9			
3	1	2	3	6	5			8	7	10	11			4	9			
4	1	2	3	6	5	4	7	8	9	10		11						
5	1	2	3	6	5	4	7	8	9	10		11						
6	1	2	3	6	5	4	11	8	7	10					9			
7	1	2		6	5	4	7	8	9	10		11	3					
8	1	2	3	6*	5	4	7		9	10	11	8		12				
9	1	2	3	6	5		7		4	10	11	8			9			
10	1	2	3	6	5	4	7		9	10	11	8						
11	1	12	3	6		4	7	8	9	10	11*	2		5		10*		
12	1	12	3	6	5	4	7	8	9		11	2				10*		
13	1	2	3		5	6	7	8		10		11		4	9			
14	1	2	3		5	6	7	8	9	10	11			4				
15	1	2	3		5		7	8	9	10	11	6		4				
16	1	2	3	4	5		7	8	9	10	11	6						
17	1	2	3	4	5		7	8	9	10	11	6						
18	1	2	3	4	5		7	8	9	10	11	6						
19	1	2	3	4	5	7		8	9	10	11	6						
20	1	2	3	4	5	7		8	9	10*	11	6						12
21	1	2	3	4	5	8	7		9	10	11	6	12					
22	1	2	3	4	5	6	7		9	10		8		11				
23	1	2	3	4	5	6	7		9	10	11	8						
24	1	2	3	4	5	6	7*		9	10		8		12		11		
25	1	2*	3	4	5	6	7	12	9	10	11	8						
26	1	2	3	4	5	6	7		9	10	11	8						
27	1	2	3	4	5	6	11	7	9	10		8						
28	1	2	3	4	5	6	11	7	9	10		8						
29	1	2	3	4	5		11	7	9	10	6	8						
30	1	2	3	4	5		11	7	9	10	6	8						
31	1	2	3	4	5	6	11	7	9	10		8						
32	1	2	3	4	5	6	11	7	9		10	8						
33	1	2	3	4	5	6	11	7	9*		10	8						12
34	1	2	3	8	5	6	11	7			10			4	9			
35	1	2	3	8	5	6	11	7	10					4	9			
36	1	2		8	5	6	11	7	9	10	3			4				
37	1	2		8*	5	6	11	7	9	10	3			4		12		
38	1	2	3	4	5	6		7	9	10	11	8						
39	1	2	3	4	5	6		7	9	10	11	8						
40	1	2	3	4	5	6*	12	7	9	10	11	8						
41	1	2	3	4	5	6		7	9	10	11	8						
42	1	2	3	4	5	6	7	8	9	10	11							
App	42	40	39	39	41	33	33	33	39	37	17	29	16	13	6	4	1	0
Sub		2					1	1					1	1	1	1		2
Gls			3			7	8	12	16	4	12	3	2		3	3		

177

1978-79

1	Aug	19	(a)	Derby C	D 1-1	Kidd	26,480
2		22	(h)	Arsenal	D 1-1	Kidd	39,506
3		26	(h)	Liverpool	L 1-4	Kidd	46,710
4	Sep	2	(a)	Norwich C	D 1-1	Channon	18,607
5		9	(h)	Leeds U	W 3-0	Palmer (2), Watson	40,125
6		16	(a)	Chelsea	W 4-1	R.Futcher (3), Channon	29,980
7		23	(h)	Tottenham H	W 2-0	R.Futcher, Owen	43,472
8		30	(a)	Manchester U	L 0-1		55,317
9	Oct	7	(a)	Birmingham C	W 2-1	R.Futcher, Kidd	18,378
10		14	(h)	Coventry C	W 2-0	Owen (2)	36,723
11		21	(a)	Bolton W	D 2-2	Palmer, Owen	32,249
12		28	(h)	West Brom A	D 2-2	Channon, Hartford	40,521
13	Nov	4	(a)	Aston Villa	D 1-1	Owen	32,724
14		11	(h)	Derby C	L 1-2	Owen	37,376
15		18	(a)	Liverpool	L 0-1		47,765
16		25	(h)	Ipswich T	L 1-2	Hartford	38,527
17	Dec	9	(h)	Southampton	L 1-2	Power	33,450
18		16	(a)	Q.P.R.	L 1-2	Channon	12,902
19		23	(h)	Nottingham F	D 0-0		37,012
20		26	(a)	Everton	L 0-1		46,996
21		30	(a)	Bristol C	D 1-1	R.Futcher	25,253
22	Jan	13	(a)	Leeds U	D 1-1	Kidd	36,303
23		20	(h)	Chelsea	L 2-3	Power, R.Futcher	31,876
24	Feb	3	(a)	Tottenham H	W 3-0	Channon, Kidd, Barnes	32,037
25		10	(h)	Manchester U	L 0-3		46,151
26		24	(a)	Coventry C	W 3-0	Channon (2), Kidd	20,116
27		27	(h)	Norwich C	D 2-2	Owen (2)	29,852
28	Mar	3	(h)	Bolton W	W 2-1	Owen, Channon	41,127
29		24	(a)	Arsenal	D 1-1	Channon	35,041
30		27	(a)	Wolves	D 1-1	Channon	19,998
31		31	(a)	Ipswich T	L 1-2	Silkman	20,773
32	Apr	4	(a)	West Brom A	L 0-4		22,314
33		7	(h)	Wolves	W 3-1	Channon, Silkman, Palmer	32,298
34		14	(h)	Everton	D 0-0		39,711
35		17	(a)	Middlesbrough	L 0-2		19,676
36		21	(h)	Q.P.R.	W 3-1	Owen (2), Silkman	30,694
37		24	(h)	Middlesbrough	W 1-0	Deyna	28,264
38		28	(a)	Southampton	L 0-1		19,744
39	May	1	(h)	Birmingham C	W 3-1	Deyna (2), Power	27,366
40		5	(h)	Bristol C	W 2-0	Deyna, Hartford	29,739
41		9	(a)	Nottingham F	L 1-3	opp.og	21,104
42		15	(h)	Aston Villa	L 2-3	Deyna (2)	30,028

Appearances
Sub Appnces
Goals

League Division One record: P 42   W 13   D 13   L 16   F 58   A 56   Pts 39   Pos 15th

FA Cup

3	Jan	15	(h)	Rotherham U	D 0-0	
R		17	(a)	Rotherham U	W 4-2	
4		27	(a)	Shrewsbury T	L 0-2	

League Cup

2	Aug	29	(h)	Grimsby T	W 2-0	
3	Oct	4	(a)	Blackpool	D 1-1	
R		10	(h)	Blackpool	W 3-0	
4	Nov	8	(a)	Norwich C	W 3-1	
5	Dec	12	(a)	Southampton	L 1-2	

Friendlies

None played.

Tour (to Denmark, Belgium, Holland)

1	Aug	2	(a)	Djurgaarden	D 1-1
2		3	(a)	Fredikstadt	W 5-0
3		7	(a)	Hamer	W 7-0
4		8	(a)	SC Heracles 74	W 3-2
5		11	(a)	SV Lierse	D 2-2
6		13	(a)	AZ Alkmaar	L 1-5

Tour (to Italy)

1	May	23	(a)	AC Roma	D 2-2
2		25	(a)	Avellino	W 2-0
3		27	(a)	Napoli	L 1-2

178

Corrigan	Clements	Donachie	Power	Owen	Watson	Futcher P.	Channon	Booth	Kidd	Hartford	Barnes	Viljoen	Henry	Silkman	Futcher R.	Deyna	Palmer	Bell	Ranson	Reid	Keegan	Bennett	
1	2	3	6		5	4	7		9	10	11										8		1
1	2	3	4		5	6	7		9	10	11										8		2
1	2	3	4	11		6	7	5	9	10											8		3
1	2	3	4	8		6	7	5		10	11			9									4
1	2	3	4	8	5	6	7			10	11					9							5
1	2	3		8	5	6	7			10*	11	4	12	9									6
1	2	3	11	8	5	6	7			10		4		9									7
1	2	3	4	8	5	6	7		9	10	11												8
1	2	3		8	5		7	4	6	10	11		12	9									9
1	2	3		8	5			4	6	10	11			9			7						10
1	2	3		8	5			4	9	10	11	6		12			7*						11
1	2	3		8		6	7	5	9	10		4*		12	11								12
1	2	3		8		6	7	5	9	10		4			11								13
1	2	3	6		5		7	4	9	10	11						8						14
1	2	3	6		5		7*	4	9	10	11		12				8						15
1	2*	3	6	7	5			4	9	10	11				8	12							16
1		3	6	12	5		7	4	9*	10	11	8								2			17
1		3	6	8	5	2	7	4		10	11			12		9*							18
1		3	4	8	5	6	7			10	11					9				2			19
1		3	4	8	5	6	7			10*	11					9	12			2			20
1		3	4	8	5	6	7			10	11					9				2			21
1		3	4	8	5*	6	7		12	10	11					9				2			22
1	2	3	4			6	7	5*	9	10	11			12		8							23
1	2	3	4		5*	6	7		9	10	11					12		8					24
1	2	3	4		5	6	7		9	10	11							8					25
1	2	3	4			6	7	5	9	10	11	8											26
1	2	3	4			6	7	5	9	10	11	8											27
1	2	3	4		5		7	6	9	10	11	8											28
1	2	3	11		5		7	6		10		8	9			4							29
1		3	4		5		7			10	11	8	6	9*		12				2			30
1		3*	4		5		7			10	11	6	9	12						2	8		31
1	2*	3				6	7	5		10		8	6	9		11	12						32
1		3		8		6	7*	5		10			4	9	12	11			2				33
1		3			5	2		4*		10	11	8	6	9		7					12		34
1		3			5	6				10	11	8	4	9	12		7*		2				35
1	2	3	7		5					10	11	4	9			8		6					36
1		3	11	8	5		7					4	9			10		6	2				37
1		3	11	8	5		7					4	9			10		6	2				38
1		3	11	8	5		7					4	9			10		6	2				39
1		3	11		5		7			10		4	9			8		6	2				40
1		3		11	5		7			10		4	9			8		6	2				41
1		3			5*		7			10		8	4	9	11	12		6	2				42
42	15	38	32	34	33	24	36	20	19	39	29	16	13	12	10	11	10	10	8	7	4	0	
				1					1				2		7	2	4				1		
		3	11	1			11		7	3	1			3		7	6	4					

179

1979-80

1	Aug	18	(h)	Crystal P	D 0-0		40,681
2		21	(a)	Middlesbrough	L 0-3		24,002
3		25	(h)	Brighton & H A	W 3-2	Power, Robinson, Channon	34,557
4	Sep	1	(a)	Tottenham H	L 1-2	MacKenzie	30,901
5		8	(h)	Southampton	L 0-1		34,920
6		15	(a)	West Brom A	L 0-4		22,236
7		22	(h)	Coventry C	W 3-0	Robinson (2), MacKenzie	30,869
8		29	(a)	Leeds U	W 2-1	Power, Deyna	29,592
9	Oct	6	(a)	Arsenal	D 0-0		34,668
10		10	(h)	Middlesbrough	W 1-0	Deyna	29,384
11		13	(h)	Nottingham F	W 1-0	Deyna	41,683
12		20	(a)	Norwich C	D 2-2	Bennett (2)	18,000
13		27	(h)	Liverpool	L 0-4		48,128
14	Nov	3	(a)	Crystal P	L 0-2		29,443
15		10	(h)	Manchester U	W 2-0	Henry, Robinson	50,067
16		17	(a)	Bolton W	W 1-0	Daley	25,515
17		24	(a)	Bristol C	L 0-1		18,296
18	Dec	1	(h)	Wolves	L 2-3	Palmer, Deyna	33,894
19		8	(a)	Ipswich T	L 0-4		18,221
20		15	(h)	Derby C	W 3-0	Henry, Robinson, opp.og	27,667
21		22	(a)	Everton	W 2-1	Henry, Daley	26,308
22		26	(h)	Stoke C	D 1-1	Power	36,286
23		29	(a)	Brighton & H A	L 1-4	Lee	28,093
24	Jan	12	(h)	Tottenham H	D 1-1	Robinson	34,337
25		19	(a)	Southampton	L 1-4	Power	21,422
26	Feb	2	(h)	West Brom A	L 1-3	Lee	32,904
27		9	(a)	Coventry C	D 0-0		17,114
28		16	(h)	Leeds U	D 1-1	Power	34,392
29		23	(a)	Nottingham F	L 0-4		27,255
30		27	(a)	Aston Villa	D 2-2	Robinson, Power	29,139
31	Mar	1	(h)	Norwich C	D 0-0		32,248
32		11	(a)	Liverpool	L 0-2		40,443
33		15	(h)	Arsenal	L 0-3		33,792
34		22	(a)	Manchester U	L 0-1		56,384
35		29	(h)	Bolton W	D 2-2	Tueart (2)	33,500
36	Apr	2	(h)	Everton	D 1-1	Deyna	33,473
37		5	(a)	Stoke C	D 0-0		20,451
38		7	(h)	Aston Villa	D 1-1	Power	32,943
39		12	(a)	Wolves	W 2-1	Tueart, Reeves	23,850
40		19	(h)	Bristol C	W 3-1	Deyna, Tueart, Robinson	32,745
41		26	(a)	Derby C	L 1-3	Tueart	22,572
42	May	3	(h)	Ipswich T	W 2-1	Henry, Reeves	31,648

Appearances
Sub Appnces
Goals

League Division One record: P 42   W 12   D 13   L 17   F 43   A 66   Pts 37   Pos 17th

FA Cup

3 Jan 5 (a) Halifax T   L 0-1

League Cup

2 Aug 28 (a) Sheffield W   D 1-1
R Sep 4 (h) Sheffield W   W 2-1
3   26 (h) Sunderland   D 1-1
R Oct 3 (a) Sunderland   L 0-1

Friendlies

1 Aug 4 (a) Coventry C   L 1-3
2   6 (a) Hibernian   D 1-1
3   8 (a) Hearts   D 1-1
4 Sep 11 (h) Liverpool/Everton
                        XI W 2-1

Friendlies (cont)

5 Sep 18 (a) Legia Warsaw   L 1-2
6 Oct 30 (a) Altrincham   L 0-2
7 Nov 8 (h) Werder Bremen   W 4-0
8   13 (a) Newcastle U   L 1-4
9   27 (a) Chorley   L 0-2
10 Dec 19 (a) Real Madrid   L 2-5
11 Mar 7 (a) Notts C   W 2-0
12 Apr 22 (a) Hereford U   W 2-1
13   29 (a) Kettering T   W 3-1
14 May 7 (a) Sheffield W   L 1-3

Tours (to Belgium and North America)
(see opposite page)

No.	Corrigan	Ranson	Stepanovic	Donachie	Reid	Caton	Booth	Henry	Daley	Robinson	Power	Bennett	Deyna	MacKenzie	Futcher P.	Tueart	Viljoen	Reeves	Silkman	Lee	Palmer	Shinton	Channon	Sugrue	No.
1	1	2*	3			4	5	11		9	6			10	7		12	8							1
2	1	2	3			4	5	11		9	6			10*	7		12	8							2
3	1	2	3			4	5			9	6				7		10	8				11			3
4	1	2	3			4	5	12		9	6				7		10*	8					11		4
5	1	2	3	5		4	12	10		9*	6				7			8		11					5
6	1	2	3	5		4		10		9	6*				7	12		8		11					6
7	1	2	4	3		5		8		9	10	11			7	6									7
8	1	2	4	3		5		8		9	10		11		7	6									8
9	1	2	4*			5		8		9	10		12	11	7	6						3			9
10	1	2	3			5		8		9	10	11			7	6							4		10
11	1	2	3			5				9	10		4	11	7	6	8								11
12	1	2	12	3		5				9	10		4	11	7*	6	8								12
13	1	2		10		5				9	3		4	11	7	6	8								13
14	1	2		10*		5	12	8		9	3		4		7	6			11						14
15	1	2	3		5	6	7	8		9	10		4	11											15
16	1	2	6	3			7	8		9	10		4	11											16
17	1	2	6	3	5		7	8		9	10		4	11											17
18	1	2	6*	3	5	4		10	8				7								11	12	9		18
19	1	2			5	6	7	8		9	3		4				10			11					19
20	1	2	3			5	6	7	8	9	11		4								10				20
21	1	2	3			5	4	7	8	9	10		6									11			21
22	1	2	3			5	6	7	8	9	10		4									11			22
23	1	2	3	10		5	6	7	8	9	4								11						23
24	1	2		4		5	7*	8		9	3	6		12			10	11							24
25	1	2	3	4	5	6		8	9	7				10*						11	12				25
26	1	2	3	4	5	6	7	8		9	10									11					26
27	1	2	3		5	6	4	8		9	10	11			7										27
28	1	2	3	12	5	6	4	8*			10	11			7						9				28
29	1	2	3	4	5	6	7		8	10	11										9				29
30	1	2	3	4	5	6	7	8	9	10	11														30
31	1	2		4	5	6*	7	8	9	3	11	12					10								31
32	1	2		4	5		7	8	3	11	9						10	6							32
33	1	2		4	5	6	7	12	3	11	9						10*	8							33
34	1	2	3	5	4		7	8		6	11*						10	9				12			34
35	1	2	3	5	4		7	8		6							10	9	11						35
36	1	2	3	5	4		7	8		6	9						10	11							36
37	1	2	3	5	4		7	8		6	9						10	11							37
38	1	2	3	5	4		7	8		6	9						10	11							38
39	1	2	3	5			7	8		6	9		4				10		11						39
40	1	2	3	5			7	8	11	6	9		4				10								40
41	1	2	3	5			7	8		6	9*12		4				10		11						41
42	1	2		5			6*	8		3	12		9	7	4				11				10		42
	42	40	13	19	22	42	24	29	33	29	41	23	21	17	12	11	9	9	7	6	5	5	2	1	
		1		1				3		1		2	1	2	1		2				1	2			
							4	2	8	7	2	6	2			5	2			2	1		1		

Tours (to Belgium and North America)

1	Aug 11	(a)	Beerschot	W 1-0
2	12	(a)	FC Bruges	L 2-3
3	May 17	(a)	Memphis Rouges	D 1-1
4	21	(a)	New York Cosmos	L 2-3
5	24	(a)	Vancouver W'Caps	L 0-5
6	26	(a)	AC Roma	W 3-2

181

1980-81

#	Date		Opponent	Result	Scorers	Attendance
1	Aug 16	(a)	Southampton	L 0-2		23,320
2	20	(h)	Sunderland	L 0-4		33.271
3	23	(h)	Aston Villa	D 2-2	Ranson, Tueart	30,017
4	30	(a)	Middlesbrough	D 2-2	MacKenzie, Reeves	15,761
5	Sep 6	(h)	Arsenal	D 1-1	Tueart	32,223
6	13	(a)	Nottingham F	L 2-3	Henry, Bennett	23,184
7	20	(h)	Stoke C	L 1-2	Tueart	29,507
8	27	(a)	Manchester U	D 2-2	Palmer, Reeves	55,926
9	Oct 4	(h)	Liverpool	L 0-3		41,022
10	8	(a)	Leeds U	L 0-1		19,134
11	11	(a)	West Brom A	L 1-3	Daley	19,515
12	18	(h)	Birmingham C	L 0-1		30,041
13	22	(h)	Tottenham H	W 3-1	Daley, MacKenzie, Reeves	28,788
14	25	(a)	Brighton & H A	W 2-1	Tueart (2)	18,368
15	Nov 1	(h)	Norwich C	W 1-0	Power	33,056
16	8	(a)	Leicester C	D 1-1	Tueart	19,104
17	12	(a)	Sunderland	L 0-2		23,387
18	15	(h)	Southampton	W 3-0	Bennett, Gow, Reeves	32,661
19	22	(h)	Coventry C	W 3-0	Bennett, Power, Reeves	30,047
20	29	(a)	Crystal P	W 3-2	Gow (2), Reeves	16,578
21	Dec 6	(h)	Ipswich T	D 1-1	Gow	35,215
22	13	(a)	Tottenham H	L 1-2	Boyer	23,883
23	20	(h)	Leeds U	W 1-0	Reeves	31,866
24	26	(a)	Everton	W 2-0	Gow, Power	36,194
25	27	(h)	Wolves	W 4-0	Hutchison (2), McDonald, Reeves	37,817
26	Jan 10	(a)	Coventry C	D 1-1	MacKenzie	18,248
27	17	(h)	Middlesbrough	W 3-2	Hutchison, Reeves, McDonald	30,774
28	31	(a)	Aston Villa	L 0-1		33,682
29	Feb 7	(h)	Nottingham F	D 1-1	Power	39,524
30	21	(h)	Manchester U	W 1-0	MacKenzie	50,114
31	24	(a)	Arsenal	L 0-2		24,790
32	Mar 14	(h)	West Brom A	W 2-1	McDonald, Tueart	36,581
33	18	(a)	Stoke C	L 1-2	McDonald	15,842
34	21	(a)	Birmingham C	L 0-2		16,160
35	28	(h)	Brighton & H A	D 1-1	MacKenzie	30,122
36	31	(h)	Leicester C	D 3-3	Reeves (2), Henry	26,144
37	Apr 4	(a)	Norwich C	L 0-2		17,957
38	18	(a)	Wolves	W 3-1	Bennett (2), Tueart	17,371
39	20	(h)	Everton	W 3-1	Bennett, MacKenzie, Reeves	34,434
40	25	(a)	Ipswich T	L 0-1		22,684
41	May 2	(h)	Crystal P	D 1-1	Bennett	31,017
42	14	(a)	Liverpool	L 0-1		24,462

Appearances
Sub Appnces
Goals

League Division One record: P 42   W 14   D 11   L 17   F 56   A 59   Pts 39   Pos 12th

FA Cup

3	Jan 3	(h)	Crystal P	W 4-0
4	24	(h)	Norwich C	W 6-0
5	Feb 14	(a)	Peterborough U	W 1-0
6	Mar 7	(a)	Everton	D 2-2
R	11	(h)	Everton	W 3-1
SF	Apr 11	(n)	Ipswich T	W 1-0
F	May 9	(n)	Tottenham H	D 1-1
R	14	(n)	Tottenham H	L 2-3

League Cup

2	Aug 27	(a)	Stoke C	D 1-1
2	Sep 3	(h)	Stoke C	W 3-0
3	23	(a)	Luton T	W 2-1
4	Oct 29	(h)	Notts C	W 5-1
5	Dec 3	(h)	West Brom A	W 2-1
SF	Jan 14	(h)	Liverpool	L 0-1
SF	Feb 10	(a)	Liverpool	D 1-1

Corrigan	Ranson	McDonald	Reid	Caton	Power	Booth	Tueart	Bennett	Mackenzie	Reeves	Henry	Hutchison	Gow	Daley	Boyer	Buckley	Sugrue	MacRae	Palmer	Williams	Deyna	Stepanovic	Kinsey	May	
1	2		4	3	10	5	7			11	6			8			9								1
1		2	3	10	5	7				11	6			8			9*	12				4			2
1	2		3	5	10	4	7			11	6			8			9*	12							3
	2		3	5	10	4		7		9	11	6		8					1						4
		2	5	3	4	7	10			9	11	6		8					1						5
		2	5	3	4	7	10			9	11	6		8					1						6
1		2	5	3	4	7	10	9			6*			8					12	11					7
1	2		3	5	7	4	10*			11	6			8	12		9								8
1	2		3	5	7	4				9	11	6		8			10								9
1	2		3	5	7	4				9	11	6		8			10*	12							10
1	2		3	5	7	4				9	11	6		8			10								11
1	2		4	6	3	5				10	9	11	7	8											12
1	12		2	6	3	5*	7			9	11	4		8	10										13
1	2	3	4	6	5		7			9	11		10	8											14
1	2	3	4	6	5		7	11	9				10*	8	12										15
1	2	3	4	6*	5		7	12	9	11			10	8											16
1	2	3	4		5	6	7*12	9	11				10	8											17
1	2	3	4		5	6	7	8	11				10	8											18
1	2	3	4		5	6	7*	9	11	12			10	8											19
1	2	3	4		5	6	7	9	11				10	8											20
1	2	3	4		5	6	7*		9	11			10	8	12										21
1	2	3	4		5	6		12	9*11				10	8	7										22
1	2	3	4		5	6*		9	11	12			10	8	7										23
1	2	3	4	6	5			9	11				10	8	7										24
1	2	3	4	6	5			9	11				10	8	7										25
1	2	3	4	6	5			9	11				10	8	7										26
1	2*	3	4	6	5			12	9	11			10	8	7										27
1		3			6	5	4			7	9	11	2	10	8										28
1		3			6	5	4	7		9	11	2	10	8											29
1		3	4		5	6				7	9	11	2	10	8										30
1	2	3*	4	6	5			12	7	9	11		10	8											31
	2	3	4	6	5			7		9	11	10		8*			12		1						32
1	2	3	4	12	5	6	7			9*11	10			8											33
1	2*	3			6	5	4	7	12	9	11			8	10										34
1	2	3	4	6	5			7*12	9	11				8	10										35
1	2	3	4	6	5			7	9	11				8	10										36
1	2	3	4		5	6		7	9	11	8		10												37
1		3			6*	5	4	8	7	9	11	2		12							10				38
		3	4		5	6	8	7	9	12	2			10	11*										39
1	2		4		5	6	8	7	9	11	3			10*								12			40
1	2	3			6	5		7	9	11	4	10	8												41
	2	3	4		5	6	11	7	9			10	8						1						42
37	32	28	37	29	42	30	21	20	39	38	25	24	20	14	6	4	4	3	3	2	2	1	1	0	
	1		1		1	6		1	2		1	1	2	1		2	1		1			1			
	1	4		4	8	7	6	12	2	3	5	2	1					1							

Friendlies

1. Jul 21 (a) Bath City — W 3-2
2. 25 (a) Nuneaton — W 3-1
3. Aug 12 (h) Legia Warsaw — L 1-5
4. Sep 15 (a) Lancaster C — W 9-1
5. Mar 23 (a) Bideford — W 5-0
6. Apr 27 (a) Penrith — W 2-1
7. May 20 (h) Manchester City 1969 FA Cup XI — W 9-2

Tour (to Portugal and Holland)

1. Jul 30 (a) Oporto — D 0-0
2. Aug 5 (a) Braga — W 3-1
3. 7 (a) Sporting Lisbon — W 2-1
4. 9 (a) Breda — W 3-2

Tour (to Spain and Canada)

1. May 30 (a) Real Betis — L 1-3
2. 31 (a) Beveren — L 0-4
3. Jun 3 (a) Vancouver Whitecaps — L 0-2

1981-82

1	Aug 29	(h)	West Brom A	W 2-1	Tueart, Hutchison	36,187
2	Sep 1	(a)	Notts C	D 1-1	McDonald	14,546
3	5	(a)	Stoke C	W 3-1	Francis (2), Boyer	25,256
4	12	(h)	Southampton	D 1-1	Reeves	42,003
5	19	(a)	Birmingham C	L 0-3		20,109
6	23	(h)	Leeds U	W 4-0	Tueart (2), Reeves (2)	35,077
7	26	(h)	Tottenham H	L 0-1		39,085
8	Oct 3	(a)	Brighton & H A	L 1-4	Reeves	18,300
9	10	(h)	Manchester U	D 0-0		52,037
10	17	(a)	Arsenal	L 0-1		25,470
11	24	(h)	Nottingham F	D 0-0		34,881
12	31	(a)	Everton	W 1-0	Tueart	31,305
13	Nov 7	(h)	Middlesbrough	W 3-2	Tueart, Reeves, Francis	32,025
14	21	(h)	Swansea C	W 4-0	Reeves (2), Tueart (2)	34,744
15	28	(a)	Ipswich T	L 0-2		20,476
16	Dec 5	(h)	Aston Villa	W 1-0	Tueart	32,487
17	12	(a)	Coventry C	W 1-0	Tueart	12,398
18	19	(h)	Sunderland	L 2-3	Francis (2)	29,462
19	26	(a)	Liverpool	W 3-1	Reeves, Bond, Hartford	37,929
20	28	(h)	Wolves	W 2-1	Francis, Hartford	40,298
21	Jan 9	(h)	Stoke C	D 1-1	Francis	31,941
22	30	(h)	Birmingham C	W 4-2	Reeves (2), Francis (2)	28,438
23	Feb 2	(a)	West Ham U	D 1-1	Bond	26,552
24	5	(a)	Southampton	L 1-2	McDonald	22,645
25	13	(h)	Brighton & H A	W 4-0	McDonald, Reeves, Francis, opp.og	30,038
26	20	(a)	Tottenham H	L 0-2		46,181
27	27	(a)	Manchester U	D 1-1	Reeves	57,872
28	Mar 6	(h)	Arsenal	D 0-0		30,288
29	10	(a)	Leeds U	W 1-0	Reeves	20,797
30	13	(a)	Nottingham F	D 1-1	Caton	20,927
31	20	(h)	Everton	D 1-1	Bond	33,002
32	27	(a)	Middlesbrough	D 0-0		11,709
33	Apr 3	(h)	West Ham U	L 0-1		30,875
34	10	(h)	Everton	L 0-5		40,112
35	12	(a)	Wolves	L 1-4	McDonald	14,891
36	17	(a)	Swansea C	L 0-2		19,212
37	21	(a)	West Brom A	W 1-0	Francis	11,703
38	24	(h)	Ipswich T	D 1-1	Hartford	30,329
39	May 1	(a)	Aston Villa	D 0-0		22,150
40	5	(h)	Notts C	W 1-0	Power	24,443
41	8	(h)	Coventry C	L 1-3	Francis	27,580
42	15	(a)	Sunderland	L 0-1		26,167

Appearances
Sub Appnces
Goals

League Division One record: P 42   W 15   D 13   L 14   F 49   A 50   Pts 58   Pos 10th

FA Cup

3	Jan 2	(h)	Cardiff C	W 3-1
4	23	(h)	Coventry C	L 1-3

League Cup

2	Oct 7	(h)	Stoke C	W 2-0
2	28	(a)	Stoke C	L 0-2
3	Nov 11	(h)	Northampton T	W 3-1
4	Dec 1	(a)	Barnsley	L 0-1

Friendlies

1	Aug 1	(a)	Bideford	W 4-1
2	3	(a)	Glasgow Rangers	L 0-2
3	25	(a)	AC Milan	L 0-1
4	Sep 16	(a)	Rosenberg	W 3-0
5	Nov 3	(a)	Leyland Motors	W 3-2
6	Dec 6	(a)	Cork U	W 4-0
7	Jan 12	(a)	Bordeaux	D 2-2
8	Feb 9	(h)	England XI	L 1-2
9	15	(a)	Poole T	W 6-1
10	Mar 2	(a)	Newport C	L 0-1
11	24	(a)	Burnley	D 3-3
12	31	(a)	Gothenburg	D 1-1
13	May 11	(a)	Port Vale	L 0-1
14	18	(a)	Kuwait	L 1-2

Appearance grid (shirt numbers; * denotes substitution). The final column is the match number.

Corrigan	Ranson	McDonald	Reid	Bond	Caton	Tueart	Reeves	Francis	Hartford	Hutchison	Power	Ryan	Kinsey	O'Neill	Boyer	Hareide	Gow	Jackson	Williams	May	Wilson	Booth	Elliott	Henry	#
1	2	3	4		6*	8	11			10	5			7	9								12		1
	2	3	4		6		11			10	5			7	9	8		1					12		2
1	2	3	4		5		11	9		10	6*			7	12	8									3
1	2	3	4		6		11	9		10				7	5	8									4
1			4	2	3	6	11	9		10				7	12	8			5						5
1	2	3	4		6	7	11	9		10	5*			12		8									6
1	2	3	4	12	6	7	11			10				5	9*	8									7
1	2	3	4	5	6	7	11							8	9										8
1	2		4	3	6	7	11			10	9	5		8											9
1	2		4	3	6	7	11			10	9	5		8											10
1	2		4	3	6	7	11			10	9	5		8*	12										11
1	2	3	4	5	6	7	11			12	10				9	8*									12
1	2	3	4	5	6	7	8	9	10	12	11*														13
1	2	3	4	5	6*	7	8	9	10	11					12										14
1	2	3	4	5		7	8	9	10	11			6												15
1	2	3	4	5	6	7	8	9	10	11															16
1	2	3	4	5	6	7	8	9	10	11															17
1	2	3	4	5	6	7*	8	9	10	11					12										18
1	2	3	4	5	6		8	9	10	11		7													19
1	2		4	5	6		8	9	10	11		7							3						20
1		3	4	5	6		8	9	10	11		2		7											21
1	2	3		5	6		8	9	10			11	4	7											22
1	2	3		5	6		8	9	10			11	4*	7	12										23
1	2	3		5	6		8	9			10*	11	4	7	12										24
1	2	3	4	5*	6		8	9	10			11		7	12										25
1	2	3	4	5*	6		8	9	10			11		7				12							26
1	2	3	4		6		8		10			11		7	5			9							27
1	2	3	4		6		8	9*	10			11		7	5			12							28
1	2	3	4	5	6		8					11		7	9			10							29
1	2	3	4	5	6		8		10			11*		7	12			9							30
1	2	3	4	5	6		8	9	10					7	11										31
1	2		4		6		8	9						7	11			5*	12	3	10				32
1	2	3	4		6		8		10				5	7	9			11							33
1	2	3	4	5	6		8		10					7	9						11				34
1	2	3		5			8	9	10					7	11	4	6*	12							35
	2	3	4	5	6		8	9	10						11		12	1	7*						36
1	2	3	4		6		8	9	10				6	7	11*			12							37
1	2*	3		5	6		8	9	10				4	7	11			12							38
1		3	4	5	6		8		10			11		7	12			9	2*						39
1		3	4	5	6		8		10			11	2	7	9										40
		3	4	5	6		8	9	10			11		7			1	2							41
1		3	4		6		8		10			5	2	7	9			11			12				42
39	36	36	36	32	39	15	42	26	30	20	25	19	13	12	10	9	6	6	3	3	3	1	1	0	
				1							2			3	1	2	7	2		3	1		2		
		4			3	1	9	13	12	3	1	1			1										

Tour (to West Germany and Iceland)

1	Aug	5	(a)	Werder Bremen	L 0-8
2		8	(a)	PSV Eindhoven	D 1-1
3		12	(a)	Ther Akureyric	W 5-0
4		13	(a)	Iceland National XI	W 2-1

Tour (to West Indies)

1	May	28	(a)	Trinidad	W 2-1
2		30	(a)	Trinidad	W 4-0

1982-83

1	Aug 28	(a)	Norwich C	W 2-1	Power, Cross	22,638
2	Sep 1	(h)	Stoke C	W 1-0	Cross	27,847
3	4	(h)	Watford	W 1-0	Tueart	29,617
4	7	(a)	Notts C	L 0-1		9,376
5	11	(a)	Tottenham H	W 2-1	Baker (2)	32,483
6	18	(h)	Aston Villa	L 0-1		28,650
7	25	(a)	West Ham U	L 1-4	Boyer	23,883
8	Oct 2	(h)	Coventry C	W 3-2	Baker, Caton, Cross	25,105
9	9	(a)	Everton	L 1-2	Cross	25,158
10	16	(h)	Sunderland	D 2-2	Cross, Reeves	25,053
11	23	(a)	Manchester U	D 2-2	Tueart, Cross	57,334
12	30	(h)	Swansea C	W 2-1	Tueart, Hartford	25,021
13	Nov 6	(h)	Southampton	W 2-0	McDonald, Reeves	25,115
14	13	(a)	Ipswich T	L 0-1		19,523
15	20	(h)	Birmingham C	D 0-0		23,174
16	27	(a)	Nottingham F	L 0-3		18,845
17	Dec 4	(h)	Arsenal	W 2-1	Caton (2)	23,057
18	11	(a)	Luton T	L 1-3	Cross	11,013
19	18	(h)	Brighton & H A	D 1-1	Bond	20,615
20	27	(a)	Liverpool	L 2-5	Caton, Cross	44,664
21	28	(h)	West Brom A	W 2-1	Kinsey, opp.og	25,172
22	Jan 1	(a)	Birmingham C	D 2-2	Bond, Bodak	16,362
23	3	(a)	Watford	L 0-2		20,049
24	15	(h)	Norwich C	W 4-1	Cross (2), Bond, Hartford	22,000
25	22	(a)	Aston Villa	D 1-1	Hartford	20,415
26	Feb 5	(h)	Tottenham H	D 2-2	Tueart, Cross	26,357
27	12	(a)	Coventry C	L 0-4		9,527
28	19	(h)	Notts C	L 0-1		21,199
29	26	(a)	Sunderland	L 2-3	Reeves, Caton	15,124
30	Mar 2	(h)	Everton	D 0-0		22,253
31	5	(h)	Manchester U	L 1-2	Reeves	45,400
32	12	(a)	Swansea C	L 1-4	McDonald	9,884
33	19	(a)	Southampton	L 1-4	Reeves	17,201
34	26	(h)	Ipswich T	L 0-1		21,845
35	Apr 2	(a)	West Brom A	W 2-0	Reeves, Cross	13,654
36	4	(h)	Liverpool	L 0-4		35,647
37	9	(a)	Stoke C	L 0-1		15,372
38	16	(h)	West Ham U	W 2-0	McDonald, Tueart	23,015
39	23	(a)	Arsenal	L 0-3		16,810
40	30	(h)	Nottingham F	L 1-2	Baker	23,563
41	May 7	(a)	Brighton & H A	W 1-0	Reeves	17,794
42	14	(h)	Luton T	L 0-1		42,843

Appearances
Sub Appnces
Goals

League Division One record: P 42 W 13 D 8 L 21 F 47 A 70 Pts 47 Pos 20th

FA Cup

3	Jan 8	(a)	Sunderland	D 0-0	
R	12	(h)	Sunderland	W 2-1	
4	29	(a)	Brighton & H A	L 0-4	

League Cup

2	Oct 5	(a)	Wigan A	D 1-1	
2	27	(h)	Wigan A	W 2-0	
3	Nov 10	(h)	Southampton	D 1-1	
R	24	(a)	Southampton	L 0-4	

Tour (to North America)

1	May 25	(a)	Tampa Bay Rowdies	W 1-0	
2	28	(a)	Ft.Lauderdale	W 4-2	

Friendlies

1	Sep 28	(a)	Barrow	D 2-2	
2	Oct 13	(a)	Sheffield U	D 2-2	
3	Nov 3	(a)	Tranmere R	W 5-2	
4	Apr 20	(a)	Maidstone U	W 4-2	

Tours (to Norway, Germany, Greece, Spain)

1	Aug 3	(a)	Lillestroem	L 1-2	
2	5	(a)	Valerengen	W 3-1	
3	12	(a)	Hertha Berlin	L 0-2	
4	13	(a)	VFL Bochum	W 3-1	
5	16	(a)	AEK Athens	L 0-1	
6	18	(a)	Olympiakos	L 0-2	
7	24	(a)	FC Cologne	D 1-1	
8	25	(a)	Int.Porto Al.	L 1-3	

Corrigan	Williams	Ranson	McDonald	Reid	Bond	Caton	Tueart	Reeves	Cross	Hartford	Power	Baker	Kinsey	Bodak	Hareide	May	Jones	Davies	Golac	Lomax	Boyer	Hildersley	Simpson	Park	
1		2	3		5	6		8	9	10	11	4			7										1
1		2	3		5	6		8	9	10	11	4			7										2
1*		2	3		5	6	12	8	9	10	11	4			7										3
	1	2	3		5	6	12	8	9*	10	11	4			7										4
	1	2	3		5	6	12	8		10	11	4			7	9*									5
	1	2	3*		5	6	12	8		10	11	4			7	9									6
	1	2	3*		5	6	12	8		10	11	4			7			9							7
	1	2			5	6	7	8	9	10	3	4											11		8
	1	2		4		6	7	8	9		3	5		10		11*							12		9
1		2		4		6	7	8	9	10	5		11*			3							12		10
1		2	3		4	6	7	8	9	10	5	11													11
1		2	3		4	6	7	8	9	10	5	11													12
1		2	3		4	6	7	8	9	10	5	11													13
1		2	3	12	4	6	7	8	9	10	5	11*													14
1		2	3		4	6	7	8	9	10	5	11													15
1		2	3	4	10	6	7	8	9		5			11											16
1		2	3		4	6	7	8	9	10	5	11													17
1		2	3	4	11	6	7	8	9	10	5														18
1		2	3		4	6	7	8	9*	10	5		11	12											19
1		2	3		4	6	7	8	9	10	5		11												20
1		2	3	4	6		7	8	9	10		5	11												21
1		2	3	4	6		7	8	9	10		5	11												22
1		2	3	4	6		7	8		10	5	9	11												23
1		2		4	3		7	8	9	10	5	6	11												24
1		2		4	3	6	7	8	9	10	5		11												25
1		2	3	4	5	6	7	8	9	10			11												26
	1	2	3*	4	5	6		8	9	10			11		7								12		27
1		2			5	6	7	8	9	10			11*	3			4						12		28
1		2	3		5	6	7	8		10		9	11	4											29
1		2	3	4	5	6	7	8		10		9	11												30
1		2	3	4	5	6	7	8	9	10		11*	12												31
1			3	4	5	6	7	8	9				11			12		2			10*				32
	1			4	5	6	7	8	9		10	11				12		3*	2						33
	1	2		4	5	6	12	8	9	10	3	11			7*										34
	1	2		4	5	6		8	9	10	3	11	7			12									35
	1	2		4	5	6		8	9	10	3	11*	7												36
	1	2	3	4	5	6		8	9	10	11		7												37
	1	2	3	4	5	6	7	8		10	11		9												38
	1	2*	3	4	5	6	7			10	11	8	9	12											39
	1	2	3	4	5	6	7			10	11	8	9												40
	1	2	3	4	5	6	7	8		10	11	9													41
	1	2	3	4	5	6	7	8		10	11	9*	12												42
25	17	40	32	24	40	38	30	40	31	38	33	27	12	12	8	4	3	2	2	1	1	1	1	0	
			1			6							1	2		4							2	2	
		3		3	5	5	7	12	3	1	4	1	1								1				

1983-84

1	Aug 27	(a)	Crystal P	W 2-0	May, Parlane		13,382
2	29	(a)	Cardiff C	L 1-2	Tolmie		8,899
3	Sep 3	(h)	Barnsley	W 3-2	Tolmie (2), Parlane		25,105
4	7	(h)	Fulham	D 0-0			23,356
5	10	(a)	Portsmouth	W 2-1	Parlane, Tolmie		18,852
6	17	(h)	Blackburn R	W 6-0	Parlane (3), Baker, Tolmie, May		25,433
7	24	(a)	Leeds U	W 2-1	Parlane, Baker		21,918
8	Oct 1	(h)	Grimsby T	W 2-1	Caton, Tolmie		25,080
9	8	(h)	Swansea C	W 2-1	Parlane, Davidson		23,571
10	15	(a)	Charlton A	L 0-1			7,639
11	22	(h)	Middlesbrough	W 2-1	Parlane, Tolmie		24,466
12	29	(a)	Newcastle U	L 0-5			33,588
13	Nov 5	(a)	Shrewsbury T	W 3-1	May, Caton, Kinsey		9,471
14	12	(h)	Brighton & H A	W 4-0	Baker (2), Parlane, Tolmie		24,562
15	19	(a)	Carlisle U	L 0-2			8,745
16	26	(h)	Derby C	D 1-1	Parlane		22,689
17	Dec 3	(a)	Chelsea	W 1-0	Tolmie		29,142
18	10	(h)	Sheffield W	L 1-2	Bond		41,852
19	17	(a)	Cambridge U	D 0-0			5,204
20	26	(h)	Oldham A	W 2-0	Parlane, Kinsey		35,898
21	27	(a)	Huddersfield T	W 3-1	Lomax, Baker, Kinsey		23,497
22	31	(a)	Barnsley	D 1-1	Parlane		17,148
23	Jan 2	(h)	Leeds U	D 1-1	Tolmie		34,441
24	14	(h)	Crystal P	W 3-1	Power, Baker, Kinsey		20,144
25	21	(a)	Blackburn R	L 1-2	Tolmie		18,199
26	Feb 4	(a)	Grimsby T	D 1-1	Parlane		11,986
27	11	(h)	Portsmouth	W 2-1	Tolmie, Reid		23,138
28	18	(h)	Newcastle U	L 1-2	Kinsey		41,767
29	25	(a)	Middlesbrough	D 0-0			9,343
30	Mar 3	(h)	Shrewsbury T	W 1-0	Reid		20,083
31	10	(a)	Brighton & H A	D 1-1	Hartford		14,132
32	17	(a)	Fulham	L 1-5	McNab		9,684
33	24	(h)	Cardiff C	W 2-1	Baker, Johnson		20,140
34	31	(h)	Charlton A	L 0-1			19,147
35	Apr 7	(a)	Swansea C	W 2-0	Parlane, Kinsey		7,254
36	14	(h)	Carlisle U	W 3-1	May, Smith, Parlane		20,740
37	20	(a)	Oldham A	D 2-2	Bond, McCarthy		19,952
38	23	(h)	Huddersfield T	L 2-3	Bond (2)		23,247
39	28	(a)	Derby C	L 0-1			14,470
40	May 4	(h)	Chelsea	L 0-2			21,713
41	7	(a)	Sheffield W	D 0-0			36,763
42	12	(h)	Cambridge U	W 5-0	Power, May, Baker, Tolmie, Kinsey		20,787

Appearances
Sub Appnces
Goals

League Division two record: P 42   W 20   D 10   L 12   F 66   A 48   Pts 70   Pos 4th

FA Cup

3 Jan 7 (a) Blackpool   L 1-2

League Cup

2 Oct 5 (a) Torquay U   D 0-0
R   25 (h) Torquay U   W 6-0
3 Nov 9 (a) Aston Villa   L 0-3

Friendlies

1 Aug 18 (a) Blackpool   L 1-3
2 May 14 (a) Stockport C   W 4-0

Tour (to West Germany)

1	Aug 5	(a)	FC Pofungstadt	W 4-2
2	6	(a)	FC Eppingham	W 4-2
3	7	(a)	FC Osterode	W 4-0
4	9	(a)	FC Sinsheim	W 4-1
5	10	(a)	FC Wolfsbung	W 6-0
6	12	(a)	FC Willem II	W 4-3

Williams	Ranson	May	Bond	Power	Caton	McCarthy	McNab	Baker	Parlane	Tolmie	Reid	Lomax	Kinsey	Wilson	Smith	Hartford	Davies	Dalziel	Walsh	Johnson	Davidson	Hoyland	No.
1	2	3	4	5	6		7		9	11	8					10							1
1	2	3	4	5	6		7		9	11	8		12			10*							2
1	2	3	4	5	6		7	10	9	11	8												3
1	2	3	4	5	6		7	10	9	11	8												4
1	2	7	4	5	6		10		9	11	8						3						5
1	2	3	4	5	6		7	10	9*	11	8									12			6
1	2	8*		5	6		7	10	9	11	4						3			12			7
1	2	8*		5	6		7	10	9	11	4						3						8
1	2	8*		5	6		7	10	9	11	4						3			12			9
1	2	8*		5	6		7	10	9	11	4						3			12			10
1	2	3		5	6		7	10	9	11									4	8			11
1	2	3		5	6		7	10	9	11			12						4	8*			12
1	2	3		5	6		7	10	9	11	4	8											13
1	2	8		5	6		7	10	9	11	4			3									14
1	2	8*12		5	6		7	10	9	11	4			3									15
1	2*	8	4	5	6	7			9	11				3				12				10	16
1		3	4	5		7			9	11		2	12			10		8	6*				17
1	2	6	4	5		7			9	11		3	12			10		8*					18
1		3	4	5		6	7	8	9	11		2	10										19
1		3	4	5		6	7	8	9	11		2	10										20
1		3	4	5		6	7	8	9	11		2	10										21
1	12	3	4	5		6	7	8	9	11		2	10*										22
1		3	4	5		6	7	8	9	11		2				10							23
1		3	4	5		6	7	8	9	11		2	10										24
1		3	4	5		6	7	8	9	11		2	10										25
1		3	4	5		6	7	8	9	11		2	10										26
1		3	4	5		6	7	8	9*	11	12	2	10										27
1		3	4	5		6	7	8	9*	11	2	12	10										28
1	2	9	4	5		6	7	12		11*	8	3	10										29
1		3	4	5		6	7	8	9	11*		2	10					12					30
1		3	11	5		6	8				8	4	2	9		10		7					31
1		3	4	5		6	7	8	9	11		2				10							32
1	2	3*	4	5		6	7	10	9	12					8					11			33
1	2	3	4	5		6	7*10		9	11			12							8			34
1		5	4			6		8	9	11		2	10	3	7								35
1		5	4			6		8	9	11*		2	10	3	7					12			36
1		5	4			6		8	9	12		2*10		3	7					11			37
1	2	5	4			6		8	9	12			10	3	7					11*			38
1	2	5	4			6	10	8	9*	11			12	3	7								39
1	2	7*	4	5		6		8	9	11				3	10					12			40
1	2	7	4	5		6		8	9	11				3	10								41
1	2	7	4	5		6		8	9*11				12	3	10								42
42	25	42	33	37	16	24	33	36	40	38	18	16	16	11	9	7	5	4	3	4	2	1	
	1		1							1	3	1	1	7					1	1	2	4	
		5	4	2	2	1	1	8	16	13	2	1	7		1	1			1	1			

189

1984-85

1	Aug 24	(a)	Wimbledon	D 2-2	Smith, Parlane	8,365
2	27	(h)	Grimsby T	W 3-0	Bond, Smith, Parlane	21,137
3	Sep 1	(h)	Fulham	L 2-3	Parlane (2)	21,071
4	4	(a)	Wolves	L 0-2		13,255
5	8	(a)	Carlisle U	D 0-0		6,641
6	15	(h)	Huddersfield T	W 1-0	Baker	20,201
7	22	(a)	Cardiff C	W 3-0	Smith, Cunningham, Wilson	6,089
8	29	(h)	Crystal P	W 2-1	Smith, Kinsey	20,252
9	Oct 6	(h)	Oxford U	W 1-0	Kinsey	24,755
10	13	(a)	Shrewsbury T	L 0-1		8,563
11	20	(a)	Middlesbrough	L 1-2	Kinsey	7,737
12	27	(h)	Blackburn R	W 2-1	opp.og, May	23,798
13	Nov 3	(a)	Brighton & H A	D 0-0		14,034
14	10	(h)	Birmingham C	W 1-0	Phillips	25,369
15	17	(a)	Sheffield U	D 0-0		16,605
16	24	(h)	Portsmouth	D 2-2	Kinsey, Smith	23,700
17	Dec 1	(a)	Oldham A	W 2-0	Smith, Melrose	14,129
18	8	(h)	Notts C	W 2-0	Phillips, Melrose	20,109
19	15	(a)	Charlton A	W 3-1	Phillips, Smith, Melrose	6,247
20	22	(a)	Fulham	L 2-3	Baker, Melrose	6,847
21	26	(h)	Barnsley	D 1-1	Melrose	27,131
22	29	(h)	Wolves	W 4-0	Phillips, Smith, Baker, Wilson	22,022
23	Jan 1	(a)	Leeds U	D 1-1	Melrose	22,626
24	12	(a)	Huddersfield T	W 2-0	Smith, Wilson	15,640
25	19	(h)	Wimbledon	W 3-0	Phillips, Smith, Baker	23,303
26	Feb 2	(a)	Crystal P	W 2-1	Phillips, Wilson	7,668
27	9	(h)	Carlisle U	L 1-3	Phillips	21,347
28	23	(h)	Brighton & H A	W 2-0	Phillips, Smith	20,227
29	Mar 2	(a)	Blackburn R	W 1-0	Kinsey	22,099
30	9	(h)	Middlesbrough	W 1-0	Phillips	22,399
31	16	(h)	Shrewsbury T	W 4-0	Smith, May, Power, Kinsey	20,828
32	19	(a)	Birmingham C	D 0-0		18,004
33	23	(a)	Oxford U	L 0-3		13,096
34	30	(h)	Cardiff C	D 2-2	Simpson, Kinsey	20,047
35	Apr 6	(a)	Barnsley	D 0-0		12,930
36	8	(h)	Leeds U	L 1-2	Tolmie	33,553
37	13	(a)	Grimsby T	L 1-4	Simpson	8,362
38	20	(h)	Sheffield U	W 2-0	Clements, Tolmie	21,132
39	27	(a)	Portsmouth	W 2-1	Phillips, Simpson	22,232
40	May 4	(h)	Oldham A	D 0-0		28,933
41	6	(a)	Notts C	L 2-3	Simpson (2)	17,812
42	11	(h)	Charlton A	W 5-1	Phillips (2), May, Simpson, Melrose	47,285

Appearances
Sub Appnces
Goals

League Division Two record: P 42   W 21   D 11   L 10   F 66   A 40   Pts 74   Pos 3rd

FA Cup

3	Jan 5	(a)	Coventry C	L 1-2

League Cup

2	Sep 25	(h)	Blackpool	W 4-2
2	Oct 9	(a)	Blackpool	W 3-1
3	31	(h)	West Ham U	D 0-0
R	Nov 6	(a)	West Ham U	W 2-1
4	21	(a)	Chelsea	L 1-4

Friendlies

1	Aug 3	(a)	Hibernian	D 0-0
2	5	(a)	Partick T	L 1-3

Friendlies (cont)

3	Aug 16	(h)	Tottenham H	L 0-2
4	18	(a)	Crewe A	W 5-1
5	19	(a)	Chester C	L 1-2
6	Sep 9	(a)	Q of the South	W 5-1
7	Oct 3	(a)	Elsborg	L 1-2
8	Nov 14	(h)	Australian XI	L 1-3
9	May 16	(a)	Bury	W 2-0

#	Williams	May	Power	Reid	McCarthy	Phillips	Smith	Baker	Cunningham	Melrose	Wilson	Kinsey	McNab	Clements	Simpson	McNaught	Parlane	Tolmie	Lomax	Bond	Beckford	Hoyland	Sinclair	#
1	1		3	5	2	11*	8	10		6		7				9	12		4					1
2	1		3	5	2	10	8	9		6		7					11		4					2
3	1		3	5	2	10*	8	9		4		7					11	12	6					3
4	1	2	3	4	5	6		8	9		10			7*			11	12						4
5	1	2	3	4	5	7		8	9	6	12						11	10*						5
6	1	2	3	4	5	6	7	8	9		10	12	11*											6
7	1	2	3	4	5	6	7	8*	9		10	11					12							7
8	1	2	3	4	5	6	7	8	9*		10	11					12							8
9	1	2	3	4	5	6	7*	8	9		10	11					12							9
10	1	2	3	4	5	6	7	8	9*		10	12	11											10
11	1	2	3	4	5	6	7*	8	9		10	11						12						11
12	1	2	3	4	5	6	7	8	9		10	11												12
13	1	2	3	4	5	6	7	8*	9		10	11						12						13
14	1	2	3	4	5	6	7		9	12	10	11*	8											14
15	1	5	3	4		6	7		9	11*	10		8	12		2								15
16	1	5	3	4		6	12	8	9	7	10	11											2*	16
17	1	2	3	4	5	6	7	8			9	10	11											17
18	1	2	3	4	5	6	7	8			9	10	11											18
19	1	2	3	4	5	6	7	8			9	10	11											19
20	1	2	3	4	5	6	7	8			9	10	11											20
21	1	2	3		5	6	7*	8	12		9	10	11		4									21
22	1	2	3		5	6	7	8			9	10	11		4									22
23	1	2	3		5	6	7	8			9	10	11		4									23
24	1	2	3		5	6	7	8			9	10	11		4									24
25	1	2	3		5	6	7	8	12		9*	10	11		4									25
26	1	2	3		5	6	7	8			9	10	11		4									26
27	1	2	3	12	5*	6	7	8			9	10	11		4									27
28	1	2	3	4	5	6	7	8			9					10	11							28
29	1	2	3	4	5	6	7	8*			9	11	10				12							29
30	1	8	3	4	5	6	7				9	11	10	2										30
31	1	8*	3	4	5	6	7				9	11	10	2			12							31
32	1	8	3	4	5	6	7				9	11	10	2										32
33	1	8	3	4	5	6*	7				9	11	10	2			12							33
34	1	8*	3	4	5	6					9	11	12	2	7	10								34
35	1	2	10	4	5	6		8			9	11				12	7			3				35
36	1	2	10	4	5	6		8*				11					7	12		3			9	36
37	1	3	10	8	5	6						11		4	7	9	2*				12			37
38	1	8	3	4	5	6					9*	11	12	2	7	10								38
39	1	8	3	4	5	6	10					11		2	7	9								39
40	1	8	3	4	5	6						11	10	2	7			12				9*		40
41	1	8	9	4	5	6						11	10	2	7					3				41
42	1	4	3			6					9	11	8	5	7	10	2							42
	42	39	42	31	39	42	31	29	16	23	27	33	15	11	9	7	7	7	6	3	1	1	1	
		1				1		2	1		2	3	1	1			10	1		3				
		3	1			12	12	4	1	7	4	7		1	6		4	2	1					

Tour (to Republic of Ireland)

1	Aug	8	(a)	Waterford	W 4-1
2		10	(a)	Drogheda	D 2-2
3		12	(a)	Finn Harps	W 5-0

Tour (to Singapore)

1	Jan	23	(a)	Trenggana	W 2-0
2		24	(a)	Selanger State	W 1-0
3		27	(a)	Kelantan State	W 3-0
4		29	(a)	Kedah State	W 5-0

1985-86

1	Aug 17	(a)	Coventry C	D 1-1	McIlroy	14,550
2	21	(h)	Leicester C	D 1-1	Lillis	25,528
3	24	(h)	Sheffield W	L 1-3	Simpson	26,934
4	26	(a)	West Brom A	W 3-2	Simpson, Wilson, Lillis	12,122
5	31	(h)	Tottenham H	W 2-1	Simpson, opp.og	27,789
6	Sep 3	(a)	Birmingham C	L 0-1		11,706
7	7	(a)	Southampton	L 0-3		14,308
8	14	(h)	Manchester U	L 0-3		48,773
9	21	(h)	West Ham U	D 2-2	Lillis, Malone	22,001
10	28	(a)	Oxford U	L 0-1		9,796
11	Oct 5	(h)	Chelsea	L 0-1		20,104
12	12	(a)	Watford	L 2-3	Lillis, McNab	15,418
13	19	(a)	Q.P.R.	D 0-0		13,471
14	26	(h)	Everton	D 1-1	Simpson	28,807
15	Nov 2	(a)	Arsenal	L 0-1		22,264
16	9	(h)	Ipswich T	D 1-1	Lillis	20,853
17	16	(a)	Nottingham F	W 2-0	Wilson, Simpson	15,140
18	23	(h)	Newcastle U	W 1-0	Lillis	25,179
19	30	(a)	Luton T	L 1-2	Lillis	10,096
20	Dec 7	(a)	Leicester C	D 1-1	Davies	10,289
21	14	(h)	Coventry C	W 5-1	Davies (2), Simpson (2), Lillis	20,075
22	21	(a)	Sheffield W	L 2-3	McNab, Lillis	23,177
23	26	(h)	Liverpool	W 1-0	Wilson	35,384
24	28	(h)	Birmingham C	D 1-1	McNab	24,955
25	Jan 1	(a)	Aston Villa	W 1-0	Lillis	14,215
26	11	(h)	Southampton	W 1-0	Phillips	21,674
27	18	(a)	Tottenham H	W 2-0	Lillis, Davies	17,009
28	Feb 1	(h)	West Brom A	W 2-1	Davies, Power	20,540
29	8	(h)	Q.P.R.	W 2-0	Davies, Simpson	20,414
30	11	(a)	Everton	L 0-4		30,006
31	Mar 1	(h)	Oxford U	L 0-3		20,099
32	8	(a)	Chelsea	L 0-1		17,573
33	15	(h)	Watford	L 0-1		18,899
34	22	(a)	Manchester U	D 2-2	Wilson, opp.og	52,174
35	29	(h)	Aston Villa	D 2-2	Wilson, McNab	20,935
36	31	(a)	Liverpool	L 0-2		43,316
37	Apr 5	(h)	Arsenal	L 0-1		19,590
38	12	(a)	Ipswich T	D 0-0		13,986
39	19	(h)	Nottingham F	L 1-2	Davies	19,715
40	26	(a)	Newcastle U	L 1-3	Davies	22,689
41	28	(a)	West Ham U	L 0-1		27,153
42	May 4	(h)	Luton T	D 1-1	Davies	20,361

Appearances
Sub Appnces
Goals

League Division One record: P 42   W 11   D 12   L 19   F 43   A 57   Pts 45   Pos 16th

FA Cup

3	Jan 4	(a)	Walsall	W 3-1
4	25	(h)	Watford	D 1-1
R	Feb 3	(a)	Watford	D 0-0
2R	6	(h)	Watford	L 1-3

League Cup

2	Sep 25	(a)	Bury	W 2-1
2	Oct 8	(h)	Bury	W 2-1
3	30	(h)	Arsenal	L 1-2

Full Members Cup

QR	Oct 14	(h)	Leeds U	W 6-1
QR	22	(a)	Sheffield U	W 2-1
SF	Nov 4	(h)	Sunderland*	D 0-0

*City won 4-3 on penalties

NF	Nov 26	(a)	Hull C	L 1-2
NF	Dec 11	(h)	Hull C	W 2-0
F	Mar 23	(n)	Chelsea	L 4-5

NF = Northern Final (played over two
      legs).

Nixon	Reid	Power	Clements	McCarthy	Phillips	Lillis	May	Davies	McNab	Simpson	Williams	Siddall	Barrett	Wilson	Johnson	Redmond	Baker	Beckford	Melrose	McIlroy	Kinsey	Moulden	Tolmie	Smith	#
		3	4		2	7			8	11	1			6	5					10	9				1
		3	4	5	2	7			8	11	1			6						10	9				2
		3	4	5	6*	7	2		8	11	1									10	9	12			3
			4	5	6	7	2		8	11	1			3						10	9				4
			4	5	6	7	2		8	11	1			3						10	9				5
			4	5	6		2		8	11	1			3				7*		10	9		12		6
			4	5	6	7	2		8	11	1			3					12	10*	9				7
		8	4	5	6	7	2			11	1			3					12	10	9*				8
1		8	4	5	6	7	2			11				3					9	10					9
1		3	4	5	6	7	2							8					9	10*12	11				10
1		3	4	5	6	7	2		10	11				8					9*	12					11
1		3	4	5	6	7	2	9	10	11				8											12
1	2	11		5	6	7	3	9	10				4				8								13
1	2	3	4	5	6	7		9	10	11				8											14
1	2	8	4	5	6	7	3	9	10*	11									12						15
1	2	8	4	5	6	7	3	9	10	11															16
1	2	3	4	5	6	7	8	9*	10	12			11												17
1	2	3	4	5	6	7	·8	9*	10	12			11												18
1	2	3		5	6	7	8	9	10				11*	4			12								19
1	2	3	4	5	6	7	8*	9	10	11								12							20
1	2	3	4	5*	6	7	8	9	10	11								12							21
1	2	3	4		6	7*	5	9	10	11			8					12							22
1	2	3	4	5	6		8	9	10				11					7							23
1	2	3	4	5	6	7	8	9	10	12			11*												24
1	2	3	4	5	6	7	8		10	11										9					25
1	2	3	4	5	6	7	8	9	10	11															26
1	2	3	4	5	6	7	8	9	10	11															27
1	2	3	4	5	6	7	8	9	10	11															28
1	2	3		5	6	7	8	9		11						4	10*								29
1	2	3		5	6	7	12	9	10	11						4	8*								30
1	2	3	4		6	7		9	10	11					5		8								31
1	2	3	4	5	6	7	8	9	10	11															32
1	2	3	4	5	6	7	8	9*	10	11											12				33
1	2	3	4*		6	7	8		10	12			11	5					9						34
1	2	3		5	6*	7	8		10	12			11	4					9						35
	2	3		5	6	7	8		10		1		11	4					9						36
	2	3		5	6		7	10	11		1		8	4					9						37
	2	3		5		10	7		8		1		9	4	6	11									38
	2	3		5		7	8	9*10	11		1		12	4	6										39
	2	3		5		7	8	9	10	12	1		11	4	6										40
		4		5	2	7	3	9	10	11*	1		6				12		8						41
1		4		5	6*	7	3	9	10	12	2	11					8								42
28	30	36	30	38	39	39	36	26	37	30	8	6	1	24	4	9	9	2	4	12	12	1	1	0	
	1					7					1			1			1	1	6		1	1	2	1		
	1				1	11			9	4	8			5						1	1					

Friendlies

#					
1	Jul	26	(a)	Preston N E	D 1-1
2		29	(a)	Stoke C	L 1-2
3		31	(a)	Carlisle U	W 3-0
4	Aug	1	(a)	Isle of Man XI	W 6-1

(above games played in the Isle of Man Tournament)

5	Aug	6	(a)	Hull C	L 1-2
6		9	(h)	Oldham A	W 3-1
7	Apr	6	(a)	Dundee	D 2-2

Tour (to North America)

1	May	25	(a)	Edmonton Brick	W 3-0
2		27	(a)	Seattle Storm	W 1-0
3		29	(a)	San Jose Earthquake	W 1-0
4		30	(a)	Dundee**	D 1-1
5	Jun	3	(a)	Hollywood Kickers	W 3-0
6		5	(a)	San Diego Sun	W 3-1
7		7	(a)	Los Angeles Heath	D 1-1

**In San Jose

1986-87

1	Aug	23	(h)	Wimbledon	W 3-1	Baker (2), Christie	20,756
2		25	(a)	Liverpool	D 0-0		39,989
3		30	(a)	Tottenham H	L 0-1		23,764
4	Sep	3	(h)	Norwich C	D 2-2	Christie (2)	19,122
5		6	(h)	Coventry C	L 0-1		18,320
6		13	(a)	Oxford U	D 0-0		8,245
7		20	(h)	Q.P.R.	D 0-0		17,774
8		27	(a)	Luton T	L 0-1		9,371
9	Oct	4	(h)	Leicester C	L 1-2	Hopkins	18,033
10		11	(a)	Newcastle U	L 1-3	Simpson	21,780
11		18	(a)	Chelsea	L 1-2	Varadi	12,990
12		26	(h)	Manchester U	D 1-1	McCarthy	32,440
13	Nov	1	(a)	Southampton	D 1-1	Baker	14,352
14		8	(h)	Aston Villa	W 3-1	Moulden (2), Varadi	22,875
15		15	(h)	Charlton A	W 2-1	Moulden, Simpson	20,578
16		22	(a)	Arsenal	L 0-3		29,009
17		29	(h)	Everton	L 1-3	Moulden	27,097
18	Dec	6	(a)	Nottingham F	L 0-2		19,129
19		13	(h)	West Ham U	W 3-1	Varadi (2), White	19,067
20		21	(a)	Coventry C	D 2-2	Redmond (2)	12,430
21		26	(h)	Sheffield W	W 1-0	Simpson	30,193
22		28	(a)	Charlton A	L 0-5		7,697
23	Jan	1	(a)	Watford	D 1-1	Varadi	15,514
24		3	(h)	Oxford U	W 1-0	McNab	20,724
25		17	(h)	Liverpool	L 0-1		35,336
26		24	(a)	Wimbledon	D 0-0		5,667
27	Feb	14	(a)	Norwich C	D 1-1	Brightwell	16,094
28		21	(h)	Luton T	D 1-1	Lake	17,507
29		28	(a)	Q.P.R.	L 0-1		12,739
30	Mar	7	(a)	Manchester U	L 0-2		48,619
31		14	(a)	Chelsea	L 1-2	McNab	19,819
32		21	(h)	Newcastle U	D 0-0		23,060
33		28	(a)	Leicester C	L 0-4		10,743
34	Apr	4	(a)	Aston Villa	D 0-0		18,241
35		11	(h)	Southampton	L 2-4	Stewart, Moulden	18,193
36		15	(h)	Tottenham H	D 1-1	McNab	21,460
37		18	(h)	Watford	L 1-2	McNab	18,541
38		20	(a)	Sheffield W	L 1-2	Varadi	19,769
39		25	(h)	Arsenal	W 3-0	Varadi (2), Stewart	18,072
40	May	2	(a)	Everton	D 0-0		37,541
41		4	(h)	Nottingham F	W 1-0	Varadi	21,405
42		9	(a)	West Ham U	L 0-2		18,413

Appearances
Sub Appnces
Goals

League Division One record: P 42 W 8 D 15 L 19 F 36 A 57 Pts 39 Pos 21st

FA Cup

3	Jan 10	(a)	Manchester	L 0-1

League Cup

2	Sep 23	(a)	Southend U	D 0-0
2	Oct 8	(h)	Southend U	W 2-1
3		28	(a)	Arsenal	L 1-3

Full Members Cup

2	Nov 4	(h)	Wimbledon	W 3-1
3		26	(h)	Watford	W 1-0
4	Jan 31	(h)	Ipswich T	L 2-3

Friendlies

1	Aug 19	(h)	Everton	L 1-4
2	Sep 9	(a)	Oldham A	D 3-3
3	May 11	(a)	Curzon Ashton	W 2-1

Tour (to Switzerland & Spain)

1	Jul 24	(a)	La Chaux-de-Fonds	W 1-0
2		26	(a)	Aarau	D 1-1
3		28	(a)	Solothurn	W 5-0
4		30	(a)	FC Sion	L 0-1
5	Aug 2	(a)	Lausanne Sports	D 1-1
6		8	(a)	Real Betis	D 0-0
7		10	(a)	Malaga	W 3-0

(continued on next page)

	Suckling	Gidman	Wilson	Clements	McCarthy	Redmond	May	White	McNab	Varadi	Brightwell	Simpson	Moulden	Baker	Grealish	Stewart	Barnes	Langley	Christie	Hopkins	Reid	Nixon	Davies	Lake	Beckford	McIlroy	Barrett	
	1	3	4	5	6	2		8			11*	12		10					9				7					1
	1	3	4	5	6	2		8			11	10							9				7*			12		2
	1	3	4	5	6	2*		8			11	10		12					9				7					3
	1	3		5	6	2		8				11		4					9	7		10						4
	1	11	2	5	6	3		8				12		4					9	7		10*						5
	1	3	4		6	5		8				11							9	7					10	2		6
	1	3	4	5	6	2		8*		10	11	12							9	7								7
	1	3	4	5	6	2	12	8				11							9*	7					10			8
	1	3		5	4	2	7	8				11	10						9	6								9
	1	3	4	5	6	2	7	8				11	10						9									10
	1	3	4	5	6	2	7	8	9	10	11*	12																11
	1	2	3	4	5	6	7	8	9	12	11	10*																12
	1	2	3	4	5		7*	8	9			11	12	6	10													13
	1	2	3	4	5			8	9			11	10	7	6													14
	1	2	3	4	5		12	8	9*			11	10	7	6													15
	1	2	3	4	5			9	8			11	10	7	6													16
	1	2	3	4	5			9	8	12		11*	10	7	6													17
	1	2	3	4	5		11	8	9				10	7*	6					12								18
	1	2	3	4	5	12	7	8	9			11	10		6*													19
	1	3	4	5	6		7	8	9			10						11		2								20
	1	2	3	4		6	7	8	9			11	10							5								21
	1	2	3	4		6	7	8	9			11	10							5								22
	1	2	3	4	5	6		8	9			11	10	7														23
	1	2	3	4	5	6	12	8	9			11	10*	7														24
	1	2	3	4	5	6	7	8	9									11					10					25
	1	3	4	5	6	2		8	9		12							11					7	10*				26
	1	2	3	4	5	6	12	8	9					7				11					10*					27
	1	2	3	4	5	6		8	9			12		7				11					10*					28
	1	2	3	4	5			8	9				6		7			11		10								29
	1	3	4	5		12		8	9			11	6	7	10*					2								30
	1	2	3	4	5		7	8	9	12			10		6*			11										31
	1	2	3	4	5	11*	7	8	9			12		6	10													32
	1	2*	11	5	4		7	8	9			12				10	6			3								33
	1	2	3	4	5		7	8	9	11						10	6											34
	1	2	3	4*	5		7	8	9			12	11			10	6											35
	1	2	3	4	5			8	9				7			10	11	6										36
	1		3	4	5			8	9				7	12		10	11*	6										37
		3	2	5	4		7	8	9	12	11			6*		10						1						38
		3	2	5	4	7		8	9		11					10	6					1						39
		3	2	5	4	7		8	9		11					10	6					1						40
		3	2	5	4	7		8	9		11					10	6					1						41
		3	2	5*	4	7	12	8	9		11					10	6					1						42
Apps	37	22	42	39	39	28	17	19	42	29	12	27	16	13	11	11	8	9	9	7	6	5	5	3	4	1	1	
Sub							2			5	1	4	5	4	2					1						1		
Gls			1	2	1							4	9	1	3	5	3	2			3	1	1					

Tour (continued)

8	Aug 12	(a) Valencia	L 0-2
9	14	(a) Barcelona	D 1-1
10	15	(a) Huelva	D 2-2

Tour (to United Arab Emirates)

1	Nov 17	(a) Al Ahli FC	W 3-1
2	19	(a) Al Nasr FC	D 1-1

City Against Other League Clubs

Manchester City have played 86 clubs in the Football League since 1892-3. Below is City's record against each club. Some clubs changed their names (eg Small Heath became Birmingham then Birmingham City) and some clubs modified their titles (eg Leicester Fosse became Leicester City). In all cases the last name used by each club cover all games under previous names.

	P	W	D	L	F	A
Arsenal	132	39	32	61	166	215
Aston Villa	108	37	29	42	162	175
Barnsley	18	9	9	0	44	15
Birmingham City	104	45	18	41	168	176
Blackburn Rovers	78	28	18	32	127	123
Blackpool	56	23	17	16	109	94
Bolton Wanderers	86	32	21	33	135	144
Bootle	2	1	0	1	10	5
Bradford City	20	10	2	8	39	29
Bradford	12	6	1	5	29	21
Brentford	8	4	1	3	15	10
Brighton & Hove Albion	12	6	4	2	21	14
Bristol City	22	6	6	10	31	30
Burnley	80	32	21	27	140	115
Burton Swifts	14	5	4	5	33	26
Burton United	2	2	0	0	7	0
Burton Wanderers	6	1	3	2	6	16
Bury	42	21	11	10	94	66
Cambridge United	2	1	1	0	5	0
Cardiff City	38	15	16	7	77	59
Carlisle United	8	3	2	3	9	10
Charlton Athletic	34	14	6	14	61	55
Chelsea	96	35	27	34	135	131
Chesterfield	8	7	1	0	19	5
Coventry City	46	24	12	10	82	52
Crewe Alexandra	8	5	1	2	19	11
Crystal Palace	20	11	3	6	29	19
Darlington	2	1	1	0	9	2
Darwen	12	8	0	4	40	22
Derby County	84	38	16	30	137	121
Doncaster Rovers	4	2	1	1	12	9
Everton	122	46	34	42	177	174
Fulham	30	15	5	10	69	56
Gainsborough T	10	7	1	2	31	8
Glossop North End	8	6	1	1	20	9
Grimsby Town	46	21	8	17	88	88
Hull City	8	3	4	1	14	10
Huddersfield Town	60	19	22	19	80	74
Ipswich Town	40	11	13	16	47	50
Leeds United	74	36	11	27	122	94
Leicester City	78	36	21	21	151	115
Lincoln City	18	12	0	6	46	25
Liverpool	116	33	24	59	162	210
Loughborough Town	8	6	1	1	24	7
Luton Town	28	9	8	11	38	44
Manchester United	110	31	39	40	150	155
Middlesbrough	90	41	19	30	142	140

Middlesbrough Ironopolis	2	1	0	1	6	3
Millwall	4	2	0	2	6	10
New Brighton	2	1	1	0	2	1
Newcastle United	126	40	29	57	176	199
Newport County	2	2	0	0	8	1
Northampton Town	4	1	0	3	4	6
Norwich City	28	13	12	3	53	29
Nottingham Forest	72	29	22	21	108	99
Notts County	54	26	11	17	81	59
Northwich Victoria	4	3	1	0	12	4
Oldham Athletic	28	16	5	7	47	30
Orient	14	10	2	2	44	17
Oxford United	6	2	1	3	2	7
Plymouth Argyle	10	3	3	4	15	17
Portsmouth	54	25	11	18	96	82
Preston North End	78	37	14	27	142	125
Port Vale	16	14	1	1	46	14
Queen's Park Rangers	20	8	7	5	22	17
Reading	4	2	1	1	8	3
Rotherham United	12	10	1	1	28	12
Scunthorpe United	2	2	0	0	12	3
Sheffield United	90	37	24	31	158	150
Sheffield Wednesday	82	24	21	37	126	141
Shrewsbury Town	4	3	0	1	8	2
Southampton	46	14	15	17	62	66
South Shields	4	2	1	1	7	4
Stockport County	4	4	0	0	11	2
Stoke City	68	25	17	26	82	86
Sunderland	100	43	17	40	168	160
Swansea City	20	12	2	6	44	33
Swindon Town	4	1	1	2	2	5
Tottenham Hotspur	90	39	23	27	148	119
Tranmere Rovers	2	2	0	0	14	5
Watford	6	1	1	4	5	9
Walsall	12	8	2	2	34	17
West Bromwich Albion	106	42	21	43	184	185
West Ham United	62	27	9	26	104	108
Wimbledon	4	2	2	0	8	3
Wolverhampton Wanderers	92	36	21	35	185	186

CONSOLIDATED COMPETITIVE RECORD 1892-1987

	P	W	D	L	F	A
First Division	2654	1012	644	998	4109	4089
Second Division	696	360	152	184	1495	959
Test Matches	4	1	1	2	5	15
FA Cup	245	116	50	79	443	324
League Cup	107	55	25	27	195	125
European Cup	2	0	1	1	1	2
Cup Winners' Cup	18	11	2	5	32	13
UEFA Cup	14	4	6	4	21	19
Anglo-Italian Trophy	2	0	1	1	2	3
Texaco Cup	5	1	2	2	7	10
Anglo-Scottish Cup	3	1	0	2	3	3
FA Charity Shield	7	3	0	4	10	9
Full Members' Cup	9	5	1	3	21	13
Second Division (1939-40)	3	1	1	1	6	5
TOTALS	**3769**	**1570**	**886**	**1313**	**6350**	**5589**

Tony Book holds aloft the FA Cup after City have beaten Leicester City in 1969.

City in the FA Cup

1891-2
Qualifying Round
Oct 3 v Newton Heath (a) 1-5
Pearson
Douglas; Ferguson, Robson, Pearson, Whittle, Davidson, Davies, McWhinnie, Morris, Milne, Milarvie.
Att: 10,000

1892-3
Qualifying Round
Sep 22 v Fleetwood Rangers (a) 1-1
Milarvie
Douglas; Robson, McVickers, Middleton, Russell, Hopkins, Davies, Morris, J.Angus, Bowman, Milarvie.
Att: 600
Replay
Oct 5 v Fleetwood Rangers (h) 0-2
Douglas; McVickers, Robson, Middleton, Russell, Milne, Davies, Morris, Bowman, Weir, Milarvie.
Att: 2,000

1893-4
Qualifying Round
Oct 14 v West Manchester (a) 0-3
Douglas; McVickers, Robson, Dyer, Whittle, Regan, Yates, Middleton, Steele, Morris, Milarvie.
Att: 6,000

1894-5
City did not enter

1895-6
Qualifying Round
Oct 12 v Oswaldtwistle Rovers (h) scratched

1896-7
Round 1
Jan 30 v Preston North End (a) 0-6
Williams; Harper, Ray, Mann, Holmes, McBride, Meredith, Sharples, Foster, Gunn, Lewis.
Att: 6,000

1897-8
Round 1
Jan 29 v Wigan County (h) 1-0
Gillespie
C.Williams; Read, Ray, Moffatt, B.Smith, Holmes, Meredith, Whitehead, Gillespie, S.Smith, F.Williams.
Att: 6,000
Round 2
Feb 12 v Bolton Wanderers (a) 0-1
C.Williams; Read, Ray, Moffatt, B.Smith, Holmes, Meredith, Whitehead, Gillespie, S.Smith, Leonard.
Att: 14,000

1898-9
Round 1
Jan 28 v Small Heath (a) 2-3
Meredith, Gillespie
C.Williams; Ray, Jones, Moffatt, B.Smith, Holmes, Meredith, S.Smith, Gillespie, F.Williams, Dougal.
Att: 15,399

1899-1900
Round 1
Jan 27 v Aston Villa (h) 1-1
Ross
C.Williams, Ray, Jones, Moffatt, Smith, Holmes, Meredith, Ross, Gillespie, F.Williams, Threlfall.
Att: 22,000
Replay
Jan 31 v Aston Villa (a) 0-3
C.Williams; Ray, Jones, Read, Smith, Holmes, Tonge, Meredith, Gillespie, F.Williams, Threlfall.

1900-01
Round 1
Feb 9 v West Bromwich Albion (a) 0-1
C.Williams; Read, Jones, Moffatt, Smith, Holmes, Meredith, Ross, Cassidy, F.Williams, Dougal.
Att: 16,000

1901-02
Round 1
Jan 25 v Preston North End (a) 1-1 (abandoned)
Henderson
Barrett; Orr, Slater, Smith, Hynds, Hosie, Meredith, Ross, Henderson, Jones, Threlfall.
Att: 10,000
Round 1
Jan 29 v Preston North End (h) 0-0
Barrett; Orr, Slater, Smith, Hynds, Hosie, Meredith, Morgan, Jones, Scotson, Threlfall.
Att: 7,000
Replay
Feb 3 v Preston North End (a) 4-2
Smith (3), Morgan
Barrett; Orr, Slater, Moffatt, Hynds, Hosie, Meredith, Morgan, Smith, Jones, Threlfall.
Att: 5,000
Round 2
Feb 8 v Nottingham Forest (h) 0-2
Barrett; Orr, Slater, Moffatt, Hynds, Hosie, Meredith, Morgan, Smith, Jones, Threlfall.
Att: 16,000

1902-03
Round 1
Feb 7 v Preston North End (a) 1-3
Turnbull
Hillman; Orr, Holmes, Forest, Hynds, Bevan, Meredith, Bannister, Gillespie, Turnbull, Threlfall.
Att: 8,000

1903-04
Round 1
Feb 6 v Sunderland (h) 3-2
Turnbull (2), Gillespie
Hillman; McMahon, Burgess, Frost, Hynds, Ashworth, Meredith, Livingstone, Gillespie, Turnbull, Booth.
Att: 23,000
Round 2
Feb 20 v Woolwich Arsenal (a) 2-0
Turnbull, Booth
Hillman; McMahon, Burgess, Frost, Hynds, Ashworth, Meredith, Livingstone, Gillespie, Turnbull, Booth.
Att: 30,000

City's 1904 Cup-winning team. Back row (left to right): T.E.Maley (secretary-manager), S.Frost, W.Gillespie, J.McMahon, T.Hynds, J.Hillman, S.B.Ashworth, J.Broad (trainer). Front row: H.Burgess, G.Livingstone, W. Meredith, A.Turnbull, F.Booth.

Round 3
Mar 5 v Middlesbrough (h) 0-0
Hillman; McMahon, Burgess, Frost, Hynds, Ashworth, Meredith, Livingstone, Gillespie, Turnbull, Booth.
Att: 35,000
Replay
Mar 9 v Middlesbrough (a) 3-1
Livingstone, Gillespie, Turnbull
Edmondson; McMahon, Burgess, Frost, Hynds, Holmes, Meredith, Livingstone, Gillespie, Turnbull, Booth.
Att: 33,000
Semi-final
Mar 19 v Sheffield Wednesday (at Goodison Park) 3-1
Meredith, Gillespie, Turnbull
Hillman; McMahon, Burgess, Frost, Hynds, Holmes, Meredith, Livingstone, Gillespie, Turnbull, Booth.
Att: 53,000
Final
Apr 23 v Bolton Wanderers (at The Crystal Palace) 1-0
Meredith
Hillman; McMahon, Burgess, Frost, Hynds, Ashworth, Meredith, Livingstone, Gillespie, Turnbull, Booth.
Att: 61,374

1904-05
Round 1
Feb 4 v Lincoln City (a) 2-1
Meredith, Turnbull
Hillman; McMahon, Burgess, Frost, Hynds, J.Moffatt, Meredith, Dorsett, Pearson, Turnbull, Booth.
Att: 10,000
Round 2
Feb 18 v Bolton Wanderers (h) 1-2
Gillespie
Hillman; McMahon, Burgess, Norgrove, Hynds, J.Moffatt, Meredith, Dorsett, Gillespie, Turnbull, Booth.
Att: 39,000

1905-06
Round 1
Jan 13 v Sheffield Wednesday (a) 1-4
Bannister
Edmondson; McMahon, Burgess, Frost, Hynds, Banks, Dorsett, Bannister, Thornley, Livingstone, Booth.
Att: 21,352

1906-07
Round 1
Jan 12 v Blackburn Rovers (a) 2-2
Dorsett, Thornley
Smith; Hill, Norgrove, Steele, Eadie, Buchan, Stewart, Dorsett, Thornley, Jones, Conlin.
Att: 20,000
Replay
Jan 16 v Blackburn Rovers (h) 0-1
Smith; Hill, Norgrove, Steele, Eadie, Buchan, Stewart, Dorsett, Thornley, Jones, Conlin.
Att: 30,000

1907-08
Round 1
Jan 11 v Glossop (a) 0-0
Smith; Kelso, Jackson, Buchan, Eadie, Blair, Dorsett, Wood, Thornley, Ross, Conlin.
Att: 6,500
Replay
Jan 15 v Glossop (h) 6-0
Buchan, Wood, Dorsett, Grieve, Jones, Conlin
Smith; Kelso, Jackson, Buchan, Eadie, Wood, Dorsett, Grieve, Thornley, Jones, Conlin.
Att: 20,000

Round 2
Feb 1 v New Brompton (h) 1-1
Jones
Smith; Kelso, Jackson, Buchan, Eadie, Blair, Dorsett, Thornley, Grieve, Jones, Conlin.
Att: 7,000
Replay
Feb 5 v New Brompton (a) 2-1
Buchan, Wood
Smith; Kelso, Jackson, Buchan, Eadie, Blair, Dorsett, Wood, Thornley, Jones, Conlin.
Att: 12,000
Round 3
Feb 22 v Fulham (h) 1-1
Blair
Smith; Kelso, Jackson, Buchan, Eadie, Blair, Dorsett, Wood, Thornley, Jones, Conlin.
Att: 25,000
Replay
Feb 26 v Fulham (a) 1-3
Wood
Smith; Kelso, Jackson, Buchan, Eadie, Blair, Dorsett, Wood, Thornley, Jones, Conlin.
Att: 37,000

1908-09
Round 1
Jan 16 v Tottenham Hotspur (h) 3-4
Holford (3)
Smith; Kelso, Norgrove, Buchan, Eadie, Dorsett, Stewart, Jones, Holford, Ross, Conlin.
Att: 20,000

1909-10
Round 1
Jan 15 v Workington (a) 2-1
Wynn 2
Lyall; Kelso, Jackson, Bottomley, Eadie, Dorsett, Stewart, Wynn, Holford, Jones, Conlin.
Att: 5,233
Round 2
Feb 5 v Southampton (a) 5-0
Dorsett, Stewart, Jones, Conlin, Holford
Lyall; Kelso, Jackson, Bottomley, Eadie, Dorsett, Stewart, Wynn, Holford, Jones, Conlin.
Att: 15,965
Round 3
Feb 19 v Aston Villa (a) 2-1
Stewart, Jones
Lyall; Kelso, Jackson, Bottomley, Eadie, Dorsett, Stewart, Wynn, Holford, Jones, Conlin.
Att: 45,000
Round 4
Mar 5 v Swindon Town (a) 0-2
Lyall; Kelso, Jackson, Bottomley, Eadie, Dorsett, Stewart, Wynn, Holford, Jones, Conlin.
Att: 14,429

1910-11
Round 1
Jan 10 v Stoke City (a) 2-1
J.Smith, Jones
W.Smith; Kelso, Chaplin, G.Dorsett, Eadie, Holford, Stewart, Ross, J.Smith, Jones, J.Dorsett.
Att: 29,000

City in 1907-08. Back row (left to right): R.Chatt (trainer), Buchan, Bannister, Smith, H.A.Gilgryst (referee). Third row: S.Anderson, Jackson, Norgrove, Kelso, Blair, Eadie, Davis, W.Iles (asst trainer). Second row: Mr J.Royle, Banks, Grieve, Eyres, Jones, Ross, Conlin, Callaghan. Front row: Stewart, Dorsett, Thornley, Wood, Steel.

Round 2
Feb 4 v Wolves (a) 0-1
W.Smith; Kelso, Chaplin, G.Dorsett, Eadie, Holford,
Stewart, Ross, J.Smith, Jones, Conlin.
Att: 25,000

1911-12
Round 1
Jan 13 v Preston North End (a) 1-0
Wynn
Goodchild; Henry, Fletcher, Lawrence, Eadie, Holford,
Hoad, Wynn, Young, Jones, J.Dorsett.
Att: 15,000
Round 2
Feb 3 v Oldham Athletic (h) 0-1
Goodchild; Henry, Fletcher, Lawrence, Eadie, Holford,
Hoad, Wynn, Young, Jones, .Dorsett.
Att: 45,000
1912-13
Round 1
Jan 11 v Birmingham (h) 4-0
Wynn (2), Hoad, Taylor
Smith; Henry, Fletcher, Bottomley, Eadie, Holford,
Hoad, Wynn, Taylor, Jones, Wallace.
Att: 17,442
Round 2
Feb 1 v Sunderland (h) 0-0 abandoned in extra-time
Smith; Henry, Fletcher, Hughes, Eadie, Holford, Hoad,
Wynn, Howard, Jones, Wallace.
Att: 41,709
Round 2
Feb 5 v Sunderland (a) 0-2
Smith; Henry, Fletcher, Hughes, Eadie, Holford, Hoad,
Wynn, Howard, Jones, Wallace.
Att: 27,974

1913-14
Round 1
Jan 10 v Fulham (h) 2-0
Hindmarsh, Howard
Smith; Henry, Fletcher, Hughes, Hanney, Hindmarsh,
Cumming, Taylor, Howard, Browell, Cartwright.
Att: 25,345
Round 2
Jan 31 v Tottenham Hotspur (h) 2-1
Howard, Browell
Smith; Henry, Fletcher, Hughes, Hanney, Hindmarsh,
Cumming, Taylor, Howard, Browell, Cartwright.
Att: 36,256
Round 3
Feb 21 v Blackburn Rovers (a) 2-1
Howard, Cartwright
Smith; Henry, Fletcher, Hughes, Hanney, Hindmarsh,
Cumming, Taylor, Howard, Browell, Cartwright.
Att: 41,250
Round 4
Mar 7 v Sheffield United (h) 0-0
Smith; Henry, Fletcher, Hughes, Hanney, Hindmarsh,
Cumming, Taylor, Howard, Browell, Cartwright.
Att: 35,738
Replay
Mar 12 v Sheffield United (a) 0-0
Smith; Henry, Fletcher, Hughes, Hanney, Hindmarsh,
Cumming, Taylor, Howard, Browell, Cartwright.
Att: 46,139
Second Replay
Mar 16 v Sheffield United (at Villa Park) 0-1
Smith; Henry, Fletcher, Hughes, Hanney, Hindmarsh,
Jones, Taylor, Howard, Browell, Williams.
Att: 23,000

1914-15
Round 1
Jan 9 v Preston North End (a) 0-0
Smith; Henry, Fletcher, Hughes, Hanney, Hindmarsh,
Dorsett, Browell, Howard, Barnes, Cartwright.
Att: 14,000
Replay
Jan 16 v Preston North End (h) 3-0
Barnes (2), Hughes
Smith; Henry, Fletcher, Hughes, Hanney, Brennan,
Dorsett, Taylor, Howard, Barnes, Cartwright.
Att: 19,985
Round 2
Jan 30 v Aston Villa (h) 1-0
Cartwright
Smith; Henry, Fletcher, Hughes, Hanney, Jones,
Dorsett, Taylor, Howard, Barnes, Cartwright.
Att: 29,661
Round 4
Feb 20 v Chelsea (h) 0-1
Smith; Henry, Fletcher, Hughes, Hanney, Brennan,
Cumming, Taylor, Browell, Barnes, Cartwright.
Att: 32,000

1919-20
Round 1
Jan 10 v Clapton Orient (h) 4-1
Goodwin (2), Barnes, Murphy
Goodchild; Cookson, Fletcher, Brennan, Woosnam,
Tyler, Goodwin, Crawshaw, Browell, Barnes, Murphy.
Att: 25,878
Round 2
Jan 31 v Leicester City (a) 0-3
Goodchild; Cookson, Fletcher, Brennan, Scott, Tyler,
Broad, Browell, Howard, Barnes, Murphy.
Att: 23,041

1920-21
Round 2
Jan 8 v Crystal Palace (a) 0-2
Goodchild; Cookson, Fletcher, Fayers, Woosnam,
Tyler, Broad, Carroll, Browell, Barnes, Murphy.
Att: 18,000

1921-22
Round 1
Jan 7 v Darlington (h) 3-1
Browell (3)
Blair; Cookson, Fletcher, Carroll, Woosnam, Fayers,
Kelly, Browell, Johnson, Barnes, Murphy.
Att: 23,686
Round 2
Jan 28 v Bolton Wanderers (a) 3-1
Browell (2), Kelly
Blair; Thompson, Fletcher, Fayers, Woosnam, Hamill,
Kelly, Browell, Johnson, Barnes, Murphy.
Att: 66,442
Round 3
Feb 18 v Tottenham Hotspur (a) 1-2
Kelly
Blair; Cookson, Fletcher, Fayers, Woosnam, Hamill,
Kelly, Bowell, Johnson, Barnes, Murphy.
Att: 53,000

1922-3
Round 1
Jan 13 v Charlton Athletic (a) 1-2
Johnson
Mitchell; Cookson, Wilson, Sharp, Hamill, Pringle,
Kelly, Roberts, Johnson, Barnes, Murphy.
Att: 28,445

1923-4
Round 1
Jan 12 v Nottingham Forest (h) 2-1
Roberts, Barnes
Mitchell; Cookson, Allen, Pringle, Woosnam, Hamill,
Morris, Roberts, Johnson, Barnes, Murphy.
Att: 33,849
Round 2
Feb 2 v Halifax Town (a) 2-2
Hamill, Roberts
Mitchell; Cookson, Allen, Sharp, Hamill, Pringle,
Morris, Warner, Roberts, Barnes, Murphy.
Att: 30,970
Replay
Feb 6 v Halifax Town (h) 0-0
Mitchell; Cookson, Allen, Sharp, Hamill, Pringle,
Morris, Warner, Roberts, Barnes, Murphy.
Att: 21,590
Second Replay
Feb 11 v Halifax Town (at Old Trafford) 3-0
Roberts (2), Browell
Mitchell; Cookson, Allen, Sharp, Pringle, Wilson,
Morris, Roberts, Browell, Johnson, Murphy.
Att: 28,128
Round 3
Feb 23 v Brighton & Hove Albion (h) 5-1
Browell (2), Meredith, Barnes, Sharp
Mitchell; Cookson, Fletcher, Sharp, Hamill, Pringle,
Meredith, Roberts, Browell, Barnes, Daniels.
Att: 24,734
Round 4
Mar 8 v Cardiff City (h) 0-0
Mitchell; Cookson, Fletcher, Pringle, Hamill, Wilson,
Meredith, Roberts, Browell, Barnes, Johnson.
Att: 76,166
Replay
Mar 12 v Cardiff City (a) 1-0
Browell
Mitchell; Cookson, Fletcher, Pringle, Hamill, Wilson,
Meredith, Roberts, Browell, Barnes, Johnson.
Att: 50,000

Semi-final
Mar 29 v Newcastle United (at St Andrew's) 0-2
Mitchell; Cookson, Fletcher, Hamill, Pringle, Wilson,
Meredith, Roberts, Browell, Barnes, Johnson.
Att: 50,039

1924-5
Round 1
Jan 10 v Preston North End (a) 1-4
Roberts
Mitchell; Thompson, Fletcher, Sharp, Woosnam, Pringle,
Austin, Roberts, Browell, Johnson, Hicks.
Att: 24,536

1925-6
Round 3
Jan 9 v The Corinthians (a) 3-3
Cookson, Roberts, Hicks
Goodchild; Cookson, Calderwood, Coupland, Cowan,
Pringle, Austin, Dennison, Roberts, Johnson, Hicks.
Att: 29,700
Replay
Jan 13 v The Corinthians (h) 4-0
Austin (2), Johnson, Hicks
Goodchild; Thompson, Calderwood, Elwood, Cowan,
Pringle, Austin, Dennison, Roberts, Johnson, Hicks.
Att: 42,303
Round 4
Jan 30 v Huddersfield Town (h) 4-0
Hicks (2), Browell, Roberts
Goodchild; Cookson, McCloy, Coupland, Cowan,
Pringle, Austin, Browell, Roberts, Johnson, Hicks.
Att: 74,789
Round 5
Feb 20 v Crystal Palace (h) 11-4
Roberts (5), Browell (3), Austin, Johnson, Hicks
Goodchild; Cookson, McCloy, Coupland, Cowan,
Pringle, Austin, Browell, Roberts, Johnson, Hicks.
Att: 51,630

Bolton appeal for an infringement as Tommy Browell forces his way through at Wembley in 1926. Referee J.Baker of Crewe seems unimpressed.

Round 6
Mar 6 v Clapton Orient (a) 6-1
Johnson (3), Hicks, Roberts, Browell
Goodchild; Cookson, Appleton, Pringle, Cowan,
McMullan, Austin, Browell, Roberts, Johnson, Hicks.
Att: 24,600
Semi-final
Mar 27 v Manchester United (at Bramall Lane) 3-0
Browell (2), Roberts
Goodchild; Cookson, McCloy, Pringle, Cowan,
McMullan, Austin, Browell, Roberts, Johnson, Hicks.
Att: 46,450
Final
Apr 24 v Bolton Wanderers (at Wembley) 0-1
Goodchild; Cookson, McCloy, Pringle, Cowan,
McMullan, Austin, Browell, Roberts, Johnson, Hicks.
Att: 91,547

1926-7
Round 3
Jan 8 v Birmingham (a) 1-4
Hicks
Goodchild; Cookson, Bennett, Pringle, Thompson,
McMullan, Austin, Barrass, W.Cowan, Johnson, Hicks.
Att: 39,503

1927-8
Round 3
Jan 14 v Leeds United (h) 1-0
Johnson
Gray; Ridley, McCloy, Barrass, Cowan, McMullan,
Austin, Roberts, Broadhurst, Johnson, Hicks.
Att: 50,473
Round 4
Jan 28 v Sunderland (a) 2-1
Broadhurst, Hicks
Barber; Ridley, McCloy, Barrass, Cowan, McMullan,
Austin, Roberts, Broadhurst, Johnson, Hicks.
Att: 38,658
Round 5
Feb 18 v Stoke City (h) 0-1
Gray; Ridley, McCloy, Pringle, Gibbons, McMullan,
Roberts, Allen, Broadhurst, Johnson, Hicks.
Att: 73,668

1928-9
Round 3
Jan 12 v Birmingham (a) 1-3
Austin
Barber; Ridley, McCloy, Barrass, Cowan, McMullan,
Austin, Marshall, Roberts, Johnson, Brook.
Att: 25,005

1929-30
Round 3
Jan 11 v Tottenham Hotspur (a) 2-2
Toseland, Cowan
Barber; Ridley, Felton, Barrass, Cowan, McMullan,
Toseland, Marshall, Tait, Heinemann, Brook.
Att: 37,000
Replay
Jan 15 v Tottenham Hotspur (h) 4-1
Busby (2), Toseland, Marshall
Barber; Robertson, Felton, Barrass, Cowan, McMullan,
Toseland, Marshall, Johnson, Busby, Brook.
Att: 37,716
Round 4
Jan 25 v Swindon Town (a) 1-1
Cowan
Barber; Felton, McCloy, Barrass, Cowan, Heinemann,
Toseland, Marshall, Tait, Johnson, Brook.
Att: 23,697
Replay

Jan 29 v Swindon Town (h) 10-1
Marshall (5), Tait (3), Johnson, Brook
Barber; Felton, McCloy, Barrass, Cowan, Heinemann,
Toseland, Marshall, Tait, Johnson, Brook.
Att: 46,082
Round 5
Feb 15 v Hull City (h) 1-2
Toseland
Barber; Ridley, Felton, Barrass, Cowan, McMullan,
Toseland, Marshall, Johnson, Tilson, Brook.
Att: 61,574

1930-31
Round 3
Jan 10 v Burnley (a) 0-3
Langford; Ridley, Barnett, Busby, Cowan, Bray,
Toseland, Marshall, Halliday, Tilson, Brook.
Att: 25,893

1931-2
Round 3
Jan 9 v Millwall (a) 3-2
Halliday (2), Toseland
Langford; Felton, Dale, Busby, Cowan, McMullan,
Toseland, Marshall, Halliday, Tilson, Brook.
Att: 32,091
Round 4
Jan 23 v Brentford (h) 6-1
Tilson (3), Brook (2), Halliday
Langford; Felton, Dale, Busby, Cowan, McMullan,
Toseland, Marshall, Halliday, Tilson, Brook.
Att: 56,190
Round 5
Feb 13 v Derby County (h) 3-0
Marshall (2), Brook
Langford; Felton, Dale, Busby, Cowan, McMullan,
Toseland, Marshall, Halliday, Tilson, Brook.
Att: 62,641
Round 6
Feb 27 v Bury (a) 4-3
Toseland (2), Halliday, Cowan
Langford; Felton, Dale, Busby, Cowan, McMullan,
Toseland, Marshall, Halliday, Tilson, Brook.
Att: 28,035
Semi-final
Mar 12 v Arsenal (at Villa Park) 0-1
Langford; Felton, Dale, Busby, Cowan, McMullan,
Toseland, Marshall, Halliday, Tilson, Brook.
Att: 50,337

1932-3
Round 3
Jan 14 v Gateshead (a) 1-1
Toseland
Langford; Ridley, Dale, Busby, Cowan, Bray, Toseland,
Race, Tilson, McMullan, Brook.
Att: 9,123
Replay
Jan 18 v Gateshead (h) 9-0
*Tilson (3), Cowan (2), Busby, Barrass, McMullan,
Brook*
Langford; Ridley, Dale, Busby, Cowan, Bray, Toseland,
Barrass, Tilson, McMullan, Brook.
Att: 22,950
Round 4
Jan 28 v Walsall (h) 2-0
Brook (2)
Langford; Ridley, Dale, Busby, Cowan, Bray, Toseland,
Marshall, Tilson, McMullan, Brook.
Att: 52,085

Manchester City goalkeeper, Langford (22), clears an Everton corner at Wembley in 1933. Other City players are, Cann (21) and Busby (19).

Round 5
Feb 18 v Bolton Wanderers (a) 4-2
Brook (3), Tilson
Langford; Cann, Dale, Busby, Cowan, Bray, Toseland,
Marshall, Tilson, Herd, Brook.
Att: 69,920
Round 6
Mar 4 v Burnley (a) 1-0
Tilson
Langford; Cann, Dale, Busby, Cowan, Bray, Toseland,
Herd, Tilson, McMullan, Brook.
Att: 48,717
Semi-final
Mar 18 v Derby County (at Leeds Road) 3-2
Toseland, Tilson, McMullan
Langford; Cann, Dale, Busby, Cowan, Bray, Toseland,
Herd, Tilson, McMullan, Brook.
Att: 51,961
Final
Apr 29 v Everton (at Wembley) 0-3
Langford; Cann, Dale, Busby, Cowan, Bray, Toseland,
Marshall, Herd, McMullan, Brook.
Att: 92,900

1933-4
Round 3
Jan 13 v Blackburn Rovers (h) 3-1
Toseland (2), Brook
Swift; Barnett, Dale, Busby, Cowan, McLuckie,
Toseland, Marshall, Tilson, Herd, Brook.
Att: 54,336
Round 4
Jan 27 v Hull City (a) 2-2
Herd, Brook
Swift; Barnett, Dale, Busby, Cowan, McLuckie,
Toseland, Marshall, Tilson, Herd, Brook.
Att: 28,000

Replay
Jan 31 v Hull City (h) 4-1
Tilson (2), Toseland, Marshall
Swift; Barnett, Dale, Busby, Cowan, McLuckie,
Toseland, Marshall, Tilson, Herd, Brook.
Att: 49,042
Round 5
Feb 17 v Sheffield Wednesday (a) 2-2
Herd (2)
Swift; Corbett, Dale, Busby, Cowan, McLuckie,
Toseland, Marshall, Tilson, Herd, Brook.
Att: 72,841
Replay
Feb 21 v Sheffield Wednesday (h) 2-0
Marshall, Tilson
Swift; Barnett, Dale, Busby, Cowan, McLuckie,
Toseland, Marshall, Tilson, Herd, Brook.
Att: 68,614
Round 6
Mar 3 v Stoke City (h) 1-0
Brook
Swift; Barnett, Dale, Busby, Cowan, Bray, Toseland,
Marshall, Tilson, Herd, Brook.
Att: 84,569
Semi-final
Mar 17 v Aston Villa (at Leeds Road) 6-1
Tilson (4), Herd, Toseland
Swift; Barnett, Dale, Busby, Cowan, Bray, Toseland,
Marshall, Tilson, Herd, Brook.
Att: 45,473
Final
Apr 28 v Portsmouth (at Wembley) 2-1
Tilson (2)
Swift; Barnett, Dale, Busby, Cowan, Bray, Toseland,
Marshall, Tilson, Herd, Brook.
Att: 93,258

205

1934-5
Round 3
Jan 12 v Tottenham Hotspur (a) 0-1
Swift; Dale, Barkas, Busby, Cowan, Bray, Toseland,
Heale, Toseland, Herd, Brook.
Att: 48,983

1935-6
Round 3
Jan 11 v Portsmouth (h) 3-1
Brook (3)
Swift; Dale, Barkas, McCullough, Marshall, Bray,
Toseland, Herd, Owen, Rodger, Brook.
Att: 53,340
Round 4
Jan 25 v Luton Town (h) 2-1
Herd, McLeod
Swift; Dale, Barkas, Percival, Marshall, Bray, Toseland,
Herd, McLeod, Tilson, Brook.
Att: 65,978
Round 5
Feb 15 v Grimsby Town (a) 2-3
McLeod, Tilson
Swift; Dale, Barkas, Percival, Busby, Bray, Toseland,
Herd, McLeod, Tilson, Brook.
Att: 28,000

1936-7
Round 3
Jan 16 v Wrexham (a) 3-1
Herd, Tilson, Brook
Swift; Clark, Barkas, Percival, Marshall, Bray, Toseland,
Herd, Tilson, Doherty, Brook.
Att: 20,600
Round 4
Jan 30 v Accrington Stanley (h) 2-0
Tilson, Doherty
Swift; Dale, Barkas, Percival, Marshall, Bray, Toseland,
Herd, Tilson, Doherty, Brook.
Att: 39,135
Round 5
Feb 20 v Bolton Wanderers (a) 5-0
Herd (2), Doherty, Brook, Tilson
Swift; Dale, Barkas, Percival, Marshall, Bray, Toseland,
Herd, Tilson, Doherty, Brook.
Att: 60,979
Round 6
Mar 6 v Millwall (a) 0-2
Swift; Dale, Barkas, Rogers, Marshall, Bray, Toseland,
Herd, Tilson, Doherty, Brook.
Att: 42,474

City players learn that they have been drawn at home to Accrington Stanley in the 1936-7 fourth round.

1937-8
Round 3
Jan 8 v Millwall (a) 2-2
Herd (2)
Swift; Clark, Dale, Percival, Nilson, Barkas, Toseland,
Herd, Clayton, Doherty, Wardle.
Att: 38,110
Replay
Jan 12 v Millwall (h) 3-1
Herd, Heale, Brook
Swift; Clark, Dale, Percival, Neilson, Barkas, Toseland,
Herd, Heale, Doherty, Brook.
Att: 39,559
Round 4
Jan 22 v Bury (h) 3-1
Toseland (2), opp og
Swift; Clark, Dale, Percival, Neilson, Rogers, Toseland,
Herd, Heale, Doherty, Brook.
Att: 71,937
Round 5
Feb 12 v Luton Town (a) 3-1
Doherty, Heale, opp og
Swift; Dale, Barkas, Percival, Marshall, Rogers, Toseland,
Herd, Heale, Doherty, Brook.
Att: 21,099
Round 6
Mar 5 v Aston Villa (a) 2-3
Doherty, opp og
Swift; Dale, Barkas, Percival, Neilson, Bray, Toseland,
Herd, Heale, Doherty, Brook.
Att: 75,500

1938-9
Round 3
Jan 12 v Norwich City (a) 5-0
Herd (2), Milsom (2), Doherty
Swift; Clark, Westwood, Percival, Cardwell, McDowall,
Toseland, Herd, Milsom, Doherty, Brook.
Att: 20,901
Round 4
Jan 21 v Sheffield United (a) 0-2
Swift; Sproston, Westwood, Percival, Cardwell,
McDowall, Toseland, Herd, Milsom, Doherty, Brook.
Att: 49,795

1945-6
Round 3 (1st leg)
Jan 5 v Barrow (h) 6-2
Herd (3), Constantine (3)
Swift; Clark, Barkas, P.Robinson, Cardwell, Walsh,
Pritchard, Herd, Constantine, Smith, Bootle.
Att: 19,589
Round 3 (2nd leg)
Jan 10 v Barrow (a) 2-2 (agg 8-4)
Dunkley, Hart
Swift; Clark, Barkas, Walsh, Caldwell, McDowall,
Dunkley, Hart, Constantine, Smith, Cunliffe.
Att: 7,377
Round 4 (1st leg)
Jan 26 v Bradford (a) 3-1
Smith (2), Herd
Swift; Clark, Barkas, Walsh, Caldwell, McDowall,
Dunkley, Herd, Constantine, Smith, Pritchard.
Att: 25,014
Round 4 (2nd leg)
Jan 30 v Bradford (h) 2-8 (agg 5-9)
Constantine, Smith
Swift; Clark, Barkas, Walsh, Caldwell, McDowall,
Dunkley, Herd, Constantine, Smith, Pritchard.
Att: 15,026

1946-7
Round 3
Jan 11 v Gateshead (h) 3-0
Jackson, Capel, Westwood
Swift; Sproston, Barkas, Fagan, McDowell, Emptage,
Dunkley, Smith, Jackson, Capel, Westwood.
Att: 38,575
Round 4
Jan 25 v Bolton Wanderers (a) 3-3
Black (2), Capel
Swift; Williams, Barkas, Fagan, McDowell, Emptage,
Dunkley, Smith, Black, Capel, Westwood.
Att: 41,286
Replay
Jan 29 v Bolton Wanderers (h) 1-0
Westwood
Swift; Williams, Barkas, Fagan, McDowell, Emptage,
Dunkley, Smith, Black, Capel, Westwood.
Att: 39,355
Round 5
Feb 8 v Birmingham C (a) 0-5
Swift; Sproston, Barkas, Fagan, McDowell, Emptage,
Dunkley, Smith, Black, Capel, Westwood.
Att: 50,000

1947-8
Round 3
Jan 10 v Barnsley (h) 2-1
Smith, Black
Swift; Sproston, Westwood, Walsh, Fagan, Emptage,
Linacre, Black, McMorran, Smith, Wharton.
Att: 54,747
Round 4
Jan 24 v Chelsea (h) 2-0
Linacre, Smith
Swift; Sproston, Westwood, Walsh, Fagan, Emptage,
Linacre, Black, McMorran, Smith, Wharton.
Att: 45,079
Round 5
Feb 7 v Preston North End (h) 0-1
Swift; Sproston, Westwood, Walsh, Fagan, Emptage,
Linacre, Black, McMorran, Smith, Wharton.
Att: 67,494

1948-9
Round 3
Jan 8 v Everton (a) 0-1
Swift; Williams, Westwood, Walsh, Fagan, Emptage,
Oakes, Hart, Smith, Linacre, Clarke.
Att: 63,459

1949-50
Round 3
Jan 7 v Derby County (h) 3-5
Black (2), Clarke
Powell; Phillips, Westwood, Gill, Fagan, Walsh, Oakes,
Black, Turnbull, Alison, Clarke.
Att: 53,213

1950-51
Round 3
Jan 6 v Birmingham City (a) 0-2
Trautmann; Branagan, Phillips, Paul, Fagan, Spurdle,
Gunning, Haddington, Westcott, Smith, Westwood.
Att: 30,057

1951-2
Round 3
Jan 12 v Wolverhampton Wanderers (h) 2-2
Meadows, Revie
Trautmann; Branagan, Hannaway, Spurdle, Rigby,
Paul, Meadows, Revie, Westcott, Broadis, Clarke.
Att: 54,497

Replay
Jan 16 v Wolverhampton Wanderers (a) 1-4
Clarke
Trautmann; Branagan, Hannaway, Paul, Rigby, Spurdle,
Meadows, Revie, Westcott, Broadis, Clarke.
Att: 43,865

1952-3
Round 3
Jan 10 v Swindon Town (h) 7-0
Hart (4), Williams, Cunliffe, Broadis
Trautmann; Branagan, Little, Revie, Ewing, Paul,
Gunning, Hart, Williamson, Broadis, Cunliffe.
Att: 28,953
Round 4
Jan 31 v Luton Town (h) 1-1
Broadis
Trautmann; Branagan, Little, Revie, Ewing, Paul,
Meadows, Spurdle, Williamson, Broadis, Cunliffe.
Att: 38,411
Replay
Feb 24 v Luton Town (a) 1-5
Spurdle
Trautmann; Branagan, Little, Revie, Ewing, Paul,
Meadows, Spurdle, Williamson, Broadis, Cunliffe.
Att: 21,991

1953-4
Round 3
Jan 9 v Bradford (a) 5-2
McAdams (3), Revie, Clarke
Trautmann; Branagan, Meadows, McTavish, Ewing,
Paul, Fagan, Hart, McAdams, Revie, Clarke.
Att: 22,194

Round 4
Jan 30 v Tottenham Hotspur (h) 0-1
Trautmann; Branagan, Meadows, McTavish, Ewing,
Paul, Anders, Hart, McAdams, Revie, Clarke.
Att: 50,576

1954-5
Round 3
Jan 8 v Derby County (a) 3-1
Barnes, Hayes, Revie
Trautmann; Branagan, Little, Barnes, Leivers, Paul,
Fagan, Hayes, Revie, Hart, Clarke.
Att: 23,409
Round 4
Jan 29 v Manchester United (h) 2-0
Hayes, Revie
Trautmann; Meadows, Little, Barnes, Ewing, Paul,
Fagan, Hayes, Revie, Hart, Clarke.
Att: 74,723
Round 5
Feb 19 Luton Town (a) 2-0
Clarke (2)
Trautmann; Meadows, Little, Barnes, Ewing, Paul,
Fagan, Hayes, Revie, Hart, Clarke.
Att: 23,104
Round 6
Mar 12 v Birmingham City (a) 1-0
Hart
Trautmann; Meadows, Little, Barnes, Ewing, Paul,
Fagan, Hayes, Revie, Hart, Clarke.
Att: 58,000

City players watch in horror as George Hannah hits Newcastle's third goal in the 1955 Final.

Semi-final
Mar 26 v Sunderland (at Villa Park) 1-0
Clarke
Trautmann; Meadows, Little, Barnes, Ewing, Paul,
Fagan, Hayes, Revie, Johnstone, Clarke.
Att: 58,498
Final
May 7 v Newcastle United (at Wembley) 1-3
Johnstone
Trautmann; Meadows, Little, Barnes, Ewing, Paul,
Spurdle, Hayes, Revie, Johnstone, Fagan.
Att: 100,000

Dyson restores City's lead in the 1956 Final.

1955-6
Jan 7 v Blackpool (h) 1-1 (abandoned)
Dyson
Trautmann; Leivers, Little, Barnes, Ewing, Paul, Spurdle,
Hayes, Johnstone, Dyson, Clarke.
Att: 32,577
Round 3
Jan 11 v Blackpool (h) 2-1
Johnstone, Dyson
Trautmann; Leivers, Little, Barnes, Ewing, Paul, Spurdle,
Hayes, Johnstone, Dyson, Clarke.
Att: 42,517
Round 4
Jan 28 v Southend United (a) 1-0
Hayes
Trautmann; Leivers, Little, Barnes, Ewing, Paul, Spurdle,
Hayes, Johnstone, Dyson, Clarke.
Att: 29,500
Round 5
Feb 18 v Liverpool (h) 0-0
Trautmann; Leivers, Little, Barnes, Ewing, Paul, Spurdle,
Hayes, Revie, Dyson, Johnstone.
Att: 70,640
Replay
Feb 22 v Liverpool (a) 2-1
Hayes, Dyson
Trautmann; Leivers, Little, Barnes, Ewing, Paul, Spurdle,
Hayes, Johnstone, Dyson, Clarke.
Att: 57,528
Round 6
Mar 3 v Everton (h) 2-1
Hayes, Johnstone
Trautmann; Leivers, Little, Barnes, Ewing, Paul, Spurdle,
Hayes, Johnstone, Dyson, Clarke.
Att: 76,129
Semi-final
Mar 17 v Tottenham Hotspur (at Villa Park) 1-0
Johnstone
Trautmann; Leivers, Little, Barnes, Ewing, Paul, Spurdle,
Hayes, Johnstone, Dyson, Clarke.
Att: 69,788

Final
May 5 v Birmingham City (at Wembley) 3-1
Johnstone, Hayes, Dyson
Trautmann; Leivers, Little, Barnes, Ewing, Paul,
Johnstone, Hayes, Revie, Dyson, Clarke.
Att: 100,000

1956-7
Round 3
Jan 5 v Newcastle United (a) 1-1
Johnstone
Trautmann; Leivers, Little, Barnes, Ewing, Paul, Fagan,
McAdams, Johnstone, Dyson, Clarke.
Att: 57,890
Replay
Jan 9 v Newcastle United (h) 4-5
Johnstone (2), Fagan, opp og
Trautmann; Leivers, Little, Barnes, Ewing, Paul, Fagan,
McAdams, Johnstone, Dyson, Clarke.
Att: 46,988

1957-8
Round 3
Jan 4 v West Bromwich Albion (a) 1-5
Hayes
Trautmann; Branagan, Sear, Barnes, Ewing, Warhurst,
Barlow, Hayes, Johnstone, Clarke, Fagan.
Att: 49,669

1958-9
Round 3
Jan 10 v Grimsby Town (a) 2-2
Barlow, Hayes
Trautmann; Branagan, Sear, Phoenix, Ewing, Barnes,
Barlow, Johnstone, McAdams, Hayes, Sambrook.
Att: 14,964
Replay
Jan 24 v Grimsby Town (h) 1-2
Johnstone
Trautmann; Leivers, Sear, Phoenix, Ewing, Barnes,
Barlow, Johnstone, McAdams, Hayes, Sambrook.
Att: 35,840

1959-60
Round 3
Jan 9 v Southampton (h) 1-5
Barlow
Trautmann; Branagan, Sear, Oakes, McTavish, Barnes,
Fagan, Barlow, McAdams, Hayes, Colbridge.
Att: 42,065

1960-61
Round 3
Jan 7 v Cardiff City (a) 1-1
opp og
Trautmann; Leivers, Betts, Barnes, Plenderleith,
Shawcross, Barlow, Law, Hannah, Hayes, Sambrook.
Att: 30,000

Hayes puts City 1-0 in front against Birmingham at Wembley.

Replay
Jan 11 v Cardiff City (h) 0-0
Trautmann; Leivers, Betts, Barnes, Plenderleith, Shawcross, Barlow, Law, Hannah, Hayes, Sambrook.
Att: 39,035
Second Replay
Jan 16 v Cardiff City (at Highbury) 2-0
Law, Hayes
Trautmann; Betts, Sear, Barnes, Plenderleith, Shawcross, Barlow, Law, Hannah, Hayes, Colbridge.
Att: 24,168
Round 4
Jan 28 v Luton Town (a) 6-2 (abandoned)
Law 6
Trautmann; Leivers, Betts, Barnes, Plenderleith, Shawcross, Barlow, Hannah, Baker, Law, Hayes.
Att: 23,727
Round 4
Feb 1 v Luton Town (a) 1-3
Law
Trautmann; Leivers, Betts, Barnes, Plenderleith, Shawcross, Barlow, Hannah, Baker, Law, Hayes.
Att: 15,783

1961-2
Round 3
Jan 6 (a) Notts County (a) 1-0
Young
Trautmann; Betts, Sear, Cheetham, Leivers, Kennedy, Young, Hannah, Dobing, Hayes, Wagstaffe.
Att: 25,015
Round 4
Jan 27 v Everton (a) 0-2
Trautmann; McDonald, Sear, Cheetham, Leivers, Kennedy, Young, Hannah, Dobing, Hayes, Wagstaffe.
Att: 56,980

1962-3
Round 3
Mar 6 v Walsall (a) 1-0
Harley
Dowd; Betts, Sear, Benson, Leivers, Pardoe, Dobing, Kennedy, Harley, Hannah, Wagstaffe.
Att: 11,553
Round 4
Mar 13 v Bury (h) 1-0
Harley
Dowd; Betts, Kennedy, Benson, Leivers, Oakes, Young, Dobing, Harley, Hannah, Wagstaffe.
Att: 41,575
Round 5
Mar 16 v Norwich City (h) 1-2
Oakes
Dowd; Betts, Kennedy, Benson, Leivers, Oakes, Hayes, Dobing, Harley, Hannah, Wagstaffe.
Att: 31,217

1963-4
Round 3
Jan 4 v Swindon Town (a) 1-2
Oakes
Dowd; Leivers, Sear, Kennedy, Wood, Oakes, Young, Gray, Murray, Kevan, Wagstaffe.
Att: 18,065

1964-5
Round 3
Jan 9 v Shrewsbury Town (h) 1-1
Kevan
Dowd; Bacuzzi, Sear, Kennedy, Wood, Oakes, Pardoe, Gray, Murray, Kevan, Young.
Att: 16,131

Replay
Jan 13 v Shrewsbury Town (a) 1-3
Gray
Dowd; Bacuzzi, Sear, Kennedy, Wood, Oakes, Pardoe, Gray, Murray, Kevan, Shawcross.
Att: 15,924

1965-6
Round 3
Jan 22 v Blackpool (a) 1-1
Crossan
Dowd; Kennedy, Sear, Cheetham, Heslop, Oakes, Summerbee, Crossan, Pardoe, Young, Connor.
Att: 23,937
Replay
Jan 24 v Blackpool (h) 3-1
Summerbee, Doyle, Crossan
Dowd; Kennedy, Sear, Doyle, Heslop, Oakes, Summerbee, Crossan, Pardoe, Young, Connor.
Att: 52,661
Round 4
Feb 12 v Grimsby Town (h) 2-0
Summerbee, opp og
Dowd; Kennedy, Sear, Doyle, Heslop, Oakes, Summerbee, Crossan, Pardoe, Young, Connor.
Att: 37,918.
Round 5
Mar 5 v Leicester City (h) 2-2
Young (2)
Dowd; Kennedy, Horne, Doyle, Heslop, Oakes, Summerbee, Crossan, Pardoe, Young, Connor.
Att: 56,787
Replay
Mar 9 v Leicester City (a) 1-0
Young
Dowd; Kennedy, Horne, Pardoe, Heslop, Oakes, Summerbee, Crossan, Doyle, Connor, Young.
Att: 41,872
Round 6
Mar 26 v Everton (h) 0-0
Dowd; Kennedy, Horne, Pardoe, Heslop, Oakes, Summerbee, Crossan, Young, Doyle, Connor.
Att: 63,034
Replay
Mar 29 v Everton (a) 0-0
Dowd; Kennedy, Horne, Doyle, Heslop, Oakes, Cheetham, Crossan, Summerbee, Crossan, Pardoe.
Att: 60,349
Second Replay
Apr 4 v Everton (at Molineux) 0-2
Dowd; Kennedy, Horne, Doyle, Heslop, Oakes, Pardoe, Crossan, Summerbee, Crossan, Young.
Att: 27,948

1966-7
Round 3
Jan 28 v Leicester City (h) 2-1
Doyle, Pardoe
Ogley; Book, Pardoe, Horne, Heslop, Oakes, Connor, Bell, Doyle, Crossan, Young.
Att: 38,529
Round 4
Feb 18 v Cardiff City (a) 1-1
opp og
Ogley; Book, Pardoe, Horne, Heslop, Oakes, Summerbee, Bell, Doyle, Crossan, Young.
Att: 37,205
Replay
Feb 22 v Cardiff City (h) 3-1
Bell, Young, Crossan
Ogley; Book, Pardoe, Horne, Heslop, Oakes, Summerbee, Bell, Doyle, Crossan, Young.
Att: 41,616

Round 5
Mar 11 v Ipswich Town (h) 1-1
Young
Ogley; Book, Pardoe, Horne, Kennedy, Oakes, Connor,
Crossan, Doyle, Bell, Young.
Att: 47,075
Replay
Mar 14 v Ipswich Town (a) 3-0
Summerbee (2), opp og
Ogley; Book, Pardoe, Horne, Kennedy, Oakes,
Summerbee, Crossan, Doyle, Bell, Young.
Att: 30,605
Round 6
Apr 8 v Leeds United (a) 0-1
Dowd; Book, Pardoe, Horne, Heslop, Oakes, Summerbee,
Bell, Connor, Crossan, Brand.
Att: 48,887

1967-8
Round 3
Jan 27 v Reading (h) 0-0
Mulhearn; Book, Pardoe, Doyle, Heslop, Oakes, Lee,
Bell, Summerbee, Young, Coleman.
Att: 40,343
Replay
Jan 31 v Reading (a) 7-0
Summerbee (3), Young, Coleman, Heslop, Bell
Mulhearn; Book, Pardoe, Doyle, Heslop, Oakes, Lee,
Bell, Summerbee, Young(Connor), Coleman.
Att: 25,659
Round 4
Feb 17 v Leicester City (h) 0-0
Mulhearn; Book, Pardoe, Doyle, Heslop, Oakes, Lee,
Bell, Summerbee, Young, Coleman.
Att: 51,009
Replay
Feb 19 v Leicester City (a) 3-4
Summerbee, Bell, Lee
Mulhearn; Book, Pardoe, Doyle, Heslop, Oakes, Lee,
Bell, Summerbee, Young, Coleman.
Att: 39,112

1968-9
Round 3
Jan 4 v Luton Town (h) 1-0
Lee
Dowd; Pardoe, Mann, Doyle, Booth, Oakes, Lee, Bell,
Owen, Young, Coleman.
Att: 37,120
Round 4
Jan 25 v Newcastle United (a) 0-0
Dowd; Book, Pardoe, Doyle, Booth, Oakes, Summerbee,
Lee, Owen, Young, Coleman.
Att: 55,680
Replay
Jan 29 v Newcastle United (h) 2-0
Owen, Young
Dowd; Book, Pardoe, Doyle, Booth, Oakes, Summerbee,
Lee, Owen, Young, Coleman.
Att: 60,844
Round 5
Feb 24 v Blackburn Rovers (a) 4-1
Lee (2), Coleman (2)
Dowd; Book, Pardoe, Doyle, Booth, Oakes, Summerbee,
Bell, Lee, Young, Coleman.
Att: 42,315
Round 6
Mar 1 v Tottenham Hotspur (h) 1-0
Lee
Dowd; Book, Pardoe, Doyle, Booth, Oakes, Summerbee,
Bell, Lee, Young, Coleman.
Att: 48,872

Harry Dowd, City's goalkeeper in the 1969 Final.

Semi-final
Mar 22 v Everton (at Villa Park) 1-0
Booth
Dowd; Book, Pardoe, Doyle, Booth, Oakes, Summerbee,
Bell, Lee, Young, Connor.
Att: 63,025
Final
Apr 26 v Leicester City (at Wembley) 1-0
Young
Dowd; Book, Pardoe, Doyle, Booth, Oakes, Summerbee,
Bell, Lee, Young, Coleman.
Att: 100,000

1969-70
Round 3
Jan 3 v Hull City (a) 1-0
Young
Corrigan; Book, Pardoe, Doyle, Booth, Oakes,
Summerbee, Bell, Lee, Young, Bowyer.
Att: 30,271
Round 4
Jan 24 v Manchester United (a) 0-3
Mulhearn; Book, Pardoe, Doyle, Booth, Oakes,
Summerbee(Towers), Bell, Lee, Young, Bowyer.
Att: 63,417

1970-71
Round 3
Jan 2 v Wigan Athletic (h) 1-0
Bell
Corrigan; Book, Mann, Doyle, Booth, Oakes,
Summerbee, Bell, Lee(Carrodus), Young, Jefferies.
Att: 46,212

Round 4
Jan 23 v Chelsea (a) 3-0
Bell (2), Bowyer
Corrigan; Book, Mann, Doyle, Booth, Oakes, Heslop, Bell, Summerbee(Young), Bowyer, Jefferies.
Att: 50,176
Round 5
Feb 17 v Arsenal (h) 1-2
Bell
Corrigan; Book, Mann, Doyle, Booth, Oakes, Heslop, Bell, Lee, Young, Bowyer.
Att: 45,105

1971-2
Round 3
Jan 15 v Middlesbrough (h) 1-1
Lee
Corrigan; Book, Donachie, Doyle, Booth, Oakes, Summerbee, Bell, Davies, Lee, Towers.
Att: 42,620
Replay
Jan 18 v Middlesbrough (a) 0-1
Corrigan; Book, Donachie, Doyle, Booth, Oakes, Summerbee, Bell, Davies, Lee, Towers.
Att: 37,917

1972-3
Round 3
Jan 13 v Stoke City (h) 3-2
Summerbee, Bell, Marsh
Corrigan; Book, Donachie, Doyle, Booth, Jefferies, Summerbee, Bell, Marsh, Lee, Mellor.
Att: 38,648
Round 4
Feb 3 v Liverpool (a) 0-0
Corrigan; Book, Donachie, Doyle, Booth, Jefferies, Summerbee, Bell, Marsh, Lee, Towers.
Att: 56,296
Replay
Feb 7 v Liverpool (h) 2-0
Bell, Booth
Corrigan; Book, Donachie, Doyle, Booth, Jefferies, Summerbee, Bell, Marsh, Lee, Towers.
Att: 49,576
Round 5
Feb 24 v Sunderland (h) 2-2
Towers, opp og
Corrigan; Book, Donachie, Doyle(Mellor), Booth, Jefferies, Summerbee, Bell, Marsh, Lee, Towers.
Att: 54,478
Replay
Feb 27 v Sunderland (h) 1-3
Lee
Corrigan; Book, Donachie, Doyle(Mellor), Booth, Jefferies, Mellor, Bell, Marsh, Lee, Towers.
Att: 51,782

1973-4
Round 3
Jan 5 v Oxford United (a) 5-2
Law (2), Summerbee (2), Marsh
Corrigan; Barrett, Donachie, Doyle, Booth, Towers, Summerbee, Bell, Law, Lee, Marsh.
Att: 13,435
Round 4
Jan 26 v Nottingham Forest (a) 1-4
Carrodus
MacRae; Barrett, Donachie, Doyle, Booth, Towers, Summerbee, Bell, Lee, Carrodus, Marsh(Leman).
Att: 41,472

1974-5
Round 3
Jan 4 v Newcastle United (h) 0-2
Corrigan; Hammond, Donachie, Horswill, Doyle, Oakes, Barnes(Henson), Bell, Marsh, Hartford, Tueart.
Att: 37,625

1975-6
Round 3
Jan 3 v Hartlepool (h) 6-0
Tueart (2), Booth (2), Hartford, Oakes
Corrigan; Clements, Donachie, Doyle, Watson, Oakes, Power, Booth, Royle, Hartford, Tueart.
Att: 26,863
Round 4
Jan 28 v Stoke City (a) 0-1
Corrigan; Barrett, Donachie, Doyle, Booth, Oakes, Barnes(Keegan), Power, Royle, Hartford, Tueart.
Att: 38,072

1976-7
Round 3
Jan 8 v West Bromwich Albion (h) 1-1
Kidd
Corrigan; Clements, Donachie, Doyle, Watson, Power, Owen, Kidd, Royle, Hartford, Tueart.
Att: 38,195
Replay
Jan 11 v West Bromwich Albion (a) 1-0
Royle
Corrigan; Clements, Donachie, Doyle, Watson, Power, Owen, Kidd, Royle, Hartford, Tueart.
Att: 38,195
Round 4
Jan 29 v Newcastle United (a) 3-1
Owen, Royle, opp og
Corrigan; Clements, Donachie, Doyle, Watson, Power, Owen, Kidd, Royle, Hartford, Tueart.
Att: 45,300
Round 5
Feb 26 v Leeds United (a) 0-1
Corrigan; Clements, Donachie, Doyle, Watson, Power, Conway, Kidd, Royle, Hartford, Tueart.
Att: 47,731

1977-8
Round 3
Jan 7 v Leeds United (a) 2-1
Barnes, Tueart
Corrigan; Clements, Donachie, Booth, Watson, Owen, Barnes, Bell, Kidd, Hartford, Tueart.
Att: 38,516
Round 4
Jan 31 v Nottingham Forest (a) 1-2
Kidd
Corrigan; Clements, Donachie, Booth, Watson, Owen(Channon), Barnes, Bell, Kidd, Hartford, Tueart.
Att: 38,509

1978-9
Round 3
Jan 15 v Rotherham United (h) 0-0
Corrigan; Ranson, Donachie, Power, Bell, P.Futcher, Channon, Kidd, R.Futcher, Hartford, Barnes.
Att: 26,029
Replay
Jan 17 v Rotherham United (a) 4-2
Kidd (2), Barnes, Owen
MacRae; Donachie, Power, Owen, Watson, P.Futcher, Channon, Deyna, Kidd, Hartford, Barnes.
Att: 13,758

Round 4
Jan 25 v Shrewsbury Town (a) 0-2
Corrigan; Donachie, Power, Owen, Watson, P.Futcher, Channon, Deyna(Bell), Kidd, Hartford, Barnes.
Att: 14,215

1979-80
Round 3
Jan 5 v Halifax Town (a) 0-1
Corrigan; Ranson, Power, Reid, Caton, Bennett, Henry, Daley, Robinson, Viljoen, Shinton.
Att: 12,599

1980-81
Round 3
Jan 3 v Crystal Palace (h) 4-0
Reeves (2), Power, Boyer
Corrigan; Ranson, McDonald, Reid, Power, Caton, Boyer, Gow, Mackenzie, Hutchison, Reeves.
Att: 39,347
Round 4
Jan 24 v Norwich City (h) 6-0
McDonald, Reeves, Mackenzie, Power, Gow, Bennett
Corrigan; Henry, McDonald, Booth, Power, Caton, Boyer(Bennett), Gow, Mackenzie, Hutchison, Reeves.
Att: 38,919

Round 5
Feb 14 v Peterborough United (a) 1-0
Booth
Corrigan; Henry, McDonald, Reid, Power, Booth, Bennett, Gow, Mackenzie, Hutchison, Reeves.
Att: 27,780
Round 6
Mar 7 v Everton (a) 2-2
Power, Gow
Corrigan; Ranson, McDonald, Reid, Power, Caton, Tueart, Gow, Mackenzie, Hutchison, Reeves.
Att: 52,791
Replay
Mar 11 v Everton (h) 3-1
McDonald (2), Power
Corrigan; Ranson, McDonald, Reid, Power, Caton, Tueart, Gow, Mackenzie, Hutchison, Reeves.
Att: 52,532
Semi-final
Apr 11 v Ipswich Town (at Villa Park) 1-0
Power
Corrigan; Ranson, McDonald, Reid, Power, Caton, Bennett, Gow, Mackenzie, Hutchison, Reeves.
Att: 46,537
Final
May 9 v Tottenham Hotspur (at Wembley) 1-1
Hutchison
Corrigan; Ranson, McDonald, Reid, Power, Caton, Bennett(Henry), Gow, Mackenzie, Hutchison, Reeves.
Att: 100,000

Tommy Caton brings a Garth Crooks attack to an end at Wembley in 1981.

Replay
Apr 14 v Tottenham Hotspur (at Wembley) 2-3
Mackenzie, Reeves
Corrigan; Ranson, McDonald(Tueart), Reid, Power, Caton, Bennett, Gow, Mackenzie, Hutchison, Reeves.
Att: 92,500

1981-2
Round 3
Jan 2 v Cardiff City (h) 3-1
Francis (2), McDonald
Corrigan; Ranson, McDonald, Reid, Bond, Caton, Gow, Reeves, Francis, Hartford, Hutchison.
Att: 31,547
Round 4
Jan 23 v Coventry City (h) 1-3
Bond
Corrigan; Gow(Kinsey), McDonald, Reid, Bond, Caton, Hutchison, Reeves, Francis, Hartford, Power.
Att: 31,276

1982-3
Round 3
Jan 8 v Sunderland (a) 0-0
Corrigan; Ranson, Bond, Reid, Power, Caton, Bodak, Reeves, Cross(Tueart), Hartford, Kinsey.
Att: 21,518
Replay
Jan 12 v Sunderland (h) 2-1
Cross, Hartford
Corrigan; Ranson, Bond, Reid, Power, Kinsey, Tueart, Reeves, Cross, Hartford, Bodak(McDonald).
Att: 22,356
Round 4
Jan 29 v Brighton & Hove Albion (a) 0-4
Corrigan; Ranson, Bond, Reid, Power(Bodak), Caton, Tueart, Reeves, Cross, Hartford, Kinsey.
Att: 16,804

1983-4
Round 3
Jan 7 v Blackpool (a) 1-2
opp og
Williams; Lomax(Dalziel), Walsh, Bond, Power, McCarthy, McNab, Baker, Parlane, May, Tolmie.
Att: 15,377

1984-5
Round 3
Jan 5 v Coventry City (a) 1-2
Power
Williams; Lomax, Power, May, McCarthy, Phillips, Smith(Cunningham), Baker, Melrose, Wilson, Kinsey.
Att: 15,642

1985-6
Round 3
Jan 4 v Walsall (a) 3-1
Simpson (2), Davies
Nixon; Reid, Power, Clements, McCarthy, Phillips, Lillis, May, Davies(Moulden), McNab, Simpson.
Att: 10,779
Round 4
Jan 25 v Watford (h) 1-1
Davies
Nixon; Reid, Power, Clements, McCarthy, Phillips, Lillis, May, Davies, McNab, Simpson.
Att: 31,632
Replay
Feb 3 v Watford (a) 0-0
Nixon; Reid, Power, Clements, McCarthy, Phillips, Lillis, May, Davies, McNab, Simpson(Kinsey).
Att: 19,347
Second Replay
Feb 6 v Watford (h) 1-3
Kinsey
Nixon; Reid, Power, Clements, McCarthy, Phillips, Lillis, May, Davies, McNab(Kinsey), Simpson.
Att: 27,260

1986-7
Round 3
Jan 10 v Manchester United (a) 0-1
Suckling; Gidman, Wilson, Clements, McCarthy, Redmond, White(Brightwell), McNab, Varadi, Grealish (Baker), Simpson.
Att: 54,294

Action from the 1981 FA Cup Final.

Tommy Hutchison and Chris Hughton do battle during City's most recent FA Cup Final appearance, in 1981.

City in the League Cup
(includes Milk Cup and Littlewoods Challenge Cup)

1960-61
Round 2
Oct 18 v Stockport County (h) 3-0
Law (2), Hayes
Trautmann; Betts, Sear, Barnes, Plenderleith, Shawcross, Barlow, Law, Hannah, Hayes, Sambrook.
Att: 21,065
Round 3
Nov 21 v Portsmouth (a) 0-2
Trautmann; Betts, Sear, Barnes, Plenderleith, Shawcross, Hayes, Law, Hannah, Baker, Colbridge.
Att: 10,368

1961-2
Round 2
Sep 11 v Ipswich Town (a) 2-4
Betts, opp og
Trautmann; Betts, Sear, Cheetham, Ewing, Kennedy, Barlow, Dobing, Hannah, Hayes, Wagstaffe.
Att: 14,926

1962-3
Round 2
Sep 24 v Blackpool (h) 0-0
Trautmann; Betts, Sear, Kennedy, Leivers, Chadwick, Young, Dobing, Harley, Hayes, Wagstaffe.
Att: 12,064
Replay
Oct 8 v Blackpool (a) 3-3
Harley (2), Young
Dowd; Betts, Sear, Kennedy, Leivers, Benson, Young, Dobing, Harley, Hannah, Wagstaffe.
Att: 10,508
Second Replay
Oct 15 v Blackpool (h) 4-2
Harley (2), Oakes, Dobing
Dowd; Kennedy, Sear, Benson, Leivers, Oakes, Young, Dobing, Harley, Hannah, Hayes.
Att: 12,237
Round 3
Oct 24 v Newport County (a) 2-1
Harley, Hannah
Dowd; Kennedy, Sear, Benson, Leivers, Oakes, Young, Dobing, Harley, Hannah, Hayes.
Att: 9,898
Round 4
Nov 14 v Luton Town (h) 1-0
Harley
Dowd; Kennedy, Sear, Benson, Leivers, Oakes, Young, Dobing, Harley, Hannah, Wagstaffe.
Att: 8,682
Round 5
Dec 11 v Birmingham City (a) 0-6
Fleet; Betts, Sear, Benson, Leivers, Oakes, Hayes, Dobing, Harley, Hannah, Young.
Att: 18,010

1963-4
Round 2
Sep 25 v Carlisle United (h) 2-0
Aimson, Kevan
Dowd; Leivers, Sear, Chadwick, Cheetham, Oakes, Hodgkinson, Hayes, Aimson, Kevan, Wagstaffe.
Att: 8,265
Round 3
Oct 16 v Hull City (a) 3-0
Aimson, Kevan, Young
Dowd; Betts, Sear, Kennedy, Cheetham, Oakes, Young, Gray, Aimson, Kevan, Wagstaffe.
Att: 13,880
Round 4
Nov 27 v Leeds United (h) 3-1
Kevan (2), Gray
Dowd; Leivers, Sear, Kennedy, Wood, Oakes, Young, Gray, Murray, Kevan, Wagstaffe.
Att: 10,984
Round 5
Dec 17 v Notts County (a) 1-0
Kevan
Dowd; Leivers, Sear, Kennedy, Wood, Oakes, Young, Gray, Murray, Kevan, Wagstaffe.
Att: 7,330
Semi-final (1st leg)
Jan 15 v Stoke City (a) 0-2
Dowd; Leivers, Sear, Kennedy, Wood, Oakes, Young, Gray, Panter, Aimson, Wagstaffe.
Att: 21,019
Semi-final (2nd leg)
Feb 5 v Stoke City (h) 1-0 (agg 1-2)
Kevan
Dowd; Betts, Sear, Kennedy, Leivers, Oakes, Young, Gray, Pardoe, Kevan, Wagstaffe.
Att: 16,894

1964-5
Round 2
Sep 23 v Mansfield Town (h) 3-5
Murray, Young, Kevan
Dowd; Bacuzzi, Kennedy, Shawcross, Cheetham, Oakes, Young, Gray, Murray, Kevan, Wagstaffe.
Att: 8,789

1965-6
Round 2
Sep 22 v Leicester City (h) 3-1
Murray, Pardoe, opp og
Ogley; Kennedy, Sear, Horne, Wood, Oakes, Summerbee, Gray, Murray, Pardoe, Young.
Att: 13,246
Round 3
Oct 13 v Coventry City (h) 2-3
Crossan, Pardoe
Dowd; Kennedy, Sear, Cheetham, Heslop, Oakes, Summerbee, Crossan, Pardoe, Brand, Young.
Att: 18,213

1966-7
Round 2
Sep 14 v Bolton Wanderers (h) 3-1
Bell, Murray, Pardoe
Dowd; Book, Kennedy, Horne, Heslop, Oakes,
Summerbee, Bell, Murray(Cheetham), Pardoe, Young.
Att: 9,006
Round 3
Oct 5 v West Bromwich Albion (a) 2-4
Summerbee, Young
Dowd; Book, Cheetham, Horne, Heslop, Oakes,
Summerbee, Bell, Pardoe, Crossan, Young.
Att: 19,193

1967-8
Round 2
Sep 13 v Leicester City (h) 4-0
Bowles (2), Book, Young
Dowd; Book, Pardoe, Doyle, Heslop, Oakes, Hince,
Bell, Summerbee, Young, Coleman(Bowles).
Att: 25,653
Round 3
Oct 11 v Blackpool (h) 1-1
Summerbee
Corrigan; Book, Pardoe, Horne, Heslop, Oakes, Hince,
Bell, Summerbee, Young, Coleman.
Att: 27,633
Replay
Oct 18 (a) Blackpool (a) 2-0
Summerbee, opp og
Corrigan; Book, Pardoe(Connor), Doyle, Heslop, Oakes,
Hince, Bell, Summerbee, Young, Coleman.
Att: 23,405
Round 4
Nov 1 v Fulham (a) 2-3
Oakes, Bell
Dowd; Book, Pardoe, Doyle, Heslop, Oakes, Hince,
Bell, Summerbee, Young(Horne), Coleman.
Att: 11,732

1968-9
Round 2
Sep 4 v Huddersfield Town (a) 0-0
Mulhearn; Connor, Pardoe, Doyle, Booth, Oakes,
Summerbee, Bell, Lee, Owen, Coleman.
Att: 23,426
Replay
Sep 11 v Huddersfield Town (h) 4-0
Summerbee (2), Bell, opp og
Mulhearn; Kennedy, Connor, Doyle, Heslop, Oakes,
Lee, Bell, Summerbee, Young(Bowles), Coleman.
Att: 26,948
Round 3
Sep 25 v Blackpool (a) 0-1
Mulhearn; Connor, Pardoe, Doyle, Heslop, Oakes,
Lee, Bell, Summerbee, Young, Coleman.
Att: 23,795

1969-70
Round 2
Sep 3 v Southport (a) 3-0
Oakes, Bell, Lee
Corrigan; Book, Connor, Doyle, Booth, Oakes,
Summerbee, Bell, Lee, Bowyer, Bowles.
Att: 11,215
Round 3
Sep 24 v Liverpool (h) 3-2
Doyle, Young, Bowyer
Corrigan; Book, Pardoe, Doyle, Heslop, Oakes,
Summerbee, Bell(Coleman), Lee, Young, Bowyer.
Att: 28,019

Round 4
Oct 15 v Everton (h) 2-0
Bell, Lee
Corrigan; Book, Pardoe, Doyle, Booth, Oakes,
Summerbee, Bell, Lee, Young, Bowyer.
Att: 45,643
Round 5
Oct 29 v Queen's Park Rangers (h) 3-0
Bell (2), Summerbee
Corrigan; Book, Pardoe, Doyle, Booth, Oakes,
Summerbee, Bell, Lee, Young, Bowyer.
Att: 42,058
Semi-final (1st leg)
Dec 3 v Manchester United (h) 2-1
Bell, Lee
Corrigan; Book, Pardoe, Doyle, Booth, Oakes,
Summerbee, Bell, Lee, Young, Bowyer.
Att: 55,799
Semi-final (2nd leg)
Dec 17 v Manchester United (a) 2-2 (agg 4-3)
Summerbee, Bowyer
Corrigan; Book, Pardoe, Doyle, Booth, Oakes,
Summerbee, Connor, Lee, Young, Bowyer.
Att: 63,418
Final
Mar 7 v West Bromwich Albion (at Wembley) 2-1
Pardoe, Doyle
Corrigan; Book, Mann, Doyle, Booth, Oakes, Heslop,
Bell, Summerbee(Bowyer), Lee, Pardoe.
Att: 97,963

*Glyn Pardoe, scorer of a goal in the 1970 League Cup
Final.*

217

1970-71
Round 2
Sep 9 v Carlisle United (a) 1-2
Lee
Corrigan; Book, Pardoe, Doyle(Bowyer), Booth, Oakes, Summerbee, Bell, Lee, Young, Towers.
Att: 17,942

1971-2
Round 2
Sep 8 v Wolverhampton Wanderers (h) 4-3
Bell (2), Lee, Davies
Corrigan; Book, Donachie, Doyle, Booth(Jefferies), Bell, Summerbee, Heslop, Davies, Lee, Mellor.
Att: 29,156
Round 3
Oct 5 v Bolton Wanderers (a) 0-3
Corrigan; Book, Donachie, Doyle, Booth, Towers, Summerbee, Jefferies, Davies, Lee, Hill.
Att: 42,039

1972-3
Round 2
Sep 6 v Rochdale (h) 4-0
Marsh (2), Bell, Lee
Corrigan; Book, Donachie, Bell, Booth, Towers(Oakes), Summerbee, Marsh, Davies, Lee, Jefferies.
Att: 17,222
Round 3
Oct 3 v Bury (a) 0-2
Healey; Book, Donachie, Doyle, Booth, Barrett, Summerbee(Mellor), Bell, Marsh, Lee, Towers.
Att: 16,614

1973-4
Round 2
Oct 2 v Walsall (a) 0-0
Healey; Book, Donachie, Doyle, Booth, Oakes, Summerbee. Bell, Marsh, Lee, Towers.
Att: 12,943
Replay
Oct 22 v Walsall (h) 0-0
MacRae; Pardoe, Donachie, Doyle, Booth, Oakes, Summerbee, Bell, Law, Lee, Marsh(Book).
Att: 19,428
Second Replay
Oct 30 v Walsall (at Old Trafford) 4-0
Lee (3), Bell
MacRae; Pardoe, Donachie, Doyle, Booth, Oakes, Carrodus, Bell, Summerbee, Lee, Towers.
Att: 13,646
Round 3
Nov 6 v Carlisle United (a) 1-0
Lee
MacRae; Pardoe, Donachie, Doyle, Booth, Oakes, Carrodus, Bell, Summerbee, Lee, Towers.
Att: 14,472
Round 4
Nov 21 v York City (a) 0-0
MacRae; Pardoe, Donachie, Doyle, Booth, Towers, Barrett, Bell, Summerbee, Lee, Marsh.
Att: 15,360
Replay
Dec 5 v York City (h) 4-1
Marsh (3), Lee
MacRae; Pardoe, Donachie, Doyle, Booth, Towers, Summerbee, Bell, Marsh, Lee, Leman.
Att: 17,972

Round 5
Dec 19 v Coventry City (a) 2-2
Booth, Leman
MacRae; Pardoe, Donachie, Doyle, Booth, Towers, Summerbee, Bell, Marsh, Lee, Leman.
Att: 12,661
Replay
Jan 16 v Coventry City (h) 4-2
Lee (2), Summerbee, Law
MacRae; Barrett, Donachie, Doyle, Booth, Towers, Summerbee, Bell, Lee, Law, Marsh.
Att: 25,409
Semi-final (1st leg)
Jan 23 v Plymouth Argyle (a) 1-1
Booth
MacRae; Barrett, Donachie, Doyle, Booth, Towers, Summerbee, Bell, Lee, Law(Leman), Marsh.
Att: 30,390
Semi-final (2nd leg)
Jan 30 v Plymouth Argyle (h) 2-0 (agg 3-1)
Bell, Lee
MacRae; Barrett, Donachie, Doyle, Booth, Towers, Summerbee, Bell, Lee(Leman), Oakes, Carrodus.
Att: 40,117
Final
Mar 3 v Wolverhampton Wanderers (at Wembley) 1-2
Bell
MacRae; Pardoe, Donachie, Doyle, Booth, Towers, Summerbee, Bell, Lee, Law, Marsh.
Att: 100,000

1974-5
Round 2
Sep 10 v Scunthorpe United (h) 6-0
Bell (3), Barrett, Marsh, Doyle
MacRae; Barrett, Donachie, Doyle(Keegan), Clarke, Oakes, Summerbee, Bell, Marsh, Henson, Tueart.
Att: 14,790
Round 3
Oct 9 v Manchester United (a) 0-1
MacRae; Hammond, Pardoe(Barnes), Doyle, Clarke, Oakes, Summerbee, Bell, Marsh, Hartford, Tueart.
Att: 55,225

1975-6
Round 2
Sep 10 v Norwich City (a) 1-1
Watson
Corrigan; Clements, Donachie, Doyle, Watson, Oakes, Hartford, Bell, Royle, Marsh, Tueart.
Att: 18,332
Replay
Sep 17 v Norwich City (h) 2-2
Royle, Tueart
Corrigan; Clements, Donachie, Doyle, Watson, Oakes, Hartford, Bell, Royle(Barnes), Marsh, Tueart.
Att: 29,667
Second Replay
Sep 24 v Norwich City (at Stamford Bridge) 6-1
Tueart (3), Doyle, Royle, opp og
Corrigan; Clements, Donachie, Doyle, Watson, Oakes, Hartford, Bell, Royle, Marsh, Tueart.
Att: 6,238
Round 3
Oct 8 v Nottingham Forest (h) 2-1
Bell, Royle
Corrigan; Clements, Donachie, Doyle, Watson, Oakes, Hartford, Bell, Royle, Marsh, Barnes.
Att: 26,536

Round 4
Nov 12 v Manchester United (h) 4-0
Tueart (2), Royle, Hartford
Corrigan; Clements, Donachie, Doyle, Watson, Oakes,
Barnes, Bell(Booth), Royle, Hartford, Tueart.
Att: 50,182
Round 5
Dec 3 v Mansfield Town (h) 4-2
Hartford, Royle, Tueart, Oakes
Corrigan; Clements, Donachie, Doyle, Watson, Oakes,
Barnes, Booth, Royle(Power), Hartford, Tueart.
Att: 30,022
Semi-final (1st leg)
Jan 13 v Middlesbrough (a) 0-1
Corrigan; Barrett, Donachie, Doyle, Booth, Oakes,
Barnes, Power, Royle, Hartford, Tueart.
Att: 35,000
Semi-final (2nd leg)
Jan 21 v Middlesbrough (2nd leg) 4-0 (agg 4-1)
Oakes, Keegan, Barnes, Royle
Corrigan; Barrett, Donachie, Doyle, Clements, Oakes,
Power, Keegan, Royle, Hartford, Barnes.
Att: 44,426
Final
Feb 28 v Newcastle United (at Wembley) 2-1
Barnes, Tueart
Corrigan; Keegan, Donachie, Doyle, Watson, Oakes,
Barnes, Booth, Royle, Hartford, Tueart.
Att: 100,000

*Aerial battle at Wembley between City and Newcastle
United in 1976.*

1976-7
Round 2
Sep 1 v Aston Villa (a) 0-3
Corrigan; Docherty, Donachie, Doyle, Watson, Power
(Booth), Barnes, Conway, Royle, Hartford, Tueart.
Att: 34,585

1977-8
Round 2
Aug 31 (a) Chesterfield 1-0
Kidd
Corrigan; Clements, Donachie, Doyle, Watson, Booth,
Kidd, Channon, Royle, Owen, Tueart(Barnes).
Att: 14,282
Round 3
Oct 25 v Luton Town (a) 1-1
Barnes
Corrigan; Clements, Donachie, Owen, Watson, Booth,
Barnes, Channon, Kidd, Keegan, Power.
Att: 16,443
Replay
Nov 1 v Luton Town (h) 0-0
Corrigan; Clements, Donachie, Doyle, Booth, Kidd,
Barnes, Channon, Royle, Hartford, Power.
Att: 28,254
Second Replay
Nov 9 v Luton Town (at Old Trafford) 3-2
Channon, Kidd, Tueart
Corrigan; Clements, Donachie, Doyle, Watson, Power,
Barnes, Channon, Kidd, Hartford, Tueart.
Att: 13,043
Round 4
Nov 29 v Ipswich Town (a) 2-1
Kidd, Tueart
Corrigan; Clements, Donachie, Booth, Watson, Power,
Barnes, Channon, Kidd, Hartford, Tueart.
Att: 22,645
Round 5
Jan 18 v Arsenal (h) 0-0
Corrigan; Clements, Donachie, Booth, Watson, Owen,
Barnes, Bell, Kidd, Hartford, Tueart.
Att: 42,435
Replay
Jan 24 v Arsenal (a) 0-1
Corrigan; Clements, Donachie, Booth, Watson, Owen,
Barnes(Channon), Bell, Kidd, Hartford, Tueart.
Att: 57,548

1978-9
Round 2
Aug 29 v Grimsby Town (h) 2-0
Palmer, opp og
Corrigan; Clements, Power, Keegan, Booth, P.Futcher,
Channon, Owen, R.Futcher(Viljoen), Hartford, Palmer.
Att: 21,481
Round 3
Oct 4 v Blackpool (a) 1-1
Channon
Corrigan; Clements, Donachie, Booth, Watson, Power,
Channon, Owen, Kidd, Hartford, Barnes(Palmer).
Att: 18,886
Replay
Oct 10 v Blackpool (h) 3-0
Owen (2), Booth
Corrigan; Clements, Donachie, Booth, Watson, Kidd,
Palmer, Owen, R.Futcher, Hartford, Barnes.
Att: 26,213
Round 4
Nov 8 v Norwich City (a) 3-1
Channon (2), Barnes
Corrigan; Clements, Donachie, Booth, Watson,
Viljoen(R.Futcher), Channon, Owen, Kidd, Hartford,
Barnes.
Att: 19,413

Round 5
Dec 12 v Southampton (a) 1-2
opp og
Corrigan; Donachie, Power, Booth, Watson, Owen,
Channon, Bell, Kidd, Hartford, Deyna(Barnes).
Att: 21,523

1979-80
Round 2 (1st leg)
Aug 28 v Sheffield Wednesday (a) 1-1
Viljoen
Corrigan; Ranson, Stepanovic, Caton, Booth, Power,
Mackenzie, Silkman, Robinson, Viljoen, Channon.
Att: 24,095
Round 2 (2nd leg)
Sep 4 v Sheffield Wednesday (h) 2-1 (agg 3-2)
Henry (2)
Corrigan; Ranson, Stepanovic, Caton, Booth, Power,
Mackenzie, Silkman, Robinson, Donachie, Henry.
Att: 24,074
Round 3
Sep 26 v Sunderland (h) 1-1
Robinson
Corrigan; Ranson, Donachie, Stepanovic, Caton,
Futcher, Mackenzie, Daley, Robinson, Power, Bennett.
Att: 26,181
Replay
Oct 3 v Sunderland (a) 0-1
Corrigan; Ranson, Donachie(Palmer), Stepanovic, Caton,
Futcher, Mackenzie, Daley, Robinson, Power, Deyna.
Att: 33,559

1980-81
Round 2 (1st leg)
Aug 27 v Stoke City (a) 1-1
Henry
Corrigan(Palmer); Ranson, Reid, Booth, Caton, Henry,
Tueart, Daley, Mackenzie, Power, Reeves.
Att: 13,176
Round 2 (2nd leg)
Sep 3 v Stoke City (h) 3-0 (agg 4-1)
Bennett (2), Henry
MacRae; Ranson, Reid, Booth, Caton, Henry, Bennett,
Daley, Mackenzie, Power, Reeves.
Att: 21,356
Round 3
Sep 23 v Luton Town (a) 2-1
Henry, Bennett
Corrigan; Ranson, Reid, Booth, Caton, Henry, Power,
Daley, Palmer, Bennett, Reeves.
Att: 10,030
Round 4
Oct 29 v Notts County (h) 5-1
Tueart (4), Bennett
Corrigan; Ranson, Power, Reid, Henry, Caton, Tueart,
Buckley, Mackenzie, Bennett, Reeves(Sugrue).
Att: 26,363
Round 5
Dec 3 v West Bromwich Albion (h) 2-1
Henry, Bennett
Corrigan; Ranson, Power, Reid, Booth, Henry, Tueart,
Bennett, Mackenzie, Boyer, Reeves.
Att: 35,611
Semi-final (1st leg)
Jan 14 v Liverpool (h) 0-1
Corrigan; Ranson, Henry, Reid, Power, Caton, Boyer,
Bennett, Mackenzie, Tueart, Reeves.
Att: 48,045

Semi-final (2nd leg)
Feb 10 v Liverpool (a) 1-1 (agg 1-2)
Reeves
Corrigan; Ranson, Caton, Reid, Power, Booth, Tueart,
Buckley, Mackenzie, Bennett, Reeves.
Att: 46,711

1981-2
Round 2 (1st leg)
Oct 7 v Stoke City (h) 2-0
Hartford, opp og
Corrigan; Ranson, Wilson, Reid, Bond, Caton, Tueart,
O'Neill, Hutchison, Hartford, Reeves.
Att: 23,146
Round 2 (2nd leg)
**Oct 28 v Stoke City (a) 0-2 (agg 2-2; City won 9-8 on
penalties)**
Corrigan; Ranson, Bond, Reid, Power, Caton, Tueart,
O'Neill(Hareide), Hutchison, Hartford, Reeves.
Att: 17,373
Round 3
Nov 11 v Northampton Town (h) 3-1
Tueart (2), McDonald
Corrigan; Ranson, McDonald, Reid, Bond, Caton,
Tueart, Reeves, Francis, Hartford, O'Neill(Hutchison).
Att: 21,139
Round 4
Dec 1 v Barnsley (a) 0-1
Corrigan; Ranson, McDonald, Reid, Bond, Caton,
Tueart, Reeves, Boyer, Hartford, Hutchison.
Att: 33,792

1982-3
Round 2 (1st leg)
Oct 5 v Wigan Athletic (a) 1-1
Tueart
Williams; Ranson, Power, Baker, Bond, Caton, Tueart,
Reeves, Cross, Hartford, Boyer.
Att: 12,194
Round 2 (2nd leg)
Oct 27 v Wigan Athletic (h) 2-0 (agg 3-1)
Power (2)
Corrigan; Ranson, McDonald, Bond, Power, Caton,
Tueart, Reeves, Cross, Hartford, Baker.
Att: 16,083
Round 3
Nov 10 v Southampton (h) 1-1
Tueart
Corrigan; Ranson, McDonald, Bond, Power, Caton,
Tueart, Reeves, Cross, Hartford, Baker.
Att: 17,463
Replay
Nov 24 v Southampton (a) 0-4
Corrigan; Ranson, McDonald, Reid, Power, Caton,
Bond, Reeves, Cross, Hartford, Baker.
Att: 13,298

1983-4
Round 2 (1st leg)
Oct 5 v Torquay United (a) 0-0
Williams; Ranson, Davies, Reid, Power, Caton, Sullivan,
May, Parlane, Baker, Tolmie.
Att: 6,439
Round 2 (2nd leg)
Oct 25 v Torquay United (h) 6-0 (agg 6-0)
Parlane (3), Tolmie (2), Hoyland
Williams; Ranson, May, Walsh, Power, Caton, McNab,
Davidson, Parlane(Hoyland), Baker, Tolmie.
Att: 14,021

Round 3
Nov 9 v Aston Villa (a) 0-3
Williams; Ranson, May, Reid, Power, Caton, McNab, Kinsey(Walsh), Parlane, Baker, Tolmie.
Att: 23,922

1984-5
Round 2 (1st leg)
Sep 25 v Blackpool (h) 4-2
Cunningham (2), McCarthy, Wilson
Williams; Lomax, Power, Reid, McCarthy, Phillips, Smith(Tolmie), Baker, Cunningham, Wilson, Kinsey.
Att: 13,344
Round 2 (2nd leg)
Oct 9 v Blackpool (a) 3-1 (agg 7-3)
Tolmie (2), Smith
Williams; May, Power, Reid, McCarthy, Phillips, Smith, Baker, Cunningham, Wilson, Kinsey(Tolmie).
Att: 10,966
Round 3
Oct 31 v West Ham United (h) 0-0
Williams; May, Power, Reid, McCarthy, Phillips, Smith(Beckford), Baker, Cunningham, Wilson, Kinsey.
Att: 20,510
Replay
Nov 6 v West Ham United (a) 2-1
Cunningham, Kinsey
Williams; May, Power, Reid, McCarthy, Phillips, Smith, McNab, Cunningham, Wilson, Kinsey.
Att: 17,461
Round 4
Nov 12 v Chelsea (a) 1-4
Smith
Williams; Sinclair, Power, Reid, May, Phillips, Smith, McNab, Cunningham, Wilson, Kinsey.
Att: 26,354

1985-6
Round 2 (1st leg)
Sep 25 v Bury (a) 2-1
Wilson, Melrose
Nixon; May, Power, Clements, McCarthy, Phillips, Lillis, Wilson, Melrose, McIlroy, Simpson.
Att: 11,377
Round 2 (2nd leg)
Oct 8 v Bury (h) 2-1 (agg 4-2)
Lillis, Melrose
Nixon; May, Power, Clements, McCarthy, Phillips, Lillis, Baker, Melrose, McNab, Simpson.
Att: 9,799
Round 3
Oct 30 v Arsenal (h) 1-2
Davies
Nixon; Reid, Power, Clements, McCarthy, Phillips, Lillis,Baker(Melrose), Davies, McNab, Simpson.
Att: 18,279

1986-7
Round 2 (1st leg)
Sep 23 v Southend United (a) 0-0
Suckling; May, Wilson, Barrett, McCarthy, Redmond, Hopkins, Baker(Moulden), Christie, Brightwell(White), Simpson.
Att: 6,182
Round 2 (2nd leg)
Oct 8 v Southend United (h) 2-1 (agg 2-1)
McNab, Simpson
Suckling; Clements, Wilson, Redmond, McCarthy, Hopkins, White, McNab, Davies, Moulden, Simpson.
Att: 9,373
Round 3
Oct 28 v Arsenal (a) 1-3
Simpson
Suckling; Gidman, Wilson, Clements, McCarthy, Redmond, White, McNab, Varadi, Brightwell(Baker), Simpson.
Att: 21,604

City goalkeepers Alex Williams (left), Eric Nixon (centre) and Perry Suckling.

221

City in Europe

European Cup

1968-9
Round 1 (1st leg)
Sep 18 v Fenerbahce (h) 0-0
Mulhearn; Kennedy, Pardoe, Doyle, Heslop, Oakes, Lee, Bell, Summerbee, Young, Coleman.
Att: 38,787
Round 1 (2nd leg)
Oct 2 v Fenerbahce (a) 1-2 (agg 1-2)
Coleman
Mulhearn; Connor, Pardoe, Doyle, Heslop, Oakes, Lee, Bell, Summerbee, Young, Coleman.
Att: 45,000

European Cup-winners' Cup

1969-70
Round 1 (1st leg)
Sep 17 v Atletico Bilbao (a) 3-3
Booth, Young, opp og
Corrigan; Book, Pardoe, Doyle, Booth, Oakes, Summerbee, Bell, Lee, Young, Bowyer.
Att: 45,000
Round 1 (2nd leg)
Oct 1 v Atletico Bilbao (h) 3-0 (agg 6-3)
Bowyer, Bell, Oakes
Corrigan; Book, Pardoe, Doyle, Booth, Oakes, Summerbee, Bell, Lee, Young, Bowyer.
Att: 49,664
Round 2 (1st leg)
Nov 12 v SK Lierse (a) 3-0
Lee (2), Bell
Corrigan; Book, Pardoe, Doyle(Heslop), Booth, Oakes, Summerbee, Bell, Lee, Young, Bowyer.
Att: 19,000
Round 2 (2nd leg)
Nov 26 v SK Lierse (h) 5-0 (agg 8-0)
Bell (2), Lee (2), Summerbee
Mulhearn; Book, Pardoe, Doyle, Booth, Oakes, Summerbee, Bell, Lee, Jefferies, Bowyer(Towers).
Att: 26,486
Round 3 (1st leg)
Mar 4 v Académica Coimbra (a) 0-0
Corrigan; Book(Heslop), Mann, Doyle, Booth, Oakes, Pardoe, Bell, Summerbee, Lee, Young.
Att: 15,000
Round 3 (2nd leg)
Mar 18 v Académica Coimbra (h) 1-0 (agg 1-0)
Towers
Corrigan; Book, Mann, Booth, Heslop(Towers), Oakes, Doyle, Bell(Glennon), Lee, Young, Pardoe.
Att: 36,338
Semi-final (1st leg)
Apr 1 v Schalke 04 (a) 0-1
Corrigan; Book, Pardoe, Doyle, Jefferies, Oakes, Booth, Bell, Lee, Young, Summerbee.
Att: 38,000

Neil Young (left) and Colin Bell found the net regularly as City went on to win the European Cup-winners' Cup.

Semi-final (2nd leg)
Apr 15 v Schalke 04 (h) 5-1 (agg 5-2)
Young (2), Bell, Lee, Doyle
Corrigan; Book, Pardoe, Doyle(Heslop), Booth, Oakes, Towers, Bell, Lee, Young, Summerbee(Carrodus).
Att: 46,361
Final
Apr 29 v Gornik Zabrze (in Vienna) 2-1
Lee, Young
Corrigan; Book, Pardoe, Doyle, Booth, Oakes, Heslop, Bell, Lee, Young, Towers.
Att: 10,000

1970-71
Round 1 (1st leg)
Sep 16 v Linfield (h) 1-0
Bell
Corrigan; Book, Pardoe, Doyle, Booth, Oakes, Summerbee, Bell, Lee, Young, Towers.
Att: 25,184
Round 1 (2nd leg)
Sep 30 v Linfield (a) 1-2 (agg 2-2; City won on away-goals rule)
Lee
Corrigan; Book, Pardoe, Doyle, Jefferies, Oakes, Summerbee, Bell, Lee, Young, Towers.
Att: 24,000
Round 2 (2nd leg)
Oct 21 v Honved (a) 1-0
Lee
Corrigan; Booth, Pardoe, Doyle, Heslop, Jefferies, Summerbee, Bell, Lee, Hill, Towers.
Att: 14,000
Round 2 (2nd leg)
Nov 4 v Honved (h) 2-0 (agg 3-0)
Bell, Lee
Corrigan; Book, Pardoe, Doyle, Heslop, Oakes, Summerbee(Bowyer), Bell, Lee, Hill, Towers.
Att: 28,770

Round 3 (1st leg)
Mar 10 v Gornik Zabrze (a) 0-2
Corrigan; Book, Towers, Doyle, Booth, Oakes, Summerbee, Bell, Lee, Young, Jefferies.
Att: 100,000
Round 3 (2nd leg)
Mar 24 v Gornik Zabrze (h) 2-0 (agg 2-2)
Mellor, Doyle
Healey; Connor, Towers, Doyle, Booth, Donachie, Jefferies, Bell, Lee, Young(Mann), Mellor(Bowyer).
Att: 31,950
Replay
Mar 31 v Gornik Zabrze (in Copenhagen) 3-1
Booth, Lee, Young
Healey; Connor, Towers, Doyle, Booth, Donachie, Jefferies, Bell, Lee, Young, Hill.
Att: 12,100
Semi-final (1st leg)
Apr 14 v Chelsea (a) 0-1
Corrigan; Book, Connor, Towers, Booth, Donachie, Johnson, Hill, Lee, Young, Mann.
Att: 45,955
Semi-final (2nd leg)
Apr 28 v Chelsea (h) 0-1 (agg 0-2)
Healey; Book, Connor, Towers, Heslop, Jefferies, Summerbee(Carter), Lee, Bowyer, Young, Johnson(Donachie).
Att: 43,663

UEFA Cup

1972-3
Round 1 (1st leg)
Sep 13 v Valencia (h) 2-2
Mellor, Marsh
Corrigan(Healey); Jefferies, Donachie, Doyle, Booth, Oakes, Mellor, Bell, Marsh, Lee, Towers.
Att: 21,698
Round 1 (2nd leg)
Sep 27 v Valencia (a) 1-2 (agg 3-4)
Marsh
Healey; Book, Barrett, Doyle, Booth(Mellor), Oakes, Summerbee, Bell, Marsh, Lee, Towers.
Att: 35,000

1976-7
Round 1 (1st leg)
Sep 15 v Juventus (h) 1-0
Kidd
Corrigan; Docherty, Donachie, Doyle, Watson, Conway, Barnes(Power), Kidd, Royle, Hartford, Tueart.
Att: 36,955
Round 1 (2nd leg)
Sep 29 v Juventus (a) 0-2 (agg 1-2)
Corrigan; Docherty, Donachie, Doyle, Watson, Booth, Keegan(Lester), Kidd, Royle, Hartford, Tueart.
Att: 55,000

1977-8
Round 1 (1st leg)
Sep 14 v Widzew Lodz (h) 2-2
Barnes, Channon
Corrigan; Clements, Donachie, Owen, Watson, Booth, Barnes, Channon, Kidd, Hartford, Keegan(Royle).
Att: 33,695

Round 1 (2nd leg)
Sep 28 v Widzew Lodz (a) 0-0 (agg 2-2; City lost on away-goals rule)
Corrigan; Doyle(Clements), Power, Owen, Watson, Booth, Barnes, Kidd, Royle, Hartford, Tueart.
Att: 40,000

1978-9
Round 1 (1st leg)
Sep 13 v Twente Enschede (a) 1-1
Watson
Corrigan; Clements, Power, Viljoen, Watson, Futcher, Channon, Owen, Palmer, Hartford, Barnes.
Att: 12,000
Round 1 (2nd leg)
Sep 27 v Twente Enschede (h) 3-2 (agg 4-3)
Kidd, Bell, opp og
Corrigan; Clements, Power, Viljoen(Bell), Watson, Futcher, Channon, Owen, Kidd, Hartford, Barnes.
Att: 29,330
Round 2 (1st leg)
Oct 18 v Standard Liège (h) 4-0
Kidd (2), Palmer, Hartford
Corrigan; Clements, Donachie, Booth, Watson, Viljoen(Keegan), Palmer, Bell, Kidd, Hartford, Barnes.
Att: 27,489
Nov 1 v Standard Liège (a) 0-2 (agg 4-2)
Corrigan; Clements, Donachie, Booth, Watson, Owen, Channon, Bell, Kidd, Hartford, Palmer.
Att: 25,000
Round 3 (1st leg)
Nov 23 v AC Milan (a) 2-2
Power, Kidd
Corrigan; Clements, Donachie, Booth, Watson, Power, Viljoen(Keegan), Bell, Kidd, Hartford, Palmer.
Att: 40,000
Round 3 (2nd leg)
Dec 6 v AC Milan (h) 3-0 (agg 5-2)
Kidd, Booth, Hartford
Corrigan; Keegan, Donachie, Booth, Watson, Power, Channon, Viljoen, Kidd, Hartford, Barnes.
Att: 38,026
Round 4 (1st leg)
Mar 7 v Borussia Mönchengladbach (h) 1-1
Channon
Corrigan; Donachie, Power, Reid, Watson, Booth, Channon, Viljoen, Kidd, Hartford, Barnes.
Att: 39,005
Round 4 (2nd leg)
Mar 20 v Borussia Mönchengladbach (a) 1-3 (agg 2-4)
Deyna
Corrigan; Donachie, Power, Viljoen, Watson, Booth, Channon, Reid(Deyna), Henry, Hartford, Barnes.
Att: 30,000

FA Charity Shield

1934-5
Nov 28 v Arsenal (a) 0-4
Swift; Dale, Barnett, Busby, Cowan, Bray, Toseland, McLuckie, Tilson, Heale, Brook.
Att: 10,888

1937-8
Nov 4 v Sunderland (h) 2-0
Herd, Doherty
Swift; Dale, Barkas, Percival, Marshall, Bray, Toseland, Herd, Tilson, Doherty, Brook.
Att: 20,000

1956-7
Oct 24 v Manchester United (a) 0-1
Savage; Leivers, Little, Revie, Ewing, Paul, Fagan, Hayes, Johnstone, Dyson, Clarke.
Att: 30,495

1968-9
Aug 3 v West Bromwich Albion (h) 6-1
Lee (2), Owen (2), Young, opp og
Mulhearn; Connor, Pardoe, Doyle, Heslop, Oakes, Lee, Bell, Summerbee, Owen, Young.
Att: 35,510

1969-70
Aug 2 v Leeds United (a) 1-2
Bell
Corrigan; Book, Pardoe, Doyle, Booth, Oakes, Summerbee, Bell, Lee, Young, Coleman(Connor).
Att: 39,535

1972-3
Aug 5 v Aston Villa (a) 1-0
Lee
Corrigan; Book, Donachie(Jefferies), Doyle, Booth, Bell, Summerbee, Lee, Davies(Mellor), Marsh, Towers.
Att: 34,859

Manchester City squad in 1969-70 that went on to win the Football League Cup. Back row (left to right): A.Oakes, C.Bell, M.Doyle, G.Pardoe, A.Book. Middle row: M.Allison (asst manager & coach), A.Mann, T.Booth, J.Corrigan, H.Dowd, G.Heslop, D.Ewing (trainer). Front row: I.Bowyer, R.Owen, N.Young, A.Coleman, F.Lee, M.Summerbee, D.Connor.

1973-4
Aug 18 v Burnley (h) 0-1
Corrigan; Book, Donachie, Doyle, Booth, Oakes, Summerbee, Bell, Law, Lee, Marsh.
Att: 23,988

Anglo-Scottish Cup

1975-6
Group One
Aug 2 v Blackpool (a) 0-1
Corrigan; Donachie, Oakes, Doyle(Leman), Watson, Booth, Henry, Royle, Marsh, Hartford, Tueart.
Att: 11,091
Group One
Aug 6 v Blackburn Rovers (a) 0-1
Corrigan; Donachie, Oakes, Doyle, Watson, Booth, Keegan, Royle, Marsh, Hartford, Tueart.
Att: 10,612
Group One
Aug 9 v Sheffield United (h) 3-1
Royle, Marsh, Leman
Corrigan; Hammond, Donachie, Booth, Watson, Oakes, Telford(Leman), Royle, Marsh, Hartford, Tueart.
Att: 11,167

Tennent-Caledonian Cup
(Four-club KO tournament played in Scotland)

1976-7
Aug 2 v Southampton (n) 1-1 (after each side had scored 11 penalties Southampton won by toss of coin)
Tueart
Corrigan; Docherty, Donachie, Doyle, Watson, Hartford, Barnes(Power), Keegan, Royle, Kidd(Lester), Tueart.
Att: 30,000
Play-off for Third Place
Aug 3 v Partick Thistle (n) 4-1
Kidd (2), Hartford, Tueart
Corrigan; Docherty, Donachie, Doyle, Watson, Hartford, Leman, Power, Royle, Kidd, Tueart.
Att: 35,000

Anglo-Italian Cup

1970-71
Round 1 (1st leg)
Sep 2 v Bologna (a) 0-1
Corrigan; Book, Pardoe, Doyle, Booth, Oakes, Summerbee, Bell, Lee, Young, Towers.
Att: 28,000
Round 1 (2nd leg)
Sep 23 v Bologna (h) 2-2 (agg 2-3)
Heslop, Lee
Corrigan; Book, Pardoe, Doyle, Heslop, Oakes, Hill, Bell, Lee, Young, Towers(Summerbee).
Att: 25,843

227

Texaco Cup

1971-2
Round 1 (1st leg)
Sep 15 v Airdrieonians (h) 2-2
Mellor, Doyle
Healey(Corrigan); Book, Donachie, Doyle(Lee), Booth, Jefferies, Summerbee, Towers, Davies, Brennan, Mellor.
Att: 15,033
Round 1 (2nd leg)
Sep 27 v Airdrieonians (a) 0-2 (agg 2-4)
Healey; Connor, Donachie, Towers, Hanvey, Jefferies, Carter, Johnson, Brennan, Henson, Hill.
Att: 13,700

1974-5
Group One
Aug 3 v Blackpool (a) 1-1
Tueart
Corrigan; Barrett, Donachie, Doyle, Booth, Oakes, Summerbee, Bell, Lee, Marsh, Tueart.
Att: 12,342
Group One
Aug 6 v Sheffield United (a) 2-4
Summerbee, Law
Corrigan; Barrett, Donachie, Doyle, Booth, Oakes, Summerbee, Bell(Henson), Law, Marsh, Tueart.
Att: 9,358
Group One
Aug 10 v Oldham Athletic (a) 2-1
Lee, Tueart
MacRae; Barrett, Donachie, Doyle, Booth, Oakes, Lee, Bell, Marsh, Law(Daniels), Tueart.
Att: 13,880
City failed to qualify.

City in 1974-5. Back row (left to right): Jeff Clarke, Mike Doyle, Colin Bell, Francis Lee, Keith McRae, Joe Corrigan, Tommy Booth, Alan Oakes, Willie Donachie, Mike Horswill. Front row: Denis Leman, Colin Barrett, Dennis Tueart, Denis Law, Mike Summerbee, Rodney Marsh, Phil Henson, Glyn Pardoe.

Full Members Cup

1985-6
Group Three
Oct 14 v Leeds United (h) 6-1
Davies (3), Baker, Lillis, Power
Nixon; Reid, Power, Clements, Johnson, May, Lillis, Baker, Davies(Melrose), McNab, Simpson(Tolmie).
Att: 4,029
Group Three
Oc 22 v Sheffield United (a) 2-1
Phillips, Baker
Nixon; May, Power, Reid, Johnson, Phillips, Lillis, Baker, Davies, McNab, McIlroy(Simpson).
Att: 3,420
Semi-final
Nov 4 v Sunderland (h) 0-0 (City won 5-4 on penalties)
Nixon; Reid, May, Clements, Johnson, Phillips, Lillis, Melrose(Smith), Davies(Moulden), Power, Simpson.
Att: 6,642
Northern Final (1st leg)
Nov 26 v Hull City (a) 1-2
Phillips
Nixon; Reid, Power, Clements, McCarthy, Phillips, Melrose(Simpson), May, Davies, McNab, Wilson.
Att: 5,213
Northern Final (2nd leg)
Dec 11 v Hull City (h) 2-0 (agg 3-2)
Phillips, Melrose
Nixon; Reid, Power, Clements, McCarthy, Phillips, Lillis, May, Davies, McIlroy, Simpson(Melrose).
Att: 10,180
Final
Mar 23 v Chelsea (at Wembley) 4-5
Lillis (2), Kinsey, opp og
Nixon; Reid(Baker), Power, Redmond, McCarthy, Phillips(Simpson), Lillis, May, Kinsey, McNab, Wilson.
Att: 68,000

1986-7
Round 2
Nov 4 v Wimbledon (h) 3-1
Moulden (2), Clements
Suckling; May, Wilson, Clements, McCarthy, Redmond, Moulden, White, Varadi, Grealish, Simpson.
Att: 4,914
Round 3
Nov 26 v Watford (h) 1-0
Moulden
Suckling; Gidman(May), Wilson, Redmond, McCarthy, Grealish, Baker, McNab, White, Moulden, Simpson.
Att: 6,393
Round 4
Jan 31 v Ipswich Town (h) 2-3
Varadi (2)
Suckling; Gidman, Wilson, Clements, McCarthy, Grealish, Simpson, McNab, Varadi, Lake, Barnes.
Att: 16,094

City in the FA Youth Cup

1953-4
Round 1
Oct 7 v Bolton Wanderers (h) 5-5
Mycock (2), Compston (2), McDonald
Replay
Oct 14 v Bolton Wanderers (a) 4-3
Croft, Compston, Hayes, Rucher
Round 2
Oct 29 v Yorkshire Amateurs (h) 8-0
Croft (2), Compston (2), Rucher(2), Hempson (2)
Round 3
Nov 9 v Oldham Athletic (h) 2-1
Croft, Rucher
Round 4
Dec 28 v Leeds United (a) 1-3
Compston

1954-5
Round 1
Oct 23 v Everton (a) 3-1
Chandley, Lamb, Anderson
Round 2
Nov 17 v Manchester United 1-2
Anderson

1955-6
Round 2
Nov 2 v Blackpool (h) 1-2
Heil

1956-7
Round 1
Sep 19 v Bolton Wanderers (h) 2-4
Lister (2)

1957-8
Round 1
Oct 15 v Leeds United (a) 0-2

1958-9
Round 1
Oct 18 v Southport (a) 2-1
Mullen (2)
Round 2
Nov 15 v Huddersfield Town (a) 3-1
Oakes Shawcross, Richardson
Round 3
Dec 15 v Manchester United (h) 0-4

1959-60
Round 1
Oct 12 v Bury (h) 4-4
Oakes (2), Wagstaffe (2)
Replay
Oct 27 v Bury (a) 2-2
Oakes, Aimson
Second Replay
Nov 10 v Bury (a) 3-2
Pearson (2), Aimson
Round 2
Nov 18 v Everton (h) 2-0
Oakes, Aimson
Round 3
Dec 16 v Bolton Wanderers (h) 4-2
Oakes, Fletcher, Aimson, Darlington
Round 4
Jan 20 v Aston Villa (a) 0-2

1960-61
Round 1
Oct 4 v Preston North End (a) 1-5
Davies

1961-2
Preliminary Round
Sep 11 v Leeds United (h) 3-1
Goodwin, Young, opp og
Round 1
Oct 7 v Burnley (a) 3-2
Pardoe (2), Young
Round 2
Nov 30 v Manchester United (a) 0-3

1962-3
Round 2
Dec 12 v Sunderland (a) 1-0 (abandoned)
Doyle
Round 2
Dec 19 v Sunderland (a) 0-4

1963-4
Round 1
Nov 18 v Oldham Athletic (h) 4-1
Clay (2), Frost, Pardoe
Round 2
Dec 16 v Burnley (h) 4-1
Frost, Pardoe, Jones, McAlinden
Round 3
Jan 13 v Preston North End (h) 0-0
Replay
Jan 20 v Preston North End (a) 2-3 (abandoned)
Jones, McAlinden
Replay
Jan 29 v Preston North End (a) 3-1
Jones (2), McAlinden
Round 4
Feb 12 v Middlesbrough (h) 6-1
Jones (3), Pardoe (2), McAlinden
Round 5
Mar 4 v Leeds United (a) 4-3
Pardoe (2), Jones, McAlinden
Semi-final (1st leg)
Apr 8 v Manchester United (a) 1-4
Pardoe
Semi-final (2nd leg)
Apr 20 v Manchester United (h) 3-4 (agg 4-8)
McAlinden (2), Pardoe

1964-5
Round 2
Dec 1 v Blackburn Rovers (a) 1-2
Clay

1965-6
Round 2
Dec 13 v Manchester United (h) 0-5

1966-7
Round 1
Nov 4 v Oldham Athletic (h) 4-3
Mason (2), Moss, Hoare
Round 2
Dec 5 v Liverpool (a) 2-2
Glennon, Moss

Replay
Dec 13 v Liverpool (h) 3-1
Bowles, Moss, Glennon
Round 3
Jan 11 v Barnsley (a) 4-1
Hoare, Walker, Moss, Mason
Round 4
Feb 8 v Manchester United (h) 0-3

1967-8
Round 2
Nov 27 v Oldham Athletic (h) 5-0
Jackson (2), Glennon (2), Booth
Round 3
Jan 2 v Burnley (a) 3-4
Hatton, Glennon, Bowyer

1968-9
Round 2
Nov 26 v Everton (a) 0-1

1969-70
Round 1
Oct 27 v Blackpool (h) 4-0
Towers, Trunkfield, Cater, opp og
Round 2
Dec 2 v Burnley (a) 1-3
Towers

1970-71
Preliminary Round
Nov 2 v Blackpool (a) 1-0
Clark
Round 1
Dec 1 v Everton (h) 2-2
Curtin, McBeth
Replay
Dec 8 v Everton (a) 1-0
Clarke
Round 2
Dec 22 v Preston North End (h) 1-3
McBeth

1971-2
Round 1
Nov 3 v Tranmere Rovers (a) 2-2
Johnson, Kevanagh
Replay
Nov 9 v Tranmere Rovers (h) 6-0
Johnson (3), Gannon (2), Smith
Round 2
Nov 30 v Burnley (a) 0-1

1972-3
Round 1
Nov 20 v Bury (a) 3-2
Madeley, Gannon, opp og
Round 2
Nov 28 v Burnley (a) 1-1
Gannon
Replay
Dec 19 v Burnley (h) 1-4
Leman

1973-4
Round 1
Oct 29 v Blackburn Rovers (h) 1-0
Black
Round 2
Nov 26 v Wrexham (a) 5-2
Ward, Coyne, Black, Burrows, Barnes

Round 3
Dec 17 v Liverpool (a) 1-1
Coyne
Replay
Jan 3 v Liverpool (h) 1-3
Keegan

1974-5
Round 1
Oct 29 v Rochdale (h) 1-1
Burrows
Replay
Nov 2 v Rochdale (a) 5-2
Lambert (3), Burrows, Barnes
Round 2
Nov 19 v Huddersfield Town (h) 1-3
Lambert

1975-6
Round 1
Oct 29 v Shrewsbury Town (h) 3-0
Owen (2), Jackson
Round 2
Nov 26 v Oldham Athletic (h) 1-2
Palmer

1976-7
Round 1
Nov 9 v Blackpool (h) 5-1
Bennett (3), Palmer, Garmary
Round 2
Dec 20 v South Liverpool (h) 8-1
Palmer (3), Bennett (2), Evans (2), Garmary
Round 3
Jan 10 v Shrewsbury Town (h) 7-1
Palmer (2), Bennett, Coughlin, Evans, Clarke, O'Shea
Round 4
Feb 7 v Sunderland (a) 2-1
Garmary, opp og
Round 5
Mar 21 v Derby County (a) 1-2
Palmer

1977-8
Round 2
Dec 6 v Burnley (h) 1-2
Bennett

1978-9
Round 2
Dec 11 v Oldham Athletic (a) 1-0
opp og
Round 3
Jan 22 v Newcastle United (a) 0-0
Replay
Feb 5 v Newcastle United (h) 3-0
Wilson (2), McClure
Round 4
Feb 20 v Crystal Palace (a) 2-1
Buckley, Kinsey
Round 5
Mar 12 v Luton Town (h) 1-1
Reid
Replay
Mar 26 v Luton Town (a) 3-1
McClure, Kinsey, Leigh
Semi-final (1st leg)
Apr 19 v Southampton (h) 1-0
Fitzgerald
Semi-final (2nd leg)
Apr 26 v Southampton (a) 3-0 (agg 4-0)
Leigh (2), Kinsey

Final (1st leg)
May 16 v Millwall (h) 0-0
Williams; Fitzgerald, Cunningham, Reid, Caton,
McGinn, McClure, Leigh, Wilson, Kinsey, Glendon.
Att: 2,952
Final (2nd leg)
May 21 v Millwall (a) 0-2 (agg 0-2)
Williams; Fitzgerald, Cunningham, Reid, Caton,
McGinn, McClure, Leigh, Wilson, Kinsey, Glendon.
Att: 5,653

1979-80
Round 2
Nov 28 v Grimsby Town (a) 1-0
Bees
Round 3
Jan 5 v Lincoln City (h) 4-2
Bees (2), May, McGinn
Round 4
Feb 4 v Sunderland (a) 2-0
May, Bees
Round 5
Mar 4 v Sheffield Wednesday (a) 1-1
McGinn
Replay
Mar 11 v Sheffield Wednesday (h) 3-2
Mackenzie, Bees, Parkinson
Semi-final (1st leg)
Mar 31 v Manchester United (a) 0-0
Semi-final (2nd leg)
Apr 21 v Manchester (h) 3-1 (agg 3-1)
Mackenzie, Wilson, Kinsey
Final (1st leg)
Apr 21 v Aston Villa (h) 1-3
Mackenzie
Williams; May, Cunningham, G.Bennett, Caton,
McGinn, Parkinson, Mackenzie, Bees, Kinsey, Wilson.
Att: 8,532
Final (2nd leg)
Apr 30 v Aston Villa (a) 1-0 (agg 1-4)
Wilson
Williams; May, Cunnıngham, G.Bennett, Caton,
McGinn, Parkinson, Mackenzie, Bees, Kinsey, Wilson.
Att: 13,500

1980-81
Round 2
Dec 8 v Barnsley (h) 2-1
Kinsey, Parkinson
Round 3
Jan 6 v Middlesbrough (a) 3-0
Kinsey, Parkinson, Bees
Round 4
Jan 27 Newcastle United (h) 5-2
Jackson (2), Kinsey (2), Elliott
Round 5
Mar 4 v Birmingham City (h) 2-0
Elliott (2)
Semi-final (1st leg)
Mar 24 v West Ham United (a) 0-5
Semi-final (2nd leg)
Apr 7 v West Ham United (h) 1-2 (agg 1-7)
Parkinson

1981-2
Round 2
Dec 2 v Everton (h) 0-1

1982-3
Round 2
Nov 22 v Leeds United (a) 2-3
Adams, Milligan

1983-4
Round 1
Nov 1 v Oldham Athletic (h) 3-1
Simpson (2), Hoyland
Round 2
Dec 6 v Middlesbrough (a) 2-1
Beckford, Beresford
Round 3
Jan 4 v Burnley (a) 1-3
Beckford

1984-5
Round 1
Nov 12 v Preston North End (h) 6-0
Beckford (3), White (2), Moulden
Round 2
Dec 9 v Billingham (a) 10-1
*Beckford (3), White (3), Scott, Moulden, Beresford,
Thackery*
Round 3
Jan 15 v Nottingham Forest (h) 8-0
Beckford (3), White (2), Moulden, Scott, Redmond
Round 4
Feb 11 v Newcastle United (a) 1-2
Scott

Darren Beckford

1985-6
Round 1
Nov 5 v Tranmere Rovers (a) 7-1
White (2), Redmond, Moulden, Lake, Scott, Boyd
Round 2
Nov 28 v Blackburn Rovers (h) 7-1
Moulden (3), Thackery, Lake, Scott, opp og
Round 3
Jan 7 v Blackpool (a) 1-0
Scott
Round 4
Jan 30 v Leicester City (h) 4-1
Moulden (2), Redmond, Thackery

Round 5
Mar 8 v Fulham (a) 3-0
Redmond (2), Lake
Semi-final (1st leg)
Apr 16 v Arsenal (a) 0-1
Semi-final (2nd leg)
Apr 22 v Arsenal (h) 2-1 (agg 2-2; City won 5-4 on penalties)
Moulden (2)
Final (1st leg)
Apr 24 v Manchester United (a) 1-1
Lake
Crompton; Mills, Hinchcliffe, Brightwell, Redmond, Thackery, White, Moulden, Lake, Scott, Boyd.
Att: 7,602
Final (2nd leg)
Apr 29 v Manchester United (h) 2-0 (agg 3-1)
Moulden, Boyd
Crompton; Mills, Hinchcliffe, Brightwell, Redmond, Thackery, White, Moulden, Lake, Scott, Boyd.
Att: 18,164

1986-7
Round 2
Jan 5 v Wigan Athletic (a) 2-2
Lake, Curry
Replay
Jan 10 v Wigan Athletic (h) 2-1
Cutts, Coward
Round 3
Jan 26 v Newcastle United (h) 2-1
Lake, Melville
Round 4
Feb 7 v Liverpool (h) 2-1
J.Beckford, Clarke
Round 5
Mar 2 v Leeds United (h) 3-0
J.Beckford (2), Clarke
Semi-final (1st leg)
Mar 25 v Coventry City (a) 0-1
Semi-final (2nd leg)
Apr 2 v Coventry City (h) 1-0
Lake
Replay
Apr 10 v Coventry City (a) 0-3

Manchester City 1977-8. Back row (left to right): Paul Power, Colin Bell, Joe Corrigan, Keith MacRae, Willie Donachie, Peter Barnes. Middle: Tony Book, Tony Henry, Kenny Clements, Tommy Booth, Dave Watson, Joe Royle, Bill Taylor. Front: Roy Bailey, Jimmy Conway, Gerard Keegan, Brian Kidd, Mike Doyle, Gary Owen, Dennis Tueart, Asa Hartford, Freddie Griffiths.

City in the Lancashire Youth Cup

1972-3
Round 1
Oct 23 v Blackburn Rovers (h) 1-0
McBeth
Semi-final (1st leg)
Mar 13 v Burnley (a) 3-1
Coyne, Clements, Leman
Semi-final (2nd leg)
Apr 12 v Burnley (h) 3-0 (agg 6-1)
Gannon, Leman, McBeth
Final (1st leg)
Apr 25 v Manchester United (h) 2-0
Gannon, Berry
Final (2nd leg)
Apr 30 v Manchester United (a) 3-0 (agg 5-0)
Berry, Leman, McBeth

1973-4
Round 2
Nov 21 v Bolton Wanderers (h) 2-1
Black (2)
Semi-final
May 8 v Oldham Athletic (a) 1-2
Barnes

1974-5
Round 2
Nov 12 v Manchester United (h) 1-2
Lambert

1975-6
Round 2
Dec 10 v Stockport County (h) 5-1
Palmer, Henry, Fowler, Sherlock, opp og
Semi-final (1st leg)
Mar 29 v Manchester United (a) 0-1
Semi-final (2nd leg)
Apr 5 v Manchester United (h) 4-4 (agg 4-5)
Palmer (2), Henry, Halford

1976-7
Round 2
Stockport County withdrew. City won outright.
Semi-final (1st leg)
Mar 28 v Bolton Wanderers (h) 2-1
Ranson, Palmer
Semi-final (2nd leg)
Apr 19 v Bolton Wanderers (a) 2-1 (agg 4-2)
Palmer, Garmary
Final (1st leg)
May 18 v Oldham Athletic (h) 3-1
McCormick (2), Palmer
Final (2nd leg)
May 23 v Oldham Athletic (a) 1-1 (agg 4-2)
Bennett

1977-8
Round 2
Nov 22 v Manchester United (a) 2-3
McCormick, Coughlin

1978-9
Round 2
Oct 30 v Rochdale (h) 6-2
Reid, Gregory, Kinsey, McClure, Buckley, opp og
Semi-final
Apr 9 v Manchester United (a) 0-3

1979-80
Round 2
Nov 12 v Manchester United (h) 3-2
Caton, May, Mackenzie
Semi-final
Jan 26 v Burnley (h) 3-1
Kinsey (2), Mackenzie
Final
Mar 19 v Blackpool (h) 2-1
Mackenzie, Bees

1980-81
Round 2
Nov 18 v Bury (a) 3-3
Cunningham, Bees, Kinsey
Replay
Dec 16 v Bury (h) 4-1
Kinsey (2), May, Mumford
Semi-final
Feb 3 v Bolton Wanderers (a) 0-0 (City won 4-3 on penalties)
Final
Apr 13 v Manchester United (h) 0-2

1981-2
Round 2
Dec 8 v Bury (a) 4-0
Parkinson (2), Jackson, Elliott
Semi-final
Mar 24 v Blackpool (a) 3-1
Hildersley, Parkinson, Elliott
Final
Apr 29 v Bolton Wanderers (h) 2-1
Hildersley, Elliott

1982-3
Round 2
Oct 27 v Bolton Wanderers (a) 3-1
Hildersley, P.Bell, Adams
Semi-final
Apr 7 v Burnley (h) 6-0
M.Bell (2), Simpson, Hoyland, Webb, Jackson
Final
May 13 v Manchester United (a) 2-1
Simpson (2)

1983-4
Round 2
Feb 23 v Rochdale (h) 4-0
Beckford (2), Conroy, Simpson
Semi-final
Mar 3 v Manchester United (a) 4-0
Beckford (2), Scott, Simpson
Final
Apr 9 v Bolton Wanderers (a) 3-0
Scott, Beckford, Redmond

1984-5
Round 1
Dec 13 v Burnley (h) 2-1
White, Beckford
Semi-final
Apr 18 v Manchester United (a) 3-1
Scott, White, Beckford
Final
May 21 v Wigan Athletic (a) 5-1
Boyd (2), Scott, White, Moulden

1985-6
Round 1
Oct 17 v Oldham Athletic (a) 12-0
Lake (3), Scott (2), Boyd (2), White (2), Moulden (2), Thackery
Semi-final
Aug 13 v Blackpool (a) 1-3
J.Beckford

1986-7
Round 2
Mar 9 v Oldham Athletic (h) 4-1
Lake (2), J.Beckford, Kelly
Semi-final
Apr 21 v Bolton Wanderers (a) 2-2 (City lost on penalties)
Coward (2)

Clive Wilson

Andy May

Abandoned Matches
(League games unless otherwise stated)

1895-6
Dec 14 v Burslem Port Vale (h) 1-0
McBride
Williams; Read, Robson, Mann, Chapman, McBride,
Meredith, Finnerhan, Rowan, Morris, Hill.
Att: 3,000
Dec 21 v Burslem Port Vale (a) 0-0
Williams; Read, Robson, Mann, Chapman, McBride,
Davies, Finnerhan, Rowan, Morris, Hill.
Att: 2,000

1898-9
Dec 31 v Grimsby Town (a) 0-0
C.Williams; Ray, Jones, Moffatt, W.'Buxton' Smith,
Holmes, Meredith, W.'Stockport' Smith, Gillespie,
F.Williams, Dougal.
Att: 300

1901-02
Dec 21 v Stoke (a) 0-2
Barrett; Orr, D.Jones, Smith, Hynds, Hosie, Meredith,
Ross, Bevan, R.Jones, Hurst.
Att: 6,000
Jan 25 v Preston North End (a) 1-1*
Henderson
Barrett; Orr, Slater, Smith, Hynds, Hosie, Meredith,
Ross, Henderson, R.Jones, Threlfall.
Att: 10,000
*FA Cup match.

1902-03
Oct 25 v Barnsley (h) 5-0
Meredith, Gillespie, Drummond, Threlfall, opp.og
Hillman; Orr, Davidson, Frost, Hynds, McOustra,
Meredith, Miller, Gillespie, Drummond, Threlfall.
Att: 16,000
Jan 10 v Small Heath (h) 0-0
Hillman; McMahon, Davidson, Moffatt, Hynds,
McOustra, Meredith, Bannister, Gillespie, Turnbull,
Threlfall.
Att: 35,000

1912-13
Jan 11 v Sunderland (h) 0-0*
Smith; Henry, Fletcher, Hughes, Eadie, Holford, Hoad,
Wynn, Howard, Jones, Wallace.
Att: 41,709
*FA Cup match.

1920-21
Feb 9 v Everton (h) 0-0
Goodchild; Cookson, Fletcher, Fayers, Woosnam,
Hamill, Broad, Woodcock, Browell, Barnes, Murphy.
Att: 30,000

1936-7
Nov 28 v Brentford (h) 0-0
Swift; Dale, Barkas, Percival, Marshall, Bray, Toseland,
Herd, Rodger, Doherty, Brook.
Att: 20,000

1955-6
Jan 7 v Blackpool (h) 1-1*
Dyson
Trautmann; Leivers, Little, Barnes, Ewing, Paul, Spurdle,
Hayes, Johnstone, Dyson, Clarke.
Att: 32,577
*FA Cup match.

1957-8
Feb 15 v Birmingham City (h) 1-1
McAdams
Trautmann; Leivers, Sear, Barnes, Ewing, Warhurst,
Barlow, Hayes, Johnstone, McAdams, Sambrook.
Att: 23,461

1960-61
Aug 27 v Manchester United (h) 2-2
Law, Hayes
Trautmann; Betts, Sear, Barnes, Plenderleith, Oakes,
Barlow, Law, Hannah, Hayes, Colbridge.
Att: 51,927
Jan 28 v Luton Town (a) 6-2*
Law 6
Trautmann; Leivers, Betts, Barnes, Plenderleith,
Shawcross, Barlow, Hannah, Baker, Law, Hayes.
Att: 23,727
*FA Cup match.
Jun 7 v Torino (a) 1-1*
Law
Trautmann; Betts, Sear, Cheetham, Plenderleith, Oakes,
Barlow, Law, Baker, Hayes, Colbridge.
Att: 25,000
*Tour match.

1962-63
Dec 22 v Aston Villa (a) 1-0
Dobing
Dowd; Betts, Sear, Benson, Leivers, Oakes, Young,
Dobing, Harley, Hannah, Wagstaffe.
Att: 21,264

1965-6
Sep 9 v Norwich City (h) 1-1
Young
Dowd; Bacuzzi, Connor, Doyle, Oakes, Gray, Summer-
bee, Crossan, Murray, Pardoe, Young.
Att: 13,235

1968-9
Feb 1 v Newcastle United (h) 1-1
Owen
Dowd; Book, Pardoe, Doyle, Booth, Oakes, Summerbee,
Lee, Owen, Young, Coleman.
Att: 30,160

CITY IN WARTIME

IN World War One, Manchester City competed in the Lancashire Section of the Football League's regional competition, which took the place of the suspended League Football. City enjoyed some success, winning both the Lancashire Section and the Subsidiary Tournament in the first season. Thereafter they were always in the top five each season.

When Germany invaded Poland in September 1939 and Britain declared war a few days later, football was immediately called to a halt, and the League was abandoned after only three matches of the new season. Once more regional football was arranged; at first City were in the Western Regional League, but this was to last only the first season, and for 1940-41 season until 1945-6 they played in the North Regional Section.

City, in common with other clubs, had often to rely on guest players to make-up the team sheet each week. More often than not they lost many of their own star players to other clubs and, of course, the forces teams which played a lot of representative matches. People like Frank Swift, Peter Doherty, Eric Westwood and Bert Sproston seemed to play many more matches for either the Army or R.A.F. XI's than they did for their own club. Another player, Les McDowall, went on loan for the whole of the war period to St Mirren, only returning to play in the 1945-6 season for City.

The wartime regional Leagues were quite complicated structures, with some games counting double, and even treble, in the League and Cups. There were two championships, one played to Christmas, and one to the end of the season. The second championship were also qualifying games for the League War Cups which involved two-legged affairs in the knockout stages which followed. For the 1945-6 season they resumed the more familiar 42-match programme, and also the F.A. Cup and Central Leagues returned in this season, so it was more or less back to normal.

Jack Milsom (left), the former Bolton player, ended his City career during World War Two. Bert Sproston (above) was one of several City men who seemed to play more guest matches for other teams.

1915-16

1	Sep	4	(h)	Stockport C	W 3-1	P.Fairclough, Wynn, Barnes	12,000
2		11	(a)	Liverpool	W 1-0	Cruse	15,000
3		18	(h)	Bury	W 5-4	Barnes (3), Cruse, Wynn	8,000
4		25	(a)	Manchester U	D 1-1	Barnes	20,000
5	Oct	2	(h)	Blackpool	W 3-0	Barnes (3)	5,000
6		9	(a)	Southport C	W 2-0	Barnes, Hughes	7,000
7		16	(h)	Oldham A	D 2-2	A.Fairclough, Barnes	13,000
8		23	(a)	Everton	L 2-4	Barnes (2)	22,000
9		30	(h)	Bolton W	L 1-2	Barnes	5,000
10	Nov	6	(a)	Rochdale	W 2-0	Barnes (2)	1,000
11		13	(a)	Stoke	L 0-1		7,000
12		20	(h)	Burnley	W 1-0	Hughes	15,000
13		27	(a)	Preston N E	L 2-3	Howard, P.Fairclough	3,000
14	Dec	4	(a)	Stockport C	D 1-1	Howard	10,000
15		11	(h)	Liverpool	W 2-1	Howard, Barnes	3,000
16		18	(a)	Bury	W 3-0	Howard, Dorsett, opp.og	2,000
17		25	(h)	Manchester U	W 2-1	Taylor, Barnes	20,000
18	Jan	1	(a)	Blackpool	L 0-2		10,000
19		8	(h)	Southport C	W 5-0	Taylor (3), Barnes (2)	12,000
20		15	(a)	Oldham A	W 2-1	Taylor (2)	4,000
21		22	(h)	Everton	W 2-1	Taylor, Barnes	20,000
22		29	(a)	Bolton W	L 2-4	P.Fairclough, Barnes	15,000
23	Feb	5	(h)	Rochdale	W 4-1	P.Fairclough, Barnes (2), Cartwright	8,000
24		12	(h)	Stoke	W 4-2	P.Fairclough (2), Taylor, Barnes	10,000
25		19	(a)	Burnley	L 1-3	P.Fairclough	12,000
26		26	(h)	Preston N E	W 8-0	A.Fairclough (5), Barnes (2), Cartwright	6,000

Lancashire Section record: Appearances
P 26   W 16   D 3   L 7   F 61   A 35   Pts 35   Pos 1st   Goals

27	Mar	4	(a)	Stockport C	L 0-2		9,000
28		11	(h)	Liverpool	D 1-1	Barnes	10,000
29		18	(a)	Everton	D 1-1	Meredith	14,000
30		25	(a)	Manchester U	W 2-0	Taylor, Cartwright	15,000
31	Apr	1	(h)	Oldham A	D 4-4	Barnes (3), Cartwright	8,000
32		8	(h)	Stockport C	W 3-2	Brennan, Jones, Barnes	10,000
33		15	(a)	Liverpool	W 2-0	Taylor, Barnes	10,000
34		21	(a)	Oldham A	L 3-4	Taylor (2), Barnes	9,000
35		22	(h)	Everton	W 5-4	Barnes (2), Taylor, Jones, Meredith	24,000
36		29	(h)	Manchester U	W 2-1	Barnes, opp.og	18,000

Subsidiary Tournament (Southern Section) record: Appearances
P 10   W 5   D 3   L 2   F 23   A 19   Pts 13   Pos 1st   Goals

Friendly

| 1 | May | 6 | (h) | Manchester U | D 2-2 | | |

Goodchild	Henry	Fletcher	Hughes	Henderson	Brennan	Broad	Taylor	Howard	Fairclough P.	Barnes	Cartwright	Fairclough A.	Jones W.L.	Dorsett	Wynn	Bottomley	Allen	Gartland	Howe	Smith	Jones F.	Lewis	Cruse	Tomlinson	Meredith	Corcoran	
1	2	3	4	5	6	7			9	10				11	8												1
1	2		4	5	6	7				10				11	8		3						9				2
1		3		5	6	7				10			11		8	4	2						9				3
1	2	3	4	5	6	7			9	10			11		8												4
1	2	3	4	5	6	7	8		9	10			11														5
1	2	3	4		6	7	8			10		9	11			5											6
1	2	3	4	5	6	7	8			10		9	11											9			7
1	2	3	4	5	6	7	8			10				11									9				8
	2	3	4	5	6	7	8			10				11					1								9
1	2	3	4	5	6	7	8	9		10	11																10
1		3	4	5	6	7	8	9		10	11						2										11
1	2	3	4	5	6	7	8	9		10	11																12
1		3	4	5	6	7	8	9	10		11							2									13
1	2	3	4	5	6	7	8	9		10	11																14
1	2	3	4	5	6	7	8	9		10	11																15
1	2	3	4	5	6	7	8	9	10					11													16
1	2	3	4	5	6	7	8		11	10						9											17
1	2	3	4	5	6	7	8			10	11					9											18
1	2	3	4		6	7	8		9	10	11					5											19
1	2	3	4		6	7	8		9	10	11					5											20
1	2	3	4	5	6	7	8		9	10	11																21
1	2	3	4	5	6	7	8		9	10	11																22
1	2		4	5	6	7	8		9	10	11							3									23
1	2	3	4	5	6	7	8		9	10				11													24
1	2	3	4	5	6	7	8		9	10			11														25
1	2	3	4	5	6	7	8			10	11	9															26
25	23	24	25	23	26	26	22	7	13	24	13	3	6	6	4	6	3	2	1	0	0	0	3	1	0	0	
			2				8	4	7	26	2	6		1	2								2				

Goodchild	Henry	Fletcher	Hughes	Henderson	Brennan	Broad	Taylor	Howard	Fairclough P.	Barnes	Cartwright	Fairclough A.	Jones W.L.	Dorsett	Wynn	Bottomley	Allen	Gartland	Howe	Smith	Jones F.	Lewis	Cruse	Tomlinson	Meredith	Corcoran	
1	2	3	4	5	6	7	8		9	10	11																27
1	2		4	5	6		8			9	11		10					3							7		28
1		3	4	5	6				9	10	11		8					2							7		29
1		3	4	5	6	7	9			10	11		8					2									30
1		3	4	5	6		8			10	11										2				7	9	31
1		3	4	5	6	7	9			10	11		8									2					32
1		3	4	5	6	7	9			10	11		8					2									33
1		3	4	5	6	7	9			10	11		8					2									34
		3	4	5	6		9			10	11		8					2		1					7		35
1		3	4	5	6				9	10	11				8			2							7		36
9	2	9	10	10	10	5	8	0	3	10	10	0	7	0	1	0	0	7	0	1	1	1	0	0	5	1	
					1		5			10	2		2												2		

1916-17

1	Sep	2	(a)	Stoke	L 0-1		6,000
2		9	(h)	Southport C	D 0-0		8,000
3		16	(a)	Blackburn R	L 1-2	P.Fairclough	3,000
4		23	(h)	Blackpool	W 4-0	Barnes (3), Brennan	10,000
5		30	(h)	Everton	W 4-1	Barnes (3), Hoare	14,000
6	Oct	7	(a)	Rochdale	D 2-2	Barnes, Brennan	1,000
7		14	(h)	Bolton W	W 1-0	P.Fairclough	8,000
8		21	(a)	Port Vale	W 1-0	P.Fairclough	6,000
9		28	(h)	Oldham A	W 2-1	Cartwright, Waldon	9,000
10	Nov	4	(a)	Preston N E	D 2-2	Wynn, Barnes	3,000
11		11	(h)	Burnley	W 2-1	Wynn, Meredith	14,000
12		18	(a)	Manchester U	L 1-2	Hoad	10,000
13		25	(h)	Liverpool	D 1-1	Barnes	10,000
14	Dec	2	(a)	Stockport C	D 0-0		6,000
15		9	(h)	Bury	D 1-1	Meredith	5,000
16		23	(a)	Southport C	D 0-0		1,000
17		25	(h)	Stoke	W 1-0	Wynn	12,000
18		30	(h)	Blackburn R	W 8-0	Capper (5), Nelson (2), Davies	10,000
19	Jan	6	(a)	Blackpool	L 1-3	Cartwright	4,000
20		13	(a)	Everton	W 2-0	P.Fairclough, Barnes	8,000
21		20	(h)	Rochdale	W 2-1	Wynn, Barnes	7,000
22		27	(a)	Bolton W	D 2-2	Tavo, W.Newton	2,000
23	Feb	3	(h)	Port Vale	W 2-0	Barnes (2),	6,000
24		10	(a)	Oldham A	L 1-2	Tyler	3,000
25		17	(h)	Preston N E	W 5-1	Tyler (2), Goddard (3)	7,000
26		24	(a)	Burnley	W 1-0	Barnes	4,000
27	Mar	3	(h)	Manchester U	W 1-0	Barnes	15,000
28		10	(a)	Liverpool	L 0-3		14,000
29		17	(h)	Stockport C	L 1-3	Barnes	14,000
30		24	(a)	Bury	D 0-0		3,000

Lancashire Section record: Appearances
P 30   W 14   D 9   L 7   F 49   A 29   Pts 37   Pos 4th   Goals

31	Mar	31	(h)	Port Vale	W 1-0	Wynn	3,000
32	Apr	6	(h)	Stoke	W 1-0	McIlvenney	12,000
33		7	(a)	Manchester U	L 1-5	H.Newton	15,000
34		9	(a)	Stoke	L 0-5		8,000
35		14	(a)	Port Vale	D 0-0		5,000
36		21	(h)	Manchester U	L 0-1		15,000

Subsidiary Tournament record: Appearances
P 6   W 2   D 1   L 3   F 3   A 11   Pts 5   Pos 3   Goals

Friendlies

1	Dec	26	(a)	Manchester U	L 0-1
2	Jan	1	(h)	Manchester U	D 0-0
3	Apr	28	(a)	Hurst	D 2-2

Goodchild	Gartland	Fletcher	Bottomley	Tyler	Brennan	Parker	Wynn	Fairclough P.	Barnes	Cartwright	Newton H.	Jones	Scott	Newton W.	Wray	Hoad	Smith	Broad	Meredith	Davies	Nelson	Miller	Goddard	Tavo	Walden	Lomas	Armstrong	McIlvenney	Clegg	Match
1	2	3	4		6				10	11		8							7	5										1
	2	3	4		6				10	11		8					1		7	5										2
		3	4	5	6			9	10	11		8				7	1			2										3
1		3		5	6			9	10	11		8	4						7	2										4
1		3	4		6				10	11		8							7	2										5
1		3	4	5	6		8	9	10	11									7	2										6
1		3	4	2	6		8	9	10	11									7	5										7
1		3	4	2	6		8	9	10	11									7	5										8
1		3	4	2	5		8		10	11									7	6					9					9
		3	4	2	5		8	9	10	11							1		7	6										10
		3	4	2	6		8		10	11							1		7	5	9									11
1	6	3	4	2			8	9	10	11									7	5										12
1		3	4	2	5		8		10	11									7	6					9					13
1	2	3	4	5	6		8		10	11									7	9										14
1		3	4	2	5	6	8		10	11									7											15
1	2	3		5	6			9	10	11									7	4		8								16
1	2	3		5	6		8		10	11									7	4		9								17
1		3	4	2	6		8			11									7	5	9									18
1		3	4	2	6		8	9		11									7	5			10							19
1	2	3	4	5	6		8		10	11									7	9										20
1	2	3	4	5			8		10	11				6					7	9										21
1	2	3	4	5					10	11				6					7	9		8								22
1	2	3	4	5			8		10	11				6					7	9										23
	2	3	4				8	9		11				5	6				7				10							24
1	2	3		5			8	9		11			4		6				7				10							25
1	2	3	4		6		8	9	10	11				5					7											26
1	2	3			6		8	9	10	11			4	5					7											27
1	2	3	4		6		8	9	10	11				5					7											28
1	2	3	4				8		10	11				5					7	6	9									29
1	2	3	4		6				10	11				5					7	8										30
25	19	29	23	22	12	16	18	20	18	23	0	8	8	5	5	3	4	2	27	18	6	4	3	2	2	0	0	0	0	
				3	2		3	4	16	2				1	1	1			2	1	2		3	1	1					
1		3					2		5			8	6						7							4	9	10		31
1		3					2							8					5							4	11	9	10	32
		3			6		2			11				5			1		7							4		9		33
		3			6		2		11					8			1		7							4		9		34
1	2	3		5			8		10	11									7							4				35
1	2	3	4	5	6		8	9	10										7								11			36
4	2	6	1	6	1	2	2	4	0	4	4	1	1	2	1	0	2	0	6	0	0	0	0	0	0	5	4	2	2	
								1							1															

Match 1: Cruse (9)
Match 2: Taylor (9)
Match 5: Hanney (5); Hoare (9; 1 gl)
Match 15: Geddes (9)
Match 18: Capper (10; 5 gls)
Match 24: Kite (1)
Match 30; Sheldon (9)
Match 33: Woodhouse (10)
Match 34: Hargreaves (5)
Match 35: Malone (6); Lee (9)

1917-18

1	Sep	1 (h)	Stockport C	W 2-1	Tyler, Thorpe	12,000
2		8 (a)	Stockport C	W 1-0	opp.og	7,000
3		15 (h)	Oldham A	D 2-2	Thorpe, Moses	13,000
4		22 (a)	Oldham A	D 0-0		10,000
5		29 (h)	Manchester U	W 3-1	Lomas (2), Jones	20,000
6	Oct	6 (a)	Manchester U	D 1-1	Lomas	10,000
7		13 (h)	Bury	W 3-1	Lomas 2, Watson	9,000
8		20 (a)	Bury	W 5-2	Lomas 2, Meredith, Jones, Taylor	8,000
9		27 (a)	Stoke	L 3-4	Lomas 2, Watson	9,000
10	Nov	3 (h)	Stoke	W 1-0	Lomas	20,000
11		10 (a)	Liverpool	L 0-2		18,000
12		17 (h)	Liverpool	D 1-1	Thompson	15,000
13		24 (a)	Southport C	D 0-0		8,000
14	Dec	1 (h)	Southport C	W 5-0	Lomas (2), Tyler, Meredith, Wynn	10,000
15		8 (a)	Burnley	W 4-0	Lomas (3), Jones	1,000
16		15 (h)	Burnley	W 4-1	Tyler, Lomas, Jones, Watson	8,000
17		22 (h)	Blackburn R	W 1-0	Cartwright	12,000
18		29 (h)	Blackburn R	W 4-0	Meredith, Lomas, Cope, Cunningham	3,000
19	Jan	5 (h)	Rochdale	D 1-1	Tyler	9,000
20		12 (a)	Rochdale	W 4-1	Thompson (2), Barnes, Watson	6,000
21		19 (h)	Everton	L 0-2		13,000
22		26 (a)	Everton	D 0-0		20,000
23	Feb	2 (h)	Port Vale	W 5-1	Broad (2), Lomas (2), Thompson	11,000
24		9 (a)	Port Vale	W 2-0	Lomas, Cunningham	1,000
25		16 (a)	Bolton W	L 0-1		12,000
26		23 (h)	Bolton W	L 0-1		10,000
27	Mar	2 (a)	Preston N E	W 2-0	Lomas, Thompson	9,000
28		9 (h)	Preston N E	L 1-2	Lomas	10,000
29		16 (a)	Blackpool	L 0-1		9,000
30		23 (h)	Blackpool	D 2-2	Royle, Thompson	11,000

Lancashire Section record: Appearances
P 30   W 15   D 8   L 7   F 57   A 28   Pts 38   Pos 5th   Goals

31	Mar	29 (h)	Manchester U	W 3-0	Fletcher, Royle, Mann	10,000
32		30 (a)	Port Vale	W 4-1	Royle (2), Thompson, P.Fairclough	8,000
33	Apr	1 (a)	Manchester U	L 0-2		10,000
34		6 (h)	Port Vale	W 1-0	Fletcher	10,000
35		13 (a)	Stoke	D 1-1	Fletcher	9,000
36		20 (h)	Stoke	W 2-0	Woodcock, opp.og	11,000

Subsidiary Tournament record:
P 6   W 4   D 1   L 1   F 11   A 4   Pts 9   Pos 3rd

Friendlies

1	Dec	25 (h)	Manchester U	L 0-2	
2	Jan	1 (a)	Manchester U	L 0-2	
3	Apr	27 (h)	Leeds C	W 3-0*	
4	May	4 (h)	Stockport C	W 1-0*	
5		11 (a)	Stockport C	W 4-1*	

*Played in aid of National War Fund

Goodchild	Sugden	Fletcher	Hughes	Tyler	Fairclough P.	Jones	Murphy	Brennan	Broad	Taylor	Barnes	Royle	Parker	Sharp	Ollerenshaw	Meredith	Lomas	Moses	Thompson	Thorpe	Cunningham	Cope	Woodcock	Watson	Elliott	Mann	Gartland	Crowther	
1	2	3		9	10			6	8							7	4				5			11					1
1	2	3	5	6	10				8							7	4							11					2
1	2	3	4	11	10	5										7	8	9	6										3
1	2	3	4	5	6	10										7	8	9						11					4
1		3	4	5	6	10										7	8	9						11			2		5
1		3	4	2	6	10	5									7	8	9						11					6
1	2	3	4	5	6	10										7	8	9						11					7
1		3	4	2	6	10	5	9								7	8							11					8
1		3	4	2	6		5									7	8	9						11					9
1	2	3	4	5	6	10										7	9						8	11					10
1	2	3	4	5		10							6			7	8		9					11					11
1	2	3	4	5		10							6			7	9		8					11					12
1	2		4	3	11	5							6			7	8		10										13
1		3	4	5		10										7	9							11					14
1	2	3	4		6	10							5			7	9		8					11					15
1	2	3	4	5	6	10										7	9		8					11					16
1	2	3	4	5									6			7	9		8										17
1	2	3	4	5	6											7	9		8			10		11					18
1	2	3	4	5		6			10							7	9		8					11					19
1	2	3	4	5	6				10							7	9		8					11					20
1	2	3	4	5	6											7	9		8			10		11					21
1	2	3	4	5	6											7	8		9					11					22
1	2	3	4	5	6		11	8								7	9		10										23
1	2	3	4	5	6		11	8								7	9				10								24
1		3	4	5			11									7	8		9		10						2		25
1	2	3	4	5	6		11									7	8		10		9								26
	2	3	4	5	6		11								1	7	8		10									9	27
			4	5	6		11		8						1	7	10												28
1	2	3	4	5	9		11	6								7	8		10										29
1	2	3		4	6					11	9		5			7	8		10										30
28	23	28	27	28	24	13	8	9	5	1	2	1	5	0	2	30	30	6	15	2	5	4	1	17	0	0	2	1	
							4		4		2	1	1	1		3	21	1	6	2	2	1		4					
1	2	3		5								6		8		7	4		10						9	11			31
1	2	3		5								6		8		7	4		10						9	11			32
1	2	3					11	6				9	5	8			4		10		7								33
	2	3		5			11	9				6		8	1	7	4		10										34
1	2	3		5				9				6				7	4		10		11								35
1	2	3		5			11					6				7	4		10		8		9						36
5	6	6	0	5	4	0	3	2	0	0	0	5	1	2	1	5	6	0	6	0	3	0	1	0	2	2			
							3						1				3				1		1						

Match 2: McRay (9).
Match 9: Roberts (10).
Match 13: Scott (9).
Match 14: Osmond (2); Hanney (6); Wynn (8; 1gl)
Match 17: Lloyd (10); Cartwright (11; 1gl)
Match 22: James (10).
Match 25: Hargreaves (6).
Match 28: Brierley (2); Allen (3); Brown (9).
Match 35: Wray (8).

243

1918-19

1	Sep	7	(a)	Stoke	L 0-3		8,000
2		14	(h)	Stoke	L 0-2		10,000
3		21	(a)	Bury	W 1-0	Moses	8,000
4		28	(h)	Bury	W 7-0	Browell (3), Brennan, P.Fairclough, Moses, Kenyon	12,000
5	Oct	5	(a)	Manchester U	W 2-0	Kenyon, Cartwright	10,000
6		12	(h)	Manchester U	D 0-0		15,000
7		19	(a)	Blackpool	W 3-0	Kenyon, Moses, Browell	9,000
8		26	(h)	Blackpool	W 4-0	Lievesley (2), Cartwright, Browell	15,000
9	Nov	2	(h)	Stockport C	W 1-0	Lievesley	12,000
10		9	(a)	Stockport C	D 1-1	Browell	3,000
11		16	(h)	Liverpool	L 0-2		25,000
12		23	(a)	Liverpool	L 0-2		20,000
13		30	(h)	Burnley	W 2-1	Lievesley, Smith	12,000
14	Dec	7	(a)	Burnley	L 1-2	Leivesley	9,000
15		14	(h)	Southport V	L 0-1		10,000
16		21	(a)	Southport V	L 0-2		6,000
17		28	(h)	Preston N E	W 2-0	Wynn, Browell	13,000
18	Jan	11	(h)	Rochdale	D 1-1	Lievesley	12,000
19		18	(a)	Rochdale	W 5-4	Barnes (2), Dorsett (2), Smith	5,000
20		25	(h)	Everton	W 1-0	Murphy	25,000
21	Feb	1	(a)	Everton	L 0-3		31,000
22		8	(h)	Oldham A	W 3-0	Lievesley (2), Barnes	18,000
23		15	(a)	Oldham A	W 3-0	Browell, Barnes, Murphy	10,000
24		22	(h)	Blackburn R	W 5-1	Barnes (3), Johnson, Browell	22,000
25	Mar	1	(a)	Blackburn R	L 1-2	Browell	8,000
26		8	(a)	Port Vale	W 6-1	Johnson (3), Browell (2), Barnes	14,000
27		15	(a)	Port Vale	W 5-1	Barnes (3), Browell, A.Fairclough	8,000
28		22	(h)	Bolton W	L 1-2	Browell	20,000
29		29	(a)	Bolton W	L 1-3	Barnes	30,000
30	Apr	10	(a)	Preston N E	L 1-2	Barnes	12,000

Lancashire Section record: Appearances
P 30 W 15 D 3 L 12 F 57 A 36 Pts 33 Pos 5th   Goals

31	Apr	5	(h)	Stoke	W 1-0	A.Fairclough	25,000
32		12	(a)	Stoke	D 1-1	Barnes	14,000
33		18	(h)	Manchester U	W 3-1	Barnes (2), Wynn	35,000
34		19	(a)	Port Vale	W 1-0	Browell	8,000
35		21	(a)	Manchester U	W 4-2	Barnes (2), Browell, Lomas	35,000
36		26	(h)	Port Vale	W 4-1	Browell (2), Barnes (2)	20,000

Subsidiary Tournament record: Appearances
P 6 W 5 D 1 L 0 F 14 A 4 Pts 11 Pos 1st   Goals

Lancashire Senior Cup

City qualified as winners of Group C for
which results in the Subsidiary Tournament
counted.

SF May 24 (h) Oldham A   D 1-1
R   27 (a) Oldham A   L 0-1

Friendlies

1	Dec	25	(h)	Manchester U	W 2-1
2	Jan	1	(a)	Manchester U	L 0-2
3	May	3	(h)	Sheffield U*	W 1-0
4		10	(a)	Sheffield U*	L 2-3

*Played in aid of the National War
Fund

Goodchild	Tyler	Brierley	Fletcher	Brennan	Fairclough P.	Browell	Lievesley	Barnes	Cartwright	Murphy	Newton W.	Sugden	Johnson T.	Howarth	Hughes	Broad T.	Jones	Blackwell	Bottomley	Wynn	Meredith	Smith A.W.	Moses	Kenyon	Catlow	Lingard	Lomas	Cope	Tomkins	Voysey	Spruce	Match
9		3	5	6						2											7									4		1
1	5	2		6	10					3											7							8		4		2
1	5	2		4	6					3											7		9	8	11				10			3
1	5	2		4	6	10			11	3											7		9	8								4
1	5	2		4	6	10			11	3						9					7			8								5
1	5	2	3	4	6	10															7		9	11	8							6
1	5	2	3	4	6	10															7		9	8		11						7
1	5	3			6			9	10							11					7	8										8
1	5	2	3		6			9	10							11					7	8	4									9
1	5	2	3	4	6			9	10							11					7	8										10
1	2	3	4		6				10												7	8	9	11								11
1	2	3	4		6			9	10						11						7											12
1	5	3	4		6			9	10			2									7	8										13
1	5	2	3	4	6			9	10							8					7				11							14
1	2	3	4		6	8			10							11					7								5			15
1	5	2	3	4	6	8			10							11				9	7											16
1	2	3	5		6			9					4			11	8				7											17
1	5		3	4	6	8			10							11			2		7								9			18
1	2		3	5	6			9	10				4			11					7	8										19
1	2		3	5	6	8			10				4			11					7	9										20
1	2		3	5	6	8			10				4			11					7	9										21
1	2		3	4	6	8			10	9						11					7								5			22
1	2		3	5	6	8			10	9			4			11					7											23
1	2		3	5	6	8			10			9	4			11					7											24
1	2		3	5	6	8			10			9	4			11					7											25
1	2		3	5		8			10	11		9	4						6		7											26
1	2		3	5		8			10	11								6	4		7											27
	2		3	5	6	8			10	11		9	4								7	1										28
1	5			4	6	8			10	11		3	2	9							7											29
1	5		3	4	6	8			10			2				11					7											30
28	30	10	25	28	28	27	10	13	8	12	6	4	5	4	3	3	2	2	2	1	28	7	5	4	4	3	2	2	2	2	2	
			1	1	14	8		13	2	2			4								1			2	3	3						
1	5		3	4	6	8			10	11		2									7											31
1	5		3	4	6	8			10			2				11					7											32
1	5		3	4	6			9	10			2				11				8	7											33
1			3	4	6	8			10	9		5	2			11					7											34
1			3	5	6			9	10			2				11				8	7				4							35
1			3	5	6			9	10			2				11				8	7				4							36
6	3	0	6	6	6	6	1	6	1	0	1	6	0	0	0	5	0	0	0		6	0	0	0	0	0	2	0	0	0	0	
						4		7								1											1					

Match 1: Ollerenshaw (1); H.Newton (10); A.Johnson (11); Kelly (8)
Match 2: Petrie (9); Connor (11)
Match 8: Osmond (2); Duffy (4)
Match 11: Hanney (5)
Match 12: Knowles (5); Brown (8)
Match 13: Fielding (11)
Match 15: Royle (9)
Match 17: Wray (8)
Match 19: Dorsett (7; 2gls)
Match 27: A.Fairclough (9; 1 gl)
Match 28: A.W.Smith (1)
Match 30: J.Broad (9)
Match 31: A.Fairclough (9; 1 gl)
Match 32: A.Fairclough (9)

1939-40

					Appearances	
1	Aug 26	(a)	Leicester C	L 3-4	Dunkley, Doherty, Brook	12,000
2	30	(h)	Bury	D 1-1	Doherty	20,000
3	Sep 2	(h)	Chesterfield	W 2-0	Milsom (2)	15,000

Football League programme abandoned upon outbreak of World War Two.   Appearances
Above games played in Division Two before League closed down.   Goals

4	Oct 21	(a)	Manchester U	W 4-0	Herd, Heale, Doherty, Brook	7,000
5	28	(h)	Wrexham	W 6-1	Doherty (2), Pritchard (2), Heale, Brook	4,000
6	Nov 11	(a)	Everton	L 1-3	Heale	5,000
7	18	(h)	Stoke C	D 1-1	Percival	5,000
8	25	(a)	New Brighton	W 3-1	Herd, Doherty (2)	3,500
9	Dec 2	(h)	Stockport C	D 6-6	Heale (5), Wright	5,744
10	9	(h)	Chester	W 4-1	Blackshaw (2), Heale, Doherty	3,000
11	23	(a)	Crewe A	W 2-1	Herd (2)	5,000
12	Jan 6	(h)	Liverpool	L 3-7	Doherty (2), Rudd	5,000
13	Feb 10	(h)	Manchester U	W 1-0	Herd	5,000
14	24	(a)	Wrexham	L 2-3	Heale, Rudd	4,000
15	Mar 9	(h)	Everton	D 2-2	Heale, Rudd	5,000
16	16	(a)	Stoke C	L 1-2	Herd	5,000
17	23	(h)	New Brighton	L 2-3	Doherty, Westwood	6,000
18	30	(a)	Stockport C	D 1-1	Herd	7,000
19	Apr 6	(a)	Chester	W 3-0	Herd (2), Emptage	2,500
20	13	(h)	Tranmere R	W 5-1	Currier (2), Bray, Herd, Emptage	3,000
21	May 4	(a)	Tranmere R	W 6-1	Currier (4), Herd, Doherty	2,500
22	11	(h)	Port Vale	W 5-2	Currier (4), Bray	2,000
23	13	(h)	Crewe A	W 6-2	Herd (4), Burdett, Doherty	1,300
24	18	(h)	Port Vale	W 7-0	Herd (4), Currier, Doherty, Pritchard	2,000
25	25	(a)	Liverpool	L 2-3	Pritchard, Doherty	2,000

Western regional League record: Appearances
P 22   W 12   D 4   L 6   F 73   A 41   Pts 28   Pos 4th   Goals

League War Cup*

1	Apr 20	(a)	Manchester U	W 1-0	Worsley	21,874
1	27	(h)	Manchester U	L 0-2		21,596

*played on two-legged home and away basis.   Appearances
                                                                         Goals

Football League Jubilee Fund match

1	Aug 19	(a)	Manchester U	D 1-1		20,000

Friendlies

1	Sep 16	(a)	Bury	W 4-2		9	Dec 26	(a)	Manchester U	L 1-3
2	23	(a)	Preston N E	L 0-3		10	Jan 1	(h)	Stockport C	W 7-2
3	30	(a)	Manchester U	W 3-2		11	13	(a)	Blackburn R	W 2-1
4	Oct 7	(a)	Stockport C	W 5-0		12	Feb 17	(h)	Sheffield W	W 3-1
5	14	(a)	Bolton W	D 2-2		13	Mar 2	(h)	Burnley	W 3-1
6	Nov 4	(h)	Preston N E	D 2-2		14	22	(h)	Blackpool	W 5-3
7	Dec 16	(a)	Burnley	W 2-0		15	25	(a)	Blackpool	W 3-0
8	25	(h)	Manchester U	D 1-1						

Swift	Sproston	Westwood	McDowall	Cardwell	Bray	Dunkley	Herd	Heale	Milsom	Doherty	Brook	Clark	Barkas	Percival	Bray	Blackshaw	Pritchard	Rudd	Wright	Walsh	Emptage	Robinson	Neilson	Smith G.	Davenport	Worsley	Currier	Toseland	Burdett	McIntosh	Smith L.	#
1	2	3	4	5	6	7	8	9		10	11																					1
1	2	3	4	5	6	7	8	9		10	11																					2
1	2	3	4	5	6	7	8		9	10	11																					3
3	3	3	3	3	3	3	3	2	1	3	3																					app
								1	2	2	1																					gls
1				5	6		8	9		10	11	2	3	4		7																4
1	3			5	6		8	9		10	11	2		4		7																5
1				5	6		8	9		10	11	2	3	4														7				6
	3			5	6		8	9		10		2		4		7				11		1										7
1	2			5	6		8	9		10	11		3	4		7																8
1	2	3		5	6			9		10				4		7	11							8								9
1	2	3		5	6		8	9		10				4		7	11															10
1	2	3		5	6		8	9		10				4		7	11															11
1	3			5	6		8	9		10		2		4		7	11															12
1				5	6		8	9		10		2	3	4		7															11	13
	2			5	6		8	9		10			3	4			11		7	1												14
	3			5			8	9		10		2		4			11	6	7	1												15
1	3			5			8	9		10		2		4		7	11	6	10													16
1	11			5	6			9		10		2	3	8		7			4													17
1	3						8					2		4		7		6						5	10					11		18
1	2	9		5	6		8						3	4		7	11				10											19
1	2			5	6		8						3	4			11				10	7					9					20
1	2	11		5	6		8			10			3			7			4								9					21
1				5	6		8			10		2					11	4	7				3				9					22
1	3			5	3		8			10		2		4			11	6	7										9			23
1	3			5	6		8			10		2		4			11		7								9					24
1	2			5	6		8			10			3			9	11	4	7													25
19	10	12	0	21	19	0	21	13	0	18	4	15	8	19	0	8	11	6	3	9	9	3	2	2	1	0	4	1	1	1	1	Tot
	1			2			19	11		3	2			1			2	4	3	1	2						11			1		gls
1	2	11		5	6		8	9					3								4						7	10				C1
1	2			5	6		8			10			3				11				4					9	7					C2
2	2	1	0	2	2	0	2	0	1	1	0	2	0	0	0	0	1	0	0	2	0	0	0	1	0	2	1	0	0	0	0	Tot
																											1					gls
1	2	3	4	5	6	7	8		9	10	11																					key

Match 18: Tilson (9; 1 gl)

1940-41

1	Aug 21 (h) Everton	D 0-0		4,000
2	Sep 7 (a) Everton	L 0-1		3,000
3	14 (h) New Brighton	W 5-2	Doherty (2), Herd (2), Currier	4,000
4	21 (a) Leeds U	D 0-0		5,000
5	28 (h) Manchester U	W 4-1	Doherty (2), Brown, Currier	10,000
6	Oct 5 (a) Manchester U	W 2-0	Currier, McShane	10,000
7	12 (h) Huddersfield T	W 3-1	Currier (2), Brown	4,000
8	19 (a) Liverpool	W 4-0	Currier (4)	7,000
9	26 (h) Blackburn R	D 1-1	Brown	5,000
10	Nov 2 (a) Doncaster R	W 4-0	Herd (2), Currier, Doherty	2,000
11	9 (h) Liverpool	W 5-1	Herd (3), Pritchard, Currier	3,000
12	16 (a) Blackburn R	D 2-2	Currier, Doherty	2,000
13	23 (h) Preston N E	L 1-2	Brown	4,000
14	30 (a) Preston N E	D 4-4	Brown (2), Currier, Doherty	2,500
15	Dec 7 (a) Oldham A	L 0-1		3,000
16	14 (a) Stockport C	W 9-1	Herd (4), Currier (3), Bray, opp.og	1,200
17	21 (h) Stockport C	W 7-2	Currier (3), Doherty (3), Emptage	3,000
18	25 (a) Burnley	D 2-2	Currier, McShane	8,300
19	28 (a) Huddersfield T	L 0-2		2,689
20	Jan 4 (h) Rochdale*	W 9-1	Currier (5), Doherty (2), Mulraney, Pritchard	2,000
21	11 (a) Rochdale*	W 6-1	Currier (5), Mulraney	1,000
22	18 (h) Blackpool*	L 2-4	Boothway, Bray	1,000
23	25 (a) Blackpool*	L 1-2	Currier	12,000
24	Feb 1 (h) Oldham A	W 5-4	Walsh, Mutch, Currier, Doherty (2)	2,000
25	8 (a) Oldham A	W 5-2	Currier (2), Bray, Mulraney, Doherty	2,000
26	Apr 12 (h) Leeds U	D 1-1	Boothway	3,000
27	14 (h) Manchester U	L 1-7	Currier	7,000
28	19 (h) Wrexham	W 5-0	Reid (2), Percival, Boothway, Pritchard	2,000
29	26 (h) Blackpool	W 2-0	Currier, Pearson	4,000
30	May 3 (a) Blackpool	D 1-1	Currier	6,000
31	10 (a) Wrexham	D 0-0		3,000
32	17 (a) Bolton W	D 1-1	Brooks	1,500
33	24 (h) Bolton W	W 6-4	Currier (3), Herd, Carey, Pritchard	1,500
34	31 (a) Bury	W 3-2	Herd (2), Dunkley	1,371
35	Jun 7 (h) Bury	W 3-2	Currier (2), Walsh	3,000

North Regional League record: Appearances
P 35   W 18   D 10   L 7   F 104   A 55   Pts 46   Pos 3rd   Goals

League War Cup

1	Feb 15 (a) Blackpool	W 4-1	Currier (2), Doherty (2)	15,000
2	22 (h) Blackpool	L 0-1		8,967
3	Mar 1 (h) Blackburn R	W 5-2	Sproston (2), Herd (2), Boothway	6,000
4	8 (a) Blackburn R	W 4-2	Bray, Pritchard, Currier, Doherty	5,000
5	15 (a) Everton	D 1-1	Currier	12,000
6	22 (h) Everton	W 2-0	Herd, Currier	10,000
7	29 (h) Preston N E	L 1-2	Boothway	15,304
8	Apr 5 (a) Preston N E	L 0-3		14,000

                                                           Appearances
                                                             Goals

Friendly (in aid of charity)

1	Aug 24 (h) RAF XI	W 2-0	Eastham, Pritchard	4,922

Swift	Robinson J.	Sproston	Eastwood	Clark	Walsh	Neilson	Bray	Pritchard	Herd	Doherty	Emptage	Percival	Boothway	Dunkley	Fagan	Jackson	Pearson	Cardwell	Barkas	Currier	McShane	Turner	Brown,	Mulraney	Walker	Mutch	Carey	Rudd	Watt	
1	2	3	4		6	11	8	10	7						5					9										1
1	2	3	4		6		8	10	11						5					9				11						2
1	2	3	4		6		8	10	11						5					9										3
	1	2	4	3	7		8	10	6						5					9	11									4
1	2	3	4		6		8	10							5					9	11	7								5
1	2	3	4	5	6		8	10	7											9	11									6
1	2	3	4	5	6		8	10												9	11	7								7
1	2	3	4	5	6		8	10												9	11	7								8
1	2	5	4		6			10	7											9	11	8								9
1	2	3	4	5	6	7		10												9	11	8								10
1	2	3	4	5	6	7	8	10												9	11									11
1	2	3	4	5	6	7	8	10												9	11									12
1		3	6	5	7		8			4										9	11	2	10							13
1		3	4		6	7		10						5						9	11	2	8							14
1	2			5	6	7		10		4									3	9	11									15
1		3	4	5	6	7	8	10												9	11	2								16
1		3		5	6	7		10												9	11	2	8							17
1		3	4	5	6	7		10												9	11	2	8							18
1		3	4	5	6		8	10												9		2								19
1	2	3	4	5		7		10		6										9	11		8							20
1		3	4	5	6	7		10												9	11	2	8							21
1		3		5	6	7		10		4										9	11	2	8							22
1			4	5	6	7		10											3	9	11	2	8							23
		3			6	11		10		4									5	9		2	7	8						24
1		3	4	5	6	11		10												9		2	7	8						25
1		3		5	6	11		10		4										9		2		8						26
1		3		5	6	7				4										9		2	10	8			11			27
1	2	3		5	6	11	8													9			10		7					28
1			4	5	6	11		10				7								9		2	8							29
1	2		4	5	6	11	8												3	9	7		10							30
1	2	3		5	6	11				4										9	7		8						10	31
1	2		4	5	6		8												3		11		10				7			32
1				5	6	11	8			4		7							3	9		2	10							33
1		3	4	5	6		8					7								9	11	2	10							34
1	2		4		6		8	10		11		7								9							3	5		35
19	**15**	**11**	**23**	**14**	**33**	**18**	**31**	**24**	**17**	**22**	**11**	**10**	**8**	**7**	**5**	**4**	**2**	**2**	**2**	**35**	**20**	**11**	**10**	**6**	**5**	**4**	**3**	**1**	**1**	
	2							3	4	14	15	1	1	3	1		1			42	2		6	3			1	1		

Swift	Robinson J.	Sproston	Eastwood	Clark	Walsh	Neilson	Bray	Pritchard	Herd	Doherty	Emptage	Percival	Boothway	Dunkley	Fagan	Jackson	Pearson	Cardwell	Barkas	Currier	McShane	Turner	Brown,	Mulraney	Walker	Mutch	Carey	Rudd	Watt	
1		2	3	4	5	6	7	8	10											9								11		1
1		2	3	4	5	6	7													9		8						11		2
1	10		2	4	5	6	7	8											3									11		3
1		5	2	4		6	7	10											3	8								11		4
	1	5	2	4		6	7	8											3	10								11		5
1		5	2	4		6	8	10											3	9	11	7								6
1		5	2	4		6	8												3	10	11	7								7
	1			6			7						4			2			9	11	8	3								8
6	**2**	**7**	**0**	**7**	**8**	**3**	**7**	**6**	**5**	**3**	**0**	**1**	**4**	**0**	**0**	**1**	**0**	**0**	**5**	**7**	**3**	**0**	**4**	**0**	**1**	**0**	**0**	**3**	**2**	
	2						1	1	3	3			2							5										

Match 3: Keeling (7)
Match 9: Davenport (3)
Match 15. Boulter (8)
Match 17: P.Robinson (4)
Match 19: Nuttall (7); Beaumont (11)
Match 24: Breedon (1)
Match 26: Henry (7)
Match 28: Reid (4; 2 gls)
Match 29: Westwood (3)
Match 32: Brooks(9; 1 gl)

League War Cup
Match 2: Thomson (10)
Match 8: Vose (5); Dickie (10)

1941-42

1	Aug 30	(a)	Tranmere R	L 2-5	Bray, Dunkley	3,500
2	Sep 6	(h)	Tranmere R	D 1-1	Doherty	3,000
3	13	(h)	Liverpool	L 3-4	Dunkley, Smith, Currier	3,000
4	20	(a)	Liverpool	L 2-4	Parlane, O'Donnell	5,000
5	27	(a)	Wrexham	W 5-3	Boothway (5)	2,000
6	Oct 4	(h)	Wrexham	W 2-0	Boothway (2)	2,000
7	11	(h)	Stoke C	W 4-3	Barkas (3), Boothway	3,000
8	18	(a)	Stoke C	L 0-5		3,000
9	25	(h)	New Brighton	D 2-2	Bray, Currier	2,000
10	Nov 1	(a)	New Brighton	L 2-3	Boothway (2)	1,500
11	8	(a)	Stockport C	W 6-4	Boothway (3), Currier (2), Emptage	3,000
12	15	(h)	Stockport C	W 2-1	Herd (2)	2,000
13	22	(h)	Everton	L 3-4	Boothway (3)	2,500
14	29	(a)	Everton	L 0-9		8,000
15	Dec 6	(a)	Chester	W 3-1	Walsh(2), Fenton	1,200
16	13	(h)	Chester	W 7-2	Dunkley (2), Fenton (2), Boothway (2), Smith	3,000
17	20	(h)	Manchester U	W 2-1	Boothway (2)	7,000
18	25	(a)	Manchester U	D 2-2	Boothway (2)	16,000

North Regional League (1st period) record: Appearances
P 18   W 8   D 3   L 7   F 48   A 54   Pts 19   Pos 17th   Goals

19	Dec 27	(a)	Blackburn R*	L 0-3		5,200
20	Jan 3	(h)	Blackburn R*	L 1-2	Currier	4,000
21	10	(a)	Burnley*	W 2-1	Bray, Fenton	4,000
22	17	(h)	Burnley*	W 5-0	Currier (2), Dunkley (2), Fenton	2,500
23	Feb 14	(h)	Rochdale*	W 5-0	Boothway (3), Walsh, Fenton	4,000
24	21	(a)	Wolves*	W 3-1	Boothway (2), Smith	6,000
25	28	(h)	Wolves*	W 4-1	Boothway (3), Fenton	5,000
26	Mar 14	(h)	Preston N E*	L 0-3		6,000
27	21	(a)	Rochdale*	L 1-3	Currier	3,200
28	28	(a)	Preston N E*	D 0-0		5,000
29	Apr 4	(h)	Blackpool**	W	Blackpool withdrew and City won outright	
30	6	(a)	Blackpool**	W	Blackpool withdrew and City won outright	
31	11	(a)	Southport**	W 4-1	Malam (2), Dellow, Currier	4,000
32	18	(h)	Southport**	W 3-0	Boothway, Dellow	5,700
33	25	(a)	Wolves**	L 0-2		15,000
34	May 2	(h)	Wolves**	W 1-0	Currier	14,715
35	9	(h)	Everton#	W 2-0	Dellow, Boothway	4,000
36	16	(a)	Everton#	L 1-6	Boothway	18,000
37	23	(h)	Manchester U	L 1-3	Stuart	6,000

North Regional League (2nd period) record: Appearances
P 17   W 9   D 1   L 7   F 33   A 26   Pts 19***   Goals

Friendly

1 Sep 8 (a) Blackpool   W 3-1

* Matches also counted towards League War Cup qualifying round.
** Matches also counted towards League War Cup KO competition (home & away, 2-legged basis).
# Matches also counted in Lancashire Senior Cup.

***City were not placed in the 'Second Championship' as they needed to have completed at
   least 18 League games to qualify. Blackpool's withdrawal from the first round proper of
   the League War Cup left City short of that figure.

250

Appearances and goals grid (numbers indicate shirt number worn; match number in right-hand column).

Robinson J.	Clark	Robinson P.	Eastwood	Bray	Walsh	Dunkley	Parlane	Boothway	Wild	Pritchard	Barkas	Kirton	Doherty	Sproston	Hogan	Stuart	Swift	Westwood	Percival	Bardsley	Smith	Davenport D.	Walker	Currier	Carey W.	Charlesworth	Fenton	Dellow	Match
	2		6	4	7			10	11														3	9					1
	2			5	6	4		11	7				10									8	3	9					2
	2			5	6	7	8											11	4	10			3	9					3
	2			5				8	9	7	6								4				3		1				4
		4		5				8	9	7			3		6										1				5
		4		5				8	9	11			7		6								3	10	1				6
	2	4	5	6				9	11			10	7					1					3	8					7
	2		5	6	4			9	11				7					1				10	3	8					8
	2		6	4	7			9	11				10	5									3	8	1				9
	2		5	6	4	7		9	11			10											3	8	1				10
	2		5	6	4			9	11				7											10	1				11
		4	5	6	7			9	11					2									3	10	1				12
		4		6				9	11		3	7								8			2	10	1	5			13
	2		4		6	7		9	11				10										3		1	5	8		14
1	2	4	3	6	10			9	11			7														5	8		15
1	2		3	6	4	7		9												10						5	8		16
1		2	6	4	7			9					7									3	10			5	8		17
1		2	6	4				9			3	10								7			11	8		5			18
4	12	5	16	12	13	8	4	17	10	4	6	6	4	4	0	0	2	1	2	2	2	2	14	13	9	6	4		
(goals)			2	2	4	1		22					3	1					2					4		3			
1			4		6	7		9			3	10											2	11		5	8		19
1			2	6	4			9	11			7											3	10		5	8		20
1	2	4	5	6				9												8			3	10		7			21
1	2		4	6		7							10										3	9		5	8		22
1		2	6	4	7			9												10			3	11		5	8		23
		4	3	6				9					2						7	10				11		5	8		24
			6	4	7			9			3									10			2	11		5	8		25
			6	4	7			9									2			8			3	11		5			26
1	2	7	5		6			9											10				3	11					27
		2	6	4				9									1			8			3	11		5		7	28
																													29
																													30
1	2		3	6	4			9												10				11		5		7	31
1	2		4	6	8			9		3										10				11		5		7	32
1	2		5	6	4			9					11							10			3	8				7	33
1	2		6	4				9		3													11	10				7	34
1	2		3	4				9					10	11									5	8				7	35
1	3		6	4				9					10	11									5	8				7	36
1	2	4	6	8									10	11	3								9	5				7	37
13	10	4	11	14	15	5	0	15	1	0	4	1	1	2	3	4	1	2	0	3	8	0	13	17	0	11	7	8	
(goals)	1			1	1	2		12					1							1							4	3	

Match 1: Crompton (1); Neilson (5); Brown (8)
Match 2: Goodall (1)
Match 3: Goodall (1)
Match 4: Kinghorn (10); O'Donnell (11; 1 gl)
Match 5: Hall (2); Devlin (10); Rudman (11)
Match 6: Hall (2)
Match 11: J.Davenport (3); Emptage (8; 1 gl)
Match 12: Herd (8; 2 gls)
Match 16: Goddard (11)
Match 17: Pearson (11)
Match 21: Rudd (11)
Match 22: Rudd (11)

Match 24: Scales (1)
Match 25: Scales (1)
Match 26: Scales (1); J.Carey (10)
Match 27: Dodd (4); Malam (8)
Match 28: Jones (10)
Match 31: Malam (8; 2 gls)
Match 34: McDowall (5); Butt (8)
Match 35: Dodd (6)
Match 36: Bacuzzi (2)

1942-43

1	Aug	29	(h)	Blackpool	L 1-3	Dellow	6,000
2	Sep	5	(a)	Blackpool	L 2-5	Dellow, Boothway	5,000
3		12	(a)	Wrexham	L 2-4	Boothway, Stuart	3,500
4		19	(h)	Wrexham	W 5-1	Malam (3), Currier, Hogan	4,000
5		26	(h)	Bolton W	W 2-0	Malam, Currier	4,000
6	Oct	3	(a)	Bolton W	L 1-2	Boothway	3,000
7		10	(a)	Crewe A	L 3-5	Bray, Bardsley, Stuart	3,000
8		17	(h)	Crewe A	W 5-1	Malam (3), Boothway (2)	4,000
9		24	(h)	Liverpool	L 1-4	Currier	6,500
10		31	(a)	Liverpool	L 1-3	Stuart	12,401
11	Nov	7	(a)	Manchester U	L 1-2	H.Clark	9,301
12		14	(h)	Manchester U	L 0-5		5,674
13		21	(h)	Chester	W 4-2	Walsh, Williamson, Currier, Jones	3,000
14		28	(a)	Chester	D 1-1	Currier	2,500
15	Dec	5	(a)	Tranmere R	W 3-1	P.Robinson, Pearson, Jones	1,000
16		12	(h)	Tranmere R	W 4-1	Jones, Currier (2), Williamson	2,500
17		19	(h)	Everton	W 7-1	King (2), Currier (2), Cox, Stuart, P.Robinson	3,000
18		25	(a)	Everton	L 3-6	King, Currier (2)	10,000

North Regional League (1st period) record: Appearances
P 18   W 7   D 1   L 10   F 46   A 47   Pts 15   Pos 30th Goals

19	Dec	26	(a)	Bolton W*	W 4-2	King, Currier, Doherty, opp.og	8,000
20	Jan	2	(h)	Bolton W*	W 2-0	Currier, Herd	3,000
21		9	(a)	Stockport C*	W 7-1	Herd (2), Welsh (2), Cox, Currier, Stuart	5,000
22		16	(a)	Stockport C*	W 5-2	Currier (3), Williamson (2)	2,500
23		23	(a)	Bury*	W 3-2	Williamson (2), Currier	4,500
24		30	(h)	Bury	W 3-2	Currier (3)	5,649
25	Feb	6	(h)	Manchester U*	D 0-0		17,577
26		13	(a)	Manchester U*	D 1-1	Herd	16,366
27		20	(a)	Liverpool*	L 2-4	King, Stuart	21,863
28		27	(h)	Liverpool*	W 3-1	Herd (2), opp.og	14,795
29	Mar	6	(a)	Manchester U**	W 1-0	Currier	28,962
30		13	(h)	Manchester U**	W 2-0	Currier, Doherty	36,453
31		20	(a)	Blackburn R**	L 0-2		15,623
32		27	(h)	Blackburn R**	W 4-0	Boothway (2), King, Currier	24,690
33	Apr	3	(a)	Blackpool**	L 1-3	Boothway	25,000
34		10	(h)	Blackpool**	D 1-1	Currier	53,205
35		17	(a)	Chesterfield	W 2-1	Boothway (2)	2,700
36		24	(h)	Chesterfield	D 1-1	Boothway	3,000
37		26	(h)	Huddersfield T	D 1-1	Currier	4,000

North Regional League (2nd period) record: Appearances
P 19   W 11   D 5   L 3   F 43   A 24   Pts 27   Pos 3rd Goals

Friendly

1 Aug 22 (h) Manchester U   L 1-5

*Matches also counted towards League War Cup qualifying round.
**Matches also counted towards League War Cup KO competition (home & away, 2-legged basis).

Appearances and goals grid (shirt numbers shown per match; totals and goals rows at foot of each block).

Robinson J.	Clark G.	Eastwood	Walsh	Bray	Clark H.	Boothway	Stuart	Scales	Robinson P.	Barkas	Doherty	McDowall	Jackson	Swift	Pearson	Bardsley	Westwood	Kenny	Pritchard	Herd	Grant	Currier	Malam	Charlesworth	Jones C.	King	Dellow	Williamson	Cox	Welsh	Match
1	2		4	6		9	11											3				10	8	5		7					1
1	2	3	4	6		9	11															10	8	5		7					2
1	2		4	6		9	11				3											10	8	5		7					3
	2	3	4	6			11	1														9	8	5		7					4
	2	3	4	6			11						1									9	8	5		7					5
1	2	3	4	6	7	9	11															10	8	5							6
1	2	3	4	6	7		11										10					9	8	5							7
	2	3	4	6	7	9	11	1														10	8	5							8
	2	3	4	6	7		11	1			10											9	8	5							9
	2	3	4		7		11	1			10											9	8	5	6						10
	2		4	6	7		11	1	3													9	8	5	10						11
	2	3	4	6		9	11	1															8	5	10		7				12
	2		5	6			11	1	4				3									9			10	7		8			13
	2		5	6			11	1	4	3					10							9						8			14
	2		5	6			11	1	4	3				7	8							9			10						15
	2		5	4	6			1		3												9			10	7		8			16
	2		5	6			11		4				1					3				9				7		8	10		17
	2	3	8	6			11	1	4	10												9				7					18
5	**17**	**16**	**18**	**13**	**6**	**6**	**17**	**11**	**5**	**5**	**3**	**0**	**2**	**2**	**2**	**1**	**1**	**1**	**0**	**0**	**0**	**17**	**12**	**12**	**7**	**5**	**5**	**3**	**1**	**0**	Apps
1	1	1	5	4		2										1	1					11	7		3	3	2	2	1		Goals

Robinson J.	Clark G.	Eastwood	Walsh	Bray	Clark H.	Boothway	Stuart	Scales	Robinson P.	Barkas	Doherty	McDowall	Jackson	Swift	Pearson	Bardsley	Westwood	Kenny	Pritchard	Herd	Grant	Currier	Malam	Charlesworth	Jones C.	King	Dellow	Williamson	Cox	Welsh	Match
	2	4	6	3			11	1			10				8							9				7					19
	2	5	4	6			11	1		3					8					10		9				7					20
	2	5	6	3			11	1	4												8	9							7	10	21
1	2	5	6				11		4	3											8	9						10	7		22
1	2	5	4	6					3						11					8	9							10			23
1	2	5		6			11		4						3					10	8	9							7		24
1	2	5		6			11		4	3												9			10			8	7		25
1		5	4	6			11			3		2									8	9							10	7	26
1	2	5	4	6			11			3										10	8	9						7			27
	2	5	6	3				4					1							10	8	9				7			11		28
1	2	5	4	6					3												8	9				7		10	11		29
1	2	5	6					4		10	3									11		9						8	7		30
1	2	5	6					4	3	10										7		9						8			31
	2	5	6	11			9		4	3	10		1								8							7			32
	2	5	4	6			9			3	10		1							11		7						8			33
	2	5	6					3	4				1								8	9						7	10		34
1	2	5	6	11			9		4	3	10										8							7			35
1	2	5	6				9	11	4	10	3										8							7			36
1	2	5	6				9			4	3		8			11				10											37
12	**18**	**19**	**17**	**13**	**0**	**5**	**9**	**3**	**10**	**11**	**5**	**6**	**3**	**4**	**0**	**3**	**2**	**0**	**1**	**10**	**6**	**19**	**0**	**0**	**1**	**8**	**0**	**9**	**8**	**1**	Apps
6	2									2										6	15					3		4	1	2	Goals

Match 4: Hogan (10; 1 gl)
Match 5: Hogan (10)
Match 14: Setters (7)
Match 16: Taylor (11)
Match 18: Cardwell (5)
Match 19: Cardwell (5)
Match 20: Barclay (7)
Match 23: Paton (7)
Match 31: Barclay (11)
Match 34: Bellis (11)
Match 37: Cassidy (7);

253

1943-44

1	Aug 28	(a)	Liverpool	L 1-4	Percival	13,600
2	Sep 4	(h)	Liverpool	W 2-1	Williamson, Boothway	10,229
3	11	(a)	Blackpool	L 2-6	Boothway, Baker	10,000
4	18	(h)	Blackpool	L 1-2	Doherty	17,500
5	25	(a)	Bolton W	L 1-4	Williamson	2,500
6	Oct 2	(h)	Bolton W	W 4-0	McDowall, Barclay, Burke, Williamson	3,000
7	9	(a)	Wrexham	W 1-0	Burke	4,500
8	16	(a)	Wrexham	W 4-1	Doherty (2), Barclay, Leech	4,000
9	23	(h)	Crewe A	W 2-0	King (2)	5,000
10	30	(a)	Crewe A	W 2-0	Doherty (2)	4,000
11	Nov 6	(h)	Manchester U	D 2-2	Burke, Boothway	15,157
12	13	(h)	Manchester U	L 0-3		8,958
13	20	(a)	Chester	W 2-1	Boothway, Barclay	3,500
14	27	(h)	Chester	W 3-0	King, Williamson, Leech	3,000
15	Dec 4	(h)	Tranmere R	D 2-2	Doherty (2)	3,700
16	11	(a)	Tranmere R	W 6-0	Doherty (3), Heale (2), King	3,000
17	18	(a)	Everton	L 0-4		10,000
18	25	(h)	Everton	L 3-5	Williamson, Doherty (2)	16,468

North Regional League (1st period) record:
P 18   W 9   D 2   L 7   F 38   A 35   Pts 20   Pos 17th

19	Dec 26	(a)	Bury*	W 4-0	Williamson (2), Heale, Doherty	7,000
20	Jan 1	(h)	Bury*	L 1-7	Heale	6,000
21	8	(h)	Oldham A*	D 0-0		6,000
22	15	(a)	Oldham A*	D 1-1	Williamson	6,000
23	22	(a)	Manchester U*	W 3-1	Boothway (2), Heale	12,372
24	29	(h)	Manchester U*	L 2-3	Williamson, Heale	18,569
25	Feb 5	(a)	Stockport C*	W 4-0	Williamson (2), Heale, Doherty	6,000
26	12	(a)	Stockport C*	L 3-4	Heale (2), Boothway	5,500
27	19	(a)	Halifax T*	W 5-3	Williamson (2), Heale (2), Doherty	4,000
28	26	(h)	Halifax T*	W 4-0	Doherty (3), Heale	7,000
29	Mar 4	(h)	Blackburn R**	W 3-0	Williamson (3)	13,897
30	11	(a)	Blackburn R**	L 2-4	Doherty (2) (90mins score 0-3)	8,000
31	18	(h)	Liverpool**	D 1-1	Heale	27,792
32	25	(a)	Liverpool**	W 3-2	Heale (2), Herd (90mins score 2-2)	41,498
33	Apr 1	(h)	Birmingham**	W 1-0	Herd	27,137
34	8	(a)	Birmingham**	D 0-0		40,000
35	10	(a)	Manchester U	W 4-1	McDowall (3), Bardsley	18,990
36	15	(a)	Blackpool**	D 1-1	Doherty	25,000
37	22	(h)	Blackpool**	L 1-2	Doherty	60,000
38	29	(a)	Bradford	L 0-5		3,724
39	May 6	(h)	Bradford	W 2-1	Bootle, Doherty	5,000

North Regional League (2nd period) record:
P 21   W 9   D 6   L 6   F 42   A 35   Pts 24   Pos 19th

Friendly

1 Aug 21 (h) Manchester U   D 2-2

*Matches also counted towards League War Cup qualifying round.
**Matches also counted towards League War Cup KO competition (home & away, 2-legged basis).

Note: Match 8 (v Wrexham) should have been a 'home' fixture but was played at Wrexham because
Maine Road was required for an international match between England and Scotland.

Matches 36 & 37 were the 2 legs of the League North War Cup semi-final.

Where extra-time was played in Cup games, 90 minutes score only counted towards League.

Swift	Clark G.	Bray	Walsh	Eastwood	McDowall	Barclay	Bardsley	Boothway	Doherty	Jackson	Chappell	Heale	Taylor	Leech	Sproston	Scales	Percival	Brown	Bootle	Worrall	Westwood	Robinson J.	Clark H.	Robinson P.	Herd	Cox	Williamson	King	Burke	Match
1		3	4	5	6	11		9		2							7										8			1
1		3	4	5	2	11		9	10																		8	7		2
		6	4	5		11		9		2						1											8	7		3
1		3	4					9	10	2																		7		4
1	2	6	4																							9	7			5
1	2	3	4	5	6	7	11	10																		8		9		6
1	2	3	4	5	6	7	11	10																		8		9		7
	2	3	4	5	6	7	8	11	10		1	9																		8
1	2	3	4	5	6			8	9	10											11							7		9
	2	3	4	5	6			8	9	10	1										11							7		10
1	2		4	5	6		8	11			3									10							7	9		11
		3	4	5	6	7	2	11			1									10						8		9		12
1		3	4	5	6	7		9				2					10									8				13
1	2	3	4	5	11	6			10					9												8	7			14
	2	3	4	5	6				10				11	9	1												7			15
1			4	5	6	11	8		10	2		9															7			16
1				5	6	7			10	2			9	11		4										8				17
1	2	3	4	5	6	7		9	10																		8			18
13	**10**	**15**	**17**	**16**	**14**	**12**	**8**	**12**	**12**	**6**	**4**	**3**	**2**	**3**	**1**	**1**	**2**	**0**	**0**	**2**	**2**	**0**	**0**	**0**	**0**	**10**	**11**	**4**		
				1	3			4	12			2		2			1									5	4	3		*(goals)*
1	2	3	4	5	6	7			10			9															8			19
	4	3	5	7	6			1				9	11		2												8			20
1	2	3	6	5	10							9			8		4									7				21
1	2	3	4	5	6							9			8											10	7			22
1	2		4	5	6		11	10				9							7			3					8			23
1	2	3		5	6		11	10				9											7	4			8			24
1		3	4	5	6		11	10				9						2	7								8			25
		4	5	6				9			2	1	10	11					7								8			26
	2	3	4	5	6				10		1	9							7								8			27
1	2	3	4	5					10			9							7								8			28
1	2	3	4	5	6	11		7	10						8												9			29
	2	3	4	5	6		11	10							8	1											9			30
	2			5	6		11	10	3			9							7			1	4				8			31
1	2		4	5	6				10			9						3	7						8					32
	2	3	4	5	6		11					9			1										8	10	7			33
1	2	3	4	5	6				10			9														11	8	7		34
	2	3	4		9	10	11	8								1		6	7											35
1	2	3	4	5	6				10			9														11	8	7		36
	2	3	4	5	6				10			9										1				11	8	7		37
	2	3	4	5	10			9					11		8				6				1	7						38
1	2	3	4	5	6				10			9	11		8												7			39
12	**18**	**16**	**20**	**21**	**19**	**4**	**2**	**9**	**14**	**3**	**3**	**17**	**5**	**0**	**6**	**3**	**3**	**2**	**9**	**0**	**1**	**3**	**2**	**2**	**2**	**4**	**14**	**7**	**0**	
		3	1		3	11				13																	1		2	11	*(goals)*

Match 1: Thomson (10)
Match 2: Dodd (6)
Match 3: Porter (3); Baker (10; 1 gl)
Match 4: Porter (5); Powell (6); Williams (8); Beattie (11)
Match 5: Butler (3); Nielson (5); Bentham (8); Iddon (10); Beattie (11)
Match 13: Hanson (11)
Match 15: Chisholm (8)
Match 16: R.Eastwood (3)
Match 17: R.Eastwood (3)
Match 18: Paton (11)

Match 20: Pearson (10)
Match 21: Paton (11)
Match 22: Paton (11)
Match 26: Poole (3)
Match 27: Grant (11)
Match 28: Emptage (6); Grant (11)
Match 30: Dunkley (7)
Match 32: Carter (11)
Match 35: Fagan (5)

1944-45

	Date		Opponent	Result	Scorers	Attendance
1	Aug 26	(h)	Tranmere R	W 4-1	Smith (3), Heale	6,000
2	Sep 2	(a)	Tranmere R	W 4-0	Sproston, Heale, Smith, Taylor	3,000
3	9	(a)	Liverpool	D 2-2	Williamson, Smith	24,009
4	16	(h)	Liverpool	D 2-2	Sproston, Smith	14,000
5	23	(a)	Stockport C	W 6-2	Williamson (3), McDowall, King, Smith	8,000
6	30	(h)	Stockport C	W 5-1	Smith (2), McDowall, Heale, King	12,000
7	Oct 7	(h)	Crewe A	D 1-1	Heale	16,000
8	14	(a)	Crewe A	W 6-1	Heale (2), Bootle (2), Walsh, Taylor	9,000
9	21	(a)	Wrexham	D 1-1	Bootle	8,854
10	28	(h)	Wrexham	W 2-1	McDowall (2)	7,000
11	Nov 4	(h)	Everton	L 1-3	Heale	30,000
12	11	(a)	Everton	L 1-4	Smith	14,000
13	18	(a)	Manchester U	L 2-3	Smith (2)	20,764
14	25	(h)	Manchester U	W 4-0	Williamson (2), Smith, Doherty	18,657
15	Dec 2	(h)	Bury	W 4-0	King (2), Bootle, Williamson	5,000
16	9	(a)	Bury	L 1-2	King	4,579
17	16	(a)	Chester	L 1-7	Bray	4,500
18	23	(h)	Chester	W 6-0	Owen (2), Doherty (2), Bootle, Smith	14,000

North Regional League (1st period) record: Appearances
P 18   W 9   D 4   L 5   F 53   A 31   Pts 22   Pos 10th   Goals

	Date		Opponent	Result	Scorers	Attendance
19	Dec 26	(h)	Blackpool	D 1-1	Smith	13,600
20	30	(h)	Bury*	W 3-2	Smith (2), Owen	10,000
21	Jan 6	(a)	Halifax T*	D 1-1	Owen	6,000
22	13	(h)	Halifax T*	L 2-3	Owen, Smith	10,000
23	27	(a)	Oldham A*	W 4-3	Dunkley, Williamson, Owen, Smith	1,432
24	Feb 3	(a)	Manchester U*	W 3-1	Herd (2), Dunkley	25,655
25	10	(a)	Manchester U*	W 2-0	Williamson, Smith	22,923
26	17	(a)	Huddersfield T*	L 1-3	King	12,937
27	24	(h)	Huddersfield T*	W 2-0	King, Williamson	24,000
28	Mar 3	(a)	Bury*	L 2-4	Smith, Taylor	10,875
29	10	(h)	Oldham A*	W 3-2	Williamson (2), King	13,000
30	17	(a)	Stockport C#	L 1-4	Williamson	4,000
31	24	(h)	Crewe A**	W 5-1	Williamson (4), King	22,560
32	31	(a)	Crewe A**	L 0-2		6,300
33	Apr 2	(h)	Stockport C#	L 1-5	Smith	18,000
34	7	(a)	Liverpool**	L 0-3		36,131
35	14	(h)	Liverpool**	L 1-3	Herd	24,905
36	21	(h)	Blackpool	L 0-1		9,500
37	28	(a)	Blackpool	L 0-4		5,000

North Regional League (2nd period) record: Appearances
P 19   W 7   D 2   L 10   F 32   A 43   Pts 16   Pos 47th   Goals

Friendly

1   Aug 19   (h)   Manchester U   D 2-2

*Matches also counted in the League War Cup qualifying round.
**Matches also counted in the League War Cup KO competition (home and away, 2-legged basis)
#Matches also counted in the Lancashire Cup.

Swift	McMillan	Clark	Bray	Walsh	Eastwood	McDowall	Bootle	Heale	Smith	Taylor	Sproston	Doherty	Owen	Hodgson	Brown	Barber	Linaker	Rudd	Robinson J.	Robinson P.	Dunkley	Grant	Bardsley	Herd	Meiklem	Williamson	King	Thorpe	Roxburgh	Jones	Match
1	2	3	4	5	6	7		9	10	11																8					1
1	2	3	4	5	6	7		9	10	11	8															8					2
	1	2	3	4	5	6	7	9	10	11																8					3
	1	2	3	4	5	6	7		10	11	8															9					4
1	2		4	5	6				8	11	3	10														9	7				5
	1	2	3	4	5			9	10	11			6													8	7				6
1	2	6	4	5				9	10	11	3															8	7				7
		3	4	5	6	7		9	8	11		10							1												8
	1	2	3	4	5	10	7	9	8	11						6															9
	1		3	4	5	6	7	9	10	11			2													8					10
1	2	3	4	5	6			9	10	11																8	7				11
1	2	3	4	5	6	7			10	11																9	8				12
1	2		4	5	6	7			10	11	3															9					13
1	2	3	4	5	6	7			8	11		10														9					14
1			3	4	5	6	7		10	11		2														9	8				15
	1	2	3	4	5	6	11		10						7											9	8				16
	1	2	10	4	5	6	7	8						9	3										11						17
	1	2	3	4	5	6	11	7	10					9												8					18
Apps 9	8	15	16	18	16	18	14	9	18	15	6	4	2	2	2	1	0	0	1	0	0	0	0	0	1	14	7	0	0	0	
Goals		1	1	4	5	7	14	2	2	3	2															7	5				
1		3	4		6	7		8	11		2	10	9																		19
		2	3	4	5	6	7		10	11			9						1			8									20
1		2	3	4	5	6			10	11			9										8					7			21
1		2	3	4	5	6			10	11			9														8	7			22
1		2	3	4	5	6	11		10				9								7					8					23
		2		4	5	6	11					10									7		8			9				1	24
1		2	3	4	5	6	11		10				8								7					9					25
1		2	3	4	5	6	7		10	11			9														8				26
		2	3	4	5	6			10	11											7					9	8			1	27
		2	3	4	5	6			10	11										1	8					9	7				28
		2		4	5	6			10												7	11				9	8			1	29
				4	5	6			10								7					11				9					30
		2	3	4	5				10											6	7	11				9	8		1		31
1		2	3	4	5				10											6	7	11				9	8				32
1			3		5				10	11						2	6	9		7		4					8				33
1		2	3	4	5				10												7		8			9	11				34
			3	4	5	6			10			2									7		8			9	11		1		35
		2	3	4	5	6	11		8						9		10				7								1		36
		2	6	4	5				10									11			7			8					1		37
Apps 9	0	16	15	19	17	16	8	0	18	8	3	2	7	1	1	2	2	2	2	3	10	5	2	3	0	12	11	2	3	2	
Goals									8	1			4									2				3	10	4			

Match 8: Ollerenshaw (2)
Match 13: Emptage (8)
Match 19: Cardwell (5)
Match 24: Westwood (3)
Match 29: Williams (3)
Match 30: Breedon (1); Jackson (2); Williams (3); Baillie (8).
Match 37: Barkas (3)

1945-46

1	Aug 25	(h)	Middlesbrough	W 2-1	Dunkley, Pearson	25,000
2	Sep 1	(a)	Middlesbrough	D 2-2	Smith (2)	14,000
3	8	(a)	Stoke C	L 0-2		15,000
4	12	(h)	Sheffield W	L 1-5	Sproston	8,000
5	15	(h)	Stoke C	L 0-2		15,000
6	22	(h)	Grimsby T	L 0-2		20,000
7	29	(a)	Grimsby T	W 2-0	Hart, Constantine	13,000
8	Oct 6	(a)	Blackpool	L 4-5	Constantine (3), Dunkley	20,000
9	13	(h)	Blackpool	L 1-4	King	32,730
10	20	(h)	Liverpool	W 1-0	Constantine	23,034
11	27	(a)	Liverpool	W 5-0	Herd (2), Pearson (2), Smith	34,941
12	Nov 3	(a)	Bury	W 3-1	Walsh, Smith, Pearson	12,216
13	10	(h)	Bury	W 4-1	Smith (2), Woodroffe, Pearson	24,600
14	17	(h)	Blackburn R	W 4-2	Constantine (2), Dunkley, Smith	22,177
15	24	(a)	Blackburn R	D 0-0		9,000
16	Dec 1	(a)	Bradford	W 3-2	Constantine (2), Smith	14,012
17	8	(h)	Bradford	W 6-0	Herd (2), Constantine (2), Wild, Dunkley	18,525
18	15	(a)	Burnley	L 0-1		10,000
19	22	(h)	Burnley	L 1-2	Constantine	21,000
20	25	(h)	Newcastle U	W 4-3	Dunkley, Constantine, Pearson, Smith	29,000
21	26	(a)	Newcastle U	D 1-1	Smith	54,495
22	29	(a)	Sheffield W	D 1-1	Wild	20,000
23	Jan 1	(h)	Huddersfield T	W 3-2	Herd (2), Constantine	25,490
24	12	(a)	Chesterfield	W 1-0	Herd	10,000
25	19	(h)	Chesterfield	W 1-0	Constantine	24,245
26	Feb 2	(a)	Barnsley	L 0-2		20,128
27	9	(a)	Everton	L 1-4	Constantine	40,000
28	16	(h)	Everton	L 1-3	Constantine	35,000
29	23	(h)	Bolton W	W 1-0	Constantine	25,000
30	Mar 9	(a)	Preston N E	L 1-3	Herd	12,000
31	13	(h)	Barnsley	L 2-3	Constantine (2)	6,662
32	16	(h)	Preston N E	W 3-0	Smith (2), Constantine	20,000
33	23	(h)	Leeds U	W 5-1	Constantine (2), Herd, Smith, Emptage	20,000
34	27	(a)	Bolton W	L 1-3	Gemmell	12,000
35	30	(a)	Leeds U	W 3-1	Herd (2), Constantine	10,000
36	Apr 6	(a)	Manchester U	W 4-1	Smith (4)	62,144
37	13	(h)	Manchester U	L 1-3	Smith	50,440
38	19	(h)	Sunderland	L 0-2		31,209
39	20	(a)	Sheffield U	W 3-2	Woodroffe, Constantine, Smith	40,000
40	22	(a)	Sunderland	L 0-4		27,650
41	27	(h)	Sheffield U	W 2-1	Dunkley, Smith	19,241
42	May 4	(a)	Huddersfield T	L 0-3		8,781

Football League North record:

P 42   W 20   D 4   L 18   F 78   A 75   Pts 44   Pos 10th

Appearances
Goals

FA Cup

3	Jan 5	(h)	Barrow	W 6-2
	10	(a)	Barrow	D 2-2
4	26	(a)	Bradford	W 3-1
	30	(h)	Bradford	L 2-8

Lancashire Senior Cup

2	Sep 5	(a)	Southport	L 2-3
	19	(h)	Southport	W 5-0
3	Apr 2	(a)	Oldham A	L 1-3
	10	(h)	Oldham A	W 4-1
SF	May 1	(a)	Manchester U	L 0-3

Swift	Clark	Sproston	Barkas	Walsh	Cardwell	McDowall	Dunkley	Herd	Constantine	Smith	Emptage	Williams	Eastwood	Woodroffe	Wild	Westwood	Bray	Fagan	Linaker	Hart	Walker	Taylor	Daniels	Robinson P.	Hodgson	Brown	Pimbley	Gemmell	Pearson	Murray	Moore	
1	3	2	4		6	7				10			5									11							9			1
1	3	2	4		6	7	8			10			5									11							9			2
1	3	2	4		6		8			10			5															9				3
	3	2	4							10			5				7	8					1		6	9		11				4
	2	8	3	4				10	9				5				7						1		6							5
1	2	3	4		5			8	9	10							6	7	11													6
1	3	2	4		6			9		10						11	7	8	5													7
1	3	2	4		6	7	8	9		10						11			5													8
	2	5		4	6	7	8	9		10					3								1									9
1	2	5	3	4	8	7			9	10							6												11			10
1	2	3	4		6		8	9		10			5	7															11			11
1	2	5	3	4	6	7	8	9		10																			11			12
1	2	3	4		6		8	9		10				7										5					11			13
1	2	3	4		6	7	8	9		10														5					11			14
1	2	3	4	5	6			9		10									8													15
1	2	3	4	5	6	7	8	9		10					11																	16
1	2	3	4	5	6	7	8	9		10					11																	17
1	2	3	4	5	6	7	8	9		10					11																	18
1	2	3	4	5	6	7		9		10																			11	8		19
1	2	3	4	5	6	7		9		10																			11	8		20
1	2	3	6	5		7			9	10							8												11	4		21
1	2	3	4	5	6	7	8	9		10					11																	22
1	2	6	5			7	8	9		10		3												4								23
1	2	3	4	5	6	7	8	9		10					11																	24
	2	3	4	5	6	7	8	9		10						11																25
1	2	3	4		6		8			10			5	7															11			26
1	2	3	4		6	7	8	9		10										5												27
1	2	5	3	4	6	7	8	9		10																			11			28
1	2	5	3	4	6		8	9		10				7															11			29
1	2	5	3	4	6	7	8	9		10						11																30
1	2		3	4	6	7	8	9		10						11	5															31
1		3	4		6	7	8	9		10	11	2	5																			32
1		3	4		6	7	8	9		10	11	2	5																			33
1		3	4		6	7	8			10	11	2	5													9						34
1		3		5	6	7	8	9		10	11	2																		4		35
1		3	4	5	6	7	8	9		10	11	2																				36
		3	4	5	6	7	8	9		10	11	2																				37
1		3	4	5	6			9		10	8	2	7																		11	38
1	2	3	4	5	6			9		10	8		7																		11	39
	2	3	4	5	6			9		10	8		7																		11	40
	2	3	4	5	6	7	8	9		10	11																					41
1	2				6	7	8				5	3										4							9			42
35	26	22	33	40	17	40	29	29	34	41	12	8	8	6	5	5	4	4	4	4	3	3	3	2	2	2	2	2	14	4	3	
		1	1			6	11	25	20	1			2	2			1												1	6		

Match 1: King (8)
Match 3: Bootle (7); Hilton (11)
Match 5: Campbell (11)
Match 9: King (11; 1 gl)
Match 15: Toseland (7); Laing (11)
Match 23: Cunliffe (11)
Match 25: Thorpe (1)
Match 26: McCormack (9)
Match 27: Pritchard (11)
Match 37: Roxburgh (1)
Match 40: Wilson (1)
Match 41: Roxburgh (1)
Match 42: Capel (10); Hope (11)

WITH THE RESERVES
LANCASHIRE COMBINATION LEAGUE

	P	W	D	L	F	A	Pts	Pos	Leading Goalscorer
1892-93	20	8	3	9	49	46	19	8th	
1893-94	16	3	3	10	18	69	9	9th	
1894-95	24	6	1	17	50	95	13	12th	
1895-96	26	10	4	12	54	53	24	9th	Tompkinson
1896-97	28	17	1	10	75	40	35	4th	
1897-98	30	15	4	11	67	68	34	7th	Hesham
1898-99	28	19	3	6	82	37	41	2nd	Patterson
1899-1900	30	18	4	8	63	49	40	5th	W.S.Smith
1900-01	34	22	4	8	108	60	48	3rd	Dartnell
1901-02	34	29	0	5	125	30	58	1st	Bevan
1902-03	34	23	7	4	84	36	53	2nd	Bevan
1903-04	34	21	7	6	90	37	49	3rd	Jones
1904-05	34	13	11	10	65	56	37	6th	Jones
1905-06	38	14	9	15	72	63	37	11th	Baldwin
1906-07	38	16	7	15	70	84	39	12th	Baldwin
1907-08	38	11	7	20	55	71	29	17th	Baldwin
1908-09	38	24	8	6	131	50	56	1st	Harrison
1909-10	38	17	9	12	65	57	43	6th	James
1910-11	38	11	9	18	49	76	31	18th	Bentley

CENTRAL LEAGUE

	P	W	D	L	F	A	Pts	Pos	Leading Goalscorer
1911-12	32	14	5	13	57	60	33	7th	Brooks
1912-13	38	12	12	14	46	54	36	12th	Kelly
1913-14	38	16	8	14	57	51	40	9th	A.Fairclough
1914-15	38	26	4	8	76	50	56	2nd	A.Fairclough
1919-20	42	17	5	20	65	77	39	14th	Lievesley, A.Fairclough
1920-21	42	12	18	12	62	57	42	11th	Johnson
1921-22	42	22	8	12	67	41	52	2nd	Crawshaw
1922-23	42	14	11	17	59	59	39	12th	Doran
1923-24	42	18	14	10	60	45	50	5th	Browell, Warner
1924-25	42	20	6	16	74	61	46	9th	Browell
1925-26	42	17	8	17	79	84	42	13th	Daniels
1926-27	42	12	4	26	82	112	28	20th	Gibson
1927-28	42	16	7	19	87	97	39	16th	Gorringe, Broadhurst
1928-29	42	13	8	21	96	98	34	21st	Tait
1929-30	42	11	6	23	73	110	28	22nd	Broadhurst
1930-31	42	21	11	10	98	71	53	2nd	Ridding
1931-32	42	24	5	13	106	66	53	4th	Syme
1932-33	42	21	7	14	81	72	49	4th	Syme
1933-34	42	22	5	15	82	66	49	7th	Wright
1934-35	42	16	10	16	81	76	42	12th	Owen
1935-36	42	9	5	28	62	108	23	22nd	McLeod
1936-37	42	9	12	21	62	93	30	19th	McLeod
1937-38	42	14	11	17	61	67	39	15th	Heale
1938-39	42	14	15	13	71	64	43	10th	McLeod, Heale
1939-40	2	1	1	0	4	1			
1945-46	40	14	11	15	72	92	39	12th	Dean
1946-47	42	20	10	12	81	66	50	4th	Jackson
1947-48	42	12	11	19	65	97	35	15th	Hart
1948-49	42	13	8	21	56	75	34	19th	McMorran
1949-50	42	16	9	17	50	56	41	11th	Jones
1950-51	42	19	7	16	77	64	45	8th	Cunliffe
1951-52	42	13	4	25	79	111	30	21st	Westcott
1952-53	42	11	7	24	51	78	29	22nd	Sowden
1953-54	42	18	9	15	76	67	45	9th	Davies
1954-55	42	18	7	17	78	82	43	11th	Davies
1955-56	42	14	4	24	72	91	32	18th	Faulkner

1956-57	42	20	10	12	90	68	50	4th	McAdams
1957-58	42	19	4	19	98	84	42	9th	Kirkman
1958-59	42	14	10	18	83	93	38	14th	Kirkman
1959-60	42	16	8	18	81	88	40	13th	Haydock
1960-61	42	15	7	20	69	91	37	15th	Pearson
1961-62	42	19	9	14	80	84	47	7th	Aimson
1962-63	42	12	8	22	58	102	32	18th	Aimson
1963-64	42	16	9	17	66	96	41	13th	Shawcross
1964-65	42	11	4	27	62	97	26	21st	Ogden
1965-66	42	13	10	19	57	77	36	17th	Jones
1966-67	42	20	2	20	75	87	42	10th	Jones
1967-68	42	19	12	11	66	54	50	6th	Jones
1968-69	42	24	3	15	66	49	51	5th	Bowles
1969-70	42	11	14	17	45	55	36	14th	Owen
1970-71	42	16	6	20	61	83	38	16th	Brennan
1971-72	42	15	12	15	59	56	42	10th	Johnson
1972-73	42	13	13	16	58	67	39	16th	Brennan
1973-74	42	19	10	13	78	52	48	6th	Daniels
1974-75	42	23	9	10	59	38	55	4th	Daniels
1975-76	42	11	16	15	47	54	38	16th	Lambert
1976-77	42	21	7	14	65	56	49	6th	Palmer
1977-78	42	27	8	7	92	40	62	1st	Palmer
1978-79	42	23	9	10	70	45	55	4th	Bennett
1979-80	42	15	15	12	62	56	45	10th	Lee
1980-81	42	17	18	7	74	51	52	5th	Deyna
1981-82	42	12	9	21	43	73	33	18th	Wiffill
1982-83*	30	13	6	11	54	40	32	6th	P.Sanderson, Wilson
1983-84†	30	15	5	10	60	36	50	4th	Simpson, Kinsey
1984-85	34	16	6	12	53	52	54	8th	Moulden
1985-86	34	16	8	10	58	40	56	5th	Moulden, Tolmie
1986-97	34	23	4	7	83	46	73	1st	D.Beckford

*Two Divisions formed with City in Division Two
†Promoted to Division One

Paul Moulden

Steve Kinsey

The £1-million roof of the Main Stand at Maine Road today.

Manchester City's Venues

TRACING the homes used by Manchester City and its forebears is to follow the club's story from its somewhat cluttered beginnings in the latter half of the last century through its rise to become one of the world's leading professional clubs.

St Mark's (West Gorton) used a rough field at Clowes Street for their first season of 1880-81; for 1881-2 they played at Kirksmanhulme Cricket Ground which was more centrally positioned in Gorton; they began their third season at Clemington Park — nicknamed 'Dobkey Common' — after the cricketers became worried about the state of their playing surface; in 1884-5, the re-named Gorton AFC played at Pink Bank Lane which they rented for £6 per annum; and in 1885-6 and, again the following season, they rented a pitch at Reddish Lane from the landlord of the Bull's Head Hotel.

All these early grounds offered problems, usually ones concerning the playing area, and the Reddish Lane venue was no different when Gorton beat West Gorton Athletic in the Manchester Cup in 1887, the pitch was in 'a very bad condition' according to one newspaper.

Attendances were becoming larger, too, so when the landlord of the Bull's Head Hotel increased the rent, Gorton AFC looked around again. The problem was solved when their captain, a Scot called K.McKenzie who worked as a moulder in Bennett's Timber Yard in Hyde Road, took a short cut to work from his Bennett Street home. Crossing some waste ground alongside some railway arches he realised that the wasteland was the ideal site for a football ground.

The Gorton committee's first thoughts might have been less enthusiastic when McKenzie showed them the site, for it was in a ghastly hinterland of industrial gloom, next to Galloway's Engineering Works and nothing more than a tip for cinders and refuse, and dreadfully uneven with a broken culvert running through it.

It was owned by the Manchester, Sheffield and Lincolnshire Railway Company and, undaunted, the Gorton committee agreed to pay £10 rent for seven months' use of the ground.

The change of venue had a fundamental effect on the club. The new location meant a change of name, to Ardwick FC, and the old church connections were left behind as Ardwick took up new ties with industry. Galloway's provided some of the material for the new ground, and a wealthy local brewer, Stephen Chester Thompson, paid for turf and a small grandstand in return for the sole right to sell alcohol on the Hyde Road ground.

Eventually, although the ground was sandwiched between the main railway line and some sidings, it housed around 40,000 people and boasted two stands. It became one of the more important football grounds and was visited by King Edward VII and by the Prime Minister, A.J.Balfour.

Yet its very short lease meant that Manchester City, as the club was now called, found it impossible to justify great expense on improving facilities and there was little shelter from the rain. That did not seem to daunt spectators, especially when really big games were staged there, but by the beginning of World War One it was increasingly obvious that a new home would have to be found.

During the war, Hyde Road was used for stabling horses and City carried on using it for their Lancashire Combination games. In March 1920, the ground had another royal visitor when King George V was one of a 40,000 crowd who saw City play Liverpool. The gates were closed half an hour before kick-off and again the need for a move was debated.

That matter was brought to a head less than eight months later when the main stand burned down and, although City carried on until the end of the 1922-3 season — having rejected a suggestion to move to Belle Vue because they wanted a bigger site — it was obvious that Hyde Road's days were numbered. Indeed, it was wanted for tramway improvements.

At the beginning of 1922-3, work began on building a new ground at Moss Side, on the site of an old brickworks. City paid £5,500 for the 16½-acres and the Manchester architect, Charles Swain, began to design the new stadium which Sir Robert McAlpine were eventually to build.

There was now the objective to build a stadium to rival Wembley, which had just been opened, and the first priority was, of course, the pitch. A steam navvy burrowed down eight feet and then cinders were laid down. On top of that was 3,000 tons of soil from nearby Wilbraham Road. Then followed some two-inch fibre pasture-land turf from Poynton, said to be 100 years old.

Prime Minister A.J.Balfour (second from left) views Hyde Road from the centre-circle during his visit in September 1900.

The architect aimed for safety and comfort and one innovation was to fill the terraces from the front via four large concrete tunnels. The only stand housed 10,000, the entire ground capacity was reputed to be between 80,000 and 90,000, and the cost was reported as anything between £100,000 and £200,000 depending on what source one wishes to believe.

Thereafter, Maine Road became the natural choice for FA Cup semi-finals. City's own Cup matches began to attract huge crowds and, on 3 March 1934, 84,569 saw the visit of Stoke and set an attendance record for any English club match outside the FA Cup Final.

Just before World War Two, the roof of the Main Stand was continued over the Platt Lane End, and during the war and immediately after it, City played host to Manchester United whose Old Trafford ground had been badly damaged by German bombs.

The general rise in football attendances saw some huge crowds at Maine Road and when the eventual Cup-winners, Derby, met Birmingham in a semi-final replay in 1946, the 80,407 crowd was the highest ever for a midweek match between two English clubs.

Manchester United attracted the highest attendance for any League match ever when 83,260 saw them play Arsenal at Maine Road in January 1948 and, 12 months later, 81,565 saw United beat non-League Yeovil 8-0 at Maine Road, another record. These huge receipts helped City improve the ground and some of the money was spent on the then innovative idea of installing seats on the Platts Lane terrace which then gave City more seats — 18,500 — than any other British club.

Floodlights were installed in 1953 — officially switched on for a game against Hearts in October that year — and in 1956, Maine Road became the first English ground to stage European Cup football when United beat RSC Anderlecht 10-0 under City's floodlights.

After City's 1956 FA Cup Final win, the club built a roof over the Kippax Street banking opposite the Main Stand, and four years later they replaced the Main Stand roof to allow a better view from the two middle blocks of seating.

The 1960s and 70s saw several alterations. New floodlights were installed in 1963-4 and a cantilever stand was built on the Scoreboard End. It became known as the North Stand, with 8,120 seats.

In 1982 the Main Stand roof was again replaced, at a cost of some £1 million which was paid for by the Supporters' Development Association. It was to have been part of a much grander redevelopment of the ground but finances did not allow its progression.

Today, Maine Road is still one of the truly great football venues. The Main Stand and North Stand would be better if they were joined into one, but that is technically impossible. The Platt Lane Stand curves away from the other end of the Main Stand, and the only area now solely for standing spectators is the Kippax Street side. The ground capacity is set at 52,600 because of safety regulations. The whole surrounds the largest football pitch in the English and Scottish Leagues and its undersoil heating has long been the envy of Manchester United.

City's club crest at Maine Road pictured before the start of the 1984-5 season.

264

Other Matches at Maine Road .....

City's ground has been used for many important matches, some of which are listed below.

2. 4.1928	Huddersfield Town v Sheffield United (FA Cup semi-final replay)
3. 2.1930	Charlton Athletic v Middlesbrough (FA Cup replay)
9.11.1932	Football League v Scottish League
16.11.1938	England v Northern Ireland
24. 8.1946	England v Scotland (Bolton Disaster Fund)
13.11.1946	England v Wales
23.12.1946	Lincoln City v Wrexham (FA Cup Replay)
12. 4.1947	Burnley v Liverpool (FA Cup semi-final)
13. 1.1948	Stockport County v Shrewsbury Town (FA Cup replay)
19.12.1949	Crewe Alexander v Oldham Athletic (FA Cup Replay)
25. 3.1950	Liverpool v Everton (FA Cup Semi-Final)
10. 3.1951	Birmingham City v Blackpool (FA Cup semi-final)
21. 3.1953	Bolton Wanderers v Everton (FA Cup semi-final)
10. 2.1954	Football League v League of Ireland
27. 3.1954	Sheffield Wednesday v Preston NE (FA Cup semi-final)
7. 2.1955	Aston Villa v Doncaster Rovers (FA Cup second replay)
19.10.1955	England 'B' v Yugoslavia 'B'
14. 1.1957	Huddersfield Town v Sheffield United (FA Cup replay)
22. 3.1958	Blackburn Rovers v Bolton Wanderers (FA Cup semi-final)
21. 9.1960	England Under-23 v Denmark XI
8.12.1966	Morecambe v York City (FA Cup tie)
29. 4.1967	Enfield v Skelmersdale (FA Amateur Cup Final replay)
18. 4.1968	West Bromwich Albion v Liverpool (FA Cup replay)

16. 2.1972	Cardiff City v Sunderland (FA Cup replay)
12.10.1973	England v Northern Ireland (Amateur International)
20. 3.1974	Football League v Scottish League
9. 4.1975	Fulham v Birmingham City (FA Cup replay)
29.11.1976	Northwich Victoria v Rochdale
29. 1.1977	Northwich Victoria v Oldham Athletic (FA Cup tie)
23. 4.1977	Liverpool v Everton (FA Cup semi-final)
27. 4.1977	Liverpool v Everton (FA Cup semi-final replay)
8. 3.1978	England Under-21 v Italy Under-21
2. 5.1978	England Under-21 v Yugoslavia Under-21
2.10.1978	Leeds United v West Bromwich Albion (League Cup replay)
16. 1.1979	Altrincham v Tottenham Hotspur (FA Cup tie)
31. 3.1979	Manchester United v Liverpool (FA Cup semi-final)
28. 4.1982	England Under-21 v Scotland Under-21
28. 3.1984	Everton v Liverpool (Milk Cup Final replay)
18. 4.1984	England Under-21 v Italy Under-21
17. 4.1985	Manchester United v Liverpool (FA Cup semi-final replay)
20.11.1985	Morecambe v York City (FA Cup replay)

The following three games were played at Hyde Road

6.11.1897	Football League v Irish League
14.10.1905	Football League v Irish League
25. 3.1906	Newcastle United v Sheffield Wednesday (FA Cup semi-final)

Manchester United protest as Tommy Browell scores for City in the 1926 FA Cup semi-final at Sheffield.

Manchester City 2   Newton Heath 5

This game was significant on two counts. It was the first Football League meeting between Manchester's two great clubs — Newton Heath would be re-formed as Manchester United in 1902 — and it was the day Billy Meredith was introduced to the Hyde Road public.

At the time, of course, no-one could know the impact Meredith would have on the City. He made his debut the previous week, at Newcastle, where City had lost 5-4 to a last-minute goal. This was his first home game.

Newton Heath, relegated from the First Division the previous season, were making a determined effort to return at the first attempt. On a dismal Manchester day, the Heathens gave City little chance of a look-in.

Once the Newton Heath inside-left, Smith, had scored twice in the first 13 minutes, City would be left with an uphill battle. They had a good spell late in the first-half, but this was interrupted by half-time.

Having lost a full-back early in the second-half, City conceded goals to Clarkin and Smith (2), thus giving Newton Heath a 5-0 lead. Late goals by Meredith and Sharples made the scoreline a little more respectable.

Manchester City: Hutchinson; H.Smith, Walker, Mann, Nash, Dyer, Meredith, Finnerhan, Rowan, Sharples, Milarvie.
Newton Heath: Douglas; McCartney, F.Erentz, Perrins, McNaught, Davidson, Clarkin, Donaldson, Dow, R.Smith, Peters.

Attendance: 14,000   *Referee: Mr Lewis (Blackburn)*

A youthful-looking Meredith on the threshold of a great career.

266

City team of the late 1890s. Billy Meredith is on the extreme left of the front row. Jimmy Ross stands to Meredith's left and 'Stockport' Smith is the player sitting next to Meredith.

Match to Remember 2   9 September 1899

Manchester City 4   Derby County 0

CITY'S first-ever League Division One game was staged in a new-look Hyde Road stadium — a new grandstand helped raise capacity to 28,000 — and proved an outstanding success for the City forwards, in particular the athletic winger, Billy Meredith, and his veteran partner, Jimmy Ross.

From the start City attacked, and Derby goalkeeper Fryer twice saved magnificently. City had to wait half an hour for the first goal. Then Fred Williams centred towards Billy Gillespie. The big cenre-forward typically won the ball from a scrimmage in front of goal and pushed it inside the near post. Before half-time, Ross had added a second with a fine low shot.

After the break City again had the better of play, exploiting Derby's weakness at half-back. Derby's legendary Steve Bloomer was completely overshadowed by the work of City's right wing. Ross fed Meredith for the third goal.

The fourth was vintage Meredith. Years later, in the *Topical Times*, he described it thus: "A free-kick had been given against us and I was quite near my own goal when I fastened on to the ball. Carrying it at my toes I galloped down the field, the whole of the Derby team hot upon my heels. Keeping the lead the whole length of the field, I found myself with only Fryer to beat. Giving a mighty kick, I let fly at the goal and the 'keeper only just managed to touch the ball before it curled itself into the corner of the net, the force sufficient to send Fryer spinning. I rather like that goal, thinking it above average, and I can remember the chase I led the field that day."

The majority of the 22,000 crowd liked it too. It was a superb effort and brought a roar of excitement. And it showed that City would feel at home in the First Division.

Manchester City: C.Williams; Read, Jones, Moffatt, Smith, Holmes, Meredith, Ross, Gillespie, F.Williams, Dougal.
Derby County: Fryer; Methven, Staley, Cox, Paterson, May, Bradbury, Bloomer, Crump, Wombwell, McQueen.

Attendance: 22,000   *Referee: T.Armitt (Leek)*

Manchester City 1   Bolton Wanderers 0

CITY'S first FA Cup Final ended triumphantly. They were worthy winners against Second Division Bolton Wanderers, but a disputed goal from Billy Meredith was all they had to show for 90 minutes' endeavour.

It was fitting the goal should be Meredith's. The famous Welsh Wizard had recently been voted the most popular player in the country by readers of *The Umpire* and railway posters advertising excursions to the game portrayed Meredith scoring the winning goal in a similar fashion to what actually occurred.

The goal came after 20 minutes. Meredith ran on to Livingstone's pass, clear of the Bolton defence, steadied himself and banged the ball well away from goalkeeper Davies. The Bolton contingent would claim offside, the City fans (and Meredith in particular) would fervently deny it. Had Gillespie or Turnbull converted other chances it might not have mattered so much. Had White equalised for Bolton in the second-half, when presented with an empty net, then disputes about the Meredith goal might have been watered down. Instead it dominated post-match discussion.

One City fan was so elated at seeing Meredith's goal that he attempted to invade the pitch and embrace the hero. At length five policemen led him away.

Another slightly disruptive incident occurred in the City dressing-room before the match. Long-serving wing-half 'Doc' Holmes threw his boots through a window, disappointed at being left out of the side after playing in the early rounds. His place was taken by the amateur Sam Ashworth.

The Cup was presented to Meredith, the City captain, by Lord Alfred Lyttelton, and Meredith made a short speech to the 60,000-plus crowd. Although this was the biggest crowd City had ever played in front of, it was below the expected crowd size for a Crystal Palace Final. The main reason was the need for fans to travel from the north. As the *Daily Graphic* put it: "It would scarcely seem like a Cup tie day now if half the people there were not speaking in a provincial dialect. On Saturday it seemed as though three-fourths of the people were speaking in it, and the remaining fourth were ineffectually trying to imitate them."

Manchester City: Hillman; McMahon, Burgess, Frost, Hynds, Ashworth, Meredith, Livingstone, Gillespie, Turnbull, Booth.
Bolton Wanderers: Davies; Brown, Struthers, Clifford, Greenhalgh, Freebairn, Stokes, Marsh, Yenson, White, Taylor.

Attendance: 61,374   *Referee: A.J.Barker (Hanley)*

Meredith bursts down the wing, outstripping two Bolton defenders in the 1904 FA Cup Final.

Twelve months after the Hyde Road heatwave, City met Woolwich Arsenal at Plumstead. This picture shows City on the defensive.

Match to Remember 4   1 September 1906

Manchester City 1   Woolwich Arsenal 4

Harry Newbold was one of the most successful secretary-managers of the 1890s and 1900s, but his first game in charge of Manchester City went badly wrong. The temperature was 90 degrees in the shade, and City players fell like ninepins in the unbearable heat.

For the opening match of the 1906-7 season — City's first after the mass suspension — City fielded virtually a new team. One by one they collapsed under the strain.

In the 30th minute, Kyle scored for Arsenal. Two minutes later City lost Irvine Thornley, who fell 'prostrate and very ill' with sunstroke. Thornley was finished for the game. He lay flat out on his back for the rest of the time.

A crowd of 18,000 saw Coleman give Arsenal a 2-0 lead. Then City lost Jimmy Conlin, despite the little winger's precaution of playing with a handkerchief over his head. At half-time it was clear that Grieve could not continue, leaving City three short.

What a problem for Harry Newbold. Only eight fit men, a new-look team, no substitutes allowed, and no sign of the heat lessening. Not a situation covered by the coaching manuals.

City's brave tactics saw them start the second-half with three forwards, three half-backs, a full-back and a goalkeeper. As City had lost three forwards this meant pushing a defender up front.

Conlin returned, Dorsett scored for City, but soon afterwards Dorsett collapsed. He had literally played himself out. City were back to eight men.

Referee A.J.Barker (Hanley) decided not to abandon the game, Arsenal scored two more, then City lost Tom Kelso...and so City were seven.

Buchan was the next to go. The Scots were finding it all too much...and then there were six.

The thin blue line held out and City's officials were left with the task of motivating the players for a Monday game at Everton. But City lost that one too...9-1.

Manchester City; Davies; Christie, Kelso, Steele, Buchan, Dorsett, Stewart, Thornley, Grieve, Jones, Conlin.
Woolwich Arsenal: Ashcroft; Cross, Sharp, Bigden, Sands, MacEachrane, Garbutt, Coleman, Kyle, Satterthwaite, Neave.

Attendance: 18,000   *Referee: A.J.Barker (Hanley)*

Manchester City 2   Sheffield United 1

THE opening of the spectacular Maine Road stadium — built at a cost of £100,000 — coincided with the visit of Sheffield United. City finally left behind the subterranean passages and confined surroundings of Hyde Road and set up home among huge, lofty stands, tiers of terracing and a beautiful playing pitch.

The City players were led on to the field by captain Max Woosnam, while the band played 'Ours is a nice house, ours is'. Councillor Cundiffe, the Lord Mayor, was introduced to the players and then kicked off, although in accordance with Football League rules the ball was actually returned to the centre for City's Tom Johnson to do the job properly.

Eli Fletcher and Sam Cookson returned to the City line-up, the former after an absence of almost a year, while City included new signing Alec Donaldson, the ex-Bolton winger. In the goalless first half, Johnson and Barnes brought good saves from goalkeeper Gough.

In the second half, with the wind behind them, City put on more pressure. After 68 minutes Donaldson centred and Horace Barnes scored the first goal at Maine Road. Three minutes later Tom Johnson made it 2-0 after Gough had saved his first attempt.

Shortly afterwards Frank Roberts became the first player to miss a penalty on the new ground, shooting straight at the goalkeeper. The Sheffield United players were compelled to stay ten yards from the ball — a change in law had introduced the penalty-arc — whereas the previous season United had instigated a clever tactic of arranging themselves in a solid phalanx on the penalty-area edge, thus restricting the penalty-taker's run-up to six yards.

With two minutes to play, Sheffield United, down to ten men, pulled back a goal through a Harry Johnson header.

Manchester City: Mitchell; Cookson, Fletcher, Hamill, Woosnam, Pringle, Donaldson, Roberts, T.Johnson, Barnes, Murphy.
Sheffield United: Gough; Cook, Milton, Pantling, Waugh, Green, Mercer, Sampy, H.Johnson, Gillespie, Tunstall.

Attendance: 56,993   *Referee: J.Rowcroft (Bolton)*

Cllr W.Cundiffe, Lord Mayor of Manchester, is introduced to the City players by Max Woosnam before the opening game at Maine Road. Left to right: L.W.Furniss, Woosnam, Johnson, Barnes, Cllr Cundiffe, Pringle, Roberts, Donaldson (shaking Hands), Cookson, Fletcher, Murphy.

Jimmy McMullan prompted City's many attacks as well as making a fine job of marking Bradford's Patterson out of the game.

Tom Johnson scored a hat-trick but it was not enough to lift City into Division One.

Match to Remember 6   7 May 1927

Manchester City 8   Bradford City 0

A HUGE crowd converged on Maine Road for the final League match of the 1926-7 season, and they experienced an afternoon of excitement and joy as City tried their utmost to clinch promotion to the First Division. In the end, however, there was only disappointment. Promotion rivals Portsmouth were scoring heavily against Preston and the outcome of a long season was settled on goal average. City's (1.7705) was marginally worse than Portsmouth's (1.7755). One more goal would have sent City up.

City scored three in the first half — Bell, Johnson and Hicks — and Blues fans were pleased to hear the news that Preston had taken the lead against Portsmouth in a game which had kicked off 15 minutes later.

In the second half City scored five more — Broadhurst, Roberts Johnson, Johnson again (from a penalty) and finally from Broadhurst in the last minute. At the final whistle the fans swarmed on to the field and rejoiced. They recognised that Portsmouth needed to score five to oust City from the second promotion spot....at least those with good arithmetic skills did.

But Portsmouth scored five and their hero, four-goal Willie Haines, was adulated with choruses of 'Farmer's Boy' and carried shoulder-high from Fratton Park. Moss Side was stunned into gloomy silence. City had won 8-0 but it had not been enough. The tightest Second Division promotion race ever had gone against them, and City would have to wait another season before they could rejoin the elite.

Manchester City: Gray; Cookson, McCloy, Pringle, Cowan, McMullan, Bell, Roberts, Broadhurst, Johnson, Hicks.
Bradford City: Boot; Russell, Watson, Knox, Bancroft, Poole, McMillan, Patterson, Alcock, Battes, Wright.

Attendance: 50,000   *Referee: A.Platts (Castleford)*

Derby County 2   Manchester City 3

THE 1933 semi-final, played at Huddersfield, started with Derby hot favourites to reach Wembley. City had to withstand a difficult early period — both Bowers and Fabian missed open goals — before asserting themselves as an attacking force.

The crucial first goal came two minutes before half-time. Eric Brook went past full-back Cooper, dashed down his left-wing and crossed on the run. Right-winger Ernie Toseland sped in to head past Kirby.

After half-time City skipper Jimmy McMullan became more prominent, scheming craftily, inspiring subtly. McMullan had switched from left-half to inside-left to retain his place in the City side, and this was to be his last season.

Against Derby, McMullan made an impact in the 49th minute, starting the move which led to City's second goal. His pass found Brook, who held the ball then lobbed it across for Fred Tilson to head in.

McMullan himself scored the third, wriggling past two defenders and the goalkeeper before shooting City into a 3-0 lead in the 70th minute.

In the next minute Fabian caught Len Langford off his line and Derby had pulled a goal back. This gave the Rams new heart and Crooks scored their second with three minutes to play. But City held on, won a memorable 3-2 victory, and afterwards learned they would be facing Everton in the Cup Final. However, Jimmy McMullan's dream of ending his career with a Cup winners' medal came unstuck at Wembley. Dixie Dean's Everton won 3-0 and McMullan was reduced to tears, a sharp contrast to the elation at Huddersfield six weeks previously.

Derby County: Kirby; Cooper, Collin, Nicholas, Barker, Keen, Crooks, Fabian, Bowers, Ramage, Duncan.
Manchester City: Langford; Cann, Dale, Busby, Cowan, Bray, Toseland, Herd, Tilson, McMullan, Brook.

Attendance: 51,961   *Referee: J.W.Lucas (London)*

Fred Tilson is foiled by Derby goalkeeper Jack Kirby. The defender is George Collin.

Young Frank Swift fainted after City had won the Cup.

Match to Remember 8   28 April 1934

Manchester City 2   Portsmouth 1

TWO late goals from Fred Tilson swung the game City's way after Portsmouth had taken a first-half lead against the run of play. For only the fifth time in 59 FA Cup Finals the team scoring first failed to win.

The game was action-packed from the start. The Portsmouth goalkeeper, Gilfillan, just beat Tilson to the ball to prevent City taking a first-minute lead. At the other end, Dale cleared from the line.

City lost Alec Herd for a few minutes, injured in a collision with Mackie, before Brook shot wide from a free-kick and Portsmouth threatened through Smith and Rutherford. It was Rutherford who put Pompey ahead in the 28th minute. His long, low shot eluded Frank Swift's dive, the goalkeeper touching the ball on its way. During the half-time interval, with Portsmouth leading 1-0, Swift conceded that he might have saved the goal had he been wearing gloves. "Tha don't need to worry," Tilson told him. "I'll plonk in two in next 'arf."

Tilson did just that. After Rutherford had missed the chance of the match, Herd hit a post and Portsmouth lost Allen with an injury, Tilson had his chance in the 75th minute. After a snaking run he flicked the ball past the advancing Gilfillan to provide City with an equaliser. With three minutes to play Brook sent Tilson clear and the centre-forward decisively swept the ball into the net. City had the lead for the first time in the game.

The minutes ticked away, the tension rose. On hearing the final whistle 19-year-old goalkeeper Frank Swift turned to collect his cap and gloves....and fainted. Afterwards an embarrassed Swift said, "Fancy a great strapping fellow like me fainting in front of all those people and the King."

Eric Brook had a much simpler message. After Sam Cowan had collected the Cup from the King, and the players were relaxing in the dressing-room, Brook stared at his medal and gave a lengthy quote to a reporter. "Champion," said Brook, with massive understatement. City were Cup winners for the first time in 30 years.

Manchester City: Swift; Barnett, Dale, Busby, Cowan, Bray, Toseland, Marshall, Tilson, Herd, Brook.
Portsmouth: Gilfillan; Mackie, W.Smith, Nichol, Allen, Thackeray, Worrall, J.Smith, Weddle, Easson, Rutherford.

Attendance: 93,258   *Referee: S.F.Rouse (Herts)*

273

Manchester City 4   Sheffield Wednesday 1

AFTER the final whistle thousands spilled over the barriers, poured across the pitch, sang 'Auld Lang Syne' and 'God Save the King', and shouted and cheered until captain Sam Barkas and chairman Bob Smith appeared. For the first time in their history City were Champions of the First Division.

It was such a contrast to when the two teams had met earlier in the season. Then, Sheffield Wednesday had thrashed City 5-1 at Hillsborough, and City were well in the lower half of the division. Now, Wednesday were seeking to avoid relegation — unsuccessfully in the end — while City were unbeaten in 20 League games.

City's start was typically tentative, but they took the lead in the 19th minute with a goal worthy of League Champions. Percival passed to Doherty who set up Brook. The winger's shot was a thunderbolt from a difficult angle. "Not so much a goal as a piece of forked lightning," wrote one reporter. It is doubtful Brook ever hit the ball harder.

Five minutes later Peter Doherty sent in Tilson for City's second. Then, on 31 minutes, came a goal from Doherty which brought the house down. Wrote Doherty in his autobiography *Spotlight on Football*: "It all started from one of Frank Swift's lofty clearances. I gained possession in just about the centre of the field, and Tilson and I went through the Wednesday defence with a rapid interchange of passes which carried us over 40 yards, and well into the Wednesday penalty area. It was a precision movement, a slick passing shuttle which the Sheffield defenders were powerless to intercept, and the ball finally came to rest in the corner of the net, after Tilson had made the final pass and I had whipped it through. It was a fine goal, a product of splendid team work, and the crowd rose to us as we left the field at half-time."

That was nothing compared to the reception at the end. Rimmer had scored for Wednesday, but Brook's last-minute goal, making it 4-1, put the crowd in just the right mood for the celebrations.

Manchester City: Swift; Clark, Barkas, Percival, Marshall, Bray, Toseland, Herd, Tilson, Doherty, Brook.
Sheffield Wednesday: Smith; Ashley, Catlin, Grosvenor, Hanford, Burrows, Luke, Robinson, Dewar, Drury, Rimmer.

Attendance: 55,000   *Referee: R.W.Blake (Middlesbrough)*

Peter Doherty (left) scored a goal which brought the house down. Eric Brook (right) netted twice, his first effort coming from a rocket of a shot.

Eric Westwood eventually settled the issue with a goal in the replay at Maine Road.

Andy Black scored twice in the first game.

Match to Remember 10   25 January 1947

Bolton Wanderers 3   Manchester City 3

CITY were chasing promotion to the First Division when they were drawn against Bolton in the fourth round of the FA Cup, and their trip to Burnden Park provided an ideal test against First Division opponents. The outcome was one of the most exciting Cup ties anyone could wish to see. Two quick goals for Bolton, a three-goal second-half rally by City, and then a Bolton equaliser in the dying minutes of the game.

Wrigglesworth scored for Bolton before a City player had touched the ball. (Reports vary on the timing of the goal but it was somewhere between 15 and 30 seconds). In the ninth minute a glorious header from Nat Lofthouse gave Bolton a two-goal lead.

City were outplayed in the first half, but their second-half fight-back amazed everyone in the ground. It was started with a goal by Andy Black in the 56th minute, the first of three goals in a 13-minute spell. Black also scored the second, with Tommy Capel adding the third.

Bolton had to wait until seven minutes from the end for their equaliser. When the ball rebounded from a post Malcolm Barrass followed up to make the score 3-3, shooting into an empty net.

Although there was a reasonably large crowd at Burnden Park there was space for 16,000 more. However, it was less than a year since the disaster on the same ground. Before a Cup tie with Stoke, 33 people were killed and over 400 injured when crush barriers collapsed.

On the Wednesday after the 3-3 draw at Burnden Park, City and Bolton met again, at Maine Road. A fourth-minute goal by Eric Westwood was sufficient to give City a place in the fifth round but Second Division opponents, Birmingham, proved five goals too strong.

Bolton Wanderers: Hanson; Banks, Hubbick, Gillies, Hamlett, Forrest, Woodward, Moir, Lofthouse, Barrass, Wrigglesworth.
Manchester City: Swift; Williams, Barkas, Fagan, McDowall, Emptage, Dunkley, Smith, Black, Capel, Westwood.

Attendance: 41,286   *Referee: L.Brown (London)*

275

Manchester City 2 West Ham United 0

MANCHESTER City took revenge over West Ham — they had lost at Upton Park the previous October — with a victory which virtually assured the Second Division Championship would come to Maine Road.

It was not an easy ground to play on, dry and bumpy, with a cross-wind making ball control difficult. On such grounds are promotion issues settled. Although the football never reached great heights, City dominated the game with a workmanlike performance and deserved the vital points.

City led 1-0 at the interval — a penalty converted by centre-half Les McDowall after Andy Black had been fouled. Not until the second half, though, did City's attack come into its own. The season's goalscoring heroes were the inside trio of Alec Herd, Andy Black and George Smith, and it was the latter who settled West Ham's fate 15 minutes from time. Smith collected a long pass from Black, dribbled into the penalty area and hit a terrific left-foot shot past Ernie Gregory. 'A picture goal' they would have called it in those days.

Although it was late-May, City's season still had three weeks to run, an extension caused by the bad winter. City lost the next two matches, but a 5-1 win against Newport County ended the season in fine style, George Smith scoring all five goals. And City had won their fifth Second Division Championship, aided by a 22-match unbeaten run which took City into the closing stages of the season.

Manchester City: Thurlow; Sproston, Barkas, Fagan, McDowall, Emptage, Dunkley, Herd, Black, Smith, Westwood.
West Ham United: Gregory; Corbett, Devlin, Cater, Walker, Small, Woodgate, Parsons, Travis, Wood, Bainbridge.

Attendance: 31,980   *Referee: G.S.Blackhall (Wednesbury)*

City's 1946-7 line-up. Back row (left to right): Mr A.Alexander (vice-chairman), L.Barnett (trainer), J.Percival, B.Sproston, F.V.Swift, Mr H.Smith (chairman), E.Westwood, L.J.McDowall, A.T.Emptage, Mr F.Jolly (director). Front row: M.E.F.Dunkley, A.Herd, A.Black, G.R.Smith, J.G.Hope, E.Eastwood.

Birmingham City 1   Manchester City 3

AFTER defeat by Newcastle in the 1955 Cup Final, City captain Roy Paul vowed that he would lead his team back to Wembley the following year and this time win the Cup. In the 1930s Sam Cowan had made the same vow, with the same outcome — runners-up one year, winners the next.

The star of the Final was Don Revie, who came in as a late replacement for Billy Spurdle. There was no place for the unlucky Johnny Hart, who had missed the previous year's Final with a broken leg.

A third-minute goal gave City a dream start. Revie swept a 43-yard pass out to the left wing and ran on to Roy Clarke's return pass, cleverly flicking the ball between his legs towards Joe Hayes. Hayes shot left-footed past Merrick's left hand. But Kinsey's equaliser, in the 15th minute, meant the teams were level at half-time, one goal each.

Midway through the second half City scored two goals in two minutes. Interpassing between Revie, Johnstone and Barnes gave Dyson a clear run on goal. He took his chance well and City had a lead they would not lose. Bobby Johnstone added the third, assisted by Dyson.

Fifteen minutes from time Bert Trautmann dived to save at Murphy's feet and was caught in the neck by the Birmingham player's knee. After receiving lengthy treatment the goalkeeper continued, courageously and obviously in great pain. Only after the match was it discovered that he had played the closing minutes with a broken neck. He would miss the next seven months and was unavailable to play for his native Germany.

Wearing City's unusual maroon-and-white-striped shirt, Roy Paul strode up the steps to the Royal Box to become the first Welshman to collect the Cup for 29 years. It was a victory for the Revie plan, the tactic whereby the centre-forward lies deep to feed the forwards, borrowed from the Hungarians but much criticised when City lost to Newcastle the previous year.

Birmingham City: Merrick; Hall, Green, Newman, Smith, Boyd, Astall, Kinsey, Brown, Murphy, Govan.
Manchester City: Trautmann; Leivers, Little, Barnes, Ewing, Paul, Johnstone, Hayes, Revie, Dyson, Clarke.

Attendance: 100,000   *Referee: A.Bond (London)*

Left: The collision in which Trautmann broke his neck. Right: The City goalkeeper receives treatment.

Manchester City 4   Newcastle United 5

THE third-round replay between City, the Cup holders, and Newcastle United, the most successful team of the 1950s, promised to be the game of the year and more than lived up to expectations. A sticky pitch favouring forwards, a large crowd and the smell of competition in the air after a thrilling 1-1 draw at Newcastle the previous Saturday. Real ingredients for Cup tie drama.

After 30 minutes, though, there was no reflection of the tension to come, for City led 3-0 and looked to be coasting into the fourth round. An own-goal by Bob Stokoe had started the scoring, then Bobby Johnstone had headed in a cross from Roy Clarke before Paddy Fagan latched on to Billy McAdams' through-ball to make it three. City's three-goal lead looked unassailable.

After half-time there was more evidence of the Cup-tie spirit which had brought the trophy to Newcastle three years in the past six. When Curry was sent sprawling in the penalty area Casey sent the penalty past Trautmann.

Newcastle were without their famous centre-forward, Jackie Milburn, but his deputy, part-timer Alex Tait, scored with 15 minutes to play, bringing United right back into the game. Four minutes remained when Curry headed the equaliser to send the game into extra-time.

City still had command. Good work by Billy McAdams and Jackie Dyson led to a goal by Bobby Johnstone, but Len White intercepted Roy Little's back pass to square the game again. Two minutes remained when White scored Newcastle's winner, though there was still time for Dyson to hit a post in City's last attack.

It was City's first defeat in ten Cup games and must have suggested Newcastle were a good bet to win the trophy. The next round, however, they went out to Third Division Millwall.

Manchester City: Trautmann; Leivers, Little, Barnes, Ewing, Paul, Fagan, McAdams, Johnstone, Dyson, Clarke.
Newcastle United: Simpson; Keith, Batty, Scoular, Stokoe, Casey, White, Davies, Tait, Curry, Mitchell.

Attendance: 46,988   *Referee: F.B.Coultas (Hull)*

Bill McAdams featured in the build-up to both of Bobby Johnstone's goals.

278

Denis Law's remarkable six-goal haul was in vain.

Match to Remember 14   28 January 1961

Luton Town 2   Manchester City 6
(abandoned after 69 minutes)

LIKE quicksilver on a quagmire, Denis Law produced a display of a lifetime to score six goals in a fourth-round FA Cup tie, only for referee Kenny Tuck to abandon the game with 21 minutes to play. A few days later Luton comfortably won the re-arranged game 3-1, leaving Law with the legacy of one of football's strangest records.

On the Saturday, on an incredibly wet and muddy pitch, Luton took a two-goal lead in the opening 18 minutes. Alec Ashworth scored both goals.

Before half-time, however, Law had completed his first hat-trick, shooting the first and heading the next two from close range.

Within 25 minutes of the second-half Law had collected a second hat-trick. The first was a perfectly-timed header, the second the merest of touches to divert a shot from Joe Hayes (a goal which was initially credited to Hayes) and the third when he strode on to a brilliant George Hannah pass in the 67th minute.

Six goals had come in 48 minutes but the conditions were worsening and referee Tuck decided that the pitch was now impossible for football, a decision which did not surprise most of the crowd. City manager Les McDowell was angry, of course, as his team looked set for the fifth round. Denis Law was left contemplating that his amazing performance had been to no avail.

A few days later Ashworth scored two more for Luton in an afternoon game and City slumped to a 3-1 defeat. No prizes for guessing who scored City's goal. Yes, it was Denis Law again.

Luton Town: Standen; McNally, Bramwell, Pacey, Groves, McGuffie, Noake, Ashworth, Turner, Brown, Fleming.
Manchester City: Trautmann; Leivers, Betts, Barnes, Plenderleith, Shawcross, Barlow, Hannah, Baker, Law, Hayes.

Attendance: 23,727   *Referee: K.R.Tuck (Chesterfield)*

City in 1967-8. Back row (left to right): Book, Horne, Heslop, Ogley, Dowd, Oakes, Pardoe, Doyle. Front row: Summerbee, Connor, Bell, Crossan, Jones, Young, Coleman.

Match to Remember 15   11 May 1968

Newcastle United 3   Manchester City 4

JUST two seasons after Joe Mercer and Malcolm Allison had steered City back into the First Division, the team were on the verge of winning the Championship. Top of the table on goal average, all that stood between City and the title was a difficult away game at Newcastle United, known for their strong home record. Nearest rivals Manchester United faced Sunderland at home on the same day — the last of the season.

City won the Championship in the most exciting manner possible. An end-to-end seven-goal game at Newcastle secured the title. The fact that Manchester United lost at home to Sunderland was irrelevant. City had won the League rather than United losing it. The margin was two points.

Mike Summerbee put City ahead that dramatic afternoon, and Bryan 'Pop' Robson equalised a minute later. After 30 minutes Neil Young scored for City, but once again Newcastle equalised swiftly, through Jackie Sinclair. At half-time the scores were level.

Further goals, from Young and Francis Lee, put City in front again, giving them the cushion of a two-goal lead. Five minutes from time John McNamee, the Newcastle centre-half, headed in a corner, and City were forced to endure a tense ending before they knew the League was theirs.

As when they first won the Championship, in 1937, City had done it in style. Mercer and Allison had attracted much media attention with their different approaches, and around £208,000 had been spent on players — big-money signings like Bell, Lee and Summerbee, and small-money signings like Tony Book, George Heslop and Tony Coleman. The value of those signings and the behind-the-scenes work was realised that afternoon at Newcastle.

Newcastle United: McFaul; Craig, Clark, Moncur, McNamee, Iley, Sinclair, Scott, Davies, B.Robson, T.Robson.
Manchester City: Mulhearn; Book, Pardoe, Doyle, Heslop, Oakes, Lee, Bell, Summerbee, Young, Coleman.

Attendance: 46,300   *Referee: R.B.Kirkpatrick (Lewiston)*

280

Neil Young cracks home his Wembley winner.

Match to Remember 16   26 April 1969

Leicester City 0   Manchester City 1

BACK at Wembley for an FA Cup Final, after an absence of 13 years, City's famous forwards were expected to annihilate a team almost certain of relegation to the Second Division. Lowly Leicester played above themselves and City's goal had some narrow escapes. In the end City were worthy winners and Leicester lost their third Final in a decade.

The game's only goal came in the 23rd minute. Mike Summerbee went down the right wing, avoided Nish and Woollett, and cut back the ball from the dead-ball line. Neil Young hit it with the outside of his famous left foot, beating Shilton at his right hand.

Leicester had their chances. Full-back Rodrigues came close at the far post, Harry Dowd saved a long-range shot from £150,000 Clarke, and Lochhead shot over from a very good position.

City had enough in reserve to hold out until the final whistle. Tony Book, joint Footballer of the Year, proudly received the Cup — the fourth City player to do so. And on three of their winning occasions City had been clad in a change strip, this time the 'continental' red-and-black striped shirts and black shorts.

Leicester, meanwhile, were on their way to the unenviable 'double' of Cup runners-up and relegation — something which had not occurred since 1926. The team on that occasion were Manchester City.

Leicester City: Shilton; Rodrigues, Nish, Roberts, Woollett, Cross, Fern, Gibson, Lochhead, Clarke, Glover(Manley).
Manchester City: Dowd; Book, Pardoe, Doyle, Booth, Oakes, Summerbee, Bell, Lee, Young, Coleman. Sub. Connor.

Attendance: 100,000   *Referee: G.McCabe (Sheffield)*

City playing staff pictured with the Football League Cup and the European Cup-winners Cup in 1970.

Match to Remember 17   7 March 1970

Manchester City 2   West Bromwich Albion 1

JUST three days after playing an important European Cup-winners' Cup tie in sunny Portugal, City tackled the snow and mud of Wembley to register their first League Cup Final win. On what Joe Mercer described as "a pig of a pitch" City conceded an early goal and fought their way through to a thrilling victory in extra-time.

West Brom's goal came in the sixth minute. Ray Wilson swung over a centre and Jeff Astle was left to head in. City could not even blame the pitch, which had been churned up by the recent Horse of the Year Show.

The early goal acted more as a spur to City than West Brom. Twin centre-halves, Tommy Booth and George Heslop, tightened their grip on the Albion forwards, and Alan Oakes and Mike Doyle began to build from midfield. But the equaliser was a long time arriving.

After Colin Suggett had missed a breakaway chance for West Brom, City won a corner. Pardoe played it into the centre, Summerbee flicked it on and Bell nodded it down to the unmarked Doyle. A first-time shot brought City level after an hour's play.

Summerbee was forced to leave the field with a hairline leg fracture, but Albion brought on Krzywicki for Asa Hartford and the newcomer's pace almost brought the winner. At the other end Francis Lee saw his fierce drive turned away.

The winning goal came in the 12th minute of extra-time and it was appropriate that Lee should start the move, chipping the ball forward to Bell. Bell back-headed to Glyn Pardoe who forced it past Osborne from the corner of the goal area.

It was the first time the League Cup had come to Lancashire, and City's success occurred in the first season all 92 League clubs had taken part in the competition.

Manchester City: Corrigan; Book, Mann, Doyle, Booth, Oakes, Heslop, Bell, Summerbee (Bowyer), Lee, Pardoe.
West Bromwich Albion: Osborne; Fraser, Wilson, Brown, Talbut, Kaye, Cantello, Suggett, Astle, Hartford(Krzywicki), Hope.

Attendance: 97,963   *Referee: V.James (York)*

Tony Book is chaired from the pitch in Vienna.

Match to Remember 18   29 April 1970

Manchester City 2   Górnik Zabrze 1

ON a damp day, dismal Vienna night, City built a 2-0 half-time lead and went on to collect their first European trophy. Two years after Malcolm Allison had warned that City would scare Europe to death, the European Cup-winners' Cup came to Maine Road.

There were almost 4,000 City fans among the 10,000 crowd in the huge Prater Stadium, and they braved a night of sheeting rain. City were missing Summerbee, and had other players nursing injuries at the end of a 60-game season.

The Poles were forced to defend, and in the 12th minute City went ahead. The goal came from Neil Young, who had been left out of the League Cup-winning team two months previously. Young followed up to score from close range after the goalkeeper had blocked Lee's shot.

Young played a key role in the second goal. He broke through the middle and was brought down by the goalkeeper. There were two minutes before half-time when Francis Lee made his cocky, sprightly run to take the vital penalty kick. He hit the ball hard, straight and into the net. It needed a close study of an action-replay to check the ball had not gone through the goalkeeper's body.

City had lost Doyle with an injured ankle, and when Ozlizlo scored for Górnik in the 68th minute there were a few tense moments. But Tony Book was soon holding aloft his side's third major trophy in 12 months.

Manchester City: Corrigan; Book, Pardoe, Doyle(Bowyer), Booth, Oakes, Heslop, Lee, Young, Bell, Towers.
Górnick Zabrze: Kostka; Latocha, Ozlizlo, Gorgan, Forenski(Deja), Szoltysik, Wilczek (Skowrone), Olek, Banas, Lubanski, Szaryniski.

Attendance: 10,000   *Referee: P.Schiller (Austria)*

Manchester City 1   Tottenham Hotspur 1

THE centenary FA Cup Final was one of the most entertaining Wembley spectacles ever — a 1-1 extra-time draw followed by an exciting replay which saw City go down by the odd goal in five.

For much of the first game City looked likely winners. Yet back in October they had no cause to think about the prospect of Wembley. City were then bottom of the First Division without a win in 12 games, and the management team of Malcolm Allison and Tony Book were on their way out.

New manager John Bond took City to halfway in the League, a League Cup semi-final and this FA Cup Final. His team included three recent signings — Gerry Gow, Bobby McDonald and Tommy Hutchison. It was Hutchison who featured in two moments of Wembley drama.

In the 29th minute the 33-year-old ex-Coventry player dived forward to head Ray Ranson's cross past Aleksic's left hand.

In the 80th minute Hutchison deflected Hoddle's free-kick for Tottenham's equaliser, thus emulating a feat of Bert Turner (Charlton) — scoring for both teams in a Cup Final.

Until that point Joe Corrigan had looked unbeatable, and eventually the City goalkeeper would be voted 'Man of the Final'. In the replay, however, Corrigan was beaten three times, twice by the Argentinian Ricky Villa, one of whose goals that night proved one of the best ever seen in a Cup Final.

Manchester City: Corrigan; Ranson, McDonald, Reid, Power, Caton, Bennett, Gow, MacKenzie, Hutchison(Henry), Reeves.
Tottenham Hotspur: Aleksic; Houghton, Miller, Roberts, Perryman, Villa(Brooke), Ardiles, Archibald, Galvin, Hoddle, Crooks.

Attendance: 99,500   *Referee: K.Hackett (Sheffield)*

Kevin Reeves celebrates his goal in the Wembley replay.

284

Programme Parade

CITY'S first match programme was published in September 1898 and was known as 'The Official Programme'. It was similar to a weekly magazine and contained much information about City and the other Manchester area clubs.

In 1900 the title was changed to simply, 'The Official' and in 1903, City at last began to publish their own programme, known as the 'Blue & White'. There were variations of the title but the 'Blue & White' tag remained until 1954 when it disappeared altogether. From 1965, the City programme design has changed almost every season.

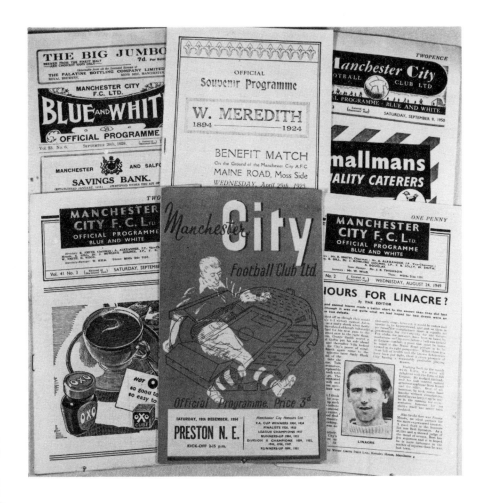

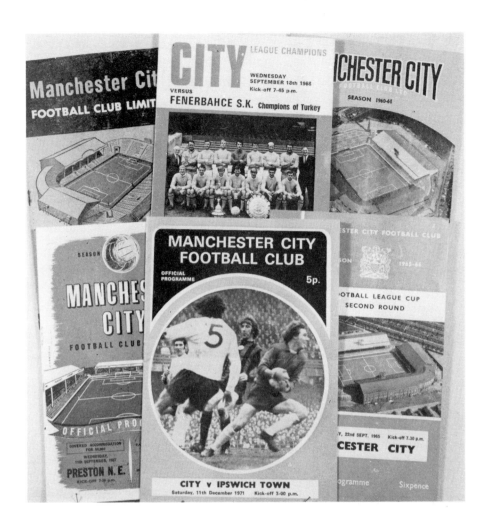

Manchester City Managers
(including secretaries with 'managerial' responsibilities)

Lawrence Furniss
1889-1893

LAWRENCE FURNISS was an amateur forward with Gorton FC and joined the embryonic City club when the two Gorton sides merged in 1883. A serious knee injury ended his career and he moved into the administrative side of football.

Furniss was the man thought by many football historians to be largely responsible for Billy Meredith joining City. Meredith was spotted playing for Northwich in a match refereed by Furniss. The City official was already well versed in the need to look further afield for players and in 1890, he and John Allison had travelled to Scotland to sign several players from north of the border. Furniss was also instrumental in bringing some of Bolton Wanderers' stars to Ardwick, the most notable being England international Davie Weir.

It was Furniss who had helped to form the Ardwick club and he was a great servant to the game in general and to Manchester City in particular, having a big hand in the club's early growth to become one of the leading sides in the country.

Although he eventually gave way to Joshua Parlby, Furniss remained with the City club for a total of 46 years. He joined the board in 1903 until 1905, then rejoined in 1915 and was club chairman from 1921 to 1928. Later he was club president.

Joshua Parlby
1893-1895

JOSHUA PARLBY had played with Stoke before becoming a member of the Potteries club committee. In 1893 he became City's first paid secretary, on a weekly wage of 50 shillings (£2.50), after previously serving the club in an *ex officio* capacity.

His short time as secretary coincided with some of the most traumatic days in the club's history — bankruptcy and a crippling defection of first-teamers in September 1894.

He was wily man — there is a story that he smuggled the hard-up City team up and down the railway system when they could not afford to travel legitimately to fulfil their fixtures; and he argued successfully for the club's election to the Football League, only a few months after Ardwick had been declared insolvent.

Parlby was no skilled tactician — rather a gifted amateur — and he would have not looked out of place in Priestley's *Good Companions*, a burly boisterous man who excelled in the art of 'wrangling'.

He, and others, aroused sufficient local support to form Manchester City Football Club Limited from the ashes of the doomed Ardwick club. Indeed, when Ardwick had been included in the League, they had no team. Later, he took up Furniss's advice and signed Billy Meredith, and was also responsible for the signing of Pat Finnerhan.

Parlby took a public house in Bolton in 1895, becoming something of an 'advisor' to City and joining the board from then until 1905. He rejoined the board in April 1909 and served until 1912, when he retired and left the area.

City directors and friends ready for the 1904 FA Cup Final. On top of the carriage (from left) are Lawrence Furniss, Josh Parlby, J.J.Bentley and Sam Ormerod. Director G.Madders is second from the left in front of the carriage.

Sam Ormerod
1895-1902

SAM ORMEROD, a player and referee in local Lancashire football, during the 1880s, hailed from Accrington and although he was not outgoing in the same manner as his predecessor, Joshua Parlby, he had a playing experience which Parlby did not.

Although he had to work as part of a three-man committee — sometimes with Parlby at his elbow — Ormerod still exercised his own influence on City's affairs and his first season with them saw City qualify for the Test matches, although they subsequently failed to win promotion.

Success, however, was not far away and after finishing sixth and then third, City at last made

First Division status in 1898-9. The team which he had moulded largely single-handedly was one built on the sturdiness of its defenders and the dash and nip of Meredith, together with his fellow forwards, Williams and Gillespie.

In the First Division, City found the going, naturally, much more difficult and they were relegated in 1901-02. Yet in the very early days of City's first season in Division One, things looked decidedly bright. City eventually finished seventh — higher than any other Lancashire club — and Ormerod was dubbed by the *Athletic News* as 'The Wizard of Longsight'.

Halfway through the 1901-02 season, however, it was obvious that the team would relinquish its place in the top section and Ormerod, whose only answer by this time was to ring the team changes, was relieved of his duties. At the club's annual meeting in June, a debt of almost £1,000 was announced and there were strong words from shareholders about the way that money had been spent, uncontrollably, on travelling expenses, bonuses and wages. The board was replaced and Sam Ormerod officially resigned.

There has been a tendency amongst students of City's early history to underrate Ormerod's time in charge; but he was unfortunate to have held the job at a time when City were still thinking in parochial terms; and he did, after all, help to lay the foundations of the team which won the FA Cup for the first time in City's history.

Tom E. Maley
1902-1906

TOM MALEY, younger brother of Celtic manager Willie Maley, had played one game in City's colours in 1896, and his appointment as secretary at Hyde Road heralded the first great era in City's history.

Within a short time of his arrival in the summer of 1902, City were on the road to national success. In his first season in charge he steered the club to the Second Division title, and then followed with the FA Cup in 1904 — and First Division runners-up spot the same season.

Maley preferred what he called 'style' football, and by that he meant Scottish syle. Not for Maley the 'kick and rush' approach of others; he liked his players to employ the close-passing game and if a footballer had skill in that direction, then he won Maley's particular admiration.

He built City's promotion and Cup-winning team with delicate but significant changes.

Some players — Meredith, Sandy Turnbull, Gillespie, Frost, 'Doc' Hynds — were on the books when he arrived. Maley switched Turnbull and Frost with great success; he found youngsters, Booth and Bannister, playing in local football; and when he spent, he spent wisely on Livingstone and Burgess.

Unlike Sam Ormerod, Maley was not overawed by Billy Meredith's reputation and he eventually found the ideal inside-right partner for Meredith in young Jimmy Bannister. He brought Turnbull back from 'exile' in Scotland and turned the man who had failed as Meredith's partner into a goal-scoring inside-left; and he gave Sammy Frost a new career as a wing-half after he, too, had been found wanting as Meredith's inside-right.

Alas, Maley became embroiled in the scandal of 1906 and was suspended *sine die* with City chairman Mr W.Forrest whilst other directors and players met with fines and lesser suspensions. For City it was the end of a great era and with it went the man largely responsible for it, Tom Maley.

Harry Newbould
1906-1912

HARRY NEWBOULD first made his sporting name as a sprinter in the Midlands and he was also a speedy outside-right with Derby St Luke's before joining Derby County as assistant-secretary in 1896. A qualified accountant, Newbould was eventually promoted to secretary and in 1900, when Derby decided to appoint their first manager, they looked no further than Newbould who combined both jobs.

Newbould was a popular figure who brought many fine players to Derby and although one of his last pieces of business was to sell the hugely popular and successful Steve Bloomer to Middlesbrough — to the dismay of Derby supporters — the Rams' directors expressed 'surprise and disappointment' when Newbould announced that he was to become Manchester City secretary-manager.

He took up his post at Hyde Road in July 1906, when City's future looked bleak after the wholesale departure of the suspended stars, but the new man continued his fine record of signing quality players.

Newbould built a new City team and after a disastrous start — City lost their first two League games of 1906-07, 4-1 and 9-1, the new men gradually forged the makings of a First Division side. Bill Eadie was signed to give City years of sterling service; the goalscoring Grieve came from Greenock Morton; and Newbould ended his first season with a forward line containing four internationals, England's Thornley and Conlin, Scottish star George Stewart, and Welshman Billy Lot Jones who was already on City's books.

In 1907-08 he steered City to third place in Division One and although relegation followed a season later, City made an immediate return as Second Division Champions in 1910. There followed another heart-stopping flirtation with relegation in 1911-12 — only a remarkable late run of 17 points from ten games saw City to safety — before Newbould ended his days at Hyde Road.

He was not, however, lost to football administration and became a key figure in the forerunner of today's PFA, serving as Players' Union secretary for a while.

Ernest Mangnall
1912-1924

ERNEST MANGNALL came to Manchester City in September 1912 having already made a fine name for himself across the city with Manchester United, whom he had guided to two League Championships and an FA Cup success.

A Bolton man, Mangnall's first taste of football administration was as a Bolton Wanderers director before he moved into his first 'managerial'job with Burnley. At Turf Moor, Mangnall learned all about the art of working on a shoestring budget and towards the end of 1903, Manchester United were sufficiently impressed to appoint him.

United won promotion in 1905-06 and two years later were League Champions. The FA Cup followed in 1909 and another League title in 1911. Ironically, Mangnall had built his United team around many of the City players suspended in 1906. He bought Meredith, Burgess, Bannister and Turnbull for what he later described as 'a mere bagatelle'.

He joined City as secretary-manager and helped keep them in Division One through a difficult period. An even more trying time followed when he somehow had to keep the club alive through the rigours of World War One, but he succeeded and by the time the directors decided not to renew his contract in May 1924, Mangnall had seen City's annual cash balance rise from £95 to £26,155.

His most notable signings for City were the crowd-pulling forwards Horace Barnes and Tommy Browell, although Billy Blyth — one youngster who was allowed a free-transfer after his first season — went on to give a decade of service to Arsenal.

Ernest Mangnall was a founder of the Central League, and the man mainly responsible for the formation of the Football Managers' Association. Awarded a Football Association medal for 21 years' service, he was granted a testimonial in 1924 when a combined Manchester team met Liverpool. Ernest Mangnall died early in 1932.

David Ashworth
1924-1926

DAVID ASHWORTH, who succeeded Ernest Mangnall as manager of Manchester City, had made his name with Liverpool. His time at Anfield coincided with one of the best periods in the Merseysiders' early history and he guided them to the First Division title in 1921-2.

Ashworth then surprised everyone by leaving the League Champions in February 1923, when they were on course for another League title, and joining bottom-of-the-table Oldham Athletic. It was from Oldham that he went to City in July 1924.

In his first season with City, Ashworth saw them score 68 goals — equal top-scorers in Division One — but finish in only a mid-table position. Supporters suggested that new players were needed to replace men like defender Eli Fletcher, who was nearing the end of his career, and Horace Barnes, who was also in his last season with the club.

In the close season of 1925, City spent £3,000 to bring Ayr United left-back Phil McCloy to Maine Road, but before Christmas it was obvious that the team was in trouble. In November 1925, Ashworth 'resigned' and was not there to see the side embark on the FA Cup run which eventually took them to Wembley and defeat by Bolton.

Ashworth later managed Stockport County and in the early post-war years was working as a scout for Blackpool. He died in the Victoria Hospital, Blackpool, on 23 March 1947, aged 79.

Peter Hodge
1926-1932

PETER HODGE joined City when they were already hurtling towards relegation, but by the time he left six years later, the club's revival was well underway.

He had been in football administration for most of his life, his first post being that of secretary to a Dumfermline boys' club. He figured with Dumfermline Reserves, became that club's secretary, and was a referee from 1900 to 1907 before taking charge of Raith Rovers who he took from the Scottish Second Division to the First.

In June 1914, Hodge came to England and took over at Stoke, then a Southern League Second Division club, before guiding them into the Football League. During the war he returned to Scotland but came back to English football in 1919. Hodge joined Leicester and yet again applied a magic touch, seeing them into the First Division before accepting Manchester City's offer in 1926.

He arrived at Maine Road at the time of City's Cup Final defeat and a week before defeat at Newcastle in their last match sent them down. Hodge then proceeded to weave his magic again and in 1927-8 he could look back on yet another promotion-winning season as City took the Second Division title.

During Hodge's reign at Maine Road, several notable players became established in the side, amongst them wingers Toseland and Brook. Tommy Johnson was moved from inside-left to centre-forward and responded with a club record 38 goals in 1928-9. That season was City's best First Division campaign since 1922-3. In 1929-30, under Hodge, City finished third but the team was still some way short of lifting the title and in 1932 the manager, attracted by a five-year contract and an increased salary, rejoined Leicester.

Wilf Wild
1932-1946

WILF WILD was appointed assistant secretary of City in 1920 and secretary four years later. It was he who had pushed hard for the idea of a full-time manager uncluttered with administrative worries — Ashworth was the first such appointment — but in 1932, when Hodge returned to Leicester, Wild found himself having to care for team matters as well.

Wild had the best possible start to his additional 'career' as City reached Wembley two years in succession — lifting the Cup in 1933 — and went on to take the League Championship title for the first time in the club's history, in 1936-7. He saw several fine players arrive at Maine Road, notably Peter Doherty, Alec Herd, Frank Swift and Sam Barkas, and, like Ernest Mangnall before him, he had to guide City through a world war.

He was still in charge when peacetime football resumed in 1946 and saw City off to a fine start in their quest for the First Division status they had lost in 1938. Then, in November 1946, Sam Cowan began his brief career as City manager and Wild reverted, perhaps thankfully, to solely secretarial duties. He was still in office when he died in December 1950. His wife Betty worked in the club's main office until the early 1960s.

Sam Cowan
1946-1947

SAM COWAN played centre-half in three FA Cup Finals for City and was a fine captain (see *A-Z of City Stars*). As a manager he enjoyed one of the most successful reigns of any City team boss, albeit also one of the briefest.

After leaving City as a player he moved to Bradford City and eventually to Brighton where he became trainer at the Goldstone Ground and subsequently set up a thriving physiotherapy practice.

In November 1946, City asked him to take over as manager and he nursed the side to the Second Division title. Even three defeats in the last seven matches of that season hardly mattered as City were already virtually assured of a return to First Division football.

Cowan continued to live in Hove and in June 1947, with the City directors expressing concern at his commuting, his days at Maine Road finally came to an end.

Jock Thomson
1947-1950

JOCK THOMSON'S two-year stay as Manchester City manager was an overall unsuccessful period in the club's history, culminating in relegation in 1950.

Thomson's great days had been as a wing-half with Everton before the war, when he won two First Division and one Second Division Championship winners' medals and an FA Cup winners' medal as well as a Scotland cap. He joined Everton in 1925, from Dundee, and stayed at Goodison until his retirement as a player in 1939.

He was appointed City manager but the team was going through a transitional period and his career did not survive the drop into the Second Division.

From then until his retirement in 1974, Thomson ran a public house in Carnoustie. He died in 1979.

Les McDowall
1950-1963

LES McDOWALL was born in India, the son of a Scottish missionary, and raised as a Scot. He became a shipyard draughtsman but was a victim of the '1930s slump' and it was whilst playing football for a team of unemployed men that he was spotted by Sunderland.

McDowall duly signed for the Roker club and in 1938 Manchester City paid well over £7,000 for his signature. McDowall, a versatile half-back, had played only 13 games in Sunderland's first team but City saw him as a player who could help in their battle against relegation.

Within 12 months McDowall was captaining a City side by now in Division Two. Then war intervened and McDowall resumed his occupation as a draughtsman, in a local aircraft factory. In the season immediately after the war he relinquished the captaincy to Barkas, who led City out of Division Two, and after a spell captaining the reserves, McDowall was appointed Wrexham manager in 1949.

Opportunities to succeed were few with so many part-time professionals on the Welsh club's books but in June 1950, City — relegated again — offered McDowall the post of manager in succession to Jock Thomson. McDowall accepted and began a 13-year spell in charge of City.

He was an innovative manager and during his time introduced some enterprising tactical moves, the most famous of which was the so-called 'Revie Plan' which involved a deep-lying centre-forward similar to that employed by the Hungarian team which humiliated England in 1953 and 1954.

McDowall's first task as City manager was to regain their First Division place and this he did in his first season. He had an infectious enthusiasm for the game and after winning promotion, City went on to two FA Cup Finals under McDowall, winning the trophy in 1956.

McDowall also signed some fine players for City, including Denis Law for whom he paid a British record fee of £55,000 in March 1960. Three years later, however, McDowall could not prevent City sliding back into Division Two and in May 1963 his career with City was over. He went to manage Oldham Athletic.

George Poyser
1963-1965

AFTER a playing career that took him to Wolverhampton Wanderers, Stourbridge, Mansfield

296

Town, Port Vale, Brentford and Plymouth, George Poyser was coach at Wolves before being appointed manager of Notts County.

In 1957 he joined Manchester City as assistant manager with a brief to organise the club's scouting system, a job which he once said took him 80,000 miles over the country each year.

In June 1963, he succeeded McDowall as manager but, although he was always a popular figure at Maine Road, he could do little to arrest the club's decline.

His first season saw City reach the New Year in high spirits with a League Cup semi-final in prospect and the possibility of a return to Division One. Poyser had signed experienced strikers Jimmy Murray (from Wolves for £30,000) and Derek Kevan (from Chelsea for £30,000).

In the second half of the season, however, things began to go wrong. Eliminated from the FA Cup third round by Swindon, and beaten by Stoke in the League Cup semi-final, City's promotion hopes also faded after crucial defeats by Leeds and Sunderland.

His second season saw the signings of Dave Bacuzzi (£20,000 from Arsenal) and Johnny Crossan (£40,000 from Sunderland), and the departure of Dave Wagstaffe (to Wolves for £30,000). It also saw City suffer a crop of injuries, a lowest-ever Maine Road attendance of just over 8,000 to see Swindon — and the Easter resignation of George Poyser as City were doomed to a mid-table position whilst, across the city, Manchester United were taking the League Championship.

Joe Mercer OBE
1965-1972

JOE MERCER was one of the game's all-time greats, both as a player and a manager, and a man whose warm personality shone through even the game's greyest days.

He began his career as a junior with Everton in 1932 and stayed with them until 1947. In that time he became one of the greatest wing-halves the game has seen, a superb tactician who won a League Championship medal in 1938-9 and whose tally of five full England caps would have been much greater but for the war. That can be seen by the fact that Mercer won 26 wartime caps, some of them as England's captain.

After the war he found his position at Goodison had changed and he moved to Arsenal where a 'second' career brought him two more League Championship medals and an FA Cup winners' medal before a broken leg forced his retirement.

Mercer went into management, first with Sheffield United and then at Aston Villa. At Villa Park he saw the club promoted from Division Two, reach the FA Cup semi-finals twice, win the League Cup, and build a new stand before his health gave.

Everyone thought his retirement was permanent but Mercer loved to be involved in football and in 1965 he came back as manager of Manchester City. His assistant was a young man called Malcolm Allison and together they restored City's pride and brought the glory days back to Maine Road.

City won the Second Division title in 1967 and the League Championship in 1968. The FA Cup followed in 1969, the League Cup and the European Cup-winners' Cup in 1970. It seemed that nothing could stop Manchester City in whose ranks the likes of Bell, Summerbee, Lee, Oakes, Booth, Corrigan, Book, Young, Coleman and company brought even the most fickle Maine Road supporters flooding back to Moss Side.

In the wake of the 1970 triumphs Allison became embroiled in a battle for boardroom control and found himself almost dismissed. Mercer stood loyally by his deputy and Allison continued his Maine Road career.

In June 1972, Mercer, himself, left City to become general manager of Coventry City. In 1977 he took temporary charge of the England team and tried, as he put it, 'to restore some laughter'. In 1981 he resigned from the Coventry board after nine years as a director at Highfield Road. In 1987, Joe Mercer is still living on his beloved Merseyside, as genial and irrepressible as ever.

Malcolm Allison
1972-1973 and 1979-1980

MALCOLM ALLISON'S success as a coach has often overshadowed the fact that he was a fine centre-half in his playing days. His first club was Charlton Athletic, for whom he signed in 1944, and he was later a member of a good West Ham team that produced several players who went on to become prominent managers and coaches.

Allison's own playing career ended in 1958 when he became ill with tuberculosis which resulted in him losing a lung. He turned to coaching and worked with the Cambridge University soccer side, then in Toronto and with Southern League Bath City before Plymouth Argyle gave him his first job in League football.

In July 1965 he joined Joe Mercer at Maine Road. He was then 37 and whilst he was a totally different character from Mercer, the then City boss had been impressed by the man who he had first met on coaching courses at Lilleshall. It was Allison's creativity that tempted Mercer to offer him the job as his assistant.

By 1972, with so many honours already won, Allison felt that he deserved more than the tag of 'assistant'. When Mercer left for Coventry, 'Big Mal' got his wish, although before the end of his first season he was off to manage Crystal Palace, saying that he could no longer motivate the City players.

There followed another spell as Plymouth manager, then periods coaching in Istanbul and in the United States before Allison returned to Maine Road in July 1979.

He became team manager, with Tony Book nominated general manager, but there were to be no fresh glory days despite City spending huge sums of money. Into Maine Road came Wolves' Steve Daley for over £1 million, Preston's Michael Robinson for £765,000, and a youngster called Steve MacKenzie for whom City paid an astonishing £250,000 despite the fact that MacKenzie still had to kick a ball in League football.

There was a humiliating FA Cup defeat by Fourth Division Halifax Town, after which City paid £1 million for Kevin Reeves only to end the season scrapping to avoid relegation. And after the first 12 League games of 1980-81 had failed to bring a single victory, Allison and Book paid the inevitable price and were dismissed.

Thereafter, Malcolm Allison took to travelling again with jobs in such diverse places as Lisbon and Middlesbrough, Willington and Kuwait. City fans, meanwhile, prefer to remember the days when Allison worked with Joe Mercer to bring the great days back to Maine Road.

Johnny Hart
1973

JOHNNY HART would be forgiven for thinking that the gods were not favourably disposed to him when he was at Maine Road. Having just established himself in the City first team (see *A-Z of City Stars*) he was forced to miss the 1955 FA Cup Final and the rest of his playing career was dogged by injuries.

And after only six months in charge of the team following Allison's dismissal in 1973, he was forced to give that up, this time through illness.

Many people were surprised when Hart was given the job of trying to make something of the team of expensive footballers that Allison had, according to his own admission, failed to motivate.

In his short spell as manager Hart was responsible for re-signing Denis Law, on a free-transfer from Manchester United, and for paying a record fee for a goalkeeper when he signed Keith MacRae from Motherwell for £100,000.

In 1987, Hart is still working at Maine Road, involved in the promotional business of the club.

Ron Saunders
1973-1974

RON SAUNDERS was an energetic, bustling, all-action centre-forward who played for Everton, Tonbridge, Gillingham, Portsmouth, Watford and Charlton, proving a particularly prolific scorer in his days at Fratton Park.

He had managed Yeovil, Oxford and Norwich (who he took to a League Cup Final) before moving to Maine Road in December 1973 to replaced Johnny Hart who had just resigned because of illness.

Saunders' reign was actually shorter than that of the man he succeeded, for after only five months as City manager he was dismissed.

His demise came in the wake of the 1974 League Cup Final defeat by Wolves when City were left with nothing but a continuing fight against relegation. During his brief stay he had negotiated a complicated deal with Sunderland which brought Horswill and Tueart to Maine Road with Towers going to Roker Park, but ultimately City's board felt that Saunders was not their man.

He has subsequently managed Aston Villa, Birmingham City and West Brom and in 1987 faced calls for his dismissal from The Hawthorns fans after recently-relegated Albion failed to make any mark on the Second Division.

Tony Book
1974-1979

TONY BOOK had an unusually late start to his League playing career but it proved to be a highly successful one (see *A-Z of City Stars*). He was passed over as manager when Allison left in 1973, and when Johnny Hart retired the same year Book found himself as Ron Saunders' assistant.

But when Saunders was dismissed, it was Book to whom the City directors finally turned in a bid to establish some stability at Maine Road. Book did not let them down and his years in charge proved successful for Manchester City.

City won the League Cup in 1976 and finished League Championship runners-up the following year. Book's qualities were really an extension of those which had made him a popular and successful captain and he has remained loyal to City even though his managerial career has seen him 'promoted sideways', dismissed and then return in an important behind-the-scenes role.

Amongst the players who came to Maine Road when he was manager were Asa Hartford, Joe Royle, Dave Watson, Brian Kidd, and Mick Channon. Perhaps Book's greatest pleasures have been from working with the younger players and he would have been delighted when City won the FA Youth Cup, for the first time, in 1986.

John Bond
1980-1983

JOHN BOND was a useful full-back who played in the same West Ham team as Malcolm Allison in the 1950s. After 17 years at Upton Park, Bond ended his playing career with Torquay United and went into management, first with Bournemouth, then Norwich, winning success for both clubs.

Bournemouth were promoted to Division Three and Norwich to Division One before Bond replaced Allison and Book at Maine Road after City's dreadful start to the 1980-81 season.

Bond introduced John Benson as his assistant and made three major signings — Tommy Hutchison and Bobby McDonald from Coventry, and Gerry Gow from Bristol City. Behind the scenes, Bond replaced Dave Ewing with Glyn Pardoe as reserve team coach, despite the fact that the reserves were top of the Central League, and Tony Scott took over from Steve Fleet as youth coach, even though City had reached the FA Youth Cup Final, for the first time, in 1979 and repeated the feat a year later.

After losing to Birmingham in mid-October to go bottom, City won ten of their next 15 League games and eventually finished 12th in Division One. The revival under Bond also saw City reach the League Cup semi-final and progress to the FA Cup Final where Spurs eventually beat them after a replay.

From the absolute doldrums Bond had dragged City up the table and on to Wembley. The £1.2 million signing of Trevor Francis in time to play in the third match of the 1981-2 season therefore sent City supporters' hopes soaring. Northern Ireland international Martin O'Neill came from Norwich for £275,000, and Bond signed his son, Kevin, from Seattle Sounders. When injuries began to bite, Bond re-signed Hartford from Everton for £350,000.

Before Christmas, City did indeed look like Championship contenders but a poor run in the second half of the season saw them finish tenth.

At the start of 1982-3, Bond and Benson refused offers to work for Benfica, but after a good start, in which Bond's new signings, Graham Baker and David Cross, did well, City began to falter away from home and after an inglorious 4-0 FA Cup defeat at Brighton, Bond resigned.

Since then he has managed Burnley, Swansea and in 1987 is Birmingham boss. John Bond has always attracted the attention of the media and in 1987 he was fined by the FA for allegedly bringing the game into disrepute following some unflattering remarks about the England coaching scene. Later there was a report that Ron Saunders, the man he had replaced as Birmingham manager, was going to sue Bond for alleged comments concerning certain aspects of the St Andrew's set-up which Bond had inherited. At the end of 1986-7, Bond's position at St Andrew's was reported to be in jeopardy and in May he was dismissed.

John Benson
1983

JOHN BENSON was given the task of trying to save Manchester City from relegation after John Bond's departure in February 1983. He failed and was dismissed in June the same year.

Born in Arbroath, Benson moved south with his family and was playing for Stockport Boys when City spotted him in 1958. He signed as an amateur, turned full-time professional in 1961 and made 44 League appearances before moving to Torquay United in June 1964 for £5,000.

Benson served Torquay well, making 233 League appearances before a £12,000 transfer to Bournemouth (93 League games) where he played under John Bond. He moved to Exeter City and then joined Bond again at Norwich (as player-coach) before returning to Bournemouth as player-manager (1975 to 1979). Another spell at Norwich — as youth coach — was followed by the move to Maine Road as Bond's assistant.

Eventually he became manager, something that he could never have thought possible when City let him go as a player almost 20 years earlier, but his task was always going to be a difficult one and he did not survive long after Luton won at Maine Road on the last day of the season and sent City into the bottom three for the first time that campaign.

Billy McNeill MBE
1983-1986

BILLY McNEILL announced his retirement as a player in 1975, following Celtic's record seventh successive Scottish Cup Final appearance.

His decison brought to an end one of the most successful club careers of any British footballer. It was a career which saw McNeill collect 23 major winners' medals including one for Celtic's 1967 European Cup Final triumph.

He appeared in a record 12 Scottish Cup Finals (seven as a winner), nine Scottish League title-winning sides, a record nine Scottish League Cup Finals (six winners' medals), and won 29 full caps for Scotland as well as appearing for the Under-23 side and the Scottish League. In 1965 he was Scottish Player of the Year and in 1974 was awarded the MBE for services to football.

Altogether he played 831 matches for Celtic before moving into management with Clyde in 1977. He stayed at Shawfield only two months before becoming Aberdeen boss in June that year. The Dons narrowly missed out on the League title and the Scottish Cup, and McNeill was the man who signed both Steve Archibald and Gordon Strachan for the Pittodrie club.

In May 1978, McNeill was on the move again, this time back to Parkhead where he took over from Jock Stein. He stayed there for five years, winning more trophies for Celtic, until he moved to Manchester City to replace John Benson.

He brought in Scottish players like Neil McNab (Brighton), Jim Tolmie (Lokeren) and Derek Parlane (Leeds), all men who were unhappy at their respective clubs. Parlane and Tolmie did well for McNeill in the early part of the season but then the goals started to dry up.

Mick McCarthy, from Barnsley, was another inspired McNeill signing but there was to be no quick return to Division One for City. Promotion was achieved in 1985, although in the early days of the following season City then looked to be heading straight back down again. Eventually they pulled up the table and also fought their way to Wembley where they met Chelsea in the new Full Members' Cup.

But there was never really a time during McNeill's stay when City could look to the game's most important honours and in September 1986 he moved to take charge of another struggling club, Aston Villa. At the end of the season Villa joined City in Division Two and McNeill was dismissed. A few days later, however, McNeill must have been one of the happiest men in football when Celtic announced he was rejoining them as manager.

Jimmy Frizzell
1986-1987

JIMMY FRIZZELL made his name by taking Oldham Athletic from the Fourth to the Second Division. He was born in Greenock and his playing career began with Morton in 1957. A wing-half or inside-forward, he moved to Oldham in 1960 and played 309 League games for them, scoring 57 goals, before becoming manager at Boundary Park in March 1970.

Oldham soon won promotion from Division Four and in 1974 they took the Third Division title. Oldham were still in the Second Division when Frizzell was sacked at the end of 1981-2 and he had been out of work for a year when he accepted Billy McNeill's offer to be his assistant at Maine Road.

When McNeill moved to Aston Villa, Frizzell was given the chance to show what he could do but he was working on a very tight financial budget and City seemed doomed to struggle. Frizzell could do little to arrest their slide and by Easter 1987 relegation was inevitable with the club firmly at the bottom of Division One. When the drop came, Frizzell was moved to the post of general manager and Mel Machin, the Norwich coach, took charge of team matters.

Outside-right Billy Austin was an expensive signing when he joined City from Norwich in May 1924 and he had a difficult job in assuming the right-wing position when many Maine Road fans could still remember, with relish, the great Billy Meredith. Austin cost City £2,000 plus a game at Norwich and he remained with them for seven years, showing good ball control and speed in his early days with the club and winning an England cap in October 1925. In 1926 Austin appeared in City's FA Cup Final team but also had the misfortune to miss a penalty which might have saved them from relegation. In 1928 he collected a Second Division Championship medal but during his last three seasons with City, played only four League games. In his entire League career he scored almost 90 goals in over 350 League appearances, and on at least three occasions he deputised for injured goalkeepers. A native of Arnold, Notts, he began his career with Arnold United and left City in December 1931 to sign for Chesterfield. *League debut for City v Bury, 30 August 1924.*

BILLY AUSTIN

	LEAGUE		FA CUP		TOTAL	
	App	Gls	App	Gls	App	Gls
1924-25	38	6	1	0	39	6
1925-26	36	12	7	3	43	15
1926-27	26	10	1	0	27	10
1927-28	18	9	2	0	20	9
1928-29	38	5	1	1	39	6
1929-30	0	0	0	0	0	0
1930-31	4	1	0	0	4	1
	160	43	12	4	172	47

JIMMY BANNISTER

Jimmy Bannister was a clever ball-player who was discovered playing in local football with Chorley. He was born at Leyland in 1881 and City manager, Tom Maley, signed him in the close season of 1902, looking on Bannister as the eventual inside-forward partner to Billy Meredith. Meredith, himself, was to heartily approve, saying in later years, "Bannister was the best partner I ever had. No one fed me better than Jimmy....he was equal to any inside-right playing in League football." In his first season Bannister helped City back to Division One, scoring 13 goals in 21 League games. Thereafter, however, his appearances were few and when he became one of the players suspended in 1906, and later moved to Manchester United, it was obvious that City had not had the best of him. He made 57 League appearances for United, scoring seven goals. *League debut for City v Stockport County, 6 December 1902.*

	LEAGUE		FA CUP		TOTAL	
	App	Gls	App	Gls	App	Gls
1902-03	21	13	1	0	22	13
1903-04	7	3	0	0	7	3
1904-05	6	3	0	0	6	3
1905-06	11	2	1	1	12	3
	45	21	2	1	47	22

Born at Tyne Dock, South Shields, Sam Barkas was a
stylish left-back who always used the ball constructively
when playing it out of defence. Barkas was one of four
brothers who played League football and he would
probably have won more than his five England caps but
for the presence of Arsenal's Eddie Hapgood on the
international scene. The fact that he was no mere big-
kicking defender was underlined when he won one cap
at inside-right, against Belgium when Ray Bowden was
injured on tour. Barkas cost City £5,000 when they
signed him from Bradford City in April 1934. He won a
League Championship medal in 1936-7, and although
his career was interrupted by war, he was still fit enough
at the age of 38 to captain City to the Second Division
Championship in 1946-7. Barkas had already won a
Third Division North Championship medal with Bradford
City. He left City in May 1947 and became Workington's
manager, later serving Wigan Athletic for a short spell
before returning to Maine Road in 1957 as a scout. He
also scouted for Leeds and then rejoined Bradford City
to run their pools scheme. His achievements are
commemorated by a bar named after him in City's main
stand. *League debut for City v Liverpool, 2 May 1934.*

SAM BARKAS

	LEAGUE		FA CUP		TOTAL	
	App	Gls	App	Gls	App	Gls
1933-34	2	0	0	0	2	0
1934-35	41	1	1	0	42	1
1935-36	39	0	3	0	42	0
1936-37	30	0	4	0	34	0
1937-38	30	0	4	0	34	0
1938-39	0	0	0	0	0	0
1945-46	-	-	4	0	4	0
1946-47	33	0	4	0	37	0
	175	1	20	0	195	1

Horace Barnes had the honour of scoring City's first
goal at Maine Road, but that was only one of his many
efforts for the club. Indeed, he had a fierce left-foot and
altogether scored 108 goals in 192 League games for
City after World War One — two of them against
Liverpool in front of King George V. Two of his goals
also helped put an end to Burnley's record-breaking run
of 30 games without defeat. Born at Whadsley Bridge,
his first League club was Derby County from whom he
signed for City in May 1914, for £2,500. He forged a fine
scoring partnership with Tommy Browell and when
they were finally split up it was not long before City's
fortunes began to fade dramatically. His career in
wartime football saw him score 56 goals in 57 League
games for City — and incur a fine from Manchester
magistrates when he absented himself from work in a
munitions factory to play against Stockport County in
September 1915. Barnes played for England in a
Victory international in 1919 and appeared twice for
the Football League in 1921-2. He moved to Preston in
November 1924, later playing for Oldham and Ashton
National. In the twilight of his career he scored six goals
in the first 30 minutes when playing for the Rest of
Cheshire against Port Vale. He died on 12 September
1961. *League debut for City v Bradford City,
1 September 1914.*

HORACE BARNES

	LEAGUE		FA CUP		TOTAL	
	App	Gls	App	Gls	App	Gls
1914-15	25	12	4	2	29	14
1919-20	39	22	2	1	41	23
1920-21	41	17	1	0	42	17
1921-22	37	20	3	0	40	20
1922-23	38	21	1	0	39	21
1923-24	23	20	7	2	30	22
1924-25	14	8	0	0	14	8
	217	120	18	5	235	125

None other than Denis Law once said that he regarded Ken Barnes as "the best uncapped wing-half who ever played in English football." Many would echo those sentiments and the skilful and consistent Barnes certainly deserved more than his reward of reserve for the Football League and three appearances for the FA XI. He was born in Birmingham and joined City in May 1950, as a 21-year-old from Stafford Rangers. He went straight into the Central League side but had to wait 16 months for his League baptism. In fact, he played one League game in his first four seasons with City, but from 1954-5 onwards he was a first-team regular and appeared in both the 1955 and 1956 FA Cup Finals. In May 1961, after more than 250 League appearances for City, he became player-manager of Wrexham and helped the Welsh club to promotion from Division Four in his first season. He returned to City in the mid-1970s, as chief scout, and has seen two sons wear the club's colours, with Peter Barnes going on to international honours. *League debut for City v Derby County, 5 January 1952.*

	LEAGUE		FACUP		FLCUP		TOTAL	
	App	Gls	App	Gls	App	Gls	App	Gls
1951-52	1	0	0	0	-	-	1	0
1952-53	0	0	0	0	-	-	0	0
1953-54	0	0	0	0	-	-	0	0
1954-55	40	0	6	1	-	-	46	1
1955-56	39	1	7	0	-	-	46	1
1956-57	31	2	2	0	-	-	33	2
1957-58	39	11	1	0	-	-	40	11
1958-59	40	4	2	0	-	-	42	4
1959-60	37	0	1	0	-	-	38	0
1960-61	31	0	4	0	2	0	37	0
	258	18	23	1	2	0	283	19

KEN BARNES

MALCOLM BARRASS

Malcolm Barrass was a more than useful player who could play equally well at either inside-forward or wing-half. He was born at Seaham Harbour and joined City from Sheffield Wednesday in July 1926. Barrass helped his new club to third place in Division Two in 1926-7 — just one more goal would have seen them promoted — and that season he scored a goal in City's famous win over Preston when they came back from 2-0 down to win 4-2. The following season he played 28 times in the team which won the Second Division Championship. For the following two seasons Barrass proved one of the mainstays of the City team as they consolidated their First Division place and finished third in 1929-30 when he missed only one League match. By 1931-2 the majority of his appearances were confined to the Central League and in the close season of 1933 he signed for Ashton National after 162 League games (14 goals) for City. *League debut for City v Fulham, 28 August 1926.*

	LEAGUE		FA CUP		TOTAL	
	App	Gls	App	Gls	App	Gls
1926-27	27	7	1	0	28	7
1927-28	28	2	2	0	30	2
1928-29	40	2	1	0	41	2
1929-30	41	1	5	0	46	1
1930-31	21	2	0	0	21	2
1931-32	2	0	0	0	2	0
1932-33	3	0	1	1	4	1
	162	14	10	1	172	15

Colin Bell's near-500 competitive games and over 150 goals for City, and his 48 England caps, are remarkable statistics and yet even they do not tell the full story of his contribution to club and international football in the late 1960s and early 70s. His effortless running, tremendous stamina — he was nicknamed 'Nijinsky' after the racehorse — and boundless enthusiasm for the game all combined to make him one of the most influential players of his day. Bell made his League debut *against* Manchester City, playing for Bury in February 1964, just before his 18th birthday. The following season he was Bury's leading scorer and in March 1966 he signed for City, making his League debut three days after putting pen to paper in City's promotion-winning season. Thereafter, his list of honours reflect the Maine Road club's great era — winners' medals for the League Championship, FA Cup, League Cup and European Cup-winners' Cup. A serious knee injury in 1976 affected his career and he missed all of 1976-7. There was time for one further honour, a Central League Championship medal in 1977-8, before the injury forced his retirement in August 1979. *League debut for City v Derby County, 19 March 1966.*

COLIN BELL

	LEAGUE		FACUP		FLCUP		EUROPE		TOTAL	
	App	Gls	App	Gls	App	Gls	App	Gls	App	Gls
1965-66	11	4	0	0	0	0	-	-	11	4
1966-67	42	12	6	1	2	1	-	-	50	14
1967-68	35	14	4	2	4	1	-	-	43	17
1968-69	39	14	5	0	3	1	2	0	49	15
1969-70	31	11	2	0	6	5	9	5	48	21
1970-71	34	13	3	4	1	0	7	2	45	19
1971-72	33	12	2	0	1	2	-	-	36	14
1972-73	39	7	5	2	2	1	2	0	48	10
1973-74	41	7	2	0	11	3	-	-	54	10
1974-75	42	15	1	0	2	3	-	-	45	18
1975-76	20	6	0	0	5	1	-	-	25	7
1976-77	0	0	0	0	0	0	0	0	0	0
1977-78	16(1)	2	2	0	2	0	0	0	20(1)	2
1978-79	10	0	1	0	1	0	3	1	15	1
	393(1)	117	33	9	40	18	23	8	489(1)	152

Malcom Allison said of Colin Bell: "At first he didn't seem to grasp his own freakish strength. He was the best, most powerful runner in the business."

BARRIE BETTS

Full-back Barrie Betts spent most of his career in the lower reaches of the Football League but he had one particularly fine season, captaining Manchester City and appearing in all 42 First Division games in 1960-61. Barnsley-born Betts played his early League soccer with the Oakwell club before moving to Stockport County. He joined City from Stockport in June 1960 and at the end of his first season was voted Player of the Year at Maine Road. Betts played only 17 times in City's relegation season of 1962-3 and in August 1964 he was given a free transfer and moved to Scunthorpe United where he ended his career after only seven games. *League debut for City v Nottingham Forest, 20 August 1960.*

	LEAGUE		FACUP		FLCUP		TOTAL	
	App	Gls	App	Gls	App	Gls	App	Gls
1960-61	42	4	4	0	2	0	48	4
1961-62	24	1	1	0	1	1	26	2
1962-63	17	0	3	0	3	0	23	0
1963-64	18	0	0	0	2	0	20	0
	101	5	8	0	8	1	117	6

Andy Black was an inside-forward whose pre-war goalscoring exploits with Heart of Midlothian won him three Scotland caps. Born in Stirling in 1917, he started his career with West End Rangers, then Shawfield Juniors. He had his first taste of English soccer when he guested for Chester and Portsmouth during World War Two. With Pompey he appeared in a London War Cup Final and once scored eight goals in a game against Clapton Orient. Black was capped a further four times in wartime internationals before joining Manchester City in June 1946. He made his League debut at the start of the first post-war season, and in 1947-8 — City's first season back in Division One — he was their top-scorer. Black, who also appeared at centre-forward, moved to Stockport County in August 1950 and made 97 appearances for the Edgeley Park club before leaving the League scene. *League debut for City v Leicester City, 31 August 1946.*

	LEAGUE		FA CUP		TOTAL	
	App	Gls	App	Gls	App	Gls
1946-47	34	13	3	2	37	15
1947-48	37	16	3	1	40	17
1948-49	35	11	0	0	35	11
1949-50	33	7	1	2	34	9
	139	47	7	5	146	52

ANDY BLACK

TONY BOOK

Tony Book's influence as captain of Manchester City was enormous, yet he was a relatively late starter in League football, making his debut one month before his 30th birthday after Malcolm Allison persuaded Joe Mercer to buy him from Plymouth Argyle for £17,000 in July 1966. He missed only one League game in his first two seasons with City before his career looked to be over following an achilles tendon injury late in 1968. However, within six months Book was accepting the FA Cup as City skipper and joint Footballer of the Year. Before he had completed his remarkable career, Book had also captained City to success in the League Cup and the European Cup-winners' Cup, adding those medals to the Second Division Championship medal he had won in 1966. According to Allison, Tony Book was one of the best and quickest defenders he had ever seen and few would disagree with that assessment. Book became assistant to Ron Saunders and when Saunders left in 1974, Book took over as City manager before himself being replaced as team manager by Allison who returned in July 1979. Book became general manager and then after a short spell away from the club, returned to Maine Road as Reserve and Youth team coach. *League debut for City v Southampton, 20 August 1966.*

	LEAGUE		FA CUP		FL CUP		EUROPE		TOTAL	
	App	Gls	App	Gls	App	Gls	App	Gls	App	Gls
1966-67	41	0	6	0	2	0	-	-	49	0
1967-68	42	1	4	0	4	1	-	-	50	2
1968-69	15	0	6	0	0	0	0	0	21	0
1969-70	38	0	2	0	7	0	9	0	56	0
1970-71	33(1)	2	3	0	1	0	7	0	44(1)	2
1971-72	40	1	2	0	2	0	-	-	44	1
1972-73	29(1)	0	5	0	2	0	1	0	37	0
1973-74	4	0	0	0	1	0	-	-	5	0
	242(2)	4	28	0	19	1	17	0	306(2)	5

A slim, lively outside-left, Frank Booth spent two spells with Manchester City. Born at Hyde, Booth — who was known as 'Tabby' — first joined City from Stockport County in April 1902. He gained his chance when Freddie Threlfall fell ill and took it to become a member of one the best teams ever to represent City. Booth inevitably gained less attention than the great Billy Meredith who was playing on the other flank, but he was nonetheless a valuable member of the team, keeping to the touchline and swinging over a succession of precise centres for his colleagues. He was one of the players sold during the 'scandal' of 1906. He moved to Bury but later took advantage of the FA amnesty and returned to Hyde Road in July 1911, from Clyde. Booth played only four more games for City, however, and was a shadow of the player who had served the club so well in the early part of the century. He died in Manchester Infirmary in June 1919, aged 37. *League debut for City v Lincoln City, 6 September 1902.*

	LEAGUE		FA CUP		TOTAL	
	App	Gls	App	Gls	App	Gls
1902-03	9	0	0	0	9	0
1903-04	24	3	6	1	30	4
1904-05	33	8	2	0	35	8
1905-06	28	7	1	0	29	7
1911-12	4	0	0	0	4	0
	98	18	9	1	107	19

FRANK BOOTH

Centre-half Tommy Booth had a meteoric rise to fame with Manchester City, scoring the winning goal against Everton in the FA Cup semi-final, in his first season. Booth, who also won an England Under-23 cap that season, was once described by Joe Mercer as being like "Stan Cullis and Neil Franklin rolled into one." He was City's first-choice centre-half for seven seasons before losing his place to big-money signing, Dave Watson. But Booth was to prove his versatility and when Colin Bell was injured he moved into midfield with good effect. Booth won several honours in his City career — FA Cup winners' medal, European Cup-winners' Cup winners' medal and two League Cup winners' medals as well as playing in a third League Cup Final. In September 1981 Booth, who hails from the Middleton estate of Langley, was transferred to Preston North End for £30,000. *League debut for City v Arsenal, 9 October 1968.*

TOMMY BOOTH

	LEAGUE		FA CUP		FL CUP		EUROPE		TOTAL	
	App	Gls	App	Gls	App	Gls	App	Gls	App	Gls
1967-68	0	0	0	0	0	0	-	-	0	0
1968-69	28	1	7	1	1	0	0	0	36	2
1969-70	41	0	2	0	6	0	9	1	58	1
1970-71	26	1	3	0	1	0	5	1	35	2
1971-72	40	4	2	0	2	0	-	-	44	4
1972-73	34	5	5	1	2	0	2	0	43	6
1973-74	40	2	2	0	11	2	-	-	53	4
1974-75	18	2	0	0	0	0	-	-	18	2
1975-76	25(1)	6	2	2	3	0	-	-	30(1)	8
1976-77	14(1)	1	0	0	0	0	1	0	15(1)	1
1977-78	39	3	2	0	6	0	2	0	49	3
1978-79	20	0	0	0	5	1	6	1	31	2
1979-80	24	0	0	0	2	0	-	-	26	0
1980-81	30	0	2	1	5	0	-	-	37	1
1981-82	1	0	0	0	0	0	-	-	1	0
	380(2)	25	27	5	44	3	25	3	476(2)	36

Full-back Ken Branagan began his career with North Salford Youth Club and soon proved his ability by winning Boys' Club international caps for England and Great Britain. He signed for City in November 1948 but then had to do 18 months National Service in the Army before making his League debut towards the end of 1950. He was a safe if unspectacular player who served City well for a number of years without winning any personal honours, missing out on the FA Cup Finals of 1955 and 1956. He had exceptional speed for a defender and scored just three League goals, one of them a 30-yard drive against Cardiff City in October 1952. Branagan moved to Oldham Athletic in October 1960, and with former City players, Bert Lister and Bobby Johnstone, helped the Boundary Park club's revival in 1962-3. In all, Branagan made 177 appearances for Oldham and his son, Jim, also played League football. *League debut for City v Sheffield United, 9 December 1950.*

	LEAGUE		FA CUP		TOTAL	
	App	Gls	App	Gls	App	Gls
1948-49	0	0	0	0	0	0
1949-50	0	0	0	0	0	0
1950-51	10	0	1	0	11	0
1951-52	32	1	2	0	34	1
1952-53	41	1	3	0	44	1
1953-54	42	1	2	0	44	1
1954-55	11	0	1	0	12	0
1955-56	15	0	0	0	15	0
1956-57	0	0	0	0	0	0
1957-58	6	0	1	0	7	0
1958-59	16	0	1	0	17	0
1959-60	23	0	1	0	24	0
1960-61	0	0	0	0	0	0
	196	3	12	0	208	3

KEN BRANAGAN

Jackie Bray cost Manchester City a £1,000 fee when they signed him from Manchester Central in October 1929. Born at Oswaldtwistle, Bray was a fast and clever wing-half who showed much imagination when prompting his attack. He made his Central League debut only three days after signing for City, against Stockport County, and his Football League debut came in a Mancunian derby match in February the following year. Bray was a natural successor to Jimmy McMullan and he went on to amass many honours from the game, playing in City's two FA Cup Finals of the 1930's with a winners' medal in 1934, and gaining a League Championship medal in 1937. In addition he won six England caps and played for the Football League three times. He played consistently for City right up to the outbreak of war and made 177 appearances in wartime League and Cup football. When City won the Second Division title in 1946-7, Bray was in his 37th year and after nine Central League games that season he moved to Watford as manager. In 1948 he became coach to Nelson, then retired from the game. *League debut for City v Manchester United, 8 February 1930.*

JACKIE BRAY

	LEAGUE		FA CUP		TOTAL	
	App	Gls	App	Gls	App	Gls
1929-30	2	0	0	0	2	0
1930-31	21	0	1	0	22	0
1931-32	20	1	0	0	20	1
1932-33	30	0	7	0	37	0
1933-34	16	2	3	0	19	2
1934-35	39	1	1	0	40	0
1935-36	38	1	3	0	41	1
1936-37	40	2	4	0	44	2
1937-38	28	2	1	0	29	2
1938-39	23	1	0	0	23	1
1939-40	3	0	-	-	3	0
	260	10	20	0	280	9

Speed and fierce shooting were just two of the hallmarks of Ivor Broadis's performances in the immediate post-war period. He was also an original and creative player, all of which attracted the England selectors and earned Broadis 14 full caps. Born in Poplar, Broadis went to a rugby-playing school in Bow before rising to prominence in wartime football as an amateur with Millwall, Spurs and Carlisle. He was only 23 when Carlisle appointed him player-manager in 1946 and three years later he created a little piece of football history by transferring himself, to Sunderland for £19,000. Two and a half years later Broadis moved to Maine Road when City broke their club transfer record by paying £25,000 for him. It was at City that Broadis quickly blossomed into an England player, playing against Austria only 10 weeks after signing for the club. In October 1953, Broadis moved to Newcastle for £20,000 and played against City in the 1955 FA Cup Final. His other honours included three appearances for the Football League. After Newcastle, he moved back to Carlisle, then played for Queen of the South before retiring from soccer to become a sports journalist. *League debut for City v Tottenham Hotspur, 6 October 1951.*

IVOR BROADIS

	LEAGUE		FA CUP		TOTAL	
	App	Gls	App	Gls	App	Gls
1951-52	31	4	2	0	33	4
1952-53	34	6	3	2	37	8
1953-54	9	0	0	0	9	0
	74	10	5	2	79	12

Manchester City pulled off an important double signing when, in March 1928, they paid £6,000 for the Barnsley forwards Eric Brook and Freddie Tilson. Both were to become vital members of the City team in the 1930s and Brook, in particular, excelled. Indeed, his 159 League goals for City puts him top of the list of all-time goalscorers for the club. Brook was an unorthodox outside-left, roaming the front ranks and not content to simply hug the touchline. He would often pop up in the centre-forward position and scored some fine goals. His versatility did not end there, either. Brook once deputised at left-back before a full-house at Old Trafford; and he went into goal for part of games against Grimsby, Arsenal and Chelsea. He stood only 5ft 6in tall, a fair-haired, energetic player who would probably have won many more England caps than his 18, had he not had the misfortune to play at the same time as Arsenal's Cliff Bastin. In 1933-4, Brook played in all four England games and scored in every one. He had a fierce shot and was a natural penalty-taker, and his cross-field passing was an exciting feature of his game. Brook made nearly 500 League and FA Cup appearances for City and his career was already drawing to a close when war was declared in 1939. The following summer, after only two wartime League games for City, Brook retired following injuries received in a motor accident. He died in March 1965, aged 57. *League debut for City v Grimsby Town, 17 March 1928.*

ERIC BROOK

	LEAGUE		FA CUP		TOTAL	
	App	Gls	App	Gls	App	Gls
1927-28	12	2	0	0	12	2
1928-29	42	14	1	0	43	14
1929-30	40	16	5	1	45	17
1930-31	42	16	1	0	43	16
1931-32	42	10	5	3	47	13
1932-33	42	15	7	6	49	21
1933-34	38	8	8	3	46	11
1934-35	40	17	1	0	41	17
1935-36	40	13	3	3	43	16
1936-37	42	20	4	2	46	22
1937-38	36	16	4	1	40	17
1938-39	34	11	2	0	36	11
1939-40	3	1	-	-	3	1
	453	159	41	19	494	178

Hull City were so keen to sign Tommy Browell in 1910 that two of their directors rowed across the Tyne to reach the colliery village where he lived. In October that year Browell, still only 18, scored three goals against Stockport and after a journalist wrote that 'ten men and a boy beat Stockport', Browell thereafter became known as 'Boy' Browell. Such scoring feats soon attracted the bigger clubs and in December 1911, Everton paid £1,650 for him. Browell responded with 12 goals in 17 games and that almost helped Everton to the title. In October 1913, Manchester City paid £1,780 for Browell's scoring prowess and he went on to forge a deadly attacking partnership with Horace Barnes. Browell had netted 32 goals in 48 appearances for Hull, and 26 in 50 games for Everton, but his best was reserved for City, for whom he netted 122 League goals in 222 games, and 17 goals in 25 FA Cup matches. His effort in the 1926 Cup Final almost rescued City when only a superhuman save by Dick Pym denied him. Browell, who surprisingly never won an England cap, transferred to Blackpool for £1,500 in September 1926 He was still playing for the Seasiders in 1930, appearing in an FA Cup tie at the age of 37. Later he became a train driver. He died in October 1955, just before his 63rd birthday. *League debut for City v Sheffield Wednesday, 8 November 1913.*

	LEAGUE		FA CUP		TOTAL	
	App	Gls	App	Gls	App	Gls
1913-14	27	13	6	1	33	14
1914-15	10	1	2	0	12	1
1919-20	30	22	2	0	32	22
1920-21	42	31	1	0	43	31
1921-22	38	21	3	5	41	26
1922-23	15	3	0	0	15	3
1923-24	14	4	5	4	19	8
1924-25	14	6	1	0	15	6
1925-26	32	21	5	7	37	28
1926-27	0	0	0	0	0	0
	222	122	25	17	247	139

TOMMY BROWELL

When Bolton goalkeeper Dick Pym made a magnificent save from Browell in the 1926 FA Cup Final, the City man reflected: "He must have left his fingernails uncut for six months to have got to that shot."

James Buchan was a half-back who joined Manchester City from Woolwich Arsenal in March 1905. Born in Perth, Buchan had made only eight appearances for the Gunners before City signed him. He made his League debut only 24 hours after putting pen to paper and after seven appearances at the end of that 1904-05 season he became a regular in the City line-up for the next five years. His first honour came in the 1906-07 Manchester Senior Cup Final when he scored City's first goal in their 2-0 win over Stockport County. In 1910, he added a second honour when he played 20 times in City's Second Division Championship winning team. Buchan played only six League games in 1910-11 before moving back to Scotland in June 1911 when he signed for Motherwell. Altogether his brief career at Hyde Road saw him make 164 League and FA Cup appearances and score ten goals. *League debut for City v Blackburn Rovers, 11 March 1905.*

JAMES BUCHAN

Early in James Buchan's City career he played in the infamous match at Villa Park which triggered off the notorious 'City Scandal'.

	LEAGUE		FA CUP		TOTAL	
	App	Gls	App	Gls	App	Gls
1904-05	7	0	0	0	7	0
1905-06	29	1	0	0	29	1
1906-07	28	0	2	0	30	0
1907-08	27	3	6	2	33	5
1908-09	38	4	1	0	39	4
1909-10	20	0	0	0	20	0
1910-11	6	0	0	0	6	0
	155	8	9	2	164	10

Herbert Burgess stood less than 5ft 5in tall, but he was still one of the finest defenders of his day. A left-back who excelled as a fierce tackler — who was also surprisingly effective in the air — he was a local man, born at Openshaw in 1883. He joined City from Glossop in July 1903 — winning an FA Cup winners' medal in his first season — and gave excellent service until he was one of the players suspended in the celebrated 1906 affair. Manchester United stepped in with a bid of £750 and Burgess went on to make 52 League and Cup appearances for them before leaving League soccer in 1910. Burgess, who made 94 League and Cup appearances for City, was one of the first British players to coach abroad and he worked in Hungary, Spain and Italy before Mussolini decreed that no foreigners should work in Italian football. In 1933, Burgess brought his family back to Britain and got a job as a labourer on a Droylsden housing estate. Winner of four England caps, Burgess also represented the Football League. *League debut for City v Stoke City, September 1903.*

HERBERT BURGESS

	LEAGUE		FA CUP		TOTAL	
	App	Gls	App	Gls	App	Gls
1903-04	27	0	6	0	33	0
1904-05	26	0	2	0	28	0
1905-06	32	2	1	0	33	2
	85	2	9	0	94	2

SIR MATT BUSBY CBE

Sir Matt Busby had two very distinct careers, serving both Manchester clubs, and Liverpool, successfully and becoming one of the greatest managers of all time. Busby was 17-years-old and ready to emigrate to the United States with his widowed mother when City manager, Peter Hodge, persuaded him to sign in February 1928. Busby, who hails from the Lanarkshire mining village of Bellshill, was a fine, contructive wing-half. He stood 5ft 10in, weighed around 11st and was superbly equipped for the midfield role. In fact, he was an inside-forward when City signed him but they soon saw his best chance of success and moulded him into a classy half-back. With City he played in the 1933 and 1934 FA Cup Finals and won his sole Scotland cap, against Wales in October 1933, before joining Liverpool in March 1936 for £8,000, after 226 League and FA Cup games for the Maine Road club. With fellow Scots, Bradshaw and McDougal, he formed one of the best half-back lines that Liverpool ever had and played 118 League games for them before war ended his League career. Busby guested for Hibernian before accepting an offer to become Manchester United manager in 1946. He built some great sides at Old Trafford — one of them after the agonies of the Munich Air Disaster, and before he retired had seen United realise his dream of European Cup triumph. *League debut for City v Middlesbrough, 2 November 1929.*

	LEAGUE		FA CUP		TOTAL	
	App	Gls	App	Gls	App	Gls
1927-28	0	0	0	0	0	0
1928-29	0	0	0	0	0	0
1929-30	11	3	1	2	12	5
1930-31	20	0	1	0	21	0
1931-32	41	1	5	0	46	1
1932-33	39	1	7	1	46	2
1933-34	39	4	8	0	47	4
1934-35	33	1	1	0	34	1
1935-36	19	1	1	0	20	1
	202	11	24	3	226	14

Roy Clarke holds the unique record of playing in three different divisions of the Football League in three consecutive League games. He turned out for Third Division Champions, Cardiff City, in their penultimate game of 1946-7 and then was transferred to Manchester City in time to play in the last game of their promotion-winning season. Clarke's next game, at the start of 1947-8, was therefore in Division One. An attacking left-winger with a powerful shot, Clarke scored many vital goals for City. He was born in Newport and his first taste of international recognition was as a Welsh Schools baseball international in 1939. During the war he worked in the coalmines and came to soccer prominence with Cardiff. For City, Clarke made 369 League and FA Cup appearances before moving to Stockport County on a free transfer in September 1958. Winner of 22 Welsh caps, he gained an FA Cup winners' medal in 1956. In 1987 he was still connected with City, running the Maine Road social club. *League debut for City v Newport County, 14 June 1947.*

	LEAGUE		FA CUP		TOTAL	
	App	Gls	App	Gls	App	Gls
1946-47	1	0	0	0	1	0
1947-48	36	5	0	0	36	5
1948-49	34	6	1	0	35	6
1949-50	37	9	1	1	38	10
1950-51	39	9	0	0	39	9
1951-52	41	9	2	1	43	10
1952-53	22	3	0	0	22	3
1953-54	35	7	2	1	37	8
1954-55	33	7	5	3	38	10
1955-56	25	6	6	0	31	6
1956-57	40	11	2	0	42	11
1957-58	6	1	1	0	7	1
	349	73	20	6	369	79

ROY CLARKE

TONY COLEMAN

Winger Tony Coleman played for several League clubs and throughout his career he was regarded as something of a 'problem boy', but at Maine Road he prospered and under Malcolm Allison's influence became first-choice for the number-11 shirt — although Allison had described his signing as "like the nightmare of a delirious probation officer." He won a League Championship medal with City in 1967-8, and an FA Cup winners' medal the following season, but after only five League appearances in 1969-70 he was transferred to Sheffield Wednesday for £20,000, his best days now behind him. Coleman was born in Liverpool and joined City from Doncaster Rovers in March 1967, for £12,000. After falling out with the club and moving to Hillsborough, Coleman never settled again and after one season with the Owls he moved again. For City he made a total of 82 complete League appearances, scoring 12 goals. Eight of them came in the Championship-winning season when he missed only four League games, and he made several goals for the likes of Young, Lee and Bell. *League debut for City v Leeds United, 18 March 1967.*

	LEAGUE		FACUP		FLCUP		EUROPE		TOTAL	
	App	Gls	App	Gls	App	Gls	App	Gls	App	Gls
1966-67	9	1	0	0	0	0	-	-	9	1
1967-68	38	8	4	1	4	0	-	-	46	9
1968-69	30	3	6	2	3	0	2	1	41	6
1969-70	5	0	0	0	0	0	0	0	5	0
	82	12	10	3	7	0	2	1	101	16

James Conlin joined Manchester City in the troubled times of 1906 and took over the outside-left position from the suspended Frank Booth. On his League debut he was one of the players who had to leave the field suffering from heat exhaustion when City finished with six men against Woolwich Arsenal in September 1906. He was a fast, direct winger who was a good crosser of the ball and he enjoyed five good seasons at Hyde Road, laying on plenty of goals for the front men. Born in Durham, Conlin won an England cap with Bradford City shortly before joining the Manchester club. In September 1911, City transferred him to Birmingham but after only one season at St Andrew's he moved back to Scottish football. Conlin enjoyed Scottish League soccer with a number of clubs, Hibernian, Falkirk, Albion Rovers and Airdrie. His honours with City were a Division Two Championship medal in 1909-10, and represented the Football League against the Irish League in October 1910. He joined the army and was killed in action in June 1917. *League debut for City v Woolwich Arsenal, 1 September 1906.*

JAMES CONLIN

James Conlin was a regular in the City side which finished third in Division One in 1908. United won the title.

	LEAGUE		FA CUP		TOTAL	
	App	Gls	App	Gls	App	Gls
1906-07	35	2	2	0	37	2
1907-08	37	6	6	1	43	7
1908-09	27	5	1	0	28	5
1909-10	35	11	4	1	39	12
1910-11	27	4	1	0	28	4
	161	28	14	2	175	30

DAVID CONNOR

Defender David Connor spent ten years at Maine Road yet made only 130 League appearances. Nevertheless, he had many admirers and turned down several moves which would have guaranteed him regular first-team football. He was something of a utility player and his best spell for City came in the late 1960s — although he managed only ten League games when City took the title in 1967-8. A local lad — he was born at Wythenshawe in 1945 — Connor joined City as an amateur in August 1962, signing professional forms one month later. After serving City in every first-team position except goalkeeper and centre-half, he finally accepted a transfer in January 1972 when he moved to Preston for £40,000, at the same time that Neil Young switched to Deepdale. In March 1974, Connor rejoined City on a free transfer — he had made only 29 appearances in three seasons with Preston — and played for City's Central League side before Macclesfield Town signed him on another free-transfer. Connor later had a spell as Macclesfield manager. *City League debut v Charlton Athletic, 22 August 1964.*

	LEAGUE		FA CUP		FL CUP		EUROPE		TOTAL	
	App	Gls	App	Gls	App	Gls	App	Gls	App	Gls
1962-63	0	0	0	0	0	0	-	-	0	0
1963-64	0	0	0	0	0	0	-	-	0	0
1964-65	24	3	0	0	0	0	-	-	24	3
1965-66	29(1)	3	8	0	0	0	-	-	37(1)	3
1966-67	20(4)	1	3	0	0	0	-	-	23(4)	1
1967-68	10(3)	1	0	0	0	0	-	-	10(3)	1
1968-69	20(1)	1	1	0	3	0	1	0	25(1)	1
1969-70	8(1)	0	0	0	2	0	0	0	10(1)	0
1970-71	11(1)	0	0	0	0	0	4	0	15(1)	0
1971-72	8	1	0	0	0	0	-	-	8	1
1973-74	0	0	0	0	0	0	-	-	0	0
1974-75	0	0	0	0	0	0	-	-	0	0
	130(11)	10	12	0	5	0	5	0	152(11)	10

Sam Cookson was a miner in the days when he played non-League football for Stalybridge Celtic and Macclesfield, joining City from the latter club in October 1918 and signing professional forms ten months later. He was a regular choice at full-back for almost eight seasons but in all that time had only one major honour to show for it — an FA Cup runners-up medal in 1926. He was often described as 'the best uncapped full-back of his time', an accolade also given to his defensive partner, Eli Fletcher. Cookson was a small, heavily-built man, and a difficult opponent for wingers who thought they could 'fly' past him. His brother, Jimmy Cookson, was also making a name for himself at the same time, as a free-scoring forward with Chesterfield and West Brom. After 306 League and FA Cup games for City, Sam joined Bradford in September 1928 and later played for Barnsley where, in his 39th year, he won a Third Division North Championship medal. He was a proud man and that honour meant as much to him as anything he had achieved in the game. After his playing days were over he returned to Manchester, the city of his birth, and died there in August 1955, aged 59. *League debut for City v Bradford City, 1 January 1920.*

SAM COOKSON

	LEAGUE		FA CUP		TOTAL	
	App	Gls	App	Gls	App	Gls
1919-20	20	0	2	0	22	0
1920-21	42	0	1	0	43	0
1921-22	39	0	2	0	41	0
1922-23	25	0	1	0	26	0
1923-24	34	0	8	0	42	0
1924-25	37	0	0	0	37	0
1925-26	35	0	6	1	41	1
1926-27	42	0	1	0	43	0
1927-28	11	0	0	0	11	0
	285	0	21	1	306	1

Joe Corrigan overcame a slow and unimpressive start to his League career to become one of the top three goalkeepers in the country and a man who would have won many more than his nine England caps had it not been for the presence of Shilton and Clemence. City have had a post-war tradition of outstanding characters between their posts and when he finally won a regular place, Corrigan was not out of place in a line which included Frank Swift and Bert Trautmann. He was born in Manchester and joined City as a junior in 1966, when he was playing for Sale FC. His early League days were fraught with inconsistency and he was always in the shadow of Dowd or Mulhearn. He fought hard to establish himself but then faced another crisis of confidence when City signed Keith MacRae for £100,000. Out of favour with manager Ron Saunders, Corrigan was transfer-listed in February 1974 but once again the goalkeeper buckled down and won back his first-team place, going on to serve City for a further seven years. He made 476 League appearances for City and a further 116 in FA Cup, League Cup and European matches. Corrigan won two League Cup-winners' medals and a European Cup-winners' medal as well as playing in the 1981 FA Cup Final defeat by Spurs. His representive honours, in addition to his full England games, included appearances for England at 'B', Under-23 and Under-21 levels and for the FA XI and the Football League. In March 1983, City transferred him to Seattle Sounders in the NASL, for £30,000, and he later played for Brighton & Hove Albion. *League debut for City v Ipswich Town, 11 March 1969.*

JOE CORRIGAN

	LEAGUE		FACUP		FLCUP		EUROPE		TOTAL	
	App	Gls	App	Gls	App	Gls	App	Gls	App	Gls
1966-67	0	0	0	0	0	0	-	-	0	0
1967-68	0	0	0	0	2	0	-	-	2	0
1968-69	4	0	0	0	0	0	0	0	4	0
1969-70	34	0	1	0	7	0	8	0	50	0
1970-71	33	0	3	0	1	0	6	0	43	0
1971-72	35	0	2	0	2	0	-	-	39	0
1972-73	30	0	5	0	1	0	1	0	37	0
1973-74	15	0	1	0	0	0	-	-	16	0
1974-75	15	0	1	0	0	0	-	-	16	0
1975-76	41	0	2	0	9	0	-	-	52	0
1976-77	42	0	4	0	1	0	2	0	49	0
1977-78	42	0	2	0	7	0	2	0	53	0
1978-79	42	0	2	0	5	0	8	0	57	0
1979-80	42	0	1	0	4	0	-	-	47	0
1980-81	37	0	8	0	6	0	-	-	51	0
1981-82	39	0	2	0	4	0	-	-	45	0
1982-83	25	0	3	0	3	0	-	-	31	0
	476	0	37	0	52	0	27	0	592	0

The story goes that Sam Cowan did not kick a football until he was 17 when he took part in a local park game at a moment's notice and wearing only one, borrowed, boot. Eight years later he was playing for England against Austria, having established himself as a fine centre-half. He was born in Chesterfield and joined City from Doncaster Rovers in December 1924. In his 12 years with the club, Cowan played in three FA Cup Finals with a winners' medal in 1934 when he collected the trophy as captain of the side. He won a Second Division Championship medal in 1927-8, was capped twice for England and also played for the Football League. His career spanned the transition to the 'stopper' centre-half and Cowan himself, was an attacking player, scoring a hat-trick of headers for Doncaster against Halifax in March 1924. His versatility showed when he won his first cap as a left-half. In October 1935 he moved to Bradford City for £2,000 and later played for Mossley and was Brighton trainer before returning to Maine Road as manager in 1945, steering City to promotion from Division Two in the first post-war League season. *League debut for City v Birmingham, 20 December 1924.*

SAM COWAN

	LEAGUE		FA CUP		TOTAL	
	App	Gls	App	Gls	App	Gls
1924-25	21	1	0	0	21	1
1925-26	38	2	7	0	45	2
1926-27	27	2	1	0	28	2
1927-28	28	0	2	0	30	0
1928-29	38	1	1	0	39	1
1929-30	40	1	5	2	45	3
1930-31	40	2	1	0	41	2
1931-32	31	3	5	1	36	4
1932-33	32	4	7	2	39	6
1933-34	32	3	8	0	40	3
1934-35	42	0	1	0	43	0
	369	19	38	5	407	24

JOHNNY CROSSAN

Johnny Crossan's career was actually furthered by a Football League ban which saw him develop his skills on the Continent. He was born in Londonderry and played Irish League football for Derry City and Coleraine before problems over a proposed move to Bristol City resulted in a 'life' suspension and a move, instead, to Sparta Rotterdam. It was with Standard Liège that his skills were brought to a wider stage when he played for the Belgian club in the European Cup. The ban lifted, Crossan signed for Sunderland for £27,000 and in January 1965 he moved to City who paid £40,000 for his midfield skills. Those skills proved vital as City returned to Division One with Crossan as their captain. He played one season for City in the First Division, taking his overall League and Cup appearances for them to 110, and then found his place threatened by the skills of Bell and Young. City sold him to Middlesbrough for £30,000 which meant they had recouped most of their fee. Crossan, who won 24 Northern Ireland caps, ten of them with City, ended his League career at Ayresome Park. *League debut for City v Derby County, 30 January 1965.*

	LEAGUE		FA CUP		FL CUP		TOTAL	
	App	Gls	App	Gls	App	Gls	App	Gls
1964-65	16	3	0	0	0	0	16	3
1965-66	40	13	8	2	1	1	49	16
1966-67	38	8	6	1	1	0	45	9
1967-68	0	0	0	0	0	0	0	0
	94	24	14	3	2	1	110	28

When full-back Bill Dale joined Manchester City from Manchester United in December 1931 he had played only 64 League games in six years at Old Trafford. Dale had considerably more success with City, making 237 League and 32 FA Cup appearances for them and winning a League Championship medal and an FA Cup winners' medal as well as playing in the losing 1933 Cup Final team. He was perhaps unlucky that there were so many fine defenders around at the time and he was passed over by the England selectors although there could have been few better full-backs when Dale was at his prime. He was Manchester-born and stood 5ft 9in tall, his 11st frame being ideal for a full-back's role. In May 1938 he moved to Ipswich Town in a complicated deal which saw Dale and Harry Rowley move to Portman Road whilst Ridding came to Maine Road with a sum of money making up the balance. *League debut for City v Portsmouth, 26 December 1931.*

BILL DALE

	LEAGUE		FA CUP		TOTAL	
	App	Gls	App	Gls	App	Gls
1931-32	21	0	5	0	26	0
1932-33	39	0	7	0	46	0
1933-34	31	0	8	0	39	0
1934-35	39	0	1	0	40	0
1935-36	41	0	3	0	44	0
1936-37	36	0	3	0	39	0
1937-38	30	0	5	0	35	0
	237	0	32	0	269	0

Peter Doherty, the flame-haired inside-forward often described as the best player ever produced by Ireland, was a complete footballer in every sense of the word. Doherty could tackle, dribble, shoot and head the ball with the best, his passing was as accurate as anyone's in the game, and he had one of the most astute tactical brains of all time. He was, quite simply, one of the truly great footballers of the 20th century. Born at Magherafelt in 1913, he played for Coleraine and Glentoran before Blackpool brought his talents to the English game in 1933, the years after he had helped Glentoran win the Irish Cup. City paid a club record £10,000 for him in February 1936 — the fee was £1,000 short of the then overall record — and Doherty proceeded to delight Maine Road fans with his artistry and seemingly boundless energy. He was a star in the 1936-7 Championship-winning team but the war interrupted his City career and after 133 League and Cup games his Maine Road career was effectively ended. The war also denied him greater international reward — 16 caps was far fewer than he deserved — but it did bring about a partnership with another legendary inside-forward, Sunderland's Raich Carter, and the two of them helped Derby win the FA Cup in 1946. Doherty later inspired Huddersfield and Doncaster (who he took to the Third Division North title) and was Northern Ireland manager when they reached the 1958 World Cup quarter-finals. *League debut for City v Preston North End, 22 February 1936.*

PETER DOHERTY

	LEAGUE		FA CUP		TOTAL	
	App	Gls	App	Gls	App	Gls
1935-36	9	4	0	0	9	4
1936-37	41	30	4	2	45	32
1937-38	41	23	5	2	46	25
1938-39	28	17	2	1	30	18
1939-40	3	2	-	-	3	2
	122	76	11	5	133	81

Few players have won more full international caps for Scotland than Willie Donachie's 35. Donachie was one of the best First Division full-backs in the 1970s and he played in the 1978 World Cup Finals and was a member of the Scotland team that beat England at Hampden in 1976. Born in Glasgow, Donachie joined Manchester City as a junior in 1968. He was a midfielder in those days but it was after City converted him to left-back that his career took off. He replaced Glyn Pardoe after that player had broken a leg and for the next seven years Donachie made the position his own. He was ever-present in the 1973-4 and 1976-7 League campaigns and played in two League Cup Finals, collecting a winners' medal in 1976. Donachie, who also played twice for Scotland Under-23s, was a full international before he was 22 and his speed and ball control made him a classy defender. In March 1980, after 347 full League appearances for City, he signed for the NASL club, Portland Timbers, for £200,000. Later he played for Norwich, Burnley and Oldham. *League debut for City v Nottingham Forest, 7 February 1970.*

WILLIE DONACHIE

	LEAGUE		FA CUP		FL CUP		EUROPE		TOTAL	
	App	Gls	App	Gls	App	Gls	App	Gls	App	Gls
1968-69	0	0	0	0	0	0	0	0	0	0
1969-70	1(2)	0	0	0	0	0	0	0	1(2)	0
1970-71	11	0	0	0	0	0	3	0	14	0
1971-72	35(2)	0	2	0	2	0	-	-	39(2)	0
1972-73	40	1	5	0	2	0	1	0	48	1
1973-74	42	0	2	0	11	0	-	-	55	0
1974-75	40	1	1	0	1	0	-	-	42	1
1975-76	40	0	2	0	9	0	-	-	51	0
1976-77	42	0	4	0	1	0	2	0	49	0
1977-78	39	0	2	0	7	0	1	0	49	0
1978-79	38	0	3	0	4	0	6	0	51	0
1979-80	19	0	0	0	3	0	-	-	22	0
	347(4)	2	21	0	40	0	13	0	421(4)	2

GEORGE DORSETT

George Dorsett joined City from West Bromwich Albion in December 1904, for a then record fee for a winger of around £450. Dorsett had made exactly 100 appearances for Albion and although it was his skills as an outside-left that attracted City, the Maine Road club eventually switched him to wing-half. In 1910 he was joined at City by his brother, Joe, who was also an outside-left with Albion and for a short time the two played together in City's first team. In May that year, George collected a Second Division Championship medal to add to his only other honour from the game, a game for the Football League against the Irish League in October 1905. Dorsett, who was born at Brownhills, retired through injury in the close season of 1912. He died in April 1943, aged 62. *League debut for City v Stoke, 7 January 1905.*

	LEAGUE		FA CUP		TOTAL	
	App	Gls	App	Gls	App	Gls
1904-05	9	5	2	0	11	5
1905-06	34	15	1	0	35	15
1906-07	32	8	2	1	34	9
1907-08	34	10	6	1	40	11
1908-09	22	9	1	0	23	9
1909-10	38	13	4	1	42	14
1910-11	23	2	2	0	25	2
1911-12	1	0	0	0	1	0
	193	62	18	3	211	65

Mike Doyle's first appearance in a City team was at centre-forward, but it was as a midfielder and defender that he made more than 500 appearances for the club. Born in Manchester, Doyle joined the City groundstaff in 1962. He was a determined performer in whatever role he was given and his influence helped City out of the Second Division in 1966 and to the top of the First in 1968. He was one of the club's finest players during their great days under Mercer and Allison, and later under Book, playing in three League Cup Finals (two winners' medals) as well as winners' medals in the FA Cup and European Cup-winners' Cup. After Rodney Marsh left Maine Road in 1975, Doyle was appointed captain. He represented England at Under-23 level before winning five full caps and also played for the Football League. Struggling to get back in the side after injury, Doyle was transferred to Stoke for £50,000 in June 1978 and later played for Bolton and Rochdale. *League debut for City v Cardiff City, 12 March 1965.*

MIKE DOYLE

	LEAGUE		FA CUP		FL CUP		EUROPE		TOTAL	
	App	Gls	App	Gls	App	Gls	App	Gls	App	Gls
1963-64	0	0	0	0	0	0	-	-	0	0
1964-65	6	0	0	0	0	0	-	-	6	0
1965-66	19(1)	7	7	1	0	0	-	-	26(1)	8
1966-67	14(2)	0	5	1	0	0	-	-	19(2)	1
1967-68	37(1)	5	4	0	3	0	-	-	44(1)	5
1968-69	40	5	7	0	3	0	2	0	52	5
1969-70	41	4	2	0	7	2	9	1	59	7
1970-71	37	5	3	0	1	0	7	1	48	6
1971-72	41	1	2	0	2	0	-	-	45	1
1972-73	38(2)	1	5	0	1	0	2	0	46(2)	1
1973-74	39	1	2	0	11	0	-	-	52	1
1974-75	42	1	1	0	2	1	-	-	45	2
1975-76	41	1	2	0	9	1	-	-	52	2
1976-77	33	1	4	0	1	0	2	0	40	1
1977-78	13(1)	0	0	0	3	0	1	0	17(1)	0
	441(7)	32	44	2	43	4	23	2	551(7)	40

BILL EADIE

Half-back Bill Eadie was one of the players who joined City in 1906, in the wake of the suspensions which cost the club the services of several key players. A Scot from Greenock, he joined City from his local side, Morton, and took over at centre-half from Tommy Hynds. He was not a particularly consistent performer but after ten appearances in the side relegated in 1908-09, he helped City return immediately to the First Division, playing in 23 League games in that promotion season. That was his only honour with City, apart from a Lancashire Combination Division Two winners' medal with the Reserves in 1908-09. In June 1914, Eadie was transferred to Derby County and made 31 appearances for the Rams in their Division Two promotion season of 1914-15. Then League football was suspended for the duration of the war and his career was over. *League debut for City v Sheffield Wednesday, 8 September 1906.*

	LEAGUE		FA CUP		TOTAL	
	App	Gls	App	Gls	App	Gls
1906-07	31	0	2	0	33	0
1907-08	29	3	6	0	35	3
1908-09	10	1	1	0	11	1
1909-10	23	2	4	0	27	2
1910-11	29	0	2	0	31	0
1911-12	26	0	2	0	28	0
1912-13	31	0	3	0	34	0
1913-14	6	0	0	0	6	0
	185	6	20	0	205	6

Albert Emptage was one of those desperately unlucky footballers whose career was gathering momentum when League soccer was suspended for the duration of war. Emptage joined City as a 19-year-old inside-forward from Scunthorpe United in February 1937 and made his League debut 11 months later. Altogether he managed only 13 first-team appearances before the war but in 1946-7, by now successfully converted to wing-half, he won a Second Division Championship medal. In October 1947, now a First Division player, Emptage won his one senior representative honour when he played for the Football League against the Irish League. That season he missed only three League games for City and was a fairly regular performer in the following two seasons before joining Stockport County, his third and final League club, in January 1951. *League debut for City v Leicester City, 15 January 1938.*

ALBERT EMPTAGE

	LEAGUE		FA CUP		TOTAL	
	App	Gls	App	Gls	App	Gls
1937-38	4	0	0	0	4	0
1938-39	9	0	0	0	9	0
1946-47	29	0	4	0	33	0
1947-48	39	0	3	0	42	0
1948-49	27	1	1	0	28	1
1949-50	27	0	0	0	27	0
1950-51	1	0	0	0	1	0
	136	1	8	0	144	1

DAVE EWING

Although Perth-born Dave Ewing took his time in gaining a first-team place — he joined City in June 1949 and did not make his League debut until January 1953 — he went on to become the anchor of the defence which helped City win the FA Cup in 1956. He came to Maine Road from Luncarty Juniors, a tall, well-built centre-half of the rugged type. In 1953-4 he was ever-present in the League team and, indeed, missed only 27 games in six seasons in the late 1950s. He was one of the toughest centre-halves in the country at that time and with Roy Paul and Ken Barnes he formed a perfectly balanced half-back line. His vocal encouragement was a particular feature of his game and he exhorted City to two Wembley Finals in successive years. After 302 League and FA Cup games for the club, Ewing joined Crewe Alexandra on a free-transfer in July 1962. After 48 appearances for Crewe he returned to City as a coach and later served Sheffield Wednesday, Bradford City and Crystal Palace in a similar capacity, and managed Hibernian, before returning to City once more. He ran the Reserves team which won the Central League title for the first time in the club's history, in 1977-8. *League debut for City v Manchester United, 3 January 1953.*

	LEAGUE		FA CUP		FL CUP		TOTAL	
	App	Gls	App	Gls	App	Gls	App	Gls
1949-50	0	0	0	0	0	0	0	0
1950-51	0	0	0	0	0	0	0	0
1952-53	19	0	3	0	-	-	22	0
1953-54	42	0	2	0	-	-	44	0
1954-55	40	0	5	0	-	-	45	0
1955-56	39	0	7	0	-	-	46	0
1956-57	34	0	2	0	-	-	36	0
1957-58	38	1	1	0	-	-	39	1
1958-59	30	0	2	0	-	-	32	0
1959-60	7	0	0	0	-	-	7	0
1960-61	9	0	0	0	0	0	9	0
1961-62	21	0	0	0	1	0	22	0
	279	1	22	0	1	0	302	1

'Paddy' Fagan, as he was inevitably known, was a versatile, crowd-pleasing winger who was at home on either flank. He won eight Republic of Ireland caps, two of them with City, and was a member of the losing 1955 FA Cup Final team. He joined City from Hull City on Christmas Eve 1953 and made his League debut on Boxing Day. Fagan started his career with Transport FC in his native Dublin. He made 153 League appearances for City before joining Derby County for £8,000 in March 1960 where he won further international honours. From Derby he moved into non-League football and played for Altrincham, Northwich Victoria and Ashton United. His father was a Shamrock Rovers player and also an Irish international. *League debut for City v Sheffield United, 26 December 1953.*

	LEAGUE		FA CUP		TOTAL	
	App	Gls	App	Gls	App	Gls
1953-54	6	0	1	0	7	0
1954-55	36	11	6	0	42	11
1955-56	16	1	0	0	16	1
1956-57	31	9	2	1	33	10
1957-58	29	7	1	0	30	7
1958-59	25	4	0	0	25	4
1959-60	10	2	1	0	11	2
	153	34	11	1	164	35

FIONAN FAGAN

In early floodlit games at Maine Road, City wore shirts with a 'satin' finish. One player complained, "They weigh a ton. We sink to our knees when we put them on." Hearts were the first floodlit visitors, in October 1953. City won 6-3 with goals from Sowden (3), Hart (2) and Broadis.

JOE FAGAN

Centre-half Joe Fagan was 17-years-old when he signed for City from Earlstown Bohemians in October 1938. War meant that he had to wait until January 1947 to make his League debut and he played 20 games in the second half of City's promotion season. Thereafter he did not miss a game for two seasons, and was absent only three times in 1949-50. He was a solid, dependable centre-half and proved his worth as City established themselves back in Division One. In August 1951, Fagan moved to Nelson but returned to League football for a short spell with Bradford. In 1953 he left Park Avenue to become trainer at Rochdale and then moved to the Liverpool training staff. At Anfield he became one of the famous 'boot-room' staff and eventually replaced Bob Paisley as manager. Liverpool won three major trophies in Fagan's first season in charge and he announced his retirement immediately before the 1985 European Cup Final. Alas, Fagan was denied his hour of final glory by the tragic events in Brussels, and he left League football in the saddest circumstances. *League debut for City v Fulham, 1 January 1947.*

	LEAGUE		FA CUP		TOTAL	
	App	Gls	App	Gls	App	Gls
1946-47	20	0	4	0	24	0
1947-48	42	1	3	0	45	1
1948-49	42	0	1	0	43	0
1949-50	39	1	1	0	40	1
1950-51	5	0	1	0	6	0
	148	2	10	0	158	2

Pat Finnerhan was spotted by City director Lawrence Furness when he was refereeing a game involving Northwich Victoria. Finnerhan was partnering Billy Meredith that day and soon the two were starring with Manchester City. Finnerhan was a clever inside-right who had the happy knack of being able to retain the ball until just the right time. Then he would release it and send a colleague on his way to goal. Finnerhan himself was no slouch in front of goal and he scored 27 in 85 League games for City — strangely, he never played in an FA Cup match for the club. He had two representative honours, playing for the Football League against the Irish League in November 1895, and for the North versus the South in March 1896. In 1895-6, when he scored nine goals in 30 games, he helped City to runners-up position in Division Two, although they were not promoted after failing in the Test matches. In May 1897, Finnerhan moved to Liverpool but made only five League appearances for them before drifting out of top-class football. *League debut for City v Bury, 1 September 1894.*

	LEAGUE		FA CUP		TEST		TOTAL	
	App	Gls	App	Gls	App	Gls	App	Gls
1894-95	30	15	-	-	-	-	30	15
1895-96	30	9	-	-	4	0	34	9
1896-97	25	3	0	0	-	-	25	3
	85	27	0	0	4	0	89	7

PAT FINNERHAN

STEVE FLEET

At first glance, goalkeeper Steve Fleet seems out of place in a gallery of Manchester City's finest servants, for in nine seasons with the club he managed a meagre five League appearances. Behind those statistics lies the fact that Fleet was, indeed, one of City's most loyal players. Born in Salford, he joined City from local amateur football in 1953, signing professional forms two years later. His League debut did not come until 1957-8 and he managed only one game that season, and for each of the next two, the 'highlight' of his City career coming in 1960-61 when he played twice. Fleet's perpetual reserve tag was because of the presence of Bert Trautmann. Fleet could have moved on but he loved the City club and only when Harry Dowd pushed him from the number-two spot did he leave. In June 1963 he signed for Wrexham on a free-transfer and made 79 appearances for the Welsh club before ending his career with Stockport County (36 appearances). Fleet returned to Maine Road and worked with the Reserves and Youth teams under Mercer and Allison when the Reserves enjoyed some of their most successful years. Fleet stayed with City until John Bond's appointment in 1981. *League debut for City v Wolverhampton Wanderers, 23 November 1957.*

	LEAGUE		FL CUP		TOTAL	
	App	Gls	App	Gls	App	Gls
1957-58	1	0	-	-	1	0
1958-59	1	0	-	-	1	0
1959-60	1	0	-	-	1	0
1960-61	2	0	0	0	2	0
1961-62	0	0	0	0	0	0
1962-63	0	0	1	0	1	0
	5	0	1	0	6	0

Full-back Eli Fletcher found his way to Manchester City from his native Staffordshire via Crewe. His first professional club was Hanley Swifts but he came to City's notice when he was a member of the Crewe team which sensationally won an FA Cup match at Bristol City in 1910. The Bristol club, then a First Division outfit, offered a £300 fee for Fletcher but he wanted to stay in the north and opted to join Manchester City in May 1911. He became a regular choice at left-back and some thought he might oust Jesse Penington from the England team at one stage, although he had to settle for three appearances for the Football League. He overcame serious injury to become one of City's longest serving players with 327 League and FA Cup games added to 133 games during World War One. In June 1926 he joined Watford as player-manager and later served Sandbach Ramblers. *League debut for City v Newcastle United, 23 September 1911.*

ELI FLETCHER

	LEAGUE		FA CUP		TOTAL	
	App	Gls	App	Gls	App	Gls
1911-12	35	1	2	0	37	1
1912-13	33	0	3	0	36	0
1913-14	36	0	6	0	42	0
1914-15	37	0	4	0	41	0
1919-20	34	1	2	0	36	1
1920-21	35	0	1	0	36	0
1921-22	38	0	3	0	41	0
1922-23	5	0	0	0	5	0
1923-24	20	0	4	0	24	0
1924-25	27	0	1	0	28	0
1925-26	1	0	0	0	1	0
	301	2	26	0	327	2

BILLY GILLESPIE

In 1934, Billy Gillespie returned to England for a holiday and spent some time at the Stretford Hotel, a public house run by Billy Meredith.

Strathclyde-born Billy Gillespie was a broad, bustling centre-forward who capitalised on the service provided by Meredith, Threlfall and later Booth. In eight years with the club Gillespie scored 132 goals in 231 League and FA Cup games and helped City to two Second Division Championship medals and an FA Cup Final victory. He joined City from Lincoln City in January 1897 and soon earned himself the reputation of a 'bad boy' on the pitch, yet his skill and good humour soon endeared him to the fans. He was their particular hero when he scored all four goals in a vital game at Blackburn's Ewood Park. In the close season of 1905 he left English football and emigrated, according to one report 'to the diamond fields of South Africa'. Even then his controversial reputation was maintained when, a year after he had sailed for Cape Town, the FA fined him £50 and suspended him following alleged transfer irregularities. His brother was Matt Gillespie, who played for rivals Newton Heath. *League debut for City v Darwen, 9 January 1897.*

	LEAGUE		FA CUP		TOTAL	
	App	Gls	App	Gls	App	Gls
1896-97	11	4	0	0	11	4
1897-98	30	18	2	1	32	19
1898-99	30	17	1	1	31	18
1899-00	28	8	2	0	30	8
1900-01	23	9	0	0	23	9
1901-02	24	15	0	0	24	15
1902-03	32	30	1	0	33	30
1903-04	24	18	6	3	30	21
1904-05	16	7	1	1	17	8
	218	126	13	6	231	132

Goalkeeper Jim Goodchild was working in the Southampton docks after being discarded by the Saints after only five League games when his career was rescued by Manchester City. Goodchild, who had joined Southampton from local club St Paul's Athletic, went on to become the one City hero in the 1926 FA Cup Final. He signed for them in December 1911 and early the following year was the star of a fine Cup win at Preston. By the time he was transferred to Guildford City, in August 1927, Goodchild had made 204 League and 13 FA Cup appearances for the Maine Road club. Goodchild was a safe if not spectacular 'keeper and in his early City career he vied with Walter Smith for the first-team spot. After World War One, during which time he made 142 appearances for City, and with Smith's League career ended, Goodchild earned himself a regular place. In 1921, City rewarded him with part of the proceeds from a game against Newcastle United. His only representative honour during his time at Maine Road was an appearance for the Central League XI against the North Eastern League in February 1920. *League debut for City v Aston Villa, 20 January 1912.*

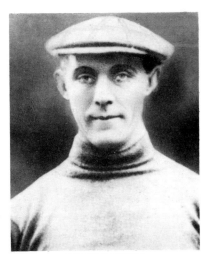

JIM GOODCHILD

	LEAGUE		FA CUP		TOTAL	
	App	Gls	App	Gls	App	Gls
1911-12	15	0	2	0	17	0
1912-13	28	0	0	0	28	0
1913-14	2	0	0	0	2	0
1914-15	1	0	0	0	1	0
1919-20	33	0	2	0	35	0
1920-21	42	0	1	0	43	0
1921-22	4	0	0	0	4	0
1922-23	20	0	0	0	20	0
1923-24	7	0	0	0	7	0
1924-25	13	0	0	0	13	0
1925-26	24	0	7	0	31	0
1926-27	15	0	1	0	16	0
	204	0	13	0	217	0

In the 1926 FA Cup Final, Jim Goodchild made some brave saves from Bolton's J.R.Smith. Goodchild was the first man Smith sought out at the final whistle. He shook the 'keeper's hand vigorously.

MICKEY HAMILL

On his City debut, Mickey Hamill found himself marking Derby's Egyptian inside-forward, Tewfik Abdallah.

Mickey Hamill spent three seasons with Manchester United under manager Mangnall before returning to his native Belfast before World War One. It was in September 1920 that Mangnall, by now manager at Hyde Road, persuaded Hamill to leave Irish League football with Belfast Celtic and return to Manchester, this time to play for City. In February 1921, Hamill was capped for Ireland against Scotland. It was his only such honour as a City player although he won seven caps altogether. He was originally an inside-forward but it was at wing-half that he enjoyed his best years. Hamill was a good all-round footballer, although some critics thought he lacked the vital spark which would have turned him into a great player. Nevertheless he was one of City's major influences in the early 1920s. In the close season of 1924 he joined the American club, Fall River, of Boston and later returned to Ireland once more, this time as manager of Distillery. Hamill's end was both tragic and mysterious when, in July 1943, his body was fished out of a river. *League debut for City v Derby County, 9 October 1920.*

	LEAGUE		FA CUP		TOTAL	
	App	Gls	App	Gls	App	Gls
1920-21	28	0	0	0	28	0
1921-22	24	0	2	0	26	0
1922-23	41	0	1	0	42	0
1923-24	25	1	7	1	32	2
	118	1	10	1	128	2

Midfield schemer George Hannah spent six years with Manchester City after scoring against City for Newcastle United in the 1955 FA Cup Final. He arrived at Maine Road via Lincoln City three years after that Wembley triumph with the Magpies and his best season was in 1960-61 when he played 30 League games, scoring three goals. Hannah cost City £20,000 and although they recouped only £2,000 of that fee when they sold him to Notts County in July 1964, he was a worthwhile signing. An industrious and skilful player, Hannah soon proved popular with the City fans. His representative honours with City were restricted to appearances with the FA XI, on tour in 1961 and against New Zealand in 1964, and he was unfortunate to play for the club at a time when they were heading for Division Two. Although born in Liverpool, Hannah began his career in Irish football after being rejected by Everton. He scored on his debut for Newcastle and throughout his career was regarded as a 'one-touch' type of player. His career ended with Bradford City and he returned to Manchester to open a newsagents' shop. *League debut for City v Arsenal, 20 September 1958.*

GEORGE HANNAH

	LEAGUE		FA CUP		FL CUP		TOTAL	
	App	Gls	App	Gls	App	Gls	App	Gls
1958-59	23	2	0	0	-	-	23	2
1959-60	26	4	0	0	-	-	26	4
1960-61	30	3	4	0	2	0	36	3
1961-62	13	1	2	0	1	0	16	1
1962-63	13	3	3	0	5	1	21	4
1963-64	9	2	0	0	0	0	9	2
	114	15	9	0	8	1	131	16

Johnny Hart was a skilful inside-right but he could be forgiven for thinking that good fortune largely passed him by at Maine Road where he spent 16 years but made only 169 League appearances largely due to injury. It was a particularly cruel blow — a broken leg at Huddersfield shortly before the 1955 FA Cup Final — that robbed him of a Wembley place after he had finally established himself in the first team. Born at Golborne, Hart joined City from local amateur football and made his senior debut in the 1945-6 wartime league. After his broken leg he never re-established his first-team claim and he was not helped by the presence of players like Bobby Johnstone who commanded regular selection yet in the 1950s Hart had found a goal-scoring touch which saw him become City's leading scorer three times (once with Revie). He retired in May 1963 and then spent a decade on the Maine Road coaching staff before becoming what many people saw as the unlikely heir to Mercer and Allison's glittering team. Hart's period as manager was not as rewarding and gave up the post after only six months because of ill-health. His 67 goals for the club was a good striking rate for the amount of games he played and both as a player and backroom servant Hart has given superb service to City, his only League club. *League debut for City v Bolton Wanderers, 10 April 1948.*

JOHNNY HART

	LEAGUE		FA CUP		TOTAL	
	App	Gls	App	Gls	App	Gls
1945-46	-	-	1	1	1	1
1946-47	0	0	0	0	0	0
1947-48	1	0	0	0	1	0
1948-49	12	1	1	0	13	1
1949-50	9	2	0	0	9	2
1950-51	27	14	0	0	27	14
1951-52	26	11	0	0	26	11
1952-53	20	9	1	4	21	13
1953-54	32	12	2	0	34	12
1954-55	31	14	4	1	35	15
1955-56	1	1	0	0	1	1
1956-57	4	0	0	0	4	0
1957-58	5	3	0	0	5	3
1958-59	0	0	0	0	0	0
1959-60	0	0	0	0	0	0
1960-61	1	0	0	0	1	0
1961-62	0	0	0	0	0	0
	169	67	9	6	178	73

Scottish international midfielder Asa Hartford will perhaps always be remembered as the player whose transfer to then First Division giants, Leeds United, was sensationally called off after a routine medical examination revealed a heart condition. That was in 1972 when Hartford was poised to move from West Brom to Elland Road for £170,000. Happily, Hartford's condition was a minor one and Manchester City had no hesitation in paying £250,000 for his skills in August 1974. Hartford, by his stamina and urgent midfield play, had swept away all doubts about his fitness and he played a major role in the glorious City era of the late 1970s. In June 1979, City sold him to Nottingham Forest for £500,000 and when they bought him back in October 1981, for £350,000 from Everton, Hartford was still a current international. In May 1984, he left Maine Road a second time, this time on a free-transfer to Fort Lauderdale Sun in the NASL. Altogether he won 50 full Scotland caps, 35 of them with City, and played in City's winning League Cup Final team of 1976. *League debut for City v West Ham United, 17 August 1974.*

ASA HARTFORD

	LEAGUE		FACUP		FLCUP		EUROPE		TOTAL	
	App	Gls	App	Gls	App	Gls	App	Gls	App	Gls
1974-75	29(1)	2	1	0	1	0	-	-	31(1)	2
1975-76	39	9	2	1	9	2	-	-	50	12
1976-77	40	4	4	0	1	0	2	0	47	4
1977-78	37	4	2	0	5	0	2	0	46	4
1978-79	39	3	3	0	5	0	8	2	55	5
1981-82	30	3	2	0	4	1	-	-	36	4
1982-83	38	3	3	1	4	0	-	-	45	4
1983-84	7	1	0	0	0	0	-	-	7	1
	259(1)	29	17	2	29	3	12	2	317(1)	36

Joe Hayes scored four goals in a trial game for City, after arriving with his boots in a brown-paper parcel, and eight weeks later was making his League debut against Tottenham Hotspur. He went on to make 331 League appearances for City, and scored 142 goals in the process, which makes him one of the club's most successful forwards of all time. He worked at a colliery and then in a cotton mill before signing for City in August 1953. Hayes overcame poor eyesight, and the fact that he stood only 5ft 8in tall, to become one of the best goal-poachers in the post-war game. He played in two FA Cup Finals, with a winners' medal at Wembley in 1956 when he scored a goal, and played for England Under-23, Young England and the FA XI. His goals tally for City would have undoubtedly been higher but for a serious knee injury sustained at Bury in 1964. In June 1965, Hayes left for Barnsley on a free-transfer and ended his career at Wigan Athletic and Lancaster City, where he was player-manager. *League debut for City v Tottenham Hotspur, 24 October 1953.*

JOE HAYES

	LEAGUE		FACUP		FLCUP		TOTAL	
	App	Gls	App	Gls	App	Gls	App	Gls
1953-54	11	0	0	0	-	-	11	0
1954-55	20	13	6	2	-	-	26	15
1955-56	42	23	7	4	-	-	49	27
1956-57	34	14	0	0	-	-	34	14
1957-58	40	25	1	1	-	-	41	26
1958-59	40	16	2	1	-	-	42	17
1959-60	41	13	1	0	-	-	42	13
1960-61	38	18	4	1	2	1	44	20
1961-62	39	16	2	0	1	0	42	16
1962-63	21	4	1	0	4	0	26	4
1963-64	3	0	0	0	1	0	4	0
1964-65	2	0	0	0	0	0	2	0
	331	142	24	9	8	1	363	152

Alex Herd had a dramatic entry into English football and within 15 months of signing for City from Hamilton Academical, he had played in two FA Cup Finals. Herd was an inside-forward who brought the ball from deep positions before using it to send his fellow strikers *en route* for goal. He was a member of one of the club's greatest-ever teams when he starred in the 1936-7 side which won the League Championship. His career stretched into wartime football — when he was capped by Scotland — and beyond, when he won a Second Division Championship medal with City in 1946-7. He made 290 League and Cup appearances for City, and a further 90 in wartime football. Herd came from a footballing family; his brother was a Hearts and Scotland player and his son, David, went on to win honours with Manchester United. Herd senior left City for Stockport County on a free-transfer in March 1948 and at Edgeley Park he turned out alongside his son in County's League team, on the last day of 1950-51 when they were Stockport's inside-forwards against Hartlepool. *League debut for City v Blackpool, 4 February 1933.*

ALEX HERD

	LEAGUE		FA CUP		TOTAL	
	App	Gls	App	Gls	App	Gls
1932-33	16	7	4	0	20	7
1933-34	37	17	8	4	45	21
1934-35	37	14	1	0	38	14
1935-36	33	10	3	1	36	11
1936-37	32	15	4	3	36	18
1937-38	35	12	5	3	40	15
1938-39	35	20	2	2	37	22
1939-40	3	0	-	-	3	0
1946-47	28	11	0	0	28	11
1947-48	4	1	0	0	4	1
	260	107	30	17	290	124

GEORGE HESLOP

Centre-half George Heslop had little success with either of his first two League clubs, making only 27 appearances for Newcastle and ten for Everton, where he spent three and a half years understudying Brian Labone. However, when Mercer and Allison took him to Maine Road, Heslop found that he had exchanged the often sterile atmosphere of Central League football for the heady air of First Division and European football. In four years with City he won Second and then First Division Championship medals, and winners' medals also in the League Cup and European Cup-winners' Cup. City signed him from Everton for only £25,000 in September 1965 and under the guidance of Allison and Mercer he shared in the great times at Maine Road as the club became a major force once more. On Christmas Eve 1971 he joined Cape Town City on loan after 159 League games for Manchester City. He spent one season in South African soccer before leaving Maine Road permanently when he was transferred to Bury for £3,000. Later he played for Bury and then became Northwich Victoria manager before taking over the licence of the Hyde Road Hotel, the original HQ of Manchester City and now the City Gates. *League debut for City v Norwich City, 15 September 1965.*

	LEAGUE		FA CUP		FL CUP		EUROPE		TOTAL	
	App	Gls	App	Gls	App	Gls	App	Gls	App	Gls
1965-66	34	0	7	0	1	0	-	-	42	0
1966-67	37	0	4	0	2	0	-	-	43	0
1967-68	41	1	4	0	4	0	-	-	49	1
1968-69	15(1)	0	0	0	2	0	2	0	19(1)	0
1969-70	6(1)	0	0	0	2	0	2	0	10(1)	0
1970-71	19(1)	0	2	0	0	0	3	0	24(1)	0
1971-72	7	0	0	0	1	0	-	-	8	0
	159(3)	1	17	0	12	0	7	0	195(3)	1

Victorian and Edwardian football was full of larger-than-life characters and England goalkeeper Jack Hillman was at home in the company of players like Billy Foulke and Billy Meredith. Indeed, Hillman was second only to the huge Sheffield United goalkeeper, Foulke, in stature; and in ability he ran goalkeeper John Sutcliffe, of Bolton and Manchester United, close. Hillman stood six feet tall and weighed 16st. He was a Devon man, born at Tavistock, and he began his League career with Burnley before playing in turn for Everton, Dundee and Burnley again. It was from Burnley that he signed for Manchester City in January 1902, and he went on to make 124 League and Cup appearances for them before switching to Millwall in January 1907. His career ended with the London club after he badly injured an elbow. Like most of the great footballers of his day, Hillman was more than simply a player of skill. The story goes that on one occasion he accepted a wager to keep goal in a charity match — and helped his team win 1-0. With City he won a Second Division Championship medal in 1903 and an FA Cup winners' medal in April 1904. *League debut for City v Notts County, 1 February 1902.*

JACK HILLMAN

	LEAGUE		FA CUP		TOTAL	
	App	Gls	App	Gls	App	Gls
1901-02	14	0	0	0	14	0
1902-03	31	0	1	0	32	0
1903-04	28	0	5	0	33	0
1904-05	32	0	2	0	34	0
1905-06	11	0	0	0	11	0
	116	0	8	0	124	0

TOM HOLFORD

When Hanley-born Tom Holford arrived at Hyde Road from Stoke in April 1908 he was in his 30th year and looked to be nearing the end of his League career, yet he helped Manchester City to win promotion from Division Two in 1909-10 when he scored 12 goals in 30 games. And he was still playing in 1924, as player-manager of Port Vale. Holford's first-class career had begun with Stoke in 1898 and it was with the Potters that he won his one England cap. His 26-year career was surpassed only by Billy Meredith at the time and during that career he played in every position except goal. He was a half-back with City and it was at centre-half that he had been capped. Occasionally in his career he had made a fair job of playing centre-forward when circumstances dictated that he be pushed up into attack. He scored 38 goals in 184 League and Cup games, and his overall figure of 479 League games was a remarkable tally when one considers that he lost four seasons to war, and that the League programme comprised fewer matches in those days. City sold him back to Stoke in the close season of 1914 and he retired whilst at Port Vale for whom he became trainer-scout. *League debut for City v Bristol City, 21 April 1908.*

	LEAGUE		FA CUP		TOTAL	
	App	Gls	App	Gls	App	Gls
1907-08	2	0	0	0	2	0
1908-09	26	12	1	3	27	15
1909-10	30	12	4	1	34	13
1910-11	29	2	2	0	31	2
1911-12	32	8	2	0	34	8
1912-13	38	0	3	0	41	0
1913-14	15	0	0	0	15	0
	172	34	12	4	184	38

William Holmes joined City from Chesterfield in July 1896, a big, strong half-back whose biting tackles made him a feared opponent. Known as 'The Doc', Holmes spent nine years with the club but they were not all happy ones. He was so disappointed at being left out of the 1904 FA Cup Final side, after playing in the quarter and semi-finals, that he threw his boots through the dressing-room window after learning that the amateur, S.B.Ashworth, was to replace him in the Cup side. In happier times he had won a Second Division Championship medal with City, in 1898-9, and represented the Football League against the Irish League in November 1897. In 1901-02, when he managed only six League games, he compensated by helping City Reserves to the Lancashire Combination title. In August 1905, after 156 League games for City, Holmes signed for Clapton Orient where he later became player-manager. *League debut for City v Notts County, 31 October 1896.*

WILLIAM HOLMES

	LEAGUE		FA CUP		TOTAL	
	App	Gls	App	Gls	App	Gls
1896-97	12	1	1	0	13	1
1897-98	29	1	2	0	31	1
1898-99	24	0	1	0	25	0
1899-00	34	0	2	0	36	0
1900-01	28	2	1	0	29	2
1901-02	6	0	0	0	6	0
1902-03	11	0	1	0	12	0
1903-04	8	0	2	0	10	0
1904-05	4	0	0	0	4	0
	156	4	10	0	166	4

'Doc' Holmes' most consistent season of 1899-1900 saw City finish higher in Division One than any other Lancashire team. He was one of four ever-presents that season.

TOM HYNDS

Tom Hynds joined Manchester City from Glasgow Celtic in September 1901 and in his five seasons with the club, before he became embroiled in the scandal of 1906, he missed only 16 League games and never appeared in any side other than the first team. He was, without doubt, the best centre-half that had ever played for City up to that time and he won a Second Division Championship medal in 1902-03 and an FA Cup winners' medal in 1904. Altogether Hynds made 172 League and FA Cup appearances for City, scoring nine goals, before being suspended and fined £75 for his part in the illegal payments sensation which saw 17 City players banned until 1 January 1907. When the players were put up for sale at the Queen's Hotel in Manchester, Woolwich Arsenal took Hynds to Plumstead where he continued his League career. Hynds later coached in British Columbia and Italy. *League debut for City v Bolton Wanderers, 12 October 1901.*

	LEAGUE		FA CUP		TOTAL	
	App	Gls	App	Gls	App	Gls
1901-02	29	2	4	0	33	2
1902-03	31	1	1	0	32	1
1903-04	32	4	6	0	38	4
1904-05	33	2	2	0	35	2
1905-06	33	0	1	0	34	0
	158	9	14	0	172	9

In 1904, Tom Hynds received wages of £6.10s (£6.50p) per week from City, more than they were paying Billy Meredith.

Dalton-in-Furness-born Thomas Clark Fisher Johnson — 'Tosh' to his colleague and supporters — still stands as the record League goalscorer for Manchester City in a single season. His 38 goals in 1928-9, in City's first season back in Division One, is the best-ever by a City player; and his overall League tally of 158 goals puts him in second place, behind Eric Brook, in the list of all-time City scorers. Apparently it was defender Eli Fletcher who insisted that City must sign Johnson from Dalton Casuals in early 1919. Fletcher threatened not to re-sign unless the club moved for the talented youngster who was turning out some eye-catching performances for his local club. City took note and Johnson repaid them instantly, scoring on his debut in a Lancashire Section match before the League got underway again after World War One, and then hitting a hat-trick on his second appearance. In 11 years with Manchester City, Johnson played 328 League matches. He won two England caps, played in the 1926 FA Cup Final, and helped City to promotion from Division Two in 1927-8. In addition he played for the Football League and the FA XI. Although he was nearly 30 when City transferred him to Everton for £6,000 in March 1930, there were plenty of Maine Road supporters who criticised the club for letting him go; and to underline their case, Johnson was in the Everton side which beat City in the 1933 FA Cup Final. Still worse for City fans, Johnson won three more England caps and collected Second and First Division Championship medals whilst at Goodison Park. He later played a few games for Liverpool before ending his career with Darwen. Johnson died in January 1973, aged 72. *League debut for City v Middlesbrough, 18 February 1920.*

TOM JOHNSON

	LEAGUE		FA CUP		TOTAL	
	App	Gls	App	Gls	App	Gls
1919-20	10	5	0	0	10	5
1920-21	12	5	0	0	12	5
1921-22	20	5	3	0	23	5
1922-23	35	14	1	1	36	15
1923-24	30	9	5	0	35	9
1924-25	41	12	1	0	42	12
1925-26	38	15	7	5	45	20
1926-27	38	25	1	0	39	25
1927-28	35	19	3	1	38	20
1928-29	39	38	1	0	40	38
1929-30	30	11	4	1	34	12
	328	158	26	8	354	166

Within 14 months of signing for Manchester City, Bobby Johnstone became the first man to score in successive Wembley FA Cup Finals, his second effort helping City to lift the trophy by defeating Birmingham City. Johnstone was born in Selkirk and he came to prominence with the fine Hibernian team of the immediate post-war era. Playing alongside such Scottish internationals as Gordon Smith, Reilly, Ormond and Turnbull, Johnstone made his name in the Hibs side which did so well in the early 1950s. His versatile forward skills induced City to pay £22,000 for his signature in March 1955 and after Clarke and Hart were injured, City supporters had special reason to bless the men who brought him to Maine Road. Besides his FA Cup success, Johnstone won four Scotland caps with City — he was honoured 17 times altogether — and represented Great Britain against the Rest of Europe in August 1955, a few months after joining City. In September 1959, Johnstone returned to Hibs for £7,000 but a year later was back in Lancashire to spark off the revival of Oldham Athletic. He scored 35 goals in 143 League games for the Boundary Park club, adding to his 42 goals in 124 League games for City. A keen cricketer, he played for Saddleworth. *League debut for City v Bolton Wanderers, 2 March 1955*

BOBBY JOHNSTONE

	LEAGUE		FA CUP		TOTAL	
	App	Gls	App	Gls	App	Gls
1954-55	8	2	2	1	10	3
1955-56	31	12	7	4	38	16
1956-57	31	16	2	3	33	19
1957-58	33	7	1	0	34	7
1958-59	18	4	2	1	20	5
1959-60	3	1	0	0	3	1
	124	42	14	9	138	51

331

Di Jones was already an international star when he arrived at Hyde Road at the start of the 1898-9 season. As a member of the fine Chirk team he had gained a Welsh Cup winners' medal in 1888, and then joined Bolton Wanderers where he spent a decade and, with goalkeeper Sutcliffe and full-back Somerville, he became part of a famous League rearguard. The Trotters made Jones, who was born in Trevonai, their captain and he skippered them in the 1894 FA Cup Final. His debut for City at Luton in October 1898 was their first away victory of that promotion season. He won two Welsh caps with City and 15 overall, a figure that would have been greater but for the fact that the unselfish Jones often put his club's welfare before personal international honours. Jones, who had taken over the City captaincy at a particularly crucial time in the club's history, had a sad and untimely death. In August 1902, during a pre-season friendly game, he fell and gashed his knee. Within a week the wound had turned septic and Jones was dead, such was the ignorance surrounding such injuries at the time. *League debut for City v Luton Town, 8 October 1898.*

DI JONES

	LEAGUE		FA CUP		TOTAL	
	App	Gls	App	Gls	App	Gls
1898-99	27	1	1	0	28	1
1899-00	34	0	2	0	36	0
1900-01	33	0	1	0	34	0
1901-02	20	0	0	0	20	0
	114	1	4	0	118	1

When he was a Bolton player, Di Jones tried to persuade Billy Meredith to sign for the Trotters.

BILLY LOT JONES

When Billy Meredith's sports shop went bankrupt in 1909, one of the creditors was Billy Lot Jones.

Forward Billy Lot Jones was one of a select band of players who formed the backbone of the Welsh international side from the turn of the century. He was born at Chirk and played for that famous team and for Druids before City signed him in January 1903. He played in most forward positions for the club, although his best days were as part of the left-wing triangle with Blair and Conlin, and his 281 League games for the club brought him 69 goals. He won a Second Division Championship medal with City as well as 19 of his 20 Welsh caps. His only downfall, despite those 69 League goals, seems to have been his shooting and one journalist wrote that he was 'one of the trickiest footballers and worst shots I have ever seen'. In 1908 his benefit game against Middlesbrough raised £835 and he was still playing for City in wartime football. In August 1919, Jones signed for Southend and later played for Aberdare, Wrexham and Oswestry before returning to his native Chirk as player-manager. *League debut for City v West Bromwich Albion, 9 April 1904.*

	LEAGUE		FA CUP		TOTAL	
	App	Gls	App	Gls	App	Gls
1903-04	1	1	0	0	1	1
1904-05	12	2	0	0	12	2
1905-06	25	6	0	0	25	6
1906-07	27	11	2	0	29	11
1907-08	24	4	5	2	29	6
1908-09	29	6	1	0	30	6
1909-10	37	12	4	2	41	14
1910-11	34	6	2	1	36	7
1911-12	24	7	2	0	26	7
1912-13	37	9	3	0	40	9
1913-14	14	4	1	0	15	4
1914-15	17	1	1	0	18	1
	281	69	21	5	302	74

Full-back Tommy Kelso joined Manchester City from Third Lanark in August 1906, aged 24. He was a big man, standing 6ft 2in, and he made good use of his rangy physique. Kelso was born in Renton and came from a well-known footballing family, his uncle Bob Kelso being a famous Scottish international. Tommy Kelso stayed with City for over six years, during which time he won a Second Division Championship medal in 1910. He made 151 League and FA Cup appearances altogether and appeared in two international trials for the Anglo Scots against the Home Scots. Yet his one Scotland cap was won after he moved to Dundee in February 1913. He had actually been on trial with the Scotish League club from the previous October. Kelso later moved to Rangers for one season, 1914-15. *League debut for City v Woolwich Arsenal, 1 September 1906.*

TOMMY KELSO

	LEAGUE		FA CUP		TOTAL	
	App	Gls	App	Gls	App	Gls
1906-07	24	0	0	0	24	0
1907-08	25	0	6	0	31	0
1908-09	21	0	1	0	22	0
1909-10	28	0	4	0	32	0
1910-11	31	0	2	0	33	0
1911-12	9	3	0	0	9	3
1912-13	0	0	0	0	0	0
	138	3	13	0	151	3

In January 1912, City missed three penalties against Newcastle who led 1-0 at the time. Eli Fletcher missed the first two but turned down the chance of a hat-trick. Thornley stepped up and missed but this time George Wynn scored from the rebound.

BOBBY KENNEDY

Wing-half and full-back Bobby Kennedy overcame a serious illness, which kept him out of the game for eight months, and went on to play in two Scottish Cup Finals with Kilmarnock and win a League Championship runners-up medal with the Rugby Park club. In July 1961, City paid £45,000 for his signature, a fee which was then a record for a wing-half. A Scottish Under-23 international, Kennedy spent eight years at Maine Road and although he was unlucky to play for the club when they were going through a particularly bad time, he eventually helped them back to Division One in 1965-6 when he had been converted to full-back. In March 1968 he left to become player-manager of Grimsby Town, and he was also manager at Bradford City where he enjoyed some success before losing the job amid some controversy in January 1978. *League debut for City v Leicester City, 19 August 1961.*

	LEAGUE		FA CUP		FL CUP		EUROPE		TOTAL	
	App	Gls	App	Gls	App	Gls	App	Gls	App	Gls
1961-62	42	6	2	0	1	0	-	-	45	6
1962-63	41	0	3	0	5	0	-	-	49	0
1963-64	26	0	1	0	5	0	-	-	32	0
1964-65	38	1	2	0	1	0	-	-	41	1
1965-66	35	1	8	0	2	0	-	-	45	1
1966-67	20(1)	1	2	0	1	0	-	-	23(1)	1
1967-68	4(2)	0	0	0	0	0	-	-	4(2)	0
1968-69	10	0	0	0	1	0	1	0	12	0
	216(3)	9	18	0	16	0	1	0	251(3)	9

Brian Kidd was the epitome of the local boy made good. Born in Manchester, he played for both City and United and almost all his 150-plus League goals were scored in the First Division. He first burst into prominence on his 19th birthday when he scored a goal in Manchester United's 1968 European Cup Final victory over Benfica. He was transferred to Arsenal for £110,000 in 1974, with 70 goals in 264 games for United to his name and two full England caps. Kidd signed for City two years later, for £100,000, and continued to score regularly. He hit four goals against Leicester in January 1977 and his overall City haul of 57 goals in 127 full matches is a creditable figure, coming as it did in one of the game's most dour defensive periods. In March 1979 Kidd moved to Everton for £150,000 and a year later became only the second player since the war to be sent off in an FA Cup semi-final. Later Kidd played for Bolton, in the NASL with Atlanta Chiefs and Fort Lauderdale, and then signed non-contract forms for Preston, becoming manager at Deepdale for a short while. *League debut for City v Leicester City, 21 August 1976.*

BRIAN KIDD

	LEAGUE		FACUP		FLCUP		EUROPE		TOTAL	
	App	Gls	App	Gls	App	Gls	App	Gls	App	Gls
1976-77	39	21	4	1	0	0	2	1	45	23
1977-78	39	16	2	1	7	3	2	0	50	20
1978-79	19(1)	7	3	2	4	0	6	5	32(1)	14
	97(1)	44	9	4	11	3	10	6	127(1)	57

DENIS LAW

When Manchester City paid £55,000 for striker Denis Law in March 1960, they surpassed the previous British transfer record by £10,000. Law had joined Huddersfield Town from his home-town of Aberdeen as a pale, bespectacled boy whose appearance belied the fact that he would one day become one of the most famous footballers in the world. City fans who could remember the great Peter Doherty recalled some similarities between the great Irish star and the young Scot. Law was a lethal finisher, and he would tackle and harry all afternoon and all over the pitch. On 13 July 1961 the Italian giants, Torino, paid £125,000 for Law's skills. It was the first time that a British club had been involved in a six-figure transfer. Twelve months later he joined Manchester United when they became the first British club to pay over £100,000 for a player. Law, winner of 55 Scotland caps, enjoyed his greatest years at Old Trafford. There he won League Championship medals and an FA Cup winners' medal, although he was in hospital when United won the European Cup. In July 1973 he rejoined City — the club for whom he had once scored six goals in an FA Cup match at Luton only to see the game abandoned — and his last goal in League football was the one which relegated United when City beat them in April 1974. He retired in August 1974. *League debut for City v Leeds United, 19 March 1960.*

	LEAGUE		FACUP		FLCUP		TOTAL	
	App	Gls	App	Gls	App	Gls	App	Gls
1959-60	7	2	-	-	-	-	7	2
1960-61	37	19	4	2	2	2	43	23
1973-74	22(2)	9	1	2	4	1	27(2)	12
	66(2)	30	5	4	6	3	77(2)	37

Francis Lee had his first taste of League football much earlier than most players. As a 16-year-old he made his debut for Bolton Wanderers, in 1960-61, and his right-wing partnership with the Trotters' Freddie Hill caught the attention of several First Division clubs before Manchester City beat off the attentions of the others to sign Lee in October 1967, when he was 23, for £60,000. Lee soon became a firm favourite with the Maine Road fans and he was one of the major successes of a City team that enjoyed one of the greatest eras in the club's history. Lee was not a tall player but his solid physique and bustling style brought him a rich harvest of goals —112 in 248 League games for City alone. He won a host of honours whilst with City, including winners' medals for the League Championship, FA Cup and League Cup. Capped 27 times for England, Lee also played for the Football League XI and a United Kingdom XI. He was a penalty expert and in 1971-2 scored a record 15 for City. In August 1974, Dave Mackay made one of his best managerial signings by taking Lee to Derby County for £110,000. Lee won a second Championship medal at the Baseball Ground and added 24 League goals to his overall tally. Lee, by now a wealthy businessman, retired in 1976 with 229 goals from 500 League games to his name. In 1987, having obtained a licence in 1986, he is a successful owner-trainer of racehorses. *League debut for City v Wolverhampton Wanderers, 14 October 1967.*

FRANCIS LEE

	LEAGUE		FA CUP		FL CUP		EUROPE		TOTAL	
App Gls	App	Gls	App	Gls	App	Gls	App	Gls		
1967-68	31	16	4	1	0	0	-	-	35	17
1968-69	37	12	7	4	3	0	2	0	49	16
1969-70	36	13	2	0	7	3	9	6	54	22
1970-71	38	14	2	0	1	1	9	4	50	19
1971-72	42	33	2	1	2	1	-	-	46	35
1972-73	35	14	5	1	2	1	2	0	44	16
1973-74	29(1)	10	2	0	11	8	-	-	42(1)	18
	248(1)	112	24	7	26	14	22	10	320(1)	143

BILL LEIVERS

Centre-half Bill Leivers was playing in the Third Division North with Chesterfield when City paid £10,500 for him in November 1953. By the time he moved to Doncaster, on a free transfer in July 1964, Leivers had made exactly 250 League appearances for City and won an FA Cup winners' medal in 1956. His only representative honour was a game for the FA XI against The Army in November 1956, but his defensive skills and commitment deserved greater reward. He had to wait a few months for his League debut for City and it was as a right-back that he established himself and won his Cup medal. Later in his career Leivers reverted to the number-five shirt but City's team was by then in decline. Leivers, who suffered a remarkable catalogue of injuries including breaking his nose five times, became player-manager of Doncaster and resigned after steering them to the top of Division Four. Leivers was manager of Cambridge United when they climbed from the Southern League to the Third Division and he also managed Chelmsford City and Cambridge City. *League debut for City v Preston North End, 21 August 1954.*

	LEAGUE		FA CUP		FL CUP		TOTAL	
	App	Gls	App	Gls	App	Gls	App	Gls
1953-54	0	0	0	0	-	-	0	0
1954-55	2	0	1	0	-	-	3	0
1955-56	25	0	7	0	-	-	32	0
1956-57	42	0	2	0	-	-	44	0
1957-58	36	0	0	0	-	-	36	0
1958-59	34	1	1	0	-	-	35	1
1959-60	28	1	0	0	-	-	28	1
1960-61	9	0	3	0	0	0	12	0
1961-62	24	1	2	0	0	0	26	1
1962-63	35	1	3	0	6	0	44	1
1963-64	15	0	1	0	5	0	21	0
	250	4	20	0	11	0	281	4

Manchester-born Roy Little joined City from Greenwood Victoria, signing professional forms in August 1949. A full-back whose defensive qualities helped City to two FA Cup Finals in successive seasons, Little managed only two goals in 168 League games — and they both came in the same season, in 1953-4 against Huddersfield and Sheffield Wednesday. His nine years at Maine Road brought him a Cup winners' medal in 1956 and in October 1958 he was transferred to Brighton and Hove Albion. Although a Lancashire lad, Little seemed to enjoy life in the South-East and after a spell with Crystal Palace he became player-manager of Dover in the Southern League. *League debut for City v Liverpool, 17 January 1953.*

	LEAGUE		FA CUP		TOTAL	
	App	Gls	App	Gls	App	Gls
1949-50	0	0	0	0	0	0
1950-51	0	0	0	0	0	0
1951-52	0	0	0	0	0	0
1952-53	3	0	3	0	6	0
1953-54	31	2	0	0	31	2
1954-55	38	0	6	0	44	0
1955-56	42	0	7	0	49	0
1956-57	37	0	2	0	39	0
1957-58	16	0	0	0	16	0
1958-59	1	0	0	0	1	0
	168	2	18	0	186	2

ROY LITTLE

GEORGE LIVINGSTONE

Inside-forward George Livingstone was one of the stars of City's first great team and his skills were especially appreciated by the legendary Billy Meredith who enjoyed some fine service from the Scotsman. Livingstone was born in Dumbarton in 1876 and came to City in May 1903 after serving numerous clubs including Dumbarton, Everton, Hearts, Sunderland, Celtic and Liverpool. With City he won an FA Cup winners' medal in 1904 and the first of two Scotland caps. His previous honours had been an appearance for the Scottish League when with Celtic, for whom he also appeared in the Scottish Cup Final. It was Livingstone's long, raking pass to Meredith in the English Cup Final at The Crystal Palace which sent Meredith away to score the only goal of the game against Bolton. He was one of the City players suspended in 1906 (he was fined £100) and in January 1907 he signed for Rangers and went on to win his second cap. Livingstone later returned to Manchester to play for United, his last club before he retired during World War One. He later managed Dumbarton and was also trainer at Bradford City and Rangers. *League debut for City v Stoke, 5 September 1903.*

	LEAGUE		FA CUP		TOTAL	
	App	Gls	App	Gls	App	Gls
1903-04	29	5	6	1	35	6
1904-05	26	7	0	0	26	7
1905-06	26	7	1	0	27	7
	81	19	7	1	88	20

Billy McAdams had a memorable start to his career with Manchester City when, in only his second game, he scored three times in a 5-2 FA Cup win over Bradford. An inside-forward who was more of a goal-scorer than a 'schemer', McAdams was born in Belfast and joined City from Irish League club, Distillery, in December 1953. Despite his rapid rise to the headlines, McAdams was dogged by injury and he failed to establish a place in time to play in either the 1955 or 1956 FA Cup Final. It was 1957-8 before he became a regular, although he had been a Northern Ireland international for some years. Altogether he won 15 caps — five with City — and in 1959-60 had his best First Division season when his 21 goals in 30 games made him City's top scorer. In September 1960, McAdams was transferred to Bolton for £15,000 and in his first season at Burnden Park hit 18 goals in 27 League games. McAdams later played for Leeds, Brentford, QPR and Barrow and continued his scoring touch in the lower divisions. *League debut for City v Sunderland, 2 January 1954.*

BILLY McADAMS

	LEAGUE		FA CUP		TOTAL	
	App	Gls	App	Gls	App	Gls
1953-54	17	8	2	3	19	11
1954-55	19	6	0	0	19	6
1955-56	0	0	0	0	0	0
1956-57	12	4	2	0	14	4
1957-58	28	19	0	0	28	19
1958-59	21	4	2	0	23	4
1959-60	30	21	1	0	31	21
1960-61	0	0	0	0	0	0
	127	62	7	3	134	65

PHILIP McCLOY

It was Philip McCloy's full-back partnership with Jock Smith for Ayr United which resulted in both men being selected for Scotland's 1924 clash with England at Hampden. Both men played well in the 1-1 draw and it was inevitable that they would attract the attentions of English clubs. Smith moved to Middlesbrough for £2,000 in 1926 and McCloy transferred to Manchester City, for £3,000, in August 1925. Their partnership had been an interesting one — Smith was the 'dashing' defender, despite his weighty build, whilst McCloy was a cool, calculating full-back who rarely looked troubled. With City he appeared in the 1926 FA Cup Final and won a Second Division Championship medal in 1928. After 147 League appearances and ten goals he moved to Chester in the close season of 1930 and then had a spell in Irish football before joining non-League Kidderminster Harriers in January 1935. He died in 1972, in his 76th year. *League debut for City v Cardiff City, 29 August 1925.*

	LEAGUE		FA CUP		TOTAL	
	App	Gls	App	Gls	App	Gls
1925-26	37	0	4	0	41	0
1926-27	30	0	0	0	30	0
1927-28	38	0	3	0	41	0
1928-29	31	0	1	0	32	0
1929-30	11	0	2	0	13	0
	147	0	10	0	157	0

Full-back Johnny McMahon joined Manchester City from Preston North End in November 1902 and went on to make exactly 100 League appearances for the Hyde Road club before being one of the City players suspended and transferred in the aftermath of the 1906 illegal payments scandal. McMahon made his League debut for City in the Mancunian 'derby' game on Christmas Day 1902 and by the end of that season he had won a Second Division Championship medal with 17 appearances in the title-winning side. Twelve months later McMahon was in the honours again, this time as a member of the City team which beat Bolton in the FA Cup Final at The Crystal Palace. Although he appeared in a Scottish trial match in March 1903, McMahon never won a cap. Bury paid £450 for his signature after his suspension. He later became a successful publican in Manchester and in 1929 was one of several local businessmen, along with Billy Meredith, who made an abortive attempt to bring League football to Belle Vue stadium with the formation of Manchester Central FC. *League debut for City v Manchester United, 25 December 1902.*

JOHNNY McMAHON

	LEAGUE		FA CUP		TOTAL	
	App	Gls	App	Gls	App	Gls
1902-03	17	0	0	0	17	0
1903-04	27	0	6	0	33	0
1904-05	31	0	2	0	33	0
1905-06	25	1	1	0	26	1
	100	1	9	0	109	1

JIMMY McMULLAN

Left-half Jimmy McMullan was already a seasoned Scottish international when Manchester City signed him from Partick Thistle, for £4,700 in February 1926. Indeed, McMullan's career prior to joining City had been particularly interesting. He was born in Denny and won a Scottish Cup winners' medal with Partick Thistle in 1921. Partick then turned down a £5,000 offer from Newcastle for McMullan's signature and the player, determined to play in English football, signed for non-League Maidstone United in the 1921 close season. In the summer of 1923 he returned to Partick and two and a half years later, City signed him. He was arguably the greatest Scottish half-back of his day, captaining the 'Wembley Wizards' when they beat England 5-1 in 1928. With City, McMullan won eight Scotland caps — he won 16 overall — and played in two FA Cup Finals, being on the losing side both times. He did win a Second Division Championship medal in 1927-8, however. In May 1933, after 242 League and Cup appearances for City, McMullan joined Oldham Athletic as player-manager. He was later Aston Villa's first-ever manager and also managed Notts County and Sheffield Wednesday. *League debut for City v Liverpool, 27 February 1926.*

	LEAGUE		FA CUP		TOTAL	
	App	Gls	App	Gls	App	Gls
1925-26	10	0	3	0	13	0
1926-27	35	3	1	0	36	3
1927-28	38	4	3	0	41	4
1928-29	38	0	1	0	39	0
1929-30	25	2	3	0	28	2
1930-31	27	0	0	0	27	0
1931-32	21	1	5	0	26	1
1932-33	26	0	6	2	32	2
	220	10	22	2	242	12

Not every City fan was convinced that the club had spent wisely when they laid out £200,000 for the enigmatic skills of Rodney Marsh in March 1972. More than anything else Marsh was an entertainer, and whilst everyone agreed that his sort was what the game needed overall, some Maine Road devotees argued that the style of the current City team had been disturbed by the individual and impulsive play of Marsh. He was certainly an imaginative and inventive footballer and in the first League Cup Final to be held at Wembley he had produced a typically mazy dribble to equalise for then Third Division QPR to set up an historic victory over First Division West Brom. Marsh was born in Hatfield, Hertfordshire, and his first League club was West Ham, for whom he played as an amateur before making his debut in senior soccer with Rangers. His time with City saw him play eight times for England — he had made his international debut as a Rangers player — and he appeared in the 1974 League Cup Final. In January 1976, Marsh joined the NASL club, Tampa Bay Rowdies, for £45,000 and later returned to Fulham where he ended his League career. *League debut for City v Chelsea, 18 March 1972.*

	LEAGUE		FA CUP		FL CUP		EUROPE		TOTAL	
	App	Gls	App	Gls	App	Gls	App	Gls	App	Gls
1971-72	7(1)	4	0	0	0	0	-	-	7(1)	4
1972-73	37	14	5	1	2	2	2	2	46	19
1973-74	23(1)	5	2	1	8	3	-	-	33(1)	19
1974-75	37	9	1	0	2	1	-	-	40	10
1975-76	12	4	0	0	4	0	-	-	16	4
	116(2)	36	8	2	16	6	2	2	142(2)	56

RODNEY MARSH

BOBBY MARSHALL

Bobby Marshall, a native of Hucknall in Nottinghamshire, made almost 200 League appearances for Sunderland, his first League club, before joining Manchester City in March 1928. Marshall went on to become a member of a fine City team and he appeared in consecutive FA Cup Finals — with a winners' medal in 1934 — and in the side which lifted the League Championship for the first time in the club's history, in 1937-8. In his early years at City Marshall starred as an inside-forward who possessed brilliant ball-control and who could also find his way to goal regularly. In 1934 he received a £650 benefit and after converting to centre-half in an emergency he began virtually a 'second career' which he crowned with that League Championship medal. Marshall made 355 League and FA Cup appearances for City before transferring to Stockport County in March 1939. He later managed Stockport as well as Chesterfield. *League debut for City v Blackpool, 3 March 1928.*

	LEAGUE		FA CUP		TOTAL	
	App	Gls	App	Gls	App	Gls
1927-28	14	7	0	0	14	7
1928-29	33	7	1	0	34	7
1929-30	31	15	5	6	36	21
1930-31	37	10	1	0	38	10
1931-32	34	13	5	2	39	15
1932-33	33	9	3	0	36	9
1933-34	34	4	8	2	42	6
1934-35	19	3	0	0	19	3
1935-36	21	2	2	0	23	2
1936-37	38	0	4	0	42	0
1937-38	31	0	1	0	32	0
1938-39	0	0	0	0	0	0
	325	70	30	10	355	80

Welsh international outside-right Billy Meredith was one of the greatest figures in the game — and one of the most controversial. Born at Chirk in 1874, Meredith started his career with that famous Welsh club and after making his bow in League football with Northwich Victoria, he signed for Manchester City in October 1894, turning professional in January the following year. He had two quite distinct careers with City, the first from 1894 until 1905, after which he was the major figure in the bribes and then illegal payments sensations which all but ripped the heart out of the club; the second when he was well into the veteran stage after World War One, when he played in an FA Cup semi-final in his 50th year. Meredith was one of the great attractions of Edwardian football, with his bandy legs and toothpick making him a cartoonists' delight. He was a deadly opponent, whether he was slinging over pin-point centres for others, or cutting inside to score. Indeed, although he ranks alongside Sir Stanley Matthews as a right-winger of heroic stature, unlike Matthews he had a fine cutting edge and scored 145 League goals for City alone. He won two Second Division Championship medals and an FA Cup winners' medal with City; and when Manchester United snapped him up, when he was banned for playing for the Hyde Road club, he added a second FA Cup winners' medal and two League Championship medals. Meredith returned to City as a guest player during World War One and after a row with United over wages he came back to City on a permanent transfer. Meredith was a leading light in the fight to form a credible players' union and was always a champions of footballers' rights. His international career of 48 caps for Wales — 22 of them whilst a City player — spanned 25 years and after ending his 29-year League career he became a publican in Manchester. Meredeith died in April 1958, aged 83, and is still revered in Manchester and his native Wales. *League debut v Newcastle United, 27 October 1894.*

BILLY MEREDITH

	LEAGUE		FA CUP		TEST		TOTAL	
	App	Gls	App	Gls	App	Gls	App	Gls
1894-95	18	12	0	0	-	-	18	12
1895-96	29	12	0	0	4	1	33	13
1896-97	27	10	1	0	-	-	28	10
1897-98	30	12	2	0	-	-	32	12
1898-99	33	29	1	1	-	-	34	30
1899-00	33	14	2	0	-	-	35	14
1900-01	34	7	1	0	-	-	35	7
1901-02	33	8	4	0	-	-	37	8
1902-03	34	22	1	0	-	-	35	22
1903-04	34	11	6	2	-	-	40	13
1904-05	33	8	2	1	-	-	35	9
1905-06	suspended							
1906-07	suspended until transfer, 5.12.06							
1921-22	25	0	0	-	-	0	25	0
1922-23	1	0	0	0	-	-	1	0
1923-24	2	0	4	1	-	-	6	1
	366	145	24	5	4	1	394	151

"I had to travel to Manchester and then to Newcastle so that I did not make my debut under the best conditions. I was working in the pit on Friday and had to take the train at two o'clock in the morning. I was travelling until eleven o'clock, played the game and set off for home again, getting back at half-past ten on Sunday morning. The same night I had to go back to work in the mine so I had a somewhat strenuous weekend."
Billy Meredith's memoirs, Topical Times, October 1919.

Half-back Bobby Moffatt, a native of Dumfries, joined Manchester City in August 1895, from Scottish League club, St Mirren. He was a great provider to Billy Meredith and sent the legendary Welsh winger on many of the thrilling runs which brought goals for City. Yet Moffatt had the misfortune to have effectively ended his first-team career with the club before City's first great team came together. His sole honour in 156 League games for them was a Second Division Championship medal in 1898-9. His brother, Jimmy, also joined City from St Mirren in May 1903, when Bobby's first-team days were over, but after only 20 appearances in three years Jimmy signed for Kilmarnock in the close season of 1906. From 1903 to 1907, Bobby Moffatt was player-coach to City's reserve team, after which he joined the coaching staff at Kilmarnock. *League debut for City v Crewe Alexandra, 19 October 1895.*

	LEAGUE		FA CUP		TOTAL	
	App	Gls	App	Gls	App	Gls
1895-96	2	0	0	0	2	0
1896-97	11	0	0	0	11	0
1897-98	30	0	2	0	32	0
1898-99	34	4	1	0	35	4
1899-00	25	2	1	0	26	2
1900-01	32	1	1	0	33	1
1901-02	21	0	2	0	22	0
1902-03	1	0	0	0	1	0
1903-04	0	0	0	0	0	0
1904-05	0	0	0	0	0	0
1905-06	0	0	0	0	0	0
1906-07	0	0	0	0	0	0
	156	7	7	0	162	7

BOBBY MOFFATT

WILLIAM MURPHY

Like so many who shared his surname, Billy Murphy was invariably known as 'Spud'. Born in St Helen's, Murphy joined City from Alexandra Victoria in February 1918 after beginning his career with Peasley Cross Juniors. He was an outside-left whose main attribute was perhaps his speed. He was renowned for his quickness and it was said that local pigeon fanciers paid him to convey the birds' arrival times to headquarters. Murphy also had plenty of long-distance stamina too, and when Pleasley disbanded at the start of World War One he took to cross-country running before resurrecting his soccer career with Victoria. In seven seasons with City he played in 220 League and FA Cup games, scoring 31 goals, before transferring to Southampton in August 1926. He was described at the time as 'cute, quick and clever' and he gave Saints three seasons' service (79 appearances and four goals) before moving to Oldham Athletic in 1929. *League debut for City v Bolton Wanderers, 13 September 1919.*

	LEAGUE		FA CUP		TOTAL	
	App	Gls	App	Gls	App	Gls
1919-20	36	5	2	1	38	6
1920-21	40	8	1	0	41	8
1921-22	42	9	3	0	45	9
1922-23	32	1	1	0	33	1
1923-24	26	2	4	0	30	2
1924-25	24	3	0	0	24	3
1925-26	9	2	0	0	9	2
	209	30	11	1	220	31

The part that Alan Oakes played in the history of Manchester City cannot be over-estimated. For a start, he played more competitive first-team games for the club — 668 — than any other player, and he was one of the most consistent peformers during the heady days of the late 1960s and early 1970s. Oakes was born in Winsford and joined City as an amateur in April 1958 before signing professional forms in September the following year. His formative years in League football were spent in a poor City side in the early 1960s, but the fair-haired midfielder held on and was rewarded with honours galore in later years. He won Second and then First Division Championship medals, two League Cup winners' medals, an FA Cup winners' medal and a European Cup-winners' Cup medal as City carried all before them. His only representative honour was an appearance for the Football League against the Scottish League in March 1969, yet Oakes was that kind of player — a quiet, unassuming and gentle man who did a thoroughly professional job without fuss. Certainly, more flamboyant but less talented players won England caps whilst Oakes was going about his business for City. Coleman and Young, in particular, benefitted from his surging runs and penetrating passes. Oakes played over 100 matches for City in Cup football alone and his overall tally is remarkable. In July 1976, having helped City to yet another Wembley triumph, he signed for Chester, for £15,000, and became player-manager at Sealand Road. *League debut for City v Chelsea, 14 November 1959.*

	LEAGUE		FACUP		FLCUP		EUROPE		TOTAL	
	App	Gls	App	Gls	App	Gls	App	Gls	App	Gls
1958-59	0	0	0	0	-	-	-	-	0	0
1959-60	18	0	1	0	-	-	-	-	19	0
1960-61	22	0	0	0	0	0	-	-	22	0
1961-62	25	1	0	0	0	0	-	-	25	1
1962-63	34	3	2	0	4	1	-	-	40	4
1963-64	41	3	1	1	6	0	-	-	48	3
1964-65	41	4	2	0	1	0	-	-	44	4
1965-66	41	1	8	0	2	0	-	-	51	1
1966-67	39	2	6	0	2	0	-	-	47	2
1967-68	41	2	4	0	4	1	-	-	49	3
1968-69	39	0	7	0	3	0	2	0	51	0
1969-70	40	3	2	0	7	1	9	1	58	5
1970-71	30	1	3	0	1	0	4	0	38	1
1971-72	31(1)	0	2	0	0	0	-	-	33(1)	0
1972-73	13(1)	1	0	0	0	0	2	0	15(1)	1
1973-74	28	0	0	0	5	0	-	-	33	0
1974-75	40	2	1	0	2	0	-	-	43	2
1975-76	38(1)	3	2	1	9	2	-	-	49(1)	6
	561(3)	26	41	2	46	5	17	1	665(3)	33

Alan Oakes' debut season of 1959-60 saw him help City in a fight against relegation which was avoided only in the 40th match when Barlow's goal secured victory over Preston.

Alan Oakes was rewarded with a testimonial match against Manchester United in 1972. To mark his 500th appearance he was presented with a silver salver before the game against Stoke City on 9 November 1974.

ALAN OAKES

Glyn Pardoe is a cousin of Alan Oakes and he too has given Manchester City fine service as a player, with 303 League games between 1961-2 and 1974-5 before becoming an equally dedicated servant as youth team coach. Pardoe had the same pedigree as Oakes — born at Winsford and a graduate of the Mid-Cheshire Boys team — before signing amateur forms for City in July 1961 and turning professional in June 1963. He went on to play for the club in every position except goalkeeper and centre-half and was the regular left-back when City won the League Championship for only the second time in their history in 1967-8. Then he broke a leg in the Mancunian 'derby' game in December 1970 and, apart from 1973-4, when he made 31 League appearances, he never regained a regular place. There was, however, at least one glorious memory for Pardoe before that unfortunate injury. It came at Wembley in March 1970 when he accepted Bell's flick to score the winning goal in the League Cup Final. An England Under-23 international, Pardoe shared in most of City's triumphs in that era with Second and First Division Championship medals, FA Cup and League Cup winners' medals. *League debut for City v Birmingham City, 11 April 1962.*

	LEAGUE		FACUP		FLCUP		EUROPE		TOTAL	
	App	Gls	App	Gls	App	Gls	App	Gls	App	Gls
1961-62	4	0	0	0	0	0	-	-	4	0
1962-63	5	0	1	0	0	0	-	-	6	0
1963-64	20	2	0	0	1	0	-	-	21	2
1964-65	14	3	2	0	0	0	-	-	16	3
1965-66	40(1)	9	8	0	2	2	-	-	50(1)	11
1966-67	40	2	6	1	2	1	-	-	48	4
1967-68	41	0	4	0	4	0	-	-	49	0
1968-69	39	1	7	0	2	0	2	0	50	1
1969-70	38	0	2	0	6	1	9	0	55	1
1970-71	19	0	0	0	1	0	4	0	24	0
1971-72	0	0	0	0	0	0	-	-	0	0
1972-73	6	0	0	0	0	0	0	0	6	0
1973-74	31(1)	0	0	0	7	0	-	-	38(1)	0
1974-75	6	0	0	0	1	0	-	-	7	0
1975-76	0	0	0	0	0	0	-	-	0	0
	303(2)	17	30	1	26	4	15	0	374(2)	22

GLYN PARDOE

Ex-coal-miner Roy Paul shared at least one distinction with Billy Meredith — he was a Welshman who captained Manchester City to success in the FA Cup Final. Paul's triumph came in 1956, 12 months after he had collected a losers' medal against Newcastle United. Paul, a native of the Rhondda, joined City from Swansea Town in July 1950, for £25,000, and he was regular throughout his career at Maine Road, with 293 League and FA Cup appearances in only seven seasons. He was a hard-working and talented half-back who won Welsh caps at right, left and centre-half. Paul's first taste of senior soccer came in 1939, in a wartime League game for Swansea, and in 1946-7 he was a member of their side which won the Third Division (South) title. He looked closely at the situation in Colombia, when other British players like Neil Franklin and Charlie Mitten went to Bogota in search of soccer fortune, but elected to stay in Britain. Paul missed only one game in the 1950-51 promotion season and was a star performer as City returned to Division One. In June 1957 he joined Worcester City on a free-transfer and became their player-manager. In all he won 33 Wales caps. *League debut for City v Preston North End, 19 August 1950.*

ROY PAUL

	LEAGUE		FA CUP		TOTAL	
	App	Gls	App	Gls	App	Gls
1950-51	41	3	1	0	42	3
1951-52	35	1	2	0	37	1
1952-53	38	0	3	0	41	0
1953-54	39	0	2	0	41	0
1954-55	41	1	6	0	47	0
1955-56	36	1	7	0	43	1
1956-57	40	3	2	0	42	3
	270	9	23	0	293	8

343

Paul Power was signed for Manchester City by Harry Godwin and he was still a student at Leeds Polytechnic when playing Central League football for expenses only. In July 1975, Power signed professional forms for City and it was Tony Book who gave him his First Division debut the following month. Malcolm Allison handed Power the captaincy in October 1979 and the player celebrated by leading City to a surprise win over Nottingham Forest. The bulk of Power's career at Maine Road was spent on the left side of midfield, but he was also used at left-back. He appeared for City in the 1981 FA Cup Final defeat by Tottenham Tottenham after scoring from a free-kick in the semi-final against Ipswich Town. Power's second Wembley appearance for City was in the 1986 Full Members Cup Final defeat at the hands of Chelsea. His one representative honour came in 1981 with an appearance in the England-Spain 'B' international. In three seasons from 1982-3, Power experienced relegation and promotion with City but in June 1986, Howard Kendall took him away from the ups and downs of life at Maine Road and gave him a place in Everton's League Championship side. *League debut for City v Aston Villa, 27 August 1975.*

	LEAGUE		FA CUP		FL CUP		EUROPE		TOTAL	
	App	Gls	App	Gls	App	Gls	App	Gls	App	Gls
1972-73	0	0	0	0	0	0	0	0	0	0
1973-74	0	0	0	0	0	0	-	-	0	0
1974-75	0	0	0	0	0	0	-	-	0	0
1975-76	14(5)	1	2	0	2	0	-	-	18(5)	1
1976-77	27(2)	2	4	0	1	0	0	0	32(2)	2
1977-78	29	3	0	0	4	0	1	0	34	3
1978-79	32	3	3	0	3	0	6	1	44	4
1979-80	41	7	1	0	4	0	-	-	46	7
1980-81	42	4	8	5	7	0	-	-	57	9
1981-82	25	1	1	0	1	0	-	-	27	1
1982-83	33	1	3	0	4	2	-	-	40	3
1983-84	37	2	1	0	3	0	-	-	41	2
1984-85	42	1	1	1	5	0	-	-	48	2
1985-86	36	1	4	0	3	0	-	-	43	1
	358(7)	26	28	6	37	2	7	1	430(7)	35

PAUL POWER

Charlie Pringle was a bustling, tenacious wing-half who joined Manchester City from St Mirren in June 1922 when he was already a Scottish international, having been capped against Wales in 1921. He had also appeared for the Scottish League. Pringle, who was born in Nitshill, went on to captain City and, despite his lack of inches — he stood 5ft 7in — also had occasional success at centre-half. He played for City in the 1926 FA Cup Final and played 22 games when they won the Second Division title in 1927-8. He married Lily Meredith, eldest daughter of Billy Meredith and it was perhaps a unique situation when Pringle turned out in the City team as his father-in-law during the twilight years of Meredith's career. In the close season of 1928, Pringle left City to become a leading figure in the attempt to establish Manchester Central as a League club. Later he played for Bradford and Lincoln City and won a Third Division (North) Championship medal with Lincoln. He captained each of his three Football League clubs. *League debut for City v Sheffield United, 26 August 1922.*

CHARLIE PRINGLE

	LEAGUE		FA CUP		TOTAL	
	App	Gls	App	Gls	App	Gls
1922-23	42	0	1	0	43	0
1923-24	28	0	8	0	36	0
1924-25	35	0	1	0	36	0
1925-26	36	0	7	0	43	0
1926-27	34	1	1	0	35	1
1927-28	22	0	1	0	23	0
	197	1	19	0	216	1

Nicky Reid was given a tough first-team baptism for Manchester City when he was thrust into the side which met Borussia Moenchengladbach at Maine Road in the 1978-9 UEFA Cup. He was yet another product of the fine City youth policy of the 1970s and his deceptively slender build belied the hard-tackling, hard-running midfielder or defender that City fans came to admire. A 'veteran' England Under-21 international with six caps at that level, Reid began in the back-four but when Kevin Bond was signed by his father, John Bond, Reid found himself moved to the midfield. He did not greatly enjoy the early experience but was lifted by the support which the Maine Road fans showed their local favourite who hails from Daveyhulme, Manchester. He came to City from Whitehall Juniors and, apart from a spell with Seattle Sounders in the NASL, has remained a one-club man since signing for City. Reid appeared in the 1981 FA Cup Final defeat by Spurs. *League debut for City v Ipswich Town, 31 March 1979.*

	LEAGUE		FA CUP		FL CUP		EUROPE		TOTAL	
	App	Gls	App	Gls	App	Gls	App	Gls	App	Gls
1978-79	7	0	0	0	0	0	2	0	9	0
1979-80	22(1)	0	1	0	0	0	-	-	23(1)	0
1980-81	37	0	7	0	7	0	-	-	51	0
1981-82	36	0	2	0	4	0	-	-	42	0
1982-83	24(1)	0	3	0	1	0	-	-	28(1)	0
1983-84	18(1)	2	0	0	2	0	-	-	20(1)	2
1984-85	31(1)	0	0	0	5	0	-	-	36(1)	0
1985-86	30	0	4	0	1	0	-	-	35	0
1986-87	6(1)	0	0	0	0	0	-	-	6(1)	0
	211(5)	2	17	0	20	0	2	0	250(5)	2

NICKY REID

Don Revie was one of the 'big-money' players of the early post-war period and will be remembered by older City fans for the so-called 'Revie Plan' which involved Revie playing a deep-lying centre-forward role in a manner similar to that which had helped bring success to the brilliant Hungarian team in the early 1950s. Revie's second career, as a manager, was also successful but dogged by controversy. He was born in Middlesbrough and began his League career with Leicester, then Hull. Hull paid £20,000 for him in 1949 and City had to pay a reported £25,000 for his signature two years later. He won Football League and England 'B' honours before the 1954-5 season, which was his best. The new role he adopted helped City to the FA Cup Final and Revie himself won the first of his six full England caps and was elected Footballer of the Year. In 1956 he returned to Wembley to help City lift the Cup. He was not assured of a Final place but a brilliant performance against Birmingham redeemed his apparently faltering career. In November 1956 he moved to Sunderland, for £24,000, and then became player-manager of Leeds. Revie revived the ailing Elland Road club, taking them from the lower reaches of Division Two to glory in the First Division and Europe. His reign as England manager was nowhere near as successful and he resigned in controversial circumstances. *League debut for City v Burnley, 20 October 1951.*

DON REVIE

	LEAGUE		FA CUP		TOTAL	
	App	Gls	App	Gls	App	Gls
1951-52	26	5	2	1	28	6
1952-53	32	6	3	0	35	6
1953-54	37	12	2	1	39	13
1954-55	32	8	6	2	38	10
1955-56	21	4	2	0	23	4
1956-57	14	2	0	0	14	2
	162	37	15	4	177	41

Manchester City laid out a considerable sum of money, £3,400, when they signed Bolton Wanderers forward, Frank Roberts, in October 1922. Roberts repaid City with an average of better than a goal every other game and although Bolton had made quite a profit on the deal — they had signed him from Crewe for £200 in 1914 — they must have occasionally regretted letting him go, especially when he won his first England cap, against Belgium in 1924. That season proved the peak of his career as he revelled in the Maine Road mud, scoring 31 goals in 38 League games that season, as well as representing the Football League. Born at Sandbach, Roberts went on to win four England caps altogether and he played for City in the 1926 FA Cup Final and helped them win the Second Division Championship in 1927-8. In June 1929 he was transferred to Manchester Central and later played for Horwich RMI. *League debut for City v Preston North End, 21 October 1922.*

FRANK ROBERTS

	LEAGUE		FA CUP		TOTAL	
	App	Gls	App	Gls	App	Gls
1922-23	32	10	1	0	33	10
1923-24	41	14	8	4	49	18
1924—25	38	31	1	1	39	32
1925-26	38	21	7	9	45	30
1926-27	27	14	0	0	27	14
1927-28	26	20	3	0	29	20
1928-29	14	6	1	0	15	6
	216	116	21	14	237	130

CLIFF SEAR

Cliff Sear was a stylish left-back who captained the Welsh Under-23 side in the late 1950s, although he won only one full cap, against England in 1962. Sear was born at Rhostyllan and when a miner at Bershaw Colliery he was on City's books as an amateur but found the travelling too much. City, however, kept him in mind and in January 1957 they signed him on professional forms. His League debut came less than four months later and he settled into the side as a regular during one of the more difficult periods in the club's history. He was a slim, 'footballing' defender and his presence gave the City rearguard much-needed stability. In April 1968, Sear signed for Chester after almost 250 League games for City, and he added 50 appearances for them before retiring to become youth-team coach, teaming up with his former City colleague, Alan Oakes, when Oakes became manager at Sealand Road. *League debut for City v Birmingham City, 27 April 1957.*

	LEAGUE		FA CUP		FL CUP		TOTAL	
	App	Gls	App	Gls	App	Gls	App	Gls
1956-57	1	0	0	0	-	-	1	0
1957-58	29	0	1	0	-	-	30	0
1958-59	31	0	2	0	-	-	33	0
1959-60	25	0	1	0	-	-	26	0
1960-61	33	0	1	0	2	0	36	0
1961-62	35	0	2	0	1	0	38	0
1962-63	33	0	1	0	6	0	40	0
1963-64	35	0	1	0	6	0	42	0
1964-65	7	0	2	0	0	0	9	0
1965-66	19	1	3	0	2	0	24	1
1966-67	0	0	0	0	0	0	0	0
1967-68	0	0	0	0	0	0	0	0
	248	1	14	0	17	0	279	1

George Smith was an inside-forward who began his City career in wartime football and missed only four League games when City won the Second Division Championship in 1946-7. He was actually signed by City in the close season of 1938 but war intervened after a handful of games for City in the war league, and some guest appearances for Hearts, he went abroad in the services. A gunshot wound sustained in South Africa left him with an injured hand but that obviously did not detract from his footballing ability and when peace was restored, Smith picked up his career. He scored all four goals in a wartime league game against Manchester United in April 1946 and collected five against Newport a year later when the Football League resumed. In October 1951 he was transferred to Chesterfield for £5,000 and enjoyed some good years at Saltergate. *League debut for City v Leicester City, 31 August 1946.*

	LEAGUE		FA CUP		TOTAL	
	App	Gls	App	Gls	App	Gls
1938-39	0	0	0	0	0	0
1946-47	38	23	4	0	42	23
1947-48	39	13	3	2	42	15
1948-49	32	12	1	0	33	12
1949-50	15	6	0	0	15	6
1950-51	39	21	1	0	40	21
1951-52	3	0	0	0	3	0
	166	75	13	5	179	80

GEORGE SMITH

WALTER SMITH

Walter Smith's benefit match against Blackburn in 1911 could hardly have been better timed. City had just won a good point at Sunderland and were also fielding two new players. A Leicester man, Smith always seemed to perform well against his home-town club.

Walter Smith was small for a goalkeeper, standing only 5ft 7in tall, but he was already reputed to be one of the best 'keepers in the Second Division when City signed him from Leicester Fosse in July 1906. Smith had made 79 appearances for Leicester and at Hyde Road he followed a line of consistent goalkeepers which included Charlie Williams and Jack Hillman. Smith spent 14 years with City but in that long career he won only two honours, when selected for an England XI against a Scottish team in April 1914, and for the Football League against the Scottish League in March 1915. When City won the Second Division title in 1909-10, Smith had lost his place to John Lyall and managed only three appearances. Smith bounced back the following year and was the regular goalkeeper in the two seasons prior to the League's suspension in World War One. He guested for Leicester and in October 1920 he was transferred to Port Vale but in three seasons made only 14 appearances before retiring. Smith collected £1,000 from a benefit match against Blackburn in 1911. *League debut for City v Bolton Wanderers, 24 November 1906.*

	LEAGUE		FA CUP		TOTAL	
	App	Gls	App	Gls	App	Gls
1906-07	22	0	2	0	24	0
1907-08	38	0	6	0	44	0
1908-09	34	0	1	0	35	0
1909-10	3	0	0	0	3	0
1910-11	31	0	2	0	33	0
1911-12	12	0	0	0	12	0
1912-13	10	0	3	0	13	0
1913-14	36	0	6	0	42	0
1914-15	37	0	4	0	41	0
1919-20	9	0	0	0	9	0
	232	0	24	0	256	0

Full-back Bert Sproston won his first England cap when he was 21-years-old, and by the time City bought him from Tottenham Hotspur in November 1938, almost £20,000 had changed hands for his services. Spurs paid Leeds £9,500 when they signed him from Elland Road, and City laid our £10,000 to bring him from White Hart Lane. It was at Leeds that he had blossomed into an England player but Leeds were desperately short of money and had to sell their young star. Sproston's time in London was short and unhappy. He could not settle in the south and four months after leaving Leeds he was a City player. He travelled to Manchester with his Spurs teammates, signed for City and turned out against his now former Tottenham colleagues the following day. Sproston won two England caps with City but war was declared before they could make best use of him and the young international star, in whom they had invested a near-record British fee, was a veteran of 30 before he could settle down. Nevertheless, Sproston won a Second Division Championship medal and was a regular until he joined Ashton United in August 1950. He later became trainer, then scout for Bolton Wanderers. *League debut for City v Tottenham Hotspur, 5 November 1938.*

	LEAGUE		FA CUP		TOTAL	
	App	Gls	App	Gls	App	Gls
1938-39	20	2	1	0	21	2
1939-40	3	0	-	-	3	0
1946-47	38	2	2	0	40	2
1947-48	37	0	3	0	40	0
1948-49	25	1	0	0	25	1
1949-50	5	0	0	0	5	0
	128	5	6	0	134	5

BERT SPROSTON

MIKE SUMMERBEE

Mike Summerbee was a member of the Swindon Town team which won promotion for the first time in that club's history, in the early 1960s. His father, George Summerbee, played alongside Joe Mercer in Aldershot's star-studded wartime team and Mercer had followed young Mike's progress. Indeed, he made the young striker his first signing when taking over at City in 1965. In those days Summerbee was a more traditional outside-right but he eventually began to assume a more versatile role and shared in City's triumphant rise to new greatness with winners' medals for the First and Second Division Championships, FA, League and European Cup-winners' Cups. He won eight full England caps amongst his many representative honours and although he was never a great goalscorer, his sheer presence created havoc in opposing defences and, therefore, many chances for his colleagues. A fashionable dresser in the 'Swinging Sixties', he was part-owner of a boutique with George Best. He made over 350 League appearances for City before joining Burnley, for £25,000, in June 1975. His career later took in Blackpool and the player-manager's job at Stockport where his career ended after more than 700 League appearances. *League debut for City v Middlesbrough, 21 August 1965.*

	LEAGUE		FACUP		FLCUP		EUROPE		TOTAL	
	App	Gls	App	Gls	App	Gls	App	Gls	App	Gls
1965-66	42	8	8	2	2	0	-	-	52	10
1966-67	32	4	4	2	2	1	-	-	38	7
1967-68	41	14	4	4	4	2	-	-	49	20
1968-69	39	6	6	0	3	2	2	0	50	8
1969-70	32(1)	3	2	0	7	2	7	1	48(1)	6
1970-71	26	4	2	0	1	0	6	0	35	4
1971-72	40	3	2	0	2	0	-	-	44	3
1972-73	38	2	4	1	2	0	1	0	45	3
1973-74	39	1	2	2	11	1	-	-	52	4
1974-75	26(1)	2	0	0	2	0	0	0	28(1)	2
	355(2)	47	34	11	36	8	16	1	441(2)	67

348

Frank Swift was a huge man in every respect, a player who stood 6ft tall and whose finger-span of almost 12 inches meant that he could easily grasp a football in one hand; and a cheery, larger-than-life character who dominated any gathering graced with his presence. He was also a very fine goalkeeper, the first to captain England, and Manchester City were fortunate that they were his only League club. Swift was born in Blackpool and signed for City in the autumn of 1932, from Fleetwood. He made his League debut the following year, on Christmas Day, and even though the war took seven seasons out of his career, he still managed almost 400 League and FA Cup appearances. Beginning with his first full season in the League side, Swift was ever-present for four consecutive seasons and missed only one game in 1938-9. Swift was a spectacular 'keeper who often elected to throw the ball to a colleague rather than opt for the usual aimless punt downfield most used in those days. Swift won 19 full England caps and played in many wartime internationals as well as gaining First and Second Division Championship medals and an FA Cup winners' medal (in his first season). Although he retired in September 1949, the year after captaining England against Italy, Swift's registration was held by City until May 1955. He was tragically killed in the Munich Air Disaster, when accompanying Manchester United as a newspaper reporter. *League debut for City v Derby County, 25 December 1933.*

FRANK SWIFT

	LEAGUE		FA CUP		TOTAL	
	App	Gls	App	Gls	App	Gls
1932-33	0	0	0	0	0	0
1933-34	22	0	8	0	30	0
1934-35	42	0	1	0	43	0
1935-36	42	0	3	0	45	0
1936-37	42	0	4	0	46	0
1937-38	42	0	5	0	47	0
1938-39	41	0	2	0	43	0
1939-40	3	0	-	-	3	0
1946-47	35	0	4	0	39	0
1947-48	33	0	3	0	36	0
1948-49	35	0	1	0	36	0
1949-50	4	0	0	0	4	0
	341	0	35	0	376	0

Centre-forward Irvine Thornley was such a popular figure at Hyde Road that he was the first player to receive £1,000 for his benefit. A butcher by trade, Thornley joined City from Glossop, his home-town club, in April 1904 for £800 although the FA later discovered some 'irregularities' concerning his transfer from the Derbyshire club. He was a wholeheaded and tireless player who scored 92 League goals in 195 League games for City. He was also something of a controversial figure who had more than one brush with authority. He was suspended for a year, and in January 1912, when captaining City shortly after returning to the side following an eye injury, he was sent off at Aston Villa. Yet there were plenty of highspots, too. Thornley was capped by England against Wales in March 1907 and twice played for the Football League, against the Scottish and Irish Leagues. He won a Second Division Championship medal in 1909-10 before signing for South Shields in August 1912. He scored over 60 goals for the Tynesiders in 1914-15 and ended his senior career in the Scottish League with Hamilton Academical. *League debut for City v Sunderland, 9 April 1904.*

	LEAGUE		FA CUP		TOTAL	
	App	Gls	App	Gls	App	Gls
1903-04	4	0	0	0	4	0
1904-05	4	2	0	0	4	2
1905-06	36	21	1	0	37	21
1906-07	29	13	2	1	31	14
1907-08	31	14	6	0	37	14
1908-09	32	18	0	0	32	18
1909-10	23	12	0	0	23	12
1910-11	18	6	0	0	18	6
1911-12	18	6	0	0	18	6
	195	92	9	1	204	93

IRVINE THORNLEY

Fred Tilson forged an exciting left-wing partnership with Eric Brook at Barnsley and the pair soon attracted the notice of Manchester City who paid a joint-fee of £6,000 for them both in March 1928. Tilson was badly injured at Old Trafford and that slowed down his progress with City. Eventually he succeeded Halliday at centre-forward and soon repaid City with four goals in one match. Tilson's career was dogged with injury and he missed an England Schoolboy cap through a bad knock. In 1933 he was injured in a League game shortly before that season's FA Cup Final and missed the Wembley game. He was, however, in the team 12 months later when City won the trophy and he scored four goals in that year's semi-final, and both City's goals at Wembley. That summer Tilson won the first of four England caps (scoring six goals) and in 1936-7 he won a League Championship medal. In November 1938 he moved to Northampton Town and later played for York City. He returned to Maine Road to serve successively as coach, assistant manager and chief scout. Tilson died in November 1972, aged 69. *League debut for City v Grimsby Town, 17 March 1928.*

	LEAGUE		FA CUP		TOTAL	
	App	Gls	App	Gls	App	Gls
1927-28	6	0	0	0	6	0
1928-29	22	12	0	0	22	12
1929-30	11	7	1	0	12	7
1930-31	17	4	1	0	18	4
1931-32	37	13	5	3	42	16
1932-33	29	17	6	6	35	23
1933-34	21	12	8	9	29	21
1934-35	34	18	1	0	35	18
1935-36	32	11	2	1	34	12
1936-37	23	15	4	3	27	18
1937-38	13	1	0	0	13	1
	245	110	28	22	273	132

FRED TILSON

Ernie Toseland was a flying winger whose 11 goals in only 22 games for Coventry City went a long way to persuading Manchester City to sign him in March 1929. Thereafter, Toseland missed very few games until he was transferred to Sheffield Wednesday in March 1939. Toseland won an FA Cup winners' medal and a League Championship medal with City, but his only representative honour was an appearance for the Football League against the Irish League in September 1929. Many people expressed surprise that he never won an England cap but there were many fine wingers around in the 1930s. After 409 League and FA Cup appearances, and 75 goals, he moved to Hillsborough but managed only 15 appearances for the Owls before war curtailed the League. He returned to guest for City and as late as 1945-6 was still playing in the Cheshire County League. *League debut for City v Bury, 20 April 1929.*

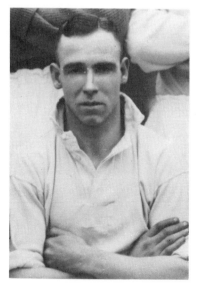

ERNIE TOSELAND

	LEAGUE		FA CUP		TOTAL	
	App	Gls	App	Gls	App	Gls
1928-29	3	1	0	0	3	1
1929-30	42	2	5	3	47	5
1930-31	38	10	1	0	39	10
1931-32	40	5	5	3	45	8
1932-33	42	9	7	2	49	11
1933-34	40	6	8	4	48	10
1934-35	32	5	1	0	33	5
1935-36	41	10	3	0	44	10
1936-37	42	7	4	0	46	7
1937-38	30	3	5	2	35	5
1938-39	18	3	2	0	20	3
	368	61	41	14	409	75

Bremen-born Bert Trautmann had to overcome a considerable amount of hostility from the fans when Manchester City signed him to replace Frank Swift after that hugely popular goalkeeper retired in 1949. The supporters resentment was perhaps understandable, given the climate at the time. The war was still fresh in people's memories and as a former German paratrooper and ex-PoW, Trautmann could hardly have expected the warmest Lancashire welcome. Yet he soon won the hearts of City's followers and went on to make over 500 League appearances for the club, breaking his neck in City's cause in the 1956 FA Cup Final. Trautmann arrived in England in April 1945 and it was at a PoW camp at Ashton-in-Makerfield that he first tried his hand at goalkeeping. He later said that his training as a paratrooper had helped him to cushion the ball as he fell. After being released Trautmann worked on a farm and played for St Helens, later marrying the club secretary's daughter. City signed him in November 1949 and he went straight into the League side. Besides two FA Final appearances, Trautmann won Football League representative honours and was the 1956 Footballer of the Year. Trautmann had to overcome personal tragedy later that year when his five-year-old son was killed in a road accident. A crowd of almost 48,000 saw his testimonial match in 1964 and Trautmann later served non-League Wellington Town, and Stockport County as general-manager before going to coach abroad. *League debut for City v Bolton Wanderers, 19 November 1949.*

BERT TRAUTMANN

	LEAGUE		FACUP		FLCUP		TOTAL	
	App	Gls	App	Gls	App	Gls	App	Gls
1949-50	26	0	0	0	-	-	26	0
1950-51	42	0	1	0	-	-	43	0
1951-52	41	0	2	0	-	-	43	0
1952-53	42	0	3	0	-	-	45	0
1953-54	42	0	2	0	-	-	44	0
1954-55	40	0	6	0	-	-	46	0
1955-56	40	0	7	0	-	-	47	0
1956-57	21	0	2	0	-	-	23	0
1957-58	34	0	1	0	-	-	35	0
1958-59	41	0	2	0	-	-	43	0
1959-60	41	0	1	0	-	-	42	0
1960-61	40	0	4	0	2	0	46	0
1961-62	40	0	2	0	1	0	43	0
1962-63	15	0	0	0	1	0	16	0
1963-64	3	0	0	0	0	0	3	0
	508	0	33	0	4	0	545	0

Dennis Tueart's spectacular goal for City against Newcastle United in the 1976 League Cup Final at Wembley is a memory which will stay with those who saw it for many a long day. Back to goal, Tueart hooked the ball over his right shoulder to restore City's lead and leave United a beaten side. It was not Tueart's first taste of Wembley glory. As a Sunderland player he had been in the Wearsiders' Second Division team which caused a shock by winning the FA Cup in 1972. Tueart, a former Newcastle Boys player who hails from Tyneside, joined City from Sunderland for £275,000 in March the following year. He had two spells with City, playing in the star-studded New York Cosmos team between 1978 and 1980. City sold him to the NASL club for £250,000 and bought him back for £150,000. Tueart won a League Cup-winners' medal with City in 1976, and played in the 1981 FA Cup Final. He won six full England caps, all with City, and his sole appearance in the Under-23 team was also as a City player. Tueart also played for the Football League. He was one of the best forwards of his era, a fine striker whose polished play excited crowds wherever he played. In July 1983 he went to Stoke on a free-transfer. *League debut for City v Manchester United, 13 March 1974.*

DENNIS TUEART

	LEAGUE		FACUP		FLCUP		EUROPE		TOTAL	
	App	Gls	App	Gls	App	Gls	App	Gls	App	Gls
1973-74	8	1	0	0	0	0	-	-	8	1
1974-75	39	14	1	0	2	0	-	-	42	14
1975-76	37(1)	14	2	2	7	8	-	-	46(1)	24
1976-77	38	18	4	0	1	0	2	0	45	18
1977-78	17	12	2	1	5	2	1	0	25	15
1979-80	11	5	0	0	0	0	-	-	11	5
1980-81	21(1)	8	2	0	5	4	-	-	28(1)	12
1981-82	15	9	0	0	4	2	-	-	19	11
1982-83	30(6)	5	2	0	3	2	-	-	35(6)	7
	216(8)	86	13	3	27	18	3	0	259(8)	107

Inside-forward Alex Sandy Turnbull was one of four City players transferred to Manchester United after the illegal payments scandal of 1906. Turnbull enjoyed two quite separate and successful careers with the Manchester clubs, winning FA Cup winners' medals with both. A small, burly Scot, he joined City from Hurlford in July 1902 and he was the man most linked with Billy Meredith. He was one of the great stars of the day, a player who could strike the ball with either foot; he even scored goals with his head, despite the fact that he was only 5ft 5in tall. With City he won a Division Two Championship medal in 1902-03 and an FA Cup winners' medal in 1904. At United he played in two League Championship winning teams and scored the goal which won the 1909 FA Cup Final. He scored 53 goals in 110 League games for City and 90 in 220 League games for United. Turnbull played for United until the outbreak of war and was killed at Arras on 3 May 1917, serving with the Manchester Regiment. *League debut for City v Bristol City, 15 November 1902.*

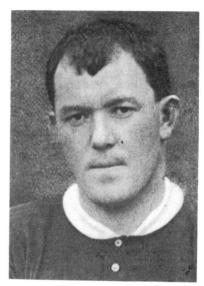

	LEAGUE		FA CUP		TOTAL	
	App	Gls	App	Gls	App	Gls
1902-03	22	12	1	1	23	13
1903-04	32	16	6	5	38	21
1904-05	30	19	2	1	32	20
1905-06	26	6	0	0	26	6
	110	53	9	7	119	60

SANDY TURNBULL

In 1946-7, Maine Road saw 2.2 million people pass through its turnstiles. The FA Cup semi-final replay between Liverpool and Burnley, and the Rugby League Challenge Cup Final were both played at City' home ground.

WILLIAM WALSH

Dublin-born half-back William Walsh began as an amateur with Manchester United before joining City in May 1936. He signed professional for City two years later but had to wait until League football resumed in 1946 to make his debut in first-class soccer. By then, however, Walsh was already a veteran, having appeared for City in 242 wartime games. Yet he missed out on a Second Division Championship medal in 1946-7, playing in 13 games as City returned to the top flight. Walsh was one the players who played for both the Republic of Ireland and Northern Ireland, when the Ulstermen could select, for Home International matches, players born in the south. In 1951 he signed for Chelmsford City on a free-transfer. *League debut for City v Arsenal, 31 August 1946.*

	LEAGUE		FA CUP		TOTAL	
	App	Gls	App	Gls	App	Gls
1938-39	0	0	0	0	0	0
1939-40	0	0	-	-	0	0
1946-47	13	1	0	0	13	1
1947-48	30	0	3	0	33	0
1948-49	39	0	1	0	40	0
1949-50	27	0	1	0	28	0
1950-51	0	0	0	0	0	0
	109	1	9	0	118	1

Eric Westwood was that surprising rarity — a Manchester-born man who played for both City and United. He was an amateur with United before moving across to Maine Road in November 1937. He made his City debut on the same day as Bert Sproston and after playing 30 League games in 1938-9, the last full season before the war, he could not pick up his career until seven seasons later. His wartime appearances for City were few, only 23, but he guested for Chelsea and played for them in the 1944 War Cup Final. Westwood was a skilful full-back who won Football League and England 'B' representative honours as well as a Second Division Championship medal with City. In May 1953 he was given a free-transfer and signed for Altrincham Town. *League debut for City v Tottenham Hotspur, 5 November 1938.*

ERIC WESTWOOD

	LEAGUE		FA CUP		TOTAL	
	App	Gls	App	Gls	App	Gls
1937-38	0	0	0	0	0	0
1938-39	30	0	2	0	32	0
1939-40	3	0	-	-	3	0
1946-47	28	2	4	2	32	4
1947-48	42	0	3	0	45	0
1948-49	42	0	1	0	43	0
1949-50	40	0	1	0	41	0
1950-51	37	1	1	0	38	1
1951-52	7	0	0	0	7	0
1952-53	22	0	0	0	22	0
	251	3	12	2	263	5

On 14 June 1947, Manchester City played their final game of the season — which had been extended because of bad weather — against relegated Newport County. Roy Clarke was making his debut but he was overshadowed by George Smith who equalled a club record with all City's goals in their 5-1 win.

CHARLIE WILLIAMS

When Billy Meredith had a benefit match in 1912 he received good wishes from Charlie Williams who was then coaching Rio Grande do Sol of Brazil.

Goalkeeper Charlie Williams' best claim to fame is perhaps his huge clearance at Sunderland which resulted in a goal for City. He was also a very fine 'keeper who might have won England honours had he possessed a more orthodox style. He stood 5ft 11in, weighed 12st, and had a few quite interesting theories about the art of defending his goal. He won a Second Division Championship medal with City in 1896-7 and played for the Football League against the Irish League in April 1899, and won a Lancashire Combination Championship winners' medal in 1901-02. Williams was born in Welling and joined City from Woolwich Arsenal in June 1894. He left in the close season of 1902, for Tottenham Hotspur, and also played for Norwich, Brentford, and managed the French club Lille. He died in South America in 1952, aged 76. *League debut for City v Bury, 1 September 1894.*

	LEAGUE		FA CUP		TEST		TOTAL	
	App	Gls	App	Gls	App	Gls	App	Gls
1894-95	23	0	0	0	-	-	23	0
1895-96	30	0	0	0	4	0	34	0
1896-97	30	0	1	0	-	-	31	0
1897-98	23	0	2	0	-	-	25	0
1898-99	33	0	1	0	-	-	34	0
1899-1900	34	1	2	0	-	-	36	1
1900-01	33	0	1	0	-	-	34	0
1901-02	15	0	0	0	-	-	15	0
	221	1	7	0	4	0	232	1

Max Woosnam, who played centre-half for City in the years immediately after World War One, was an all-round sportsman in the truest sense — Cambridge Blue at soccer, golf and lawn tennis, 12th man for the cricket team, and a Wimbledon doubles champion and Olympic gold-medallist at tennis. He was the son of a former Canon of Chester and had himself been born in Newtown, Liverpool, although his family home was in North Wales. He played for Chelsea and signed for City in November 1919. His employers helped him all they could so that he could play for City — something which Woosnam fitted in around all his other commitments. For instance, he missed the start of the 1921-2 season because he was in Britain's Davies Cup team. He was the archetypal amateur of his day, well-groomed, a player of classic style and a member of the famous Corinthians. He was a popular captain of City and he also captained England. His full international appearance came against Wales in March 1922. His City appearances were restricted by a collision with a wooden fence around the Hyde Road pitch and in October 1925 he signed for Northwich Victoria. *League debut for City v Bradford City, 1 January 1920.*

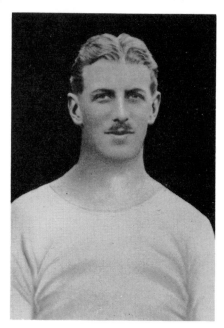

MAX WOOSNAM

	LEAGUE		FA CUP		TOTAL	
	App	Gls	App	Gls	App	Gls
1919-20	16	0	1	0	17	0
1920-21	34	0	1	0	35	0
1921-22	33	3	3	0	36	3
1922-23	0	0	0	0	0	0
1923-24	1	0	1	0	2	1
1924-25	2	1	1	0	3	1
	86	4	7	0	93	5

GEORGE WYNN

Welsh international inside-forward George Wynn served City well during the years leading up to World War One. He was born at Oswestry but his first club was the famous Chirk side. Wynn then joined Oswestry United and won a Welsh Cup winners' medal with them in 1907. His next club was Wrexham before he signed for City in April 1909, waiting until Christmas Day that year for his League debut. In May 1910 he collected a Second Division Championship medal and during his City career he won eight of his 12 Welsh caps. His career was interrupted by war and after 30 games and nine goals for City in wartime soccer, he managed only four more League appearances before Coventry City paid £300 for him in November 1919. Wynn later played for Halifax and Mansfield. *League debut for City v Bradford, 25 December 1909.*

	LEAGUE		FA CUP		TOTAL	
	App	Gls	App	Gls	App	Gls
1908-09	0	0	0	0	0	0
1909-10	20	10	4	2	24	12
1910-11	20	9	0	0	20	9
1911-12	31	17	2	1	33	18
1912-13	31	14	3	2	34	16
1913-14	12	3	0	0	12	3
1914-15	1	0	0	0	1	0
1919-20	4	1	0	0	4	1
	119	54	9	5	128	59

Inside-left Neil Young was a star amongst stars in the City forward line which helped the club win the League Championship in 1967-8. He was the player who always seemed to have something to spare and was top-scorer in both City's Second and First Division title-winning sides. An apprentice professional at Maine Road — he was locally-born, at Fellowsfield — Young signed full-time professional forms in February 1961 and made his League debut the following November. In his early days, when City were going through a difficult time, Young was switched around the forward line, but when Mercer and Allison moved him permanently to the number-10 spot, he blossomed. Besides his Championship medals, Young won European Cup-winners' Cup and FA Cup winners' medals with City and it was his splendid left-foot shot that won the 1969 Wembley Final against Leicester. His only representative honour was in the England Youth team and it was surprising that he was not considered at Under-23, or even full levels. In January 1972, City sold him to Preston for £48,000 and Young later played for Rochdale. *League debut for City v Aston Villa, 25 November 1961.*

NEIL YOUNG

	LEAGUE		FACUP		FLCUP		EUROPE		TOTAL	
	App	Gls	App	Gls	App	Gls	App	Gls	App	Gls
1960-61	0	0	0	0	0	0	-	-	0	0
1961-62	24	10	2	1	0	0	-	-	26	11
1962-63	31	5	1	0	6	1	-	-	38	6
1963-64	37	5	1	0	5	1	-	-	43	6
1964-65	31	8	1	0	1	1	-	-	33	9
1965-66	35	14	7	3	2	0	-	-	44	17
1966-67	38	4	5	2	2	1	-	-	45	7
1967-68	40	19	4	1	4	2	-	-	48	22
1968-69	40	14	7	2	2	0	2	0	51	16
1969-70	29	6	2	1	5	1	8	4	44	12
1970-71	24	1	2	0	1	0	7	1	34	2
1971-72	3(2)	0	0	0	0	0	0	0	3(2)	0
	332(2)	86	32	10	28	7	17	5	409(2)	108

Manchester City Football Club, season 1965-6. Back row (left to right): V.Gomersall, D.Bacuzzi, R.Cheetham, H.Dowd, D.Doyle, R.Kennedy, A.Oakes, J.Clay. Front row: N.Young, G.Pardoe, J.Murray, J.Crossan, D.Connor, A.Ogley.

International & Representative Honours with City

Many players won additional caps with other clubs but the totals given here are for appearances made whilst Manchester City players. Before 1924 there was only one 'Ireland' team, then the Republic began separate matches and that position is reflected here. The date given is the year in which the match was played.

ENGLAND

Austin S.W. 1925 v Northern Ireland (1).

Barkas S. 1936 v Belgium; 1937 v Scotland, Northern Ireland, Wales, Czechoslovakia (5).

Barnes P.S. 1977 v Italy, 1978 v West Germany, Brazil, Wales, Scotland, Hungary, Denmark, Republic of Ireland, Czechoslovakia; 1979 v Northern Ireland (twice), Scotland, Bulgaria, Austria (14).

Bell C. 1968 v Sweden, West Germany, Bulgaria; 1969 v France, Wales, Uruguary, Brazil, Holland, Portugal; 1970 v Holland, Northern Ireland, Brazil, Czechoslovakia, West Germany, Greece; 1972 v West Germany, Wales, Northern Ireland, Scotland, Yugoslavia, West Germany, Wales; 1973 v Wales, Scotland, Northern Ireland, Wales, Scotland, Czechoslovakia, Poland, Austria, Poland, Italy; 1974 v Wales, Northern Ireland, Scotland, Argentina, East Germany, Bulgaria, Yugoslavia, Czechoslovakia, Portugal; 1975 v West Germany, Cyprus (twice), Northern Ireland, Scotland, Switzerland, Czechoslovakia (48).

Booth F. 1905 v Ireland (1).

Bray J. 1934 v Wales; 1935 v Northern Ireland, Germany; 1936 v Wales, Scotland; 1937 v Scotland (6).

Broadis I.A. 1951 v Austria; 1952 v Scotland, Italy; 1953 v Scotland, Argentina, Chile, Uruguay, USA (8).

Brook E.F. 1929 v Northern Ireland; 1933 v Switzerland, Northern Ireland, Wales, France; 1934 v Scotland, Hungary, Czechoslovakia, Wales, Italy; 1935 v Northern Ireland, Scotland, Northern Ireland; 1936 Wales, Scotland, Hungary; 1937 v Northern Ireland, Wales (18).

Burgess H. 1904 v Wales, Ireland, Scotland; 1906 v Scotland (4).

Channon M.R. 1977 v Switzerland (1).

Corrigan J.T. 1976 v Italy; 1978 v Brazil; 1979 v Wales; 1980 v Northern Ireland, Australia; 1981 v Wales, Scotland; 1982 v Wales, Iceland (9).

Cowan S. 1926 v Belgium; 1930 v Austria; 1931 v Belgium (3).

Doyle M. 1976 v Wales, Scotland, Brazil, Italy; 1977 v Holland (5).

Francis T.J. 1981 v Norway; 1982 v Northern Ireland, Wales, Scotland, Finland, France, Czechoslovakia, Kuwait, West Germany, Spain (10).

Johnson T.C.F. 1926 v Belgium; 1929 v Wales (2).

Lee F.H. 1968 v Bulgara; 1969 v France, Northern Ireland, Wales, Scotland, Mexico, Uruguay, Holland, Portugal; 1970 v Holland, Belgium, Wales, Colombia, Ecuador, Rumania, Brazil, West Germany, East Germany; 1971 v Greece, Malta, Northern Ireland, Wales, Scotland, Switzerland (twice), Greece; 1972 v West Germany (27).

Marsh R.W. 1972 v West Germany (twice), Wales, Northern Ireland, Scotland, Yugoslavia, Wales; 1973 v Wales (8).

Meadows J. 1955 v Scotland (1).

Mitchell J.F. 1924 v Northern Ireland (1).

Reeves K.P. 1980 v Northern Ireland (1).

Revie D.G. 1954 v Northern Ireland; 1955 v Scotland, France, Denmark, Wales; 1956 v Northern Ireland (6).

Roberts F. 1924 v Belgium; 1925 v Wales, Scotland, France (4).

Royle J. 1976 v Northern Ireland, Italy, Finland; 1977 v Luxembourg (4).

Sproston B. 1938 v Norway (1).

Summerbee M.G. 1968 v Scotland, Spain, West Germany; 1971 v Switzerland; 1972 v West Germany, Wales, Northern Ireland; 1973 v USSR (8).

Swift F.V. 1946 v Northern Ireland, Republic of Ireland, Wales, Holland; 1947 v Scotland, France, Switzerland, Portugal, Belgium, Wales, Northern Ireland, Sweden; 1948 v Scotland, Italy, Denmark, Northern Ireland, Wales; 1949 v Scotland, Norway (19).

Thornley I. 1907 v Wales (1).

Tilson F.S. 1934 v Hungary, Czechoslovakia, Wales; 1935 v Northern Ireland (4).

Tueart D. 1974 v Cyprus, Northern Ireland; 1976 v Finland; 1977 v Northern Ireland, Wales, Scotland (6).

356

Watson D.V. 1975 v Switzerland, Czechoslovakia, Portugal; 1977 v Holland, Luxembourg, Northern Ireland, Wales, Scotland, Brazil, Argentina, Uruguay, Switzerland, Luxembourg, Italy; 1978 v West Germany, Brazil, Wales, Northern Ireland, Scotland, Hungary, Denmark, Republic of Ireland, Czechoslovakia; 1979 v Northern Ireland, Wales, Scotland, Bulgaria, Northern Ireland, Sweden, Austria (30).
Woosnam M. 1922 v Wales (1).

SCOTLAND

Busby M.W. 1933 v Wales (1).
Donachie W. 1971 v Peru, Northern Ireland, England, Yugoslavia, Czechoslovakia, Brazil, Denmark; 1973 v England, Wales, Northern Ireland; 1974 v Northern Ireland; 1975 v Rumania; 1976 v Wales, Northern Ireland, England, Finland, Czechoslovakia, Wales; 1977 v Sweden, Wales, Northern Ireland, England, Chile, Argentina, Brazil, East Germany, Wales; 1978 v Bulgaria, Wales, England, Iran, Holland, Austria, Norway, Portugal (35).
Hartford R.A. 1975 v Denmark, Rumania; 1976 v Northern Ireland, Czechoslovakia, Wales; 1977 v Sweden, Wales, Northern Ireland, England, Chile, Argentina, Brazil, East Germany, Czechoslovakia, Wales; 1978 v Bulgaria, Wales, England, Peru, Iran, Holland, Austria, Norway, Portugal; 1979 v Wales, N.Ireland, England, Argentina, Norway; 1981 v Northern Ireland, Portugal; 1982 v Spain, Northern Ireland, Wales, England, Brazil (36).
Johnstone R. 1955 v England, Northern Ireland, Wales; 1956 v England (4).
Law D. 1959 v England, Poland, Austria, Northern Ireland; 1961 v England; 1973 v Czechoslovakia (twice), West Germany; 1974 v West Germany, Northern Ireland, Zaire (11).
Livingstone G.T. 1906 v England (1).
McLuckie J.S. 1933 v Wales (1).
McMullan J. 1926 v England, Wales; 1927 v England, Wales; 1928 v England, Wales; 1929 v Northern Ireland, England (8).
Plenderleith J.B. 1960 v Northern Ireland (1).
Stewart G. 1907 v Wales, England (2).

WALES

Chapman T. 1896 v England (1).
Clarke R.J. 1948 v England; 1949 v Scotland. Belgium; 1950 v Northern Ireland, Scotland, England; 1951 v Northern Ireland, Portugal, Switzerland, England, Scoland, United Kingdom; 1952 v Northern Ireland, Scotland, England; 1953 v England, Scotland; 1954 v Northern Ireland, Yugoslovia, Scotland, England; 1956 v Northern Ireland (22).
Davies G. 1986 v Saudi Arabia, Republic of Ireland (2).
Davies J. 1890 v Ireland; 1896 v England (2).
Davies W.R. 1972 v England, Scotland, Northern Ireland (3).
Gray A. 1927 v England, Scotland; 1928 v Scotland, England, Northern Ireland; 1929 v Scotland (5).
Hughes E. 1913 v Scotland, England; 1914 v Ireland (3).
Jones D. 1900 v Ireland, England (2).
Jones W.L. 1905 v England, Ireland; 1906 v Scotland, England, Ireland; 1907 v Ireland, Scotland, England; 1908 v Scotland; 1909 v Scotland, England, Ireland; 1910 v England; 1911 v England; 1913 v Scotland, England; 1914 v Ireland, Scotland (18).
Lewis W. 1897 v Scotland, England (2).
Meredith W.H. 1895 v Ireland, England; 1896 v Ireland, England; 1897 v Ireland, Scotland, England; 1898 v Ireland, England; 1899 v Englnd; 1900 v Ireland, England; 1901 v England, Ireland; 1902 v Scotland, England; 1903 v England, Scotland, Ireland; 1904 v England; 1905 v Scotland, England (22).
Morris H. 1896 v England (1).
Paul R. 1950 v Scotland, England; 1951 v Northern Ireland, Portugal, Switzerland, England, Scotland, United Kingdom; 1952 v Northern Ireland, Scotland, England; 1953 v Northern Ireland, France, Yugoslavia, England, Scotand; 1954 v Northern Ireland, Yugoslavia, Scotland, England; 1955 v England, Scotland, Austria; 1956 v Northern Ireland (24).
Phillips D.O. 1984 v Spain, Iceland; 1985 v Scotland, Spain, Norway, Scotland, Hungary; 1986 v Saudi Arabia, Republic of Ireland, Uruguay (10).
Sear C.R. 1962 v England (1).
Wynn G.A. 1910 v England; 1911 v Ireland; 1912 v Scotland, England; 1913 v Scotland, England; 1914 v Scotland, England (8).

NORTHERN IRELAND (and Ireland before 1924)

Crossan J.A. 1965 v Holland (twice), Wales, Albania, Scotland, Albania, England; 1966 v West Germany, England, Scotland (10).
Doherty P.D. 1936 v England; 1937 v Wales, England, Scotland; 1938 v England, Wales (6).
Hamill M. 1921 v Scotland (1).
Kelly P. 1920 v England (1).
McAdams W.J. 1954 v Wales, Scotland; 1956 v England; 1957 v Scotland; 1957 v Italy (5).
McCourt F.J. 1951 v England; 1952 v Wales, England, Scotland, France; 1953 v Wales (6).
McCullough K. 1935 v Scotland; 1936 v Scotland, England (3).
McIlroy S. 1985 v Turkey, Rumania, England; 1986 v France, Denmark, Morocco, Algeria, Spain, Brazil (9).
Mulligan J. 1921 v Scotland (1).
O'Neill M.H.M. 1981 v Scotland (1).
Walsh W. 1947 v Scotland, England; 1948 v Wales, England, Scotland (5).

REPUBLIC OF IRELAND

Conway J.P. 1977 v Poland (1).
Dunne L. 1935 v Switzerland, West Germany (2).
Fagan F. 1954 v Norway; 1959 v Sweden (2).
McCarthy M. 1984 v Poland, China, Mexico, Denmark; 1985 v Italy, Israel, England, Spain, Switzerland (twice), USSR; 1986 v Wales, Uruguay, Iceland, Czechoslovakia, Scotland, Poland; 1987 v Scotland, Bulgaria, Belgium (20).
Walsh W. 1946 v England; 1947 v Spain, Portugal; 1948 v Portugal, Spain; 1949 v Belgium, England, Sweden; 1950 v Belgium (9).

NORWAY

Hareide A. 1981 v England, Denmark; 1982 v Finland, West Germany, Denmark, Sweden, Wales, Yugoslavia, Bulgaria (9).

ENGLAND XI (Unofficial internationals)

Bell C. 1968 v Young England (1).
Bray J. 1935 v Scotland *(Jubilee Match)* (1).
Corrigan J.T. 1981 v Athletic Bilbao (1).
Dorsett J.H. 1914 v Scottish XI (1).
Doyle M. 1976 v Team America (1).
Smith W. 1901 v German XI (1).
Smith W.E. 1914 v Scottish XI (1).
Summerbee M.G. 1967 v Young England (1).
Swift F.V. 1946 v Scotland (*Bolton Disaster Fund*); 1947 v Switzerland 'B'; 1948 v Switzerland 'B', Schaffhausen XI (4).

ENGLAND 'B'

Bell C. 1970 v Colombia 'B', Ecuador 'B' (2).
Corrigan J.T. 1978 v West Germany 'B', Malaysia, New Zealand (3 games), Singapore, Czechoslovakia 'B'; 1979 v Austria 'B'; 1980 v Spain 'B'; 1981 v Spain 'B' (10)
MacKenzie S. 1981 v Spain 'B' (1).
Owen G. 1978 v W.Germany 'B', Malaysia, Christchurch, Otago, New Zealand (3 games), Singapore. (8)
Power P. 1981 v Spain 'B'. (1)
Reeves K.P. 1980 v U.S.A; 1981 v Spain 'B'. (2)
Revie D.G. 1954 v Scotland 'B' (1).
Tueart D. 1975 England 'B' XI v Arsenal (unofficial) (1).
Westwood E. 1949 v Finland, Holland (2).

WARTIME INTERNATIONALS

ENGLAND
Brook E.F.G. 1939 v Wales (1).
Sproston B. 1939 v Wales; 1940 v Scotland (2).
Swift F.V. 1939 v Wales; 1941 v Scotland; 1943 v Scotland (twice), Wales; 1944 v Wales, Scotland (twice); 1945 v Scotland (twice) (10).

SCOTLAND
Herd A. 1942 v England (1).

VICTORY INTERNATIONALS

ENGLAND
Barnes H. 1919 v Wales (1).
Swift F.V. 1945 v Northern Ireland; 1946 v Belgium, Scotland, Switzerland (4).

WALES
Hughes E. 1919 v England (twice) (2).
Wynn G.A. 1919 v England (1).

NORTHERN IRELAND
Doherty P.D. 1945 v England (1).

YOUNG ENGLAND

Doyle M. 1968 v England XI (1).
Hayes J. 1958 v England XI (1).

GREAT BRITAIN XI

Johnstone R. 1955 v Rest of Europe (1).
Swift F.V. 1947 v Rest of Europe (1).

Peter Doherty

COMMON MARKET CELEBRATION MATCH

Bell C. 1973 (The Three v The Six) (1).

UNITED KINGDOM XI

Lee F.H. 1969 v Wales (1).

ENGLAND AMATEUR INTERNATIONALS

Mitchell J.F. 1923 v Ireland, Wales (2).

REPUBLIC OF IRELAND 'B'

Fagan F. 1957 v Rumania 'B' (1).

J.F.Mitchell

359

UNDER-23 INTERNATIONALS

ENGLAND
Bell C. 1968 v Scotland, Hungary (2).
Booth T.A. 1969 v Portugal; 1971 v Switzerland ; 1972 v Wales, Scotland (4).
Corrigan J.T. 1969 v USSR (1).
Doyle M. 1968 v Hungary (twice), Italy, West Germany; 1969 v Portugal (twice), Holland, Belgium (8).
Dyson J. 1957 v Scotland (1).
Hayes J. 1958 v Scotland, Wales (2).
Jeffries D. 1972 v East Germany (1).
Pardoe G. 1968 v Hungary; 1969 v Portugal (twice), Belgium (4).
Shawcross D.F. 1961 v West Germany (1).
Summerbee M.G. 1966 v Turkey (1).
Towers A.M. 1972 v USSR; 1973 v Denmark, Czechoslovakia (3).
Tueart D. 1974 v Scotland (1).

WALES
Sear C. 1958 v Scotland; 1959 v Scotland (2).

SCOTLAND
Donachie W. 1972 v West German Olympic XI, Wales , England (3).
Law D. 1961 v Army XI; England (2).

UNDER-21 INTERNATIONALS

ENGLAND
Barnes P.S. 1976 v Wales; 1977 v Scotland, Finland , Norway, Finland; 1978 v Italy (twice), Norway; 1978 v Yugoslavia (9).
Caton T. 1981 v Norway, Hungary; 1982 v Poland (twice), Scotland, West Germany (twice); 1983 v Greece; 1983 v Denmark, Hungary (10).
Corrigan J.T. 1978 v Italy (twice), Yugoslavia (3).
Futcher P. 1978 v Denmark (1).
Keegan G.A. 1976 v Wales (1).
May A.M. 1986 v Italy (1).
Owen G. 1977 v Scotland, Finland (twice), Norway (twice); 1978 v Italy (twice), Yugoslavia , Denmark; 1979 v Wales (10).
Ranson R. 1979 v Bulgaria; 1980 v East Germany, Rumania , Switzerland; 1981 v Rumania, Switzerland, Hungary; 1982 v Poland, (twice), Scotland, West Germany (11).
Reeves K.P. 1980 v East Germany (1).
Reid N.S. 1981 v Hungary (twice); 1982 v Poland (twice), Scotland (twice) (6).
Simpson P.D. 1986 v Denmark, Yugoslavia (2).
Suckling P. 1986 v Yugoslavia, Sweden; 1987 v Spain, Turkey (4).

SCOTLAND
Hartford R.A. 1977 v Switzerland (1).

FOOTBALL LEAGUE

Barkas S. 1935 v Irish League; 1937 v Scottish League, Irish League (3).
Barnes H. 1921 v Irish League; 1922 v Scottish League (2).
Barnes P.S. 1977 v Glasgow Select (1).
Bell C. 1967 v League of Ireland; 1968 v Irish League; 1973 Scottish League; 1974 v Scottish League (4).
Bray J. 1934 v Scottish League; 1935 v Scottish League; 1936 v Irish League; 1937 v Scottish League, Irish League (5).
Broadis I.A. 1952 v Irish League; 1953 v League of Ireland, Scottish League (3).

Brook E.F.G. 1929 v Scottish League; 1933 v Irish League; 1934 v Irish League, Scottish League; 1935 v Scottish League; 1936 v Irish League; 1937 v Irish League (7).
Browell T. 1919 v Irish League (1).
Burgess H. 1904 v Scottish League, Irish League; 1905 v Scottish League, Irish League; 1906 v Scottish League (5).
Chapman T. 1895 v Irish League (1).
Clements K.H. 1977 v Glasgow Select (1).
Conlin J. 1910 v Irish League (1).
Corrigan J.T. 1977 v Glasgow Select (1).
Cowan S. 1934 v Irish League (1).
Dorsett G. 1905 Irish League (1).
Doyle M. 1972 v Scottish League; 1976 v Scottish League (2).
Emptage A.T. 1947 v Irish League (1).
Finnerhan P. 1895 v Irish League (1).
Fletcher E. 1912 v Southern League; 1913 v Scottish League; 1919 v Burnley (3).
Frost S. 1903 v Irish League; 1904 v Scottish League (2).
Holmes W.M. 1897 v Irish League (1).
Johnson T.C.F. 1928 v Irish League; 1929 v Scottish League (2).
Law D. 1960 v Irish League, Italian League (2).
Lee F.H. 1969 v League of Ireland (1).
Meadows J. 1954 v Irish League (1).
Oakes A. 1969 v Scottish League (1).
Owen G.A. 1977 v Glasgow Select (1).
Revie D.G. 1954 v League of Ireland, League of Ireland (2).
Roberts F. 1925 v Scottish League (1).
Royle J. 1977 v Glasgow Select (1).
Smith W.E. 1915 v Scottish League (1).
Summerbee M.G. 1969 v League of Ireland (1).
Thornley I. 1907 v Scottish League, Irish League (2).
Tilson F.S. 1934 v Irish League, Scottish League; 1935 v Scottish League (3).
Toseland E. 1929 v Irish League (1).
Trautmann B.C. 1960 v Irish League, Italian League (2).
Tueart D. 1974 v Scottish League; 1976 v Scottish League; 1977 v Glasgow Select (3).
Watson D.V. 1977 v Glasgow Select (1).
Westwood E. 1949 v Scottish League, League of Ireland (2).
Williams C.A. 1897 v Irish League (1).

FA XI

Barnes K.H. 1955 v RAF; 1957 v Army; 1960 v RAF (3).
Bell C. 1967 v Leon Mexico, Borussia Dortmund (2).
Birtwhistle W.J. 1932 v Universities Union (1).
Brook E.F.G. 1939 v South Africa (twice), South African Province teams (5 games) (7).
Corrigan J.T. 1981 v London FA XI (1).
Dyson J. 1956 v Army (1).
Hannah G. 1961 Far East Tour (11 games); 1964 v New Zealand (12).
Hayes J. 1957 v Army (1).
Johnson T.C.F. 1929 v Combined Universities (1).
Leivers W.E. 1956 v Army (1).
Meadows J. 1954 v The Army (1).
Roberts F. 1924 v Manchester University (1).
Sharp S. 1924 v Manchester University (1).
Sproston B. 1945 v Belgium (1).
Summerbee H.G. 1967 v Leon Mexico, First Vienna (2).
Swift F.V. 1944 v France, Belgium; 1945 v Switzerland (twice) (4).
Woodcock W. 1920 v South African XI (twice) (2).

REPUBLIC OF IRELAND FA XI

McCarthy M. 1984 v University of Japan, SC Internacional (Brazil) (twice) (3).

TRIAL MATCHES

ENGLAND
Barkas S. 1935 The Rest v England; 1936 Probables v Possibles; 1937 Possibles v Probables; Probables v Possibles.
Booth F. 1905 The North v The South.
Bray J. 1935 England v The Rest; 1937 Probables v Possibles (twice).
Brook E.F.G. 1930 The Rest v England; 1934 The Rest v England; 1935 The Rest v England; 1937 Probables v Possibles (twice).
Burgess H. 1904 The North v The South.
Cowan S. 1931 The Rest v England.
Finnerhan P. 1896 Professionals v Amateurs.
Johnson T.C.F. 1926 The Rest v England.
Jones W.L. 1909 Professionals v Amateurs.
Roberts F. 1925 The Rest v England.
Sharp S. 1925 The North v the South.
Swift F.V. 1935 The Rest v England.
Tilson F.S. The Rest v England; 1937 Probables v Possibles.
Wood J. 1908 The North v The South.
Woosnam M. 1922 The North v England XI.

SCOTLAND (Anglo-Scots v Home Scots)
Blair J. 1909 & 1910.
Blair T. 1922.
Kelso T. 1909 & 1910.
Livingstone G.T. 1906.
Lyall J. 1909 & 1910.
McMahon J. 1903.
McMullan J. 1928.
Stewart G. 1907.
Turnbull A. 1903 .

Frank Swift

Herbert Burgess

CITY CAREER RECORDS

Below are the career records for all City players in major competitions since 1892. They include the three matches of the 1939-40 season but exclude abandoned matches. Football League Test matches are under 'Europe' column and indicated thus*.

Player	Played	LEAGUE App	LEAGUE Gls	FA CUP App	FA CUP Gls	LG CUP App	LG CUP Gls	EUROPE App	EUROPE Gls	TOTAL App	TOTAL Gls
ABBOTT J.A.	1913-1915	3	2	0	0	0	0	0	0	3	2
ALBINSON G.	1921-1922	3	0	0	0	0	0	0	0	3	0
AIMSON P.E.	1958-1960	16	4	0	0	3	2	0	0	19	6
ALISON J.	1949-1952	19	0	1	0	0	0	0	0	20	0
ALLAN J.	1927-1928	8	1	1	0	0	0	0	0	9	1
ALLEN A.J.	1915-1924	52	0	4	0	0	0	0	0	56	0
ALLMARK J.J.	1937-1938	1	0	0	0	0	0	0	0	1	0
ANDERS H.	1953-1956	32	4	1	0	0	0	0	0	33	4
ANGUS H.	1892-1893	2	0	0	0	0	0	0	0	2	0
ANGUS J.W.	1892-1893	7	3	1	0	0	0	0	0	8	3
APPLETON F.	1924-1929	2	0	1	0	0	0	0	0	3	0
ARMITT G.G.H.	1892-1893	1	0	0	0	0	0	0	0	1	0
ASHWORTH S.B.	1903-1904	18	0	4	0	0	0	0	0	22	0
AUSTIN S.W.	1924-1931	160	43	12	4	0	0	0	0	172	47
BACON A.	1928-1929	5	1	0	0	0	0	0	0	5	1
BACUZZI D.R.	1964-1966	56/1		2	0	1	0	0	0	59/1	0
BAKER G.	1960-1961	37	14	1	0	1	0	0	0	39	14
BAKER G.	1982-1987	114/3	19	2/2	0	13/1	0	0	0	129/6	19
BAKER J.	1893-1895	3	1	0	0	0	0	0	0	3	1
BALDWIN W.	1904-1908	2	0	0	0	0	0	0	0	2	0
BANKS W.	1905-1908	25	1	1	0	0	0	0	0	26	1
BANNISTER C.	1896-1897	18	2	0	0	0	0	0	0	18	2
BANNISTER E.	1907-1910	1	0	0	0	0	0	0	0	1	0
BANNISTER J.	1902-1906	45	21	2	1	0	0	0	0	47	22
BARBER L.F.	1927-1932	92	0	7	0	0	0	0	0	99	0
BARKAS S.	1934-1947	175	1	20	0	0	0	0	0	195	1
BARLOW C.J.	1956-1963	179	78	8	2	2	0	0	0	189	80
BARNES H.	1914-1924	217	120	18	5	0	0	0	0	235	125
BARNES K.H.	1950-1961	258	18	23	1	2	0	0	0	283	19
BARNES P.S.	1972-1979 1986-1987	116/7	15	7	2	16/4	4	9	1	148/11	22
BARNETT L.H.	1930-1936	84	0	8	0	0	0	0	0	92	0
BARR A.M.	1936-1940	4	2	0	0	0	0	0	0	4	2
BARRASS M.W.	1926-1933	162	14	10	1	0	0	0	0	172	15
BARRETT C.	1970-1976	50/3		3/1		8	1	1	0	62/4	1
BARRETT E.	1983-1987	2/1	0	0	0	1	0	0	0	3/1	0
BARRETT F.	1901-1902	5	0	4	0	0	0	0	0	9	0
BATTY M.	1960-1966	13	0	0	0	0	0	0	0	13	0
BECKFORD D.	1984-1987	7/4	0	0	0	0/1	0	0	0	7/5	0
BEEBY A.R.	1911-1912	11	0	0	0	0	0	0	0	11	0
BELL C.	1966-1979	393/1	117	33/1	9	40	18	23/1	8	489/3	152
BELL P.N.	1926-1928	42	7	0	0	0	0	0	0	42	7
BENNETT A.	1893-1896	12	6	0	0	0	0	0	0	12	6
BENNETT D.A.	1976-1981	43/9	9	5	1	7	5	0	0	55/9	15
BENNETT E.T.	1926-1929	19	0	0	0	0	0	0	0	19	0
BENSON J.H.	1958-1964	44	0	3	0	5	0	0	0	52	0
BENTLEY H.	1910-1912	1	0	0	0	0	0	0	0	1	0
BENZIE R.	1925-1928	13	0	0	0	0	0	0	0	13	0
BETTS B.J.	1960-1964	101	5	8	0	8	1	0	0	117	6
BEVAN F.T.	1901-1903	8	1	1	0	0	0	0	0	9	1
BLACK A.	1946-1950	139	47	7	5	0	0	0	0	146	52
BLACKSHAW W.	1937-1946	3	0	0	0	0	0	0	0	3	0
BLAIR J.	1906-1910	76	0	5	1	0	0	0	0	81	1
BLAIR T.	1920-1922	38	0	3	0	0	0	0	0	41	0
BLEW H.	1906-1907	1	0	0	0	0	0	0	0	1	0
BODAK P.	1983-1984	12/2	1	2/1	0	0	0	0	0	14/3	1
BOND K.	1981-1984	108/2	11	6	1	8	0	0	0	122/2	12
BOOK A.K.	1966-1974	242/2	4	28	0	19/1	1	17	0	306/3	5
BOOTH F.	1902-1906 1911-1912	98	18	9	1	0	0	0	0	107	19
BOOTH T.A.	1965-1981	380/2	25	27	5	44/2	3	25	3	476/4	36
BOOTLE W.	1943-1950	5	0	1	0	0	0	0	0	6	0

Player	Played	LEAGUE		FA CUP		LG CUP		EUROPE		TOTAL	
		App	Gls	App	Gls	App	Gls	App	Gls	App	Gls
BOTTOMLEY W.	1908-1919	98	2	5	0	0	0	0	0	103	2
BOWLES S.	1965-1970	15/2	2	0	0	2/2	2	0	0	17/4	4
BOWMAN W.W.	1892-1900	47	3	2	0	0	0	0	0	49	3
BOWYER I.	1966-1971	42/8	13	4	1	6/2	2	5/2	1	57/12	17
BOYER P.J.	1980-1983	17/3	3	2	1	4	0	0	0	23/3	4
BRADFORD L.J.	1925-1926	5	1	0	0	0	0	0	0	5	1
BRANAGAN K.F.	1948-1960	196	3	12	0	0	0	0	0	208	3
BRAND R.L.	1965-1967	20	2	1	0	1	0	0	0	22	2
BRAY J.	1929-1947	260	10	20	0	0	0	0	0	280	10
BRENNAN J.	1914-1922	56	0	4	0	0	0	0	0	60	0
BRENNAN M.	1968-1973	1/3	0	0	0	0	0	0	0	1/3	0
BRIGHTWELL I.	1985-1987	12/4	1	0/1	0	2	0	0	0	14/5	1
BROAD T.	1915-1921	42	0	2	0	0	0	0	0	44	0
BROADHURST C.	1927-1930	33	25	3	1	0	0	0	0	36	26
BROADIS I.A.	1951-1953	74	10	5	2	0	0	0	0	79	12
BROOK E.F.G.	1928-1940	453	159	41	19	0	0	0	0	494	178
BROOKS G.	1911-1912	3	1	0	0	0	0	0	0	3	1
BROOMFIELD H.	1908-1909	4	0	0	0	0	0	0	0	4	0
BROWELL T.	1913-1926	222	122	25	17	0	0	0	0	247	139
BROWN H.R.	1910-1911	2	0	0	0	0	0	0	0	2	0
BROWN J.P.	1908-1910	6	0	0	0	0	0	0	0	6	0
BUCHAN J.	1905-1911	155	8	9	2	0	0	0	0	164	10
BUCKLEY F.C.	1907-1909	11	0	0	0	0	0	0	0	11	0
BUCKLEY G.	1977-1981	4/2	0	0	0	2	0	0	0	6/2	0
BURGESS C.	1908-1911	32	0	0	0	0	0	0	0	32	0
BURGESS H.	1903-1906	85	2	9	0	0	0	0	0	94	2
BUSBY M.W.	1928-1936	202	11	24	3	0	0	0	0	226	14
CAINE J.	1892-1894	1	0	0	0	0	0	0	0	1	0
CALDERWOOD J.C.	1922-1927	35	0	2	0	0	0	0	0	37	0
CALLAGHAN T.	1907-1909	2	0	0	0	0	0	0	0	2	0
CALVEY M.	1894-1895	7	5	0	0	0	0	0	0	7	5
CANN S.T.	1930-1935	42	0	4	0	0	0	0	0	46	0
CAPEL T.A.	1941-1947	9	2	4	2	0	0	0	0	13	4
CARDWELL L.	1938-1947	42	0	6	0	0	0	0	0	48	0
CARRODUS F.	1969-1974	33/9	1	1/1	1	3	0	0/1	0	37/11	2
CARROLL F.	1920-1925	18	0	2	0	0	0	0	0	20	0
CARSON A.	1893-1894	9	3	0	0	0	0	0	0	9	3
CARTER S.C.	1968-1972	4/2	2	0	0	0	0	0/1	0	4/3	2
CARTWRIGHT J.E.	1913-1921	38	1	9	2	0	0	0	0	47	3
CASSIDY J.	1900-1901	31	14	1	0	0	0	0	0	32	14
CASSIDY J.A.	1935-1937	3	0	0	0	0	0	0	0	3	0
CATON T.	1979-1983	164/1	8	12	0	21	0	0	0	197/1	8
CHADWICK G.	1959-1964	12	0	0	0	2	0	0	0	14	0
CHANNON M.R.	1977-1979	71/1	24	3/1	0	11/1	4	7	2	92/3	30
CHAPELOW H.	1909-1911	7	0	0	0	0	0	0	0	7	0
CHAPLIN J.F.	1910-1913	15	0	2	0	0	0	0	0	17	0
CHAPMAN T.	1895-1896	26	3	0	0	0	0	2*		28	3
CHAPPELL T.	1896-1900	8	0	0	0	0	0	0	0	8	0
CHEETHAM R.A.	1955-1968	127/5	4	4	0	6/1	0	0	0	137/6	4
CHRISTIE J.	1904-1907	10	0	0	0	0	0	0	0	10	0
CHRISTIE T.	1986-1987	9	3	0	0	1	0	0	0	10	3
CLARE T.	1897-1899	1	0	0	0	0	0	0	0	1	0
CLARK G.V.	1936-1947	55	0	9	0	0	0	0	0	64	0
CLARKE R.J.	1947-1958	349	73	20	6	0	0	0	0	369	79
CLARKE J.D.	1971-1975	13	0	0	0	2	0	0	0	15	0
CLAY J.H.	1962-1968	1/1	0	0	0	0	0	0	0	1/1	0
CLAYTON R.	1935-1938	3	2	1	0	0	0	0	0	4	2
CLEMENTS K.H.	1971-1979										
	1985-1987	196/4	1	12	0	23	0	6	0	237/4	1
CLIFFORD H.	1895-1896	4	1	0	0	0	0	0	0	4	1
CODLING R.	1910-1911	5	0	0	0	0	0	0	0	5	0
COLBRIDGE C.	1959-1962	62	12	2	0	1	0	0	0	65	12
COLEMAN A.G.	1967-1969	82	12	10	3	7/1	0	2	1	101/1	16
COMRIE M.	1932-1934	17	1	0	0	0	0	0	0	17	1
CONLIN J.	1906-1911	161	28	14	2	0	0	0	0	175	30
CONNOR D.R.	1962-1972										
	1974-1975	130/11	10	12	0	5/1	0	5	0	152/12	10
CONSTANTINE J.	1945-1947	18	12	4	4	0	0	0	0	22	16
CONWAY J.P.	1976-1978	11/2	1	1	0	1	0	1	0	14/2	1
COOKSON S.	1918-1928	285	0	21	1	0	0	0	0	306	1
CORBETT F.W.	1930-1936	15	0	0	0	0	0	0	0	15	0
CORBETT V.	1933-1935	5	0	1	0	0	0	0	0	6	0

364

Player	Played	LEAGUE App	Gls	FA CUP App	Gls	LG CUP App	Gls	EUROPE App	Gls	TOTAL App	Gls
CORRIGAN J.T.	1966-1983	476	0	37	0	52	0	27	0	592	0
COUPE D.	1908-1910	1	0	0	0	0	0	0	0	1	0
COUPLAND C.A.	1925-1927	24	2	3	0	0	0	0	0	27	2
COWAN S.	1924-1935	369	19	38	5	0	0	0	0	407	24
COWAN W.D.	1926-1927	22	11	1	0	0	0	0	0	23	11
COWIE A.	1898-1899	11	3	0	0	0	0	0	0	11	3
COX W.	1900-1901	1	0	0	0	0	0	0	0	1	0
CRAWSHAW R.	1919-1922	25	6	1	0	0	0	0	0	26	6
CROSS D.	1982-1983	31	12	3	1	4	0	0	0	38	13
CROSSAN J.A.	1965-1967	94	24	14	3	2	1	0	0	110	28
CUMMING J.F.	1913-1920	35	3	6	0	0	0	0	0	41	3
CUNNINGHAM A.	1984-1985	16/2	1	0/1	0	5	3	0	0	21/3	4
CUNLIFFE R.A.	1945-1956	44	9	4	1	0	0	0	0	48	10
CUNLIFFE R.	1960-1965	3	1	0	0	0	0	0	0	3	1
DALE W.	1931-1938	237	0	32	0	0	0	0	0	269	0
DALEY S.	1979-1981	47/1	4	1	0	5	0	0	0	53/1	4
DALZIEL G.	1983-1984	4/1	0	0/1	0	0	0	0	0	4/2	0
DANIELS A.W.C.	1920-1926	31	1	1	0	0	0	0	0	32	1
DANIELS B.J.	1973-1975	9/4	2	0	0	0	0	0	0	9/4	2
DARTNELL H.	1900-1901	4	0	0	0	0	0	0	0	4	0
DAVIDSON A.	1900-1901	7	1	0	0	0	0	0	0	7	1
DAVIDSON D.	1951-1958	1	0	0	0	0	0	0	0	1	0
DAVIDSON D.	1983-1984	2/4	1	0	0	1	0	0	0	3/4	1
DAVIDSON R.	1902-1904	32	0	0	0	0	0	0	0	32	0
DAVIES F.	1906-1909	6	0	0	0	0	0	0	0	6	0
DAVIES G.E.	1951-1957	13	5	0	0	0	0	0	0	13	5
DAVIES G.	1985-1986	31	9	4	2	1	1	0	0	36	12
DAVIES J.	1891-1894										
	1895-1896										
	1900-1901	35	13	2	0	0	0	2*	1	39	14
DAVIES I.	1982-1984	7	0	0	0	1	0	0	0	8	0
DAVIES R.	1911-1912	6	0	0	0	0	0	0	0	6	0
DAVIES W.R.	1971-1972	45	8	2	1	2	1	0	0	49	10
DEARDEN R.	1901-1907	21	0	0	0	0	0	0	0	21	0
DELLOW R.W.	1935-1936	10	4	0	0	0	0	0	0	10	4
DENNISON J.	1903-1906	1	2	0	0	0	0	0	0	1	2
DENNISON R.	1925-1926	8	4	2	0	0	0	0	0	10	4
DEYNA K.	1978-1981	34/4	12	2	0	2	0	0/1	1	38/5	13
DITCHFIELD J.C.	1895-1896	12	1	0	0	0	0	3*		15	1
DOBING P.	1961-1963	82	31	5	0	7	1	0	0	94	32
DOCHERTY M.	1976-1977	8	0	0	0	1	0	2	0	11	0
DOHERTY P.D.	1936-1945	122	76	11	5	0	0	0	0	133	81
DONACHIE W.	1968-1980	347/4	2	21	0	40	0	13/1	0	421/5	2
DONALDSON A.P.	1923-1924	7	0	0	0	0	0	0	0	7	0
DONNELLY R.	1935-1937	37	1	0	0	0	0	0	0	37	1
DORAN J.F.	1922-1924	3	1	0	0	0	0	0	0	3	1
DORSETT G.	1904-1912	193	62	18	3	0	0	0	0	211	65
DORSETT J.H.	1910-1920	132	17	6	0	0	0	0	0	138	17
DOUGAL G.	1898-1901	75	13	2	0	0	0	0	0	77	13
DOUGLAS W.	1890-1894	36	0	3	0	0	0	0	0	39	0
DOWD H.	1958-1970	181	1	22	0	16	0	0	0	219	1
DOYLE M.	1962-1978	441/7	32	44	2	43	4	23	2	551/7	40
DRUMMOND J.	1902-1904	28	5	0	0	0	0	0	0	28	5
DUNKLEY M.E.F.	1938-1947	54	6	7	1	0	0	0	0	61	7
DUNNE L.	1933-1935	3	0	0	0	0	0	0	0	3	0
DYER F.	1893-1898	36	3	1	0	0	0	0	0	37	3
DYSON J.	1951-1961	63	26	9	3	0	0	0	0	72	29
EADIE W.P.	1906-1914	185	6	20	0	0	0	0	0	205	6
EASTWOOD E.	1935-1947	16	0	0	0	0	0	0	0	16	0
EDELSTON J.	1920-1921	6	0	0	0	0	0	0	0	6	0
EDEN J.	1911-1912	1	0	0	0	0	0	0	0	1	0
EDGE A.	1893-1894	1	0	0	0	0	0	0	0	1	0
EDMONDSON J.H.	1902-1906	38	0	2	0	0	0	0	0	40	0
EGAN W.	1893-1894	7	0	0	0	0	0	0	0	7	0
ELLIOTT A.	1980-1982	1	0	0	0	0	0	0	0	1	0
ELWOOD J.H.	1924-1927	31	0	1	0	0	0	0	0	32	0
EMPTAGE A.T.	1937-1951	136	1	8	0	0	0	0	0	144	1
ESPIE J.	1896-1897	1	0	0	0	0	0	0	0	1	0
ETHERINGTON R.	1921-1924	12	0	0	0	0	0	0	0	12	0
EWING D.	1949-1962	279	1	22	0	1	0	0	0	302	1
EYRES S.	1907-1908	1	1	0	0	0	0	0	0	1	1

Player	Played	LEAGUE App	Gls	FA CUP App	Gls	LG CUP App	Gls	EUROPE App	Gls	TOTAL App	Gls
FAGAN F.	1953-1960	153	34	11	1	0	0	0	0	164	35
FAGAN J.F.	1938-1951	148	2	10	0	0	0	0	0	158	2
FAIRCLOUGH A.	1913-1920	5	1	0	0	0	0	0	0	5	1
FAIRCLOUGH P.	1913-1920	5	0	0	0	0	0	0	0	5	0
FARRELL T.	1905-1908	3	0	0	0	0	0	0	0	3	0
FAULKNER R.V.	1952-1957	7	4	0	0	0	0	0	0	7	4
FAYERS F.	1920-1923	73	5	4	0	0	0	0	0	77	5
FELTON W.	1929-1932	73	0	10	0	0	0	0	0	83	0
FERGUSON A.	1894-1895	2	0	0	0	0	0	0	0	2	0
FIDLER D.J.	1956-1960	5	1	0	0	0	0	0	0	5	1
FINNERHAN P.	1894-1897	85	27	0	0	0	0	4*	0	89	27
FINNIGAN R.J.	1926-1927	8	0	0	0	0	0	0	0	8	0
FISHER A.	1906-1907	5	2	0	0	0	0	0	0	5	2
FLEET S.	1953-1963	5	0	0	0	1	0	0	0	6	0
FLETCHER E.	1911-1926	301	2	26	0	0	0	0	0	327	2
FLETCHER L.	1932-1935	5	1	0	0	0	0	0	0	5	1
FORD A.	1921-1922	4	0	0	0	0	0	0	0	4	0
FORRESTER T.	1892-1894	10	2	0	0	0	0	0	0	10	2
FOSTER C.L.	1927-1928	3	0	0	0	0	0	0	0	3	0
FOSTER H.A.	1896-1898	7	1	1	0	0	0	0	0	8	1
FRANCIS T.J.	1981-1982	26	12	2	2	1	0	0	0	29	14
FREEMAN R.H.	1935-1939	4	1	0	0	0	0	0	0	4	1
FROST R.A.	1962-1965	2	1	0	0	0	0	0	0	2	1
FROST S.	1901-1907	103	4	9	0	0	0	0	0	112	4
FURR G.M.	1909-1910	3	0	0	0	0	0	0	0	3	0
FUTCHER P.	1978-1980	36/1	0	3	0	3/2	0	2	0	44/3	0
FUTCHER R.	1978-1979	10/7	7	1	0	2	0	0	0	13/7	7
GARNER W.	1912-1919	5	0	0	0	0	0	0	0	5	0
GARTLAND P.	1914-1917	1	0	0	0	0	0	0	0	1	0
GAUGHAN W.B.	1914-1919	10	0	0	0	0	0	0	0	10	0
GIBBONS S.	1927-1930	10	0	1	0	0	0	0	0	11	0
GIBSON T.D.	1926-1927	2	2	0	0	0	0	0	0	2	2
GIDMAN J.	1986-1987	22	0	1	0	1	0	0	0	24	0
GILL R.	1947-1951	8	0	1	0	0	0	0	0	9	0
GILLESPIE W.J.	1897-1905	218	126	13	6	0	0	0	0	231	132
GILLIES R.	1895-1896	3	0	0	0	0	0	2*	0	5	0
GLENNON C.D.	1965-1971	3/1	0	0	0	0	0	0/1	0	3/2	0
GODFREY J.	1919-1920	9	1	0	0	0	0	0	0	9	1
GODWIN V.	1948-1949	8	3	0	0	0	0	0	0	8	3
GOLAC I.	1982-1983	2	0	0	0	0	0	0	0	2	0
GOMERSALL V	1958-1966	39	0	0	0	0	0	0	0	39	0
GOODCHILD A.J.	1911-1927	204	0	13	0	0	0	0	0	217	0
GOODWIN E	1919-1921	20	3	1	2	0	0	0	0	21	5
GORRINGE F.C.	1926-1928	1	2	0	0	0	0	0	0	1	2
GOULD W.	1909-1912	8	2	0	0	0	0	0	0	8	2
GOW G.	1980-1982	26	5	10	2	0	0	0	0	36	7
GRATRIX R.	1964-1965	15	0	0	0	0	0	0	0	15	0
GRAY A.	1927-1930	68	0	2	0	0	0	0	0	70	0
GRAY G.	1919-1922	3	0	0	0	0	0	0	0	3	0
GRAY M.	1963-1967	87/4	21	3	1	7	1	0	0	97/4	23
GREALISH A.P.	1986-1987	11	0	1	0	0	0	0	0	12	0
GREGG W.	1937-1938	9	0	0	0	0	0	0	0	9	0
GREGORY C.F.	1930-1934	21	2	0	0	0	0	0	0	21	2
GREGORY J.	1905-1906	3	0	0	0	0	0	0	0	3	0
GREENWOOD J.E.	1946-1949	1	0	0	0	0	0	0	0	1	0
GRIEVE R.	1906-1911	44	18	2	1	0	0	0	0	46	19
GUNN J.	1896-1897	21	4	4	1	0	0	0	0	25	5
GUNNING J.M.	1950-1954	13	0	2	0	0	0	0	0	15	0
HADDINGTON R.W.	1950-1951	6	4	1	0	0	0	0	0	7	4
HALL J.E.	1913-1915	1	0	0	0	0	0	0	0	1	0
HALL W.	1906-1907	11	0	0	0	0	0	0	0	11	0
HALLIDAY D.	1930-1933	76	47	6	4	0	0	0	0	82	51
HALLOWS H.	1900-1901	1	0	0	0	0	0	0	0	1	0
HAMBLETT G.	1905-1908	1	0	0	0	0	0	0	0	1	0
HAMILL M.	1920-1924	118	1	10	1	0	0	0	0	128	2
HAMMOND G.	1974-1976	33/1	2	1	0	1	0	0	0	35/1	2
HANNAH G.	1958-1964	114	15	9	0	8	1	0	0	131	16
HANNAWAY J.	1950-1957	64	0	2	0	0	0	0	0	66	0
HANNEY E.T.	1913-1919	68	1	10	0	0	0	0	0	78	1
HAREIDE A.	1981-1983	17/7	0	0	0	0/1	0	0	0	17/8	0
HARGREAVES J.	1893-1895	8	0	0	0	0	0	0	0	8	0

366

Player	Played	LEAGUE App	Gls	FA CUP App	Gls	LG CUP App	Gls	EUROPE App	Gls	TOTAL App	Gls
HARLEY A.	1962-1963	40	23	3	3	6	6	0	0	49	32
HARPER J.	1895-1898	33	0	1	0	0	0	1*	0	35	0
HARPER W.	1923-1924	4	0	0	0	0	0	0	0	4	0
HARRISON J.R.	1929-1930	2	1	0	0	0	0	0	0	2	1
HART J.P.	1944-1963	169	67	9	6	0	0	0	0	178	73
HARTFORD R.A.	1974-1979										
	1981-1984	259/1	29	17	2	29	3	12	2	317/1	36
HARVEY H.	1900-1901	7	1	0	0	0	0	0	0	7	1
HAYDOCK W.E.	1959-1961	3	1	0	0	0	0	0	0	3	1
HAYES J.	1953-1965	331	142	24	9	8	1	0	0	363	152
HEALE J.A.	1934-1945	86	39	5	2	0	0	0	0	91	41
HEALEY R.	1967-1974	30	0	0	0	2	0	4/1	0	36/1	0
HEDLEY F.	1930-1931	2	2	0	0	0	0	0	0	2	2
HEINEMANN G.H.	1928-1931	21	0	3	0	0	0	0	0	24	0
HENDERSON J.	1914-1920	5	0	0	0	0	0	0	0	5	0
HENDERSON J.	1901-1902	5	1	1	1	0	0	0	0	6	2
HENDREN E.H.	1908-1909	2	0	0	0	0	0	0	0	2	0
HENRY A.	1974-1981	68/11	6	3/1	0	7	6	1	0	79/12	12
HENRY W.A.	1911-1920	143	1	15	0	0	0	0	0	158	1
HENSON A.M.	1969-1975	12/4	0	0/1	0	1	0	0	0	13/5	0
HERD A.	1933-1948	260	107	30	17	0	0	0	0	290	124
HESHAM F.	1896-1901	3	0	0	0	0	0	0	0	3	0
HESLOP G.	1965-1972	159/3	1	17	0	12	0	7/3	0	195/6	1
HICKS G.W.	1923-1928	123	40	12	8	0	0	0	0	135	48
HIGGS F.	1932-1933	1	0	0	0	0	0	0	0	1	0
HILDERSLEY R.	1981-1984	1	0	0	0	0	0	0	0	1	0
HILL F.	1970-1973	28/7	3	1	0	2	0	4	0	35/7	3
HILL P.	1906-1909	38	0	2	0	0	0	0	0	40	0
HILL R.	1895-1897	21	9	0	0	0	0	1*	0	31	0
HILLMAN J.	1902-1906	116	0	8	0	0	0	0	0	124	0
HINCE P.F.	1966-1968	7	4	0	0	4	0	0	0	11	4
HINDMARSH J.	1912-1919	28	1	7	1	0	0	0	0	35	2
HITCHCOCK E.	1908-1909	1	0	0	0	0	0	0	0	1	0
HOAD S.J.	1911-1920	64	1	5	1	0	0	0	0	69	2
HODGKINSON D.	1961-1964	1	1	0	0	1	0	0	0	2	1
HODGSON R.	1944-1947	1	0	0	0	0	0	0	0	1	0
HOGAN W.J.	1942-1949	3	0	0	0	0	0	0	0	3	0
HOLFORD T.	1908-1914	172	34	12	4	0	0	0	0	184	38
HOLMES W.M.	1896-1905	156	4	10	0	0	0	0	0	166	4
HOPE J.G.	1939-1947	7	0	0	0	0	0	0	0	7	0
HOPKINS R.	1986-1987	7	1	0	0	2	0	0	0	9	1
HOPKINS W.	1891-1894	23	0	1	0	0	0	0	0	24	0
HORNE A.	1928-1929	11	2	0	0	0	0	0	0	11	2
HORNE S.F.	1965-1969	48/2	0	11	0	4/1	0	0	0	63/3	0
HORRIDGE P.	1951-1959	3	0	0	0	0	0	0	0	3	0
HORSWILL M.F.	1974-1975	11/3	0	1	0	0	0	0	0	12/3	0
HOSIE J.	1901-1902	39	3	4	0	0	0	0	0	43	3
HOWARD F.J.	1912-1920	79	40	12	3	0	0	0	0	91	43
HOWE F.	1938-1939	6	5	0	0	0	0	0	0	6	5
HOYLAND J.	1982-1986	2	0	0	0	0/1	1	0	0	2/1	1
HUGHES E.	1912-1920	77	2	12	1	0	0	0	0	89	3
HUGHES J.	1894-1895	2	0	0	0	0	0	0	0	2	0
HUMPHREYS R.	1910-1912	3	0	0	0	0	0	0	0	3	0
HUNTER R.	1898-1903	7	0	0	0	0	0	0	0	7	0
HURST D.J.	1901-1902	15	0	0	0	0	0	0	0	15	0
HUTCHINSON G.W.	1894-1896	7	0	0	0	0	0	0	0	7	0
HUTCHISON T.	1980-1982	44/2	4	10	1	3/1	0	0	0	57/3	5
HYNDS T.	1901-1906	158	9	14	0	0	0	0	0	172	9
INGHAM T.W.	1921-1923	2	1	0	0	0	0	0	0	2	1
JACKSON B.H.	1907-1911	91	0	10	0	0	0	0	0	101	0
JACKSON G.	1981-1985	6/2	0	0	0	0	0	0	0	6/2	0
JACKSON H.	1946-1947	8	2	1	1	0	0	0	0	9	3
JAMES F.E.	1909-1910	2	0	0	0	0	0	0	0	2	0
JARVIS H.	1919-1921	2	0	0	0	0	0	0	0	2	0
JEFFRIES D.	1966-1973	64/9	0	8	0	2/1	0	9	0	83/10	0
JOBLING L.W.	1912-1913	2	0	0	0	0	0	0	0	2	0
JOHNSON D.E.	1983-1984	4/2	1	0	0	0	0	0	0	4/2	1
JOHNSON J.D.	1970-1974	4/2	0	0	0	0	0	2	0	6/2	0
JOHNSON N.M.	1985-1987	4	0	0	0	0	0	0	0	4	0
JOHNSON T.C.F.	1919-1930	328	158	26	8	0	0	0	0	354	166
JOHNSTONE R.	1955-1959	124	42	14	9	0	0	0	0	138	51

Player	Played	LEAGUE		FA CUP		LG CUP		EUROPE		TOTAL	
		App	Gls	App	Gls	App	Gls	App	Gls	App	Gls
JONES A.	1893-1894	2	1	0	0	0	0	0	0	2	1
JONES C.H.	1982-1983	3	0	0	0	0	0	0	0	3	0
JONES C.M.N.	1962-1968	6/1	2	0	0	0	0	0	0	6/1	2
JONES D.	1898-1902	114	1	4	0	0	0	0	0	118	1
JONES R.S.	1894-1895	18	0	0	0	0	0	0	0	18	0
JONES R.T.W.	1901-1902	9	2	4	0	0	0	0	0	13	2
JONES W.J.B.	1948-1951	3	0	0	0	0	0	0	0	3	0
JONES W.L.	1903-1919	281	69	21	5	0	0	0	0	302	74
KEARY A.	1911-1912	8	1	0	0	0	0	0	0	8	1
KEEGAN G.A.	1971-1979	32/5	2	0/1	0	4/1	1	3/2	0	39/9	3
KELLY P.	1920-1923	25	1	4	2	0	0	0	0	29	3
KELLY W.B.	1911-1913	10	0	0	0	0	0	0	0	10	0
KELSO T.	1906-1913	138	3	13	0	0	0	0	0	151	3
KENNEDY R.	1961-1969	216/3	9	18	0	16	0	1	0	251/3	9
KERR A.	1959-1960	10	0	0	0	0	0	0	0	10	0
KEVAN D.T.	1963-1965	67	48	3	1	7	6	0	0	77	55
KIDD B.	1976-1979	97/1	44	9	4	11	3	10	6	127/1	57
KINSEY S.	1979-1986	87/14	15	4/3	1	6	1	0	0	97/17	17
KIRKMAN A.J.	1955-1959	7	6	0	0	0	0	0	0	7	6
KNOWLES F.	1919-1920	2	0	0	0	0	0	0	0	2	0
LAKE P.	1985-1987	3	1	0	0	0	0	0	0	3	1
LAMBIE W.	1890-1893	3	1	0	0	0	0	0	0	3	1
LAMPH T.	1919-1920	11	0	0	0	0	0	0	0	11	0
LANGFORD L.	1930-1934	112	0	13	0	0	0	0	0	125	0
LANGLEY K.	1986-87	9	0	0	0	0	0	0	0	9	0
LAW D.	1960-1961										
	1973-1974	66/2	30	5	4	6	3	0	0	77/2	37
LAWRENCE V.	1911-1913	20	0	2	0	0	0	0	0	22	0
LEE F.H.	1967-1974	248/1	112	24	7	26	14	22	10	320/1	43
LEE F.S.	1979-1980	6/1	2	0	0	0	0	0	0	6/1	2
LEIGH P.	1957-1961	2	0	0	0	0	0	0	0	2	0
LEIVERS W.E.	1953-1964	250	4	20	0	11	0	0	0	281	4
LEMAN D.	1970-1976	10/7	1	0/1	0	2/2	1	0	0	12/10	2
LEONARD P.	1897-1898										
	1899-1900	16	5	1	0	0	0	0	0	17	5
LESLIE A.J.	1923-1925	1	0	0	0	0	0	0	0	1	0
LESTER M.J.	1973-1977	1/1	0	0	0	0	0	0/1	0	1/2	0
LEWIS W.	1896-1897	12	4	1	0	0	0	0	0	13	4
LEYLAND J.	1920-1922	3	0	0	0	0	0	0	0	3	0
LIEVESLEY E.F.	1919-1922	2	0	0	0	0	0	0	0	2	0
LILLIS M.	1985-1986	39	11	4	0	3	1	0	0	46	12
LINACRE W.	1947-1949	75	6	4	1	0	0	0	0	79	7
LISTER H.F.	1954-1960	2	0	0	0	0	0	0	0	2	0
LITTLE R.	1949-1958	168	2	18	0	0	0	0	0	186	2
LITTLE T.	1894-1896	16	5	0	0	0	0	0	0	16	5
LIVINGSTONE G.T.	1903-1907	81	19	7	1	0	0	0	0	88	20
LLOYD N.	1932-1935	3	0	0	0	0	0	0	0	3	0
LOMAX G.	1981-1985	23/2	1	2	0	1	0	0	0	26/2	1
LYALL J.	1909-1911	40	0	4	0	0	0	0	0	44	0
LYON W.J.	1903-1904	6	0	0	0	0	0	0	0	6	0
McADAMS W.J.	1953-1960	127	62	7	3	0	0	0	0	134	65
McALINDEN R.J.	1962-1965	1	0	0	0	0	0	0	0	1	0
McBRIDE J.	1894-1897	70	1	1	0	0	0	4*	1	75	2
McCABE A.	1895-1896	1	0	0	0	0	0	0*	0	1	0
McCARTHY M.	1983-1987	140	2	7	0	10	1	0	0	157	3
McCLELLAND J.B.	1953-1958	8	2	0	0	0	0	0	0	8	2
McCLOY P.	1925-1932	147	0	10	0	0	0	0	0	157	0
McCONNELL T.	1896-1897	2	0	0	0	0	0	0	0	2	0
McCORMACK M.	1946-1947	1	0	0	0	0	0	0	0	1	0
McCOURT F.J.	1950-1954	61	4	0	0	0	0	0	0	61	4
McCOURT J.	1924-1925	4	0	0	0	0	0	0	0	4	0
McCULLOUGH K.	1935-1938	17	1	1	0	0	0	0	0	18	1
McDONALD R.	1956-1963	5	0	1	0	0	0	0	0	6	0
McDONALD R.W.	1980-1983	96	11	10/1	4	5	1	0	0	111/1	16
McDOWALL L.J.	1938-1949	120	8	9	0	0	0	0	0	129	8
McDOWELL A	1893-1895	4	0	0	0	0	0	0	0	4	0
McGUIRE P	1912-1916	15	0	0	0	0	0	0	0	15	0
McILROY S	1985-1987	13	1	0	0	1	0	0	0	14	1
MacKENZIE S	1979-1981	56/2	8	8	2	10	0	0	0	74/2	10
McLEOD E	1938-1940	4	2	0	0	0	0	0	0	4	2

368

Player	Played	LEAGUE App	Gls	FA CUP App	Gls	LG CUP App	Gls	EUROPE App	Gls	TOTAL App	Gls
McLEOD J.S.	1935-1937	12	9	2	2	0	0	0	0	14	11
McLUCKIE J.S.	1933-1934	32	1	5	0	0	0	0	0	37	1
McMAHON J.	1902-1906	100	1	9	0	0	0	0	0	109	1
McMORRAN E.J.	1947-1949	33	12	3	0	0	0	0	0	36	12
McMULLAN J.	1926-1933	220	10	22	2	0	0	0	0	242	12
McNAB N.	1983-1987	127/3	9	6	0	8	1	0	0	141/3	10
McNAUGHT K.	1984-1985	7	0	0	0	0	0	0	0	7	0
McOUSTRA W.	1902-1907	65	6	0	0	0	0	0	0	65	6
MacRAE K.A.	1973-1981	56	0	1	0	13	0	0	0	70	0
McREDDIE W.	1894-1895	31	12	0	0	0	0	0	0	31	12
McTAVISH J.R.	1952-1960	93	0	3	0	0	0	0	0	96	0
McVICKERS J.	1892-1894	26	0	3	0	0	0	0	0	29	0
MALEY W.	1894-1896	1	0	0	0	0	0	0	0	1	0
MANN A.F.	1968-1972	32/3	0	4	0	1	0	3/1	0	40/4	0
MANN G.W.	1894-1897	59	5	1	0	0	0	4*	0	64	5
MANSFIELD E.	1908-1909	1	0	0	0	0	0	0	0	1	0
MARSDEN K.	1955-1959	14	1	0	0	0	0	0	0	14	1
MARSH R.W.	1972-1976	116/2	36	8	2	16	6	2	2	142/2	46
MARSHALL R.S.	1928-1939	325	70	30	10	0	0	0	0	355	80
MAY A.M.	1980-1987	141/9	8	6	0	10	0	0	0	157/9	8
MEADOWS J.	1951-1957	130	30	11	1	0	0	0	0	141	31
MEECHAN P.	1900-1901	6	0	0	0	0	0	0	0	6	0
MELLOR I.	1967-1973	36/4	7	3/1	0	1/1	0	2/1	2	42/7	9
MELROSE J.	1984-1986	27/7	8	1	0	2/1	2	0	0	30/8	10
MEREDITH W.H.	1894-1906										
	1921-1924	366	145	24	5	0	0	4*	1	394	151
MIDDLETON H.	1892-1894	36	4	3	0	0	0	0	0	39	4
MILARVIE R.	1891-1896	50	9	4	0	0	0	0	0	54	9
MILLER J.	1895-1896	2	0	0	0	0	0	2*	0	4	0
MILLER J.	1902-1903	8	2	0	0	0	0	0	0	8	2
MILNE J.	1890-1894	18	3	1	0	0	0	0	0	19	3
MILSOM J.	1938-1940	33	22	2	2	0	0	0	0	35	24
MITCHELL J.F.	1922-1926	99	0	10	0	0	0	0	0	109	0
MOFFAT J.	1903-1906	20	4	2	0	0	0	0	0	22	4
MOFFAT R.	1895-1907	156	7	7	0	0	0	0	0	163	7
MOONEY F.	1892-1895	9	4	0	0	0	0	0	0	9	4
MORGAN H.	1901-1902	12	1	3	1	0	0	0	0	15	2
MORRIS H.	1891-1893										
	1895-1896	44	21	3	0	0	0	4*	0	51	21
MORRIS H.	1922-1924	57	0	4	0	0	0	0	0	61	0
MOULDEN P.	1984-1987	17/5	0	0/1	0	1/2	0	0	0	18/8	5
MULHEARN K.J.	1967-1971	50	0	5	0	3	0	3	0	61	0
MULLIGAN J.	1920-1923	3	0	0	0	0	0	0	0	3	0
MUNDY J.H.	1966-1971	2/1	0	0	0	0	0	0	0	2/1	0
MUNN S.	1897-1901	20	0	0	0	0	0	0	0	20	0
MUNRO J.F.	1947-1950	25	4	0	0	0	0	0	0	25	4
MURPHY W.	1918-1926	209	30	11	1	0	0	0	0	220	31
MURRAY H.	1954-1960	1	0	0	0	0	0	0	0	1	0
MURRAY J.R.	1963-1967	70	43	3	0	5	3	0	0	78	46
MURRAY W.	1947-1950	20	1	0	0	0	0	0	0	20	1
NASH J.	1894-1895	17	1	0	0	0	0	0	0	17	1
NAYLOR J.	1932-1933	1	0	0	0	0	0	0	0	1	0
NEILSON R.	1935-1947	16	1	4	0	0	0	0	0	20	1
NELSON J.H.	1911-1912	8	0	0	0	0	0	0	0	8	0
NEWTON W.A.A.	1916-1920	2	0	0	0	0	0	0	0	2	0
NICHOLLS J.H.	1932-1934	16	0	0	0	0	0	0	0	16	0
NIXON E.	1983-1987	33	0	4	0	3	0	0	0	40	0
NORGROVE F.	1904-1912	94	1	4	0	0	0	0	0	98	1
OAKES A.	1958-1976	561/3	26	41	2	46/1	5	17	1	665/4	34
OAKES J.	1948-1951	77	9	2	0	0	0	0	0	79	9
OAKES T.	1947-1948	1	0	0	0	0	0	0	0	1	0
O'BRIEN J.	1893-1894	2	0	0	0	0	0	0	0	2	0
OGDEN T.	1963-1965	9	3	0	0	0	0	0	0	9	3
OGLEY A.	1963-1967	51	0	5	0	1	0	0	0	57	0
O'NEILL M.H.M.	1981-1982	12/1	0	0	0	3	0	0	0	15/1	0
ORR W.	1901-1903	36	0	5	0	0	0	0	0	41	0
OWEN G.A.	1974-1979	101/2	19	7	2	9	2	5	0	122/2	23
OWEN R.	1968-1970	18/4	3	3	1	1	0	0	0	22/4	4
OWEN W.	1934-1936	9	3	1	0	0	0	0	0	10	3
OXFORD K.	1947-1948	1	0	0	0	0	0	0	0	1	0

Player	Played	LEAGUE App	Gls	FA CUP App	Gls	LG CUP App	Gls	EUROPE App	Gls	TOTAL App	Gls
PALMER R.N.	1975-1980	22/9	9	0	0	3/2	1	4	1	29/11	11
PANTER D.	1960-1964	1	0	0	0	1	0	0	0	2	0
PARDOE G.	1961-1976	303/2	17	30	1	26	4	15	0	374/2	22
PARK T.	1982-1983	0/2	0	0	0	0	0	0	0	0/2	0
PARLANE D.	1983-1985	47/1	16	1	0	3	3	0	0	51/1	19
PATTERSON W.	1896-1897	1	0	0	0	0	0	0	0	1	0
PAUL R.	1950-1957	270	9	23	0	0	0	0	0	293	9
PAYNE J.F.	1931-1934	4	1	0	0	0	0	0	0	4	1
PEARSON F.	1903-1905	7	2	1	0	0	0	0	0	8	2
PEARSON H.	1921-1923	1	0	0	0	0	0	0	0	1	0
PENNINGTON J.	1955-1961	1	0	0	0	0	0	0	0	1	0
PERCIVAL J.	1932-1947	161	8	12	0	0	0	0	0	173	8
PERCIVAL P.	1931-1935	2	0	0	0	0	0	0	0	2	0
PHILLIPS D.O.	1984-1986	81	13	5	0	8	0	0	0	94	13
PHILLIPS E.	1947-1951	80	0	2	0	0	0	0	0	82	0
PHILLIPS J.R.	1925-1927	1	0	0	0	0	0	0	0	1	0
PHOENIX R.J.	1950-1960	53	2	2	0	0	0	0	0	55	2
PICKFORD E.	1893-1894	8	3	0	0	0	0	0	0	8	3
PLATT J.W.	1896-1897	1	0	0	0	0	0	0	0	1	0
PLENDERLEITH J.B.	1960-1963	41	0	4	0	2	0	0	0	47	0
PORTEOUS T.S.	1895-1896	5	0	0	0	0	0	0	0	5	0
POWELL R.W.H.	1948-1952	12	0	1	0	0	0	0	0	13	0
POWER P.	1973-1986	358/7	26	28	6	37/1	2	7/1	1	430/9	35
PRINGLE C.R.	1922-1928	197	1	19	0	0	0	0	0	216	1
PRITCHARD H.J.	1938-1947	22	5	3	0	0	0	0	0	25	5
RACE H.	1930-1933	10	3	1	0	0	0	0	0	11	3
RAMSEY J.D.	1909-1910	1	0	0	0	0	0	0	0	1	0
RANKIN B.	1907-1907	2	0	0	0	0	0	0	0	2	0
RANSON R.	1976-1984	181/2	1	12	0	22	0	0	0	215/2	1
RAY R.	1896-1900	83	3	6	0	0	0	0	0	89	3
READ T.H.	1895-1902	115	2	4	0	0	0	0	0	119	2
REDMOND S.	1986-1987	28/2	2	1	0	3	0	0	0	32/2	2
REEVES K.P.	1980-1983	129/1	34	13	4	15	1	0	0	157/1	39
REGAN E.J.	1893-1894	21	0	1	0	0	0	0	0	22	0
REGAN R.H.	1936-1937	4	0	0	0	0	0	0	0	4	0
REID J.E.	1919-1920	3	1	0	0	0	0	0	0	3	1
REID N.S.	1977-1982										
	1982-1987	211/6	2	17	0	20	0	2	0	250/6	2
REVIE D.	1951-1956	162	37	15	4	0	0	0	0	177	41
RIDDING W.	1930-1931	9	4	0	0	0	0	0	0	9	4
RIDLEY J.G.	1927-1933	174	0	10	0	0	0	0	0	184	0
RIGBY J.	1946-1954	100	0	2	0	0	0	0	0	102	0
ROBERTS C.L.	1931-1932	8	2	0	0	0	0	0	0	8	2
ROBERTS F.	1922-1929	216	116	21	14	0	0	0	0	237	130
ROBERTSON D.	1893-1894	7	3	0	0	0	0	0	0	7	3
ROBERTSON G.	1927-1933	14	0	1	0	0	0	0	0	15	0
ROBERTSON J.	1895-1896	3	2	0	0	0	0	0	0	3	2
ROBINSON J.J.	1937-1946	2	0	0	0	0	0	0	0	2	0
ROBINSON L.G.	1896-1897	3	2	0	0	0	0	0	0	3	2
ROBINSON M.J.	1979-1980	29/1	8	1	0	4	1	0	0	34/1	9
ROBINSON P.	1940-1947	1	0	1	0	0	0	0	0	2	0
ROBINSON R.B.	1893-1894	4	2	0	0	0	0	0	0	4	2
ROBINSON W.S.	1902-1905	1	0	0	0	0	0	0	0	1	0
ROBSON D.	1890-1894										
	1894-1896	86	1	3	0	0	0	4*	0	93	1
RODGER C.	1935-1938	19	7	1	0	0	0	0	0	20	7
ROGERS J.H.	1935-1938	11	1	3	0	0	0	0	0	14	1
ROSS D.	1907-1912	61	19	4	0	0	0	0	0	65	19
ROSS J.D.	1899-1902	67	21	3	1	0	0	0	0	70	22
ROWAN A.	1894-1896	45	23	0	0	0	0	3*	2	48	25
ROWLEY H.B.	1931-1933	18	4	0	0	0	0	0	0	18	4
ROYLE J.	1974-1977	98/1	23	6	2	12	6	3/1	0	118/2	31
ROYLE S.	1919-1922	1	0	0	0	0	0	0	0	1	0
RUDD J.J.	1938-1947	2	0	0	0	0	0	0	0	2	0
RUSSELL D.	1892-1893	17	3	2	0	0	0	0	0	19	3
RYAN J.	1982-1983	19	0	0	0	0	0	0	0	19	0
SADDINGTON H.	1893-1894	6	0	0	0	0	0	0	0	6	0
SALT G.O.	1911-1913	1	0	0	0	0	0	0	0	1	0
SAMBROOK R.	1958-1962	62	13	4	0	1	0	0	0	67	13
SAVAGE J.A.	1953-1958	30	0	0	0	0	0	0	0	30	0
SCOTSON J.	1898-1903	8	3	1	0	0	0	0	0	9	3

Player	Played	LEAGUE		FA CUP		LG CUP		EUROPE		TOTAL	
		App	Gls	App	Gls	App	Gls	App	Gls	App	Gls
SCOTT S.	1913-1921	15	0	1	0	0	0	0	0	16	0
SEAR C.	1955-1968	248	1	14	0	17	0	0	0	279	1
SHADWELL W.J.	1933-1936	2	0	0	0	0	0	0	0	2	0
SHARP S.	1918-1929	176	0	6	1	0	0	0	0	182	1
SHARPLES J.	1894-1897	39	20	1	0	0	0	0	0	40	20
SHAWCROSS D.F.	1956-1965	47	2	5	0	3	0	0	0	55	2
SHINTON R.T.	1979-1980	5	0	1	0	0	0	0	0	6	0
SIDDALL B.	1985-1986	6	0	0	0	0	0	0	0	6	0
SILKMAN B.	1979-1980	19	3	0	0	2	0	0	0	21	3
SIMPSON A.	1921-1923	1	0	0	0	0	0	0	0	1	0
SIMPSON P.D.	1982-1987	67/15	17	5	2	6	2	0	0	78/15	21
SINCLAIR G.	1984-1984	1	0	0	0	1	0	0	0	2	0
SLATER P.	1900-1904	20	0	4	0	0	0	0	0	24	0
SMELT T.	1927-1928	2	1	0	0	0	0	0	0	2	1
SMITH F.E.	1952-1953	2	1	0	0	0	0	0	0	2	1
SMITH G.R.	1938-1951	166	75	13	5	0	0	0	0	179	80
SMITH G.D.	1984-1986	42/2	12	1	0	5	2	0	0	48/2	14
SMITH H.E.	1894-1895	18	0	0	0	0	0	0	0	18	0
SMITH J.W.	1909-1914	18	6	2	1	0	0	0	0	20	7
SMITH R.	1920-1924	6	0	0	0	0	0	0	0	6	0
SMITH W. ('Buxton')	1897-1902	144	5	10	3	0	0	0	0	154	8
SMITH W. ('Stockport')	1897-1900	54	22	3	0	0	0	0	0	57	22
SMITH W.E.	1906-1920	232	0	24	0	0	0	0	0	256	0
SOWDEN W.	1949-1954	11	2	0	0	0	0	0	0	11	2
SPITTLE A.	1893-1894	1	1	0	0	0	0	0	0	1	1
SPOTTISWOOD J.	1913-1914	6	0	0	0	0	0	0	0	6	0
SPROSTON B.	1938-1950	128	5	6	0	0	0	0	0	134	5
SPURDLE W.	1950-1956	160	32	12	1	0	0	0	0	172	33
STEELE A.	1906-1908	30	1	2	0	0	0	0	0	32	1
STEELE F.	1892-1894	17	1	1	0	0	0	0	0	18	1
STENSON J.	1893-1894	2	0	0	0	0	0	0	0	2	0
STEPANOVIC D.	1979-1981	14/1	0	0	0	4	0	0	0	18/1	0
STEWART G.	1906-1911	93	11	9	2	0	0	0	0	102	13
STEWART P.	1986-1987	11	2	0	0	0	0	0	0	11	2
STOBART B.	1964-1965	14	1	0	0	0	0	0	0	14	1
STONES H.	1892-1894	12	0	0	0	0	0	0	0	12	0
SUCKLING P.	1986-1987	37	0	1	0	3	0	0	0	41	0
SUGDEN F.A.	1917-1920	6	0	0	0	0	0	0	0	6	0
SUGRUE P.	1980-1981	5/1	0	0	0	0/1	0	0	0	5/2	0
SULLIVAN D.	1983-1984	0	0	0	0	1	0	0	0	1	0
SUMMERBEE M.G.	1965-1975	355/2	47	34	11	36	8	16	1	441/2	67
SWANN J.W.	1909-1912	1	0	0	0	0	0	0	0	1	0
SWIFT F.V.	1932-1949	341	0	35	0	0	0	0	0	376	0
SYME R.G.	1930-1934	11	2	0	0	0	0	0	0	11	2
TAIT D.	1896-1897	4	2	0	0	0	0	0	0	4	2
TAIT T.	1928-1930	61	43	3	3	0	0	0	0	64	46
TAYLOR H.G.	1912-1921	91	27	10	1	0	0	0	0	101	28
TAYLOR K.V.	1954-1960	1	0	0	0	0	0	0	0	1	0
TELFORD W.A.	1975-1976	0/1	0	0	0	0	0	0	0	0/1	0
THOMPSON F.	1921-1927	33	0	3	0	0	0	0	0	36	0
THOMPSON G.H.	1956-1957	2	0	0	0	0	0	0	0	2	0
THOMPSON J.	1920-1921	2	0	0	0	0	0	0	0	2	0
THORNLEY I.	1904-1912	195	92	9	1	0	0	0	0	204	93
THRELFALL F.	1898-1907	67	8	7	0	0	0	0	0	74	8
THURLOW A.C.E	1946-1950	21	0	0	0	0	0	0	0	21	0
TILSON F.S.	1928-1938	245	110	28	22	0	0	0	0	273	132
TOLMIE J.	1983-1986	46/15	15	1	0	3/2	4	0	0	50/17	19
TOMPKINSON H.	1894-1899	6	1	0	0	0	0	0	0	6	1
TONGE J.	1896-1900	4	0	1	0	0	0	0	0	5	0
TOSELAND E.	1929-1939	368	61	41	14	0	0	0	0	409	75
TOWERS A.M.	1967-1974	117/5	10	7/1	1	14	0	13/1	1	151/7	12
TOWNLEY W.J.	1896-1897	3	0	0	0	0	0	0	0	3	0
TRAUTMANN B.C.	1949-1964	508	0	33	0	4	0	0	0	545	0
TUEART D.	1974-1978										
	1980-1983	216/8	86	13/2	3	27	18	3	0	259/10	107
TURNBULL A.	1902-1906	110	53	9	7	0	0	0	0	119	60
TURNBULL R.W.	1949-1951	30	5	1	0	0	0	0	0	31	5
TURNER H.A.	1892-1893	1	0	0	0	0	0	0	0	1	0
TYLER H.E.	1916-1921	44	0	3	0	0	0	0	0	47	0
UTLEY G.	1922-1923	1	0	0	0	0	0	0	0	1	0

Player	Played	LEAGUE		FA CUP		LG CUP		EUROPE		TOTAL	
		App	Gls	App	Gls	App	Gls	App	Gls	App	Gls
VARADI I.	1986-1987	29/1	9	1	0	1	0	0	0	31/1	9
VILJOEN C.	1978-1980	25/2	0	1	0	2/1	1	7	0	35/3	1
WAGSTAFFE D.	1958-1964	144	8	6	0	11	0	0	0	161	8
WALKER J.	1894-1895	19	1	0	0	0	0	0	0	19	1
WALL L.J.	1910-1913	41	2	0	0	0	0	0	0	41	2
WALLACE A.	1894-1895	6	1	0	0	0	0	0	0	6	1
WALLACE W.	1911-1914	43	9	4	0	0	0	0	0	47	9
WALMSLEY C.	1931-1932	2	0	0	0	0	0	0	0	2	0
WALSH M.T.	1983-1984	3/1	0	1	0	1/1	0	0	0	5/2	0
WALSH W.	1936-1951	109	1	9	0	0	0	0	0	118	1
WARDLE W.	1937-1939	6	0	1	0	0	0	0	0	7	0
WARHURST R.	1957-1959	40	2	1	0	0	0	0	0	41	2
WARNER J.	1921-1926	76	15	2	0	0	0	0	0	78	15
WATSON D.V.	1975-1979	146	4	9	0	18	1	12	1	185	6
WATSON L.S.	1901-1902	1	0	0	0	0	0	0	0	1	0
WEBB C.	1908-1909	22	3	0	0	0	0	0	0	22	3
WEBB G.W.	1912-1913	2	0	0	0	0	0	0	0	2	0
WEBSTER E.	1952-1953	1	0	0	0	0	0	0	0	1	0
WEIR D.	1890-1893	14	8	1	0	0	0	0	0	15	8
WESTCOTT D.	1950-1952	72	37	3	0	0	0	0	0	75	37
WESTWOOD E.	1937-1953	251	3	12	2	0	0	0	0	263	5
WHARTON J.E.	1947-1948	23	2	3	0	0	0	0	0	26	2
WHELAN A.M.	1973-1974	3/3	0	0	0	0	0	0	0	3/3	0
WHITE D.	1986-1987	19/5	1	1	0	2/1	0	0	0	22/6	1
WHITE H.K.	1970-1973	1	0	0	0	0	0	0	0	1	0
WHITEHEAD J.	1897-1899	24	7	2	0	0	0	0	0	26	7
WHITEFIELD K.	1953-1954	13	3	0	0	0	0	0	0	13	3
WHITTAKER J.H.	1904-1906										
	1907-1908	6	1	0	0	0	0	0	0	6	1
WHITTLE D.	1890-1894	30	3	1	0	0	0	0	0	31	3
WILKINSON J.	1906-1912	31	2	0	0	0	0	0	0	31	2
WILLEY W.	1893-1894	1	0	0	0	0	0	0	0	1	0
WILLIAMS A.	1978-1987	114	0	2	0	9	0	0	0	125	0
WILLIAMS C.A.	1894-1902	221	1	7	0	0	0	4*	0	232	1
WILLIAMS D.	1951-1954	1	0	0	0	0	0	0	0	1	0
WILLIAMS E.	1945-1951	38	0	3	0	0	0	0	0	41	0
WILLIAMS F.	1896-1902	125	38	5	0	0	0	0	0	130	38
WILLIAMSON J.	1949-1956	59	18	3	1	0	0	0	0	62	19
WILSON C.	1979-1987	107/2	9	2	0	10	2	0	0	119/2	11
WILSON J.	1897-1898	1	0	0	0	0	0	0	0	1	0
WILSON W.	1921-1927	48	0	5	0	0	0	0	0	53	0
WOOD A.E.H.	1961-1966	24/1	0	4	0	4	0	0	0	32/1	0
WOOD J.	1907-1909	28	6	5	3	0	0	0	0	33	9
WOODCOCK W.	1920-1922	15	2	0	0	0	0	0	0	15	2
WOODROFFE L.C.	1945-1947	9	1	0	0	0	0	0	0	9	1
WOOSNAM M.	1919-1925	86	4	7	0	0	0	0	0	93	4
WOOSNAM P.A.	1951-1954	1	0	0	0	0	0	0	0	1	0
WRIGHT N.	1933-1935	3	1	0	0	0	0	0	0	3	1
WRIGHTSON F.L.	1930-1932	22	4	0	0	0	0	0	0	22	4
WYNN G.A.	1909-1919	119	54	9	5	0	0	0	0	128	59
YATES J.	1892-1893	20	9	1	0	0	0	0	0	21	9
YOUNG A.	1911-1912	13	2	2	0	0	0	0	0	15	2
YOUNG J.	1905-1907	1	0	0	0	0	0	0	0	1	0
YOUNG N.J.	1959-1972	332/2	86	32/1	10	28	7	17	5	409/3	108
YUILL J.G.	1906-1909	3	1	0	0	0	0	0	0	3	1

TOP TWENTY LEAGUE APPEARANCES			TOP TWENTY OVERALL APPEARANCES		
1	Alan Oakes	561/3	1	Alan Oakes	665/3
2	Bert Trautmann	508	2	Joe Corrigan	592
3	Joe Corrigan	476	3	Mike Doyle	551/7
4	Eric Brook	453	4	Bert Trautmann	545
5	Mike Doyle	441/7	5	Eric Brook	494
6	Colin Bell	393/1	6	Colin Bell	489/1
7	Tommy Booth	380/2	7	Tommy Booth	476/2
8	Sam Cowan	369	8	Mike Summerbee	441/2
9	Ernie Toseland	368	9	Paul Power	430/7
10	Billy Meredith	366	10	Willie Donachie	421/4
11	Paul Power	358/7	11	Ernie Toseland	409
12	Mike Summerbee	355/2	12	Neil Young	409/2
13	Roy Clarke	349	13	Sam Cowan	407
14	Willie Donachie	347/4	14	Billy Meredith	394
15	Frank Swift	341	15	Frank Swift	376
16	Neil Young	332/2	16	Glyn Pardoe	374/2
17	Joe Hayes	331	17	Roy Clarke	369
18	Tom Johnson	328	18	Joe Hayes	363
19	Bob Marshall	325	19	Bob Marshall	355
20	Glyn Pardoe	303/2	20	Tom Johnson	354

Alan Oakes

City 1935. Back row (left to right): T.Chorlton (trainer), W.Dale, M.Busby, S.Cowan, F.V.Swift, R.Donnelly, J.Bray, J.Percival, S.Barkas, L.H.Barnett (asst trainer). Front row: R.W Dellow, R.S.Marshall, E.Toseland, A.Herd, J.A.Heale, S.F.Tilson, E.F.Brook.

TOP TWENTY LEAGUE GOALSCORERS			TOP TWENTY OVERALL GOALSCORERS		
1	Eric Brook	159	1	Eric Brook	178
2	Tom Johnson	158	2	Tom Johnson	166
3	Billy Meredith	145	3	Colin Bell	152
4	Joe Hayes	142	4	Joe Hayes	152
5	Billy Gillespie	126	5	Billy Meredith	151
6	Tom Browell	122	6	Francis Lee	143
7	Horace Barnes	120	7	Tom Browell	139
8	Colin Bell	117	8	Fred Tilson	132
9	Frank Roberts	116	9	Billy Gillespie	132
10	Francis Lee	112	10	Frank Roberts	130
11	Fred Tilson	110	11	Horace Barnes	125
12	Alex Herd	107	12	Alex Herd	124
13	Irvine Thornley	92	13	Neil Young	108
14	Dennis Tueart	86	14	Dennis Tueart	107
15	Neil Young	86	15	Irvine Thornley	93
16	Colin Barlow	78	16	Peter Doherty	81
17	Peter Doherty	76	17	Colin Barlow	80
18	George Smith	75	18	George Smith	80
19	Roy Clarke	73	19	Bob Marshall	80
20	Bob Marshall	70	20	Roy Clarke	79

Eric Brook

City Wartime Appearances and Scorers

WORLD WAR ONE

	League		Subsid		TOTAL	
Allen A.J.	4	0	0	0	4	0
Armstrong	0	0	4	0	4	0
Barnes H	57	56	16	17	73	73
Blackwell E.E.	2	0	0	0	2	0
Bottomley W	31	0	1	0	32	0
Brennan J	75	3	19	1	94	4
Brierley H	11	0	0	0	11	0
Broad T	36	2	10	0	46	2
Broad J	1	0	0	0	1	0
Browell T	27	14	6	4	33	18
Brown A.E.	2	0	0	0	2	0
Capper	1	5	0	0	1	5
Cartwright J.E.	45	7	15	2	60	9
Catlow	4	0	0	0	4	0
Clegg J	0	0	2	0	2	0
Connor	1	0	0	0	1	0
Cope	6	1	0	0	6	1
Corcoran	0	0	1	0	1	0
Crowther	1	0	0	0	1	0
Cruse	4	2	0	0	4	2
Cunningham	5	2	3	0	8	2
Davies A	18	1	0	0	18	1
Dorsett J.H.	7	3	0	0	7	3
Duffy	1	0	0	0	1	0
Elliott	0	0	2	0	2	0
Fairclough A	4	7	2	1	6	8
Fairclough P	85	12	17	1	102	13
Fielding	1	0	0	0	1	0
Fletcher E	106	0	27	3	133	3
Gartland P	23	0	9	0	32	0
Geddes R	1	0	0	0	1	0
Goddard H	3	3	0	0	3	3
Goodchild A.J.	106	0	24	0	130	0
Hanney E.T.	3	0	0	0	3	0
Hargreaves R	1	0	1	0	2	0
Henderson J	23	0	10	0	33	0
Henry W.A.	23	0	2	0	25	0
Hoad S.J.	3	1	0	0	3	1
Hoare G	1	1	0	0	1	1
Howard F.J.	7	4	0	0	7	4
Howarth J.T.	4	0	0	0	4	0
Howe G.A.	1	0	0	0	1	0
Hughes E	55	2	10	0	65	2
James	1	0	0	0	1	0
Johnson A	1	0	0	0	1	0
Johnson T.C.F.	5	4	0	0	5	4
Jones F	0	0	1	0	1	0
Jones W.L.	29	4	8	2	37	6
Kelly	1	0	0	0	1	0
Kenyon	4	3	0	0	4	3
Kite P	1	0	0	0	1	0
Knowles F	1	0	0	0	1	0
Lee M	0	0	1	0	1	0
Lewis T.E.	0	0	1	0	1	0
Lievesley E.F.	10	8	1	0	11	8
Lingard	3	0	0	0	3	0
Lloyd	1	0	0	0	1	0
Lomas W	32	22	13	1	45	23
McIlvenney F	0	0	2	1	2	1
McRay	1	0	0	0	1	0
Malone	0	0	1	0	1	0
Mann	0	0	2	1	2	1
Meredith W.H.	85	5	22	2	107	7
Miller	4	0	0	0	4	0
Moses	11	4	0	0	11	4
Murphy W	20	2	3	0	23	2
Nelson	6	2	0	0	6	2
Newton H	1	0	4	1	5	1
Newton W.A.A.	11	1	3	0	14	1
Ollerenshaw E	2	0	1	0	3	0
Osmond J.E.	2	0	0	0	2	0
Parker F	21	0	3	0	24	0
Petrie C	1	0	0	0	1	0
Roberts	1	0	0	0	1	0
Royle S	2	1	5	3	7	4
Scott S	9	0	1	0	10	0
Sharp S	0	0	2	0	2	0
Skeldon	1	0	0	0	1	0
Smith A.W.	7	2	0	0	7	2
Smith W.E.	5	0	3	0	8	0
Spruce	2	0	0	0	2	0
Sugden F.A.	27	0	12	0	39	0
Tavo J.D.	2	1	0	0	2	1
Taylor H.G.	24	9	8	5	32	14
Thompson J	15	6	6	1	21	7
Thorpe	2	2	0	0	2	2
Tomkins	2	0	0	0	2	0
Tomlinson	1	0	0	0	1	0
Tyler H.E.	80	7	14	0	94	7
Voysley	2	0	0	0	2	0
Waldon H	2	1	0	0	2	1
Watson	17	4	0	0	17	4
Woodcock W	1	0	1	1	2	1
Woodhouse	0	0	1	0	1	0
Wray J	6	1	2	0	8	1
Wynn G.A.	24	7	6	2	30	9

WORLD WAR TWO

	League		WarCup		TOTAL	
Bacuzzi J	1	0	0	0	1	0
Baillie M	1	0	0	0	1	0
Baker H.V.	1	1	0	0	1	1
Barber E	3	0	0	0	3	0
Barclay C.E.	13	3	5	0	18	3
Bardsley L	13	2	8	0	21	2
Barkas S	56	3	19	0	75	3
Beattie A	2	0	0	0	2	0
Beaumont L	1	0	0	0	1	0
Bellis A	0	0	1	0	1	0
Bentham S	1	0	0	0	1	0
Blackshaw W	8	2	0	0	8	2
Boothway J	49	39	27	18	76	57
Bootle W	20	6	12	0	32	6
Boulter L	1	0	0	0	1	0
Bray J	121	9	56	2	177	11
Breedon J	2	0	0	0	2	0
Brook E.F.G.	4	2	0	0	4	2
Brooks H	1	1	0	0	1	1
Brown A.R.J.	11	6	4	0	15	6
Brown E	7	0	0	0	7	0
Burdett T	1	1	0	0	1	1
Burke R.J.	4	3	0	0	4	3
Butler M.P.	1	0	0	0	1	0
Butt L	0	0	1	0	1	0
Campbell J	1	0	0	0	1	0

Capel T.A.	1	0	0	0	1	0	McShane H	20	2	3	0	23	2
Cardwell L	42	0	3	0	45	0	Malam A	12	7	2	2	14	9
Carey J.J.	3	1	1	0	4	1	Meiklem R.C.	1	0	0	0	1	0
Carey W.J.	9	0	0	0	9	0	Milsom J	0	0	1	0	1	0
Carter D.F.	0	0	1	0	1	0	Moore B	3	0	0	0	3	0
Cassidy L	1	0	0	0	1	0	Mulraney A	6	3	0	0	6	3
Chappell F.G.	4	0	3	0	7	0	Murray W	4	0	0	0	4	0
Charlesworth S	19	0	10	0	29	0	Mutch G	4	1	0	0	4	1
Chisholm K.M.	1	0	0	0	1	0	Neilson R	22	0	3	0	25	0
Clark G.V.	120	0	60	0	180	0	Nuttall E	1	0	0	0	1	0
Clark H	7	1	1	0	8	1	O'Donnell H	1	1	0	0	1	1
Constantine J	34	25	0	0	34	25	Ollerenshaw J	1	0	0	0	1	0
Cox F.J.A.	1	1	12	1	13	2	Owen E.L.	4	2	5	4	9	6
Crompton J	1	0	0	0	1	0	Paton J	3	0	2	0	3	2
Cunliffe R.A.	1	0	0	0	1	0	Paton T.J.	0	0	1	0	1	0
Currier J	75	69	38	15	113	84	Parlane J	4	1	0	0	4	1
Daniels D	3	0	0	0	3	0	Pearson S	5	2	1	0	6	2
Davenport D.W.	2	0	0	0	2	0	Pearson W.G.	14	6	0	0	14	6
Davenport J	3	0	0	0	3	0	Percival J	33	3	4	0	37	3
Dellow R.W.	8	3	5	2	13	5	Pimbley D.W.	2	0	0	0	2	0
Devlin J	1	0	0	0	1	0	Poole B	0	0	1	0	1	0
Dickie P	0	0	1	0	1	0	Porter W	2	0	0	0	2	0
Dodd L	2	0	1	0	3	0	Powell I.V.	1	0	0	0	1	0
Doherty P.D.	66	45	23	15	89	60	Pritchard H.J.	41	8	7	1	48	9
Dunkley M.E.F.	45	11	15	4	60	15	Reid J.D.	1	2	0	0	1	2
Eastwood E	104	0	59	0	163	0	Robinson J.J.	35	0	25	0	60	0
Eastwood R	2	0	0	0	2	0	Robinson P	17	2	15	0	32	2
Emptage A.T.	33	5	1	0	34	5	Roxburgh A.W.	2	0	3	0	5	0
Fagan J.F.	10	0	0	0	10	0	Rudd J.J.	9	3	5	0	14	3
Fenton B.R.V.	4	3	7	4	11	7	Rudman K	1	0	0	0	1	0
Gemmell E	2	1	0	0	2	1	Scales G	13	0	8	0	21	0
Goddard W.G.	1	0	0	0	1	0	Sellers W.E.	1	0	0	0	1	0
Goodall E.I.	2	0	0	0	2	0	Smith G.R.	68	38	22	7	90	45
Grant W	1	0	12	0	13	0	Smith L.G.F.	1	0	0	0	1	0
Hall B.A.C.	2	0	0	0	2	0	Sproston B	57	3	17	2	74	5
Hanson A.J.	1	0	0	0	1	0	Stuart D	21	5	9	2	30	7
Hart J.P.	4	1	0	0	4	1	Swift F.V.	102	0	31	0	133	0
Heale J.A.	26	20	16	13	42	33	Taylor J	25	2	9	1	34	3
Henry G.R.	1	0	0	0	1	0	Thomson A	1	0	0	0	1	0
Herd A	68	46	22	14	90	60	Thomson J	0	0	1	0	1	0
Hilton J	1	0	0	0	1	0	Thorpe W.F.	3	0	0	0	3	0
Hodgson R	5	0	0	0	5	0	Tilson F.S.	1	0	0	0	1	0
Hogan W.J.	5	1	0	0	5	1	Toseland E	2	0	0	0	2	0
Hope J.G.	1	0	0	0	1	0	Turner H	11	0	0	0	11	0
Iddon H	1	0	0	0	1	0	Vose G	0	0	1	0	1	0
Jackson L	14	0	6	0	20	0	Walker C.E.	21	0	12	0	33	0
Jones C.W.	7	3	1	0	8	3	Walker S	3	0	0	0	3	0
Jones J.T.	0	0	2	0	2	0	Walsh W	162	7	67	1	229	8
Jones L.J.	0	0	1	0	1	0	Watt A	1	0	0	0	1	0
Keeling A.J.	1	0	0	0	1	0	Welsh D	0	0	1	2	1	2
Kenny F	1	0	0	0	1	0	Westwood E	23	1	6	0	29	1
King F.A.B.	28	13	23	7	51	20	Wild A	15	2	1	0	16	2
Kinghorn W.J.D.	1	0	0	0	1	0	Williams E	9	0	1	0	10	0
Kirton T.W.	6	0	1	0	7	0	Williams J	1	0	0	0	1	0
Laing R	1	0	0	0	1	0	Williamson W.M.J.	28	15	34	24	62	39
Leech H	3	2	0	0	3	2	Wilson F	1	0	0	0	1	0
Linaker J.E.	6	0	0	0	6	0	Woodroffe L.C.	6	2	0	0	6	2
McCormack C.J.	1	0	0	0	1	0	Worrell J	2	0	0	0	2	0
McDowall L.J.	82	8	32	0	114	8	Worsley H	0	0	2	1	2	1
McIntosh J.M.	1	0	0	0	1	0	Wright T.B.	3	1	0	0	3	1
McMillan J	8	0	0	0	8	0							

City Transfer Trail

Below is a list of every player to have appeared in a first-team match for Manchester City, showing (where known) birthplace, date and club from which the player joined City, date and club for which the player left. The date of signing is always the *first* signing, whether that was as an amateur, apprentice, full-time professional or non-contract and irrespective of what status the player later adopted. The abbreviation 'cs' means close-season.

NAME	Pos	BIRTHPLACE	FROM	TO
ABBOTT, J	F	Patricroft	Eccles Borough, 25.4.13	cs1915
AIMSON, P	F	Macclesfield	Stafford Boys, 11.11.58	York City, 6.7.64
ALBINSON, G	HB	Manchester	Manchester Utd, 19.5.21	cs1922
ALISON, J	F	Falkirk	Falkirk, 8.12.49	Aldershot, 18.7.52
ALLAN, J	F	Glasgow	9.3.27	Scottish Interim Lge, cs1928
ALLEN, A	FB	Manchester	Glossop, cs1915	Southport, June 1924
ALLMARK, J	F	Liverpool	Colwyn Bay, 6.1.37	New Brighton, cs1938
ANDERS, H	F	St Helens	Preston NE, 6.3.53	Port Vale, 28.7.56
ANGUS, H	F		West Manchester, Mar 1892	cs1893
ANGUS, J	F		Third Lanark, 21.8.92	Soton St Marys, Dec 1892
APPLETON, F	FB	Hyde	Marple FC, 10.7.24	cs1929
ARMITT, C	F		Blackburn R, 11.2.93	cs1893
ASHWORTH, S	HB	Fenton, Stoke	Stoke City, cs1903	Everton, 23.9.04
AUSTIN, S	F	Arnold, Notts	Norwich C, 6.5.24	Chesterfield, 9.12.31
BACON, A	F	Tupton, Derbys	Derby Co, 7.12.28	Reading, 1.6.29
BACUZZI, D	FB	London	Arsenal, 24.4.64	Reading, 9.9.66
BAKER, G	F	New York	St Mirren, 2.11.60	Hibernian, 17.11.61
BAKER, G	M	Southampton	Southampton, 13.8.82	
BAKER, J	HB		5.3.93	cs1895
BALDWIN, W	F		Sale Holmfield, 27.3.04	Reading, cs1908
BANKS, W	HB	Hurlford	Kilmarnock, 13.12.05	Atherton Canbee, cs1908
			Alberta, Canada, 8.6.11	Kilmarnock, 23.11.11
BANNISTER, C	HB	Burton-on-Trent	Newtown, cs1896	Lincoln City, Mar 1897
BANNISTER, E	HB		Buxton, cs1907	Preston NE, cs1910
BANNISTER, J	F	Leyland	Chorley, cs1902	Manchester U, 5.12.06
BARBER, L	G	Wombwell	Halifax T, 6.6.27	Retired, cs1932
BARKAS, S	FB	Wardley	Bradford C, 20.4.34	Workington T, May 1947
BARLOW, C	F	Manchester	Tarporley Boys Club, 2.3.56	Oldham A, 30.8.63
BARNES, H	F	Wadsley Bridge	Derby Co, 14.5.14	Preston NE, 11.11.24
BARNES, K	HB	Birmingham	Stafford Rangers, 6.5.50	Wrexham, 3.5.61
BARNES, P	F	Manchester	Manchester Boys, 31.7.72	West Brom A, 17.7.79
			Manchester U, 13.1.87	
BARNETT, L	FB	Bramley	Blackpool, 15.5.30	Retired, Apr 1936
BARR, A	F	Ballymena	Glentoran, 7.5.36	cs1940
BARRASS, M	F	Seaham Harbour	Sheffield Wed, 31.7.26	Ashton National, cs1933
BARRETT, C	FB	Stockport	Cheadle Heath N, 11.5.70	Nottingham F, 9.4.76
BARRETT, E	D	Rochdale	Youth Training Scm, 23.4.84	
BARRETT, F	G		New Brighton T, 13.9.01	Dundee, 6.11.02
BATTY, M	HB	Manchester	Schools, 12.5.60	Rhyl, Aug 1966
BECKFORD, D	F	Longsight	Schools, 16.4.84	
BEEBY, A	G	Ashbourne	Liverpool, May 1911	cs1912
BELL, C	MF	Heselden	Bury, 16.3.66	Retired, 21.8.79
BELL, P	F	Chilton, Darlington	Raith R, 17.9.26	Falkirk, 20.7.28
BENNETT, A	F		6.10.93	cs1896
BENNETT, D	F	Manchester	Schools, 20.8.76	Cardiff C, 19.9.81
BENNETT, E	FB	Bristol	Wrexham, 4.5.26	Norwich C, 9.5.29
BENSON, J	HB	Arbroath	Stockport Boys, 31.7.58	Torquay U, 15.6.64
BENTLEY, H	HB	Knutsford	Macclesfield, May 1910	cs1912
BETTS, B	FB	Barnsley	Stockport C, 23.6.60	Scunthorpe U, 12.8.64
BENZIE, R	HB	Greenock	Doncaster R, 23.4.25	Welsh League, cs1928
BEVAN, F	F	Hackney	Millwall, 4.5.01	Reading, cs1903
BLACK, A	F	Stirling	Hearts, 6.6.46	Stockport C, 3.8.50
BLACKSHAW, W	F	Ashton-under-Lyne	Audenshaw U, 3.5.37	Oldham A, July 1946
BLAIR, J	HB		Woolwich Arsenal, 23.11.06	Bradford C, May 1910
BLAIR, T	G	Glasgow	Kilmarnock, 15.7.20	Canada, cs1922
BLEW, H	FB	Wrexham	Wrexham Victoria, 11.9.06	Wrexham Victoria, 30.9.06
BODAK, P	F	Birmingham	Manchester U, 18.1.83	Seiko, Hong Kong, 11.10.83
BOND, K	D	West Ham	Seattle Sounders, 7.9.81	Southampton, 24.9.84
BOOK, A	FB	Bath	Plymouth A, 20.7.66	Retired, 30.11.74
BOOTH, F	F	Hyde	Stockport C, 13.4.02	Bury, 7.12.06
			Clyde, 25.7.11	Retired, cs1912

NAME	Pos	BIRTHPLACE	FROM	TO
BOOTH, T	D	Manchester	Middleton Boys, 11.9.65	Preston NE, 4.10.81
BOOTLE, W	F	Ashton	16.6.43	Wigan A, July 1950
BOTTOMLEY, W	HB	Mossley	Oldham A, 12.5.08	Retired, 30.9.19
BOWLES, S	F	Moston	Schools, 30.7.65	Crewe Alex, 22.9.70
BOWMAN, W	HB	Canada	Accrington, 25.8.92	cs1900
BOWYER, I	MF	Ellesmere Port	Mid-Cheshire Boys, 30.7.66	Orient, 11.6.71
BOYER, P	F	Nottingham	Southampton, 28.11.80	Retired, 19.2.83
BRADFORD, L	F	Eccles	Hurst FC, 9.5.25	Ashton-National, cs1926
BRANAGAN, K	FB	Salford	North Salford YC, 5.11.48	Oldham A, 1.10.60
BRAND, R	F	Edinburgh	Glasgow Rangers, 11.8.65	Sunderland, 11.8.67
BRAY, J	HB	Oswaldwistle	Manchester Central, 16.10.29	Watford, cs1947
BRENNAN, J	HB	Manchester	Bradford C, 16.7.14	Rochdale, cs1922
BRENNAN, M	F	Salford	Lanc's Schools, 23.7.68	Rochdale, 1.10.73
BRIGHTWELL, I	MF	Lutterworth	Midas Jnr Club, 1.7.85	
BROAD, T	F	Stalybridge	Bristol C, Mar 1915	Stoke C, 26.5.21
BROADHURST, C	F	Moston	Ashton-National, 17.3.27	Blackpool, 6.2.30
BROADIS, I	F	Poplar	Sunderland, 5.10.51	Newcastle U, 29.10.53
BROOK, E	F	Mexborough	Barnsley, 16.3.28	Retired, cs1940
BROOKS, G	HB	Radcliffe, Lancs	Longfield AFC, 1.1.11	Bury, 3.4.12
BROOMFIELD, H	G	Audlem	Manchester U, 11.7.08	cs1909
BROWELL, T	F	Walbottle	Everton, 31.10.13	Blackpool, 15.9.26
BROWN, H	HB		Crewe Alex, 6.10.10	Tredager, cs1911
BROWN, J	F		Orrell, 1.9.08	Stoke, Aug 1910
BUCHAN, J	HB	Perth	Woolwich Arsenal, 10.3.05	Motherwell, Jun 1911
BUCKLEY, F	HB	Urmston	Manchester U, 2.9.07	Birmingham, July 1909
BUCKLEY, G	F	Manchester	Salford Boys, 30.5.77	Preston NE, 3.10.81
BURGESS, C	FB	Talke, Staffs	Stoke, cs1908	cs1911
BURGESS, H	FB	Openshaw	Glossop, 30.7.03	Manchester U, 5.12.06
BUSBY, M	HB	Bellshill	Denny Hibs, 11.2.28	Liverpool, 11.3.36
CAINE, J	HB		16.3.92	Newton Heath, cs1894
CALDERWOOD, J	HB	Busby, Lanark	Manchester Calico Ptrs, 19.4.22	Grimsby T, 5.7.27
CALLAGHAN, T	F		Glossop, 14.6.07	Partick T, Aug 1909
CALVEY, M	F		Blackburn R, 21.5.94	Baltimore, USA, 13.10.94
CANN, S	FB	Torquay	Torquay U, 13.3.30	Charlton A, 7.6.35
CAPEL, T	F	Manchester	Droylsden, 5.11.41	Chesterfield, 24.10.47
CARDWELL, L	HB	Blackpool	Blackpool, 16.9.38	Netherfield, 2.2.47
CARRODUS, F	F	Manchester	Altrincham, 3.11.69	Aston Villa, 31.7.74
CARROLL, F	F	Beesbrook	Belfast Celtic, 5.11.20	Newry T, cs1925
CARSON, A	F		Newton Heath, 15.3.93	Liverpool, 28.2.94
CARTER, S	F	Great Yarmouth	Norfolk Schools, 29.7.68	Notts Co, 25.3.92
CARTWRIGHT, J	F	Warrington	Northwich Victoria, cs1913	Crystal Pal, 29.6.21
CASSIDY, J	F	Motherwell	Newton Heath, 20.4.1900	Middlesbrough, 8.5.01
CASSIDY, J	F	Lurgan	Newry T, 12.10.35	Tranmere R, 30.6.37
CATON, T	D	Kirkby	Liverpool Boys, 6.7.79	Arsenal, 1.12.83
CHADWICK, G	HB	Oldham	Manchester Boys, 5.9.59	Walsall, 31.7.64
CHANNON, M	F	Orcheston	Southampton, 25.7.77	Southampton, 8.9.79
CHAPELOW, H	F		Chorley, 21.5.09	Middlesbrough, Aug 1911
CHAPLIN, J	FB	Dundee	Dundee, 14.11.10	Leeds City, Nov 1913
CHAPMAN, T	HB	Newtown	Newtown, 30.6.95	Grimsby T, May 1896
CHAPPELL, T	G		West Manchester, 14.3.96	cs1900
CHEETHAM, R	HB	Eccles	Manchester Boys, 12.7.55	Detroit Cougers, 2.1.68
CHRISTIE, J	FB		Manchester U, 5.5.04	Bradford, Sept 1907
CHRISTIE, T	F	Newcastle	Derby County, 7.8.86	Walsall, 16.10.86
CLARE, T	FB	Congleton	Stoke, 8.5.97	Port Vale, 27.8.99
CLARK, G	FB	Guisborough	Denaby U, 22.1.36	Hyde U, Apr 1947
CLARKE, J	D	Pontefract	Schools, 12.12.71	Sunderland, 13.6.75
CLARKE, R	F	Newport	Cardiff C, 23.5.47	Stockport C, 19.9.58
CLAY, J	MF	Stockport	Stockport Boys, 16.7.62	Macclesfield T, 13.7.68
CLAYTON, R	F	Retford	Retford, 18.1.35	Bristol C, 13.6.38
CLEMENTS, K	D	Manchester	Youth Club, 22.7.71 Oldham A, 1.6.85	Oldham A, 12.9.79
CLIFFORD, H	HB		Stoke, 4.7.95	Mar 1896
CODLING, R	HB	Durham	Croydon Common, 19.8.10	cs1911
COLBRIDGE, R	F	Hull	Crewe Alex, 5.5.59	Wrexham, 13.2.62
COLEMAN, T	F	Liverpool	Doncaster R, 16.3.67	Sheffield W, 1.10.69
COMRIE, M	F	Denny	Brentford, 30.7.32	Burnley, 4.5.34
CONLIN, J	F	Durham	Bradford C, 13.7.06	Birmingham C, 29.9.11
CONNOR, D	MF	Wythenshawe	Manchester Boys, 8.8.62 Preston NE, 5.3.74	Preston NE, 21.1.72 Macclesfield T, cs1975
CONSTANTINE, J	F	Ashton-under-Lyne	Rochdale, 19.4.45	Bury, 29.8.46
CONWAY, J	MF	Dublin	Fulham, 10.8.76	Portland Timbers, 17.1.78
COOKSON, S	FB	Manchester	Macclesfield T, Oct 1918	Bradford, 28.9.28
CORBETT, F	FB	Birmingham	Torquay U, 13.3.30	Lincoln C, 21.7.36

NAME	Pos	BIRTHPLACE	FROM	TO
CORBETT, V	FB	Birmingham	Hereford U, 12.5.33	Southend U, 8.5.35
CORRIGAN, J	G	Manchester	Sale FC, 24.9.66	Seattle Sounders, 25.3.83
COUPE, D	FB		Worksop, 22.1.08	cs1910
COUPLAND, C	HB	Grimsby	Mansfield T, 25.3.25	Grimsby T, 5.7.27
COWAN, S	HB	Chesterfield	Doncaster R, 12.12.24	Bradford C, 17.10.35
COWAN, W	F	Edinburgh	Newcastle U, 11.5.26	St Mirren, 14.5.27
COWIE, A	F	Lockee	Gravesend U, 6.8.98	Queen's Park R, cs1899
COX, W	G	Southampton	Millwall, 8.5.1900	Bury, cs1901
CRAWSHAW, R	F	Manchester	Stockport C, June 1919	Halifax T, 17.7.22
CROSS, D	F	Heywood	West Ham U, 31.7.82	Vancouver Whitecaps, 26.4.83
CROSSAN, J	F	Londonderry	Sunderland, 22.1.65	Middlesbrough, 23.8.67
CUMMING, J	F	Alexandria	Clydebank Jnr, 2.4.13	West Ham U, 3.3.20
CUNNINGHAM, T	F	Kingston, Jamaica	Sheffield W, 11.7.84	Newcastle U, 5.2.85
CUNLIFFE, R	F	Manchester	Apprentice, 27.7.60	York City, 14.6.65
CUNLIFFE, RA	F	Bryn	Garswood St Andrew's, 25.9.45	Chesterfield, 29.6.56
DALE, W	FB	Manchester	Manchester U, 23.12.31	Ipswich T, 22.5.38
DALEY, S	MF	Barnsley	Wolves, 5.9.79	Seattle Sounders, 24.2.81
DALZIEL, G	F	Motherwell	Glasgow Rangers, 1.12.83	Partick T, 10.9.84
DANIELS, A	F	Mossley	Mossley, 27.8.20	Watford, 22.5.26
DANIELS, B	F	Salford	Ashton U, 30.3.73	Chester, 9.7.75
DARTNELL, H	F		Wellingborough, 10.4.1900	Barnsley, 17.12.01
DAVIDSON, A	F	Beith, Ayrshire	Glossop, 23.3.1900	Reading, cs1901
DAVIDSON, D	F	Elgin	Sea Bees(Hong Kong), 2.9.83	Highland League, 31.7.84
DAVIDSON, D	HB	Govan Hill	Glentyne Thistle, 29.8.51	Workington, 3.7.58
DAVIDSON, R	FB	West Calder	Glasgow Celtic, 13.8.02	Airdrie, Oct 1904
DAVIES, F	G		Glossop, 2.6.06	Oct 1909
DAVIES, GE	F	Manchester	Ashton U, 6.12.51	Chester, 28.5.57
DAVIES, GJ	F	Merthyr Tydfil	Chelsea, 10.10.85	Fulham, 30.10.86
DAVIES, I	D	Bristol	Newcastle U, 1.8.82	Carlisle U, 17.5.84
DAVIES, J	F	Chirk	Chirk, 19.2.91	Sheffield U, 24.1.94
			Sheffield U, 7.11.95	Millwall, cs1896
			Reading, cs1900	Stockport C, cs1901
DAVIES, R	HB		Stafford Rangers, 26.8.11	Pontypridd, 9.6.12
DAVIES, W	F	Caernarvon	Newcastle U, 2.8.71	Manchester U, 14.9.72
DEARDEN, R	HB		Leyland, 24.6.01	Mar 1907
DELLOW, R	F	Crosby	Mansfield T, 26.1.35	Tranmere R, 12.3.36
DENNISON, J	F		Sale Holmfield, 16.2.03	Oct 1904
DENNISON, R	F	Arnold	Brighton & HA, 6.5.25	Clapton Orient, 26.8.26
DEYNA, K	F	Starsgrad, Poland	Legia, Warsaw, 21.11.78	San Diego, 28.1.81
DITCHFIELD, J	FB		Rossendale, 26.12.95	Nov 1896
DOBING, P	F	Manchester	Blackburn R, 17.7.61	Stoke C, 15.8.63
DOCHERTY, M	FB	Preston	Burnley, 29.4.76	Sunderland, 31.12.76
DOHERTY, P	F	Magharafelt	Blackpool, 19.6.36	Derby County, 6.12.45
DONACHIE, W	FB	Glasgow	Glasgow Amateurs, 23.10.68	Portland Timbers, 19.3.80
DONALDSON, A	F	Barrhead	Sunderland, 18.5.23	Crystal P, 24.5.24
DONNELLY, R	FB	Craigneak	Partick T, 24.6.35	Morton, 11.7.37
DORAN, J	HB	Belfast	Brighton & HA, 7.8.22	Crewe Alex, 16.1.24
DORSETT, G	F	Brownhills	West Brom A, 8.12.04	Retired, cs1912
DORSETT, J	F	Brownhills	West Brom A, 31.8.10	Southend U, cs1920
DOUGAL, G	F		Hibernian, 8.3.98	Glossop, cs1901
DOUGLAS, W	G		Dundee OB, May 1890	Newton Heath, 26.1.94
DOWD, H	G	Manchester	ICI Blackley, 10.1.58	Oldham A, 1.12.70
DOYLE, M	HB	Manchester	Stockport Boys, 11.5.62	Stoke C, 5.6.78
DRUMMOND, J	F		Glasgow Celtic, 3.2.02	Partick T, cs1904
DUNKLEY, M	F	Kettering	Northampton T, 11.3.38	Kettering T, cs1947
DUNNE, L	FB	Dublin	Drumoronda, 18.8.33	Hull C, cs1935
DYER, F	FB	Bishopbriggs	Woolwich Arsenal, 15.8.93	Retired, May 1898
DYSON, J	F	Oldham	Nelson, 15.10.51	Stirling Albion, 30.3.61
EADIE, W	HB	Greenock	Morton, 16.8.06	Derby County, 30.6.14
EASTWOOD, E	HB	Heywood	Heywood St James, 14.4.35	Port Vale, 27.3.47
EDELSTON, J	HB	Appley Bridge	Hull C, 8.6.20	Fulham, 18.11.20
EDEN, J	FB		13.10.11	cs1912
EDGE, A	F		Northwich Victoria, 15.1.94	cs1894
EDMONDSON, J	G	Accrington	Accrington, 2.5.02	Bolton W, 8.12.06
EGAN, W	F		Fairfield, 15.11.93	Burnley, Mar 1894
ELLIOTT, A	M	Ashton	Derby Boys, 2.4.80	Sligo Rovers, cs1982
ELWOOD, J	HB	Belfast	Glentoran, 13.3.24	Chesterfield, 26.7.27
EMPTAGE, A	HB	Grimsby	Scunthorpe U, 2.3.37	Stockport C, 6.1.51
ESPIE, J	HB		Burnley, 23.2.96	cs1896
ETHERINGTON, R	F	Manchester	Leyland, 27.8.21	Rotherham C, 6.6.24
EWING, D	HB	Perth	Luncarty Jnrs, 10.6.49	Crewe Alex, 7.7.62
EYRES, S	F	Droylsden	Failsworth, 26.4.07	Colne, 30.9.08

NAME	Pos	BIRTHPLACE	FROM	TO
FAGAN, F	F	Dublin	Hull C, 24.12.53	Derby County, 15.3.60
FAGAN, JF	HB	Liverpool	Earlstown Bohemians, 8.10.38	Nelson, 2.8.51
FAIRCLOUGH, A	F	St Helens	Eccles Borough, 23.4.13	Southend U, cs1920
FAIRCLOUGH, P	F	St Helens	Eccles Borough, 23.4.13	cs1920
FARRELL, T	F	Earlstown	Woolwich Arsenal, 1.9.05	Airdrie, 22.1.08
FAULKNER, R	F	Manchester	Juniors, 3.12.52	Walsall, 8.9.57
FAYERS, F	HB	Kings Lynn	Stockport C, 9.5.20	Halifax T, 11.5.23
FELTON, W	FB	Felling-on-Tyne	Sheffield W, 15.3.29	Tottenham H, 16.3.32
FERGUSON, A	FB		Preston NE, 2.4.94	Baltimore, USA, 13.10.94
FIDLER, D	F	Stockport	Manchester U, 28.11.56	Port Vale, 2.6.60
FINNERHAN, P	F	Northwich	Northwich Victoria, 10.6.94	Liverpool, 5.3.97
FINNIGAN, R	G	Wrexham	Connah's Quay, 4.5.26	Accrington S, 23.5.27
FISTER, A	F		Brighton, 29.6.06	Bradford, cs1907
FLEET, S	G	Salford	Manchester Boys, 10.8.53	Wrexham, 21.6.63
FLETCHER, E	FB	Tunstall, Staffs	Crewe Alex, 18.5.11	Watford, 2.6.26
FLETCHER, L	F	Helsby	25.11.32	Watford, 31.5.35
FORD, A	F	Sunderland	Spen Black & White, 14.5.21	Seaton Delaval, cs1922
FORRESTER, T	F		5.10.92	cs1894
FOSTER, C	F	Rotherham	Morecambe, 28.4.27	Oldham A, 26.4.28
FOSTER, H	F		12.8.96	Darwen, Mar 1898
FRANCIS, TJ	F	Plymouth	Nottingham F, 3.9.81	Sampdoria, 30.7.82
FREEMAN, R	F	Droitwich	Bromsgrove R, 4.11.35	Exeter C, cs1939
FROST, R	F	Hazel Grove	Stockport Boys, 24.7.62	Kettering T, 30.6.65
FROST, S	HB	Poplar	Millwall, 4.5.01	Millwall, Mar 1907
FURR, G	F		Watford, 8.5.09	Watford, Nov 1910
FUTCHER, P	D	Chester	Luton T, 1.6.78	Oldham A, 31.7.80
FUTCHER, R	F	Chester	Luton T, 22.8.78	Minnesota Kicks, 14.4.79
GARNER, W	HB	Manchester	Heaton Park, 20.8.12	Southport, cs1919
GARTLAND, P	FB	Seaham	Seaham Harbour, 21.3.14	Retired, cs1917
GAUGHAN, W	F	Cardiff	Cardiff C, 9.6.14	Newport C, 28.7.19
GIBBONS, S	HB	Darlaston, Staffs	Cradley Heath, 14.4.27	Fulham, 12.5.30
GIBSON, T	F	Glasgow	Bridgetown Waverley, 5.7.26	South Shields, 16.5.27
GIDMAN, J	D	Liverpool	Manchester U, 21.10.86	
GILL, R	HB	Manchester	15.10.47	Chester, 6.6.51
GILLESPIE, W	F	Strathclyde	Lincoln C, 7.1.97	South Africa, cs1905
GILLIES, R	F		Bolton W, 2.2.96	Hearts, cs1896
GLENNON, C	F	Manchester	Manchester Boys, 13.8.65	Northwich Victoria, 23.7.71
GODFREY, J	HB		Coventry C, 21.11.19	Merthyr Town, cs1920
GODWIN, V	F	Blackpool	Blackburn R, June 1948	Stoke C, 4.6.49
GOLAC, I	FB	Yugoslavia	Bournemouth, 8.3.83	Bijelasica, Yugoslavia, 9.4.83
GOMERSALL, V	FB	Manchester	Juniors, 8.5.58	Swansea T, 13.8.66
GOODCHILD, A	G	Southampton	Southampton Comm, 2.12.11	Guildford City, 18.8.27
GOODWIN, E	F	Manchester	Leeds City, 17.10.19	Rochdale, 27.5.21
GORRINGE, F	F	Salford	Manchester Docks, 4.9.26	Lincoln C, 27.1.82
GOULD, W	F	Burton-on-Trent	Bradford C, 21.5.09	cs1912
GOW, G	M	Glasgow	Bristol C, 23.10.80	Rotherham U, 27.1.82
GRATRIX, R	HB	Salford	Blackpool, 18.9.64	Toronto, Canada, 27.4.65
GRAY, A	G	Tredegar	Oldham A, 6.1.27	Coventry C, 6.8.30
GRAY, G	HB	Bolton	June 1919	cs1922
GRAY, M	F	Renfrew	Third Lanark, 26.2.63	Port Elizabeth, 17.4.67
GREGG, W	FB	Woodhouse	Accrington S, 16.4.37	Chester, 11.11.38
GREALISH, T	M	Paddington	West Brom A, 23.10.86	
GREENWOOD, JJ	HB	Manchester	12.9.46	Exeter C, 20.6.49
GREGORY, C	HB	Doncaster	Doncaster R, 4.3.30	Reading, 1.3.34
GREGORY, J	FB		Bury, 21.5.05	Bolton W, cs1906
GRIEVE, R	F		Morton, 16.8.06	Accrington, 5.11.11
GUNN, J	F		Bolton W, 22.10.96	Clyde, Apr 1897
GUNNING, J	F	Helensburgh	Hibernian, 22.11.50	Barrow, 21.7.54
HARDINGTON, R	F	Scarborough	Oldham A, 3.11.50	Stockport C, 14.12.51
HALL, J	FB	Boldon	Barnsley, 15.5.13	cs1915
HALL, W	G		Bolton W, 6.9.06	Crystal P, Mar 1907
HALLIDAY, D	F	Dumfries	Arsenal, 20.11.30	Clapton Orient, 29.12.33
HALLOWS, H	HB		Southport Central, 2.5.1900	Southport Central, cs1901
HAMBLETT, G	HB		St Francis Gorton, cs1905	St Helens Rangers, cs 1908
HAMILL, M	HB	Belfast	Belfast Celtic, 29.9.20	Fall River, Boston, cs1924
HAMMOND, G	FB	Sudbury	Ipswich T, 20.10.74	Charlton A, 4.7.76
HANNAH, G	F	Liverpool	Lincoln C, 19.9.58	Notts Co, 10.7.64
HANNAWAY, J	FB	Bootle	Seaforth Fellowship, 26.4.50	Gillingham, 17.6.57
HANNEY, E	HB	Reading	Reading, 26.11.13	Coventry C, 19.11.19
HAREIDE, A	FB	Norway	Molde FK, 1.10.81	Norwich C, 7.7.83
HARGREAVES, J	F		Northwich Victoria, 9.2.93	Blackburn R, 3.9.95

379

NAME	Pos	BIRTHPLACE	FROM	TO
HARLEY, A	F	Glasgow	Third Lanark, 24.8.62	Birmingham C, 14.8.63
HARPER, J	FB		Newtown, 31.8.95	Chatham, cs1898
HARPER, W	G	Bothwell	Sunderland, 15.5.23	Crystal P, 24.5.24
HARRISON, J	F	Rhyl	Rhyl, 14.2.29	Sheffield U, 11.6.30
HART, JP	F	Golborne	Loughton YC, 8.12.44	Retired, 4.5.63
HARTFORD, A	MF	Clydebank	West Brom A, 13.8.74	Nottingham F, 27.6.79
			Everton, 1.10.81	Fort Lauderdale, USA, 8.5.84
HARVEY, H	F		Burslem Port Vale, 5.1.1900	Burton U, May 1901
HAYDOCK, B	F	Salford	Buxton T, 6.3.59	Crewe Alex, 8.3.61
HAYES, J	F	Kearsley	Bolton Sunday Lge, 28.8.53	Barnsley, 30.6.65
HEALE, J	F	Bristol	Bristol C, 24.1.34	Retired, cs1945
HEALEY, R	F	Manchester	Manchester Boys, 28.7.67	Cardiff C, 6.5.74
HEDLEY, F	F	Monkseaton	Nelson, 6.3.30	Chester, 7.7.31
HEINEMANN, G	HB	Stafford	Stafford Rangers, 19.10.28	Coverntry C, 29.5.31
HENDERSON, J	HB	Cowdenbeath	St Barnard's, 27.4.14	Southend U, cs1920
HENDERSON, J	F		Abercorn, 1.11.01	cs1902
HENDREN, E	F	Turnham Green	Brentford, 31.3.08	Coventry C, 22.10.09
HENRY, A	M	Houghton	Durham Boys, 29.7.74	Bolton W, 17.9.81
HENRY, W	FB	Glasgow	Leicester Fosse, 25.11.11	St Barnard's, July 1920
HENSON, P	M	Manchester	Brookdale YC, 26.5.69	Sheffield W, 6.2.75
HERD, A	F	Bowhill	Hamilton A, 1.2.33	Stockport C, 16.3.48
HESHAM, F	F	Manchester	Nov 1896	Crewe Alex, cs1901
HESLOP, G	HB	Wallsend	Everton, 14.9.65	Bury, 11.8.72
HICKS, G	F	Salford	Droylsden, 18.11.23	Birmingham, 24.10.28
HIGGS, F	G	Wellington-on-Tyne	Barnsley, 6.6.32	Aldershot T, cs1933
HILDERSLEY, R	F	Kirkcaldy	Kirkcaldy Schools, 8.6.81	Chester C, 30.6.84
HILL, F	MF	Sheffield	Halifax T, 4.5.70	Peterborough U, 25.5.73
HILL, P	FB		Everton, 9.11.06	Airdrie, Nov 1909
HILL, R	F		Sheffield U, 7.11.95	cs1897
HILLMAN, J	G	Tavistock	Burnley, 21.1.02	Millwall, 24.12.06
HINCE, P	F	Manchester	Local Amateurs, 2.6.66	Charlton A, 8.2.68
HINDMARSH, J	HB	Whitburn	Stockport C, 4.12.12	Newport C, Sept 1919
HITCHCOCK, E	F		Aston Villa, 11.3.09	cs1909
HOAD, S	F	Eltham	Blackpool, 22.5.11	Rochdale, cs1920
HODGKINSON, D	F	Banwell	Margate, 19.8.61	Stockport C, 12.6.64
HODGSON, R	HB	Birkenhead	Tranmere R, 25.10.44	Southport, 20.6.47
HOGAN, WJ	F	Salford	6.5.42	Carlisle U, 31.8.49
HOLFORD, T	HB	Henley	Stoke, 18.4.08	Stoke, cs1914
HOLMES, W	HB	Matlock	Chesterfield, July 1896	Clapton Orient, 19.8.05
HOPE, JG	F	East Wemyss	Ardear Recreation, 4.2.39	Queen of the South, Feb 1947
HOPKINS, R	F	Birmingham	Birmingham C, 1.9.86	West Brom A, 16.10.86
HOPKINS, W	HB		Derby County, cs1891	cs1894
HORNE, A	F	Birmingham	Southend U, 14.3.28	Preston NE, 20.9.29
HORNE, S	HB	Clanfield	Aston Villa, 24.9.65	Fulham, 21.2.69
HORRIDGE, P	FB	Manchester	Newton Heath Parish, 28.10.51	Crewe Alex, 2.6.59
HORSWILL, M	M	Annfield Plain	Sunderland, 11.3.74	Plymouth A, 14.7.75
HOSIE, J	HB	Glasgow	Blackburn R, 23.1.01	Stockport C, 31.10.02
HOWARD, F	F	Walkden	Walkden Wed, 18.9.12	New Brighton, cs1920
HOWE, F	F	Bredbury	Liverpool, 21.6.38	Grimsby T, 6.10.38
HOYLAND, J	M	Sheffield	Schools, 5.7.82	Bury, 31.7.86
HUGHES, E	HB	Wrexham	Wrexham, 16.12.12	Aberdare Ath, cs1920
HUGHES, J	F		20.3.94	cs1895
HUMPHREYS, R	FB	Oswestry	Oswestry T, 8.5.10	cs1912
HUNTER, R	FB		22.3.98	Stockport C, Mar 1903
HURST, D	F		Blackburn R, May 1901	Manchester U, 30.5.02
HUTCHINSON, G	G		24.9.94	cs1896
HUTCHISON, T	MF	Cardenden	Coventry C, 22.10.80	Bulova, Hong Kong, 1.7.82
HYNDS, T	HB	Hurlford	Glasgow Celtic, 27.9.01	Woolwich Arsenal, 7.12.06
INGHAM, T	F	Manchester	6.12.21	cs1923
JACKSON, B	FB	Manchester	Luton T, 1.5.07	Stalybridge Celtic, cs1911
JACKSON, G	M	Swinton	Schools, 20.7.81	Exeter C, Sept 1985
JACKSON, H	F	Blackburn	Burnley, 18.6.46	Preston NE, Dec 1947
JAMES, F	F		Halesowen, 1.7.09	Exeter C, July 1910
JARVIS, H	HB	Manchester	25.10.19	cs1921
JEFFRIES, D	D	Longsight	Manchester Boys, 22.7.66	Crystal P, 24.9.73
JOBLING, L	F	Sunderland	Norwich C, 14.2.12	Hartlepool U, cs1913
JOHNSON, D	F	Liverpool	Everton, 21.3.84	Tulsa Roughnecks, 31.5.84
JOHNSON, N	D	Rotherham	Rotherham U, 10.6.85	
JOHNSON, J	M	Cardiff	Welsh Schools, 10.8.70	Crystal P, 22.1.74
JOHNSON, T	F	Dalton-in-Furniss	Dalton Casuals, 22.2.19	Everton, 5.3.30
JOHNSTONE, R	F	Selkirk	Hibernian, 2.3.55	Hibernian, 22.9.59

NAME	Pos	BIRTHPLACE	FROM	TO
JONES, A	F	Llandudno	Small Heath, July 1893	cs1894
JONES, CH	F	Jersey, Channel Islands	Tottenham H, 23.8.82	Crystal P, 25.11.82
JONES, CM	F	Altrincham	Cheshire Boys, 8.12.62	Swindon T, 25.7.68
JONES, D	FB	Trevonei	Bolton W, 28.9.98	Died, Aug 1902
JONES, RS	HB		Everton, 3.6.94	South Shore, cs1895
JONES, RT	F	London	Millwall, 4.5.01	Millwall, cs1902
JONES, WJB	F	Liverpool	3.5.48	Chester, 12.6.51
JONES, WL	F	Chirk	Rushton Druids, 19.1.03	Southend U, Aug 1919
KEARY, A	F	Liverpool	Liverpool Dominion, 3.5.11	Port Vale, cs1912
KEEGAN, G	MF	Bradford	Schools, 6.8.71	Oldham A, 2.2.79
KELLY, P	F	Kilco, N Ireland	Belfast Celtic, 4.10.20	West Ham U, 4.7.23
KELLY, W	F	Newcastle	Newcastle U, 2.11.11	Blyth Spartans, Aug 1913
KELSO, T	FB	Renton	Third Lanark, 17.8.06	Dundee, 18.2.13
KENNEDY, B	FB	Motherwell	Kilmarnock, 20.7.61	Grimsby T, 3.3.69
KERR, A	F	Lugar, Ayr	Partick T, 15.5.59	Kilmarnock, 24.12.59
KEVAN, D	F	Ripon	Chelsea, 22.8.63	Crystal P, 29.7.65
KIDD, B	F	Manchester	Arsenal, 7.7.76	Everton, 29.3.79
KINSEY, S	F	Gorton	Manchester Boys, 30.5.79	Minnesota Kicks, 11.10.86
KIRKMAN, A	F	Bolton	Bacup Borough, 20.10.55	Rotherham U, 27.2.59
KNOWLES, F	HB	Manchester	Manchester U, 6.10.19	Stalybridge Celtic, cs1920
LAKE, P	M	Denton	Blue Star, 1.7.85	
LAMBIE, W	F	Larkhall	Queen's Park, Dec 1890	Queen's Park, cs1893
LAMPH, T	HB	Gateshead	Leeds City, 17.10.19	Derby County, 11.3.20
LANGFORD, L	G	Alfreton	Nottingham F, 4.6.30	Manchester U, 1.6.34
LANGLEY, K	M	St Helens	Everton, 26.3.87	
LAW, D	F	Aberdeen	Huddersfield T, 15.3.60	Torino, 13.7.61
			Manchester U, 2.7.73	Retired, 26.8.74
LAWRENCE, V	HB	Arbroath	Forfar Ath, 5.7.11	Oldham A, 31.5.13
LEE, FH	F	West Houghton	Bolton W, 9.10.67	Derby County, 14.8.74
LEE, S	F	Manchester	Stockport C, 5.9.79	Portland Timbers, 21.3.80
LEIGH, P	FB	Altrincham	Stamford Lads, 15.3.57	Crewe Alex, 16.6.61
LEIVERS, WE	FB	Bolsover	Chesterfeld, 27.11.53	Doncaster R, 10.7.64
LEMAN, D	F	Newcastle	Newcastle Boys, 13.7.70	Sheffield W, 31.12.76
LEONARD, P	F		St Mirren, 19.5.97	New Brompton, cs1898
			Thames Ironworks, May 1899	cs1900
LESLIE, A	HB	Methil, Greenock	25.1.23	Tranmere R, 31.7.25
LESTER, MJ	F	Manchester	Oldham A, 5.11.73	Washington Dip, 22.3.77
LEWIS, W	F		Chester, 10.9.96	Chester, Sept 1897
LEYLAND, J	HB	Northwich	Witton Albion, 31.8.20	Manchester NE, 1.12.22
LIEVESLEY, E	F	Netherthorpe	Staveley, May 1919	Southend U, 29.6.22
LILLIS, M	F	Manchester	Huddersfeild T, 7.8.85	Derby County, 7.8.86
LINACRE, B	F	Chesterfield	Chesterfield, 24.10.47	Middlesbrough, 10.9.49
LISTER, H	F	Manchester	25.12.54	Oldham A, 30.9.60
LITTLE, R	FB	Manchester	Greenwood Victoria, 6.8.49	Brighton & HA, 18.10.58
LITTLE, T	F		Derby County, 27.6.94	Baltimore, USA, 13.10.94
			Baltimore, USA, Nov 1894	Wellingborough, cs1896
LIVINGSTONE, G	F	Dumbarton	Liverpool, 13.5.03	Glasgow Rangers, Jan 1907
LLOYD, N	HB	Manchester	Manchester Central, 13.5.32	cs1935
LOMAX, G	FB	Droylsden	Schools, 24.7.81	Carlisle U, 5.12.85
LYALL, J	G	Dundee	Sheffield W, 15.9.09	Dundee, Apr 1911
LYON, W	HB	Clanchuscudden	Bristol R, 25.5.03	Preston NE, 4.3.04
McADAMS, B	F	Belfast	Distillery, 6.12.53	Bolton W, 2.9.60
McALINDEN, RJ	F	Salford	Salford Boys, 21.3.62	Toronto, Canada, 13.5.65
McBRIDE, J	HB		Liverpool, 16.11.94	Ashton NE, Sept 1897
McCABE, A	F		Rotherham T, 26.1.96	Rochdale, cs1896
McCARTHY, M	D	Barnsley	Barnsley, 14.12.83	Glasgow Celtic, May 1987
McCLELLAND, JB	F	Bradford	Manchester YMCA, 9.9.53	Lincoln C, 20.9.58
McCLOY, P	FB	Uddington	Ayr U, 27.8.25	Irish League, 4.8.32
McCONNELL, T	F		Moss End Swifts, July 1896	Woolwich Arsenal, cs1897
McCORMACK, M	F	Glasgow	Glasgow Rangers, Apr 1947	Blackpool, July 1947
McCOURT, FJ	HB	Portadown	Bristol R, 30.11.50	Colchester U, 17.6.54
McCOURT, J	HB	Glasgow	Sheffield U, 15.8.24	Dykehead, 21.10.25
McCULLOCH, K	HB	Larne	Belfast Celtic, 26.10.35	Northampton T, 11.3.38
McDONALD, RW	D	Aberdeen	Coventry C, 22.10.80	Oxford U, 9.9.83
MacDONALD, R	FB	Old Kilpatrick	Vale of Leven, 6.9.56	Bournemouth & BA, 12.8.63
McDOWELL, A	FB		28.7.93	cs1895
McDOWELL, LJ	HB	India	Sunderland, 14.3.38	Wrexham, 11.6.49
McGUIRE, P	FB	Manchester	Hurst FC, 15.8.12	Killed in Action, 25.10.16
McILROY, S	MF	Belfast	Stoke C, 1.8.85	Bury, 5.3.87
MacKENZIE, S	M	Romford	Crystal P, 27.7.79	West Brom A, 13.8.81
McLEOD, E	F	Glasgow	East Fife, 17.11.38	Hibernian, 30.8.40
McLEOD, J	F	Glasgow	Larne, 2.12.35	Millwall, 7.7.37

NAME	Pos	BIRTHPLACE	FROM	TO
McLUCKIE, J	HB	Stonehouse	Hamilton A, 1.2.33	Aston Villa, 5.12.34
McMAHON, J	FB		Preston NE, 17.11.02	Bury, 7.12.06
McMORRAN, EJ	F	Larne	Belfast Celtic, 31.7.47	Leeds U, 18.1.49
McMULLAN, J	HB	Derry	Partick T, 10.2.26	Oldham A, 15.5.33
McNAB, N	MF	Greenock	Brighton & HA, 20.7.83	
McNAUGHT, K	D	Kirkcaldy	West Brom A, 21.12.84	West Brom A, 4.3.85
McOUSTRA, W	HB		Glasgow Celtic, 31.1.02	Blackpool, 9.10.07
MacRAE, K	G	Glasgow	Motherwell, 17.10.73	Portland Timbers, 4.3.81
McREDDIE, W	F		Stoke, 3.10.94	Bolton W, 28.12.95
McTAVISH, JR	HB	Glasgow	Dalry Thistle, 12.6.52	St Mirren, 2.11.60
McVICKERS, J	FB		Accrington, 25.3.92	Macclesfield, cs1894
MALEY, W	HB		Glasgow Celtic, 30.10.94	Glasgow Celtic, Mar 1896
MANN, AF	FB	Burntisland	Hearts, 25.11.68	Notts C, 6.7.72
MANN, G	HB		Blackburn R, 2.7.94	Bristol C, Aug 1897
MANSFIELD, E	F		Northern Normads, 18.3.09	cs1909
MARSDEN, K	HB	Darley Dale	Chesterfield, July 1955	Accrington S, 25.6.59
MARSH, R	F	Hatfield	Queen's Park R, 8.3.72	Tampa Bay Rowdies, 12.1.76
MARSHALL, R	F	Hucknall	Sunderland, 1.3.28	Stockport C, 22.3.39
MAY, A	MF	Bury	Schools, 23.5.80	
MEADOWS, J	FB	Bolton	Southport, 16.3.51	Retired, 17.10.57
			Retirement, 16.3.61	Retired, 30.6.61
MEECHAN, P	FB		Southampton, 15.9.1900	Barrow, cs1901
MELLOR, I	F	Sale	Wythenshawe Schs, 13.11.67	Norwich C, 7.3.73
MELROSE, J	F	Glasgow	Glasgow Celtic, 7.11.84	Charlton A, 24.3.86
MEREDITH, W	F	Chirk	Chirk, 19.10.94	Manchester U, 5.12.06
			Manchester U, 25.7.21	Retired, cs1924
MIDDLETON, H	HB		Derby Junction, 19.3.92	Loughborough T, Feb 1894
MILARVIE, R	F		Newton Heath, cs1891	cs1896
MILLER, J	HB		Bolton W, 11.3.96	Bolton W, cs1896
MILLER, J	F		Hamilton A, 18.8.02	South Africa, Oct 1903
MILNE, J	HB		Bolton W, cs1890	cs1894
MILSOM, J	F	Bristol	Bolton W, 25.2.38	Retired, cs1940
MITCHELL, J		Manchester	Preston NE, 9.5.22	Leicester C, 6.10.26
MOFFATT, J	HB	Paisley	St Mirren, 20.5.03	Kilmarnock, cs1906
MOFFATT, R	HB	Dumfries	St Mirren, 17.8.95	Kilmarnock, cs1907
MOONEY, F	F		Bootle, 15.11.92	Bury, June 1895
MORGAN, H	F		Newton Heath, 31.7.01	Accrington, cs1902
MORRIS, H	F	Chirk	Chirk, March 1891	Sheffield U, 1.12.93
			Sheffield U, 7.11.95	Grimsby T, May 1896
MORRIS, H	F	Hardgate	Clyde, 16.8.22	Nottingham F, 6.7.24
MOULDEN, P	F	Bolton	Bolton Boys, 4.6.84	
MULHEARN, KJ	G	Liverpool	Stockport C, 21.9.67	Shrewsbury T, 10.3.71
MULLIGAN, J	FB	Belfast	Belfast Celtic, 20.11.20	Southport, 10.9.23
MUNDY, J	F	Wythenshawe	Ashland Rovers, 16.8.66	Bangor C, 20.6.71
MUNN, S	HB	Glasgow	Grimsby T, 23.11.97	cs1901
MUNRO, JF	F	Garmouth	Waterford, 24.11.47	Oldham A, 16.3.50
MURPHY, W	F	St Helens	Alexandra Victoria, 2.2.18	Southampton, 18.8.26
MURRAY, H	F	Drybridge	Dalry Thistle, 4.4.54	Altrincham, June 1960
MURRAY, JR	F	Elvington	Wolves, 5.11.63	Walsall, 3.5.67
MURRAY, W	F	Burnley	Arbroath, 29.1.47	Macclesfield T, 1.8.50
NASH, J	HB		Nelson, 5.6.94	cs1895
NAYLOR, J	HB	Crompton	Newcastle U, 6.10.32	Oldham A, 16.2.33
NEILSON, R	HB	Blackhall	Dawdon Colliery, 26.9.35	Droylsden, cs1947
NELSON, J	F	Manchester	31.1.11	cs1912
NEWTON, W	FB	Romiley	Droylsden, 16.2.16	Southend U, cs1920
NICHOLLS, J	G	Bilston	Bilston U, 12.5.32	Brentford, 14.5.34
NIXON, E	G	Harpurley	Curzon Ashton, 13.10.83	
NORGROVE, F	FB	Hyde	Glossop, 15.4.04	cs1912
OAKES, A	HB	Winsford	Mid-Cheshire Boys, 9.4.58	Chester, 17.7.76
OAKES, J	F	Hamilton	Blackburn R, 12.6.48	Queen of the South, 11.6.51
OAKES, T	F	Manchester	Manchester U, 14.4.47	Goslings FC, cs1948
O'BRIEN, J	F		15.9.93	Walsall Town S, Nov 1893
OGDEN, TREVOR	F	Culcheth	24.10.63	Doncaster R, June 1965
OGLEY, A	G	Barnsley	Barnsley, 27.7.63	Stockport C, 21.9.67
O'NEILL, M	MF	Kilrea, N Ireland	Norwich C, 24.6.81	Norwich C, 29.1.82
ORR, W	FB		Glossop, 12.7.01	Fulham, cs1903
OWEN, GA	MF	Whiston	Manchester Boys, 5.8.74	West Brom A, 30.5.79
OWEN, R	F	Bolton	Bury, 18.7.68	Carlisle U, 29.6.70
OWEN, W	F	Llanfairfechan	Northwich Victoria, 22.6.34	Tranmere R, 12.3.36
OXFORD, K	G	Manchester	Ardwich LC, 5.11.47	Derby County, 31.12.48

NAME	Pos	BIRTHPLACE	FROM	TO
PALMER, RN	F	Manchester	Manchester Boys, 26.5.75	Oldham A, 19.11.80
PANTER, D	F	Blackpool	Chorlton Lads, 15.10.60	Torquay U, 18.5.64
PARDOE, G	FB	Winsford	Mid-Cheshire Boys, 26.7.61	Retired, 30.4.76
PARK, T	F	Liverpool	Stockport C, 11.1.83	Bury, 31.5.83
PARLANE, D	F	Helensburgh	Leeds U, 20.7.83	Swansea C, 18.1.85
PATTERSON, W	F		Hibernian, June 1896	Stockport C, cs1897
PAUL, R	HB	Ton Pentre	Swansea T, 18.7.50	Worcester C, 8.6.57
PAYNE, J	F	Southall	Brentford, 5.1.31	Brighton & HA, cs1934
PEARSON, F	F	Manchester	Preston NE, 6.6.03	Chelsea, 2.10.05
PEARSON, H	F		Bredbury, 23.3.21	cs1923
PENNINGTON, J	F	Golborne	Juniors, 6.12.55	Crewe Alex, 8.3.61
PERCIVAL, J	HB	Low Patrington	Durham C, 20.10.32	Bournemouth & BA, 23.5.47
PERCIVAL, P	F	Reddish	Ashton-National, 15.12.31	Sheffield W, 10.5.35
PHILLIPS, D	MF	Wegberg, W Germany	Plymouth A, 26.7.84	Coventry C, 30.5.86
PHILLIPS, E	FB	North Shields	South Shields, 30.5.47	Hull C, 9.11.51
PHILLIPS, J	G	Weston Rhyn	Chirk, 25.3.25	Retired, cs1927
PHOENIX, RJ	HB	Stretford	Humphrey Park, 11.3.50	Rochdale, 9.6.60
PICKFORD, E	F		13.9.93	cs1894
PLATT, J	F		May 1896	cs1897
PLENDERLEITH, JB	HB	Bellshill	Hibernian, 3.7.60	Queen of the South, 5.9.63
PORTEOUS, T	FB		Rotherham T, 22.1.96	Rotherham T, Mar 1896
POWELL, RWH	G	Knighton	Knighton T, 20.11.48	Chesterfield, 13.6.52
POWER, P	MF	Openshaw	Manchester Boys, 11.8.73	Everton, 27.6.86
PRINGLE, C	HB	Nitshill	St Mirren, 21.6.22	Manchester Central, cs1928
PRITCHARD, HJ	F	Meriden	Crsytal P, 9.3.38	Southend U, 10.2.47
RACE, H	F	Evenswood	Liverpool, 2.8.30	Nottingham F, 27.6.33
RAMSEY, D	HB		Wishaw, 11.5.09	cs1910
RANKIN, B	F	Glasgow	West Brom A, 2.2.07	Luton T, cs1907
RANSON, R	FB	St Helens	15.7.76	Birmingham C, 15.11.84
RAY, D	FB	Newcastle-under-Lyme	Burslem Port Vale, May 1896	Non-League, cs1900
			Non-League, 24.9.02	Stockport C, cs1903
READ, T	FB	Manchester	Stretford, 31.8.95	Manchester U, 28.8.02
REDMOND, S	HB	Liverpool	Liverpool Boys, 1.7.84	
REEVES, KP	F	Burley	Norwich C, 11.3.80	Burnley, 8.7.83
REGAN, E	HB		May 1893	Burslem Port Vale, cs1894
REGAN, R	F	Falkirk	Partick T, 20.8.36	Dundee, 9.7.37
REID, J	HB	Hebburn-on-Tyne	South Shields, cs1919	Stockport C, 19.10.20
REID, NS	MF	Davyhulme	Whitehall Juniors, 30.4.77	Seattle Sounders, 10.5.82
			Seattle Sounders, 4.10.82	
REVIE, D	F	Middlesbrough	Hull C, 18.10.51	Sunderland, 10.11.56
RIDDING, W	F	Heswell	Tranmere R, 6.3.30	Manchester U, 23.12.31
RIDLEY, J	FB	Mickley	South Shields, 13.6.27	Reading, 28.6.33
RIGBY, J	HB	Golborne	Bryn Boys Brigade, 12.12.46	Peterborough U, 14.3.54
ROBERTS, C	F	Halesowen	Brentford, 5.1.31	Exeter C, 26.2.32
ROBERTS, F	F	Sandbach	Bolton W, 18.10.22	Manchester Central, 14.6.29
ROBERTSON, D	F		18.10.93	cs1894
ROBERTSON, G	HB	Failsworth	Ashton-National, 17.3.27	Southend U, 1.8.33
ROBERTSON, J	F		Stoke, 28.2.96	cs1896
ROBINSON, J	G	Oswaldtwistle	Accrington S, 16.4.37	Bury, 26.11.46
ROBINSON, L	F		Notts C, June 1896	cs1897
ROBINSON, MJ	F	Leicester	Preston NE, 25.6.79	Brighton & HA, 13.7.80
ROBINSON, P	HB	Manchester	Juniors, 7.5.40	Chesterfield, 24.10.47
ROBINSON, R	F		cs1893	Wolves, 8.1.94
ROBINSON, W	HB	Prescott	Bolton W, 2.10.02	Hull C, 16.5.05
ROBSON, D	FB		Ayr U, May 1890	Wolves, 8.1.94
			Wolves, 30.11.94	Millwall, cs1896
RODGER, C	F	Ayr	Ayr U, 2.12.35	Northampton T, 11.3.38
ROGERS, J	HB	Normanton	Oswestry T, 9.2.35	Chesterfield, 28.5.38
ROSS, D	F	Over-Darwen	Norwich C, 14.2.07	Dundee, 11.7.12
ROSS, J	F	Glasgow	Burnley, 24.2.99	Died, 12.6.02
ROWAN, A	F		Burton Swifts, 5.8.94	cs1896
ROWLEY, H	F	Bilston	Manchester U, 23.12.31	Oldham A, 16.2.33
ROYLE, J	F	Liverpool	Everton, 24.12.74	Bristol C, 15.12.77
ROYLE, S	F	Manchester	Heaton Chapel, cs1918	cs1922
RUDD, JJ	F	Hull	Teremure Ath, 25.1.38	York C, 17.3.47
RUSSELL, D	HB		Nottingham F, 21.7.92	Hearts, cs1893
RYAN, J	MF	Lewisham	Sheffield U, 7.1.82	Stockport C, 1.7.83
SADDINGTON, H	F		cs1893	cs1894
SALT, G	F		21.1.11	cs1913
SAMBROOK, R	F	Wolverhampton	Coventry C, 2.1.58	Doncaster R, 20.6.62
SAVAGE, JA	G	Bromley	Halifax T, 17.11.53	Walsall, 17.1.58

NAME	Pos	BIRTHPLACE	FROM	TO
SCOTSON, J	F		16.5.98	Stockport C, 15.9.03
SCOTT, S	HB	Macclesfield	Northwich Victoria, 1.5.13	Norwich C, 14.6.21
SEAR, C	FB	Rhostyllen	Oswestry T, 7.6.55	Chester, 25.4.68
SHADWELL, J	HB	Bury	Turton, 24.5.33	Exeter C, 13.7.36
SHARP, S	HB	Manchester	Bolton W, 18.4.18	Crewe Alex, 29.6.29
SHARPLES, J	F	Blackburn	Rossendale, 9.6.94	Wigan Co, cs1897
SHAWCROSS, D	HB	Stretford	Manchester Boys, 27.7.56	Stockport C, 10.6.65
SHINTON, B	F	West Bromwich	Wrexham, 2.6.79	Newcastle U, 6.3.80
SIDDALL, B	G	Ellesmere Port	Stoke C(loan), 26.3.86	Stoke C, 6.5.86
SILKMAN, B	F	London	Plymouth A, 29.3.79	Brentford, 29.7.80
SIMPSON, A	F	Salford	13.5.21	cs1923
SIMPSON, P	F	Carlisle	Cumbria Boys, 26.7.82	
SINCLAIR, G	FB	Paisley	Glasgow Celtic, 16.11.84	Glasgow Celtic, 30.11.84
SLATER, P	FB		Blackburn R, 9.5.1900	Bury, cs1904
SMELT, T	F	Rotherham	Morecambe, 28.4.27	Oldham A, 26.4.28
SMITH, FE	F	Draycott	Sheffield U, 10.5.52	Grimsby T, 17.9.52
SMITH, GR	F	Fleetwood	Salford Adelphi LC, cs1938	Chesterfield, 18.10.51
SMITH, G	F	Kilwinning	Brighton & HA, 21.3.84	Oldham A, 10.2.86
SMITH, H	FB		Blackburn R, 25.5.94	Stalybridge R, cs1895
SMITH, J	F	Burton-on-Trent	Burton U, 4.11.09	South Shields, 13.3.14
SMITH, R	HB	Walkden	Walkden, 30.9.20	Pontypridd, cs1924
SMITH, Walter(St'prt)	F		Stockport C, cs1897	Stockport C, 23.8.1900
SMITH, Walter	G	Leicester	Leicester Fosse, 4.7.06	Port Vale, 19.10.20
SMITH, Wlm(Buxton)	HB		Buxton, 24.4.97	cs1902
SOWDEN, W	F	Manchester	Greenwood Victoria, 16.4.49	Chesterfield, 29.11.54
SPITTLE, A	F		27.9.93	cs1894
SPOTTISWOOD, J	F	Carlisle	Carlisle U, 28.8.13	Bury, 7.5.14
SPROSTON, B	FB	Sandbach	Tottenham H, 4.11.38	Ashton U, Aug 1950
SPURDLE, W	F	Guernsey, CI	Oldham A, 21.1.50	Port Vale, 23.11.56
STEELE, A	HB		Ayr U, 17.1.06	Tottenham H, 27.8.08
STEELE, F	FB		11.10.92	cs1894
STENSON, J	HB		21.9.93	cs1894
STEPANOVIC, D	D	Rekovac, Yugoslavia	Wormatia, W Gmny, 14.8.79	Wormatia, W Gmny, Jly '81
STEWART, G	F	Wishaw	Hibernian, 5.5.06	Partick T, June 1911
STEWART, P	F	Manchester	Blackpool, 19.3.87	
STOBART, B	F	Doncaster	Wolves, 14.8.64	Aston Villa, 13.11.64
STONES, H	G	Manchester	22.9.92	Newton Heath, cs1894
SULLIVAN, D	MF		Galsgow Celtic, 12.9.83	Morton, 20.10.83
SUGDEN, F	FB	Gorton	Droylsden, cs1917	Tranmere R, cs1920
SUGRUE, P	F	Coventry	Nuneaton Boro, 18.2.80	Cardiff C, July 1981
SUCKLING, P	G	Hackney	Coventry C, 30.5.86	
SUMMERBEE, MG	F	Cheltenham	Swindon T, 20.8.65	Burnley, 13.6.75
SWANN, J	G	Broughton	Northern Nomads, 16.10.09	cs1912
SWIFT, FV	G	Blackpool	Fleetwood, 21.10.32	Retired, Sept 1949
SYME, R	F	Sth Queensferry	Dunfermline, 8.8.30	Burnley, 13.7.34
TAIT, D	HB		Renton, May 1896	Darwen, Mar 1897
TAIT, T	F	Hetton-le-Hole	Southport, 7.3.28	Bolton W, 28.11.30
TAYLOR, H	F	Burslem	Huddersfield T, 1.6.12	cs1921
TAYLOR, KV	FB	Manchester	Manchester Trans, 26.8.54	Buxton, July 1960
TELFORD, WA	F	Carlisle	Burnley, 7.8.75	Peterborough U, 8.9.75
THOMPSON, F	FB	Egerton	Atherton, 27.2.21	Swindon T, 17.8.27
THOMPSON, GH	G	Swallow Nest	Preston NE, 30.7.56	Carlisle U, 13.6.57
THOMPSON, J	F		Oldham A, 19.8.20	Stalybridge Celtic, 11.6.21
THORNLEY, I	F	Glossop	Glossop, 7.4.04	South Shields, 12.8.12
THRELFALL, F	F		23.6.98	Fulham, 9.6.07
THURLOW, ACE	G	Depwade	Huddersfield T, 26.9.46	Retired, June 1950
TILSON, SF	F	Barnsley	Barnsley, 14.3.28	Northampton T, 11.3.38
TOLMIE, J	F	Glasgow	Lokeren, Belgium, 25.7.83	
TOMPKINSON, H	F		Longsight St Johns, 8.9.94	cs1899
TONGE, J	F		17.10.96	cs1900
TOSELAND, E	F	Northampton	Coventry C, 11.3.29	Sheffield W, 15.3.39
TOWERS, AM	MF	New Moston	Manchester Boys, 24.7.67	Sunderland, 11.3.74
TOWNLEY, W	F	Blackburn	Darwen, 20.8.96	Mar 1897
TRAUTMANN, BC	G	Bremen, W Germany	St Helens T, 2.11.49	Retired, 10.5.64
TUEART, D	F	Newcastle	Sunderland, 11.3.74	New York Cosmos, 13.2.78
			New York Cosmos, 31.1.80	Stoke C, 9.7.83
TURNBULL, S	F	Hurlford	Hurlford, 27.7.02	Manchester U, 5.12.06
TURNBULL, RW	F	Newbiggin	Sunderland, 9.9.49	Swansea T, 24.1.51
TURNER, H	F		Stoke, 26.1.1893	cs1893
TYLER, HE	HB	Sheffield	Sheffield W, cs1916	Stalybridge Celtic, 21.5.21
UTLEY, G	HB	Elscar	Sheffield U, 20.9.22	Bristol C, cs1923

NAME	Pos	BIRTHPLACE	FROM	TO
VARADI, I	F	Paddington	West Brom A, 16.10.86	
VILJOEN, C	MF	Johannesburg	Ipswich T, 15.8.78	Chelsea, 13.3.80
WAGSTAFFE, D	F	Manchester	Manchester Boys, 30.8.58	Wolves, 26.12.64
WALKER, J	FB		Everton, 3.10.94	Leicester Fosse, 26.5.95
WALL, LJ	HB	Shrewsbury	Glossop, 8.10.10	Dundee, Nov 1913
WALLACE, A	F		Blackpool, 5.6.94	Baltimore, USA, 13.10.94
WALLACE, W	F	Blaydon-on-Tyne	Newburn, 2.10.11	Bolton W, cs1914
WALMSLEY, C	G	Burnley	Burnley, 12.9.31	Reading, 30.5.32
WALSH, M	D	Blackley	Fort Lauderdale, 14.10.83	Blackpool, 31.1.84
WALSH, W	HB	Dublin	Manchester U, 5.5.36	Chelmsford C, 11.4.51
WARDLE, W	F	Houghton-le-Spring	Southport, 14.10.37	Grimsby T, 14.7.39
WARHURST, R	HB	Sheffield	Birmingham C, 3.6.57	Crewe Alex, 16.3.59
WARNER, J	F	Woolwich	Custorn House, 5.4.21	Watford, 22.5.26
WATSON, DV	D	Stapleford	Sunderland, 13.6.75	Werder Bremen, 21.6.79
WATSON, L	F		Southport Central, 18.7.01	Blackburn R, 14.10.02
WEBB, C	F		Dundee, 6.3.08	Airdrie, June 1909
WEBB, GW	F	East London	West Ham U, 18.7.12	Retired, Nov 1912
WEBSTER, E	HB	Manchester	16.2.52	30.6.53
WEIR, D	F	Aldershot	Bolton W, May 1890	Bolton W, 26.1.93
WESTCOTT, D	F	Wallasey	Blackburn R, 14.2.50	Chesterfield, 13.6.52
WESTWOOD, E	HB	Mancheser	Manchester U, 13.11.37	Altrincham, 10.6.53
WHARTON, JE	F	Bolton	Preston NE, 8.3.47	Blackburn R, 12.6.48
WHELAN, AM	F	Salford	Manchester U, 15.3.73	Rochdale, 1.7.74
WHITE, D	F	Urmston	Salford Boys, 4.6.84	
WHITE, HK	HB	Timperley	Cheshire Boys, 28.8.70	Bangor C, 22.6.73
WHITEHEAD, J	F	Church	Blackburn R, 12.9.97	Retired, cs1899
WHITFIELD, K	F	Bishop Auckland	Wolves, 27.2.53	Brighton & HA, July 1954
WHITTAKER, J	F		Barnsley, 2.2.04	Clapton Orient, cs1906
			Clapton Orient, 16.1.07	Clapton Orient, 15.8.08
WHITTLE, D	HB		Halliwell, cs1890	Bolton W, Aug 1894
WILKINSON, J	HB	Darlington	Darlington St Agnes, 28.11.06	cs1912
WILLEY, W	F		22.12.93	cs1894
WILLIAMS, A	G	Moss Side	Manchester Boys, 11.7.78	Port Vale, 23.1.87
WILLIAMS, CA	G	Welling	Royal Arsenal, 5.6.94	Tottenham H, cs1902
WILLIAMS, D	G	Mold	Mold A, May 1951	Wrexham, cs1954
WILLIAMS, E	FB	Manchester	Brindle Heath, 10.3.45	Halifax T, Oct 1951
WILLIAMS, F	F	Manchester	South Shore, 24.11.96	Manchester U, 4.6.02
WILLIAMSON, J	F	Manchester	Manchester Transport, 25.8.49	Blackburn R, 14.3.56
WILSON, C	MF	Greenheys	Moss Side Ams, 5.12.79	Chelsea, 19.3.87
WILSON, J	FB		Lincoln C, 10.12.97	cs1898
WILSON, W	HB	Middlesbrough	Hurst FC, 11.5.21	Stockport C, 10.8.27
WOOD, AEH	F	Macclesfield	Apprentice, 25.7.61	Shrewsbury T, 25.6.66
WOOD, J	F		Derby County, 14.6.07	Plymouth A, cs1909
WOODCOCK, W	F	Manchester	Manchester U, 5.5.20	Stockport C, cs1922
WOODROFFE, LC	F	Portsmouth	26.10.45	Watford, 16.6.47
WOOSNAM, M	HB	Newtown	Corinthians, 8.11.19	Northwich Victoria, Oct 1925
WOOSNAM, PA	F	Caersws	Bangor C, July 1951	Sutton U, July 1954
WRIGHTSON, FW	F	Sheldon	Darlington, 14.3.30	Fulham, 16.3.32
WRIGHT, N	F	Ushaw Moor	Accrington S, 20.5.33	Watford, 31.5.35
WYNN, GA	F	Oswestry	Wrexham, 21.4.09	Coventry C, 19.11.19
YATES, J	F		Burnley, 5.11.92	Sheffield U, 1.12.93
YOUNG, A	F		Tottenham H, 4.11.11	Sth Liverpool, cs1912
YOUNG, J	HB		Port Glasgow Ath, 6.10.05	Glasgow League, cs1907
YOUNG, NJ	F	Fellowsfield	Manchester Boys, 15.5.59	Preston NE, 21.1.72
YUILL, JG	F		Northern Nomads, 9.3.06	Stockport C, 17.6.07
			Stockport C, 8.1.09	cs1909

Matt Gray

Wyn Davies

Roy Donnelly

Jack Heale

Jimmy Murray

Asa Hartford scores a goal against Arsenal at Highbury in October 1975.

David Wagstaffe   Dave Watson

Joe Royle

Peter Barnes

Mick Channon

Trevor Francis (left) became the first British player to feature in two £1-million transfer deals when he signed for Manchester City in time for the third match of 1981-2. He came to Maine Road for £1.2 million and left in the close season of 1982 for the Italian club, Sampdoria, for a reported loss to City of half a million pounds. Add to that the player's wages, reported to be £2,000 per week, and City paid a high price for Francis' 12 League goals in 26 games. After recovering from an injury early in the season, Francis had been quite successful for City in the short term but his spell at Maine Road was, nonetheless, another example of a big-money signing which failed to reap even bigger rewards.

City v United

The Manchester 'derby' game has always been one of soccer's biggest occasions. The following lists every competitive first-team game played between the two clubs in peacetime.

Football League

1894-5
City 2   Newton Heath 5
Newton Heath 4   City 1

1895-6
Newton Heath 1   City 1
City 2   Newton Heath 1

1896-7
City 0   Newton Heath 0
Newton Heath 2   City 1

1897-8
Newton Heath 1   City 1
City 0   Newton Heath 1

1898-9
Newton Heath 3   City 0
City 4   Newton Heath 0

1902-03
United 1   City 1
City 0   United 2

1906-07
City 3   United 0
United 1   City 1

1907-08
United 3   City 1
City 0   United 0

1908-09
City 1   United 2
United 3   City 1

1909-10
United 2   City 1
City 1   United 1

1911-12
City 0   United 0
United 0   City 0

1912-13
United 0   City 1
City 0   United 2

1913-14
City 0   United 2
United 0   City 1

1914-15
United 0   City 0
City 1   United 1

1919-20
City 3   United 3
United 1   City 0

1920-21
United 1   City 1
City 3   United 0

1921-2
City 4   United 1
United 3   City 1

1925-6
City 1   United 1
United 1   City 6

1928-9
City 2   United 2
United 1   City 2

1929-30
United 1   City 3
City 0   United 1

1930-31
City 4   United 1
United 1   City 3

1936-7
United 3   City 2
City 1   United 0

1947-8
City 0   United 0
United 1   City 1

1948-9
City 0   United 0
United 0   City 0

1949-50
United 2   City 1
City 1   United 2

1951-2
City 1   United 2
United 1   City 1

1952-3
City 2   United 1
United 1   City 1

1953-4
City 2   United 0
United 1   City 1

1954-5
City 3   United 2
United 0   City 5

1955-6
City 1   United 0
United 2   City 1

1956-7
United 2   City 0
City 2   United 4

1957-8
United 4   City 1
City 2   United 2

1958-9
City 1   United 1
United 4   City 1

1959-60
City 3   United 0
United 0   City 0

1960-61
United 5   City 1
City 1   United 3

1961-2
United 3   City 2
City 0   United 2

1962-3
United 2   City 3
City 1   United 1

1966-7
United 1   City 0
City 1   United 1

1967-8
City 1   United 2
United 1   City 3

1968-9
City 0   United 0
United 0   City 1

1969-70
City 4   United 0
United 1   City 2

1970-71
United 1   City 4
City 3   United 4

1971-2
City 3   United 3
United 1   City 3

1972-3
City 3   United 0
United 0   City 0

1973-4
City 0   United 0
United 0   City 1

1975-6
City 2   United 2
United 2   City 0

1976-7
City 1   United 3
United 3   City 1

1977-8
City 3   United 1
United 2   City 2

1978-9
United 1   City 0
City 0   United 3

1979-80
City 2   United 0
United 1   City 0

1980-81
United 2   City 2
City 1   United 0

1981-2
City 0   United 0
United 1   City 1

1982-3
United 2   City 2
City 1   United 2

1985-6
City 0   United 3
United 2   City 2

1986-7
City 1   United 1
United 2   City 0

FA Cup

1925-6
United 0   City 3

1954-5
City 2   United 0

1969-70
United 3   City 0

1986-7
United 1   City 0

League Cup

1969-70
City 2   United 1
United 2   City 2

1974-5
United 1   City 0

1975-6
City 4   United 0

FA Charity Shield

1956-7
United 1   City 0

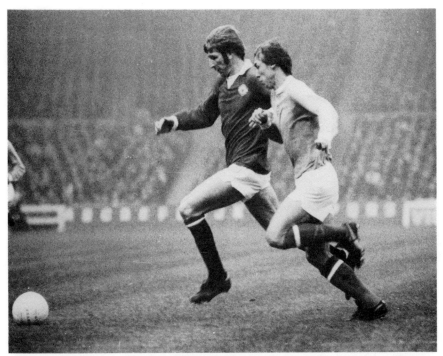

Above: Derek Jeffries (City) and Wyn Davies (United) battle for the ball during the Manchester derby of November 1972. Below: Joe Jordan (United) tussles with Dave Watson (City) in September 1978.

Graham Baker

Kenny Clements

Mick McCarthy

Neil McNab

SUBSCRIBERS

4 Ray Goble	53 John Watson	102 Donald Jepson
5 Andrew Ward	54 John Cocking	103 David J Miller
6 John A Harris	55 Stephen E Messenger	104 Alan Corr
7 Derek Hyde	56 Joseph Harkin	105 H B Ford
8 Philip Zech	57 Roger G Major	106 I Pawlett
9 Andrew Milarvie	58 Paul Devine	107 Julie Manns
10 Graham Ward	59 Roger Whitworth	108 Eric Mellor
11 Michael W Doherty	60 Chas Spencer	109 H Crabtree
12 Brendan Gahan	61 B Ganley	110 Jason Allcroft
13 A & J A Waterman	62 H V Dixon	111 E Howell
14 Stanley Ratcliffe	63 Neville Walker	112 William Dugdale
15 Stanley Ratcliffe	64 Alan Lockett	113 Arthur Moores
16 John Terence Dillon Casey	65 Karen Gillespie	114 P Hangle
17 Kåre M Torgrimsen	66 John Hughes	115 Christopher Anthony Butler
18 William Needs	67 H Lane	116 George H Reece
19 Harald Lohr	68 John Hopkinson	117 F Broadbent
20 Peter Pickup	69 John Wragg	118 R J Clarke
21 John Qvarnberg	70 James J Murphy	119 A Corbishley
22 R G Woolman	71 Robert John Passmore	120 Stephen King
23 M Swart	72 T Whitworth	121 Ian Bunting
24 Richard Stocken	73 J F J Burgess	122 Douglas Mellon
25 Harry Thompson	74 Stephen Quinn	123 Christopher Roberts
26 Mark Southwell	75 Michael Sheldon	124 Michael Milton
27 Christian Bastianelli	76 Grahame Michael Lutley	125 Roderick Hall
28 J Gardiner	77 David J Sheppard	126 Brian Tabner
29 Carsten Grønning	78 Raymond Keith Caukill	127 Matthew Traverse
30 Domenico Polimeno	79 Thomas Foran	128 Ronald Beggs
31 David Alexander Hurst	80 Arthur A Richardson	129 Pat McDonagh
32 Ian Griffiths	81 Arthur A Richardson	130 Peter Rogers
33 G Protheroe	82 David Maycock	131 Thomas Muir
34 Roger Hudson	83 Robert Gillespie	132 Imteaz Akhtar
35 Derek T Bryant	84 Daivd I Henshaw	133 Dave Royle
36 George Walker	85 J T Finnigan	134 Kevin Fowles
37 Gary James	86 Albert Evans	135 Martin Wakeling
38 Arnold Victor	87 Anthony Farrar	136 Alan Bates
39 Bert Eaton	88 Mark Lever	137 J Davies
40 Colin MacBean	89 John McDermott	138 Kevin T Lawman
41 W Phillips	90 Alan Worthington	139 Peter Horridge
42 Darren Storey	91 Ray Gillespie	10 Philip Gibbons
43 Maurice E Cummings	92 John A Gillespie	141 Stephen Gibbons
44 Austin N Fletcher	93 Sidney Horton	142 P Flanagan
45 David Moores	94 William Paul Barry	143 G Flanagan
46 William Burns	95 Steven J Wilson	144 B Flanagan
47 Thomas Mills	96 John Brownhill	145 Michael Crook
48 Alfred McClughan	97 Simon John Brownhill	146 Stephen O'Mara
49 Leslie McDonald	98 A T Morrison	147 Mattew Grandin
50 Michael Maybury	99 Brian Wainwright	148 Martin David Hurst
51 Kenneth McDonald	100 Alan Robert Benson	149 David J B Holgate
52 Neville A Phillips	101 Kevin Dermody	150 Philip M Holgate

151	Ian P Hitchen	208	I R Gerrard	265	Glyn Lloyd Edwards
152	William Charles Catchpole	209	R J Derbyshire	266	Mrs G Mackie
153	Nigel D Baguley	210	H Makin	267	Peter James McDonald
154	John Huxstep	211	Graham Waring	268	D J Nelson
155	Garry John Turner	212	Keith Lowe	269	Jack Conway
156	G Dyer	213	H Carrington	270	Larry Wilson
157	Barry Salt	214	F R Genders	271	Kevin Newburn
158	J R M Fielden	215	Alan Taylor	272	Geoff Thomas
159	G C Richbell	216	Gordon John Hyslop	273	M Tidswell
160	Paul Whiteside	217	Harry Hyslop	274	Duncan McDermott
161	John Rennie	218	Howard McCarthy	275	Paul Metcalfe
162	George Thomas Greenhalgh	219	Christer Svensson	276	Paul Denny
163	Richard Bracha	220	J Musgrove	277	R A J Chauhan
164	Dr Christopher Gordon	221	Harry Callister	278	Philip Michael Walker
165	Frank Gordon	222	Martin Lewis	279	David M Roy
166	David John Smith	223	Paul Latham	280	William Anthony Brunt
167	Colin Hudson	224	Juri Pawlovich Lukosiak	281	Sean & Jane Riley
168	Thomas Riley	225	Geir Juva	282	Stephen W Stenson
169	K Derbyshire	226	Keith Coburn	283	K P Wood
170	David Wilson	227	Michael Nolan	284	John Wardle
171	Adnan Tayyab	228	Richard D N Wells	285	M D Ricketts
172	Stanley Brophy	229	Peter Summerton	286	Paul Sunderland
173	Jack Mills	230	T S Wright	287	Brian Lowndes
174	Ian McKay	231	Anthony Roy Billington	288	Mrs Jacqueline Heap
175	Neil McKay	232	Wayne M Seaton	289	Philip J Gallier
176	J Wattam	233	David Alan Lunt	290	John E Bailey
177	Dennis A Reilly	234	William Perks	291	Neville John Blakeley
178	Clifford Ogden	235	A G Howard	292	Barry Hirst
179	John Motson	236	M D Howard	293	Kevin Dillon
180	Colin Mundy	237	William Garnett	294	J G Dixon
181	Ralph Mortimer	238	Stephen Gisborne	295	Colin Ogden
182	John Weir	239	V Boyle	296	Raymond G Law
183	Duncan Watt	240	Mark Saxon	297	Damion Shaw
184	Joe Waters	241	Steven Carruthers	298	Ronald Blackburn
185	Stephen J Painter	242	Tony Griffiths	299	David Carruthers
186	Peter A Newton	243	Mark Darren Sim	300	Brian Yardley
187	Jack Avery	244	Stephen Locke	301	Roy Wolstenholme
188	Stephen Avery	245	Alan Bell	302	Steve Brierley
189	Keith Roberts	246	Jonathan Buchan	303	D A Ansbro
190	Mark Dowsett	247	Mrk Buchan	304	Anthony Flitcroft
191	Phil Soar	248	P Duce	305	David Williams
192	Gordon Small	249	George Hamilton	306	Alan Galley
193	Frederick J Lee	250	Kevin A Leather	307	Brian B Williams
194	John Treleven	251	David Lambley	308	Albert Davison
195	Ian Clarke	252	Ken Borne	309	Mark A Emberton
196	Colin Smith	253	Bob Coalbran	310	Barry A Emberton
197	Douglas Lamming	254	Kenneth A Thomas	311	Allan C Gibbon
198	B H Standish	255	Helen M Maybury	312	Stanley Thorp
199	P L M Lunn	256	Martin Larah	313	R L Blair
200	William Hackland	257	David Woodyatt	314	G B Maltby
201	Robert Meehan	258	Mike Billington	315	J D Niemand
202	David Downs	259	Frank Newton	316	Bernard Griffin
203	S P Tomlin	260	Paul Howarth	317	Martin Colyer
204	Stewart Fell	261	Gary Pickles	318	Paul Ashton
205	Glyn Jones	262	Tony Holland	319	Paul Taylor
206	R Turbitt	263	Peter Higgins	320	John D Kandel
207	Colin Hughes	264	John S Dinsdale	321	Mike & Dave Brierley

398

322 John Gee	379 Miss Angela M Hodge	436 Dave Hillam
323 Mark Billings	380 Colin James Thompson	437 Søren Skafte Jensen
324 Neil R Billings	381 Philip Brown	438 Gareth Hamer
325 J B Garfield	382 Frank H Lord	439 Sandra Buck
326 Andrew Caiger	383 Leslie Purkis	440 Peter Brazier
327 Chris Doherty	384 Simon Curtis	441 D Coughlan
328 Shaun Michael Crowley	385 Andrew Lawson	442 John Logan Petch
329 David Keats	386 Miss P A Bouette	443 Jeremy St John Harrison
330 Adam Watkins	387 Robert Braid	444 John Jennings
331 Eric Chadwick	388 R P C Martin	445 F W Humphreys
332 Dennis Chapman	389 D J Musker	446 Dr S J Clarke
333 Stephen Charles Handley	390 John Shaughnessy	447 Danny McManus
334 Mark Simpson	391 Peter Gregory	448 D J Harrison
335 Peter S Wilson	392 Moira & Frederick Furness	449 Mrs Rita K Martyniak
336 Roy Garde	393 D Lang	450 Steve Mingle
337 Simon Artingstall	394 C Carlin	451 William Michael Misiewicz
338 Tony Hobson	395 Peter Baxter	452 Simon Weigh
339 Tony Hobson	396 Matthew Donovan	453 Paul Dyson
340 David Leonard	397 Harry Holland	454 David W Roberts
341 T Tomkins	398 Peter Wilkinson	455 Howard J Frost
342 John K Duncan	399 Stephen Kirkby	456 J Lindley
343 Leslie McCormick	400 Michael David Woodcock	457 A W Burns
344 Ian B Rankin	401 Paul Arthur Simmonds	458 Roy Astil
345 Leon S Phillips	402 Bernie Taylor	459 Alan Allcock
346 The Carr Family	403 Malcolm Hartley	460 Paul Worrall
347 Paul Ramsden	404 Peter Aldcroft	461 Steve R Reeves
348 Harry M Anderton	405 P A Thomson	462 Leo Skyner
349 S Fox	406 G E Pattison	463 Steve Bone
350 Anne Langley	407 Graham S Bohanna	464 J Ringrose
351 Gary Garlick	408 I J H Welch	465 Ian McCleverty
352 Raymond A Kelly	409 David A Wallace	466 G A Shawcross
353 Corrado Callero	410 Harold Taylor	467 Cyril George
354 Peter Womersley	411 Christopher Brady	468 Angus W Rodger
355 Gordon R Clark	412 Andrew Winn	469 R McDonald
356 Duncan Golding	413 James McDonnell	470 John Pickup
357 Stephen E Roberts	414 Martin John Stephens	471 K T Ellison
358 Neville Roughsedge	415 Paul William Ashton	472 Colin Jose
359 Allan Morris	416 John Harrison	473 L A Zammit
360 A C Wignall	417 Terry Frost LCIOB	474 Mark Burton
361 Peter T Chapman	418 D Wheatley	475 Peter Dowse
362 Lawrence O'Brien	419 Tom Bolaberger	476 Peter Vallom
363 N Ford	420 G J Carter	477 Stephen A Fowell
364 Ronald Whitfield	421 Julian Wood	478 Philip Alcock
365 Wilfred Hornby	422 Martin Poulter	479 George Ernest Wiles
366 Bernard Holding	423 Michael John Parker	480 Carsten Grønning
367 C M Butler	424 Glynne Davies	481 Kevin Cummins
368 Stephen Adams	425 Derek Skegg	482 Roger H Spruce
369 H & B J Calder	426 Simon Wilde	483 Nick Naylor
370 Gareth Jones	427 Ivan Turner	484 Mark Nicholas Savage
371 Steven Holmes	428 Donald Noble	485 Alexander W Forbes
372 Barry Roberts	429 A Wheatley	486 Rob Thomas
373 Ian Drew	430 John D Ansbro	487 A E Waldron
374 Carl David Heald	41 Greg M Smith	488 Robert Lilliman
375 R A Ball	432 Andy Cantor	489 Dag Roar Fordal
376 Gary Phillips	433 P J Drewett	490 Arve Stubberud
377 Lars-Olof Wendler	434 Jon Goddard	491 Bjørn Langerud
378 Paul W Richardson	435 Andrew Hendry	492 Bjarne Rasmussen

493	Sem Lima	521	Martin Simons	550	R C Huyton
494	Neil A Shaw	522	Mark Raphael	551	Stephen Spurgeon
495	Alfred Price	523	G H Mellor	552	Kevin Stephen Newton
496	Alan Williamson	524	Graham Corless	553	Iain Richardson
497	Simon Paul Edwards	525	Michael A Pidoux	554	Andreas Larsson
498	John Northcutt	526	Duncan Lewis Thomas	555	Andrew James Burgoyne
499	Brian Rogerson	527	Jason M Bullock	556	Gary Kenneth Johnson
500	R A C Smith	528	Michael J Gyves	557	Phil Durbin
501	Ian Stuart Fletcher	529	Anthony McKenna	558	David T Geraghty
502	Colin Cameron	530	Vic Morley	559	Bernard Newton
503	Alan Davies	531	Donna Margaret Heath	560	Ron Smith
504	Chris Elton	532	Robert Ian Wilson	561	Paul Hattersley
505	Christopher Catchpole	533	Philip Woodward	562	David Michael Woods
506	Brian Butler	534	Jimmy White	563	C J Kennington
507	N Green	535	Rob Dunford	564	Phillip Booth
508	Mike Purkiss	536	Anthony C Kemp	565	Stephen David Bardsley
509	Peter Andrew Oliver	537	Tim Chadwick	566	Andrew Pass
510	Ian D Goodwin	538	Steven F Thomas	567	Daniel Forster
511	Andrew Hemingway	539	Paul W J Millward	568	G R Remond
512	Nigel Peter Gregory	540	Michael M Brown	569	G A Remond
513	Mr Ernest Toseland, Manchester City FC, 1929-1939	541	David Robert Wakefield	570	Les Gold
		542	John Foran	571	Damian O'Mara
514	Gavina Ann Jones	543	Nicholas Booth	572	Neil James Hartle
515	Mark Frederick Jones	544	Edward James G Williams	573	Kenneth Griggs
516	Colin John Nowell	545	Roy Kenneth Jackson	574	Mark Jackson
517	Ian Harraden	546	R Anderton	575	Ian Shorrock
518	Simon John Kirby	547	Derek Jones	576	I Harman
519	R L Burge	548	Eric Palmer	577	Philip Sanders
520	Julian Tomlinson	549	Michael Horwich	578	Joe Mercer OBE